ROUGH NOTES ON INDIAN OOLOGY AND ORNITHOLOGY

ROUGH NOTES ON INDIAN OOLOGY AND ORNITHOLOGY

ALLAN HUME

GYAN

Published by

Gyan Publishing House
5, Ansari Road
Daryaganj, New Delhi-110002
Phone: 011-47034999, 9811692060
E-mail: books@gyanbooks.com

Distribution Network
gyanbooks.com
India, USA, Canada, UK, Australia

ISBN: 978-93-7169-580-0 (HB)

First Published, 1869

2nd Impression 2025

Printed at: Gyan Press, Delhi.

ROUGH NOTES ON INDIAN OOLOGY AND ORNITHOLOGY

Author: ALLAN HUME

MY SCRAP BOOK:

OR

ROUGH NOTES

ON

INDIAN OOLOGY AND ORNITHOLOGY.

EDITED BY

ALLAN HUME.

CALCUTTA:

PRINTED BY C. B. LEWIS, BAPTIST MISSION PRESS.

1869.

TO

E. BLYTH, Esq.

AND

Dr. T. C. JERDON,

Who, between them, have done more for Indian Ornithology, than all other modern observers put together,

This Ornithological Scrap Book,

All unworthy as it is of their notice or acceptance,

Is affectionately inscribed

BY

Their friend and pupil,

THE EDITOR.

NOTE TO READERS AND CONTRIBUTORS.

Please address all corrections of, or additions to, the matter of this present part, and all contributions to, or notes for, the forthcoming parts, to me at AGRA. All information will be thankfully received; and will be embodied in the present or next edition, according to the time at which it may be received; and please remember that this is eminently a case of BIS DAT QUI CITO DAT.

ALLAN HUME.

PREFACE.

THESE rough notes are merely intended as a sort of nucleus, round which future observations, (which it is hoped that they may somewhat tend to systematize) may, as it were, crystallize. In them, I have thrown together all the information in regard to Indian Oology and Ornithology, supplementary to my friend Dr. Jerdon's excellent work, that I have happened to collect.

Much of this information is original, the result of recent observations of my own, or of the different gentlemen who have kindly communicated it, and whose names are duly recorded *in loco*, but much has also been extracted from the pages of the Ibis, Yarrell, Bree, Gould, &c., works with which every ornithologist ought to be acquainted, but which no working Indian field naturalist, (for whose use these notes are chiefly designed), can possibly carry about with him.

My object in now *printing* these avowedly miserably imperfect and disjointed scraps is, primarily, to enable my numerous coadjutors, in different parts of India, to ascertain what I have already on record, and what portion of the information they may happen to possess, will help to fill in many of the woeful blanks remaining in that record.

Hereafter* I propose, (D. V.,) to republish these notes in a revised form, in which I shall embody all the additional in-

* I have not, in the present notes, offered any general remarks on oology, nor attempted, as I shall hereafter do, to show how peculiarities, both in the eggs themselves and in nest architecture, are reproduced, not only in representative *species*, but even in representative genera, in distant portions of the globe. I reserve these subjects for a future edition, when, with ampler materials before me, I may hope to generalize both more usefully and more safely.

formation that their circulation may elicit, and I earnestly entreat all who can to aid me* in gathering together materials, for a really satisfactory account of the nidification† and eggs of our Indian Birds.

* To enable me to select good characteristic type specimens for figuring, it is absolutely necessary to have before one a large series of the eggs of each species.—Moreover safe and useful generalizations can seldom be made, or in many cases useful descriptions written from only a few specimens.—I therefore trust that all those who have it in their power, will favour me not only with particulars as to the nidification, but also with as many specimens as they conveniently can of the eggs of all those species, of which the text shows that these are still desiderata. Those disposed to assist, should address me direct at Agra.

† So few, even of professed ornithologists, in India, at all realize the importance of oology as an element in classification, that I venture to reproduce some pregnant remarks on this subject, which appeared in the Ibis of 1867, from Mr. Tristram's pen.

"There are two very distinct tides of sylviad immigration in Palestine. In October and November, thousands of the hardier species pour down into the lowlands and *wadys*, where they remain till February or March. Then, for a month, the land is left almost deserted till in April and May the spring arrivals commence, and every thicket is tenanted by species either strange to our shores, or known only by the occasional capture of a straggler. Such are *S. Orphea*, *Aedon Galactodes*, *Hypolais Elaica* and *H. Upcheri*. We were especially fortunate in our opportunities of watching the nidification of the less known species, and I believe there is no class of birds in which the style of architecture, with the coloration and form of the egg, casts more light on the true grouping of species and the arrangement of genera. Possessed of a good series of the eggs of the *Luscinidæ*, we might classify the species accordingly, and find that we had scarcely in one instance diverged from the recognized order of our best systematists. Thus the unique egg of *Cettia Sericea* separates it at once from all our other Palæarctic warblers, and points out its affinities to the long-tailed *Prinia* group of the Indian region. Then the the eggs of Savi's, and the grasshopper warbler, group them apart and link them to the very similar eggs of the Australian *Megalurus* and *Calamanthus*, *Cisticola* and *Drymœca*, varying, as they do still vary, within the same limits as the oriental *Prinia* and *Orthotomus*, to which we must admit their affinities. The egg of *Aedon* stands out alone, steadily demanding a distinct and isolated position, which all who are familiar with its manners and note will readily grant, but approaching in habit, as in its eggs, the Indian *Thamnobiæ*.

The great group of *Calamoherpe*, from whatever part of the world they come, have but one unmistakeable character of egg, sharply defined from all the other groups. The beautiful and fragile eggs of every member of the genus *Hypolais*, though each distinct in markings and in ground-colour, from the richest salmon hue to pale ashy white, but all of a peculiar rough texture, are a group almost as isolated and peculiar as *Pycnonotus*, with no affinities approaching *Phyllopneuste*. These again, though infinitely varying within themselves, disclaim alliance with any of the other sylviads. We then have the genus *Sylvia* as restricted by Bonaparte, of which our white throat is the type, with its greenish ground colour and the spotting

If I be blamed for the innumerable errors and defects certain to occur in these notes, I can only plead—

1*st.* That they were jotted down in those rare leisure moments, that the control of a vast public department (whose operations extend over nearly 2,00,000 square miles, and whose employés number nearly 14,000 officers and men), leaves me for recreation, and

2*nd.* That they contain, I believe, some little new and useful matter which I am unwilling should be lost, and that life being so uncertain, as it is in India, and I, having absolutely *no* time to work up the materials I have collected, and separate the wheat from the chaff, just print the whole as it is, so that, even if *I* do not live to do so, others at least may hereafter utilize whatever little good there is in it.

different in each species, while *Melizophilus* and *Pyrrhophthalmus* are evidently aberrant members of the same family. Next we may take the *Curruca*, as restricted by Bonaparte, with the eggs always of a whitish or brownish white ground, and the markings set each in a nimbus of fainter colour, as in our black cap and garden warblers; while *Nisoria Undata*, a good genus, comes next them by its ground colour, but wants the spots.

The Redbreast, pugnacious as he always is, stands aloof from any entangling alliances, and asserts an independent position as *Erythacus*, which introduces us to Mr. Gray's sub-family of *Luscininæ* comprising all the remaining sylviads. Here we find a character, pervading almost the whole sub-family, in the coloration of the eggs, which is never found in the first sub-family *Sylvinæ*, *viz.* the blue or bluish white ground colour; *Copsychus*, *Myiomela*, *Saxicola*, *Ruticilla*, *Thamnobia*, and all their subdivisions, have this common feature. The most aberrant are the genera *Luscinia* and *Cyanecula* with their uniform olive green coloration, but, as we well know, the nightingale's egg is not unfrequently blue, and the identity of the colour in the eggs of the blue throats attests their affinity to the nightingale. All the innumerable species of *Saxicolinæ* lay blue eggs, either plain or spotted, and frequently, as in the *Turdinæ*, we find two closely affined species laying one a plain the other a spotted egg; while, occasionally, the eggs of comparatively distant members of the family are identical, as in the case of *Saxicola Œnanthe* and *S. Isabellina*. Of the five species of the sub-genus *Dromolæa*, of which I have taken the eggs, four are of the faintest bluish white with ruddy spots, and the fifth a rich blue ground with similar spots. From these we are led on to *Ruticilla*, the eggs of which are never spotted, though the ground colour varies from pure white in the single instance of *R. Tithys*, to the most delicate white with the faintest tinge in *R. Moussieri*, up to the very dark blue of *R. Semirufa*, a bird most closely allied to *R. Tithys*. Finally, we have the spotless blue of *Sialia* and *Accentor*, with which last I find much difficulty in grouping Mr. Grays *Acanthiza*, or the *Siurus* of the new world."

Gentle reader, if these notes chance to be of the slightest use to you, use them; if not, burn them, if it so please you, but do not waste your time in abusing me or them, since no one *can* think more poorly of them than I do myself.

ALLAN HUME.

ROUGH NOTES

ON

Indian Oology and Ornithology.

No.* 1. Vulture Monachus, Lin.

†The Cinereous Vulture.

I have been unable to obtain certain information as to the breeding of this noble bird within our limits, but it most certainly *does* breed in the Himalayas, as I have seen a perfect egg, which was extracted from the oviduct of a female, shot in March, 1865, between Dalhousie and Murree. Nests are likely to be found anywhere in precipitous places, in the Himalayas, or perhaps in large trees, in the Sub-Himalayan ranges, west of the Ganges. Eastwards of this, the species seems to have far fewer representatives; though Dr. Jerdon has seen it at Darjeeling, and specimens have been obtained in Assam and Bhotan.

The following particulars of its nidification, in the Pyrenees, are derived from Dr. Bree's work. The breeding season is not mentioned. The bird breeds in isolated pairs, and not in society as *Fulvus* (verus), *Auricularis*, *Indicus* and *Bengalensis* all appear to do. It builds, Dr. Bree says, among the most inaccessible rocks, making a large nest of branches, boughs and small sticks.

* The numbers are those of Dr. Jerdon's work. Although I differ widely from him on many points of classification, I yet think it will, for obvious reasons, be most convenient in these present notes to adopt his arrangement. Where the scientific name, adopted by Dr. Jerdon, has been shown, by Mr. Blyth and others, liable to supersession by some other name, on the score of the priority of this latter, or for any other good cause; I have, while retaining the NUMBER, made the necessary alteration in the name.

† Where, as not unfrequently happens, Dr. Jerdon departs from the pre-established English names, calling, for instance, the "Cinereous Vulture," the great brown Vulture, "the Griffon," the Large Tawny Vulture, and the like, I have reverted to the original English names. Where I have neglected any corrections of the nature referred to in the present, or preceding note, I hope my error may be pointed out to me, for rectification in forthcoming editions.

It lays, it is said, two eggs in the Pyrenees, but with us, would probably, like other species of this family, lay normally, only one; just as, in another family, *Circætus Gallicus*, which in some parts of the world always lays two, here (I speak from the experience of over 20 nests, in several of which the egg was nearly ready to hatch off), apparently, *never* lays more than one egg. In colour, the eggs vary from a more or less pure white, with scarcely a trace of markings, and this I take to be the normal type, to a reddish or fulvous white, richly spotted and marked with reddish brown, or brownish red. In shape, they are said to be "pointed alike at both ends," but the egg I saw, (and Dr. Bree's figure corresponds in shape) was a very blunt, slightly pyriform oval, one end being decidedly smaller than the other. In texture, they are coarse and rough; more so I think in the specimen I saw, than those of either *Bengalensis* or *Calvus*. The lining I omitted to notice, or, if I did notice it, have now forgotten its colour; but it is probably greenish as in other vultures. The egg figured by Dr. Bree, from Thienemann, measures 3.48 by 2.75, but I should guess this to be a small egg, as *Bengalensis* and *Calvus*, both smaller birds, often lay larger eggs than this.

Dr. Jerdon had probably never seen much of this bird, when he wrote his account of it. In no single specimen, of the numbers that I have killed (or watched with binoculars, from within 100 yards greedily devouring some carcass) were the "bill with the cere red mixed with ashy," nor "the naked parts of the neck ashy red," nor the "legs dusky yellow." Such may be the colouring of individuals in confinement, but it has not been that of any one of the fifty odd wild birds that I have closely examined. My measurements, made in the flesh, moreover scarcely agree with his, and so for purposes of comparison I insert my own notes taken from numerous freshly killed specimens.

Length,* 42 to 45. Expanse from 96 to 118. Wing, from 29·5 to 32; the 3rd primary the longest, the 1st from 3 to 4 shorter, and the 2nd from ·5 to 1 shorter. Tail, from vent, from 13 to 16; the outer tail feathers from 1·5 to 3 shorter than the central ones. Tarsus, 4.8 to 5·5. Tibia, 8 to 8·75. Foot, greatest length, 8 to 9; greatest width, 5·75 to 6·6; mid toe (to root of claw), 3·7 to 4·25; its claw, along the curve, 1·4 to 1·75; hind toe, 1·5 to 1·9, its claw along the curve 1·75 to nearly 2; inner toe 1·6 to 2, its claw along the curve 1·7 to 2. Bill from gape 3·6 to 4·0; width at gape 2·2 to 2·5; bill straight from edge of cere to point 2·3 to 2·7; along curve from margin of cere, 3 to 3·25; length of cere on culmen,

* All dimensions are in English inches and decimals of ditto.

1·16 to 1·28; height of bill at margin of cere, 1·2 to 1·3. Wings when closed, reach to within from 1 to 4 inches of end of tail. Lower tail coverts generally reach to within 4 or 5 inches of end of tail. Weight from 12 lbs to nearly 20 lbs; 14 lbs being the average for males, and the females being considerably heavier.

The tarsus is covered in front, and on the sides, for more than half its length, with a dense, almost silky fur, which in *one place* almost meets behind. The bare portion of the tarsus and the feet* are, in some, a clear, slightly creamy white, on others, a pearl white, with here and there a barely perceptible pink tinge. Scutellation reticulate, scales slightly prominent; with commonly 5 rather large transverse scutæ at the end of the middle toe, and 4 at the ends of the others; outer and centre toes connected by a membrane as far as the 2nd joints. Traces of a membraneous connection between inner and mid toe. Terminal pads of hinder and inner toes very large. Inner toe claw as large and at times even slightly larger than the hind toe claw, outer toe and claw, especially the latter, very feeble.

Irides brown, lower eyelid creamy white, (often with a faint delicate lilac or even purplish shade) pinkish at margin, and with a row of thick short eyelash feathers; upper lid, and bare eye-shelf pinkish, at times with a lilac shade. Cere, gape and base of lower mandible a pale mauve, at times tinged in places with pink. Bill horny, blackish brown, darker on upper mandible and tip of lower ditto, palest at sides of base of upper mandible, and of lower ditto. Tongue thick and fleshy, round ended, slightly emarginate at the tip, hastate as a whole, and fringed at the back, not merely *grooved* down the centre, but the sides curving regularly up from the middle, so as to give a semicircular section. The lores, cheeks, forehead, crown, occiput, chin and throat, and a patch on the lower mandible, covered with dark brown fur-like feathers, growing lighter towards the occiput. This fur is sparse and rather harsh on the cheeks, chin and throat, but very dense and soft on the upper portions of the head. The naked skin at the back and sides of neck, and the bare patch over the articulation of the jaws, (generally continued as a ring upwards, behind and over the dark fur border of the ear aperture, to within one half an inch or so of the posterior angle of the eye,) creamy, or in some, delicate bluish white, occasionally with a shade of pink.

The whole body and wings are a rich, very dark, chocolate brown, (the under surface being darker than the upper,) the quills and tail

* What does Dr. Bree mean by saying "Feet covered with feathers above?" The whole of the feet and the lower portion of the tarsus, are as perfectly nude as feet and legs can be.

being almost black. The feathers of the lower part of the back and sides of the neck, are of a loose texture, elongated and of a slightly lighter hue than the back, and form a conspicuous ruff. Feathers of the upper breast lengthened, acutely pointed, somewhat rigid, and often with the webs a good deal separated. The tail feathers are remarkably stiff, with the tips much abraded, and naked, tipped with extremely stiff hard projecting shafts, reminding one much of the tail feathers of many woodpeckers. I do not know if the fact has been noticed, but I have repeatedly seen this vulture use its tail for a fulcrum, much as a woodpecker does, tearing out the entrails of a dead camel with claws firmly dug into, and tail hard pressed against the carcass, nay I have seen it, when on the ground, tearing to pieces lumps of flesh which it held down between its two feet, always as it lifted its head, tearing away morsel by morsel, firmly pressing its tail against the ground.

To return, the lower tail coverts are of a slightly lighter hue than any other part except the occiput. The first 5 quills are strongly notched on the inner web and the 2nd to the 6th are emarginate on the outer webs; both notches and emarginations are very high up and near the bases of the feathers.

Dr. Jerdon says that this bird "is found, though rarely, in the Himalayas, occasionally descending to the plains;" but this scarcely conveys a correct idea. Throughout the upper Doab, the Punjab and Northern Rajpootana, it is found during the cold weather; even as low as Etawah, I used to see at least a dozen and shoot at least 2 or 3 (and in Etawah it is very wary) every year. Further north, in the Sirsa district for instance, it is one of the commonest vultures during the cold weather, and I have seen 20 of this species with a few of the large plains representative of *Fulvus* (our *Fulvescens* No. 3 bis), all busy over a single camel. In localities where they are plentiful, they are by *no means* difficult to approach; at any rate when feeding, I have twice killed two at a shot with a single barrel of an ordinary No. 12 fowling-piece with No. 3 loose shot, and Mr. Parsons of Sirsa, in shooting for me, (I happened to be on horseback at the moment and he on foot,) an imperial eagle busy with a dead calf, knocked over one of these vultures with the same shot that killed the eagle. I have never found any difficulty in getting up to within 50 or 60 yards of them in the upper Punjaub, when feeding on the ground; and from a distance of from 80 to 100 yards, they will let you stare at them through binoculars as long as you like. Near Murree in October, I saw a large group of them devouring some dead animal in a khud (valley) below the road. I saw several at Rawulpindee and at Lahore, and generally, I should say, that this species is very nearly as common in the cold weather in the northern portion of the Punjab as even *Gyps Bengalensis.*

The youngest birds, that I have seen, had the legs dingy yellow, and were of a dull pale brown, the wing coverts and scapulars centred darker, and with a sort of faint pinkish or ruddy tint on the upper surface, very conspicuous, when rising close in front of one along with young and adults of our *Fulvescens* (No. 3 bis). I once shot one, but was unable to preserve it, and so can now give no exact description.

Between this, comparatively, very light plumage and the deep chocolate brown, that at a short distance looks perfectly black, every shade of plumage is observable.

The claws of *Vultur Monachus* are, on the whole, sharper than those of any other species of Indian Vulture and contrast in this respect strongly with those of our hills, and plains, representatives of *Gyps Fulvus,* (No. 3 and No. 3 bis); as a rule too they are not only much sharper but considerably more powerful.

The Rev. H. B. Tristram, in his ornithology of Palestine, (*Ibis* 1865) gives an interesting account of a "successful attack" on an Eyrie of this Vulture.

"On the 27th of February, Mr. Upcher, while walking with me from the plain of Gennesaret to Tiberias, shot a Bonelli's eagle under the cliffs overhanging the sea of Galilee. I saw a vulture dash from the small cave just behind him, at the report of the piece, but it wheeled round a corner before we had more than a glimpse of it. We were unable, at the time, to climb up and examine the cave; but returned in the afternoon, reinforced by Messrs. Shepherd and Bartlett to lay siege to it. We easily mounted to a ledge about twelve feet under the cave, but no bird appeared; while we were talking, a sudden rush, like the beating of the branches of a tree was heard, and a huge dark object dashed close over our heads, at a distance of not more than six feet. In wheeling circles it continued to return, and swept as near to us as prudence permitted, while Mr. Shepherd climbed up to the cavern and in a few seconds returned with one white egg, a little larger than the ordinary run of Griffon's, but of exactly the same texture. It was rather soiled and proved to be hard set. The nest was scanty, consisting chiefly of large tufts of grass with the roots laid on the floor of the cave. I have seen eggs stated to belong to this vulture very much spotted and coloured with rufous, but not more so than those of the Griffon occasionally are, but the only other egg of the species I ever obtained (in Africa) was white, like this, and perceptibly thicker than the Griffon's. This eyrie near Tiberias was by no means difficult of access, and was about two miles distant from the immense colony of Griffons in the wady Hamoun."

The nest, however, is not always on rocks, nor does the egg appear to be always pure white or larger than that of the Griffon, as may be seen from the following extracts from a paper of Lord Lilford's, which appeared in the *Ibis* for 1866.

"The result this evening was, a nest with five eggs of the blue Magpie, and an egg of the cinereous vulture, which last, the boys assured me, they had found on the ground at a spot much frequented by this species, which breeds in the pine-forests close at hand, and is by far the most common vulture in the Castiles. This egg is slightly smaller than those of *Gyps Fulvus* in my collection, and is of a uniform clouded reddish-pink colour, very much resembling some varieties of the egg of *Aquila Chrysaetus*. I have no hesitation in ascribing this egg to *Vultur Monachus*, as, although I was unfortunately too late to find the eggs *in situ* myself, the fragments of egg-shells found in and below several nests of this vulture, exactly corresponded with this specimen, and I found that *Gyps Fulvus*, of which species a few pairs used in former years to nest in a range of cliffs near the village, is now comparatively scarce in the district."

"The nest (of *Vultur Monachus*) was situated at the top of one of the tallest pines, and visible from some distance with the male bird seated close to it. He allowed us to approach almost to the foot of the tree, and sailed off apparently unhurt by a volley of our four barrels. Agapo was soon up to the nest, in which was a young bird of about the size of a Dorking-cock. A more unsightly specimen of the great class *Aves*, I never before beheld, he was covered with brownish grey down, with a bright pink cere and very pale yellow legs and feet; part of the trachea of a sheep or goat, perfectly hard and dry, completely encircled one leg; and altogether his appearance presented a combination of the absurd and repulsive, almost impossible to describe. The nest was composed of large boughs externally, and was lined with twigs and a few fragments of wool. In the foundation of the nest, which was unusually deep for that of a raptor, a pair of tree creepers, (*Certhia Familiaris*), had established their abode, and were rearing a family of five or six young."

Further interesting particulars of this bird's nidification, are given in Mr. C. Farman's notes on the birds of prey of central Bulgaria, which appeared in the *Ibis* for 1868. He says "In central Bulgaria, this is by no means a common species. I have noticed these birds only during the spring and summer, they certainly do not remain during the winter, and they are therefore (in some degree at least) migratory; nidification with this species commences early in March, somewhat earlier than with the Griffon Vulture, in proof of which I may state that on the 30th of April, 1865, I found three young birds in three successive nests of the first, whereas on the same day, I took several eggs of the Griffon Vulture fresh enough to be easily blown, while in no case did I find the eggs hatched. My experience of the following year confirmed me in this opinion, as I invariably found the young of *Vultur Monachus* a full fortnight, and in some cases more, in advance of *Gyps Fulvus*. Dr. Bree (B. Eur. I. P. 8) says of the Cinereous Vulture that "it builds among the most inaccessible rocks." This, however, I have not found to be the case, I have invariably seen the nest placed on a tree, and generally on one of no great size. In April, 1865, as just mentioned, I observed several nests of this bird, in the thickly wooded country, lying to the right of the Pravidy valley, within about three miles of the town of that name; and they were all, without exception, placed on trees at an average height of about twenty feet from the ground. Unfortunately I have nearly always been too late for the eggs of this bird, and have only been able to secure a single example; I am inclined to think that it does not usually lay more than one, as I never found but one young bird in a nest. It is also probable that birds of this species return to the same nest year after year, as I found the nests of 1865 tenanted when I visited them in 1866."

That this bird does breed in the Dhoon seems probable from the following remarks furnished by my friend Captain Hutton :—

"Vultur Monachus. Lin. *V. Cinereus*, young. *Monarchus* in Hardwicke's Illustrations is a misprint for *Monachus*.—Of this bird, Jerdon says, "It is found, though rarely, in the Himalaya, occasionally descending to the plains;" at Mussooree about 5,500 feet of elevation it cannot be called rare, although at the same time, it is by no means abundant.—It is seen all the year through, coursing about in company with *G. Bengalensis*, *G. Fulvus* and *Otogyps Calvus* in search of carrion, all descending upon the same carcass.—In the Dehra Dhoon, it is not so common as in the lower hills, but one was seen in the Eastern Dhoon, near Hurdwar, in January, sitting on the branch of a lofty tree beside a large nest made of dry sticks and branches of goodly size; the nest was rather a deep bowl, rather deeper that is, than those of *G. Bengalensis;* the sides and especially the bottom were of great thickness and the diameter fully 2½ feet. At that time the nest was not completed within. The branches with which the nest was constructed were not merely laid one upon another in simple platform fashion, but were strongly interwoven like loose basket work.—In the end of February, the spot was again visited, and the nest was found to be finished; the lining being of somewhat finer sticks, with bits of rag and a few feathers apparently rubbed from the body of the bird which had evidently been sitting in it; it was, however, still empty, and no bird was seen.—In the early part of March, the nest was again visited, but there were neither eggs nor birds; several nests were seen in the neighbourhood but all alike were abandoned, as the jungle grass had been fired beneath the trees, and even the branches of many trees had been lopped off to feed the herds of cattle. —Although therefore we felt tolerably certain that the nest where the bird had been seen was that of *V. Monachus*, yet we have no certain proof that such was in reality the case.

No. 2. **Vultur Calvus,** Scop.

The Indian King Vulture.

Breeds from the latter end of January to the middle of April; but, so far as my experience goes, by far the majority lay in March. In fact, as a rule, this bird hardly begins to lay until every *G. Bengalensis* has hatched off.

I once found a nest with a fresh egg in November, but this was a most exceptional case. The nest I have invariably found on *trees*. It is said, Dr. Jerdon remarks, to breed on inacessible cliffs; but at Ajmere, where on the Taragurh hill, there are numerous suitable precipices, many of which are occupied by *Gyps Indicus*, I found a pair, the only ones I met with, breeding on a large Peepul tree at the foot of the hill. As far as my experience goes, the nests are always on large trees, commonly on the very top of Peepul (*Ficus Religiosus*) and Banian (*Ficus Indicus*) trees, at least 30 or 40 feet from the ground. Mr. W. Blewitt, however, informs me that he obtained an egg of this bird on the 20th February, from a large nest, (constructed of Acacia twigs and lined with leaves and straw) placed on the top of a Keekur bush (*A. Arabica*), in the Dhoona Beer near Hansie, at a height of about 13 or 14 feet only, from the ground. I have never found two pairs breeding near each other. The tree they commonly select is one standing altogether apart, in the middle of some Dhak (*Butea Frondosa*) jungle, or waste place; but I have taken their eggs from trees, belonging to groups situated in cultivated land, and on the 1st March, 1867, I found a nest, (from which I shot the female and took the egg,) on a Peepul tree, situated right in the centre of the village of Deopoora, zillah Mynpooree. The nest is a huge flat platform, more often oval or oblong than circular, chiefly composed of sticks, varying from one inch to half an inch in diameter, loosely put together, but still from their aggregate weight and the manner in which they interlace, forming a very solid structure. They always have a lining towards the centre, often of numerous strips, from 6 to 10 inches long and from 1 to 3 broad, of the fan leaves of the Toddy palm, (*Borassus Flabelliformis*), but not uncommonly of Peepul, Banyan or Neem (*Melia Azedirukhta*) leaves, or of slender twigs of these trees to which the leaves are attached.

The nest varies from 2½ to 4 feet in length and breadth and is often more than a foot in thickness. Though I have no positive proof of it, native hunters assure me that, when not molested, they breed year after year during long periods in the same nest, and the materials of one nest that I demolished, weighed over 8 Indian maunds (over 6 hundred weight) and proved to have at least 3 distinct layers and to have been used many times. As however *I know* that this bird sometimes, (like *Ketupa Ceylonensis, vide infra*) takes possession of old nests of *Haliætus Leucoryphus* (of which bird there were several pairs in the neighbourhood) I cannot be certain, that these vultures had really, as the nest seemed to indicate and the villagers declared, bred in this same nest during many successive seasons.

They lay a single egg; I have heard it asserted that they sometimes lay two, but of the numbers of nests that I have personally examined, I never found one that contained more than a single egg or a single young one, and in upper India, I feel quite sure that *one* is the normal number.

The eggs, when first laid, are usually a nearly unsullied pale greenish white, but as incubation proceeds, they become greatly stained and discolored by the droppings of the parent bird. I have taken only one egg at all marked, and this showed numerous *very faint* dingy purplish streaks and spots, but possibly higher coloured examples may occur.

In shape, the eggs vary from rather long ovals to nearly spheres; but the normal type I consider to be a round oval.

The texture is moderately fine, the shell *very* strong and as a rule glossless, but I have found eggs with a faint gloss.

The egg-lining is green.

The eggs vary in size from 3·5 to 3·2 in length, and from 2·8 to 2·45 in breadth: of 24 eggs measured, the *average* length and breadth was 3·34 and 2·6.

Mr. W. Blewitt tells me that, besides the nest already alluded to, he found no less than 7 nests of this Vulture, in the neighbourhood of Hansee, between the 6th and 24th March;

each contained a single egg. Four of the eggs were quite fresh, two partly incubated, and one ready to hatch off, those taken on the 22nd and 24th March, being quite fresh. Two nests were not above fourteen feet from the ground, and no nest, (this is not a part of the country where trees run high,) was above 25 feet from the ground. Two were on Keekur trees, two (the two low ones) on old *Heense shrubs (Capparis Aphylla)* and three on Peepul, Burgot and Seeshum trees. The nests varied from 19 to 25 inches in diameter, and from 5 to 8 inches in thickness, and were all dense masses of thorny twigs of the Ber *(Zisyphus Jujube)* Khyr *(Acacia Catechu)* and Keekur *(Acacia Arabica)*. They were lined, some thickly, some thinly, with leaves or straw, and in one the egg was regularly bedded in leaves and straw. This is not altogether in accordance with my own experience; but in this, as in other cases, Mr. Blewitt sent me all the eggs, and more than one of the parent birds, and there can be no doubt as to the accuracy of his observations. The same gentleman took a fresh egg of this species, as late as April 13th, 1868. The nest was placed upon a Peepul tree, at the height of about 30 feet from the ground, measured about 16 inches in diameter by 6″ in depth, and was composed of Keekur twigs, lined with fine straw and a few leaves. This was also in the Hansee district.

About Etawah, the native fowlers call this the "Bhaour Gidh." I rather suspect that these birds pair in the air. Just before the breeding season, a pair may be seen to tower, and then, one apparently getting on the back of the other, both come with plunges and flappings of the wings nearly to the ground, when separating they sail away slowly towards some large tree where they both rest. Mr. R. Thompson and myself have observed something very similar in the Lammergeyer. Perhaps this is only ante-nuptial play and is not the real consummation of matrimony. As regards the colour of the neck, legs and *conspicuous bare thigh patch* (which last Dr. Jerdon does not notice) I have remarked that it becomes much brighter, and more vivid, towards the breeding season, and is always at this time brighter in the male than in the female.

The head of the young bird (which latter has the black of the adult everywhere replaced by a more or less dark brown) is pretty thickly covered with down, (that of the adult is bare) and looks almost like a miniature *V. Monachus*. In its oval narines too, *Calvus* approximates to the round ones of *Monachus*, so different from the slit-like nostrils of our 4 species of *Gyps*. *Vultur Occipitalis* of S. Africa is a sort of representative of *Calvus*, but in this species, to judge from the specimen in my valued friend Colonel Tytler's museum, (to which I owe many opportunities of comparing foreign and Indian types,) the adult *always* retains the down on the head as in *Monachus*. The narines in this bird *(Occipitalis)* are more oval than in *Calvus*, but all 3 species are closely related to each other, and the genus *Otogyps* scarcely appears to me worthy of retention.

Gyps Indicus (verus) and *Gyps Bengalensis* may doubtless give place to this bird in feeding; but it is our bird that has to give way, when it comes into the company, as I have so often seen it, of *V. Monachus* and *G. Fulvescens* (nobis, No. 3 bis).

The following are exact dimensions taken from several specimens. Length, 30 to 33. Expanse, 80 to 88. Weight, 8·5 lbs. to 11 lbs. Wing, 22·5 to 24; the third primary is the longest, the first is from 2 to 3 inches shorter, and the second from 2 to 4. Tail of 14 feathers, from 9·8 to 11. Tarsus, 4·3 to 4·6. The greatest length of the foot is from 7 to 8 inches, the greatest width, 5 to 5·5; the mid toe from 3·4 to 3·8; its claw along curve from 1·3 to 1·5, hind toe, 1·2 to 1·45; its claw along curve, 1·5 to 1·68; inner toe, 1·25 to 1·6; its claw along curve, 1·6 to 1·75. Bill, straight from edge of cere to point, 1·9 to 2; ditto along curve, 2·3 to 2·55; from gape, 2·6 to 3; width at gape, 1·8 to 1·95; height at margin of cere, 1 to 1·1, length of cere, 0·9 to 1·15. The closed wings fall short of the end of the tail by 2 to 3·25. The lower tail coverts by from 3 to 5·5.

Mr. Salvin, I think, tells us how a young *Gyps Fulvus* devoured a half pound pot of arsenical soap, without seeming much the worse for its indigestible meal, the following remarks by Captain Hutton tend to show that Vultures generally are but little liable to injury from poisonous food. He says, " There is a curious fact which applies not only to all these Vultures, but likewise to *Leptoptilus Javanicus* our rain Adjutant, which it may be as well to record. In order to procure good specimens of Mammalia, I have occasionally been in the habit of placing out a carcass of some large animal, well poisoned with Strychnia, and have thus procured Foxes, Jackals, Leopards, Bears, Kites, Jays, Crows and *Aquila Imperialis*, but never in any instance was a Vulture or an Adjutant affected, although greedily devouring the flesh of the poisoned carcass. The eagles ate greedily for about five minutes, scarcely more, then they suddenly ceased, but instead of flying off, they stood as if rooted to the ground, and then fell prone with outstretched neck and half open wings upon the spot where they had stood; after a few convulsive croakings and gaspings they were dead. The Vultures after feeding, either soared away or sat upon the neighbouring trees, yet none ever fell, as did the smaller birds, nor did they appear to be in the least affected. A medical officer at Dehra told me he had observed the same in regard to the Adjutant above mentioned. The natural way to account for this is, the power of such foul feeders to resist the effects of things that would poison most other animals ; feeding as do the vultures upon the most putrid and disgusting substances, they may be said habitually to feed upon poison. I found, however, that deer, such as the Kakur and Goral, which are any thing but foul feeders, could eat poisoned bread without being affected by the drug, so that the matter seems to require further investigation. *Aquilæ Imperiales* do not touch the putrid entrails in which the vultures delight, but confine themselves to the solid and non-poisonous flesh, so that they might well be supposed not to possess the same power of resisting poison rubbed into their food."

No. 3. Gyps Fulvus, Gmel.

(Gyps Himalayensis, nobis.)

The Griffon.*

The large Himalayan Vulture, which Dr. Jerdon and Mr. Blyth identify with *Fulvus* of Europe and Africa, and which I provisionally *(vide infra)* designate as *Himalayensis*, breeds in January, February and March. The nest, a huge platform of sticks, (at times the property in past years of some eagle or falcon, which the early nesting vultures have seized upon, long before the rightful owners have even begun to think of their annual matrimonial duties,) is placed, I believe invariably, on a rocky ledge of some bold precipice in the Himalayas, at least 3000 feet above the sea. I have never yet heard of their nesting on trees. Though generally gregarious in their breeding habits, large numbers rarely appear to breed together. Six is the greatest number of nests I have yet known of, in one single locality. In this respect, they differ from *G. Indicus*, of which usually from 10 to 30 pairs breed close alongside each other.

The bird lays a single egg ; as indeed *all* true Vultures here invariably seem to do.

The eggs of this species, are larger than those of any of our other Indian Vultures. The two I have, both of which I owe to Captain Cock are ovals : the one a rather long, and the other a broad oval. The texture of the shell appears coarser

* Should the Himalayan species prove distinct, it should be called the "Himalayan Griffon."

than that of the eggs of either *Indicus*, *Fulvescens*, *Bengalensis*, or *Calvus*. The ground colour is the usual greenish or greyish white of all the true vultures. The one egg is unspotted, the other is richly blotched and mottled, chiefly towards the small end, with brownish red. The eggs measure* 3·98 × 2·85, and 3·78 × 2·8. I have always myself been too late to get the eggs, though I have often seen the empty nests, and I therefore give Captain Cock's interesting account of the taking of the two eggs I have above described.

"In April, 1867, I was at a pic-nic in the Kumara slate quarries (near Dhurmsala), and there noticed a nest of *Gyps Fulvus ;* the old bird was sitting at the time ; the nest was a mass of sticks and dirt, placed on a shelf of rock under an overhanging precipice. Some idea of the magnitude of the precipice I can give you. When standing at the foot I could not nearly fling a stone up to where the nest was, and yet it was more than half way down from the top. I got long ropes and hill-men, and a venturous plain's-man ! (hill-men would not look at it) went over. After dangling in mid air for some time, he contrived to get hold of a creeper with his toes, and by means of that, pulled himself on to the ledge ; then creeping along the ledge, he got to the nest, and went quite close to it ; the vulture at last flew off, leaving a young one covered with dingy yellow down, and looking like a huge gosling. I left the young one, and took measures for securing the eggs in 1868. On the 25th February, I went out, and saw that this year there were two nests on the ledge. I then on the 28th February, got long ropes reaching from the top of the precipice to the bottom, and with the aid of a long bamboo with a bag at the end, we fished the eggs out of the nests ; a man having been pulled up from below for that purpose. There was only one egg in each nest." Captain Cock found the birds breeding earlier in 1869 than in the previous year. On the 20th February he found 4 nests, one had an egg, in the other three the old birds were sitting close. Next day, taking ropes and men, he visited the nests. In No. 1, the egg had hatched off, No. 2 contained a young one of some 5 or 6 days old, and No. 4 one fully a week old, No. 3 alone contained an egg, and that even would have hatched off, probably in another day, and contained a live fully-formed chick.

It seems, even to myself, a piece of presumption on my part to say so, but it is nevertheless, I believe, an incontestible fact, that both Mr. Blyth and Dr. Jerdon have erred in giving us only 3 Indian species of *Gyps* instead of 4, as there really are.

* A third egg since obtained in Kotegurh measured 3·83 × 2·85.

It *does* seem at first sight absurd to assert, that after all these years, during which ornithology has been studied in India, a species of such a genus should have escaped notice, but both Mr. Blyth and Dr. Jerdon give us only 3 species, while clearly, and unmistakeably there are 4. Our four vultures of the genus *Gyps* are these :—

1*st*.—The large Pale Himalayan Bird, which is usually identified with *Fulvus*, but from which, it seems to me that, (if there be any faith in figures and descriptions) it materially differs. This, however, will be settled when the specimens I am sending home have been compared with European examples. For the moment I provisionally designate it as G. HIMALAYENSIS.*

2*nd*.—The large fulvous vulture of the *plains* which, though smaller, approaches *V. Monachus* or *G. Himalayensis* in size, and which I need scarcely therefore say, is *not* the true *G. Indicus* of Scop. and Lath. (*V. Tenuiceps et Tenuirostris*, Hodgson.) This is the bird which possibly Dr. Jerdon has measured as "*Gyps Indicus*, the long-billed brown Vulture," the measurements given by him for that bird, being much too large. The *true G. Indicus*, is a bird but little exceeding *G. Bengalensis* in size, though differing from it widely in structure. The large fulvous Vulture of the plains, (which I have shot all over the N. W. Provinces, Punjab and Rajpootana) is, as already remarked, decidedly a somewhat smaller bird than *G. Himalayensis*, and the plumage differs, *toto cœlo*, as I shall hereafter notice.

The bill of the plains bird is decidedly shorter and stouter than that of its Himalayan congener. As regards the claws, when I had only a few specimens of each before me, I thought that those of the plains bird were decidedly less curved ; but in these, as well as other species, the comparison of large series, shows that the variation, in the comparative thickness, bluntness, sharpness and curvature of the claws, in different examples of the same species, is too great to render any useful generalization in regard to them possible.

This plains bird more resembles the descriptions of the true *Fulvus*, than does *Himalayensis*, especially in the much greater quantity of down on the head, face and neck, but it almost entirely wants the white down ruff running round the back of the neck, the lanceolate fulvous feathers springing almost directly out of the bare back of the neck. This, however, may have little significance, because, figures are generally taken from individuals in confinement ; and birds of this family, well fed in confinement, on good food, notoriously throw out finer ruffs, and

* Colonel Tytler tells me that he has written and talked of this as "*Simlaensis*."

assume in many cases a finer plumage than those in a wild state. But altogether the bird strikes me as far more *rufous* and less stoutly built, than the true Griffon, and until, by the identification of the specimens which I send home, the matter can be settled, I provisionally designate our bird as G. FULVESCENS. This may be the bird (I have never seen the figure) figured by Temminck (Pl. Col. 26) as *G. Indicus;* but if so, the name having been, *previously*, I believe, appropriated to the species, which I shall next notice, *(Gyps Indicus, Scop.)* it cannot stand. Perhaps our Bird is identical with *G. Rueppelli* from Abyssinia, or *G. Vulgaris* of Savigny (if these be, as I believe, synonymous); or with *G. Kolbii*, which, however, both Mr. Gurney and Mr. Blyth, I believe, unite with true *Fulvus*; or it may be some other already known African species. In the absence of European and African specimens to compare it with, I am unable to decide, but so far as I can make out, it has not hitherto been discriminated *in India*, as a separate species, and therefore, for the moment, I designate it G. FULVESCENS.

3rd.—Gyps Indicus (Verus) Scop. The real slender-billed, or long-billed, brown Vulture, a bird with 14 rectrices it is true, like the preceding, but little larger than, and only about the same weight as *G. Bengalensis.* I cannot help thinking that Dr. Jerdon has described the immature bird of this species, as the young of Bengalensis. He says, p. 10, vol. I. "The young is lightish brown above, the feathers centred paler, quills, tail, and scapulars blackish brown, beneath light brown, the feathers *broadly centred with whitish.*" Now this is an exact description of the *immature* (I do not mean *quite* young, but not adult) *Gyps Indicus.* The young of Bengalensis, is really always a more or less *dark* brown above and below, and the feathers of the lower parts, are *narrowly*, and *never broadly centred with whitish.*

4th.—Gyps Bengalensis, of which no more need here be said.

I now proceed to furnish exact measurements and a detailed description of G. HIMALAYENSIS, which, if really distinct from *Fulvus*, well deserves the specific name I have proposed, I having observed it myself in, or received specimens of it from, all parts of the Himalayas, from Cabool to Bhootan.

Length, 46 to 49 inches. Expanse, 106 to 110 inches. Wing, 38 to 31. Tail, 15 to 17. Tarsus, 4·25 to 4·8. Mid toe, 4·3, its claw, along curve, 1·5 to 1·9. Inner toe, 2·4; its claw, 1·51 to 1·9. Hind toe, 1·75, its claw, 1·5 to 1·9. Bill, from gape, 3·1 to 3·44; straight, from edge of cere to point, 2·15 to 2·25; along curve, from edge of cere to point, 2·56 to 2·7; height at edge of cere, ·98 to 1·1; width at gape, 1·8 to 2. Length of cere, 1·13 to 1·2; Length of Gonys, 1·25. Weight, 18 to 20 lbs.

The legs and feet are a dingy greenish grey or white. The claws, pale brown. The bill very pale horny green; dusky just at tip. Cere, rather pale brown. Skin of cheeks and chin pale brownish grey, or dove colour, with a pure blue tinge round the lower half of the eye. The closed wings fall short of the end of the tail, by from 3·5 to 5 inches. The lower tail coverts fall short of ditto by about 2·8 to 4·0 inches.

The 4th primary is the longest. The first falls short of it by from 4 to 5 inches, and the 2nd by from 1 to 2 inches. The shortest tail feathers, (the external ones) fall short of the longest, (the central ones) by from 1·5 to 3 inches. The adult bird has the whole head, cheeks, chin and throat rather closely covered with yellowish white hair-like feathers. The nape, and upper two-thirds of the back, and sides, of the neck, are somewhat thickly covered with yellowish white down. The basal one-third of the back and sides of the neck were bare in all the specimens I have examined, and the front of the neck sparsely studded with star-like tufts of down. The large crop patch, some 8 inches long by 6 in breadth, is densely clothed with small close-sitting pale wood brown feathers. At the base of the back of the neck, rising in all the instances I have seen out of the bare skin, is a ruff of linear lanceolate feathers, about 3 inches in length with very loose, separated, filamentous webs, of dingy buffy white. Upper back, shorter scapulars and wing coverts, (except the larger row), a nearly unichromous pale brown, or whitey brown, many of the feathers inconspicuously paler centred. Mid back pure white, but some of the feathers with a fawn-coloured tinge. Rump and upper tail coverts, more or less fulvous, buffy, or fawny white, (the hue seems to vary in different individuals) some of the longer feathers, much tinged towards the tips, with brownish fawn colour. Longer scapulars and largest wing coverts, deep umber brown, tipped (in the scapulars broadly) with fulvous fawn, and more or less centred towards the tips with the same colour. Quills and tail feathers (the secondaries a shade less deep) deep umber brown; freshly moulted ones having a purplish gloss, and being perhaps best described as of a deep chocolate brown. The whole of the lower parts, including wing lining, and lower tail coverts, a *very* pale dingy brown, or fulvous white, some of the feathers especially on the sides, with ill-defined, moderately broad, somewhat paler centres, passing imperceptibly into the tint of the rest of the web.

The tarsus is clad in *front*, for nearly, or in some cases *fully*, the upper half, with slightly fulvous white down. The whole of the rest of the tarsus, and the back of the joint are quite bare.

In the distribution of the down on the neck, in the somewhat elongated bill, in the paler under-parts, with (in the adult) inconspicuous broad paler centerings to the feathers, and in the more pointed character of the feathers of the back, this species approaches the true *G. Indicus.* As compared with the next species, *(Fulvescens apud nos)* the somewhat greater size, the sparseness and star-like character of the down tufts about the throat and neck, the paler under surface devoid in the adult of conspicuous narrow pale centerings to the feathers, the looser ruff, longer upper tail coverts, more pointed back feathers, more powerful feet, with more prominent scutæ and reticulations, serve amongst other differences to distinguish it.

The young bird differs much in its plumage from the adult. Seen flying at a little distance, it appears of a pale bronze colour, and on the wing, might possibly be mistaken for the young of *Monachus.* When in the hand, however, there is no mistaking it. In the arrangement of down about the neck and throat, in the colour of the bill, bare skin and feet, and quill and tail feathers, it exactly resembles the adult, but the prevailing hue of all the rest of the plumage is a rich brown, very deep above, somewhat paler below ; *every* feather, except the greater wing-coverts and larger scapulars, with a broad, central, yellowish brown or fulvous stripe. As in the adult, there is a pure white patch on the upper back extending to the sides of the middle back, but this is usually hidden by the scapulars. The crop patch is a warm brown, much deeper and darker than in the adult. The down-patch on either side of the crop-patch, and the downy covering of the upper half of the tarsus, and the tibia, pure white. The striped appearance above described, extends to the wing-lining, and ruff of *linear* lanceolate feathers, at the base of the neck behind.

The later secondaries are at all ages very long, and the wings very broad. When the wings are closed in the fresh bird, the longest primaries are surpassed by the longest secondaries.

As far as my experience goes, the feet are always dingy pearly white or dingy greenish white, in this particular, although in none other, approximating to *V. Monachus*, and differing, apparently, from the *G. Fulvus* of Europe, the legs and feet of which are given by Yarrell as lead-coloured.

Whether our Himalayan bird be really identical with the *G. Fulvus* of Europe, Africa and Palestine or not, some notes on the nidification of this latter, which is at any rate a very nearly allied species, will be interesting. Mr. O. Salvin in his 5 months' bird-nesting in the eastern Atlas, has the following remarks on the Griffon Vulture.

"In one instance only did we find an egg and a young one in the same nest; in all other cases, one egg, or one young one, was the invariable number. The eggs appear to be laid in the month of February, as most of the nests contained young in the beginning of April. During the time of incubation, one of the parent birds sits constantly, and if frightened off, returns immediately. The nest is composed almost entirely of sticks, which are used in greater or less abundance, as the situation requires. The eggs obtained from wild birds, generally show indications of natural colouring, in addition to the blood and dirt with which they are usually stained. This colouring is dispersed in faint spots of a reddish hue sometimes all over the egg, but generally at the larger or smaller end. Of the four eggs in my collection, three exhibit traces of this marking. The eggs usually placed in collections are laid by birds kept in confinement, and this colouring is not observable."

The Rev. H. B. Tristram tells us that "The numbers of the Griffon Vultures in every part of Palestine are amazing; they are found at all seasons of the year. I do not think that I ever surveyed a landscape without its being enlivened by the circling of a party of Griffons. Many colonies of eyries came under our observation in the gorge of the wady Kelt, (the supposed Cherith) near Jericho; in the cliffs near Heshbon, under Mount Nebo, in the ravine of the Jabbok, in a gorge near Ammam, the ancient Rabbah; two large colonies inhabit wadys on the north and east sides of Mount Carmel, whence we procured several eggs, but the most populous of all, were the 'Griffouries' in the stupendous cliffs of the wady Hamam, 'the Robber's Caves' to the south-west and in the deep glen of the wady Leimem at the north-west of the plain of Gennesaret. We collected about twenty eggs. In no nest did we ever find more than a single egg, or young bird."

Mr. Tristram further points out the interesting fact, that the Hebrew word "nesher" rendered in our version of the Scriptures "eagles," really, like the Arabic "nissr," refers to the Griffon Vulture, "the most majestic of birds" he remarks "in action and appearance, and the type of the Assyrian deity Nisroch. The expression "who enlargeth thy baldness as an eagle's" *(nesher)* evidently applies only to the Griffon."

No. 3 *(bis)*. **Gyps Fulvescens,** (Sp. Nov.)

The Bay Vulture.

This bird, of which a description and measurements will be found below, breeds, as far as I yet know, in February, and the first half of March. Its nest, a huge platform of sticks, was placed, in the only 3 instances which I know of, near the top of very large Peepul (*Ficus Religiosa*) trees. Both nests, that I found, were solitary, as was that found by Mr. C. H. T. Marshall. The nests are between 2·5, and 3 feet in diameter, some 6 to 10 inches in depth, constructed of sticks and twigs, and without any lining. The nests, that I found on the 12th and 21st of March, contained a single young bird each. It is to Mr. C. Marshall that I owe the only egg I possess. He says "the nest was found on the 14th of March on the top of a large Peepul tree, (some 40 feet from the ground), in the Shahbaloul gardens near Lahore. It contained a single egg nearly ready to hatch off, the bill of the young one being actually protruding."

The egg is a very perfect oval, a good deal larger than that of *Calvus* or *Bengalensis*, and the texture appears to be finer than that of the eggs of any of our other Indian Vultures. No positive conclusion, however, can be arrived at from the examination of a single egg.

The egg is of the usual Vulturine type, pale bluish white, but with a faint gloss; it is altogether unspotted, but was extensively soiled and discoloured from the droppings of the parent bird. It measures 3·5 × 2·8. I have found this bird very common throughout the Punjaub, northern Rajpootana and the North-Western Provinces, north and west of Etawah, and Colonel Tytler has a young bird from Oraiee. I will now give exact measurements, and descriptions, taken from freshly killed specimens.

Length, 41 to 47 inches. Expanse, 94 to 106 inches. Wing, 27 to 29·5; the 3rd is the longest primary; the 1st is from 2 to 4 inches shorter, and the 2nd from 0·3 to 0·85. Tail, of 14 feathers, 12 to 13·5 inches. Tarsus, 3·88 to 4·2. Foot, mid toe, 3·75 to 4·5, its claw along curve, 1·3 to 1·8; inner toe, 1·8 to 2, its claw, 1·6 to 1·9; hind toe, 1·4 to 1·65, its claw, 1·55 to 1·8. Bill from gape, 3 to 3·2; length of cere, 1·03 to 1·13; straight, from edge of cere to point, 1·9 to 2; along curve, from edge of cere to point, 2·15 to 2·4; height at edge of cere, 1· to 1·1; length of gonys, 1·13. Weight, 12 to 18 lbs.

The top of the head, cheeks, chin and throat, are covered with dingy, yellowish white, hair-like feathers, so closely set upon the top of the head, chin and throat, and with such an admixture of down, that the dark skin, which in the hill bird (*G. Himalayensis*) shows so plainly through the scant covering, is, in this species, completely hidden. The nape and the whole of the neck, (except the back and side of the basal one fifth or less, which are bare or nearly bare,) are closely covered with dense, short, fur-like white, or dingy yellowish white, down. The crop patch is about the same colour as in the hill bird, (vide supra) but somewhat more rufous, and the whole of the rest of the plumage is a far more rufous, and deeper fawn or buffy brown than in *G. Himalayensis.* The lower plumage is in the adult of a rich rufous brown, bay, or even dull chesnut, conspicuously white shafted, whilst the mantle is a warm sandy brown, unlike the colouring of any of our other Indian Vultures. The feathers of the ruff are almost linear, (the web not so much separated as in the hill bird,) usually of a warm wood brown or rufous fawn, the feathers conspicuously paler centered. In one specimen, the old female shot by Mr. Marshall on the nest from which he took the egg, the ruff feathers differ in being of a uniform dingy white, faintly tinged with rufous. The upper back, the whole of the upper wing coverts, and all but the longest scapulars are a warm, wood brown, or brownish rufous fawn, yellower and sandier in some, deeper and more of a bay colour in others. The secondaries, tertials and longer scapulars umber- (but *not* dark umber-) brown, the latter (*viz.* the longer scapulars) more or less tipped with the rufous or sandy colour of the upper back, which colour, in some specimens, more or less extends to the tips and outer webs of the tertiaries. Lower back, rump and upper tail coverts, the same colour as the upper back, but of a considerably lighter tint, in some mingled with brown, and in some altogether of a pure pale bay. The primaries and tail feathers are very dark brown, in some not so dark as the corresponding feathers in *G. Himalayensis,* but in others of an intense chocolate brown. Lower parts a rich sandy or rufous fawn or even a deep bay, (the tint varies in different stages of plumage) each feather conspicuously paler shafted, and most of them (in the younger birds) conspicuously, though narrowly paler centred. The lineated appearance of the lower parts alone, at once distinguishes this species from the preceding one.

The feathering of the tarsus is similar to that of *G. Himalayensis.* This species, and not his *Fulvus,* (our *Himalayensis,*) as Dr. Jerdon surmises, is doubtless the one to which Adams refers, under the name of *G. Indicus,* and though his dimensions slightly exceed those of any specimens I have measured,* the differences are too small to be of much consequence.

From the true *G. Indicus*, this species differs (amongst other things) 1st in its much greater size, often weighing fully half as much again; 2nd, in the bright rufous tinge of the lower parts, and the conspicuous narrow pale centerings of the feathers there; 3rd, in the far more rufous tint of the mantle; 4th, in the thick whitish down covering of the nape and whole upper part of the neck, back and front, and the *comparatively* greater abundance of down on the rest of neck. Altogether, the bird is infinitely more massive than *Indicus*, but the feet and claws are most conspicuously so, the latter being like those of some giant, *G. Bengalensis*, immeasurably blunter and *stumpier*, (if I may use such a word,) than those of *Indicus*. In several particulars, the distribution of down on the neck, the lineation of the lower plumage, and the greater stoutness and lesser elongation of bill, our *G. Fulvescens* approximates to *G. Bengalensis*, while, as already noticed, the hill bird and the true *Indicus* are in similar matters more nearly allied.

The younger birds are sandier and paler than above described, but the older they grow, the more richly rufous they become. With noble series' of each of our four species of *Gyps* before me, the marked distinctness of this, in India at any rate, hitherto undescribed species, is very striking, the general colour of some of the older birds being precisely that of the back and train of *Buphus Coromandus* in breeding plumage.

In its habits and mode of feeding, it differs in no way from *Gyps Indicus* and *Bengalensis*, with both of which, as well as with *V. Monachus*, it closely associates. As far as I can yet judge, it is essentially the Vulture of the desert. In richly cultivated tracts, far from any sandy wastes it is rare, but in the barer portions of the North Western Provinces and the Punjaub, it is common, and in and on the borders of Bhawulpoor, Bikaneer, Jodhpoor and Northern Jaipoor, it abounds.

No. 4. **Gyps Indicus,** (Scop.)

The long billed Vulture.

This bird breeds in the latter part of December, January, and possibly the early part of February; by the end of March every egg has been hatched off. It always selects, as far as

* Mr. Marshall I should note, gives the length of the old female shot on the nest as 51 inches, and the weight 19·5 lbs. I have never met with any specimen so heavy or large as this; but he may be right.

my experience goes, nearly inaccessible and precipitous cliffs to breed on, but as I have only yet found it breeding in two places, *viz.* at the Taragurh hill near Ajmere, and the Gaimookh cliffs on Mt. Aboo, I cannot speak positively. Jerdon, however, mentions, that the present species breeds on "some of the cliffs bounding the valley, in which are situated the celebrated caves of Ajunta."

The nest, placed on some ledge of the cliff's face, consists only of coarse sticks and twigs. When the eggs are first laid, there may be some lining of leaves, as in those of many other kinds of vultures and eagles, but when I examined a number of the nests, the young were all hatched, and the nest so coated with their droppings, that it was impossible to trace any lining. The nest is nothing more than a thin, flat, irregularly circular, pad of sticks, from 2 to 3 feet in diameter, and from 3 to 6 inches in depth. As a rule they only lay a single egg; of all the 50 odd to which, with extreme difficulty, I made my way, not one contained more than a single young one, and not one could boast even a single addled egg. Captain Repton, Deputy Commissioner of Ajmere, very kindly secured for me a noble series of eggs from these very nests, ten months after I had visited them. The eggs' normal type is a very long oval. Taken as a body, they are very much larger than those of *Calvus* or *Bengalensis*, and their texture is, if anything, somewhat finer than that of either of these two species; as a rule, they are of an unspotted, very pale greyish or greenish white, but some are thinly spotted and blotched with pale reddish brown, or in some cases faint purplish brown. One only that I possess is *richly* blotched and mottled, chiefly, however, towards the smaller end, with somewhat pale brownish and purplish red, about equally intermingled; this is the handsomest Vulture's egg, I have yet seen. They vary in length from 3·9 to 3·48, and in breadth from 2·85 to 2·62, the average dimensions of 21 eggs were 3·61 × 2·72.

The breeding places of this species, (they appear always to breed in society,) are very picturesquely situated. The Taragurh hill which overlooks and almost overhangs the city of Ajmere and the beautiful Ana Sagur Lake, may be about 2,900 feet high. On precipitous faces of this hill, specially where succeeding overlapping ledges make the place as nearly inaccessible as may be, colonies of this Vulture breed. One of these breeding-haunts, which I minutely examined, was a cliff face some 100 feet high by 300 wide, all broken up into irregular ledges, of which the highest overhung all the rest. In amongst the ledges were a few dwarf banyan trees, whose long bare roots and rootlets hung down, here and there, in dense, grey, giant skeins; all the ledges, but the uppermost, when looked at from below, seemed garnished with heavy white fringes, the white droppings of the birds having run down in close parallel lines in a wonderfully symmetrical fashion, over the weather smoothed edges of the terraces. Seen from a distance, the whole cliff face seemed mottled with huge patches of white-wash. Bleached bones, and dusky quills strewed every little plateau, and nestled in every cranny. It was on the 30th of March, 1867 that I laid siege to this natural fortress. With the assistance of two sporting Mahomedan faqeers, two of the best cragsmen I ever saw, having duly removed my boots, I crept to the lowest ledge, a work of extreme difficulty, owing to the excessive slipperiness of the white crusted rocks. To my intense disgust, a little apart from the nest, on the bare stone, sat a huge unwieldy mass of yellow fluffy down, opening a vast mouth and cackling and hissing at me in the most hostile manner. The unfortunate little wretch was too fat and heavy to stand firmly on its stumpy legs, and could only stand up for a second, stagger a few inches, and then plump down exhausted. It was really touching to see how every moment in the midst of its vain efforts to intimidate us, the little fellow kept looking anxiously around and above for its parents. But it was about 10 A. M. and all the old ones were away procuring food, and during the two hours we remained about the rocks, only one of them at all closely approached the place, although before we left, the whole community, I should say nearly 60 in number, had collected in the valley, (in one side of which the cliff was situated) and kept wheeling and circling round above their homes, but at a distance of fully a quarter of a mile. We left the dingy little tenant of the first nest in peace, doubtless congratulating himself on the fact that his valorous demonstrations had driven us away, and slowly and painfully made our way, (at what risk I hardly care to think of now) to one after another of the nest-filled ledges. Every where we found the nests empty, but in the case of about half the number, a more or less advanced young one of from a week to a month old, was squatting on the bare rock a few feet from the nest. Those nests near which no young one was seen, had obviously not been tenanted. At the time I fancied that these belonged to birds that had not yet laid, but I had the place closely watched for nearly a month without any one of them being used, so that I presume that the birds often find their first nest unsuitable in some way, and construct a second, in which to incubate their egg. It could not be, that any considerable number of the pairs were barren, for we saw quite as many young ones as pairs of old birds, and by the time we left, (nearly 1 P. M.) I feel confident that the whole colony must have assembled.

Other smaller colonies were subsequently visited, but not one single egg rewarded our perseverance. The Faqeers assured me, that the young birds were from 2 to 3 months before they were able to leave the nest.

The following are the dimensions of this species. Length, 37 to 40.—Expanse, 88 to 92. Wing, 23·5 to 22·5; the 3rd and 4th, or 4th primaries are the longest; the 1st is from 2·5 to 2·35 shorter, and the 2nd 0·5 to 1 shorter. Tail, of 14 feathers, from 10 to 11; the longest tail feathers exceeding the shortest, by from 0·5 to 2. Tarsus, from 3·5 to 4. Foot, greatest length, 7·75 to 8·5; greatest width, 6·5 to 7; mid toe, 3·75 to 4·2, its claw, along curve, 1·15 to 1·45; hind toe, 1·25 to 1·6, its claw, along curve, 1·25 to 1·75; inner toe, 1·55 to 1·9, its claw, along curve, 1·25 to 1·75. Bill, straight, from edge of cere to point, 1·68 to 1·8; along curve, 2 to 2·25; from gape, 2·6 to 2·85; width at gape, 1·12 to 1·32; height at margin of cere, 0·8 to 0·92; length of cere, 0·9 to 1·12.

Lower tail coverts reach to within 3 of end of tail. The legs and feet are dusky cinereous. The irides are brown. The weight varies from 11 to 14 lbs.

In the perfect adult, brownish white hair-like feathers are thinly sprinkled over the head, nape, cheeks, and throat. The upper half of the back and sides of the neck, and whole of the front of the neck are excessively thinly studded with small star-like tufts of down. The lower half of the back, and sides, of the neck are perfectly bare. The crop patch is closely covered with silky, tight fitting, dark hair brown feathers. The whole of the rest of the lower surface is a pale whity brown, becoming almost a pure white towards the vent and lower tail coverts. The ruff is full, soft and pure white, of very downy feathers, the webs much disintegrated. The whole mantle is pale earthy brown, the centres of the lesser, and all but the tips and margins of the larger scapulars, being dark, hair brown.

The lower back, rump and upper tail coverts white, tinged with pale earthy brown, many of the feathers, however, especially of the longer tail coverts, being brown at the base, but so broadly tipped and margined with the paler colour, that little of the brown shows. The primaries and tail feathers are deep chocolate brown. The secondaries and tertiaries hair brown, more or less suffused, on their outer webs, with pale, dingy earthy or fulvous brown.

A quite young bird has the top and back of the head, and upper part of the back of the neck, thickly covered with white down. The rest of the head and neck, as in the adult. The crop patch much lighter than in the adult, is covered with pale, dove-coloured, brown feathers. The rest of the lower surface is pale brown, becoming albescent towards the vent, each feather broadly centered, (most conspicuously so, on the sides and breast), with dingy white. The ruff, of long linear lanceolate feathers, is a very pale fulvous white, faintly margined with brown. The mantle, a somewhat pale hair brown, every feather, *narrowly* but *conspicuously*, centred with fulvous white. The quill feathers and tail feathers chocolate brown, darkest on the primaries and rectrices. The lower back, rump, and upper tail coverts, are nearly pure white, only a few of the longest of the latter, being tinged with brown.

In an intermediate stage, the crop patch is intermediate in colour, between that of the adult and of the young, as is also the colour and character of the ruff, and indeed of the whole plumage.

This bird differs at all ages from *Bengalensis*, not only in having 14 instead of 12 rectrices, and in the greater length and slenderness* of the bill, especially the ceral portion, but in many other points. In colour the adults of course differ as black from white, but even the youngest *Bengalensis* is every where of a darker and dingier hue, than the young even, of *Indicus*. Then the appearance of the plumage of the back differs in the two species. In *Bengalensis* the feathers are more broad and rounded, and have a more of a squamated appearance, whilst those of *Indicus* are more pointed and narrower. Again, the true *Indicus* differs from the young of *Bengalensis* in the pale rump, (that of the latter being dark although in the adult it is white,) in the comparative absence of pale centerings to the feathers of the under-parts, and in such pale centerings being in *Indicus* very *broad* and *inconspicuous*, while in *Bengalensis* they are *narrow, almost linear* and *very conspicuous*. Further, there is a quantity of nearly pure white down on the nape

* I contrast the dimensions of 3 average specimens, but in these birds, dimensions vary much in different individuals :

	Gyps Indicus.	*G. Bengalensis Y.*	*G. Bengalensis adult.*
Bill, from gape, ...	2·94	2·63	2·69
Length of cere, ...	·94	·73	·81
Length, straight, from edge of cere to point, ...	1·88	1·78	1·81
Height, at margin of cere, ...	·88	·94	·97
Length of gonys, ...	1·01	·94	·97

and upper neck of all but the quite adult *Indicus*, while that on the neck of the young *Bengalensis* is darkish brown. The basal half of the back of the neck of *Indicus* is quite bare; in the young *Bengalensis*, it is more or less covered with down; lastly the sides and front of the neck in *Indicus*, are sparsely dotted with star-like tufts of white down, (herein much resembling *G. Himalayensis*,) while these parts in the young of *Bengalensis* are somewhat thickly sprinkled with double *hair-like* feathers, such as in *Indicus* occur only on the chin, throat, face and head. The colour of the claws and cere is also much paler in *Indicus* than in the young of *Bengalensis*.

The close similarity of the plumage of the young of *Himalayensis* and *Indicus*, is another indication of the close relationship that these two species bear to each other. Both moreover breed in rocks, (and not on trees as *Fulvescens* and *Bengalensis* do). The plumage of the adults moreover is nearly as similar as that of the young, and the character, extent and distribution of the down, on the head and neck, in both, is identical.

No. 5. **Gyps Bengalensis**, (Gmel.)

The Indian white-backed Vulture

Breeds from the latter end of November, to the early part of March, but the majority I think lay during the month of January. The nest, as far as my personal experience goes (and I have seen many hundreds), is always placed upon trees, even where convenient cliffs and precipices are close at hand. Banyan and Peepul are their favourite trees, I think, but I have found them breeding on the Neem, Tamarind, Arjun *(Terminalia Arjúna)* and others; in every case, however, on *large* trees. As a rule they prefer to nest near each other, in the outskirts of some populous town, like Binderabund for instance, where ancient groves with suitable trees abound, and I have seen as many as fifteen nests on one single Peepul tree, and as many as a hundred on a group of trees lying within a circle of two or three hundred yards in diameter. It is not, however, uncommon to find a solitary nest, high up on some huge Peepul tree, standing isolated in the midst of cultivated land or scanty jungle; but I have an idea that these are always the nests of young birds, and that while the clustered nests are tenanted by the same species year after year (in one case that I know of, for certainly the last fifty years), these solitary nests are rarely if ever re-occupied by this Vulture, who, after the first year, abandons them to other tenants. On two occasions, I have found nests of this bird that I had robbed one year, occupied the next by the Grey eagle owl, *(Ascalaphia Coromanda)*, and once I found a lordly king Vulture in possession of its plebeian brother's former residence.

The nest is a large irregular platform of sticks, sometimes quite at the top of the tree, often wedged in a fork, averaging probably nearly 3 feet in diameter and 6 inches in thickness, but often far exceeding this latter dimension, especially where a deep fork has to be filled in. Not far from Puhpoondh, I made a man measure one in my presence, which was an irregular cone, (the apex downwards) by pushing an iron ramrod through it, and found the depth to be 22 inches! The materials of the nest appear to be heaped on at random, but in reality they are so carefully overlaid, that it is very difficult to pull out one of the sticks that compose the nest, without pulling the whole fabric to pieces. The shape of the nest depends upon the locality, and is more generally oblong or oval, than truly circular. There is only a slight depression, as a rule, towards the centre of the nest, but I found one nest near Hodul which was a regular deep cup, in which I really think a moderate-sized sheep might have been stowed away. They always line the centre of the nest more or less with leaves, and the peepul seems their favourite. These leaves are green and fresh when the egg is first laid, and before you blow it, you can pretty well guess how long the egg has lain in the nest, by the condition of the lining leaves.

They lay normally a single egg. That 2 eggs *may* have been found in one nest I will not take upon myself to deny, but I have before me now, notes of eighty odd nests, and besides these, I have had many others examined of which I took no note at the time, and yet I never met with more than a single egg or a single young one *in any* nest. In colour, the eggs when fresh are dull white, with an excessively pale bluish green tinge. As a rule they are unmarked, but at times they are a good deal tinged and speckled, or even blotched, with darker or lighter shades of reddish brown, most usually I think chiefly towards the large end. The eggs of this species vary to an amazing extent; whether in reality these eggs vary more than those of the other Vultures, or whether it is, that the enormous series of over a a hundred eggs, which I have myself collected, makes the variations more conspicuous, I cannot say, but the fact remains that I have the eggs, of my own taking, of almost (for such a bird) every conceivable size and shape. The cubic contents of one egg (the largest) is certainly 2½ times that of the smallest. One is a perfect pear, another so long an oval, as to be almost cylindrical, and one or two are almost spherical; the normal type, however, appears to be a somewhat broad oval, slightly compressed or pointed towards one end. As a body, they are more oval and less round than those of *Calvus*, while they are rounder and less oval than those of *Indicus*. As above remarked, the majority, though often much soiled and discoloured, as incubation proceeds,are of the usual pale greyish or greenish white colour, and unspotted; but a certain number, perhaps about 1 in 5, are more or less speckled, spotted and blotched, always chiefly towards one end, with pale reddish brown. One egg only, out of more than a hundred that I have, is richly and extensively blotched and clouded, in fact almost capped at the large end with reddish and purplish brown. So discoloured do the eggs sometimes become before they are hatched, that I have one egg, an addled one, stained throughout an almost uniform earth-brown. The texture varies a good deal, but is generally moderately fine, a few exhibit a slight gloss, but mostly they are glossless.

The shell is very thick and strong, and, like that of most other large bird's eggs, (especially those of Cranes and game birds) often has pimply lumps and crease-like folds at the small end. The lining is a rich green. The eggs measure from 3·05 to 3·85 inches in length, and from 2·25 to 2·8 in breadth, but of 68 eggs measured, 3·26 by 2·42 inches are the average dimensions.

Though the birds are plentiful all over the N. W. P. Rajpootana, and the major portion of the Punjab, they only affect particular localities for breeding. Where large trees abound, and where either cattle are numerous, or a large village ensures a continual supply of offal, their nests will generally be found, but in treeless tracts, like much of the upper Punjab, where cattle are few, and population scant, although the birds (whose powers of flight are, like those of all their kindred, very great), may themselves often be seen, you may search many hundred square miles without meeting with a single nest.

Mr. W. Theobald makes the following note of this bird's breeding in the neighbourhood of Pind Dadan Khan and Katas in the Salt Range. "Lay in the 1st and 2nd weeks of March, eggs, one only, shape, ovate pyriform, size, 3·36 inches by 2·62 inches; colour, dull white. Nest, of sticks and twigs; in large trees."

I give exact measurements taken from several birds and description of a fine male, which I shot on a nest on the 8th March, thus proving that the males participate in the labour of incubation. The female in this case did not return for some hours and when she did, she was apparently so enraged, at finding her egg (which was much incubated) gone, and her husband missing, that she tore the upper part of the nest to pieces, scattering the sticks and leaf lining, here and there, and making a wonderful snorting and hissing all the while. This is not the only instance I have witnessed, of birds tearing their own nests to pieces, in anger at the loss of their eggs, (vide *Grus Antigone*, No. 833, and for a somewhat similar incident, Falco Jugger, No. 11.)

Length, 33 to 37 inches. Expanse 83 to 88. Wing, 22 to 24; the 3rd primary the longest, the 1st about 2·5 inches, the 2nd about 0·5, and the 4th about 0·13 shorter than the 3rd. Tail of 12 feathers; length from vent, 9 to 11; Tarsus, (in some feathered in front for about half its length, in some for less than ⅕th), 3·5 to nearly 4 inches. Foot, greatest length, 7·5 to 8·5; greatest width, 5 to 5·5; mid toe, 3·6 to 4·2; its claw, straight, 1 to 1·09, along the curve, 1·13 to 1·31; inner toe, 1·69 to 1·9; its claw, straight 1·13, along the curve, 1·44; outer-toe, 1·88, its claw, straight 0·81, along the curve, 1·06; hind toe, 1·38 to 1·7, its claw, straight 1·09 along the curve, 1·3 to 1·5. Bill, straight, from edge of cere to point, 1·8 to 1·9; along curve, 2·19 to 2·31; from gape, 2·65 to 2·9; width at gape, 1·44; height, at margin of cere, 0·87 to 0·97; length of cere, 0·75 to 0·81; gonys, 0·97. Weight 9 to 13 lbs. Wings, when closed, reach just to the end of the tail, and the lower tail-coverts reach to within from 1·5 to 2·25 of end of ditto.

The legs and feet are nearly black, but in the live bird are always more or less incrusted with dirt, so as to appear of a dry mud colour, except where on the smooth surfaces of the scales, the horny black shows through. Claws, massive and very blunt, that of mid toe *little*, of hind toe *well* curved, in colour blackish horny. Scutellation, reticulate except on ridges of toes, that of mid toe nearly all, and of other toes the terminal half or more, with transverse scales, larger and more strongy marked as they approach the claws. The lateral toes are nearly equal, the outer being only a little longer, and both are conspicuously short as compared with the central one, outer toe claw as usual very feeble. Irides, brown, eyelids, very pale plumbeous or greyish white, each with a row of short black lashes. Bill, with a trace of two festoons in edge of upper mandible; cere, short and prominent, horny black, hard, and polished like the bill itself. Greater part of upper mandible, greyish white, with bluish grey tips, and edges dusky. Lower mandible, dingy plumbeous at base, dusky at tip.

The whole head, face, chin, throat and front and sides of the upper two-thirds of the neck, dusky plumbeous with sparse inconspicuous, brownish hairs, which, however, are longer, denser and more conspicuous on the occiput. The upper half of the back of the neck densely clad with soft, velvetty, white feathers. Below this, a prominent white ruff on the back of the neck, extending rather further forward towards the front of the neck than the above mentioned white, velvetty feathers do. The base of the neck, where it joins the back, shoulders, scapulars, tail and upper tail coverts, primaries, and wing coverts, a dull blackish brown. The secondaries, and tertiaries, paler and much tinged, especially on the outer webs, with brownish grey, a trace of which is also visible on the later primaries. The 2nd to the 7th primary, emarginate on the outer web, and the 1st to the 6th, conspicuously notched on the inner web. The rump, and lower back, pure white. The centre of the upper breast, and the lower part of the front of the neck, in fact what is commonly known in vultures as the crop patch, clad with very close, blackish brown, furlike feathers, with a white border of long down on either side, which extends into a sort of triangular patch at each side, at the base of the neck, nearly in the centre of which is a small, round, and quite bare spot, of a dull pinkish hue; sides, lower breast, and abdomen, and longer axillaries, dark brown, or blackish brown, each feather with a linear or narrow central white stripe, most conspicuous towards the tips. The shorter axillaries, and a patch in the axilla, pure white; edge of the wing, and all the smallest of the lower wing coverts blackish brown; the rest of the wing lining, pure white. Thigh coverts and lower tail coverts, very dark brown; feathers of interior of thigh, pure white. In a younger bird, the corneous portion of the bill was horny black, paler on the culmen, and towards the edge of the cere. The lores and cheeks were bluish, a patch over the eye, the chin and skin on sides of lower mandible, a sad dove colour, or plumbeous brown. The rest of the bare skin, dingy greenish white, here and there spotted with leaden brown.

The Ibis (1865) notices a paper of Dr. Salvadori, the object of which was to prove the specific distinctness of the white backed Vultures of India and Africa. "The chief differences are thus summarised."

Gyps Bengalensis. (ex Asia).	*Gyps, sp.* (ex Africa)
Beak, thick, yellowish, at the thickest part, at the tip.	Beak, compressed, elongated, quite black.
General colour, black cinereous.	General colour, greyish cream.

The name *Gyps Africanus*, is accordingly bestowed upon the latter by the author, but it appears probable that this application must give way to that of *Moschatus*, which, according to Von Heuglin (Sitzungsb. A Kad Wien, 1856, p. 256) had been previously bestowed upon it by Duke Paul of Wurtemberg." It appears to me that the so-called *G. Africanus* must closely resemble, if it be not identical with, our *G. Indicus*.

Dr. Jerdon informs me, that he noticed our bird pairing, in December in the Bijnour district. These birds, he tells me, *pair* on trees and utter a hoarse roar at the time, which, had he not himself watched them, he could never have believed to have been uttered by a bird; a sound of great volume and sui generis.

There is one point about *all these* vultures in regard to which I should be glad of information, as although I have closely examined some hundreds of birds, I have not yet been able to satisfy myself thoroughly on the subject. Some specimens of vultures have ruffs of *long*, very narrow, pointed *feathers* springing out of the base of the back of the neck, others of the same species, have ruffs of comparatively short thick *down*, without a trace of a single long pointed feather. I used to think, that these latter were signs of nonage, but I have seen quite young birds, on two occasions, with full down ruffs, and I have several birds manifestly adults, with the long pointed ruff feathers. I cannot make out that it depends on sex, nor that the change is seasonal; but doubtless the real explanation is well known to naturalists, although I have failed to find any mention of it.

No. 6. **Neophron Ginginianus,** (Lath.)

The white Scavenger Vulture,

Breeds from the latter end of February to the end of April, but the majority I think lay towards the end of March. They nest indifferently, it appears to me, on rocky precipices, earthen cliffs, parapets or cornices of buildings and large trees. I have often found the nests in ledges of the clay cliffs of the Jumna, close to nests containing the young of Bonelli's eagle, or the Jugger Falcon. At Etawah, a pair yearly build on the church tower, at the base of the steeple. On the rocky headland known as the *Mata Pahar*, which juts out from the southern shore of the Sambhur lake, whose blue waters it overlooks, I found a nest in a cleft of the rock from which I was able to take the eggs, without leaving the pathway, and within two feet of the head of the sitting bird, was a nest containing 3 eggs of *Ptionoprogne Concolor*. They are far from seeking retirement. They build commonly in trees in the suburbs of towns. Neem, Tamarind, Peepul and Burgut, alike furnishing them with homesteads, and for several years I have noticed a pair building, on a comparatively small tree, in the centre of the busy grain market at Etawah.

The nests are clumsy, ragged, stick structures; platforms slightly depressed towards the centre, loosely put together and lined with any soft substance they can most readily meet with. Old rags are a great stand by. In many parts of the country, way-farers as they pass particular trees, have a semi-religious custom of tearing a strip off their clothes to hang thereon. Who puts the first strip, and why they do it, I have never clearly been able to ascertain, but, once a beginning is made, "one fool makes many" and the tree (usually a *Babool*) soon becomes loaded with rags and tatters. These are a perfect god-send to the Neophrons of the neighbourhood, whom I have more than once watched robbing these rural "shrines" of their trophies by the score. Sometimes the rags of various colours are laid out neatly in the nest, as if an attempt had been made to please the eye, sometimes they are irregularly jumbled up with the materials of the nest. Cotton wool, old and dirty, stolen I suspect from the old "rizais" or padded coverlids, thrown with half burnt dead bodies into the river, occurs occasionally in great lumps in the nest; and I have several times found nests lined entirely with masses of human hair, which in a country where near relatives shave their heads as a part of the funeral ceremonies, often lies thick in the environs of villages and towns. Sometimes the birds line their nests with green leaves, much as *Eutolmaetus Bonelli* and many other eagles do. In size, the nests vary from 2 to 3 feet in diameter, and from 4 to 10 inches in depth. Normally they lay 2 eggs, but I have repeatedly found birds incubating a single egg, twice I have found 3 eggs in the same nest, but, in each of these latter cases, one of the 3 eggs was much smaller and feebler coloured than the other two.

In shape, size, and colour these eggs vary much. I have one egg an excessively long pear, another for all the world like a goose's egg, while others again are as round as an egg of the Honey Buzzard's, but the normal shape is certainly a rather broad oval, somewhat compressed towards one end. The texture varies a good deal, in some it is coarser than that of any Vulture's egg, and in some there is almost a gloss, but as a rule the eggs are dull, and of a rather coarse somewhat chalky texture, less compact and indurated than in any of the true vultures. They never have any *real* gloss, but some exhibit a sort of surface glaze which they lose by washing; as indeed they are apt to do much of their richest colouring. I have seen a very handsome, richly coloured, boldly marked, egg, reduced, by the misguided energy of a fair advocate for soap water, and a nail brush, to a uniform, dull dirty brown.

It cannot be too strongly impressed upon egg-collectors that, with the exception of pure white ones, no egg should ever be washed externally, if it can possibly be avoided. Water removes the colour in many eggs, deadens it in most, and in all renders it more liable to fade.

In colour, the eggs of the present species vary from pure greyish or rufous white, with only a few minute reddish brown specks at one end, to a uniform deep but dingy blood-red, recalling some of the deeper coloured falcon eggs. Between these two extremes, every variation in shade, extent and intensity of markings is found. Every possible shade of brownish red and reddish brown is met with, and every degree of markings from a few distinct scattered *specks*, to streaks and blotches nearly confluent over the greater portion of the egg's surface or forming a conspicuous cap at one (more commonly the larger) extremity.

There is a common type with a pinkish white ground, minutely freckled and speckled all over with dull brownish red, and then richly blotched and clouded towards one end, (at which the markings are often almost or quite confluent,) with a deep brownish red. Other eggs are uniform pale brownish pink, almost salmon colour, without any deeper coloured markings, while others of the same type have the colour deepening towards one end, or are richly and boldly, or in others feebly and faintly blotched, streaked or clouded with a deeper shade. Some eggs when fresh are excessively handsome and are coloured quite like a honey Buzzard's egg: one I have which might pass, so far as colouring goes, for the Osprey's egg figured by Hewitson, Pl. VI. 1.

They measure from 2·28 to 2·82 in length and from 1·8 to 2·1 in breadth, but the average of 45 eggs measured was 2·6 × 1·98.

I have seen this species fully 8,500 feet high in the Himalayahs. Mr. R. Thompson says: "The Neophrons are to be found breeding in numbers along the precipices which crown the river Kosilla from Khyrna upwards. On the sandstone precipices of the Sewaliks, and those of the Kamaon and Ghurwal outer ranges, numberless nests may be found. One pair breeds yearly on a precipice south-east of Nynee Tal."

Mr. W. Theobald makes the following note of this bird's breeding in the neighbourhood of Pind Dadan Khan and Katas in the Salt Range. "Lay in the 3rd week of March, eggs two only, shape long oval, size 2·53 to 2·75 inches in length and from 1·84 to 1·90 in breadth. Colour, pale brownish red, thickly blotched with dark brownish red; nest, a few twigs placed in holes of cliffs and difficult to approach." Mr. W. Blewitt records taking some 20 nests of this species in the neighbourhood of Hansee between the 20th of March and the end of April 1868. The nests were all on trees, Peepul, Sheeshum, Burgot, Neem and Keekur, none were more than 21 feet from the ground and one was at a height of only 12 feet. They varied from 12 to 18 inches in diameter, and from 3 to 7 inches in thickness; some were slightly, some densely, put together, and were composed in almost every instance of small branches and twigs of the Ber and Keekur, both thorny trees. One nest had no lining, the others were more or less lined with straw, feathers, leaves, and rags, one or all, while in many instances rags were plentifully incorporated in the body of the structure. Two was the number of eggs in each nest, some of those taken at the end of April were still quite fresh.

There can be little doubt, I think, that the egg figured by Dr. Bree as belonging to Bonelli's eagle, was really a Neophron's.

Dr. Jerdon says that this vulture is common in Egypt, but Mons. Jules Verreaux long ago wrote out to Colonel Tytler, that the Egyptian species *(N. Percnopterus)* was distinct from our Indian bird, which therefore stands as *N. Ginginianus*; and Mr. Blyth remarks (Ibis, 1866), "In the gardens of the Zoological Society there were lately four white Rachamas or Neophrons, one from Africa, and three from India. They were evidently of two distinct specific races. The African (Lev. Ois d'afr. t. 14; Viellot gal. des ois. t. 2; Jard, and Selb. Ill. orn. pl. 23; Gould's B. Eur. pl. 3) is larger and more robust, the tarsi and toes conspicuously so. The corneous portion of the bill is black, and the ceral portion is of a reddish yellow, different from the purer yellow of the cheeks; the talons also are black, and the cuneate tail passes the tips of the closed wings by an inch or more.

In the three Indian birds, the corneous portion of the bill is a pure yellowish flesh colour, as are also the talons; the ceral portion of the bill is of the same yellow as the cheeks, the points of the closed wings just reach to the tail tip; and a conspicuous fold of skin is continued from beneath the ear to the throat underneath, which is little more than indicated in the

African example; moreover the throat is quite bare in the Indian species, thinly clad with short white feathers in *N. Percnopterus* and with short black feathers in *N. Pileatus*.

The last appertains properly to the Ethiopian region (south of the Great Desert) the second to the southern half of the Eastern Atlantic region and the first to the Indian region; other African white Rachamahs I find to have black bills and claws, but not any Indian; and referring to *Vultur Meleagris* of Pallas, I remark, that he describes the black billed race as a scarce bird in the Tauric Chersonesus (Crimea); while the Indian race is that figured in the collection of drawings presented by Mr. Hodgson to the British Museum. This bird appears to be the *Vultur Ginginianus* of Latham (Ind. orni. I. p. 7, and Gen. Hist. B. I. p. 27, pl. 5), founded on the "Vautour de Gingi" of Sonnerat (Voy. Ind. II. p. 187)."

I think this matter requires looking into more closely. Since I first saw Mr. Blyth's remarks, I have procured one adult Indian bird with the claws horny black (a peculiarity which he describes as characteristic of *N. Percnopterus)* and not at all pale yellowish flesh colour; also a *young* bird with the corneous portion of the bill *almost black*, horny black in fact. In Colonel Tytler's Museum, there are two birds, one adult, the other young, *also* with black claws, and the young with a black bill. True, these latter are dried specimens, and the colours of these parts, may have faded and darkened, but I hardly can believe that the claws have ever been "pale yellowish flesh colour," since the colours of these only change to a certain extent, and not from pale yellow to black. Observers should look closely into this matter, and besides noting these points of colour, &c., record exact and detailed measurements, weight, &c., of every specimen they shoot.

Mr. Tristram, when speaking of birds mentioned in the Bible, remarks "The Hebrew "*ráchám*" (Arabic "*rakhma*") is translated 'Gier-eagle,' but is the universal and exclusive name of the Egyptian Vulture *(Neophron Percnopterus)* throughout Africa and Western Asia."

No. 7. **Gypaetus Barbatus,** (Lin.)

The Lammer Geyer or Bearded Vulture.

This species lays in December and January, and perhaps in the early part of February also. It breeds, in India of course, only in the Himalayahs.

The nest is commonly placed in almost inaccessible situations in the face of some bold cliff; a ledge of rock, above which some other ledge projects, is commonly chosen.

The only eyries, I have been able to inspect, were shapeless heaps of sticks, nearly a cart load I should say, strewed on ledges of rock, (over a space of some three to five feet long by 2 or 3 broad), intermingled with rags, huge feathers and large bones, and plentifully besprinkled with the droppings of the birds. Altogether they were not dainty spots, nor, it must be confessed, peculiarly pleasing to the olfactory nerves. I could see no trace of there having been any lining at any time to the nest; but I saw them, it must be remembered, in August, September and October, months after the eggs had been hatched and the young had flown, although the old birds still roosted there.

Captain Cock was more fortunate, and I cannot do better I think, than quote his account of an eyrie to which he not long since laid successful seige. "On the 4th December, 1868, I found the nest of *Gypaetus Barbatus*, in a hollow on the face of a steep precipice, situated in a range of hills, some six miles off the Grand Trunk road, 2 marches from Rawulpindee on the Peshawur side. I was out after nests, with but little hope of finding any at that time of year, when the shikaree I had with me, told me that some years before, when out with some sportsmen after Ourial, they had frightened a large bird off its nest, and he volunteered to show me where it was. We accordingly went to a steep gorge in the hill, very narrow, but with a tremendous precipice on each side. From the top, where I was standing, to the opposite side, might have been some ninety yards across, and the precipice was some 180 feet in depth. About half way down, in what seemed a sheer wall of rock, was a hollow, some six feet in height and five feet in depth and breadth. In this was placed the Lammergeyer's nest.

'The old bird was on her nest, and I looked at her for some time with the glass; she took alarm at once, and advancing to the edge of her nest stood up and looked at me with her neck stretched out and head turned sideways, bringing one eye to bear on me. She was a most noble looking bird, her large yellow eye, setting off her appearance. Flinging some stones down into the gorge to frighten her, she soon glided off her nest, and I could see two eggs. I now sat down to reconnoitre and plan some way of getting her eggs. By means of a shelf of rock I could crawl to within 15 feet of her nest, but there it ended. I had 3 long ropes with me, but they would only just reach down to the nest from the top; one of my fellows, a young light lad of 15, offered to go over the precipice with the rope round him. We made the rope fast to a tree above, and the boy's brother, a sturdy Pathan, payed out the rope, and the young fellow went over most gallantly. Both Lammergeyers now came flying round, but did not evince any great courage, for after I had hurled some bits of rock at them, the male went off altogether, and the female only hovered about at some distance. The young Pathan now got into the nest and walked about in it. It was a large structure of sticks and completely filled up the hollow, or cave, in which it was placed. It was lined with locks of the hair of hill goats, on which the eggs were placed; there was also one piece of cloth in the nest, some blue cotton stuff, by which I was reminded of this bird's relationship to Neophron. The eggs were set, I should think, from 15 to 18 days."

The only 2 eggs that I, as yet, possess of this species, I owe to Captain Cock, and these were taken as above described. They are excessively like one of the common types of the eggs *Neophron Gingimianus*, but of course immensely larger. Both eggs are a rather broad oval, somewhat pointed towards one end. The length of the bird's tail and wings, give it an appearance of size which would lead one to expect a very large egg, and Captain Cock was disappointed at finding the eggs so much smaller than those of *Gyps Himalayensis*. The fact is, however, that *Gyps Himalayensis* averages some 20 lbs in weight, while the Lammergeyer may average 12 or 13 lbs; and the eggs of this latter are fully as large as average eggs of *Gyps Bengalensis*, which bird averages about the same in weight. The texture of the 2 eggs I have, is rather coarse, but the shells are more compact, and less chalky than those of the Neophron.

Neither of the eggs has the slightest gloss. Both have a nearly uniform pale salmon buff ground, here and there mottled paler. One is devoid of all markings, the other is somewhat thinly blotched, clouded, and spotted, in all parts, with pale reddish brown, not much darker than the ground colour. Doubtless, to judge from the analogy of the Neophron, far more highly coloured examples occur. The colour of the shell, when held up against the light, is pale dingy yellow, as in Neophron, thereby further exhibiting the close affinities of these two species, and separating them from the true Vultures, all of whose shells, when seen against the light, are, to the best of my belief, a more or less dark sea green.

The eggs measure $3{\cdot}43 \times 2{\cdot}68$ and $3{\cdot}05 \times 2{\cdot}52$.

It seems probable that, as in the case of the Egyptian Vulture, two is the number of eggs most commonly laid, and that three may, not very unfrequently, be found.

At present only two distinct species of *Gypaetus*, are commonly admitted; *viz. G. Barbatus*, of Europe, northern and western Africa, the Taurus, Persia, Cabool and the Himalayahs, and *G. Meridionalis* from Abyssinia, Arabia and the Cape; which latter has the lower part of the tarsus bare. On the principle, however, that *constant* differentiæ, even though small, constitute a separate species, I am inclined to think that the Cabool and Himalayan bird should be specifically separated.

Captain Hutton named the Afghan bird, so common in the Bolan pass and at Quetta in the Shawl valley, *G. Hemachalanus*, distinguishing it chiefly I believe by its dark pectoral band or gorget. Col. Tytler who was with Captain Hutton in Afghanistan, and who shot these birds there, assures me that the specimens procured at Simla and elsewhere in the Himalayahs, both by himself and myself, have the pectoral band fully as well marked as in the Cabool birds.

Dr. Jerdon says that our bird is said to differ from the European bird in the dark gorget, more tawny hue of the lower surface, and in the 1st quill being 3·5 inches shorter than the 3rd; whilst in the European bird it is said only to be a very little shorter. I have only seen a single specimen of the European bird, shot in 1847 in the Bernese Alps. This one has scarcely a trace of any gorget, and has the chin, throat and sides of neck, which in our bird are always, in the adult, (at least in all the 20 odd specimens I have examined) a rusty *red* (often very bright and deep,) a pale rusty *white*. The talons too appear less curved and powerful in the European than in our bird. As regards the length of the primaries, the European bird had the first primary fully 2 inches shorter than the third, while in six adult Himalayan birds the 1st primary varied from 4 to 5·75 inches shorter than the 3rd, while the 2nd, which in the European bird (I refer to the single specimen that I have examined) is almost equal to the 3rd, in these Indian birds varied from 1·5 to 0·5 shorter than this latter. Again Dr. Bree gives the length of the European bird at 4 feet 7 inches. I have as yet succeeded in obtaining no individual (and I have killed some superb adults) exceeding 4 feet 1 inch in length. Adult males average 44 inches, females 47 and 48.

In Europe it would seem to carry off children, and to bear away Foxes, Lambs, and the like, but in the Himalayahs (rejecting good Bishop Heber's story, which the present native inhabitants of Almora altogether discredit), I have heard no authenticated instance, of its carrying off anything larger than a Marmot or a Kitten, or of its being as a rule other than a carrion or offal eater. Let a cow or goat die anywhere, and the Lammergeyers are down as soon as the Vultures, and, by no means behave, as Dr. Bree says of the European bird, in a cowardly fashion. On the contrary the Lammergeyer holds its own against all comers, including a stray Adjutant or two, which are often to be seen in the summer and autumn, even as high up in the Himalayahs as Simla. It is only proper, however, to note here, what Dr. Stoliczka says on this subject: "The Bearded Vulture is common all through the Sutlej valley and through W. Tibet; it generally retires in winter from the northern part of W. Tibet to the more southern hills, but permanently resides about Chini. The Chukor, *Caccabis Chukor*, and other partridges are its favourite meal. It is, however, well known, that this bearded eagle often accepts any other refuse of bones and meat, being very often seen near the houses of hill stations."

"When marching through Lahul, in 1865, the people assured me that it very often carries off lambs and kids, and is very bold at the time of breeding. The natives of Kulu, about Plash and the eastern districts, prize the meat very highly, which is not only eaten by the low class, the Kolies, but also by the higher class the Kaists. They generally tie a *Chukor*, on a short string, and stick four or five sharpened spears in the ground crossing each other, so as partially at least to cover the bird, and at the same time to radiate with their points in differend directions. The eagle is watched from some distance and as soon as it throws itself with its usual great force and velocity upon the prey, it is overpowered with large clubs before it can extricate the spears from its body."

This account surprises me, I have always observed the Lammergeyer descend very gingerly, a few feet off anything it fancied and then *walk* up to its food; perhaps, when after living game it *may* be less careful and sluggish.

I am not the only person who considers the popular accounts of the daring and ferocity of the Lammergeyer gross exaggerations: our two best Himalayan observers come to precisely the same conclusion.—I will first quote what Captain Hutton writes to me: "These birds are common in the hills, from the Doon to the snowy range; it breeds for several seasons together in the same nest, sometimes giving the old nest a few repairs. The spots selected at Mussooree are of the most dangerous description, and often perfectly inaccessible, while even in the least dangerous spots, a man must be lowered down over the rock by a stout rope to ascertain if there are either eggs or young ones in the nest; since that, being generally placed in a wide fissure in the perpendicular face of the cliff, is not visible from above.

"One nest was found on the 30th March, and a boy was lowered down over the rock, but found that the cleft and nest of two years previously had been abandoned, and a new nest had been made in another cleft lower down, and in which was one young bird partially fledged. Not being prepared to rob the nest at that time, the nestling was left, especially as the old birds were near, and their movements somewhat threatening. On the following morning, the lad was again persuaded to descend, and as the old birds were absent, he secured his prize. The nest was built on a ledge of rock within a cleft, and was composed of a thick bed of sticks, lined with grass, old rags, bones and what appeared to have been a portion of a sheet. There was nothing in the shape of food, except part of the wing of some large bird.

"During the present year (1869) a nest was prepared in the very same spot, and was finished on the 24th February; on the 10th of March it was visited, the old birds being at hand, but no eggs were found. It was visited again once after this and found to be deserted. Towards the end of March, another nest was visited, but it had been blown off the rock in a gale of wind.

"The young bird captured three or four years ago, had the bill of a horn colour; pupil of eye black, with a broad hazel brown iris bordered by a narrow dull red ring; down, pale fulvous brown, the feathers on the shoulders and tail, dark black; those of the back, buff-coloured; top of the head, flat and black; legs and feet dull leaden, with strong black, and shining sharp pointed claws. A short pointed black beard of bristles, depending from the angle beneath the lower mandible. One of the toes of the right foot had a bunch or tuft of feathers on it.

This individual grew up to be a fine bird, and truly astonishing was it to see the quantity, and the great size of the bones it swallowed. At last when fully fledged, as I did not want the bird, I gave it its liberty; but go it would not. One night it would roost upon the ridge of the bungalow, another night on a neighbouring tree or outhouse; then he took a fancy to a bazar close at hand: there he stayed the greater part of the day and returned home at night. Being at last driven from the bazar, he became a kind of highwayman, sitting upon the public roads, until some Goorkha sepoys at last seized him, and took him to Dehra.

"Marvellous, indeed, are the stories told both by natives and Europeans of the destructive habits of this bird, and both accounts, I fully believe, have scarcely a grain of truth in them: all

all I can positively say upon the point however, is, that I have known the bird well in its native haunts for thirty years and more, and never once, in all that time, have I seen it stoop to anything but a dead carcase; as to carrying off hens, dogs, lambs or children, I say the feat would be utterly impossible, for the creature does not possess the strongly curved sharp pointed claws of the Eagle, but the far straighter and perfectly blunt talons of the Vulture. Day after day, I have seen them sweeping by along the face of the hill like the wandering albatross at sea, and like it, ever in search of offal, and even that, when found, is not swept off the ground after the manner of the kite, but the bird alights upon it, as it would upon a bullock, and then, if the morsel is worth having, devours it on the spot, and again launches itself upon its widespread wings and sails away as before. There is no sudden stooping upon a living prey as with the Falcon tribe, but its habits and manners in this respect are, as far as I have seen, entirely Vulturine. There seems to be some difference between our bird and the Alpine one of Europe in the selection of a breeding-place; for, while in the Alps, the bird is said to breed within the higher and more inaccessible mountains; here at Mussooree, they frequent the outer and less solitary mountain glens, and often the immediate vicinity of a village; yet never do the people complain of the loss of either lambs or fowls or attacks on children. Sometimes if a native finds that you are anxious to obtain information, he will at once, as in other matters, spin a yarn clean off the reel without there being an atom of truth in it. This, however, must be regarded simply as one of the idiosyncracies of this intelligent people! Notwithstanding the weight of authority against me! I still persist in regarding our bird as distinct from the European *G. Barbatus*."

Mr. R. Thompson writes that "This species breeds from November to February, late in which latter month the young may sometimes be seen; it selects ledges of precipices, at elevations of 5,000 feet and upwards. The nest, a huge platform, some four or five feet in diameter, is constructed of small sticks and thick twigs, placed so as to form a footing for the young, and is lined with pieces of cloth, rags, &c. I have frequently noticed parent birds with only a single young one following them, and I am inclined to think that they seldom *rear* more.

"I have been a close and constant observer of the habits of these birds for the last 12 years, and I confess I never saw the bearded Vulture attack or come down to a living animal

They have repeatedly sailed past close to my nets, when I have had live fowls and pigeons picketed as lures for Hawks and Eagles. They have passed within a few feet of these, without once showing a desire to pick up any of the birds, and this too on the tops of high mountains, in a perfectly wild country, with no human habitation within miles. Surely, if the birds had a natural desire for such food, it was temptingly laid out for them. On the contrary, the Lammergeyer will at once come down on a well-cleaned carcass, a heap of bones, or the skeletons of smaller mammalia. I once killed one that was picking up, and swallowing soup bones behind my cook-house. I have sometimes seen them stop in their quarterings of a hill side, and settling down, pick up a bone, swallow it, and fly off again, recommencing their careful survey of the hill side, doubtlessly, for more bones. At Paoree, in the interior of Ghurwal, in the height of winter when snow lay on the ground, I had the carcasses of several bears thrown out on a little ridge not far from my house. Invariably after the vultures had cleaned them, they were attacked by the Lammergeyer, some of which I shot in the act of tugging at the tough sinews and tendons left by the other Vultures. In Ghurwal, the Lammergeyer is known to the natives as the *Hârrphoor*, *i. e.* bone-breaker. A name well borne out by a habit of the bird, which I have verified by actual observation. It picks up a rather large-sized bone with which it soars high up into the air, and then by dropping it on a ledge of rock smashes it, when it descends, picks up the fragments and swallows them. It is only two years since I saw this again done under my own eye at Khoorpa Tal.

"The Lammergeyer is naturally of a very shy disposition, though when its object is to secure some tempting morsel, it will pass within a few feet of one.

"In the commencement of the breeding season, *i. e.*, when the birds first begin to pair, they may be seen swooping at each other and turning over on their backs. Sometimes one darts up towering to a considerable height with a graceful sweeping curve, when the other comes down from a greater height, and meets it at the apex of its ascent. So on the pair continue till lost to sight in the azure of the sky. I have usually observed this kind of courtship to commence after the breaking up of the rainy season, and continue to about the end of October.

"There must be, of course, some foundation for the many statements that have been put forth as to the rapacious character of this bird. But this foundation, I believe, to consist in the natives constantly attributing the depredations committed by

Entolmætus Bonellii, Limnætus Nipalensis, and Aquila Chrysætus to the Lammergeyer. The first and second of these will carry of fowls, ducks, pigeons, and other poultry readily, and do so whenever and wherever they can get at them. Aquila Chrysætus will kill and carry off young deer and kids, as I have myself seen. Entolmætus Bonellii will, as readily, knock over a young deer, full grown hare, or snap up a monkey, as he will a duck or hen, indeed I have myself seen them do it. In all such cases the poor *Hârrphoor* is always put forward as the guilty party by the Shikaris who, at times, will frame the most exaggerated charges against the finest yet most harmless of our hill birds.

"The structure of the Lammergeyer's feet, hardly I think, admits of its killing and carrying off living prey. I believe that a great deal of what has been absurdly written about its depredations might well be refuted by studying the anatomical structure of its feet."

On the whole, I am at present inclined to think we ought to separate our Indian bird as a distinct species; if so, Hutton's name *G. Hemachalanus* will I fancy stand.

Mr. Gurney says that the young birds from the Himalayahs, have a row of small feathers running down the outer side of the mid toe, half way down the first joint. I have been able to find no trace of this in any of the five this year's birds that I have recently examined, and I would direct the attention of Indian observers to this alleged peculiarity.* It may prove to have been only a monstrosity in Mr. Gurney's specimen.

Some natives at Almora first drew my attention to the fact noticed above by Mr. Thompson that the Lammergeyer habitually drops large bones from a considerable height, on to the rocks, with the object, they assert, of breaking them and getting at the marrow. I myself, on one occasion, actually saw one of these birds drop a large shin bone of an ox in this way; *but*, whether it was my presence or what, I cannot say, he made no attempt to follow up the operation, but sailed straight away, having I thought at the time merely dropped the bone, (which though fresh was quite bare), *because* he found it to be clean picked. One thing is certain, *viz.* that this bird sometimes devours what it has in its claws, as it flies, much as kites will do. This I have twice myself witnessed, and Captain Hutton has recorded the same fact, it *may* be that they pick the bones as they go along, and drop them when nothing remains on them; by no means invariably descending on the fragments. If, however, they only occasionally do this, and this Mr. Thompson proves, it would

* But see Capt. Hutton's remarks, *supra*.

be sufficient to account for the belief, (above noticed), which I have found prevalent in many parts of the Himalayahs, and which is general to this day in Europe.

Mr. Tristram says, "Incidentally as natural history is mentioned in Holy Scripture, yet even there we have ten distinct Hebrew names for raptoral birds, several of which are at once recognizable in the vernacular Arabic of the country. They are first, "*peres*" *i. e.* 'the breaker,' translated in our version. 'Ossifrage,' a name, admirably adapted to express the remarkable and well-known habit of the Lammergeyer, of dropping its prey, whether mammals, serpents, but especially tortoises, from great heights to break their bones or shells."

"Although the name has been applied in modern scientific nomenclature to one of the eagles, there can be no doubt but that the *Ossifraga* of the Latin authors, and of the authorized version, is to be identified with the Gypaete."

In the Himalayahs, these birds are not difficult to snare. Mr. R. Thompson mentions that he has often caught them, and that quite recently, seeing a pair come down, to the carcase of a cow, he went and laid a few snares round it and caught both birds in little more than an hour.

Even if our bird *be* specifically different from the European one, it is so closely allied to it, that anything in regard to the nidification of the latter, must be interesting to us. Dr. Bree gives us the following account:—

"The Lammergeyer builds in places equally inaccessible to naturalists, and bullets! Its nest is ingenious; the substratum is formed of a mass of straw, fern and stalks, lying upon a number of sticks and branches laid cross ways one upon another. The nest, which rests upon the under-layer, is composed of branches woven into the shape of a wreath, and lined with down and moss, and the contents of this part alone, would fill the largest hay cloth. Very early in the year, the female lays three or four large white eggs, spotted with brown, of which only two generally are hatched. The young birds are covered with a whitish down, and their huge ill-proportioned crops and maws, give them an ugly and shapeless appearance."

I must confess that I regard the moss and down, and wreath of branches, (why not of "*roses*" at once?) in the above extract as somewhat apocryphal. I cannot say that I have, as yet, met with any Vulturine birds of prey indulging in this goldfinch type of architecture. I also doubt the four eggs, although it is *possible* that, according to the Rev. H. Tristram's hypothesis (that where particular birds are very rare, they lay more eggs than where they are common), European

Lammergeyers (which now alas are becoming yearly, "few by degrees and sorrowfully fewer") *may* have taken to laying double the number of eggs that their *confreres* (I ought perhaps says *consœurs*) lay elsewhere.

I don't know, by the way, that I quite understand this theory of Mr. Tristram's. Is it supposed that the poor things, viewing sadly the approaching extinction of their long descended race, make extra philoprogenitive exertions to avert such a catastrophe? or is it that the struggle for existence diminishing, the birds get such unusual rations, that excessive fecundity is superinduced?

In the Eastern Atlas, *one*, seems the normal number of eggs laid. Mr. Salvin tells us (Ibis, 1859), "The first opportunity I had of observing this finest of birds, was in the neighbourhood of Sonk Harras in the first week in April. In a ramble in search of a spot for our encampment we discovered an eyrie in one of the stupendous cliffs that characterize that district. It was quite inaccessible, and we had to bear our disappointment, as well as a good wetting, and return to the hotel (if the house where we put up may be designated by such a title), after an almost fruitless day. We were not then aware that the eggs of this species had long been hatched. It would appear that this bird, like the Gyps Fulvus, *seldom, if ever, lays more than one egg;* no instance of more than one young has ever occurred in the nests visited."

Mr. Simpson, in his ornithological notes from Mesolonghi and southern Etolia, tells us of an unsuccessful attack on a Lammergeyer's nest which, on the 1st of March, contained an egg, supposed to be near hatching.

In the Ibis for 1862, it is mentioned that Herr Meves had, by a simple chemical test, ascertained the red colouring in this bird's feathers, as also the rustiness observable at times in the feathers of the common Crane, (*Grus Cinerea*) to be due to a *superficial* deposit of oxide of iron; as also, that the colouring matter on the eggs, arose from the same cause. Herr Meves suggested, that the stain on the feathers might be owing to the birds *bathing* in water containing iron in solution; but my belief is, that the Lammergeyer is a very dirty bird, (it swarms with vermin to such a degree, that cats and the like will seldom touch it when dead,) and *never* washes! I have been watching this bird, off and on, for the last twenty years, and I have never yet seen it bathe; nor have I ever yet met with any one, amongst the numerous intelligent native sportsmen whom I have had to do with in the Himalayahs, who has witnessed such an operation. Certainly iron *does* enter into the composition of the colouring matter of the feathers, (I have tested it myself) as also into the red colouring on Neophron's and kite's eggs, but my idea is, that in both cases the iron is derived from the blood, and not from any ferruginous streams. Many birds, notably the grey goose and the common teal, very often have the feathers of the lower parts strongly tinged with rusty, and here too an oxide of iron enters into the composition of the colouring matter. How it gets there, is a question well worthy of investigation.

The Lammergeyer, as Mr. Brookes remarks, has a habit of quartering the side of a hill, and working it backwards and forwards, as steadily and regularly as a good pointer will a turnip field, and these are the times when they can easily be shot, since if you notice carefully *how* they are beating, and then when they are away on the opposite side of the tract they are working, sit quietly down in some bush or beside some rock, in the line of their next tack, they will come past you unsuspiciously, and often within twenty yards. They are birds that, flying towards you, take away an incredible amount of the heaviest shot in their deep breasts; but once on the top of Deo Dhoura (Kumaon) coming to the edge of a little cliff which overhung two tiny Buddhist temples, on the stone (so called) umbrella of one of which, some twenty yards below me sat a fine male, I knocked him over dead with a loose charge of No. 10 shot, as, altogether unaware of my presence, he sat (his back towards me) proudly overlooking the vast valley that lay beneath us.

I consider that in its habits, and gait, (especially in its manner of walking about and holding its tail &c., when feeding on the ground,) this bird is more closely allied to the Neophrons than to any other Vulturine type. Dr. Jerdon fully concurs with me in this matter, and had independently noted it. I may remark that one of those shot by me at Simla had gorged itself on human ordure.

The structure of the nest and the eggs, which, except in size, are, as already noticed, precisely similar to those of some types of the Neophrons, further confirms the close relationship of these two genera.

While on the subject of affinities, I cannot help alluding to the strong resemblance that *Gypætus* externally bears to *Attagen*. This may be merely superficial, (and the weak, half-webbed feet of *Attagen*, and slender larine (?) bill would lead us to believe such to be the case), but still I should like to see skeletons of the two types compared. In their method of sailing, I must note, that on the only occasion on which I saw an *Attagen* (*Ariel*, I believe) on the wing, I fancied that there was a strong resemblance between the two genera.

As one difference between the European and Indian bird appears to consist in the smaller size of the latter. I give exact measurements derived from a number of specimens procured in various parts of the Himalayahs.

Length, from 44 to 49. Expanse, 99 to 110. Weight, 10 lbs. to 16 lbs., average about 12 lbs., Wing, from 30 to 34; the 3rd primary, sometimes the 2nd and 3rd, sometimes the 4th and 3rd the longest. 1st primary from 3 to 5 shorter, *never* less; 2nd primary from 1 shorter to sub-equal, 4th at times sub-equal generally from 1 to 2, shorter. Tail of 12 feathers. Length of tail from vent, from 21 to 25; longest tail feathers exceed shortest by from 5 to 8. Tarsus 3·9 to 4·7. Foot, greatest length, from 6·8 to 8; greatest width, from 5·2 to 6·3; mid toe from 3 to 3·6; its claw, along curve, from 1 to 1·6; hind toe, from 1·4 to 2; its claw along curve, from 1·45 to 2·1; inner toe from 1·5 to 2; its claw along curve, from 1·5 to 2·05. Bill straight from edge of cere from 1·9 to 2·4. Bill, along curve from edge of cere, from 2·5 to 3·2; from gape from 4 to 4·7; width at gape, from 2·5 to 2·9; height at margin of cere, from 0·85 to 1; length of cere, from 1·35 to 1·6. Distance by which the closed wings fall short of end of tail, from 4 to 6. Distance by which lower tail coverts fall short of tail, from 8·9 to 10·5.

Of a fine adult male killed, September 3rd, the feet were plumbeous, the claws pale greenish horny. The eyelids dark plumbeous brown. The irides bright, very pale orange. (In some I have found them straw-coloured, but I have never seen them white without either a red or yellow tinge.) The bill was bluish horny at gape, greenish horny beyond, and dusky on point. Sclerotic membrane blood red. *Above;* Lores, nareal bristles, a patch over the eye and a line joining the hinder portions of these patches, black. The top of the head white, with a tinge of rufous, and a few of the feathers black. Back of the head and neck and sides of latter pale ferruginous; feathers about gape whitish mixed with black; a black stripe from gape about 1·5 long. Lower neck, (behind), upper back and lesser wing coverts, a rich brown, white shafted and conspicuously centered with white, or in some, fawn colour; lower back and upper tail coverts deep brown. Tail, quills, and larger coverts, deep brown, with white shafts, many of the feathers powdered as it were with silver grey. Scapulars dark brown, more or less frosted with silver grey. *Below;* a conspicuous tuft of black bristles, (the longest fully 1 inch in length,) on the chin. General hue, *bright* ferruginous, richest on throat, neck, middle of breast and abdomen, and paling, (becoming in places almost white), on sides, flanks, vent and lower tail coverts. A few feathers of the throat and lower chin, dark brown. A conspicuous, but somewhat imperfect, pectoral gorget, formed by many of the feathers being broadly tipped with dark brown. Larger axillaries dark brown, white-shafted, with a broad central white stripe, which, in the smaller axillaries, leaves only a very narrow brown margin. Tail, beneath, deep brown, quills greyish brown, under wing-coverts conspicuously white shafted and with a narrow stripe on each side of the shaft also white; which stripe expands at the tip into a sort of spot or drop; a small patch of rufous on the carpal joint.

The young birds are all hatched, by the 1st of April, many by the beginning of March or even earlier, and towards the close of August or during September, they assume their first fresh plumage. I have seen no description of the freshly moulted young bird, although the plumage is very characteristic, and widely different from that, of any other stage of plumage. The legs, feet, claws and bill, are much as in the adult, but the irides are a pale yellowish brown. The whole head and neck *all* round, is deep blackish brown; on the nape and cheeks positively black, but in the lores, cheeks, forehead, and sides of lower mandible, some tiny whitish feathers are intermingled, and some of the feathers have white bases which, showing through, give a mottled appearance to those parts. A few of the feathers, distributed over a triangular crop patch, are yellowish brown, tipped pale buffy yellow. The whole of the upper back presents a mottled appearance: some of the feathers being deep purplish brown, white shafted, some being a rather pale clove brown, also white shafted, some being white, and some buffy white, and some a mixture of these colours. The lower back and upper tail coverts, a nearly uniform moderately dark clove brown. The scapulars, quills, winglet, and greater coverts, deep chocolate brown, with a purplish gloss, all white shafted, the quills and tail conspicuously so. The outer webs of many of the quills towards the base, brushed with buffy white, and similarly, both webs of the centre tail feathers, and the outer webs of some of the lateral tail feathers, much streaked and clouded with buffy white towards the bases. Lesser and median coverts, a somewhat less deep brown than the rest of the wings, all pale shafted; many of them with a minute fulvous white tipping, and three or four in each wing with broad, pure white tips. Beneath, the whole of the breast, sides, flanks, abdomen, thigh coverts, and lower tail coverts, a pale somewhat clove coloured brown, contrasting strongly with the black of the throat and neck, a few of the breast feathers tinged with a darker brown, and broadly tipped with fulvous white; several of the flank feathers, and upper thigh coverts, broadly tipped with pure white. The whole wing lining, a uniform, somewhat dark brown.

No. 8. **Falco Peregrinus,** Gmel.

The Peregrine.

Of the breeding of this bird in India, little is known. "Mr. Layard," I quote Dr. Jerdon, "mentions the Peregrine as breeding in Ceylon in January, and Dr. Adams says, that he found the nest on a tree on the banks of the Indus, below Ferozpoor, but I imagine," continues Dr. Jerdon, "that in both cases an old *Laggar* (*F. Jugger*) has been mistaken for the *Bhyri*." As to Ceylon, I can offer no opinion, although it is difficult to mistake a Peregrine for a *Laggar* at *any* stage, but as regards the Indus, I think Dr. Adams was very likely correct. When marching between Ferozpoor and Mooltan, I saw a trained Peregrine, which the owner assured me, had been taken from a nest on the banks of the Indus near Leia; and I have been informed by an officer well acquainted with our bird, that it breeds on the banks of the Cabool and Swat rivers, close to the Peshawur valley. I have also a nestling bird just able to fly, shot by a native shikaree somewhere in the interior of the Himalayahs, not far from Koteguru; proving that the bird does breed in the Hills. Further observations are necessary. I should say that our birds laid in May, or not earlier than the later part of April, because of a fine pair that I shot early in April at the Sambhur lake; (where there were several,) neither ovaries, nor testicles were at all developed; and the native sportsmen of the place assured me, that they rarely left the lake before the middle of April. The migratory ducks leave earlier, all had left when I was there, but Gulls, Terns and Flamingoes were there in myriads, and these and the Peregrines all leave, I was assured, together; and my informants, though wholly uneducated were good observers, as they pointed out, even on the wing, the difference between *Xema Brunneicephala* and *Ridabunda*; both of which, with *Chroicocephalus Ichthyætus*, were very plentiful about the lake.

In Europe, they build on rocks and cliffs; by preference along the sea coast. They form a large nest of sticks, and lay,

Yarrel says, four eggs, averaging about two inches in length, by 1·67 in breadth; mottled all over with pale reddish brown. Those that I have seen, varied nearly as much in depth, and intensity of colouring, as do those of *Falco Jugger*.

Although I have reasons, as above explained, for believing that some of our birds *do* breed in the far North-West, and in the Himalayahs, I yet do not doubt that the majority of them go further north. The Peregrine is rather a northern bird, not rare, for instance right up to the north cape, as Old Bushman informs us; and I should guess that many of our birds breed in the neighbourhood of the Caspian Sea.

Captain C. H. T. Marshall says, "Do you know that the Bhyri, about the time of its migration, always sleeps facing the north? It sits in that direction even during the day time, if possible; but at night, it invariably keeps its head pointing northwards." I cannot say that I place much faith in this native story communicated by my friend Captain C. Marshall, but I am bound to confess, that the two Peregrines that I shot at Sambhur, in the dusk of the evening, on the trees where they always roosted, certainly were sitting facing the north, although what little wind was blowing came from the south-west.

I have (both in Col. Tytler's museum and elsewhere,) had opportunities of comparing a number of European and Indian specimens, and must add my feeble testimony to Mr. Blyth's dictum, that they are clearly, all referrible, to one, and the same species. I would say more. I cannot agree with Mr. Blyth, that the adults are *always* distinguishable at a glance. I have before me two adult males, one shot in England, the other near Umballa, which are undistinguishable. I do *not* find, after comparing a large series, either that the European bird has *always* more rufous on the lower parts than the Indian, or that the cross bars are always much larger and stronger, or that the breast is more conspicuously spotted: all these points vary in both races, the two latter solely, as I believe, according to age. But the fact I suspect is, that in Europe, Peregrines are rarely allowed to live to any great age, being there continually shot at, and in many places I might almost say, hunted down; while in Asia, except by a few "misguided Europeans," Peregrines are never shot; and though numbers are caught for hawking purposes, they are commonly turned loose again after one, or more years; and thus, while the large majority of European specimens exhibit more or less traces of nonage, a fair proportion of our Indian specimens are of really *old* birds, in which the whole chin, throat, and upper breast, are spotless white; the spots on the thigh coverts reduced to mere triangular dots; the abdomen, with only a few scattered dots here and there; the sides, axillaries, and under-wing coverts, with the markings reduced to narrow arrow-head bars, rarely extending quite to the margins of the webs; and with the lower tail coverts spotless, with only, perhaps here and there, a faint trace of where a bar *has* been.

In the next younger stage, (and this is that, in which the so-called adult birds appear to be generally shot in England and western Europe,) the chin and throat are spotless, but the whole breast has very narrow, linear, lanceolate, dark, central stripes to the feathers; the abdomen is well marked with pretty large black brown spots; the thigh coverts are barred with narrow transverse bars, far more conspicuous and closer than even in the axillaries of the older stage; while the sides, axillaries, and under-wing coverts are firmly barred with bars, broader and darker than in the older bird, and which moreover, extend quite to the margins of the feathers. The lower tail coverts are all distinctly barred, but the bars are very narrow, and in colour they are greyish brown. In the first described stage moreover, the head and nape are blacker, and the white markings on the inner webs of the primaries, much broader than in the second. From the large number of specimens, obtained in upper India, in stages intermediate between these two, as compared with those exactly answering these descriptions, I conclude that the bird, probably takes a long time, perhaps many years, to pass from one to the other. In the next younger stage, each feather of the breast has an ovato-lanceolate, clove-brown drop near the tip. The feathers of the whole of the abdomen, have large brown subterminal spots, and many of them a broad bar above this. The thigh coverts are far more broadly and decidedly barred, than even in the last described stage, while in the sides, axillaries, and lower wing coverts, (especially the two latter,) the brown bars are as broad as the interspaces, and the lower tail coverts are much more strongly, though not more closely barred, than in the preceding. In both the first described stages, the central tail feathers are slatey blue, tipped white, with a subtipping and margin of blackish brown, and bars of the same colour, or traces of them, projecting inwards, towards, but usually not extending quite to, the centre of the feathers; but in the youngest of the three stages, the central tail feathers are deep brown, tipped with rufous, with well-marked transverse grey bars, most conspicuous towards the base. Other younger stages are well known.

I have not above alluded to the difference in the amount of rufous, observable on the lower parts of different individuals.

I have come to the conclusion, that this has no necessary connection, with the age of the bird; but varies, according either to season, (in relation to the state of the reproductive organs) or climate, (with reference to temperature and moisture) or food, or perhaps all combined. Certain it is, that, with numerous specimens before one, no rule about the more rufous character of the English bird can be absolutely maintained. Col. Tytler has an undoubted English specimen, with less rufous than any of the numerous Indian ones, that I have seen, and I have in my own collection an old female, shot near Lahore, fully as rufous as any of the six European birds that I have compared it with, and more rufous than any, but one of these. It is said that northern specimens run larger, than those of lower latitudes; but this too I question, and for facility of comparison, I subjoin exact measurements of a fine, but not old Indian female, which to judge from Yarrell and Old Bushman, cannot fall far short of even Scandinavian examples.

Length, 20·25 inches. Expanse, 39. Wing, 13·25; (the second and third primaries equal and longest, 1st 0·25 shorter, 4th 0·73 shorter.) Tail, 6·75 (exterior feathers 0·62 shorter than central feather.) Tarsus, (feathered in front for nearly 1 inch) 2·12. Foot, greatest length 4·62; greatest width 2·75; mid toe 2·06, its claw 0·81; hind toe 1·0, its claw 0·94. Bill, straight 1·12; along curve 1·37; from gape 1·31; width at gape 1·25; height at front at edge of cere 0·5; length of cere 0·25. Weight, 1 lb 13 oz.

I also add a full description, as that will show exactly, the stage of European bird with which it should be compared. Legs and feet, pale yellowish brown. Claws black, *outer* toe claw larger than mid, or interior toe claw. Irides deep brown. Bill, pale blue at base of upper mandible, greenish at base of lower mandible, bluish black at both tips; cere, dingy yellowish.

The whole of the top of the head, back of the neck, and a broad patch below the eye, covering almost the whole of the cheek, a very deep slatey blue, almost black on the cheek stripe, the whole of the back of the neck, upper back scapulars, and upper surface of the wings slatey blue, all the feathers obscurely barred with a lighter hue, and many of them tipped and margined somewhat paler; middle and lower back, rump and upper tail coverts, bluish grey, conspicuously barred with broad arrow head bars, of darker, or slatey blue. Tail feathers all conspicuously tipped with white, centre tail feathers, and outer webs of the rest dingy blue, or grey, with from seven to nine broad, transverse, dark slatey blue bars. Inner webs of lateral tail feathers, of a paler ground colour, contrasting more strongly therefore, with the bars, which are similar on both webs, though possibly, somewhat darker on the inner webs. Inner webs of the quills with numerous long oval patches, or incomplete transverse bars, of whiter greyish, or rufous white. Chin, throat, upper breast, and a patch over the terminal half of the ear-coverts, beside or behind the dark ear-patch, white with a buffy, or even pinkish tinge, some few of the feathers having a trace of linear, dark brown, central stripes. Lower breast, and middle of abdomen, still more rufous, each feather having a conspicuous subterminal transverse spot of dark brown, smaller on the upper, larger on the lower feathers. The whole of the lining of the wing, axillaries, sides, flanks, sides and lower part of abdomen, thigh coverts, and lower tail coverts, white, conspicuouly barred with dark brown, the bars being most numerous, and marked on the axillaries and sides, and least conspicuous, on the lower tail, and thigh coverts.

Dr. Jerdon, I may here note, informs me, that he cannot help suspecting, that specimens shot on the eastern sea coast, are *larger*, than those procured in the North West. It would be interesting to obtain accurate measurements in the flesh, of numerous specimens, from both localities.

Tyros continually complain, that they are unable, from Dr. Jerdon's descriptions, to discriminate our various species of Indian falcons; I must confess that I think his descriptions clear enough; but I will note a few points, by which, independent of any detailed description, the five species may be generally distinguished.

First, the Sacer so far exceeds all the others in size, that this alone would be sufficient to identify it. The wings average from 15 to 16 inches,* against 14·0 in *F. Jugger*, and *F. Peregrinus*, and 13·0 in *Perigrinator* and *Babylonicus*. Then, while the central tail feathers of *Peregrinus*, *Perigrinator*, and *Babylonicus* are all barred, (in different degrees according to age) and those of *Jugger* are unbarred, those of *Sacer*, in most of the specimens I have seen, are marked with *roundish*† *spots*, (more

* These dimensions differ somewhat from Dr. Jerdon's. I am aware he is not likely to be wrong, *but* this much I can say, that mine are taken from numerous specimens in the flesh, and have all been most carefully recorded.

† Dr. Bree *figures* the Sacer with *bars*, but gives in his specific characters, "spots white, ovoid and round on the tail." Of more than a dozen specimens that *I have*, or have seen, not one had the central feathers barred, all but one, had round, or ovoidal spots on each web of the central feathers. That *one*, a very young bird, had the central tail feathers, just like Jugger, unspotted and unbarred. Is this really a young Sacer? I think there is no doubt that our Falcons want re-examining. I allow what I have above written to stand, but I have since had reason to believe, that instead of five true Falcons, we have *eight* in India, and that it will be necessary, carefully to re-write the discrimi-

or less broad ovals on the laterals). Then again, the *Sacer* never has much, and commonly shows scarcely any sign, of a cheek stripe, while in all the others it is well marked. Further, the Peregrine is distinguished at all times from the Jugger, by its huge broad cheek patch, which in the Laggar is at most, about a quarter of an inch broad, and by the entire absence of barring on the centre tail feathers in *F. Jugger*, which absence equally distinguishes this latter from both *Perigrinator* and *Babylonicus*. From *Babylonicus*, both *Perigrinator* and *Peregrinus* differ in the cheek stripe, which is narrow in the former, as in the *Jugger*, but very broad and strongly marked in the two latter; but *Babylonicus*, as far as my experience goes, is not of the *Jugger* type of *brown* plumage, the old birds becoming slatey, or greenish *blue*, as do both *Perigrinus* and *Perigrinator*,* while the oldest Jugger, is never more than slatey brown.

Then as to *Perigrinator*, and *Peregrinus*, the comparatively rich rufous colouring at all ages, of the under parts, and the very dark head and nape of the former, (whence, and *not* as Jerdon says by corruption from Kohi, comes I believe the native name of *Koella*, "charcoal") at once separate the two species. There are other distinguishing points, which I shall notice hereafter; but these are sufficient, I think, to enable any one to discriminate the five species, at present admitted.

Since the above was written, I have met with the following remarks: As to the specific identity of all the Peregrines, (of the northern Hemisphere at any rate,) in the Ibis for 1868. The writer, Mr. J. H. Gurney is, I believe, unquestionably the first living authority, in regard to raptorial birds.

"I have for many years made a point of examining, as carefully as I have been able, as many specimens as possible of the Peregrine Falcon, from all parts of both hemispheres, where that widely-spread species occurs, and I have found myself entirely unable to detect, any constant specific difference that may be relied on, between the three supposed species: *Falco Peregrinus*, *F. Anatum*, and *F. Nigriceps*.

In this case, as in that of the Osprey, specimens from the Pacific Coast, (where this Falcon ranges from Vancouver's Island northward, to Chili southward) appear to be of a slightly smaller average size, than those found in the countries of North

native points. I hope all who can, will send me Falcons. Most assuredly, two species are now confounded under *Sacer*, and two under *Perigrinator*.

* This may be wrong, and the Shaheen, which becomes blue like a Peregrine, but has a black head, may be entitled to separation as *F. Atriceps* (nobis) q. v.

America, lying towards the Atlantic Ocean; but I cannot think that there is sufficient variation in this respect, to admit of specific separation.

South of Chili, in the southern part of Patagonia, and about the straits of Magellan, a really distinct race *does* occur, closely allied to *F. Melanogenys* of Australia, from which indeed, it only differs in its slightly larger size. It is worthy of remark, that the three southern races of Peregrine Falcons, *viz.* this Magellan race, to which, I believe, no specific name has yet been given, *F. Melanogenys* of Australia, and *F. Minor* of South Africa, all agree between themselves, and differ from the true *F. Peregrinus* in having much narrower spaces, than occur in that bird, between the dark, transverse, abdominal bars, which characterize the adult plumage of all these Falcons."

Although South Africa has a peculiar race of its own, (the *F. Minor* mentioned above) the real Peregrine occurs there also, and undoubted specimens of this latter species, have been obtained at Natal, and at the Cape of Good Hope; eastward of India, the true Peregrine occurs in Java, Sumatra, China, and Japan, but only rarely, Mr. Wallace tells us, in the western islands of the Archipelago.

No. 9. **Falco Perigrinator**, Sundwall.

The Shaheen Falcon.

I have, as yet, no detailed information as to the breeding of this species. The bird most commonly known as the Shaheen, in upper India, at any rate in the Himalayahs, is distinct, I believe, from the true *Perigrinator* (Sund.), and to it I have, provisionally, applied the name of *F. Atriceps*, (No. 9 *(bis)* q. v.). The true *Perigrinator*, doubtless occurs in upper India, but its real habitat is, I believe, Southern and Central India, *F. Babylonicus*, Gurney, and *F. Atriceps*, nobis, being its representatives in the North West.

Dr. Jerdon mentions, that the true Shaheen breeds on steep and inaccessible cliffs, and that he has seen three eyries, one on the Neilgherries, another, at the celebrated Hill fort of Antoor, and the third, at the great water-fall at Mhow. It lays its eggs, he remarks, in March and April, and the young fly in May and June, when they are caught by falconers.

The only other Indian Falcons, for which *Perigrinator* could be mistaken, are *Perigrinus* and *Atriceps*, and how it may be at once distinguished from the former of these two, I have indicated when speaking of this bird. But there are other differences, which, so far as the limited number of specimens that I have examined, enables me to judge, are constant. In the first place, the Shaheen is smaller, I have four average males before me, two of each species, and I find the wings of the Peregrine, 12·25, and 12·87, while those of the *Shaheen* are only 11·47 and 11·64. Then not only are the head, nape and upper back almost black, far blacker than in any Peregrine that I have ever seen; but the cheek stripe also is blacker, and proportionably to the size of the bird, longer. Then, on the nape, a number, (greater or less) of buffy patches are always seen, owing to the feathers there, being buffy, with broad blackish tips, and the buffy bases showing through. Lastly, the white bars on the inner web of the first primary, are more numerous, and age for age, narrower in *Perigrinator*, than in *Peregrinus*. Thus in two specimens, one of each species, both males, and as I take it, of much the same age, *Perigrinator* has thirteen white bars, each averaging 0·15, on the first primary of a wing 11·47; while *Peregrinus* has only eleven bars, averaging 0·23, on the first primary of a wing measuring 12·5.

From *Atriceps*, to which it is more closely allied, it differs in three important points. This latter is never quite so rufous beneath, as *Perigrinator* often is. It has *no* separate cheek stripe, but has this, the cheeks, ear-coverts, head and neck, black, all in one; and whereas, the true adult *Perigrinator* has the rest of the upper parts, slatey blue, almost unbarred, *Atriceps* has them closely and clearly barred with dusky slatey, as in *Peregrinus*.

I mentioned, when talking of the primary differences between *Peregrinus*, and *Perigrinator*, the rufous tinge on the lower parts of the latter bird, but it must not be supposed, that *all* specimens show this, as markedly as others. I have one specimen, an adult too, the whole lower part of which, including chin and throat, are a pure *bright* (but not deep) chestnut. On the other hand, Col. Tytler has a fine specimen; an undoubted *Perigrinator*, which has the chin, throat, and neck, in front, pure white; ear-coverts, and sides of neck, with only a *faint* salmon coloured tinge, towards the tips of the feathers; breast, some feathers pure white, others, chiefly towards the sides, with a decided, but not deep, salmon tinge; centre of abdomen alone, pure salmon colour; vent feathers, yellowish, and only a very very faint yellowish salmon tinge on sides, flanks, thigh coverts, and lower tail coverts. But the head, nape, and upper back of this bird, are positively black; there are the buffy patches on the nape, and the numerous narrow primary bars, so the bird is an unmistakeable *Perigrinator*, though, (if I except the salmon coloured patch, in the centre of the abdomen,) I have seen many Peregrines more rufous. This bird of Col. Tytler's, in common with most that I have seen, (but not all) has an obscure pale frontal band.

Mr. R. Thompson sends me the following note, but I am by no means sure, whether his remarks, and those which he quotes from Major Radcliffe, H. M.'s 88th, really apply to this species, or to *F. Atriceps.*

"In the Field newspaper of the 2nd of May, 1868, Major E. D. Radcliffe, 88th Regiment, gives some interesting accounts of the Shaheen and its habits. Amongst others, having described one that had been kept, and moulted for fourteen years, flying still in capital style, and killing vast quantities of game of a miscellaneous description, he goes on to notice a habit of the wild ones, of catching Bats, after having gone to roost with full crops. This the Shaheen will often do, and I have known of an instance, when the Falcon *eat* the Bat it had just caught. It was apparently still hungry. The Shaheen is not the only bird of prey that will do this, I have seen the Shikra, *Micronisus badius* catch and kill Bats, sometimes eating, at other times throwing them down dead. My Goshawks often fluttered at Bats, which happened to pass close over where they were picketted, to enjoy the cool of the evening.

"The Shaheen is an early bird. In the first gleam of daylight one may just see it shoot past, like an arrow, at some unlucky early bird. Late in the evenings, it will often sit and watch for returning flocks of Mynas, and Parrots, and having selected one, will dash at it, surely nailing a victim, which it will carry back to its perch and devour. It takes the *Turtur risorius* more than any other bird, though Pigeons are not safe from it. I once saw one dash into a vertical net set with a small quail for a bait, it was late in the evening, and the Shaheen was on a tree not a hundred yards from the net.

"When used to take Pigeons, it becomes very destructive to dove cots, usually selecting the highest mounted and best flyer of the flock.

"After a full meal in the daytime, or early morning, the Shaheen will retire to some tank or rivulet, and there enjoy a good bath. It remains for hours seated on a tree, cleaning and drying its feathers after its ablutions.

"I have lately seen one, an adult, doing its *best* with a small flock of wild Pigeons, without succeeding in striking a single bird. I have seen this once or twice before, but the Falcons in those instances were young birds, this one was an adult."

I append exact dimensions of a male. Length, 14·87. Wing,

11·49; (second primary the longest, 1st 0·35 shorter, 3rd 0·5 shorter. Tail, 6; exterior tail feathers, 0·4 shorter than central ones.) Tarsus, 1·85. Foot, greatest length, 3·3; greatest width, 3·2; mid-toe, 1·7; its claw on curve, 0·8; hind toe, 0·75; its claw on curve, 1·1; outer toe 1·2; its claw, 0·75; inner toe, 1; its claw, 0·87. Bill, straight from margin of cere, 0.72; on curve, from cere, 0·87; from gape, 1·1; width at gape, 0·89; height, at margin of cere, 0·4; width of cere, 0·3.

"This bird," Mr. Blyth mentions, "is *F. Ruber Indicus (Aldrovandi)* and *F. Communis indicus*, Gmel. and undoubtedly *F. Sultaneus*, Hodgson. Mr. Layard obtained this species in Ceylon."

No. 9. (bis). **Falco Atriceps**, Sp. Nov.

The Black Cap Falcon.

The species to which I have provisionally given the above name, closely resembles *Perigrinator* in size, flight and habits, but is, I believe, distinct. I have as yet only obtained adults, (one of which is now with my friend Mons. Jules Verreaux,) and I can therefore only indicate the differences between full grown birds of this and the preceding species. The whole head, nape, cheek stripe, cheeks and sides of the head, are black, forming one unbroken cap, and showing no separate cheek stripe, as all our other Indian Falcons do. In this latter respect, it differs from these, just as the Indian Hobby, (*H. Severus*, Horsf.) does from the European; the cheek stripe, cheeks, and ear coverts being confluent or very nearly so. The whole of the rest of the upper parts, are a clear Peregrine slatey blue, closely and conspicuously barred, as in the Peregrine, with dusky slatey, and differing in this respect from the adult *Perigrinator*, which has these parts nearly free from bars. Beneath, it is never so rufous as *Perigrinator usually* (but *not* invariably) is, and it has the thigh coverts, and under wing coverts closely, though narrowly, barred, while in the old *Perigrinator*, the lower parts are nearly spotless. The bars in the inner webs of the primaries are narrow and close, as in *Perigrinator* and, in this respect, differ conspicuously from those of the Peregrine's wing.

Dr. Jerdon, to whom I showed specimens of this species, entertained no doubt as to their differing from any of the true *Perigrinator*, that he had seen in Central and Southern India, and remarked that, "if distinct, this is probably the *Neela Shaheen* of native falconers, and may be identical with one of

Hodgson's undescribed species; possibly his *F. Micrurus*, the Javali Kooee."

Although I have not been able to examine the specimens, I have little doubt, that the two birds referred to by Dr. Jerdon, (Vol. I. p. 26) as probably hybrids between the Peregrine and the Shaheen, belong to this species.

Mr. Blyth remarks in the Ibis, "Mr. J. H. Gurney has called our attention to the fact that an adult female, attributed to this species, in the British Museum, believed to be from Nepaul, and an adult male in the Norwich Museum from Northern India, have a much lighter colouring on the under parts, than has hitherto been figured or described as being the case in *F. Perigrinator*. If it be not that this peculiarity is due to old age, Mr. Gurney supposes the two specimens, just mentioned, may belong to an undescribed species." I cannot help thinking that these birds also may belong to our new *Atriceps*. Again, Mr. Blyth says, that, *F. Sultaneus*, Hodgson, is *undoubtedly* the true *F. Perigrinator*, "though a figure in one of his drawings represents, I suspect, a stray individual of the Australian *F. Melanogenys;* and such also may be Dr. Jerdon's supposed hybrid falcons." I cannot doubt that Mr. Hodgson's figure, thus referred to, represents *F. Atriceps*, since this latter, though to my notion unmistakably distinct, has a great general resemblance to the Australian species.*

Mr. R. Thompson says, "I must say that I agree with Mr. Hume, in thinking that we have another species; which he names, in his catalogue, *F. Atriceps*. I remember shooting an adult male with a perfectly black head, the cheek stripe represented by a deep, dark, band, confluent with the ear coverts. By way of illustrating this, I would recommend comparison with an adult *Lanius Nigriceps*. I think the latter fully gives an idea of the Falcon I killed, as regards the plumage of the bird's neck and head. In the south of the Mirzapoor district, one swept close past me the other day, which I recognized as identical with the black headed *Perigrinator*, which I shot a few years ago."

This species if, as I conceive, really distinct, is common in the Himalayahs, more so, I believe, than any other of the genus *Falco*, as restricted in Dr. Jerdon's work, and it is this species I think, to which my friend Mr. Thompson refers, when he

* I have, however, only a single Australian specimen, which is not, I think, adult, so that a further comparison *may* require me to modify my views, but if *Atriceps* and *Melanogenys* should (which seems in *the highest* degree improbable) prove to be identical, then the latter is no *straggler* to, but a common resident in, the Himalayahs.

remarks that it "begins to breed in March, some laying as late as the commencement of May; during the whole breeding season, the screaming and noise the birds make, betray the situation of the nest. This latter is usually found in lofty precipices of the lower Himalayan ranges; it is placed on a ledge of rock, often inside the hole left by the falling out from the softer sandstone matrix, of a water worn boulder, or nodule of igneous rock. I know several eyries to which the birds yearly resort; one in the Kotree Dhoon, another in the gorge of the Ramgunga, where it first leaves the hills, and a third close to Khoorpa Tal, near to and below Nynee Tal. I have noticed the young birds following their parents late in June, and early in July."

To my friend, Capt. Cock of Dhurumsalla, I owe the eggs, and an undoubted specimen of the female of this bird. He gives a most interesting account of his operations. He found the nest on a ledge of rock on the face of a most dangerous precipice. The nest had for many years been occupied by the Black Cap, but in 1868, one of the large Himalayan Vultures, *G. Fulvus*, or if distinct, *G. Himalayensis*, (vide supra No. 3,) laid there, and had to surrender its eggs to Captain Cock. This year (1869) the Falcons again took possession, and on the 10th of March, this gentleman again visited it. "I went," he says, "to the Falcon's nest, and found the female sitting close: with great difficulty I got her off by throwing stones down from above, but even then she did not fly, but only shifted her position on the ledge, so as to show me two eggs in the nest. I got men and ropes, and a friend, Captain Duff, to shoot her as she left the nest, but though I, with great difficulty, induced a man to descend and take the eggs, (after I had all but gone over the precipice myself, a tuft of grass, having given way under my foot at the very verge,) the female got off scathless or but slightly wounded, owing to the height of the precipice. Captain Duff who has a house hard by, tells me that the birds are always killing the blue rock Pigeons under his very nose. Both birds showed themselves, but neither came sufficiently within shot to enable us to bag them, though we fired at the female." On the 17th March, he returned to the nest where the female was again sitting, on driving her off he saw that another egg had been laid, and he again fired at the old bird, but owing to the hazardous position in which he was standing at the time, again missed her. On the 20th he revisited the eyrie. "I was sitting under the cliff when a Lammergeyer came sailing by and the male Falcon dashed at him, and then returned to the nest, the female flying out in pursuit. As she returned I shot her; the male then sat on the egg, (there was still only one) for some time, when by sending a man up above, to throw down stones, he (the Falcon *not* the man) flew off and I got a shot at, and wounded him. He managed to get on to a tree over-hanging the precipice, and though I got as near to him as I could and took a pot shot, he was too far off, and sailed away down the *khud* (valley)." Subsequently he took the third egg.

The extraordinary boldness exhibited by the female bird is very characteristic.

The nest, as may be guessed from its age, and from having once at least served our larger Himalayan Vulture (No. 3) as a laying place, was a large irregular mass of sticks. Two eggs were taken the first, and one the second time, but probably the normal number is four. I have seen two of the eggs, these are very beautiful—broad, very perfect ovals, slightly larger than the eggs of *F. Jugger*, and with shells of a somewhat finer and closer texture than those of these latter. The ground colour in both is a rich brick red, here and there faintly blotched and spotted with a darker shade, and with a few bold blotches and splashes, specks and spots of the deepest liver-colour ; strange to say, there are one or two pure white spots on the ground colour, and a white spot or blotch in the middle of almost every one of the larger liver-coloured blotches. In my whole series of Jugger's eggs, I have none at all like these, although the eggs of both species are emphatically of the true Falcon type. The eggs appear to me fully as big as the average run of Peregrines.

They measure 2·1 in length, by 1·66 and 1·68 in breadth. "The female measured," (Captain Cock tells me,) "in the flesh : Length 18. Wing 13·5. Tail 6·5. The bill was light blue, dark at the tip ; cere and orbits light yellow ; legs and feet a rather brighter yellow ; irides deep brown.

"Top, back and sides of head, nape, and upper back, *very* deep blackish brown, actually black on the sides of the head. On the nape, a few feathers dashed with fulvous red. From this point downwards towards the tail, gradually lighter and slatey, (slatey-*blue* I should call it) lightest on the rump and every where barred with dusky. From the base of the tail the slatey colour darkens, the end tipped with light rufous or fulvous, the inner webs barred light fulvous, and the visible surface barred like the back. The quills very dark brown, nearly black at the tips, the inner webs barred with fulvous, and each with a narrow fulvous edge, whiter in the secondaries and tertiaries. Shoulders slatey, barred as in the back. Underneath the throat, and two long scallops into the blackish brown sides of the neck, white changing into fulvous. The crop or upper breast chestnut, spotted with dark brown; lower breast, abdomen and lower tail coverts rufous white, or very light rufous, barred with brown. Tibial feathers light chestnut underneath, above darker and closely barred." This specimen, though not of quite so old a bird as I have sent to Paris, and with less *blue* therefore in the mantle, is a very characteristic one, the whole side of the head for nearly an inch below the eye, embracing what in *Perigrinator* would be the cheek or moustachial stripe, the cheeks, ear coverts, and sides of the base of the skull, uniform unbroken black, confluent with, and only slightly darker than the lores, top and back of the head and nape.

No. 10. **Falco Sacer,** Schlegel.

The Saker.

I have as yet been able to learn nothing certain of the breeding of this noble bird within our limits. I have been assured by natives who know it well and train it for hawking, that it breeds in Cabool, the Huzara country, and Cashmere, but none of the many sportsmen whom I have enquired from, and who have spent one or more summers in Cashmere, appear to have noticed it there. The Ameer of Cabool when recently (March, 1869) on his visit to the Governor-General, brought with him some well trained specimens of this species and mentioned, that they bred in Afghanistan, and that he was himself acquainted with several eyries. It is this bird I believe, which is the *F. Biarmicus* of Vigne's list noticed (I quote Mr. Blyth) as being "common in the plains under the Alpine Punjaub." It has been repeatedly shot, as low down as Umballa and even Dehli; while west of the Sutledge and towards the Peshawur valley, it almost replaces Jugger, being at any rate more common there than the latter species. *Babylonicus* which also occurs there, is far rarer, while on the other hand, this latter is more common about, and north of Umritsur.

Of the breeding of the Sacer elsewhere, Mr. W. H. Simpson has given an interesting account in the Ibis for 1860.

"On the evening of the 29th, another fortunate discovery was made by the same party, and this time of the nest of a bird (*F. Sacer*) whose eggs it was believed were almost unknown previously in authentic cabinets. We were strolling on a low flat island in the Danube, the edge of which is well covered with tall Poplars and other trees. A nest of *Milvus Ater* had occupied us for a short time; but on getting close to the river again, in a place where the trees are very tall, and not thickly grouped, my friend and *Cicerone* drew our attention to a good sized nest which was placed about one-third of the way up a tallish Poplar. The nest was resting upon a large branch close to the bole of the tree, and appeared exceedingly easy of access. The nest was not very much larger than those of the numerous Hooded Crows we had already examined, but was deep and comfortably lined, appearing, however, from the outside as like a large Crow's nest as one bundle of sticks is like another. The eggs, four in number, were slightly incubated. In size they seem to be intermediate between those of the Peregrine and Geir Falcon, being, however, longer in proportion to their breadth. Two of them are light in colour, the other two much darker."

The one figured, measures 2·2 in length, by 1·6 in breadth. An egg of this bird figured by Dr. Bree from a specimen in the British Museum, measures 2·13 by 1·7.

Mr. C. Farman, in his notes on the birds of prey of Central Bulgaria (Ibis 1868) gives the following valuable information relative to this species.

"This noble Falcon, although not so plentiful as some others of its tribe, is in this country by no means a very rare bird. From April to October, it is pretty generally to be met with on the barren wastes which stretch from Hasique to Kushetchen. Whether it remains here during the winter, is a question about which I am not absolutely decided; but I am inclined to think it does. Some specimens I certainly have seen during the depth of winter; but they seem scarcer during the severe cold which freezes the mighty Danube.

"In the spring of 1865, my friend Mr. Robert Barkley, when residing at Shitangick, in charge of the Railway works in that district, obtained a pair of young Sakers from a nest situated on a tree, about a quarter of a mile from the Railway works at Shitangick. He kept these birds in confinement for several months, and they appeared to thrive; but, if I recollect rightly, they ultimately succumbed to the carelessness of native servants.

"The following year (1866) I had the good fortune to be residing at Shitangick, and I carefully watched the habits of this species. Towards the middle of March I observed two pair of these Falcons frequenting the neighbourhood; and at the end of the month I found one of these pairs were repairing the old nest from which Mr. R. Barkley, the preceding spring, had taken the young. In the first week of April I found the nest of the second pair at a distance of about two miles from that of the first. The nest was placed on a solitary tree in close proximity to which, there was a little corn growing; but the general character of the surrounding country is that of wild undulating moor, with a few shrubs at long intervals, and an occasional tree or two.

"On approaching within about two hundred yards of the place, one of the birds flew from the tree in an anxious manner, as though leaving the nest, and I was much disappointed at not being able to get a shot at it. However, I ascended the tree; and when within a few feet of the nest, off flew another bird, at which of course I was unable to shoot. I found the nest quite finished, but no eggs in it. It was about eighteen inches in external diameter, neatly put together; and unlike most Falcon's nests, it was by no means flat, but, on the contrary, was much hollowed in the middle, in the form of a bowl; it was composed of large sticks at the base, the upper part being made of smaller and more pliable twigs, and lined inside with tender twigs, a little coarse grass, and a few pieces of wool interwoven together.

"On the 12th of April I again paid a visit to this nest; but this time I took a friend with me, being determined, if possible, to secure one of the birds. We approached very stealthily and quietly to within about one hundred and fifty yards of the tree, when, as before, one of the parent birds left the tree. Being, however, mindful of what happened on my former visit, I kept myself in readiness for the other bird. On coming to the foot of the tree, we stationed ourselves on either side of it, shouted and made a great noise, but all to no purpose; no second bird appeared, nor could I distinguish anything like a bird on the nest. I began to think that the birds had been too wise to trust again to their former device; however, to make quite sure of the fact before ascending the tree, my friend fired, when to our no little surprise out flew a bird like an arrow; and as it came my way, I had the satisfaction of bringing it down. On ascending the tree, I found that the nest contained two eggs, which with the female bird I had shot, I brought away with me, being well satisfied with the result of my morning's walk.

"The eggs are of a slightly elongated oval form, and differ from the generality of Falcon's eggs in being decidedly more pointed at the smaller end. The two eggs taken by me from the same nest, as before described, are similar in form, but they differ much in markings; of one, the ground colour is light red covered all over with small spots and blotches of bright red; the blotches being larger and darker at the larger end; the other egg has a ground-colour of dirty reddish white, covered with small spots and rather large blotches of a dirty red, the blotches being fewer, larger and more distinct than on the other egg."

In the Ibis for 1864, Mr. J. H. Cochrane describes how, on the 26th March, 1868, he obtained a nest with four eggs of a red-headed Falcon, on the south side of the third or small pyramid of Ghizeh. The nest was a few feathers and still fewer sticks, in a hollow on one of the steps, about 30 feet from the top. He failed to procure the parent, and so remained uncertain of the species; he figures one of the eggs so obtained, it is of the yellow brown, Falcon type, and measures 2·17 by 1·71 in breadth. But he obtained a second nest from a very similar situation.

"On the 3rd April following, on my return from a fortnight's trip down the Rosetta branch of the Nile, the same Bedouin whom I had asked to look out for nests for me, brought me a fine living female, *Falco lanarius*, and three eggs, which he had taken on the Dashoor Pyramid. The eggs were much incubated, and I unfortunately broke one in blowing it. The Bedouin said, he had taken the bird by throwing a cloth over it at night, and in so doing had broken one of the eggs, which originally had been four in number. These eggs much resemble those before mentioned."

He figures one of the eggs obtained in the latter nest: it is of the clouded, brownish red, Falcon type, and measures 2·13 by 1·55.

In a later number of the Ibis, this latter egg is put down as pertaining to *F. Lanarius* (*verus*, I conclude, for Schlegel had long previously discriminated between this species and the "*Saqr*,") and the former to "*Barbarus*." Now, although the living bird said by the Bedouin to have been captured with the eggs, is stated to be "alive in the gardens of the Zoological Gardens," and to be "*F. Lanarius*," I confess that I altogether disbelieve that these eggs belonged to the two species indicated, and entertain little doubt that they pertained to our present bird, *F. Sacer*. In the first place, the size of these eggs agrees well, with the authentic egg obtained by Mr. Simpson. In the second, there seems an incompatibility between the size of the supposed parents and of the eggs. *F. Peregrinus* is *a much larger* bird than *F. Lanarius*, but how seldom do its eggs reach the dimensions above given. *F. Jugger* again, is a much larger bird than *Lanarius*, but of the hundreds of its eggs that have passed through my hands, the very largest only measured 2·15 by 1·65, and they average 2·01 by 1·57. *F. Barbarus* to which curiously enough the largest egg is assigned, is the smallest of this group of Falcons, and Mr. Salvin gives the following dimensions of authentic eggs of this species taken by himself in the Eastern Atlas: 1·91 by 1·62, 1·87 by 1·5, and 2·04 by 1·56. Again the eggs of the Eleonora Falcon, a bird fully as long as, though slighter built than, the true Lanner, I find figured from 1·7 to 1·85 in length, and from 1·3 to 1·4 in breadth. I submit that Mr. Cochrane's two nests of large eggs: 1stly. Certainly belonged to Falcons; 2ndly. Did not, as he says, belong to *Peregrinus*, *Perigrinator* &c. which have *not* red or reddish heads;* 3rdly. Could not, on account of their size, have belonged to either *Barbarus* or *Lanarius*, which *have* red heads; and 4thly. Did, considering the locality, most probably belong to *Falco Sacer*. Lower Egypt is quite within the range of *Sacer*, I have seen a specimen shot, not far from the pyramids, and Mr. E. C. Taylor procured a fine female near Girgeh. It is common in northern Arabia, and was observed by the Rev. H. Tristram once in the oak forests of Bashan; although, as he says, it prefers the wide plains and deserts to the cliffs of the Jordan valley, and he adds: "The sheikhs of the Beni Sakk'r (sons of the Falcon) make it a point of distinction to possess *several* of these birds trained for the chase of the Gazelle, and the distinction between it and the Lanner is well known to all the Arabs."

In his notes on the birds observed in his first visit to Palestine, the Rev. H. B. Tristram had remarked (Ibis for 1859):

"On one occasion while riding with an Arab guide, I observed a Falcon of large size rise close to us. The guide, when I pointed it out to him, exclaimed '*Tair sakqr*.' *Tair*, the Arabic for 'bird' is universally throughout North Africa and the East, applied to those Falcons which are capable of being trained for hunting, *i. e.* 'the bird,' *par excellence*. *Tair el Hohr*, 'the noble bird,' is the common appellation of the Peregrine and its congeners. '*Sakqr*,' I have only heard applied to the very large Falcons, never to the *F. Peregrinus* or *F. Punicus*, both of which are trained by the Arabs for the chase. No doubt our specific name '*Falco Sacer*' is derived not from a Latin source, but from the Arabic trivial name of the species. There seems as yet much confusion in the nomenclature of the different larger species or races, which to the south and east of the Mediterranian take the place of the *F. Greenlandicus*, *islandicus*, and *norwegicus* of the North. The bird which I saw was nearly as large as a Jer Falcon, and had a very bright rufous head, the light colour extending to the back of the neck. How far *F. Sacer*, *lanarius*, *cervicalis*, *biarmicus*, and *cherrug* are distinct species, and what

* Adult, but not very old Sacers, appear as they fly, and even when sitting at no great distance, to have dingy fulvous red heads. I have repeatedly noticed this.

is the geographical range of each, seems a question well worthy the investigation of naturalists travelling in the East."

Though much thus indicated as requiring investigation still remains uncertain, no doubts *now* exist as to the distinctness of *Sacer* and *Lanarius*, the former of which, if I have rightly identified the bird* is fully double the weight of the latter. The identity of *Cherrug* and *Sacer* seems scarcely now to be questioned, while the distinctness of *Biarmicus* and *Cervicalis* from *Sacer* and their identity with each other is, I believe, admitted. The plumage of our Indian Sacers, however, varies so much, that it would be well if a series of them could be compared with a series of the Abyssinian ones, of which unfortunately I have never seen a specimen or even a good figure.

Mr. Blyth would place *F. Subniger*, Gray, and probably he thinks *F. Hypoleucus*, Gould, (both Australian species) in what he designates the Sakir and Lanner group, but Mr. Gurney differs from him on this point, and altogether demurs, (as I think with excellent reason,) to uniting *F. Sacer* and *F. Lanarius* in the same sub group. "*F. Sacer*," he says, "appears to me to be referable to a small distinct section of which the other members are *F. Jugger* and *F. Polyagrus*."

The cere in this species is narrower on the culmen than in either *Peregrinus* or *Perigrinator*. The "saqr" is feathered much further down the tarsus than is the Peregrine, and this latter again than the Shaheen. The white spots or oval bars on the inner webs of the saqr's primaries, are larger than in any other Indian species, I think; occupying nearly the whole surface, the ovals running into each other, so that the central portions of the brown interspaces often disappear altogether. As a rule, the 2nd quills of *F. Jugger*, *Peregrinus*, *Perigrinator* and *Babylonicus*, are longest, and there is a notch on the inner web of the 1st primary only. In *F. Sacer*, the notch is more obscure, but is present I have remarked *usually*, *on both* the 1st and 2nd primaries, while the 3rd quill is often subequal to the 2nd.

M. Schlegel, quoted by Dr. Bree, says that the adult Sacer differs from all other Falcons; its plumage, as in the young, is of more agreeable tints, and *has not transverse bands either on the upper part* of the body or on the under side. But Mr. Gurney,

* Schlegel quoted by Bree, says, "The Sacer of the falconers, is a bird of a figure rather *less strong* than the Lanner, and consequently it is intermediate in this respect between this species and the Gyr Falcon." Now the bird that I have taken to be the Lanner is *much less* than the Sacer. Bree himself gives the lengths of males and females of each species as follows: *F. Sacer*, 19 and 21 inches. *F. Lanarius* 14 and 15 inches.

Dr. Bree tells us, remarks that there was, when he wrote, a living specimen from Turkey in the gardens of the Zoological Society, (London) differing from any other specimen he had seen, its plumage being cross-barred like that of a female merlin. Mr. Gurney later found a similar specimen in the collection of the East India Company, with distinct brown transverse markings all across the back, shoulders and wing coverts, and he considered that these were indications of maturity, the bird in the Zoological Society having exhibited few if any of them when first sent there. I have seen both barred and unbarred birds from the North West, and I cannot help believing that there are at least two distinct species now included, under the specific name *Sacer*, one of which *may* prove to be the real *F. Cherrug*, but at present I have not sufficient specimens to work out the question; and, even if I had, am not in a position to decide whether the bird originally designated *Cherrug* was an example of *F. Sacer*, (*verus*) or of the nearly allied species, which I have reason to believe exists.

I give a description and measurements of two young birds, a male and a female shot in Hurriana, but whether these are true Sakers, or whether they belong to the supposed allied species, I am unable to determine.

The feet were grayish green, and the cere leaden green, but in the female, which was I think rather the older bird, there was a yellowish tinge on the feet. In both, the head was yellowish white, (tinged in the female on the cap with rufous) each feather with a dark central brown stripe, broadest in the female. The general hue of the upper parts in the male was much the same as that of the young *F. Jugger*, but slightly more rufous. The tail feathers had large round or oval white spots on each web, roundest on the central feathers, and more and more oval on the laterals as they receded from these. The feathers of the lower back, rump and upper tail coverts were broadly margined with *yellowish* white, the tertials, later secondaries and upper wing coverts with *rufous* white. The scapulars and tertials, had *scarcely* a trace of the rufous white spots or blotches so conspicuous in the female, the upper wing coverts *no* trace. Beneath (in the male) the brown of the lower breast, abdomen, sides and thigh coverts and of the lower wing coverts was pale, dull and small in extent as compared with that of the same parts of the female. This latter was of a deeper brown, and had a more rufous tinge everywhere, especially on the upper surface, where all the feathers, except the longest upper tail coverts were edged with rufous, and the larger scapulars, tertiaries, and later secondaries, as well as many of the wing coverts, had conspicuous rufous white double blotches or broad imperfect bars. In the female too, there was a trace of a pale frontal band continued as a supercilium right round the occiput, neither bird showed any sign of a cheek stripe. These were the measurements. Length M, 19·81, F, 22. Wing M, 15, F, 15·5; 2nd or 2nd and 3rd primaries the longest; 1st primary M, 0·85, and F, 0·7, shorter. Tail M, 9·2, F, 10·75. Tarsus 2·13. Foot, greatest length M, 3·55, F, 3·6; greatest width M, 3·25, F, 3·5; mid toe M, 1·9, F, 2·1; its claw, along curve, M, 0·9, F. 0·95; hind toe M, 0·85, F, 0·95; its claw along curve M, 1·2, F, 1·3; inner toe M, 1·3, F, 1·35; its claw along curve M, 1·0, F, 1·2. Bill, straight from edge of cere to point, M, 1·05, F, 1·1; along curve, M, 1·3, F, 1·38; from gape M, 1·42, F, 1·45; width at gape, M, 1·2, F, 1·25; height at margin of cere M, 0·6, F, 0·65; length of cere in both 0·25.

Dr. Jerdon in a recent note to me mentions, that the Sacer is particularly common in the desert country of Hurriana and Bhuttiana, where he has seen four or five in one morning's ride. They are said, he adds, in these parts to feed much on the Sandha Lizard (*Uromastix Hardwickii*). The old birds that Dr. Jerdon has observed, had the heads, he tells me, nearly pure white, the upper surface pale brown, and the lower parts nearly devoid of markings.

The *Cherrug* is not only trained to capture Cranes, Bustards, Houbara, Hares and the like, but also to attack and kill the common Kite, *Milvus Govinda*, which might be thought more than a match for it. Mr. R. Thompson sends me the following account of a Kite chase. "The bird mounted at a free wild *Milvus* which, before the hood was removed, was quietly sailing over a village. The hawk flew straight in the direction of the Kite. The other seeing it coming, began to mount in a series of graceful gyrations. On, and up, and up, went the two birds till they appeared like small specks in the sky. At last it was seen that the Falcon had the better of his long winged quarry, he made one stoop and struck the Kite, but not effectively, as the stroke was avoided by the latter turning over and receiving it on his claws. The chase became exciting, as the two birds began again to mount still higher. At last we saw that the Falcon was drawing away from the quarry. Some said he was going for good, but the falconer remained confident in his bird. After going away a considerable distance from his quarry and thereby acquiring, what he wanted, superior height, the Sacer resumed the chase returning downwards like a thunder-bolt on the Kite. Blow after blow was struck, and the hopeless Kite with his merciless enemy descended clutched fast together, their wings expanded, in wheeling circles to the earth, where the Kite, already half dead, was soon despatched."

Mr. Thompson mentions a remarkable fact connected with this Falcon. He had three of the same species out; one, whose successful flight has been above described, the other two, trained only to attack Herons and the like. About these latter Falcons, the Kites troubled themselves not one whit, no, not when they even flew near them, but almost the moment the hood of the first was removed, every Kite anywhere near it, began to make itself scarce. If this be correct and Mr. Thompson vouches for it, birds must be able to read the intentions of others in their eyes, and discover from the searching glances that the Falcon throws around it before starting, what kind of quarry it intends to select. The same gentleman says (though I can obtain no confirmation of the fact elsewhere. "It is admitted by most native falconers and bird-catchers that *F. Sacer* breeds in the *Bhoor* lands, or sandy and desert tracts of Western India. Many birds are brought at the beginning of October for sale; I lately saw three at the Nawaub of Rampore's in Rohilcund. They were purchased for fifteen Rupees, showing thus that the birds are easily and plentifully obtained."

No. 11. **Falco Jugger,** Gray.

The Laggar.

Lays during January, February, and March, but the majority appear to lay in the early part of February. I have never obtained an egg earlier than the 6th January, or later than the 30th March. The situation of the nest varies, it is sometimes on large trees, the Pepul being perhaps the favourite, and sometimes on ledges, or in recesses of rocky or earthy cliffs, and sometimes in the face of ancient ramparts, where one or two stones have disappeared, or on more or less inaccessible cornices of ruined buildings. I found a nest in the exterior walls of Togluck Shah's grand Egyptian-like mausoleum. Another in one of the lateral walls of the high gate of Futteh-poor Sikree. I have taken them times without number on ledges of the clay cliffs of the Jumna and Chumbul in the Etawah district, and I met with one with three full-fledged young ones on the rocks of the Mata Pahar, overlooking the Sambhur lake; still in those parts of the country with which I am best acquainted, the N. W. Provinces, Oudh, and the Punjaub, I believe the majority breed upon trees. When built on trees, the nest is usually a large and massive one, some 2 feet in diameter, if circular, or if, as is more common, oblong in shape, some 2·5 feet in length by 1·5 feet in breadth, and fully six inches in thickness.* It is composed of twigs and small sticks, at times without any lining, and at times lined with a little grass, or straw, or even leaves. Occasionally the nest is very much larger than I have described, but it will then generally be found that the bird, instead of building a nest of its own, has taken possession of, and repaired, one of some other bird. Near Bhureh on the Chumbul, a pair took possession of a nest that for the two previous years had, to my knowledge, been always occupied by our Indian ring-tail eagle (H. *Leucoryphus*) and Mr. W. Blewitt who took five nests of this species in January and February, in the neighbourhood of Hansie, remarks, that in every case, the Falcon had taken possession of, and more or less repaired, a deserted nest of the common eagle (*A. Fulvescens*). The repaired nests were all on Keekur trees (the favourite par excellence, of *A. Fulvescens*) at heights of from 17 to 24 feet from the ground. Three of these nests contained five eggs, a very unusual number. There was no mistaking either eggs or birds, all of which Mr. Blewitt kindly sent me.

Where the bird selects a recess or ledge in a cliff's face for nesting, a large nest is rarely made, a few handfuls of sticks, just enough to prevent the eggs rolling about, with a few feathers, accidentally or purposely intermingled, is all that is usually met with in such situations, and I have twice taken the eggs laid on the bare earth in a slight depression, without one particle of stick, grass or feather near them.

The normal number of the eggs is four; but, while five are occasionally found, the bird often sits on only three; and once I took two eggs, ready to hatch off, out of a very old pair's nest, that in former seasons had always contained the full number. In colour, the eggs vary much, as indeed do those of all true Falcons. The usual type is a reddish, brownish, or yellowish brown ground, very thickly speckled and spotted all over, with a darker and richer shade of the ground colour. The spots are often more crowded at one end than the other, producing occa-

* It appears to be a general rule, with birds that build sometimes on trees, and sometimes on rocky ledges, that their nests in the former situation are always deeper, more cup-like and more massive, than when in the latter.

sionally the effect of a clouded cap; some in addition to the multitudinous specks exhibit bold red blotches, or dark streaky clouds, and some again are very feebly coloured, a nearly uniform pale dingy buff, with scarcely a trace of blotches or even specks of a darker hue. In shape, the eggs are commonly a broad oval, slightly more pointed at one end, of a dull, glossless and slightly chalky, but still compact texture. The egg lining is white or slightly reddish white.

Elsewhere I have thus described the eggs: "A very great variation in shape is observable in the eggs of this species. They are all a somewhat broad, but generally very perfect oval. In texture, they are rather fine, but at the same time (if I may so express it) chalky, and they are perfectly devoid of gloss. The eggs, as a rule, are a longer oval than those of *Falco Peregrinus*, and are scarcely ever so richly coloured as the latter often are. The coloration is of course of the true Falcon type. Some eggs are of a nearly uniform pale dingy yellowish brown, blanching towards one extremity or the other, indistinctly clouded, blotched or mottled with a somewhat deeper and redder brown. Others are a nearly uniform red brown, with scarcely any traces of distinct markings; others have a nearly pure white, reddish white, pale dingy yellow, brownish yellow or reddish brown ground, more or less boldly, extensively and thickly blotched and clouded or even freckled, mottled, and streaked with more or less bright or deep brick or blood red. As a rule, the markings are not very bold or sharply defined, in but few is there any decided tendency towards capping at either end, and all have a more or less freckled and dotted appearance. These eggs fade much as time passes, but when first found many of them are, to an oologist's eye, perfect pictures."

In size they vary from 2·15 to 1·85 in length, and from 1·65 to 1·48 in breadth, but of ninety-eight eggs measured, the average size was 2·01 by 1·57. I once noticed a curious trait in this bird, somewhat similar to that related above of *Gyps Bengalensis*. On the 2nd of March, 1866 near Soj in the Mynpoorie district, I found a nest of these birds on what had been a large Peepul tree, but which, owing to the continual cutting of its branches for the elephants of the Chohan Rajahs of the neighbourhood, had become a gaunt, white spectre-like thing with two or three huge nearly bare arms, each with a dense cluster of leafy twigs near the extremity, and smaller similar clusters at odd angles of the branches. The tree stood solitary in the midst of a wide tract of land overflowed during the rains, but at the time I speak of, waste and parched, with no other vegetation for a good mile in any direction, but patches of down-trodden, withered rush.

The nest was in one of the highest clusters. The male was sitting on the broad bare bough, about 6 feet below it, tearing a Roller *(Coracias Indica)* to pieces, and I may mention, that when examined, this bird proved to have had the whole head, neck, and upper part of the body eaten; the wings, tail and lower portion of the body were altogether uninjured. I shot the male, and he fell flat on the bough. A man was sent up, who threw the male down, still there were no signs of the female, and I called to the man to search the nest for eggs. As he placed his hand at the side of the nest, which he could only just reach, the female suddenly appeared from the hollow of the nest, and stood upon its margin. The man drew back rather startled, the female turned towards the inside of the nest, gave a vicious drive at it with her bill and flew off. On taking the eggs, it appeared that she had driven her powerful bill into one of them, making a triangular hole, each side of which, measured about half an inch. The female must have seen her mate shot, and have felt, perhaps from the man still coming to the nest, after securing the male, that he intended to rob it. Did she break the egg herself in anger? The eggs were nearly ready to hatch off. Had she perchance some glimmering idea that she might let the chick out and thus save it? It is impossible to say: but a whole party of us witnessed the fact, and it seems worthy of record. What struck me fully as much in this case was, that though the male was in the act of tearing the Roller to pieces, and though the whole ground, for many yards round the tree, was strewed with feathers of Pigeons, Doves and Rollers, a pair of Doves, (*T. Risoria*) had a nest with young ones, in another leafy cluster of this same tree, and another pair were sitting calmly on two bare sprays, not 15 feet from where the male, whom they could not help seeing, was devouring his prey. Had the Roller always been his prey, one might have understood their fearlessness, but around the tree, lay the feathers of, I should say, at least fifty individuals of their own species. That the Falcons must *designedly* have spared their fellow-tenants is clear; the two birds, however wary and watchful, could never have built their nest, hatched their young, and partly reared these latter in safety, within 30 feet of the Falcons' nest, unless these latter had allowed them to do so absolutely without molestation; for had one of the pair only been once set upon or pursued, they would assuredly have deserted the nest. The natives declared that this pair of Doves, were left by the Falcons as decoys; and that the other pair were strangers, who would probably soon have fallen victims to the confidence engendered by seeing the resident birds rearing their young in security. I can really give no more plausible explanation of what seems to me a very remarkable fact. Mr. R. Thompson furnishes the following interesting remarks, in regard to this species:

"This Falcon breeds on lofty trees; usually on one, with others standing near it, in open cultivated country; even when it is a forest bird, it chooses such parts as are tolerably open, with widely spreading glades; but habitually it prefers open localities.

"A nest found in open forest country, south of Lall-dang in the Provinces of Kumaon, on the 5th February, 1868, was up to that date unfinished, though both the Falcons were present. The male, I observed carrying small twigs and roots to the female, who seemed the architect. This nest was begun in a large Semel tree (*Bombax heptaphyllum*) on the forked branch of one of the principal lateral arms, and might have been 40 feet from the ground. The nest was about 2½ feet in diameter, with the egg cavity about ten inches. The inside was lined with small fine roots and bruised dry leaves, evidently such as had been attached to the twigs, which composed the body and foundation of the nest; on the 27th March succeeding, the nest was again visited. The Falcons were out at the time, it being about the middle of the day. On a man ascending the tree, both birds quickly appeared, and the male, which appeared an old adult, made the first swoop at the man climbing, passing within a few inches of his head. The female (which appeared not to have cast her nestling plumage) then followed, making her attacks with more vigour and determination. We found three eggs, one addled and two a good deal incubated.

"The eggs were dull white, closely blotched with chocolate brown spots, very irregular in detail, coalescing in parts, and then forming stains. One egg appearing a rufous brown with an indistinct ground colour only visible.

"Size. Length, 2 inches; breadth, at greatest diameter, 1½ inches, shaped very like one of our Indian hen's eggs, to which it approximates in size. *F. Jugger*, within the sub-Himalayan tract, breeds, as has been stated before, on the open dry forest lands, skirting the lowest range of hills, and is particularly found in the vicinity of the larger, dry, sandy beds of torrents which drain them. In the Terai, however, where it is tolerably moist and swampy, I have also occasionally known the birds to breed.

"In Dehra Dhoon, many years ago, a pair always nested in a large single tree of the *Ulmus integrifolia* (*Dhoul papree* or *Kunjoo* of natives). Each year saw the couple at the same tree, and as an instance of intelligence and memory, I may mention that when as a lad I used to take my gun and Dogs out to shoot Quail (*Coturnix communis*) which abounded there in the grassy plains, and later, in March and April in the wheat fields, the Falcons always joined the party. On seeing the first Quail rise, they would fly towards us, and hover round us, until another was flushed, when they would both come down with one long well directed swoop. If the Quail were taken, both would fly off with it, if they failed they would wait for the next. When, as often happened, the Quail seeing the Falcons above, flew for a short distance only, and then suddenly dropt; they (the Quails) were invariably caught by the Dogs, as they would never rise a second time after having once been stooped at by the Falcons. This kind of sport used to last for several minutes and sometimes for half an hour, the pair of wild Falcons hovering above us all the time in perfect circles at a height considerably out of shot of my gun, though for that matter, had they come ever so close, nothing would have induced me to kill one of them. Every time I went shooting, or even to exercise the Dogs, these birds invariably appeared, and would join the party sometimes long before the first Quail was flushed. This did not happen once or twice or even during one or two seasons, it was *regularly* the case for the *four* or *five* successive years, that I remember the birds returning to their favourite tree."

This curious trait indicates pretty clearly, the manner in which the idea of training Falcons may first have arisen in the earlier and ruder ages of the world.

Tyros are always, in India, labouring under the delusion, that in the Laggar, in its different stages of plumage, they have different species. I have had *F. Jugger* in one stage or another sent me as *Peregrinus*, *Perigrinator* and *Babylonicus* (the latter *repeatedly*). I will endeavour to give such a description, as shall prevent these kind of mistakes in future.

In the young birds of the year, the whole of the upper plumage, except the nape and head, is a nearly uniform umber brown, darker on the primaries, margined paler on the wing coverts and back, and with a more or less observable tinge of bluish on the tail feathers. In young birds, the tail feathers and coverts are often much abraded and almost sandy in hue. The forehead is white, the feathers black shafted, and the white is continued more or less distinctly over the eye, for the length of about an inch and a half, as a sort of supercilium. The whole of the top of the head and occiput, have the brown feathers darker centered and faintly edged, with a more rufous brown. The lores are covered with whitish hair, in some, more or less involved in the dark stripe under the eye. Below the orbit, a dark brown streak commences, which, when most clearly seen, divides at the gape, and being prolonged backwards under and over the ear coverts, re-unites behind the ear covert, and is continued as a broad dark ill-defined half collar round the base of the neck. This is much more strongly marked in some birds than in others. The ear-coverts are white, many of the feathers dark shafted and spotted with brown or rufous brown. The chin and throat are white or creamy white, most of the feathers dark shafted and with a subterminal brown spot. The whole breast, abdomen, sides, flanks, thigh coverts, uniform unspotted umber brown, some of the feathers very faintly margined paler, and on the breast somewhat darker shafted. The vent and under tail-coverts white or dingy fawn, some of the latter with a subterminal pale brown blotch. The axillaries and lower wing coverts are mostly brown with occasional white spots or mottlings, in some almost wanting. The inner webs of the primaries, except the terminal 2 or 3 inches, conspicuously marked with transverse spots of white or buffy white. Tail feathers, albescent below; all of them except the two centre ones, more or less noticeably barred on the inner webs, towards their bases, with white or buffy white. The thighs behind and interiorly white.

In the adult, the white of the forehead is more conspicuous. The supercilium less so; the whole top of the head has a rufous cast, the feathers being brown, darker shafted and broadly margined, rufous. There is a blackish brown line under the eye, but this is no longer quite continuous with the dark brown stripe, which proceeds from the gape under the ear coverts, and this latter again no longer (as in the young bird it often appears to do) encircles the back of the ear coverts and joins into the dark collar. The dark brown stripe above the ear coverts which, in the young bird, is connected with the brown at the lower angle of the eye, in the adult no longer meets it, but commences at the hinder angle of the eye, and then produced backwards, widens into a broad ill-defined half collar, covering the whole back of the neck. The whole of the upper parts are a sort of slaty brown colour, browner on the upper back and scapulars, the feathers dark shafted and paler margined; the smallest coverts on the shoulder of the wings being often conspicuously, though very narrowly, margined with white. The dark colour of the nape which, in some specimens, is almost blackish brown, shades gradually into the slaty brown of the upper back. The chin, throat, cheeks and ear coverts, are almost perfectly pure white. The whole breast is pure white, but many of the feathers are darker shafted. The abdomen and sides are white, dark shafted, with a few linear drops of dark brown. The flanks nearly unmottled brown, the thigh coverts slaty brown, the feathers darker shafted, vent and lower tail coverts yellowish white, some of the exterior of the latter only sparsely blotched with pale brown. The lower wing coverts and axillaries are mingled brown and white, but whereas in the young, the brown greatly predominated, in the adult the white is in excess. The tail feathers are now all distinctly tipped with white, except perhaps the two centre ones, and all the feathers, but the centre ones, are distinctly marked on the inner webs to the very points, by ill-defined bars of a paler hue, in most specimens, greyish white tinged with rufous near the shaft. On the outer webs, of, at least, the three outer tail feathers on each side, there are usually paler spots corresponding to the bars on the inner webs. The legs and feet as well as the cere, have changed from a greenish hue to bright yellow. The iris, which in the young is often pale brown or brownish yellow, assumes in the adult its perfect rich brown tint.

Between these two states of plumage every possible gradation is observable. Gradually as the bird grows older, the white of the forehead becomes more conspicuous and the head more rufous. The spots on the ear coverts and throat gradually disappear, the cheek stripe grows shorter, the breast, then the abdomen become successively mottled with white, then white with conspicuous drops of brown, and lastly as in the adult, almost pure white. The upper plumage passes from a rich or umber (?) brown to almost a slaty grey, the under wing coverts and axillaries become more and more barred and mottled with white, while even the thigh coverts, participating in the general change of hue, pass from a deep rich burnt umber to a pale greyish brown. The intensity of the colours varies much in different individuals, some are in all stages less rufous on the head and less slaty on the upper plumage than others, and in some the dark colour of the base of, and back of neck is very much darker than others of apparently the same age. With an enormous series before me, I cannot discover any sexual difference of plumage: just as many of the females as of the males have very rufous heads; just as many are very grey; just as many have very dark patches in the hind neck, and just as many of each seem to be less rufous, less grey, and less dark on the neck. In the young, the colour of the legs and feet vary, from pale plumbeous to dull greenish grey, in the adult from full wax yellow to a bright almost *orange* yellow. The claws are a horny black.

The legs and feet do not appear to assume their bright yellow hue, until almost all the brown has disappeared from the throat and breast. The cere and gape are dingy greenish grey, or at times pale plumbeous in the young, bright yellow in the adult, the orbit greenish yellow in the former, bright yellow in the latter. In one stage, legs, feet, cere, orbits, are all pale primrose yellow. The corneous portion of the bill varies at base from greenish horny to greyish blue and even blue, and at tip from dark horny blue to bluish black.

Dimensions of adults. Length M, 15 to 16·5, F, 17·5 to 19. Expanse M, 37 to 41, F, 42 to 45. Weight M, 14 to 18 oz., F, 24 to 26 oz. Wing M, 12 to 13, F, 13 to 15; 2nd primary longest. Primaries fall short of longest, M, 1st, 0·62; 3rd, 0·44, F, 1st, 0·75; 3rd 0·37 (*about*, these dimensions vary). Tail from vent M, 7 to 8, F, 8 to 9; longest tail feathers exceed shortest by M, 0·7 to 0·85, F, 0·75 to 0·95. Tarsus M, 1·7 to 1·9, F, 1·75 to 2; (feathered in front for from 0·85 to 1) Foot, greatest length, M, 3·5 to 4, F, 4·25 to 4·5; greatest width, M, 3·25 to 3·7, F, 3·75 to 4; mid toe M, 1·6 to 1·75, F, 1·9 to 2; its claw, along curve M, 0·69 to 0·78 F, 0·8 to 1·05; hind toe M, 0·69 to 0·72, F, 0·8 to 0·9; its claw, along curve M, 0·75 to 0·9, F, 0·9 to 1·1. Bill straight, from edge of cere, M, 0·85 to 0·98 F, 1 to 1·1; along curve M, 1·1 to 1·19, F, 1·1 to 1·25; from gape M, 1 to 1·12, F, 1·15 to 1·37; width at gape, M, 1 to 1·12, F, 1·15 to 1·22; height at margin of cere M, 0·4 to 0·5, F, 0·47 to 0·53; Length of cere M, 0·18 to 0·22, F, 0·2 to 0·25. Distance by which the closed wings fall short of end of tail M, 1·1 to 1·2, F, 1·2 to 1·3; Distance by which lower tail coverts fall short of tail M, 3 to 3·4, F, 3·2 to 3·6.

There ought to be no confounding the *Peregrine* and the Laggar after they have once been seen together. The Peregrine is a much heavier and stouter bird, the bill is much stronger and stouter; the cheek stripe of the Peregrine is a huge broad patch, in the Laggar, at most, a line a quarter of an inch wide. Then the sides, flanks, thigh coverts, and lower tail coverts of the Peregrine exhibit in all, except in very old birds, regular transverse bars, and even in the oldest birds show traces of these. There is no barring in any age on any of these parts in the Laggar. The groundwork of the lining of the wing of the Peregrine is white, barred with brown, whereas the ground-work of the wing lining of the Laggar is dark wood brown, a good deal mottled or barred with white in the old bird. The Peregrine, as a rule, has no white frontal band, no white superciliary stripe and no rufous crown, as in the Laggar. Moreover the Peregrine has the centre tail feathers barred, whereas the Laggar has no trace of this barring; again the whole of the upper back, scapulars and upper surface of the wing in the Peregrine are at times somewhat obscurely, but yet manifestly, barred, but there is no trace of such barring at any age in the Laggar. Lastly, however old the Laggar, the general tint of the upper surface is brown or greyish brown, no doubt shaded with slaty in very old birds, but still a *brownish* slaty, whereas the whole upper surface of the old Peregrine is a pure slaty *blue* of different shades, not a trace of brown about it.

*Generally** it may be said, that if any beginner meets in India with a true Falcon of large size, without any markings on the upper surface of the centre tail feathers, it is *F. Jugger*. If there are markings, and these are large, round or oval spots, the bird is *F. Sacer* (or a nearly allied and as yet undiscriminated species). If the markings are bars, and the head and nape are nearly black, the latter, with a few rufous or buffy feathers, it is *Perigrinator*, or *Atriceps*, the distinctions between which have already been pointed out; while, if the head is brown, or in adults, deep blackish slaty (*Peregrinus*), or rufous, (*Babylonicus*) ; it is *Peregrinus* if the cheek stripe is broad and massive, *Babylonicus* if long and narrow.

No. 12. **Falco Babylonicus**, GURNEY.

THE RED-CAP FALCON.

I have, as yet, been unable to obtain any detailed account of the nidification of this species. It breeds, I know, in, or close to, the Peshawur valley, as well as in Cashmere, laying three or four eggs in March and April, but I have hitherto failed to procure the eggs. The type specimen of this bird, was obtained by Capt. Irby, in October 1858, at Nawabganj, (Barabunkee) Oudh, and is now in the Norwich Museum. In regard to this, Mr. Sclater remarked, that Capt. Irby's specimen, seemed to be referable to a new species of true Falcon, most nearly allied to *F. Barbarus* (Ibis, 1859, p. 184,) which is the *F. Peregrinoides* of Temminck. Mr. Gurney proposed the name *Babylonicus*, the *first* specimen of the bird having been obtained in Babylonia, by the Euphrates Exploring Expedition. This latter bird was in immature plumage, and was erroneously entered in the catalogue of the East India Company's Museum, where it was deposited as *F. Perigrinator*. Besides these examples, there are two adults in the Norwich Museum, one of which, is said to be from Abyssinia. The following are the dimensions given by Mr. Sclater.

* I am now doubtful whether these discriminative points are quite constant, but I let what I have written stand, for the present.

Locality.	*Length.*	*Wing.*	*Tail.*	*Tarsus.*	*Mid toe.*
Oudh,	17·3	13·0	7·0	1·95	2·05
Babylon,	17·0	12·5	6·6	1·95	1·95
Abyssinia,	18·0	12·8	6·5	2·00	1·95

I doubt whether these dimensions are altogether reliable, I expect they were taken from dry skins; under any circumstances I should suppose that all these specimens were females.

I proceed to give exact measurements, and a description (recorded from the specimen when fresh) of a young male, shot by me at Suhson in the Etawah district, and I would add, that this description, agrees very closely, with a specimen given by Dr. Jerdon (who procured it in Cashmere,) to Col. Tytler, though being a female, it is somewhat larger than my bird, having the wing, 12·6, and the tail, 7 inches.

Length, 16 inches. Expanse, 38 inches. Weight, 12 ozs. Wing, 11·87 inches; the 2nd primary the longest. Tail of 12 feathers, length from vent, 6 inches. Tarsus, (feathered for 0·5 inches, in front) 1·87 inches. Foot, greatest length, 4 inches; greatest width, 3·75 inches; mid toe, 1·94, its claw, 0·73; hind toe 0·94, its claw, 0·81. Bill, straight, 1·06; along curve, 1·25; from gape, 1·19; width at gape, 1·19; height at front, at edge of cere, 0·53; length of cere only, 0·27. Contents of stomach, portions of a *Turtur Cambaiensis*, feathers and all.

Legs and feet, bright yellow, whitish at the joints of the reticulated scales of the tarsus; soles with large pads, very conspicuous under second joint of middle, and exterior toe; claws, horn black; middle toe, very slender and elongated. Irides, dark brown; edges of the lids, greenish yellow, with tiny dark lashes; membrane of the orbits, pale greenish.

Cere, pale sea-green with only a tinge of yellow on the ridge. Bill pale bluish green; points, and culmen, horny bluish black.

Tongue, small, thick, fleshy, obtuse ended, of nearly the same size throughout, deeply divided by a groove down the centre.

Plumage. Forehead, buffy white, feathers dark shafted. Line over the eye, continued round the back of the head, whitish or fulvous white; feathers, dark shafted. Whole crown of the head, brown, a few feathers in centre, towards the front, very broadly margined, the rest very narrowly margined, with fulvous or buffy white. The nape below the white stripe, darkish brown in the centre, the feathers margined with buffy white, and with a patch of white on either side, the feathers of which have dark spots towards the tips. The whole of the rest of the back of the neck, upper back, scapulars, and wing coverts, a nearly uniform brown, with a faint tinge of slaty, and all the feathers tipped and margined with fulvous white, very narrowly towards the head, and more broadly towards the points of the scapulars. The hue of the back of the neck is slightly darker. The quills are much the same colour, but somewhat more bluish. All the quills have a number of incomplete bars, or oval spots, of rufous white on the inner web; the last five primaries, the secondaries, and the tertiaries have each two or three tiny rufous white spots, on the outer webs also; and the greater coverts of the secondaries, and tertiaries, have similar small inconspicuous spots on both webs; and all the secondaries and tertiaries, and the last few primaries, are narrowly tipped with buffy white. The rump, and lower back are a somewhat paler, and more sandy brown, margined with pale rufous; the upper tail coverts are a still more sandy brown, tipped and margined, with dingy white, and with one or more incomplete bars of fulvous white. The tail feathers are brown, paler and sandier on the centre feathers, and darker, and more slaty on the outer feathers, all narrowly tipped with dirty white, and all with six or seven $\frac{1}{4}$ inch broad transverse bars on both webs, fulvous white on the centre feathers, and rufous white on the exterior feathers. These bars are scarcely visible on the outer web of the exterior feather. Chin, and upper part of throat, pure white, a dark brown cheek stripe from under the eye, margined with pale rufous; ear coverts mingled pale brown and rufous white. Hinder portion of the cheeks white, some of the feathers tinged pale rufous; an ill-defined brown stripe (the feathers slightly tipped with fulvous white,) running backwards from the posterior angle of the eye, and dividing the white of the hind cheeks, from the white of the sides of the nape. The lower throat, and upper portion of the breast, fulvous white, each feather dark shafted, and with a narrow somewhat pear-shaped streak, of dark brown, towards the tip. The rest of the breast, sides, and upper abdomen, fulvous white; each feather with a well marked central stripe of brown, narrowest in front, broadest towards the sides. Lower abdomen, and vent, white, slightly tinged with fulvous, a few of the feathers dark shafted. Lower tail coverts, (which do not reach within two inches of the end of the tail) white, with two or three transverse, somewhat wavy bars, of pale brown. Interior thigh coverts, white. Exterior thigh coverts, white, tinged with fulvous, each feather dark shafted, and with a central lanceolate stripe of brown. Under surface of tail, and quills, greyish brown, the bars above mentioned showing through. The lower wing coverts, all reddish brown, conspicuously margined at the tip, and the longer ones barred with somewhat fulvous white.

Of Col. Tytler's female,—a slightly younger bird than mine, I think,—I have the following note, made when I examined it. "The back wings and scapulars are just like those of a young Jugger, but the upper tail coverts, and the tail, have broad, buffy, more or less imperfect bars, conspicuous on the tail. The under parts, are dirty, buffy white, palest on the chin and throat. The feathers of the breast, and abdomen, with imperfect irregular, more or less broad, central stripes of dull reddish brown. The tarsus is less feathered in front than even in *Perigrinator* I think, to which bird it seems to me to approximate not a little. The head, however, is of the Lanner type, and has a narrow, but pretty long, and well marked cheek stripe. The head is a rather warm red brown; forehead, and centre of head, a rusty red brown. There are a number of pale rufous white feathers at the back of the neck. The white bars on the primaries, are broader than in *Perigrinator*, about the same size as the Peregrine, but not so broad, as the Juggers, or *a fortiori*, those of the Sacer. According to Mr. Blyth, this bird is the *F. Peregrinoides* of Hodgson. (J. A. S. B. XXIV. 574,) Mr. Blyth also tells us, (Ibis, 1866, p. 237,) that "there is a fine specimen, of an adult female, (as adjudged) of this rare Falcon, in the Worcester Museum, alleged to be from Java, which must needs be a mistake. Its general colouring is very pallid, but I would refer the species to the Peregrine sub-group, rather than to that of the Sakir, and Lanner. The specimen in the Worcester Museum, is like an adult female Peregrine, only much paler, with all the markings considerably less developed; nape, light cinnamon rufous, marked with dusky, the moustachial streak, small, the feathers of the upper parts, cross banded, as in adult Peregrines. A recent communication from Dr. Jerdon, proves, that *F. Babylonicus* is not uncommon in Kashmere." It seems possible, that two allied species, have been confounded under this name. All the birds that I have seen of this species, are so unmistakeably of the Lanner type, white or pale foreheads, rufous heads, small cheek stripes, and slaty *brown* or grey plumage, that I cannot understand Mr. Blyth's referring this same species, to the Peregrine sub-group; and I doubt the propriety of identifying the Worcester Museum bird, with *Babylonicus*.

The adult female figured by Wolf in the Ibis, has a conspicuous white frontal band. The whole top, and back of the head, and nape, are of a warm rufous, most of the feathers dark shafted, and with dark central streaks, which, on the nape, occupy nearly the whole surface of the feather, leaving only a narrow rufous margin. The whole back, scapulars, wing coverts, and tail, slaty grey, everywhere barred with dark slaty. Many of the coverts and scapulars are obscurely tipped with pale rufous, or buffy, and the tail feathers are conspicuously, but not broadly tipped with rufous white. There is a narrow, dark brown moustachial streak, from the gape, and a narrow dark line under the eye, a trace of which is observable over and behind the ear coverts; cheeks, ear coverts, chin, throat, and centre of upper breast, unspotted white; rest of lower parts, white, slightly tinged with fulvous, each feather with a subternural brown, or rufous, and brown spot, small and dot-like in the centre of the lower breast and abdomen, and widening towards the sides, flanks, and lower tail coverts, into arrow head bars, not quite extending to the edge of the feathers. The cere, gape, and orbits, are bright wax yellow, the base of the corneous portion of the bill, is pale horny blue, the tips of the mandibles horny black. The legs and feet are yellow. I take this description from the figure—a very unsafe method in most cases—but Mr. Wolf's figures are *sui generis*, unapproached and unapproachable, to my fancy, and may, I believe, be implicitly relied on.

Since the above was written, I myself shot (on the 27th November) a fine adult female, at *Sirsa*, in the Punjaub, of which I proceed to give measurements and description taken in the flesh.

Dimensions. Length, 17·25. Expanse, 41. Tail, from vent, 7·25. Foot, greatest length, 4·5, greatest width 4. Wing 13; wings, when closed, reach to within 1·87 of end of tail. Tarsus, 1·75. Mid toe to root of claw, 1·9. Weight 1·87lbs.

Description. The irides were deep brown. The cere, gape, and orbital skin, as well as the legs, and feet, were bright yellow. The claws were black, and the corneous portion of the bill was blue, changing to horny black at the tip. The forehead, and the centre of the top of the head, were sandy rufous, each feather with a dark brown shaft. The sides of the top, and the back, of the head were a somewhat ashy or slaty brown, the feathers more or less margined with sandy rufous. A broad, rufous, half collar, ran round the back of the neck, a little mottled behind the ear coverts, and again in the centre of the back of the neck, with dusky slaty. The whole mantle was slaty grey, dark and dusky towards the base of the neck, and paling towards the rump and upper tail coverts. Most, if not all of the feathers were narrowly margined paler,—those towards the nape, with rufous, and those lower down with greyish white. Most of the feathers also were somewhat conspicuously darker shafted, and *all* exhibited broad, transverse, somewhat ill-defined, dusky slaty, bands. The rump, and upper tail coverts were pale slaty, or french grey, with brown shafts, and transverse arrow head, dusky bars. The tail feathers, were pale slaty grey, tipped with rufous, and with numerous broad, transverse, well defined, slaty brown bars, broadest towards the tips. There was a blackish line under the eye, continued downwards for about an inch and a quarter, as a narrow cheek stripe. The two cheek stripes nearly meet on the throat, about an inch and a half below the base of the lower mandible. The whole of the lower parts were a rich rufous salmon colour, somewhat paler on the chin, and centre of the throat, and deeper on the ear coverts, sides of the neck, and centre of the abdomen. The breast, chin, and throat were perfectly spotless, the abdomen, flanks, lower tail coverts and tibial plumes were regularly, but rather widely barred with slaty brown; the bars, everywhere narrow, being nearly obsolete in the centre of the abdomen, and best marked on the flanks. The under wing coverts, were of a pale salmon colour, conspicuously barred with brown.

I have never seen *Falco Biarmicus*, Temm. (p. col. T. t. 324.,) nor even Temminck's figure, but Layard's description and dimensions of this species, (Birds of South Africa, No. 27) recall to me the bird above described, and I cannot help suspecting a possible identity. Major E. Delme Radcliffe, our best Indian falconer, tells me that the back in this species becomes very pale slaty from age, the red of the head becomes slightly paler, but the rufous colour of the breast is maintained, or becomes deeper. In some, he has seen the head as red as that of the Toorumtee *(Lithofalco Chiquera)*. He found it breeding near Murree.

Dr. Jerdon gives the following dimensions, of a fresh bird, taken at Umritsur. Adult female. Length, 17, Expanse, 42. wing 12. Tail, 6·5. Mid toe, and claw, 2·5. He also sends me the following brief note.

"This is the common *Shahin* of the Punjab falconers. In the cold weather it visits the plains of the Punjab, N. W. P. and Oudh. I have had trained ones in my possession, but found it a very inferior bird for hawking, to *Falco Perigrinator*."

I believe, we may say that the Red cap occurs throughout Northern India, during the cold weather, as far south as Gwalior, being rare east of the Jumna, less rare between the Sutledge and Jumna, and decidedly common west of the Sutledge, specially in the Peshawur valley, and the tract west of the Indus, and that it breeds in Cabool and Cashmere, and throughout the southern ranges of the Himalayas, west at any rate of Dalhousi, at heights of from four to seven thousand feet; but further information in regard to this species is much required.

No. 13. **Hypotriorchis Subbuteo,** Lin.

The Hobby.

Of the breeding habits of this species in India, I as yet know nothing. Although common enough in some parts of the Himalayahs, it is a rare visitant, and then only in the cold season, to the plains, and if it breeds any where within our limits, it will be, I apprehend, in the higher ranges of the Hills. Mr. R. Thompson, writing from Kumaon, the 16th September, says, "I saw yesterday, our English Hobby, numbers of which visit India during the cold weather; every mountain top of 12,000 feet and upwards had flocks of them hunting about for insects, last September, when I was out in the interior. I am inclined to doubt whether the Hobby breeds any where in the Himalayahs, south of the snowy range."

Of the breeding of this species in England, Mr. Yarrell gives the following particulars: "The Hobby, though a well known bird, is not very numerous as a species. It chooses a high tree to make its nest on, occasionally taking to the remains of one of suitable size, that has been deserted. The female lays three or four eggs, like those of all the true Falcons in shape and colour, that is, of a short oval form, speckled all over with reddish brown, on a dirty white ground; the length, 1·67 inches; the breadth, 1·33.

Mr. Hewitson, quoting Mr. Hoy, tells us that "the Hobby is a late breeder; seldom having eggs before the first week in June; that it very rarely, if ever, builds its own nest, but takes possession of that of a Crow, or Magpie, preferring those which are placed near the tops of high trees; and that, though it may be met with, breeding in large woods, it seems to prefer isolated groves of fir, and other trees, situated in open country, where it can not only pursue small birds, but readily capture *coleopterous* and other insects on which it feeds very much. Mr. Hewitson, himself, found a nest, in Norway, in the month of June, placed upon a projecting ledge of rock, on the face of a steep precipice. The Hobby *he* tells us, lays *two* or *three* eggs.

The one he figures, has a pale salmon coloured ground, closely freckled and mottled with salmon red, and measures 1·58 by 1·26. He says that the eggs are not subject to much variety, but that specimens entirely devoid of dark markings are met with. The eggs are usually very regularly freckled, over the whole surface, and more nearly resemble (in colour) the eggs of the Iceland Falcon, than those of any other species. The darkest varieties, he adds, are rather like some lightly coloured eggs of the Kestrel, being, however, of a pinker hue, and without any large blotches of colour. Mr. R. Thompson sends me the following note on this species, "In October, on the highlands, immediately below the snow, both young and adult birds are met with in abundance. Of the young, several that I killed, appeared not to have long left the nest; they were hawking about for insects, and often swept past close to where I was standing. I think they are strictly migratory, only appearing as a rule within our territories early in October, though I have seen a few adults at Nynee Tal as early as 15th September.

"I have been a close observer of these birds for some years now, yet I cannot say, I ever saw one take a bird in the wild state. Hundreds I have seen hawking about, but taking nothing but insects. Those shot under the snows on the high bare *boogials*, had nothing but insects in their stomachs. Many, are taken in the cold weather, in the plains, and trained to fly at the Hoopoe, *Upupa Nigripennis*, affording wonderful sport; also at *Dicrurus Macrocercus* which, from their undulatory flight, are very difficult for the little Falcon to strike. The Hobby is a courageous bird, especially in self-defence. I have seen them, after being bullied by Crows, turn on these, and strike them almost to the ground, with repeated blows."

This bird seems to have a very wide range. It is found throughout Europe, in north and south Africa, (including Egypt), Palestine, and northern China.

A male in Col. Tytler's collection, answers Jerdon's description of the adult bird well enough, but the whole upper surface is *a black* brown, of much the same colour as the cheek stripe; there appears to be a broad half collar of buffy white, the feathers only narrowly tipped with the brown. The chin and throat are pure white, the breast and abdomen, deep brown, the feathers, edged with rusty white. The primaries, with a few spots, or obsolete bars, of greyish white, very slightly tinged in some with rufous. The tail, a warm, clove brown, the inner webs of the laterals, with obsolete rufous bars. What is noticeable about this bird, is, that it is neither slaty, as all adult true Hobbies are described, nor have the feathers, the pale or ferruginous edgings of the young; it is, I suppose, in an intermediate stage.

A very fine female that I procured at Kotegurh, which was only 14·5 inches long, had the wing no less than 11·5, she had the lores, narrow frontal band, and well marked supercillium, white; the cheek stripe, (which was very broad) and a broad patch behind, and below the eye, including the ear coverts, were blackish brown, and the upper portion of the head and nape, dusky slaty, each feather, rather narrowly centred with blackish brown, and some few of the feathers, with a trace of excessively narrow paler edgings; chin, throat, and upper breast, and sides of the neck, prolonged behind the ear coverts, (so as almost to meet the ends of the broad buffy half collar on the base of the back of the neck) unspotted yellowish white. The whole of the rest of the upper parts, slaty blue, dark, and tinged almost blackish, immediately below the half collar, and on the lesser wing coverts, elsewhere pale, and pure. All the feathers of the back, and the scapulars, somewhat conspicuously darker shafted, central tail feathers, and outer webs of laterals, paler slaty than the rest of the upper parts, entirely unbarred or unspotted; inner webs of laterals, with numerous transverse, rufous bars; quills a rather dusky slaty, on outer webs, and with the inner ones dark brown, with numerous long oval, transverse, imperfect, bar-like, rufous spots. Lower breast, abdomen, and sides, a mixture of buffy, and rufous white, each feather, with a broad dark brown central stripe. Thigh coverts, bright ferruginous, a few of the feathers with dark central stripes. Lower tail coverts, and vent feathers, pale ferruginous. I note that the cheek stripe is distinctly separated from the dark ear coverts, by the white of the throat; in the next species, the Indian Hobby, the cheek stripe and ear coverts are all in one.

No. 14. **Hypotriorchis Severus,** Horsf.

The Indian Hobby.

That this bird breeds in India, there can, I think, be little doubt. It is in Southern, or South Eastern Asia, the local representative of the preceding species, and not having been observed north of the Himalayahs, must of necessity breed somewhere within our limits. As yet, I have been unable to meet with any account of its nidification. Dr. Jerdon remarks, that it is said to breed on trees, and this is nearly all that I know about the matter.

A fine male, shot at Barrackpore, had the wing, 8·75; tail, 4·62. The upper plumage, deep brown, not a trace of slaty, but faint traces of a rufous half collar at the back of the neck. All the lateral tail feathers, with rufous bars, on the inner webs, extending partially on to the outer ones, and all, but centre feathers, tipped with rufous white, chin and throat rusty white; rest of lower parts, deep rusty, except feathers of the lower abdomen, vent, and under tail coverts, which are paler, and yellower. Breast, abdomen, sides, thigh coverts, and lower tail coverts with deep brown subterminial spots, or oval drops. There is a peculiar notch in the first quill's inner web, about 1·25 from the tip, which is very marked. The 2nd quill is the longest, the 1st being 0·37 shorter, the 3rd 0·5 shorter. No such strongly marked notch is observable in any of the specimens of *H. Subbuteo* before me, and none is noticeable in the 2nd quill in this species. In *L. Chequera* again, the notch is of quite a different shape, and occurs in both 1st and 2nd quills; the 3rd quill being the longest in this latter species. Proportionally, the wings of *Severus*, and *Subbuteo*, are much longer than those of *L. Chequera*.

Mr. Wallace tells us that this species is found in Macassar, Salwattee, Java, the Philippines, and most probably, occasionally in every island of the Archipelago.

Just as this species is the local representative of the common Hobby in Southern Asia, so in Southern Africa, this latter finds its local representative in *H. Cuvieri*, which Mr. Gurney considers very closely allied to the present species.

Hypotriorchis Subbuteo (Linn.) Hobby.

Hypotriorchis Cuvieri (A. Smith.) Cuvier's Hobby.

These two Hobbies, though treated by Mr. Layard as belonging to the same species, are unquestionably distinct: They both occur in South Africa, but both appear to be rare in that region.

H. Cuvieri described by Sir A. Smith, in 1830, (S. African Quarterly Journal, I. p. 392) is nearly allied to the peculiar Hobby of South Eastern Asia, *H. Severus* (Horsf.), and has been figured by Professor Schlegel (Nedeil. Tijdschr. I. p. 123, pl. 5) under the name of *Falco Boschir* (cf. Ibis, 1864, p. 398)."

Mr. Blyth, in the Ibis for 1866, makes the following interesting remarks, in regard to *Hypotriorchis Subbuteo*, and *Severus*.

"The crepuscular habits of the birds of this division, have now been noticed in *H. Eleonoræ* (Ibis, 1865, p. 333).

"*H. Severus* bears just that relationship to *H. Subbuteo*, which *Hirundo Cahirica* bears to *H. Rustica*, and *H. Hyperythra* (of Ceylon) to *H. Erythropygia*, (Sykes, which is distinct from *H. Daurica*.) In all of these cases, the deeper coloured bird is less migratory, or even permanently resident. The rufous-bellied Hobby, has not been observed northward of the Himalayahs, nor *Hirundo Hyperythra* out of Ceylon; and while neither *H. Rustica*, nor *H. Rufula* winters in Palestine, Mr. Tristram remarks of *H. Cahirica* that a few remain on the sea coast and in the Ghor, all the winter (P. Z. S. 1864, p. 443). Indeed, it would appear, that he observed them, in considerable numbers, during the winter months. (Land of Israel pp. 105, 118). It may be added, that *Falco Peregrinator* stands in the same relationship to *F. Peregrinus*, and is likewise a more subtropical species, with a comparatively limited range of distribution. Compare also the African *Tinnunculus Rupicolus* with *T. Alaudarius*, and *Athene Castanotus* of Ceylon with *A. Radiatus*."

Dr. Stoliczka remarks, that this species "is not common in the forest about Kotegurh, and Kooloo, and that, during the summer, it seems to migrate further *north*."

Mr. R. Thompson, however, a very accurate field naturalist, sends me the following notes :

"These birds regularly resort to the dense forests, on the lower ranges of Kumaon and Gurhwal, about April. In June, I watched a female bearing a small bird away, but could not follow where she took it to. I inferred from this, that she must have had a nest of fledged young ones, as there were lots of fine trees standing close to where she passed me, and where she might have stopped to pluck her quarry. Later observations, confirm that the bird breeds about April, in our lofty and dense forests. I have seen a pair constantly hovering in the valley of Dhumola ; a place of only about 2500 feet elevation.

"I lately saw, in February last, a pair sitting on a dead tree, in the Kumaon valley, Kotridhoon, Gurhwal. They were both screaming as most Falcons do when pairing."

No. 15. Lithofalco Œsalon Gmel.

The Merlin.

Of the breeding of this species, in India, we have as yet no detailed accounts. Dr. Jerdon, in a recent note to me, remarks that "the Merlin is by no means rare in the plains of the Punjab, during the cold weather, and I have had trained ones in my possession. It is chiefly flown at the Hoopoe.

"One of my falconers caught one near Delhi. It is called *Regi* and *Retul turunti* in the Punjab, and *Dooreli* by Hindustanees, which name I have, in my work, applied to the Hobby."

About Umritsur it is commonly captured and sold, by native huntsmen, for a very small price. It comes down, I am informed, in numbers into the Peshawur Valley, and is always to be met with, early in the year, in the Salt Range, it is therefore highly probable, that it breeds in Cashmere, and the neighbouring regions of the Himalayahs.

Mr. Yarrell says, "The Merlin makes its scanty nest on the ground, laying four or five eggs, measuring one inch, seven lines, in length, by one inch, three lines in breadth, mottled all over with two shades of reddish brown."

Mr. Hewitson tell us, that in England, the eggs have usually been found, deposited on the ground, chiefly upon those extensive heathy moors, which abound towards the north. On the continent of Europe, however, they are known to breed on trees; and Mr. Hewitson himself found a nest in Norway "near the top of a spruce fir," which appeared to have been newly made by the birds themselves, and not to be a repaired nest, originally the tenement (as is so common in the case of the Hobbies) of some other species. The nest was outwardly composed of sticks, thickly lined with wool. "The Merlin," he adds, "can scarcely be said to make a nest, when it deposits its eggs upon the ground, laying them either upon the bare heather, or on a small quantity of dry grass. They are four or five in number," they seem to be usually of a deep dingy red, "smaller, browner, and less bright in colour" than those of the Kestrel, "very closely freckled, not spotted, and thickly sprinkled over with small black dots." Varieties remarkable for their deep red brown vinous colouring, and others with pure white grounds, thickly blotched with crimson red, also, as he notices, occur, and I remember to have seen many intermediate types of colouration, in European cabinets.

The eggs are of the usual Falcon type, broad, oval, slightly compressed towards one end, and one I have from Europe measures 1·6 by 1·25.

Of a male, shot near Hoshiarpoor; I have the following note:

"Comparatively short wings; notch as in *Severus*, but on both, the two first quills, as in *Chiquera*. The 2nd and 3rd quills subequal; wing, 8; tail 5. The bird is a rich deep brown above, deepest towards the head; the feathers of the head, having still deeper central brown stripes; the scapulars, many of the wing coverts, and the quills, have rich rufous brown, irregular, and imperfect, transverse bars, extending as spots, on to the outer webs of the primaries. The tail, with five broad, transverse, rufous bars; (one hidden by the upper tail coverts) tip rufous white. An indistinct yellowish, imperfect collar round the base of the neck. Bill, very small, and feeble, as compared with *Severus*, *Subbuteo*, and *Chiquera*, which are all about equally strong.

The Merlin seems to be found all over Europe, in Malta, Egypt, (Lower,) Palestine, Kandehar, and, according to Mr. Swinhoe, in Pekin, Amoy, and Foochow.

No. 16. **Lithofalco Chiquera** Daudin.

The Toorumtee.

The Toorumtee breeds in February, March, April, and May; the majority, I think, laying in March. I have, as yet, obtained no egg earlier than the 15th February, or later than the 15th of May, and all those obtained in May, were from the Punjaub, where many birds breed later than in more southern parts of the country.

They nest, I believe, exclusively on trees: I have seen no record of their building on rocks, as so many of the Falcons often do, and I once took a nest in the Siwaliks, in a Peepul tree, at the foot of a cliff, full of ledges and boulder holes, which, had the bird any sort of inclination for such localities, would have been sure to have attracted it.

Where such occur, they prefer large trees, Peepul, Mango, and Tamarind, (more commonly the two latter) usually selecting one of a small group, standing by itself. In the Punjaub, and Rajpootana, where large trees are scarce, their nests may be found on mere bushes, not above 10 feet from the ground.

The nest is generally, firmly fixed in a fork near the top of the tree, and is typically a very neat, compact and characteristic structure; it is usually circular, some 12 inches in diameter, and from 6 to 9 inches in thickness, with a deep egg cavity, some 5 to 6 inches in diameter, and from 3 to 3·5 in depth; but I have seen some nests comparatively thin platforms with only a depression of 1·5 to 2 in depth, towards the centre. The lower portion of the nest is constructed of pretty stout twigs, of various kinds of wood, closely put together; the upper portion of finer twigs, still more closely interwoven. The egg cavity or depression, is lined with fine roots, or vegetable fibre, the roots of the Khus grass (*Andropogon Muricatum,*) being commonly chosen for this purpose; along with straw, a few feathers, and occasionally a shred or two of cloth. The lining being firmly intertwined, with the twigs, forming the walls of the cavity.

These birds make, I think, their own nests, fresh and fresh every year—I have repeatedly seen them building new nests, in trees containing very nice last year's nests of Crows and other birds, and though I have very often looked them up again, I have not, as yet, ever found a nest tenanted by the Toorumtee during two successive seasons. Both sexes assist in building, and they make no little fuss about the placing of each twig that is brought up. The normal number of the eggs is four, but I have found the female sitting on only three. Two nests, each containing five eggs, have been reported to me, but these are very exceptional.

The eggs vary somewhat in shape; but are generally, I think, much like those of a common hen, though perhaps slightly narrower. In colour, they vary from very pale yellowish brown, with just a few reddish brown specks, to a nearly uniform dark brownish red, obscurely mottled and blotched with a somewhat purer and darker red; typically they may be said to have a reddish white ground, so thickly freckled and speckled with dull brownish red, as to have but little of the ground colour visible. Often, they have a sort of ring of more or less feeble blotches near the large end; and at times, a zone of rather higher colour than the rest of the egg, near the middle. The eggs are normally a long oval; and with the exception of shape, which is invariably less round than those of that species, the eggs of the Toorumtee are perfect miniatures of the *Jugger's*. As far as colouring goes, every egg of the one in my collection, can be matched by some one of the other I possess. In size and colouring, they remind us not a little of the eggs of the Merlin, but, as a rule, they are somewhat narrower than these, and a greater number of them belong to the dingy, yellowish brown, Falcon type, and fewer to the deep red type.

In length, they vary from 1·6, to 1·75, and in breadth, from 1·25, to 1·32, but the average of 32 eggs measured was 1·68, by 1·27.

Mr. William Blewitt mentions taking several nests of this bird, which at Hansie is known as the *Koohee* (a name elsewhere applied to the Shaheen,) in March, April, and May. The nests were placed on Peepul and Jhand trees, at heights of from 10 to 24 feet from the ground; were most of them scantily and loosely, but one or two densely and compactly, constructed of fine *Babool* (A. Arabica) and other twigs, lined with fine straw, feathers, and a few rags; and measured from 8 to 10 inches in diameter, with a cavity from 2 to 3 inches deep. None contained more than four, and one had only three much incubated eggs.

Mr. R. Thompson communicates the following note in regard to this species.

" I do not remember ever seeing the Toorumtee circling aloft or sailing like *Falco Perigrinator* or *Jugger*. It invariably flies rapidly, in a direct horizontal line, and with very frequent flappings of its wings. The young birds are out of the nest in June; in Gurhwal I have never seen one earlier. The Toorumtee is very courageous, as remarked by Jerdon, but it does not, as he seems to think, confine its attacks to small birds. I have frequently seen it take Mynas, Starlings, Quails, and the smaller Doves. I once saw one strike a Pigeon, killing it on the spot, with the first blow. I have trained this species to be thrown from the hand, at Quails, and Partridges. The bird readily learns the lesson, and makes a good bag. The Quail, or Partridge is allowed a good start, the Toorumtee being held up, so as to eye the receding bird, and then thrown in the direction of the latter, with some force, shooting off at once, more like a dart than anything else, at the quarry, which it rarely misses. I have been told, that this bird affords peculiar sport, with *Turtur Suratensis*, striking at the quarry, several times, and even often losing it altogether, owing partly to the softness of the Dove's feathers, which give way at the least touch, and partly to its rapid dodging flight."

I remember once, after robbing a nest of this species, to have seen the parent birds fall foul of all the Crows in the neighbourhood, in the most surprising manner; the strangest thing being, that the Crows submitted very tamely, (only seeking refuge in flight) to the most vindictive buffets from the little Falcons. Mr. Brookes tells me that on a similar occasion, he witnessed a similar scene. Whether the Toorumtees conceived that the Crows, whose egg-stealing propensities all birds seem well aware of, had some hand in the robbery of their penates, or whether being afraid to attack *us*, they, on the Hindustani principle of "*Koomhar pur bus na chulla, gudhe ka kan ametha*,"* flew at the Crows whom they *did* feel equal to thrashing, I cannot pretend to decide. I have twice found portions of a Squirrel in the stomachs of these birds.

Mr. Gurney has the following note in the Ibis for 1868, on the nearly allied *Chequera Rufficollis* (Swains) of South Africa.

"Vierthaler, who met with this species, somewhat plentifully, in Sennaar, states, (*Naumannia*, 1852, Pt. II. pp. 48, 49) that it usually perches, and always breeds on the Dhelleb Dolleb, or Debbel Palm, (*Borassus æthiopicus*) and Dr. von Heughlin, who also observed this Falcon on the upper part of the Blue Nile, refers to its preference for this tree. (Ibis, 1860, p. 409.) Both Vierthaler (loc. cit.) and his companion, Dr. A. E. Brehm (J. F. C. 1858, p. 408,) remark, that *Columba Guinea* also selects the same species of Palm for its nest, and that a pair of

* This proverb is a very characteristic Indian one, it means—" He was not man enough to punch the potter's head, so contented himself with wrenching the ear of the potter's donkey;" a true picture of the manner in which natives so often revenge themselves on the helpless dependents of enemies they are afraid to attack.

these Falcons, and a pair of Guinea Pigeons, frequently have their nests on the same tree, and live as neighbours in apparent amity; both species were found thus in Sennaar in the month of January, 1851.

According to the account given by Sir Andrew Smith in the South African Quarterly Journal, (Vol. I. No. April, June, 1830, pp. 233-235) both the manner, and the season of breeding adopted by this Falcon, in South Africa, somewhat differs from its habits in these respects, as observed in Sennaar.

His account of its nidification in South Africa, is as follows:—

"Specimens of this Hawk, are not unfrequently found, along the Western Coast, and I have also met with some, about the Langikloof, at least three hundred miles to the eastward of Cape Town. In these situations, it is often seen resorting in the evenings, to the Poplar, and other trees in the vicinity of farm houses, and upon such also it often builds its nest. The latter is constructed externally of dry twigs, and within, of hair and feathers, and in it are deposited from three to four eggs, during the months of August and September. I think that Bonaparte was fully justified in assigning this species, and its Indian congener *Falco Chiquera*, (Daud) to the separate genus which he instituted (Rev. Zool. 1854, p. 535) under the title of *Chiquera*, as they appear to me to form a group generically distinct, both from the typical Falcons, and also from the various genera most nearly allied to the genus Falco."

In connection with this note, I would remark, *first*, that a native once brought me a nest, with four eggs belonging to the Toorumtee, which he declared that he had found in the crown of a *Borassus flabelliformis*, our toddy Palm, which he had ascended to search for nests of the Palm swift. This was in Bhowgaon in the Mynpooree district, where these trees are very common. At the time, I utterly disbelieved the story, but now I think that it may have been true, especially as he had no earthly object in deceiving me. Even if true, the bird here very rarely chooses this situation, most probably because the majority of these Palms, are with us, regularly *tapped* year by year, and no birds will build where they are liable to disturbance, day by day, throughout the breeding season. It will be seen, that Sir Andrew Smith's account of the breeding of the African species, agrees well enough with the habits of our bird. *Secondly*, I would note, that I fully concur with Mr. Gurney, that the Hobbies, Merlins, and Toorumtees, all require generic separation, indeed the latter differ more from the two former, than these two do *inter se;* but I have been compelled to retain the name *Lithofalco Chiquera*, from ignorance (*Valde deflendus,*) of the specific name proposed for *our Chiquera*. I append exact measurements, and a full description, (taken from the freshly killed bird) of a fine adult female.

Dimensions. Length, 13·5. Expanse, 27·25. Weight, 8·5 oz. Wing, 8·62; the 3rd primary the longest; 1st, 0·94 shorter; 2nd, 0·19; 4th, 0·56. Tail from vent, 6·13; exterior tail feather, 0·75; shorter than central ones. Tarsus, feathered in front, for half an inch, 1·63. Foot, greatest length, 3·13; greatest width, 2·8; mid toe, 1·56; its claw along curve, 0·63; hind toe, 0·63; its claw along curve, 0·69. Bill straight, 0·75; along curve, nearly 1. From gape, 0·88; width at gape, 0·88; height at front, at margin of cere, 0·34; length of cere, 0·19. Wings when closed reach to within 2·25 of end of tail,

Description. Legs and feet, pure, slightly orange, yellow; claws black; toes, long and slender, with pads, especially of penultimate joint, much developed. Scutæ of tarsus, reticulate; those of front, comparatively large; three or four scutæ at base of tarsus, over foot; and those of upper surface of toes; transverse; claws, fine and very sharp; the inner edge of mid claws, slightly dilated.

Irides, rather light brown. Orbits, yellow, brightest at the angles of the eye. Bill, greenish yellow, at base; bluish black at tips. Tongue, rather short, narrow compared with gape; nearly square-ended; emarginate at tip.

Plumage. A narrow band across forehead; not quite pure white. Lores dingy white, but with a dark brown line, running through them, and under the eye as far as the cheek stripe; and over the eye, as a narrow supercilium; and for a little distance behind the eye as an ill-defined patch, of dark brown, mingled with chestnut. The whole of the top, and back of the head, and sides and back of upper neck; a rich deep chestnut. Lower neck behind, upper back, and scapulars, a pure, uniform, pale, slaty blue, or blue grey, the shafts of the feathers being darker. The lower back, and rump similar, but slightly paler, except at the very tips of the feathers. Upper tail coverts similar, until separately examined, when they prove to be much paler, (almost white at the base) than at the tips, and white 3, 4, or 5 arrowhead, transverse, darker bars, which though, (with the exception of the terminal one, which is faint,) well marked, are concealed by the over-lapping of the feathers. The tail feathers are the same colour as the back, (the central ones being rather more dingy and the exterior ones, whiter) with greenish white tips, an inch and a half subterminal black band and above this about five somewhat imperfect, narrow, blackish, transverse bars, feeble on the central feathers, and outer webs of the rest, and well marked on the inner webs. The lesser wing coverts are the same colour as the scapulars, but the darker shafts are perhaps slightly more conspicuous, and there is a tinge of chestnut along the upper margin of the wing. The greater coverts of secondaries and tertiaries are perhaps a slightly dingier blue, with narrow, not sharply defined, transverse, blackish brown bars. The winglet, and primary greater coverts, are similar, but the blue is dingier, the brown though paler, of greater extent, covering in some, nearly the whole inner webs. The first five primaries are brown; with numerous parallel, whitish, long oval, transverse spots, or incomplete bars, from the base, to near the tip. The secondaries are blue on the outer, white or nearly so on the inner webs, with numerous transverse brown bars; narrow on the outer but wider on the inner webs. The last five primaries are intermediate in character, between the first five, and the secondaries. The 2nd and 3rd primaries are emarginate, the former noteably so on the outer web; and the 1st and 2nd are conspicuously notched on the inner webs, near the points. The chin and upper part of the throat, are pure white. From the gape, there is a chestnut cheek stripe, or moustache, about $\frac{5}{8}$th of an inch long. Between this and the chestnut of the sides of the back of the head, and back of the neck, there is a broad white band coming down from the eye. The lower part of the throat, and the uppermost portion of the breast is white, the feathers having each a single linear, central, subterminal, browner spot, or speck it should perhaps be called.

The whole of the rest of the lower parts, including axillaries, wing lining, thigh, and lower tail coverts, a bluish white, with numerous close narrowish, greyish, brown bars; most conspicuous on sides, axillaries, larger lower wing coverts and thigh coverts, and feeble and more or less obsolete, on abdomen, vent, and lower tail coverts. The bars of the body feathers, specially on the middle of breast and abdomen, have a point developed downwards at the shaft, having a tendency in fact to become arrowhead bars as they are often called.

No. 17. **Tinnunculus Alaudarius**, Briss.

The Kestrel or Windhover.

The Kestrel with us breeds in April, May and June; as far as I am yet aware, it breeds in India, only in the Himalayahs and the Dhoon; natives informed me that they had seen its nest in the Salt Range of the Punjaub near Pind Dadun Khan.

In the Himalayahs, it almost invariably breeds on rocky ledges, or small holes, in cliffs. I know no well recorded instance of its nest having been found on trees in India. The nest is round, oblong, or semicircular, according to the shape of the site chosen, and is a thicker or thinner platform from 12 to 20 inches in diameter and 2 to 6 in thickness, made of small twigs, in which grass roots, rags and, as Mr. R. Thompson informs me, at times strips of cloth, a yard and a half in length, are incorporated, and serve as lining.

The eggs are normally five in number, I believe, but two nests taken near Kotegurh, contained only four each, in both cases, considerably incubated. The eggs resemble those of the preceding species, but are slightly broader, and less uniform in their colour. In shape, they are broad ovals, more or less pointed or compressed towards one end. The ground colour is a darker or lighter brick or blood red, blotched, or mottled and freckled with a deeper shade of the same colour, the blotches being in some eggs strongly defined, and well marked, and the whole tint of the egg being, in one specimen that I have seen, browner and yellower than I have above described. The eggs are glossless, and the shell though fine and compact, has the sort of chalky texture, noticed in the eggs of *F. Jugger* and *L. Chiquera*. The eggs vary from 1·63 to 1·75 in length, and from 1·28 to 1·35 in breadth, the average of eight eggs measured, being 1·68 by 1·31.

Although I have no record of the birds actually breeding in the plains, I shot a female in the Etawah district, late in March, which was one of a pair, that I saw frequenting a cleft in the clay cliffs of the Chumbul, near Oodee. The oviduct of this bird contained a *white* egg, the size of a Dove's, and when, on seeing this, I next day examined the cleft, I found that it contained a new, nearly finished nest, such as a Kestrel would build. The native fowlers, however, by no means despicable observers, assured me positively that this bird never breeds in the district, so I hardly know what to think; especially as on another occasion (11th February, 1867) I shot a *young male* at the mouth of a similar cleft in the clay cliffs of the Jumna, below Sheregurh, in which was a new nest, apparently ready to lay in. Perhaps these birds search clefts like these for the young of other birds, but the stomachs of those I have killed, have generally contained insects, bees, black ants, beetles, and the like.

Captain Hutton remarks (in Epist.) "The Kestrel is very common, both in the outer hills and the Doon; at Mussoorie I have known it to breed upon a lofty ledge of rocks above the Superintendent's offices."

Mr. W. Theobald makes the following remark on the breeding of this bird in the valley of Kashmir. "Lays in the 3rd week of April; eggs six in number, blunt ovate pyriform; measuring from 1·51 to 1·68 inches in length, and from 1·22 to 1·27 in. in breadth. Colour, pale reddish brown, freckled and blotched with brownish red. Nest, hole in serai wall of Thanna, south of Buranegala, Shahabad, and valley generally."

It will be observed that his dimensions are smaller than those of the eggs that I have measured; and that he found the nest on a building.

Dr. F. Stoliczka remarks that "*Tinnunculus Alaudarius* is common all through the N. W. Himalaya, on the southern side as well as in W. Tibet. I found this common European Hawk breeding near Chini in narrow crevices of rocks. The eggs are dirty white, mottled and irregularly spotted with reddish brown. The young birds vary extremely in colour of their plumage; but the old ones are in every way identical with those from Europe."

Since the above was written, Capt. Cock has sent me the following: "*Tinnunculus Alaudarius.* This bird remains with us all the year round, although it retires higher up the mountain during the month of May. I noticed a pair of birds about a precipice some two or three times, and concluded that they built there. On the 27th of May, I went with a rope and found that there were three young ones only a few days old, in a niche in the precipice that was overhung with grass, rendering the entrance to the nest difficult to be seen. This nest was on the mountains at a height of 7,000 feet above the sea level, and I doubt their breeding lower down, though an officer assured me he saw a Kestrel breeding on a cliff on the banks of the Beas in February. I found another nest at about 8000 feet elevation on the 27th of May with one egg in it, I had watched the birds pairing some days before, and with the help of a rope managed to secure the solitary egg. On the 5th of June I sent up a party who got three more eggs out of this same nest.—Two of the eggs, the largest and smallest measured 1·55 by 1·16 and 1·35 by 1·14."

Mr. R. Thompson sends me the following, "The Kestrel breeds in this country, preferring the shelving of a rock to any other situation. I have seen the nest and young on the precipices of the Sewaliks. A dozen nests might be pointed out on the precipices overhanging the Kossilla river between Khyrna and the Lat bridge. In the valley here noted, it may be seen breeding in company with the Neophron."

"At Pocree in the interior of Ghurwal, a Kestrel carried off a large piece of a *pugree* belonging to one of my Shikarees and took it off to its nest, whence it was recovered by the fellow letting himself down by a rope. I was witness to the whole transaction. At Nynee Tal, two pairs breed early—one on the western precipices, the other on the south-eastern, not far from where I live."

Mr. Brookes writes to me that "the Kestrel is tolerably common in Kumaon. I saw a young bird taken from a nest near Almorah. The colours of the adult male do not appear to be so pure as those of the English bird. The grey of the head is darker, I think, and the chestnut of the back more dingy."

Dr. Jerdon tells me that "he has seen this bird breeding everywhere in the interior of the Himalayas, at heights of from 8000 to 10,000 feet, in May, June and July." (?)

Out of India Mr. Swinhoe remarks that this bird is "resident all the year at Amoy, and several pairs build on the Amoy rocks."

In Palestine (vide Ibis, 1865) Mr. Tristram writes—"The Kestrel is excessively common in every part of the country throughout the year, up to the confines of the southern desert. In the Ghor and in the eastern forests, among the ruins of Amman and Gerash, in the desolate gorges of the Dead Sea, among the luxuriant gardens of the coast, and in the sacred recesses of the mosques of Omar and Hebron, it equally abounds. It is generally gregarious, ten or twenty pairs breeding in the same ruins, and rearing their young about the end of March. It often builds its nest in the recesses of the caves which are occupied by the Griffons, and is the only bird which the Eagles appear to permit to live in close proximity to them. At Amman, too, it builds in the ruins in company with the Jackdaws; and in several places, as at Lydda and Nazareth, large colonies are mixed indiscriminately with those of the lesser Kestrel. The number of nests we came across without searching for them, was enormous."

It is found throughout Europe, in Siberia, in northern and possibly central Africa, but, in the south of that continent, seems to be replaced by the brighter coloured *T. Rupicolus.*

As regards its nidification in England, Mr. Yarrell says, "In spring the Kestrel frequently takes possession of the nest of a Crow or a Magpie, in which to deposit its eggs. Sometimes these birds build in high rocks, or on old towers, and among the ruins of buildings, laying four and occasionally five eggs, about one inch seven lines long, by one inch three lines across, mottled all over with dark reddish brown, and sometimes with blotches of reddish brown upon a pale reddish white ground.

The fifth egg has been known to weigh several grains less than either of those previously deposited and it has also less colouring matter spread over the shell than the others; both effects probably occasioned by the constitutional exhaustion the bird has sustained in her previous efforts. The young are hatched about the end of April, or the beginning of May, and are covered for some time with a yellowish white down."

In Scotland where the physical contour of the country more nearly resembles that of the tract within which in India our Kestrels breed, Macgillivray (I quote from Hewitson) says that "twenty nests of this species might be pointed out on rocks, for one in a tree." Hewitson adds that he is inclined to believe that the true Falcons very rarely make a nest for themselves, and I have no doubt that if observation be directed to this matter, it will be found that in the Himalayas, as elsewhere, the Kestrel often borrows or steals a nest originally belonging to some other bird.

Mr. Blyth (Ibis, 1866) has the following remarks—"There is a Tenasserim (Siamese province) Kestrel to which attention should be directed—*T. Saturatus*, Blyth (J. A. S. B. XXXVII. p. 277) an adult female received from Yé is noticed in my catalogue of the birds in the Calcutta Museum (No. 69) as perhaps the female of a distinct race, remarkable for the great development of the black markings of its plumage. A young female of the same race was subsequently obtained in which the cap is fuscous, with scarcely any indication of rufous margining the feathers. The fuscous colour also *predominating over the rufous* upon the whole upper plumage, and on the tail the *rufous bands are narrower than the black bands.* An adult male Kestrel, from the vicinity of Moulmain (though rather deeper coloured than usual) differed in no respect from the common *T. Alaudarius*, or perhaps, though less probably, the adult male of *T. Saturatus* may prove to be less strongly distinguished, as indeed is exemplified by *T. Japonicus* (Faun. Japon. Tab. 1 and 1 b.) *T. Saturatus* is quite distinct from *T. Molliccensis* (Hombr. et Jacq. voyage au Pôle Sud; Ois. tab. 1 and 2)."

With reference to the deeper coloured example from Moulmain I may remark, that the Southern Indian specimens in my museum, are markedly of a far deeper hue than any of the large series obtained by me in various parts of upper India. I cannot learn that the bird breeds in Southern India, but the intensity of the rufous colouring, recalling that of *T. Rupicolus* or even the American *Pœcilornis Sparverius* would from analogy lead us to suspect, a local southern race, and this should be carefully investigated by observers in Southern India.

To Dr. Jerdon's description of the adult male, we must add; that the tail is tipped with white, the breadth of the tipping increasing from the centre to the exterior feathers; the black band mentioned by him being a subterminal one; all but the two centre tail feathers have at times linear black brown spots on the inner webs; as for the quills, they are often narrowly edged and tipped with white, and the spots on their inner webs are generally more or less rufous. The cere and orbits are bright yellow, the legs and feet bright orange yellow. The bill yellowish at the base; bluish black on culmen and at tips. The claws horny black; the irides brown.

The young male is not, as Jerdon would lead one to suppose, exactly like the female; it is always in the first place more rufous I think, and there are minor differences difficult to express perhaps, but very perceptible to the practised eye. I subjoin accurate measurements and a detailed description of the young male.

Dimensions. Length, 14. Expanse, 30. Weight, 7 ozs. Wing, 9·8; the 2nd and 3rd primaries equal, and the longest; 1st 1·0 shorter; 4th, 0·8 shorter. Tail from vent, 7·5; exterior tail feathers 1·3 shorter than centre ones. Tarsus, (feathered in front for 0·5), 1·53. Foot, greatest length, 2·35; greatest width, 2·35; mid toe, 1·1; its claws straight, 0·44; hind toe, 0·5; its claws straight, 0·5. Bill, straight, 0·69; along curve, 0·88; from gape, 0·85; width at gape, 0·76; height at front at margin of cere, 0·32; cere, only 0·19. Lower tail coverts reach within about 3·38 of end of centre tail feathers. Wings, when closed, reach to within about 2 inches of the end of the centre tail feathers.

Description. Legs and feet yellow, feet slender, claws black, centre and outer toes connected by a membrane as far as the first joints.

Orbits, yellowish green. Irides, brown.

Cere and gape, yellow or pale or greenish yellow. Bill, pale greenish or bluish green at margin of the cere and base of lower mandible, pale blue beyond, deepening almost to blue black at the tips. Tongue, short, rather broad, thin and membraneous towards the tip which is slightly divided.

Plumage. Feathers of forehead, rufous white, feathers, dark shafted. Feathers of the top and back of head and nape, a somewhat vinous rufous, each with a narrow central dark brown stripe. The whole of the base of the back of the neck, the upper back, scapulars and upper wing coverts, except the greater coverts of the primaries, vinous rufous, all the feathers with conspicuous broad bars of dark brown, the bar nearest the tip, especially on the lesser wing coverts, being somewhat triangular in shape. Winglet, dark brown, narrowly margined with rufous on the outer web, and with spots or incomplete transverse bars of the same on both webs. Greater coverts of the primaries, dark brown (with a trace of or in some a well-marked paler tipping), paler towards the margins of the interior webs, and with a few blotches of the same warm rufous hue as characterizes the wing coverts on the outer webs and broad bars of the same, more or less incomplete on the inner webs. Primaries dark brown on the outer webs (which have an *excessively* narrow paler or pale rufous edging, and are unspotted, with the exception of three or four rufous spots, on those of the last two or three), and inner webs brown at the tips, white at the base; the intermediate portions being partly white and partly brown, a set of brown teeth or scallops of brown, running out from the shaft towards the margin, and a set of similar white teeth or scallops running out alternately with them from the margin towards the shaft. The tips of the white scallops deeply tinged with rufous, where they approach the shaft. In some of the primaries before the regular scallops commence, there are near the tip in the inner webs one or more oval rufous spots. The secondaries are a lighter brown, narrowly but distinctly tipped with rufous, or in some dingy, white, and barred transversely with broad rufous bars, which pale and become almost or quite pure white towards the margins of the inner webs, and this more so towards the bases, where on the inner webs, these is scarcely any rufous and less so towards the tips where there is scarcely any white. It is to be noted that in the earlier secondaries, the brown and in the latter the rufous and white predominate. The tertials connect the scapulars and secondaries and resemble both; but are more uniformly rufous and brown, and have less (if any) white on the inner webs than the later secondaries. Lower back, rump and upper tail coverts grey, with a vinous or pinkish tinge, regularly barred with pretty broad bars of brown. In some, the lower back and rump are uniform with upper back and scapulars, only slightly paler; while the upper tail coverts are fulvous white but barred as usual. The tail feathers are a vinous rufous, tipped with white most broadly so in the exterior, least broadly so, on the centre ones, and with a broad subterminal band of blackish brown usually narrower on the 2nd exterior feather, and much narrower on the exterior feathers. Above the subterminal band, each feather is conspicuously barred with transverse dark brown bars, somewhat irregular; those on the two webs, not exactly coinciding at the shaft, and somewhat incomplete, as not extending quite to the margin. The exterior feather often has a narrow and obscure white margin to the outer web, and a trace of this is also at times visible on the 2nd exterior, while all but the centre feathers are more or less whitish towards the margins of the inner webs.

The lores are white, thickly overlaid by fine, dark brown, hair-like feathers. There is a trace of a narrow brown stripe over the back of eye and ear-coverts; ear-coverts lax, mingled white (with or without a faint rufous tinge) brown or dusky; a brown cheek stripe, not very conspicuous, from the eye, past the gape, on either sides of the upper throat, with commonly a branch from the base of the lower mandible just below the gape. Chin white Upper throat unspotted rufous white, or pure white; sides of neck below ear coverts, front of neck, breast and upper abdomen, pale rufous or nearly pure white, most of the feathers with narrow central dark brown stripes, most conspicuous on sides of neck and body (where the stripes are dilated towards the tips of the feathers into broadish blotches) and least so on the upper abdomen, where they become mere specks at the tips of dark shafted feathers. Lower abdomen, vent, lower tail, and thigh coverts white or very pale rufous white, dingy about lower tail coverts and vent, at times with two or three minute dark brown specks on the thigh coverts. Axillaries white, barred with brown; lesser lower wing coverts pure white, with tiny oval subterminal spots of dark brown. Larger lower wing coverts also pure white, with subterminal heart-shaped spots of dark brown, and most of them, chiefly those of the secondaries however, with more or less incomplete bars of a somewhat lighter brown. On the under surfaces of the quills and tail feathers, the markings described on the upper surfaces show through.

No. 18. **Erythropus Cenchris,** NAUMANN.

THE LESSER KESTREL.

Dr. Jerdon tells us that he found this Falcon breeding on cliffs of the Neilgherries in May and June, and I regret to say that this is the extent of my information as to its breeeding in India.

In Greece, Sicily, Palestine, &c., it breeds gregariously, laying three, four, or occasionally five eggs, in clefts of rocks or ruins, or even under the tiles of houses. It makes, it would seem, but little or no nest. Degland, quoted by Bree, says that "the eggs are three or four in number; very short, smaller than those of the Kestrel: of a reddish white, with a great number of little points and fly spots of a brick red mingled together and mixed with small brown spots." The egg figured by Bree measures, according to the drawing, 1·42 by 1·17, and is like a light-coloured variety of common Kestrel eggs. I am rather suspicious of Dr. Bree's eggs generally, the simple faith with which he accepts, as authentic, Continental eggs with positively *no* pedigree, being more remarkable than reassuring; but this egg is so common now in Europe, that I suppose he may here be trusted.

Mr. Tristram in the Ibis for 1859 told us, that this species was "gregarious about the ruins in the plain districts. About fifteen or twenty pairs were building their nests in and about the beautiful tower of Ramleh (Arimathea) in company with a still larger number of the common Kestrel, and flew screaming round me, as I climbed the still perfect staircase of the tower."

In the Ibis for 1865, he gives a full account of its nidification in Palestine. He says, "It breeds, so far as we have observed, invariably in communities, usually in narrow fissures of the rocks or in the crevices of ruins, not generally in very inaccessible situations, but always in so narrow a cleft, and at such a depth in, that the eggs are hard to extract. I never found a colony without many of the common Kestrel breeding in the same place. The largest rookeries of this bird we met with, were in the towns of Lydda and Ramleh, and in the top of an old quarried cave (perfectly protected by prickly fern) in the town of Nazareth. Although the two species are so closely allied, there can be no difficulty in discriminating the eggs; and we found that the Arab boys knew the difference between the two species at once, calling one the black nailed and the other the white nailed '*bashik*.'"

Mr. Simpson in his notes on the birds of western Greece has the following interesting remarks on this species. "Towards the middle of March, the little Kestrel (*Falco Cenchris*) begins to arrive, and presently takes up its abode, often in considerable numbers, in the villages and ruins upon the plains.

"Whilst the common Kestrel, which occurs all the year round, dwells in the rocks and remote ruins, breeding generally in single pairs, this species prefers more inhabited places and, like the Swallow, trusts to mankind. In eastern Greece, one of its favorite localities is the renowned ruin, which crowns the Acropolis Rock at Athens. Most of the villages in the marshy plain near Mesolonghi have their colony of *F. Cenchris* and notably those in the neighbourhood of the Phidaris, where the insects abound on which they feed. Each of the favoured villages will have from half a dozen to a dozen pairs. They breed generally, under the tiles of a house sometimes in a position where it is no easy matter to introduce the hand. There is no regular nest, but the eggs (four and rarely five, is the complement) are placed in a depression upon the bare wall amongst bits of lime mixed with the hard parts of coleopterous insects. Incubation commences about the middle of May, and if the eggs are removed, they speedily lay again; the second time mostly three eggs. In size, the egg is considerably smaller than that of the common Kestrel; but it appears subject to pretty much the same varieties of colour, being on the whole perhaps somewhat lighter."

This species seems to have a very wide range; it is found throughout the south and south-east of Europe, the north of Africa, Egypt and Abyssinia, and probably all over Africa, as Layard notes it from the Cape. I have seen a specimen shot near Umballa; and Col. Tytler tells me, he killed one near Delhi. It is not uncommon in the rainy season in Bengal, and seems to reside permanently in the hilly tracts of Southern India. It does not appear to go much further east, as Wallace does not include it in the birds of the Malay Archipelago, nor do I find it noticed from Japan or China. In Australia, it seems to be represented by *E. Cenchroides*, (Vig. et Horsf.)

My friend Mr. Carter of Coimbatoor, sends me the following detailed measurements of an adult female, shot near Conoor.

Dimensions—Length, 13. Expanse, 28·5. Weight, 6·44 ozs. Wing, 9·75; the 2nd and 3rd primaries sub-equal; 2nd the longest. Tail from vent, 6·75. Tarsus, 1·81. Foot, greatest length, 2·5; greatest width, 2·38; mid toe, 1·13; its claw, straight, 0·44; hind toe, 0·5; its claw, straight, 0·5. Bill, straight, 0·69; along curve, 0·75; from gape, 0·88; width at gape, 0·88; height at front, 0·5.

He notes that the bill is plumbeous, black at the tips, and that the specimen measured had eaten nothing but locusts.

Dr. Jerdon's description of the male is not quite satisfactory; he tells us, that the wing coverts are a fine blue grey, and immediately afterwards that they are vinaceous red; quite true so far as it goes, but without explanation, not unlikely to perplex a tyro. An adult male before me has the lores, forehead, crown, occiput, nape, cheeks, ear coverts and generally the sides of the head and neck, a pure bluish ashy. Back, scapulars and lesser and median wing coverts, a deep red. Primaries and secondaries blackish brown, some of the hinder ones tinged ashy and more or less paler tipped. Tertiaries more or less ashy, margined rufous. Larger wing coverts tinged ashy. Rump and upper tail coverts, ashy blue; tail feathers tipped white, with a black subterminal band, broadest on the median, and narrowest on the external feathers; the rest of the tail nearly concolorous with the rump, but slightly darker. Chin and throat white faintly tinged with rufous. Lower tail coverts nearly pure white, rest of lower parts of body a delicate vinaceous red, the feathers with small brownish black spots and central streaks, smallest on the breast, most conspicuous on the sides and flanks. The beak, pale plumbeous, darker at the tips, and the claws, apparently *yellow*. From the ticket on the specimen, it appears that the wings, when closed, reached quite to the end of the tail and that cere, orbits, legs and feet were bright yellow.

No. 19. **Erythropus Vespertinus,** Lin.

The Ingrian Falcon, Lath.

Of the nidification of this bird in India, which in most parts of the country is rare, or at any rate owing to its crepuscular habits, difficult to procure, (so much so, that I have never yet seen a specimen) nothing is known; nay, up to this time it is uncertain whether the bird that occurs in India, and has hitherto generally been referred to this species, really belongs to it, or to a nearly allied form *E. Amurensis*, of which more anon.

In regard to the true *Vespertinus*, Mr. Yarrell tell us, that "M. Viellot in the *Faune Francaise*, says, that it builds in the hollows of trees, or takes to the nest of the Magpie, sometimes in companies like Rooks, and that it flies and hawks for its prey only in the evening."

Mr. Hewitson, on Mr. Cochrane's authority, states, that in Hungary, this species "arrives about the middle of April and have laid their eggs early in May. They make no nest for themselves, but after a fight with the lawful owners, take possession of those of the Crow, Rook, or Magpie, altering or repairing them, according to their own taste. The eggs are sometimes six in number, but most commonly four or five; at times as many as six or seven pairs breed in a single tree. "The eggs," Mr. Hewitson remarks, "most nearly resemble those of the Kestrel, being, however, for the most part considerably less; like the eggs of that bird, they are sometimes finely freckled throughout," and sometimes with more or less conspicuous blotches and spots of a darker hue. They are of course of the regular Falcon type, and so far as variation of colour goes, my description of the eggs of *F. Jugger* (*q. v.*) will, I fancy, apply more or less to those of the present and other kindred species;

according to Mr. Hewitson's *figures*, the eggs measure 1·48 and 1·59 by 1·2.

Of its breeding about Talien bay, N. China, Mr. Swinhoe had a note in the Ibis for 1861, he said—"This handsome little bird-slayer was not unfrequently met with flying along overhead or hovering, poised in air. Judging from the contents of the stomachs of two I procured, I should say it committed considerable havoc among the Larks and other field birds. It certainly caused considerable consternation whenever it appeared among them. I had an opportunity of observing the nest of this species twice; one was placed amongst the topmost boughs of a willow, the other in the leafy foliage of some umbrageous tree. The nests are large and round, and built of sticks; resembling somewhat those of the Magpie. When the old birds visited the nest, the young set up a chattering cry." It seems probable, however, that the bird here referred to, is *E. Amurensis* and not *Erythropus* (verus).

Mr. Blyth, in commenting on Dr. Jerdon's work remarked "the rufous plumage of the adult female of this species, was unknown to Dr. Jerdon. In confinement, this species and *E. Cenchris* do not thrive upon meat, but must be fed *on a mixed diet*, like that commonly given to small insectivorous birds. Dr. Jerdon, it will be observed, agrees with me in referring *E. Cenchris* and *E. Vespertinus* to the same minimum division. I cannot help thinking, that all naturalists who are familiar with the living birds, must needs be of the same opinion. These two little white clawed Kestrelets only visit lower Bengal during the rainy season (so far as I have observed), and the same remark applies to *Baza Lophotes*." The editor of the Ibis in a note to this, pointed out that it would be interesting to ascertain whether the Indian bird was true *Vespertinus*, the Western form, or *Amurensis*, the Eastern form, with light coloured under surface to the wings.

The history of this so-called Eastern form is this: Van Rodde, in the 2nd volume of his Reisen in *suden von ost Siberien*, mentioned that the red-footed Hobbies from Eastern Siberia, had the under surface of the wings either entirely white, or white barred with grey, instead of the uniform deep tint which is found in European examples, and he proposed to distinguish them as var. *Amurensis*.

This same species, next turned up in South Africa, and the following note by Mr. Gurney (Ibis, 1868) contains much interesting matter in regard to the two species.

"*Erythropus Amurensis* (Radde,) *Falco Vespertinus*, var. *Amurensis*, Radde, Reisen II. p. 102 tab. I. fig. 2; Ibis, 1866, p. 119;

Eastern red-footed *Hobby*. Iris hazel; eyelids and bare skin, orange; bill, dark orange; black at the tip; tarsi and feet, dark orange.

Numbers of these pretty Falcons may be seen during the summer months about the open downs in the neighbourhood of Maritzburg; but are not, so far as I know, found there in winter.

They hunt in company; sometimes as many as twenty together, well scanning the ground for grasshoppers, and other insects, of which their food seems almost entirely to consist; they do not generally remain long on the wing, alighting on any low plant, ant-heap, or on the level ground; in twos and threes. They are not particularly shy; one may get within fifty yards of them without much difficulty. They seem to prefer marshy ground to hunt over.

The very curious circumstance of the occurrence in southeastern Africa of this species, which had previously been known only as an inhabitant of Amuria and of Northern China, has been already mentioned in the Ibis (*loc. cit.*) where a brief reference to the specimens sent from Natal by Mr. Ayre was made.

These specimens were three in number, two males and one female, all, I believe, adult. I have also received from my friend, Mr. Anderson, an adult male obtained at the Kuysna, on the south-eastern coast of the colony of the Cape of Good Hope; and I have had the opportunity of examining a female specimen in the British Museum, procured in South Africa by Mr. Charles Livingstone, and believed to have been obtained near the River Shire.

The examples from South-east Africa appear to me to be specifically identical with specimens of both sexes in the Norwich Museum obtained in Northern China, consisting of a male and female from Yoon Ying, near Pekin, and of two males from the neighbourhood of Talien Bay.

The question whether the red-footed Hobby of India, belongs to the present species, or to its Western congener, *Erythropus Vespertinus*, is one which, in the absence of Indian specimens, I am unable to decide, and to which I would beg the attention of ornithologists resident in that country* (Ibis, 1866, p. 119).

With regard to the distribution of *E. Amurensis* in south Africa, I may add that Mr. Anderson informs me, that he has obtained one example in Damara Land; where, however, *E.*

* Since the above was written, Mr. G. R. Gray has been good enough to tell me of a specimen in the British Museum brought from Nepal, which I agree with him in considering an immature female of *E. Amurensis*.

Vespertinus is the common species, and is indeed so numerous, that in a letter, dated 16th February, 1866, Mr. Anderson writes to me, that it appears during the wet season in incredible numbers: they then come, not by thousands, but literally by tens of thousands.

Of the specific distinction between *E. Amurensis* and *E. Vespertinus* I cannot entertain the slightest doubt. The adult male of the former differs from that of the latter, in having the under wing coverts of a pure white, instead of a slaty black, as well as in the slightly darker colouring of its upper parts. The female of *E. Amurensis* differs from the female of the other species, in the absence of rufous colouring on the head, neck and under parts, except the thighs and under tail coverts, which are rufous in it, as in the female of *E. Vespertinus*, and also excepting a very slight rufous tinge on the sides of the neck and throat, and on the under wing coverts, near the carpal joint. The plumage of all the under parts in the female of *E. Amurensis*, excepting that of the throat (which is pure white) the thighs and the under tail coverts, is strongly marked with ovate and sagittate spots of dark slaty black on a white ground; which markings assume a transverse form on the under wing-coverts and lower flank feathers, and produce a general appearance of the under parts considerably resembling the front view of the adult common Hobby (*Hypotriorchis Subbuteo*)."

I have been unable to ascertain to which form our Indian species belongs, perhaps both forms occur. It is to be hoped that some of my numerous coadjutors will make a point of securing good specimens. They seem tolerably common in some localities. Mr. R. Thompson writing from Kumaon, says—

" Whilst up under the snow line in the month of September, I observed large parties of these birds hovering about catching insects, and occasionally alighting on the ledges of rock. Eight to twenty birds have been seen together hovering about like swallows. In October last year, I saw several hovering over the Nynee Tal valley, and remember later, seeing one down in the plains."

Per contra, Dr. Stoliczka writing from the Hills north and east of Simla, tells us, that this species is rarely seen in the interior of the Himalayas, and then only in the lower Hills.

There is this, however, to be said; Yarrell informs us, that this species "is a native of Russia, Poland, and Austria from whence it passes southward" and westward to the shores and islands of the Mediterranean. It undoubtedly occurs in Turkey in Asia, Palestine and northern Africa, and at least as far south on that continent as Damara Land. But I can hear nothing of its having been found in Mesopotamia, Persia, Cabool, or Kashmir and even westward of the Ganges, it seems very rare. At Darjeeling, at certain seasons, I am assured that it is common; Mr. Thompson tells us the same from Kumaon; in lower Bengal too it is reported plentiful during the rains. The bird is strictly migratory with us, coming in during and after the rains, when insect-life most abounds, and I apprehend, that it is chiefly eastward of the Ganges where vegetation is more luxuriant, and where the plains below the Hills afford a better supply of insect food than the comparatively arid tracts of the North West Presidencies, and the Punjaub, that the great mass of the birds cross the Snowy Range. Should such be the case, there is an additional probability in favour of our bird proving to be *Amurensis.*

Dr. Jerdon's descriptions of this bird are rather meagre, and I therefore proceed to quote Mr. Yarrell's, which appear unusually full and satisfactory.

"After their first change, the plumage of the males is much more uniform than that of the females. In the adult male, the base of the beak is yellowish white, the other part, dark horn colour; the cere and eyelids, reddish orange; the irides, dark brown; the head, neck, beak, upper surface of the wings and tail, the throat, breast, and belly, of a uniform dark lead colour; the thighs, vent, and under tail coverts, deep ferruginous; the legs and toes, reddish flesh colour; the claw, yellowish white, with dusky tips. The whole length of the bird eleven inches.

"The plumage of the young males, before their first change, is similar to that of young females, which will hereafter be described. At their first change, they become of a uniform pearl grey; the thighs and flanks, ferruginous; beak, cere, eyes, legs, toes, and claws, as in the old male. The vignette is taken from a young male bird, that has nearly completed his first change, but still retains a portion of the barred appearance of his first livery on the outer or distal part of the wing, on the lower part of the beak and the tail feathers, the central pair only of which are as yet mottled.

"The adult female has the beak, cere, irides, legs, &c., as in the male; the head and back of the neck reddish brown; the eye surrounded with dusky feathers almost black; the whole of the back, wing coverts, and tail feathers, blackish grey, barred transversely with bluish black; upper surface of the wing-primaries, uniform dusky black. The chin and throat nearly white; breast and all the under surface of the body, pale rufous, with dark reddish brown longitudinal streaks; the thighs and their long feathers plain rufous; under wing coverts rufous, with transverse bars of dark brown; under surface of the wing primaries, blackish grey, with numerous transverse bars of bluish grey; under surface of the tail feathers bluish grey, with nine or ten transverse bars of bluish black; the bars increasing a little in breadth as they approach the tip.

"Young females have the top of the head reddish brown with dusky streaks; the eyes encircled with black, with a small black pointed moustache descending from the anterior part of the eye; ear coverts white; upper surface of the body, dark brown, the feathers ending with reddish brown; wing primaries, dusky black; the inner edges and tips, buffy white; the tail feathers, dark brown with numerous transverse bars of reddish brown; throat, white: sides of the neck, the breast, and all the under surface of the body, pale, reddish white, with brown longitudinal streaks and patches on the breast; the thighs and their long feathers, uniform pale ferruginous; beak, cere, irides, &c., as in the adult female."

No. 20. **Hierax Eutolmus,** Hodgson.

The Red* Legged Falconet.

Nothing is known of the breeding of this species. Mr. Blyth says, that an account of the habits of the nearly allied black legged Falconet (*H. Fringillarius*) is given in the Proceedings of the Zoological Society for 1863, p. 206, but of our Indian species, I have failed to find any record.

It is not, I think uncommon, anywhere in the Himalayas east of the Ganges. I have shot it low down at Jewlee in August, and at the height of nearly 9000 feet, on the Takhil at the end of October. The first I shot, I took as it passed me, from its flight and glossy black, white and rufous plumage, to be some sort of Swallow, and so did the native with me; but on its falling to my shot, and his going to pick it up, he rapidly changed his opinion, the fierce little creature having buried its talons and the point of its beak in his hand, inflicting wounds quite surprising, when the size of the bird, scarcely so large as a Skylark, is considered.

* Three species of this genus may well be separated by the colour of their tibial plumes. The present which has these red, under the name above given. *H. Fringillarius*, Drapiez. (*H. Malayensis*, Strickland and *Falco Cærulescens*, Viellot) as the black legged, and *H. Melanoleucus*, Blyth, (of which I have only seen a drawing) as the white legged Falconets. Mr. Blyth pointed out this distinction long ago.

Mr. R. Thompson remarks—"I have observed these birds make their appearance in our Gurhwal forests in March. I have never found a nest, nor do I know when they breed.

"They are quick and lively in their motions, hawking insects with swallow-like agility, and after a long flight, betaking themselves to a tree, always getting on some high dead branch.

"Their flight is rapid, direct, and made with frequent flappings of the wing, like the Sand Martins. On one occasion at Almorah, one passed close to where I was standing; it was, I think during the month of October."

I believe this species to be migratory, spending the warmer portion of the year, from March to November, in well-wooded portions of the hilly country; between 2500 and 9000 feet altitude. They must therefore breed with us, and their first nest is a prize that I hope yet to see secured; but where do they spend the winter? As yet no one seems to have seen them in the plains or even in the Terai, and it seems pretty certain that they are not permanent residents in our territories. Do they recross the snow (as the red-footed Hobby seems to do) when the cold weather begins to set in? and if so, where do they go? Where, in the barren steppes of Central Asia, can they find food? (to judge from the specimens that I have killed, they are entirely insectivorous) or do they work eastward towards the provinces that form the head-quarters of the genus, which is essentially a south-eastern* type?

No. 21. **Astur Palumbarius,** Lin.

The Goshawk.

The Goshawk breeds in India, so far as I have been able to ascertain, only in the higher regions of the Himalayas, in the immediate neighbourhood of the snows. A pair of very young birds were brought late in July, while I was at Simla, for the Rajah of Putialla from near the Chor, and the Shikaree asserted, that he had taken them out of a nest, placed near the top of some kind of Fir or Pine tree.

Mr. R. Thompson, an enthusiastic falconer by the way, tells me that "they breed from March to June, building on trees, a

* There are *Hierax Sericeus* (Kittle) from the Philippine Islands and China. *H. Fringillarius* (Drapiez) from Malay (extending, Blyth says, sparingly into the southern Tenasserim provinces, where it meets *Eutolmus*) Malacca, Sumatra, Borneo and Java, *H. Melanoleucus* from Assam, and if distinct, *H. Erythrogenys* (Vigors), from the Philippines.

large circular nest of coarse twigs, in which they lay three or four nearly pure white eggs. They confine themselves peculiarly to the interior of the deep precipitous woody valleys, lying close to the snowy peaks. They usually, I am told, select a tree of the Birch, *Alnus Boojputtia*, or one of *Cupressus Tomentosa* to build their nests on.

"During this period, the birds are very daring, and will readily attack a man, attempting to climb up to the nest. In these woods, the Moonal Pheasant is very abundant, and no doubt affords capital quarry for these Hawks."

Of the Goshawk in Europe, Mr. Hewitson, quoting Mr. Hay, says that it "builds its own nest, and if undisturbed in its possession, will frequently occupy it for several years, making the necessary repairs. It is placed in some high tree on the outskirts of the forest, and is rarely found in the interior, except in those parts which are open and free from timber. The eggs are three or four, and are frequently hatched by the middle of May; they are, for the most part, spotless, but are sometimes indistinctly marked with brown." The one he figures is a delicate bluish white, like that of *Micronisus Badius*, and measures 2·17 by 1·72.

Mr. Yarrell tells us that "the eggs of the Goshawk are rare, the few that I have seen were in size and colour, 2·19 in length by 1·69 in breadth, of a pale bluish white, without any spots or streaks."

Compare the above with what Gould tells us of the nearly allied *Astur Approximans* of Australia.

"Its nest is usually built on a large swamp-oak (*Casuarina*) growing on the side of a brook, but I have occasionally met with it on the gum trees (*Eucalypti*) in the forest, at a considerable distance from water; it is of a large size, and is composed of sticks, and lined with gum leaves. The eggs are generally three in number, of a bluish white, smeared over with blotches of brownish buff; they are one inch and ten lines long, by one inch and five lines broad. The nesting season commences in August and continues till November."

Kaup separates this species under Uraspiza, and the eggs, as above described, appear to differ from the typical *Astur* egg, but I have to note that the man who brought the young birds from near the Chor, affirmed that he had looked down into the nest, from the distance of a few yards, when it contained eggs, and that these latter were blotched with brown like those of a kite (*M. Govinda*), except that the brown was lighter and more earthy.

Dr. Jerdon lately mentioned to me (in epist.) that "the

Goshawk is occasionally taken in the plains of the Punjab during the cold weather. I saw," he adds, "a pair in July 1864, that evidently had their nest in a wood in the Asrang valley above Chini, about 12000 feet high."

My friend, Mr. Thompson, sends me the following account of hawking with the Goshawk in the forests of Gurhwal and the Terai.

"Several are caught on the high peaks of Josheemat, Tomynaut, Tuppobund, &c. during October and November, when it would appear that the birds leave their snow-girt valleys, and betake themselves to others lower down, and free from snow. The trap consists of vertical nets six feet high, of stout thread enclosing three sides of a square and open at top. In the centre, a Pigeon is tied to the end of a small stick, which again is fastened by the other end to a peg in the ground; two other pegs, one on each side of this first peg are driven in, and from these, fine strings are carried to the point of the stick to which the Pigeon is fastened. These strings assist in keeping the stick in its place, when the man pulls another string, by which the stick is alternately raised, and then suddenly allowed to fall, thereby giving that fluttering motion to the Pigeon's wings which best serves to attract the Hawk. The trapper hides under some bushes, and as his trap is usually set on the very summit of the ridge or peak, can keep a good look out for any bird approaching, when he sees one he begins to pull at his Pigeon and watches with keen anxiety every movement of the Goshawk. The latter, as a rule, the instant he sees the Pigeon, dashes at it either from one of the enclosed sides, or through the open one, and striking against the net is enveloped in it. The nets, I should note, are supported on four slender posts firmly driven into the ground one at each corner of the square, and to these the nets are loosely hung by fine threads, or hairs from a *cow's tail!*

"The price of a young female varies from Rs. 40 to 60. Birds of first, second and third plumage, are valued at considerably less, not even a fourth of what a young bird will fetch. The males are of proportionately less value. Nearly all of the birds caught in British and foreign Gurhwal are taken to the Punjab, a few only finding their way down to Rohilcund.

"Despite of all that is said about short wing Hawks, this bird is capable of attaining a high degree of efficiency as a bold and rapid flyer,* a fagless worker, and affording decidedly the best

* As instances :—I have taken *Coturnix Communis* in the middle of April with my Goshawks flying straight off the fist at the Quail. My Goshawks have flown at Partridge and Quail 800 to 1,000 yards from where they were slipped.

sport that can be had in a forest country. When first put to the quarry, they fly with outspread wings, with a listless slow motion like that of a great Owl, admirably described in Sir John Sebwright's little pamphlet on hawking, but by every day practice, and constant flying at the black Partridge, high feeding, and carefully training it to become familiar with men, dogs, and all other objects, likely to frighten it, it becomes in about two or three months perfect at its work. The docility of the bird in the hands of a good trainer, is wonderful. Its intelligence is almost equal to that of the dogs. I have had them (and it must be said that the natives of India are the only people who seem to understand rightly the training of this bird) so docile and intelligent, that by the mere putting out of my hand, the birds have flown from the falconer's fists and settled on mine whilst seated on an elephant; and this, because I was in the habit of receiving the birds on my fists to fly at blacks.* Other birds have shown equal intelligence; one I lately had, used to be unleashed at my tent door, would fly to the nearest tree, and as the party set out through forest and glade, would fly from tree to tree, and thus keep on, quite up to the beaters and dogs, never lagging behind till a bird was flushed, but always sufficiently forward to receive the quarry as it rose. This was the best bird I ever had at taking black Partridge, which it always caught on the wing.

"It was a beautiful sight to see 'Sultana' shoot out of a tree like a cannon shot, at a Partridge just flushed, often striking it before it knew where it was. Sometimes, however, there would be a race—Partridge ahead, Sultana immediately behind, each straining every nerve, the Partridge must go on, it dare not settle in the grass, for to do this it must slacken its pace, each moment bringing the Hawk closer to it, till at last it is clutched. This, over a fine spread of grass, without much interruption to the view, is a splendid sight! Another fine flight often to be witnessed with these birds, is the taking the *Francolin* in tall heavy grass. A line of elephants are beating up the game. The flushed Partridge rising out of the grass towers straight up; the Hawk is slipped, and follows horizontally the direction of the other, until it sees it descending, when, springing up almost perpendicularly, the Hawk seizes the quarry.

"The Goshawks I have had, after a preliminary education of Partridge hunting, have generally been put at Jungle Fowl, Kalleege Pheasant, Hares, and Peacocks. At all of which

* I hasten to explain that Mr. Thompson means black Partridges and not as some of our English philanthropists (?) would certainly conclude, natives of India.

they have done well. I have taken a dozen Jungle Fowl in a couple of hours with them, using dogs to flush the birds. They have also killed Peacocks in a single flight, and Hares without ever having been booted. I have also taken Teal and Ducks in woody swamps, by appearing at the water from a point whence a distant view could be had of the Water-fowl. The Hawk, on being shown the Ducks, would fly at once to the tree nearest to them, and there wait in ambush. The beaters were then sent to flush the Fowl, one of which the Hawk caught in the air as the flock rose, almost perpendicularly, out of the water."

No. 22. **Lophospiza Trivirgatus**, Reinw.

The Crested Goshawk.

While the common Goshawk is a true Palæarctic type, never I believe finding its way far south of 30° North Latitude, the Crested Goshawk belongs essentially to the middle Palætropical or Indian Region, and while unknown north and west of Delhi, is found throughout Southern India and Ceylon, in Assam, Burmah, Java, Borneo, Sumatra and the Philippine Islands, Formosa, and probably Southern China generally.

I know nothing of the nidification of the species beyond what Layard, quoted by Jerdon, says, of its breeding on rocks in Ceylon. It is common enough on the Neilgheries, and it is to be hoped that some of my correspondents there, will make it a special study.

Swinhoe has the following note (Ibis, 1866) on "a fine female" killed in Formosa. "Length, 16·25 inches; wing, 9 inches; tail, 7·6 inches. First quill, 1·5 inches shorter than the third, which is 0·3 inch shorter than the fourth and fifth, the longest in the wing. The second to the fifth quills indented on the inner web, the first less sinuated. Tail of twelve, nearly equal feathers, rectrices barred, the outer pair with only one faint bar near the base, and an indistinct one near the tip. Legs yellow. Claws black. Tarsi about 2·75 inches long, feathered for about 1·75 inches down the front; middle toe without the claw, about 1·62 inches; claw of outer toe, about the same size as that of the middle toe, inner toe, shorter than the outer, with the claw nearly as large as that on hind toe."

Wallace in the Ibis for 1868, gives the "bill black, base, lead colour; iris and cere, orange yellow; cheeks and orbits olive; feet yellow. Length 15 inches."

No. 23. **Micronisus Badius,** GMEL.

THE SHIKRA.

The Shikra lays in April and May, building for itself a moderately sized nest on trees, large and lofty ones being, as far as my experience in the plains goes, always selected. Writing from Gurhwal, Mr. Thompson says—"This is a regular breeder in our forests, and always chooses trees standing on the edges of streams or stagnant pools. The birds are very fond of frogs, which they are constantly stooping at. They are noisy, and quarrelsome, if any large bird approaches their nest."

The nest is usually placed in a fork high up, and near the top of the tree. It is but loosely built of twigs, and smaller sticks lined with fine grass roots, is much smaller and less compact than those of the Toorumtee, (*Lithofalco Chicquera*) often are, and may average about ten inches in diameter.

The greatest number of eggs I have ever taken in a nest was four, but I am inclined to think that the generality only lay three. The eggs do not vary much in shape. They are a little shorter and stouter than those of *L. Chicquera.* They are oval or somewhat pyriform, a rather longer egg in proportion to its breadth than one expects to find in this class of bird. They belong to the Goshawk and not to the Sparrow Hawk type. Smooth, fine, glossless shells, of a pure, delicate, pale bluish white, as a rule absolutely devoid of markings; at most, thinly sprinkled all over with very faint grayish specks and spots, thus differing widely from the apparently closely allied *A. Nisus*, whose eggs are often richly, and always, I believe, more or less marked.

In size the eggs vary from 1·5 to 1·63 in length and from 1·2 to 1·26 in breadth, but the average of a dozen eggs was 1·55 × 1·24. These little Hawks take, I should say, a full month in preparing their nest, only putting on two or three twigs a day which they place and replace, as if they were *very* particular, and had a great eye for a handsome nest, whereas, after all their fuss and bother, the nest is a loose ragged looking affair, that no respectable Crow even, would condescend to lay in. I can never help thinking of the Public Works Department, when I see these Shikras busy building. All the fuss they make about scientific training, and elaborate plans, estimates, budgets and what not, and how after all, the result of their labours, is only some hideous, straight up and down, blank wall, barn-like, mud and plaster affair, with which no respectable, *unscientific* native would have ventured to disfigure the face of the earth.

M. Badius, Brachydactylus, Sphenurus, are said by Bree to be very close to each other. Length of wing and tail; length and thickness of tarsus; and length of mid toe, and proportions of primaries are what chiefly assist in discriminating these nearly allied species. Plumage, owing to its extreme variability in this family, going for little. I have recorded carefully the measurements of ten males and ten females of this species, and subjoin the result which may be useful for comparison with those of nearly allied races.

Wing F. 7·9 to 8·3; M. 6·8 to 7·3. Tail F. 6·8 to 7·2; M. 5·5 to 5·9. Tarsus F. 1·9 to 2·0; M. 1·8 to 1·9; mid toe to root of claw F. 1·25 to 1·4; M. 1·06 to 1·15. Circumference of tarsus, at middle F. 0·65 to 0·73; M. 0·6 to 0·65;

1st primary shorter than the 4th by			F. 2·5 to 2·7	M. 2·38 to 2·55
2nd	do.	do.	F. 0·9 to 1·0	M. 0·84 to 0·9
3rd	do.	do.	F. 0·12to0·25	M. 0·05 to 0·15
5th	do.	do.	F. 0·2to 0·25	M. 0·12 to 0·15

In reading remarks in regard to the various species of *Accipiters,* I often see stress laid on the absence or presence of bars on central, or outer feathers, and on the showing through or the contrary, of these bars, on the under surfaces, especially of the outer feathers. This class of characters appears to me of but little value, depending, as I believe them to do, mainly upon age. I have kept numbers of *M. Badius* for years at a time, rearing them from the nest, and from the following notes drawn up, when I had peculiar opportunities of watching the changes, it will be seen, that in this species at any rate, the presence or absence of bars on any part of the tail, is simply worthless as a specific character.

The young Shikras have (with the subnoted exception) *all* the tail feathers barred on *both* webs, with normally six bars in the female, and five in the male (though this difference is not invariable) including one near the base, hidden by the upper tail coverts, always feeble and sometimes wanting. The outer web, of the outer feather, on each side, commonly (even in very young birds) shows only a terminal and none of the other bars. At this stage, the bars show through on the under surface of *all* the feathers.

Even in the quite young birds, the bars on the inner webs of the outer feathers, are less than half the breadth of those on the other feathers, and are not unfrequently much more numerous. As they get older, the birds begin to lose all but the terminal bar on the centre tail feathers, the other bars turn into spots; then these disappear and only lighter and darker alternate patches on the shafts indicate where the bars once were, and then these also disappear, and leave the central feathers of a pure grey brown, or perhaps, I should say, brownish dove-colour in the females, and french grey in the males, narrowly tipped with white, and with one moderately broad subterminal deep brown bar, which itself soon disappears in the males, and even in the females, as time runs on, becomes more feeble, and more of a spot, and in one old female I now have, has entirely disappeared. Simultaneously, the bars on the inner web of the outer tail feather on each side, begin to show less and less on the under surface, from which after a time they altogether disappear, and having during this process, grown feeble on the upper surface too, go on fading and fading, till at last they disappear there also.

The lateral tail feathers share in the change; those immediately next the central ones, lose all bars on their outer webs, except the terminal one, which is much reduced; while in the next two, on either side, the bars on the outer webs become very faint, and though this seems exceptional in the females, I have a specimen in which *all* the lateral tail feathers have lost *all* the bars except the terminal one from their outer webs, and in the old males this seems the rule; even the terminal bar in these latter, becoming feeble and ill-defined.

Besides the minor differences pointed out in the foregoing, between the sexes and the important one of size, it should be noted that while the old male, becomes a sort of *hoary ashy blue* on the back and scapulars, the females seem never to become more than a *pale brownish ashy;* moreover, the rufous brown of the breast and upper abdomen is deeper in the adult female than in the male, and there is *more of it.*

The changes above described, do not always take place at the same period; specimens may be met with, with the back and scapulars ashy, and yet with bars on all the tail feathers, while at other times, quite brown birds that show still, here and there, faint traces of rufous margins to the back plumage, will be found to have lost most of the tail bars.

In almost every case, the chin and throat are *white* and free from longitudinal *striæ*, but have a conspicuous dark central stripe. I had, however, an adult female with plenty of these striæ, and in old males, the central stripe often grows very faint, and has entirely disappeared in one specimen in my museum. The length of wing, tarsus and mid toe, varies a good deal, as will have been seen; the thickness of the tarsus even, is not invariable, and the more I study this group, the more doubtful do I feel of the value of most of the characters relied on as specific, and on the strength of which species are at times instituted from a single specimen.

Even the colour of the iris is not invariable. Usually the irides of the adults are bright yellow, but both Mr. Brookes (who first pointed this out to me) and myself, have repeatedly shot specimens, in which the iris was the brightest ruby red, much the same colour as that of *Elanus Melanopterus* usually is. Bree, by the way, figures the iris of this latter as bright yellow, and having shot numbers, and always found the iris bright red, I conceived this to be a simple mistake; but Mr. Brookes assures me, that he has met with specimens, in which the irides really were yellow, though this, in India at least, is most exceptional.

I carefully compared a young bird, in Col. Tytler's museum, sent by Layard from the Cape, ticketed: "*A. Tachiro*, young male; Damara Land," with a series of young male *Badius*, and I was utterly unable to see how they could be separated; compared with some specimens, the tarsus was a trifle slenderer and the wings longer, but with others again, the bird was absolutely identical. Perhaps the difference is clearer in the adult or possibly (a good number of the birds sent by him are clearly wrongly named) Layard may have sent one of his old Indian birds by mistake, but if no error has been committed, the resemblance between the young of these two species, is most remarkable; so far as plumage and such dimensions as can be ascertained in the dry skin go, they seem positively identical.

Accurate and detailed measurements and descriptions taken from the flesh are often useful for comparison, and I therefore subjoin such, of a nearly fully adult male, killed on the 10th of March.

Dimensions. Length, 12·13. Expanse, 23. Weight, 4·75 oz. Wing, 6·88; the 4th primary the longest; 1st, 2·38; 2nd, 0·88; 3rd, 0·07; 5th, 0·13 shorter. Tail, from vent, 5·88; exterior tail feathers, 0·5 shorter than central ones. Tarsus, 1·88; feathered in front for 0·56. Foot, greatest length, 2·63; greatest width, 2·13; mid toe, 1·06; its claw, 0·47; hind toe, 0·59; its claw, 0·56. Bill, straight, 0·72; along curve, 0·81; from gape, 0·78; width at gape, 0·63; height at front at margin of cere, 0·31; length of cere, 0·25. Wings when closed reach to within 3 inches of end of tail. Lower tail coverts, 2·88 of ditto.

Description. Legs and feet, rather dingy greenish yellow, scutellation on front of tarsus and toes transverse, rather feeble; on sides and back of tarsus, obscure. Toes slender, 2nd joint-pad of mid and outer toes, well developed. Claws, slender, sharp-pointed, pretty well curved, black; inner edge of mid toe, claw scarcely perceptibly dilated.

Irides, yellow. Bill, blackish horny; blue at gape, base of lower, and sides of upper, mandible.

Tongue small, somewhat fleshy bluish and like lower mandible, dusky at tip; obtuse ended, with a conspicuous depression down the centre.

Plumage. The lores, cheeks, chin and throat, slightly greyish white. The ear coverts having the faintest possible shade of fulvous, and the chin and throat having just the trace of a central dark line.

The whole top and back of the head, a pale rather brownish slaty, paler just at the forehead and immediately above the eyes. Sides of the neck, behind the ear coverts, pale fulvous, or faintly reddish brown, nearly meeting on the nape; the whole of the base of the neck in front, and at sides, the breast, sides, and upper abdomen, white, with numerous, close, regular, narrow, transverse bars of the same pale faintly reddish brown, closer on the upper breast, and wider apart, and slightly feebler lower down. The base of the neck behind, shoulders, scapulars, back, rump, tail feathers, and their coverts, and whole upper surface of the wings, generally slaty. The first five primaries being dusky at the tips, and all the primaries, winglet, and anterior portion of wing, being a shade darker. In the basal portion of the scapulars probably more than half the feathers are white, though this, owing to the over-lapping of the feathers is little seen; about half the interior webs of all the quills (except the first four primaries in which the white only begins above the notches) white, all, with several incomplete moderately broad transverse dark bars in the inner webs, which are faintly visible even on the dusky tips of the early primaries. The central tail feathers have darker patches on their shafts, corresponding with the transyerse bars on the lateral feathers, but no bars, narrow white tips, or subterminal dark bands. The lateral tail feathers all with narrow white tips and an oblique patch of white on the inner webs on the basal halves, and the rest of the inner webs rather lighter than the outer. All the lateral feathers but the outermost with a pretty broad subterminal dark band, and four somewhat narrower similar dark transverse bands, traceable on both webs but *much* more conspicuous on the inner. The exterior tail feathers are browner and less slaty than the rest of the tail, have no subterminal band, and seven or eight narrow, brownish, transverse bands on the inner web only. The lower part of abdomen, vent, thigh coverts, flanks, and lower tail coverts, pure white. The lower surface of the tail, greyish white, the broad blackish bars of the four lateral feathers on each side showing through conspicuously, and the narrow bars of the outermost pair being faintly visible. The lesser and median lower wing coverts are very pale fulvous, or creamy white, with a tinge of fawn. The larger lower coverts, are nearly pure white with a few imperfect faint, narrow, grey bars. The under surface of the quills is nearly pure white, greyish at the tips of all but the earlier primaries, which are dusky, and all with the incomplete bars on the inner webs, showing through; strongly on the earlier primaries, and very feebly on the later secondaries.

NOTE.—There is another nearly allied species, *Micronisus Brevipes*, in regard to which the following remarks appeared in the Ibis for 1865 :—

"Dr. Kruper has made another valuable discovery also relating to a rare and hitherto somewhat obscure European bird of prey. In the 'Bulletin' of the Moscow Society of Naturalists for 1850 (ii pp. 234-239) M. N. Severzow described, under the name of *Astus Brevipes*, a new species of Sparrow Hawk of which he had obtained three examples from the Government of Voroney in Southern Russia; and Herr Seidensacher has communicated to the Vienna Transactions (the paper being reprinted in the Journal für Ornithologie, p. 464) the intelligence that in May 1864, Dr. Kruper found a nest with four eggs of this little-known bird near Smyrna. Dr. Sclater kindly informs us that, when he was at Vienna last autumn, he became aware that *Astur Brevipes* was no other than the *Accipiter Gurneyi*, founded on examples received from Beyrout (Ibis, 1859, p. 390) and described and well-figured by Dr. Bree (B. Eur. IV. p. 158) of which mention has before been made in this Journal (Ibis, 1863, p. 463) and Mr. Gurney has written to us to corroborate this identification. But what is still more interesting, Mr. Gurney finds that the 'specimens obtained in Galilee by Mr. Tristram, and supposed by him (P. Z. S. 1864, p. 429) to be the *A. Sphenurus* of Ruppell, also belong to this species. This discovery was made just in time to insert the right specific name in the paper on the Ornithology of Palestine' printed in our present number (*supra* p. 260) though not soon enough to admit of Mr. Tristram's there giving an explanation of the facts of the case. The species, however, as we are informed by Mr. Gurney, should be referred to the genus *Micronisus*, and accordingly will take its place as *Micronisus Brevipes* (Severzow). All we at present know of its history, may be condensed into these few words, that it occurs in Southern Russia from April to August, and probably breeds there, as it certainly does in Asia Minor, and that it has been met with once in Greece and several times in Syria. Herr Seidensacher considers *Micronisus Brevipes* to be identical with the Indian *M. Badius*, and it is probably the species referred to under this last name in Professor Blasius's List of the birds of Europe, p. 4; but Mr. Gurney is very confident that the two birds, though nearly allied, are quite distinct."

Mr. Bree's dimensions and descriptions are as follows:—

	Length.	Carpus to tip of wing.	Tarsus.	Tail.	Middle Toe.
"1. Asia, male adult, Lauretta, Beyrout,	14·2	8·5	1·8	0·7	1·4
2.* Syria, female adult, Verreaux,	14·5	9·6	0·2	0·7	1·4
3. Young female, Lauretta, Beyrout,	15·5	0·9	1·7	0·7	1·4
4. Young male, Lauretta, Beyrout,	13·3	8·3	1·8	6·5	1·2

"Description. The adult male has the upper plumage dark slaty brown, with some white spots on the nape and upper tail coverts. Primaries nearly black, and barred with lighter black on the basal half beneath. Below, the general tint is rufous, lighter on the croup; the chin and sides of the head are slaty, light slate colour; the rest of the body, thighs and under wing coverts barred with ferruginous and silvery gray; under tail coverts white. Tail above, dark slaty brown, below lighter; the two central feathers, both above and below, being rare colorous; the others silvery gray, broadly barred through the feathers with black. Beak, black; tarsi and toes yellow; claws black.

"The female has the upper plumage lighter than that of the male, and the upper tail feathers have traces of black bands, while all the under ones are barred through. Primaries nearly black, barred on their inner webs with white, the whole length of the feather, chin and sides of the head grey with light brown bars and spots. The rest of the body, under wing coverts and thighs barred with hair brown and silvery grey; under tail coverts white, slightly barred with brown. Beak black; tarsi and toes yellow.

"Young birds of the year have the head prettily striped longitudinally with rich brown of two shades and white. The upper plumage rich dark brown; the edges of the primaries, wing and upper tail coverts bordered with fawn colour. The chin is white with a few longitudinal dark streaks; the crops and chest broadly marked with brown and white longitudinal

* This female, it will be observed, is shorter than the male, though otherwise larger. This depends entirely upon the mode in which the skin has been prepared.

spots, which assume a crescentic shape and lighter colour on the abdomen, thighs, and under tail coverts; under wing coverts above fawn colour, below cream colour, barred with grey and brown on all the feathers, less distinct on the two above and below; beak horn colour; tarsi and feet yellow."

Mr. Bree further adds: "In addition to the measurements, the male adult Levant Sparrow Hawk differs from that of *A. Nisus*. 1*st*. In the darker upper plumage. 2*nd*. In the closer barring of the under plumage. 3*rd*. In the under wing coverts being lighter rufous, and less barred, and by the deep black uncolorous primaries beneath, those of *A. Nisus* being barred to the end. 4*th*. By the two first under tail feathers being uncolorous grey, while those of *Nisus* are strongly barred. 5*th*. By the primaries being black brown and uncolorous above, while those of *Nisus* are lighter and distinctly barred, and 6*th*. The cheeks of the Levant Sparrow Hawk are slight grey, while those of *Nisus* are rufous."

No. 24. **Accipiter Nisus**, Lin.

The Sparrow Hawk.

A Sparrow Hawk, but whether the present or the next species, I am unable to decide, breeds commonly enough in woody valleys in the interior of the Himalayas. I have repeatedly seen their nests and once (in May) took one about two marches on the Mussourie side of Gungootree, containing four bluish white, red blotched eggs exactly like, it seemed to me, the Sparrow Hawk's eggs I had so often taken as a boy at home. Unfortunately I was then a mere sportsman, and troubled myself little about anything but game, and therefore neither shot the parent nor preserved the eggs.

Capt. Thompson of Simla, (not Mr. R. Thompson of Gurhwal) assures me, that two pairs of the true Sparrow Hawk, breed yearly in Anandale, just below Simla, laying in May and June.

Of the breeding of this species in England Mr. Yarrell tells us that "the Sparrow Hawk generally takes possession of some old or deserted nest in a tree, most frequently that of the Crow, in which the female deposits four or five eggs, each about one inch seven lines long, by one inch four lines broad, of a pale bluish white, blotched and spotted with dark red brown. The young are covered with a delicate and pure white down, and are abundantly supplied with food."

Mr. Hewitson tells us that the eggs of this species may sometimes be found upon the ledge of some lofty cliff, but are more frequently to be met with in trees, for the most part occupying the usurped nest of a Crow or Magpie. Occasionally it would seem to make its own nest in low trees or thorn bushes, a flat shallow structure, composed of slender twigs similar to that of the Ring Dove, but larger. "The eggs of the Sparrow Hawk, although usually very readily distinguished from those of any other species, are subject to varieties, which sometimes rather resemble those of the Kestrel, but are never marked with the same rich crimson colouring. There are some specimens on which all the markings are very obscure and indistinct; and others on which all the dark blotches of colour are at the smaller instead of the larger end. I know of no egg which is so subject to this variety. Mr. Walter's collection contains one that is white, except a few black dots; another that is pointed at the small end like the egg of a Wader." The eggs he figures are *very* broad ovals, measuring 1·5 × 1·3, and 1·52 × 1·26, a whitish ground, profusely blotched and spotted, with different shades, of brownish red and reddish brown, very similar to well marked eggs of our common Kite (*M. Govinda*).

Compare in regard to the breeding of this species, what Gould tells us of *Accipiter Torquatus* a nearly allied Australian form. "The breeding season lasts from August to November, and the nest, which is rather a large structure, composed of sticks and lined with fibrous roots and a few leaves of the gum tree, is usually placed in the fork of a Swamp Oak *(Casuarina)* or other trees growing on the banks of creeks and rivers, but is occasionally to be met with in the depths of the forests. The eggs are generally three in number, of a bluish white, in some instances stained and smeared over with blotches of buff; in others, I have observed square-formed spots and a few hair-like streaks of deep brown; their medium length is one inch and six lines by one inch and two lines in breadth."

As regards the Sparrow Hawk commonly flown by native falconers, (whether the present or the next species I cannot say) Mr. R. Thompson writes as follows:

"Though a highly prized bird by the natives for its speed and courage, it does not really come up to the Besra, (*Accipiter Virgatus*) even for courage; its powers of endurance are much less and it is less easily reclaimed. Many birds appear regularly at Nynee Tal every year about October. I have had several specimens alive, sent in to me from the interior where they have been caught in traps set for the Goshawk, having readily flown at the live Pigeon bait. It is a delicate and difficult bird to keep. And with all its boasted speed, is but second to the Besra for every kind of hard field or wood work. What the Besra would do at the first throw, the other could not do till the quarry was exhausted. To hunt with the *Basha*, requires a deal of tact, you must not throw it whilst the wind is high, you must keep well within the proximity of woods and trees, and not baulk it with birds larger than it can afford to strike and clutch."

One thing is to be said, native falconers generally over-do the training of this bird, and make it too delicate—probably if more hardily reared and trained, it would do better, and turn out as tough and useful in its way as its larger relative, the Goshawk. Descriptions of the European Sparrow Hawk vary a good deal. It is very essential to have as minute a record as possible of the plumage &c., of these various *Accipiters* and I shall quote one or two descriptions of this present species from English works, the more so that this will help to show the distinctness of the species I shall next have to deal with.

Mr. Yarrell says, "The adult male measures about twelve inches in length; the beak blue, lightest at the base; the cere greenish yellow, the irides yellow; the top of the head, nape of the neck, back, wings, and wing coverts, rich dark brown, in very old males with a tinge of bluish grey; feathers of the tail greyish brown, with three conspicuous transverse bands of dark brown; the chin, cheeks, throat, breast, belly, thighs, and under tail coverts, rufous with numerous transverse bars of darker rufous brown, legs and toes, long, slender, and yellow; the claws curved, sharp and black.

"The female is generally three inches longer than the male; the beak, bluish horn colour; cere yellowish, the irides yellow; the top of the head, upper part of the neck, back, wing, and tail coverts, brown, the base of many of the feathers white, which extending beyond the edge of the feather immediately above it, causes a white spot or mark; primaries and tail feathers light brown, barred transversely with darker brown; under surface of the neck, body, wing coverts, and thighs, greyish white, barred transversely with brown; under surface of the wing and tail feathers of the same colour, but the light and dark bars much broader; the first six wing primaries emarginated; the fourth and fifth quill feathers equal, and the longest, the first quill feather the shortest; the legs and toes yellow; the claws long, curved, sharp, and black.

"The young male Sparrow Hawk resembles the female; but the brown feathers of the back and the wing coverts are edged with reddish brown; feathers of the tail reddish brown, particularly toward the base, with three conspicuous dark brown transverse bands. In other particulars like the female, and both have a collar formed by a mixture of white and brown, which extends from the sides of the neck to the nape."

From the Naturalist's Library, I quote the following—

"The male has the upper plumage of an uniform pale blackish grey; tip of the tail and nuchal collar white; quills clove brown, darkest at the tips, with clouded bars on their inner webs. Tail with a dark bar after the white tip, shading upwards, and three bars afterwards indistinct above, decidedly marked beneath. Auriculars, buff orange, darker along the shafts. Throat and chin pale ochraceous, with dark shafts; breast, belly, vent, and thighs, ochraceous; shafts dark, and thickly marked with reddish buff orange; in the centre of the belly tinted with brown, under tail coverts white. Length above twelve inches; from shoulders to tip of fifth quill, eight and a quarter.

"The female, with the upper parts clove brown, darkest on the crown, and sometimes tinted with rufous; on the tips of the auriculars, above the eyes, and on the hind head, the tips of the feathers only are dark, and the light bases appearing, produce a pale line above the eyes, and a variegation with white on the hind head; the quills and tail are barred with narrow darker bands, conspicuous on the under surface of both. The underparts are of a delicate yellowish white, on the throat and neck streaked with clove brown, sometimes tinted with rufous, and on the other parts, except the lower tail coverts, barred with the same colour, which also runs to a point on the apical bands, and sometimes along the shafts; at times these bars are much darker than at others, and shew beautifully and distinctly on the pure white breast; feet and legs gamboge yellow; irides rich safron yellow. Length from 14 to 15 inches; one shot this morning (in November, 1836) 14 inches 3 quarters; expanse of wing 24 or 25 inches. In a young female before us, the upper parts are nearly yellowish brown, tinted with grey, and have the edge of each feather ochraceous; on the head and back of the neck darker, and edged with rufous. The lower parts yellowish white, on the breast, a yellowish brown streak along the shaft of the feather, which, on the lower part of the breast, or on the belly, stretched out at the base to a bar, and produced an appearance at once both barred and streaked. On the thighs and vent, the distribution is in bars of a brownish tint. In the young Goshawk, the breast marking is all longitudinal bars, here it assumes somewhat that of the adult bird, in both the colouring of the markings in the young is brown, the adults a rich black."

No. 24 (*bis*). Accipiter Melaschistos, Sp. Nov.

The Dove Hawk.

Under the above name, I venture to draw attention to what I believe to be a perfectly distinct species, although hitherto confounded with the true *Nisus*.

The chief distinctive features are, its greater size, and the much greater intensity of the colour of the upper plumage, especially in the female.

When at Simla I examined the numerous specimens of *A. Nisus* from France and England in Col. Tytler's museum; of these, the wings and tails measured as follows:

Females. Wings 9·25—9·62. Tails 7·75 to 7·88.
Males. " 8·13—8·38. " 6·55 to 6·88.

And these measurements are much the same as those given by European authors.

Of all these birds, none of the females are ashy above, several are apparently quite adult, but all are *brown* above; a drab brown, rufous drab brown, clove brown, or what you will, dusky at times on the head, but still brown, and this seems to be insisted on by all the English describers whom I have quoted. Now the females of my new (?) species, have in the first place the wings 10·12, 10·25, 10·5, and the tails 8·25, 8·4, 8·5. They are very much darker than any of the European specimens, and of a wholly different shade; it can hardly be called brown at all, a sort of blackish slaty, or in some, inky olivaceous, especially on the head and nape (it is paler elsewhere) which reminds one of the same parts of *F. Perigrinator* or *Atriceps*. The bill appears far more powerful, the tooth or festoon larger and more conspicuous, the bars of wing and tail broader and stronger, the bars on the lower surface broader and more decided, being as broad as the white interspaces. I am aware that these characters are not absolute, that in this genus, all these points vary widely, in individuals of the same species, but taken altogether, these differences give the bird a distinctive character.

Bree's figure of the male *A. Brevipes* (A. Gurneyi, Bree. Vol. IV. p. 185) would do well enough for our females, but the difference of size is irreconcileable; he gives the following dimensions for that species.

	Length.	Wing.	Tarsus.	Tail.
Adult male,	14·2	8·5	1·8	7·0
Young male,	13·3	8·3	1·8	6·5
Adult female,	14·5	9·3	2·0	7·0
Young female,	15·5	9·0	1·7	7·0

The same dimensions for two of our birds are:

	Length.	Wing.	Tarsus.	Tail.
Young male,	15·75	9·75	2·25	8·5
Adult female,	16·5	10·5	2·35	8·7

The primaries of our bird moreover are strongly marked instead of being unicolorous, as he says. As for there being no marks on the outer laterals, which if I understand him rightly, he rather insists on, this I take it, is pretty often in this family dependent on age, the marks are very faint in one European *Nisus* before me, they wholly disappear in the old *Badius*, and are disappearing in one *Melaschistos*. Setting the minor points aside, the left hand drawing in his plate (the male) though scarcely *dark enough*, especially about the upper parts, and the description so far as colour goes, would answer well enough for our female, though the bill, as figured, is neither long enough, nor powerful enough, nor the tooth strong enough.

I think it will be admitted that this species is distinct from *Nisus*. Unfortunately I have not long enough discriminated this species to have a good series. The only specimens I know, are a pair (female adult, male in second plumage) sent by me to my friend Mons. Jules Verreaux at Paris, a young male and second plumage female, now in my museum, and two old birds both probably females in Col. Tytler's.

I proceed to give a description of these latter, sex *not* ascertained, but from the length of the wings, 10·25 and 10·5, probably females.

The head, nape, and upper back, *deep* blackish, olivaceous brown, with even a tinge of slaty on the head and nape, where there are traces of a white patch owing to the bases of the feathers showing through. The scapulars, slightly less deep, blackish brown. Lower back, rump, and upper tail coverts, somewhat slaty brown. Upper wing coverts, and quills hair brown. The secondaries, and some of the primaries, with traces of darker bars on the outer webs. Tail, greyish brown, or brownish slaty with five broad transverse dark brown bars; the upper bar hidden by the upper tail coverts. The subterminal bar broadest; a narrow white tipping, most conspicuous on the centre feathers. The lores white, a trace of a whitish streak behind the eye, cheeks rufous white, the feathers with dark brown linear central stripes. The ear coverts rufous, with dark central stripes and the longer feathers tipped blackish brown. A black line immediately under the eye running over the ear coverts and lost in the dark tips of these. Chin, and throat, rufous white, most rufous towards the sides of the neck, and each feather with a dark shaft, or narrow dark central stripe. The whole of the breast, abdomen, sides, thigh coverts, axillaries, and lining of the wing, white; conspicuously, closely and broadly barred with dark brown; many of the feathers with a rufous tinge towards the tips, and some of them especially in the flanks, with rufous more or less taking the place of the brown bar. The lower tail coverts nearest the vent, narrowly barred with paler brown; the longer tail coverts pure white. A conspicuous patch of rusty or pale chestnut on the sides. Inner webs of the primaries strongly barred white, or greyish white, and dark brown; the bars perpendicular or nearly so to the shaft, and not slanting as in the European specimens of *Nisus* that I have examined; the whole barring of the under surface is much closer and more conspicuous than in any of the nine specimens of *Nisus* from Europe, with which I have compared it, the bars being in one quite as broad, and in the other, *nearly* as broad as the white interspaces. The feet are larger; the hind toe and claw, and inner toe and claw, conspicuously so. The wings appear to be more pointed and much larger than in any of the apparently adult European specimens (females) from France, and from England with which I compared them. Of the second plumage male, which I sent to Mons. Verreaux I have no detailed notes, but the whole upper plumage, had a dark olivaceous tint, unlike anything I have ever seen in *Nisus*.

The female in second plumage, a small bird comparatively, measured. Length, 16·5. Wing, 10·12. Tail, 8·6. Expanse, 0·31. Tarsus, 2·5. Mid toe to root of claw, 1·8. The upper parts are grey brown, darker and more slaty about the head, nape and upper back, whitish about the forehead, over the eye, and with a mottled white patch (owing to the white bases of the feathers showing through) on the nape. The scapulars, lesser wing coverts, upper tail coverts and most of the feathers of the back, with darker shafts, and the longest upper tail coverts tipped white and with a dark subterminal band. Tail, a sort of dove colour slightly paler on the lateral feathers, tipped white and with five broad transverse dark brown bands (one hidden by the upper tail coverts) on both webs of all the feathers, except in the outer web, of *one* of the exterior laterals, from which the bars have nearly disappeared. The chin, throat, and sides of neck yellowish white, tinged rufous towards the sides, all the feathers dark shafted. Lores and ear coverts whitish, the latter dark shafted, tinged rufous towards the tips, and the hindermost ones tipped blackish brown. A blackish brown line through the lores, (where it is very narrow,) running under the eyes, (where it is about 0·15 wide,) and joining into the dark tips of the hinder ear coverts. The whole breast, abdomen and lower parts generally, fulvous white, regularly barred transversely with mingled dark brown and rufous, the bars on the breast being as broad as the interspaces and diminishing in width as they recede from the breast, till those on the tibial plumes, are only half as wide, and those on the lower tail coverts only average one-fourth as wide as the interspaces. There is a regularity, straightness, and closeness in the barrings of the lower parts, unlike any of the European *Nisus*, that I have been able to compare them with and unlike the figures in Yarrell and in the Naturalist's library.

The sides are much tinged with rufous, which there nearly wholly displaces the brown.

Then there is the young male in first plumage (sex ascertained by dissection) shot by my friend, Capt. Marshall, R. E., at Solon on 30th September, and measured by him in the flesh.

Dimensions. Length, 15·75. Expanse, 29·75. Wing, 9·75. Tarsus, 2·25. Mid toe to root of claw, 1·75. Foot, greatest length, 3·25; width, 2·8. Tail from vent, 8·5. Closed wings fall 3·8 short of end of tail.

Description. Irides, bright yellow. Legs and feet, dingy yellow. Upper plumage, umber brown, edged rufous and centered darker (almost black) on head and nape. Upper tail coverts (a trifle paler than the back,) dark shafted. Tail a drab brown narrowly white tipped, with five moderately broad, dark brown transverse bars, on both webs of all the feathers, except the outer webs of the external laterals, where they are indistinct, though *not* altogether *wanting*, one of the five bars being high up and hidden by the upper tail coverts. Forehead whitish, a conspicuous yellowish white band, feathers brown shafted, running backwards from top of the eye, over ear coverts, fully 1 inch long. Lores dingy white, a trace of a dark line through them to the eye-line under the eye, and terminal halves of ear coverts, reddish or umber brown, rest of ear coverts, whole chin, throat and sides of neck, pale fulvous, with conspicuous, very narrow, central stripes to feathers. Breast and upper abdomen pale buffy with numerous conspicuous narrow transverse arrow-head bars, the central portion of the bar bright rufous, the lateral portions dark brown; these bars are much the *shape* that seagulls are often represented in pictures, the head and body portion of the bar (if I may so express myself,) being rufous and the wings dark brown. The sides are very rufous. The lower abdomen and tibial plumes are buffy white with still narrower transverse arrow head brown bars. The lower tail coverts, yellowish white, each faintly tipped rufous. This is a veritable young bird, the rufous edgings to the whole upper plumage shows this, but how different it is to a young of the veritable *Nisus* sent me from Kumaon by my friend, Mr. R. Thompson. In this, the central tail feathers have four, the external laterals six instead of five throughout, as in this. The chin, throat, and breast are white with huge, central, longitudinal, umber brown streaks, the abdomen and tibial plumes have very *broad*, transverse, rufous brown bars, and the lower tail coverts, truly cordate brown spots. The wing measures 7·6; the tail, 6·4; the tarsus, 2·2; the mid toe without the claw, 1·45.

I cannot doubt the distinctness of the species, and though I am fully conscious that more specimens are required to enable us to characterize it as it should be done, I think the best way to ensure the matters being cleared up, is to insert this notice, imperfect as it is. I call this the Dove Hawk, because both specimens that I shot, had killed Doves (*T. Rupicola*); the one struck a Dove before my eyes, at the back of Jacko (Simla) and fell to my shot at the same moment, the other was perched on a bare branch, between Simla and Kalka, devouring a Dove, when I killed it. This may be accidental but I mention it, because I doubt whether the true *Nisus* (especially the male as one of mine was) would strike so large a bird.

The only specimens that I know of were shot, more or less in the interior of the Himalayas. I know nothing as yet of its nidification or breeding habits.

No. 25. **Accipiter Virgatus**, Tem.

The Besra.

Of the nidification of this species nothing seems known, Mr. R. Thompson is confident that they breed from March to May, in the Gurhwal forests, he says,—"I have never found the nest of this bird though it breeds in our forests. I have seen, caught, and shot the young birds during the rainy season: conclusive evidence, I should think, of their breeding with us." Dr. Jerdon's descriptions do not fully apply to many specimens I possess, all of which I believe to belong to this species.

First, there is a young female. Length, 13·5. Wing, 8·1. Tail, 6·5. Tarsus, 0·2. Mid toe to root of claw, 1·4. Circumference of middle of tarsus, 0·5, (the same as in others of this species), *Nisus* and *Melaschistos* have it from 0·6 to 0·75. The head, nape, mantle and upper tail coverts are umber brown, very dark on nape and upper back, all the feathers narrowly margined rufous. The tail rather pale brown, narrowly tipped with fulvous white, with six moderately broad transverse dark brown bars, on both webs of the ten central tail feathers, and seven on the interior webs only, of the external laterals one bar in each case hidden under the upper tail coverts. Behind the eye a broad white streak, the feathers centered dark brown, the whole of the chin, throat, cheeks, and ear coverts (except the tips of the hindermost of the latter which are rufous brown) white, *each* feather with a very narrow central stripe of dark brown, growing slightly broader as the feathers approach the breast. Breast, upper abdomen and sides, white; all the feathers with transverse, somewhat arrow head bars, rufous in the centre and brown laterally. Lower abdomen and tibial plumes, with narrower, cuspidate, transverse brown bars, and lower tail coverts with similar bars, but fainter, smaller and wider apart. This bird is very like *Nisus*, but the dimensions, size of bill, very slender tarsus and toes, prevent our referring it to that species. It was a female, ascertained by dissection, killed at Lahore. It cannot be *Nisoides*, for the throat is conspicuously streaked like *Nisus*, and has no central stripe. I believe it to be *Virgatus*. If it be not identical (which *I* feel sure it is) it might stand as *A. Micronisus*. I have another young female, from Gurhwal, the skin measures—Wing, 8·05. Tail, 6·42. Tarsus, 2·05. Mid toe to root of claw, 1·5. Circumference of tarsus, 0·5. This bird is a rather darker brown above, the bars below are rather broader and more rufous, and the ten central tail feathers have only five and the external lateral six bars, (one of each as in the former case hidden under the upper tail coverts) but in every other respect, this bird precisely resembles the preceding.

Then I have a very young male from Darjeeling. Length, 11·5. Wing, 6·35. Tail, 5·5. Tarsus, 1·9. Mid toe, 1·35. Circumference of tarsus, 0·42. This above is like the preceding but more rufous, and the ten centre feathers have only four, and the external laterals six bars, extending to both webs on all the feathers, the bars being broader than in the preceding. Below the chin, throat, ear coverts, breast, abdomen and tibial plumes, are white, here and there slightly tinged fulvous, each feather with a broad central stripe of dark, more or less rufous brown, smaller actually of course on the throat where the feathers are smaller, and larger on the breast, &c., where these are larger, but relatively much the same size. On the lower abdomen and tibial plumes, however, they become very drop-like. The lower tail coverts white, some faintly tinged fulvous towards the tips.

Another male, certainly not adult, but yet not very young from Murree, measured—Length 11·25. Expanse, 0·20. Wing, 6·5. Tail, 5·25. Tarsus, 1·9. Mid toe, 1·3. Circumference of tarsus, 0·5. Wings, when closed, reached to within 1·75 of end of tail. It has the head, nape, back, mantle and upper tail coverts dusky cyaneous, darkest on the head—the kind of colour you may make by mixing indigo and Indian ink—a narrow barely perceptible white streak behind the eye, and the usual white mottling on the nape. Tail slaty grey, brownish on external laterals, with seven narrow transverse bars on the inner webs of these latter, and four broad, blackish bars on both webs of the other ten feathers, ear coverts and sides of the neck, dusky, the former with traces of rufous striæ, the latter tinged cyaneous, chin and throat white, tinged fulvous towards the sides, with no striæ, but one central well-defined, blackish stripe. The breast quite deep ferruginous at the sides, the central portion, having the feathers a mixture of blackish, deep ferruginous and white, the blackish portion, a stripe more or less wide, lying on the shaft the ferruginous surrounding this and extending quite to the point, and the lateral margins being white, sides, flanks, and upper abdomen ferruginous imperfectly barred with white, the white not quite meeting at the shaft. The lower abdomen white, barred with paler ferruginous and near the vent, with slightly rufous grey. Tibial plumes, white, very closely barred with grey, slightly suffused with rusty. Lower tail coverts pure white.

The streakless white, central striped throat reminds one of "*Gularis*," but this is unmistakably of the same species as the preceding (though differing *toto cœlo* in plumage) and as the adult female from Simla, which I will next describe.

This measures in the dry skin—Wing, 8·1. Tail, 0·7. Tarsus, 2·05. Mid toe, 1·45. Circumference of tarsus, 0·5. The upper plumage closely resembles the preceding, but is somewhat paler and more slaty. The tail is slightly browner and is narrowly but conspicuously white tipped, with four bars on both webs of the ten central, and five on the inner webs of the two external feathers; the bars faint, and but little darker than the rest of the feather, on both webs of the central and the outer webs of the next three laterals on either side. The chin and throat are streakless white, slightly tinged with rufous, and no trace of any central stripe. The ear coverts, sides of neck, breast, abdomen and sides, bright ferruginous, the breast chiefly the centre, very narrowly and sparsely, and the abdomen and sides, regularly, closely and moderately, broadly barred with white. The vent and lower tail coverts pure white. The tibial plumes barred rufous white, and pale ferruginous.

There is yet another type of female, query, the oldest of all, I have no specimen by me; but quote my notes made when I had one. "Female. Umballa. Wing, 8·5. Tail, 6·5. Whole upper plumage a delicate, uniform, rather dark, french grey, white half collar (mottled) on nape. No trace of bars, except a dusky subterminal spot, on central, or outer webs of lateral tail feathers. Chin and throat white, no trace of striæ or central stripe. Sides of head and ear coverts tinged ferruginous, breast, abdomen and flanks, feathers tipped and barred, rather widely apart with pale rufous." I have been thus minute in these descriptions, in order to show how many usually deemed diagnostic points. Number, size and position of tail bands, character of throat markings and indeed of the plumage generally vary in different individuals of this species.

In all humility, I often wonder how many of the *Accipiters* of the Malay Archipelago, and is not their name legion? would lose their present supposed specific character if really large series, such as I am endeavouring to collect of all Indian birds, were available.

The shape of the tail is insisted on! Here before me lie a long row of *A. Virgatus;* some with slightly rounded, some with absolutely square, some with slightly forked tails.

In the face of the doubts I entertain, as to how far many of these small *Accipiters* have been rightly identified, I can say little, about the real distribution of *A. Virgatus*, but I may mention that Mr. Wallace gives it from Malacca, Timor, Java, and Sumatra. Noting, that the bill is black, lead colour at base, iris and cere yellow. Feet pale orange yellow. Birds killed by Mr. C. H. T. Marshall at Lahore and by myself in Kumaon, had the irides deep orange yellow.

There is a nearly allied species, *A. Gularis*, Schlegel, *A. Nisoides*, Blyth, that has of late years been the bugbear of all Indian ornithologists. I don't believe that any specimen has been procured in India (if even the species is a good one, and even that may admit of doubts) but every one is always writing that they have got it, and being told by others to whom they send the specimens, that their birds are *Virgatus* or *Nisus*. Dr. Jerdon first noticed a little Hawk known to native falconers as the Khandesra, and surmised that it was probably Blyth's *A. Nisoides*. Now we have all heard of the Khandesra, or as I believe it is more correctly called, the Khand Besra, but no one can ever get it, it is a perfect Mrs. Harris amongst birds, and I myself greatly incline to Betsy Prig's belief that "there never was no sich" bird "at all."—To return, Mr. Blyth commenting on Dr. Jerdon's work remarked, that the Khandesra Hawk was "probably *A. Nisoides*, nobis (J. A. S. B. 1845, XVI. p. 727, XXI. p. 359; ex Sumatra. *A. Fringillarius*, var. Vigors, appendix to memoir of Sir T. S. Raffles, p. 549 and *A. Gularis*, Schlegel, Faun. Japon, Aves. 1850, t. 2.) Professor Schlegel mentions a specimen of *N. Gularis* from Nepal. Dr. Jerdon writes that *A. Nisoides* is not rare in the interior of the Himalaya; but two examples received from him possibly intended for this (though I can hardly comprehend his making such a mistake) are decidedly *A. Virgatus*. In the report on Japanese ornithology accompanying the narrative of Commodore Perry's expedition, it is stated of *A. Gularis*, that the young bird is darker above than represented in the figure of the adult male, in the plate in '*Fauna Japonica*' and has the transverse bars on the under parts, much less regular and lighter coloured than in the figure of the female in the same plate."

Dr. Jerdon had clearly got hold of *A. Virgatus*. I much suspect the expedition had got hold of another form of this protean species, similar to the nearly adult male that I have above described.

My friend, Mr. R. Thompson, sent me an interesting note about this supposed species, which I reproduce as showing that possibly, the same birds in different stages of plumage and at different ages may affect different localities, and even appear to fly more or less briskly.

"I have observed what I believe to be another species or variety of the *Accipiter Virgatus*. I have had the dark plumaged one and trained it: but the light plumaged one is a larger bird with the tarsi less smooth, more robust, and toes shorter than the true Besra. I have got some specimens and would like you to look them up. I believe it is the Khandbesra mentioned in Jerdon, page 54, Vol. I. I have met the dark plumaged ones, male and female, usually on the skirts of dense forests, and observed their flight which is more feeble, with a broader and more ample expanse of wing, than the lighter coloured variety, which is met with in lofty dense forests and has a flight similar to the Shikra. That is, with sudden and rapid stoops, with an active manner of sitting suddenly in a tree when you expected the bird to shoot past it. Its motions in the tree are restless, jerking from branch to branch. Sometimes I have found them very timid, at others quite bold, and will let you approach within a few paces."

The Khand Besras, duly arrived.—They turned out to be female *Virgatus*, one in the stage I first described and the other similar, but the whole plumage, very much paler, faded and abraded, with the throat rusty white without a central stripe, and only a very few of the feathers with dark shafts, the barring of the under parts, feebler, wider apart, much less regular, paler and yellower, often incomplete, and in the breast, especially at the tips, having a cordate tendency.

No one who knows Mr. Thompson, will doubt that he has accurately described a real difference in the haunts and habits of the birds in their two stages, measurements show that structural differences do not exist; but no one I think, after looking through the series now before me, can doubt that these are true *Virgatus*.

Mr. Blyth in commenting upon Dr. Jerdon, added in a note, "My original description of *A. Nisoides* may here be quoted. 'Presumed female in mature plumage, differing only from that of *Nisus* in its much inferior size, being smaller than the male of that species, and in having the throat streak-less white, except a narrow median dark line. The usual lateral lines occur, but not conspicuously, which are observable in various species of Hawks, Eagles, &c. Length of wing, 7·25. Tail, 5·5. Tarsus, 1·75. Mid toe and claw, 1·5.' "

Now I note here that in the specimens that I have of *Virgatus*, the wing varies from 6·35 to 8·1. The tail from 5·5 to 6·7; the tarsus from 1·85 to 2·1, and the mid toe and claw from 1·6 to 1·85. There is nothing here very irreconcilable. Mr. Blyth goes on: "I have seen three nearly similar specimens of this Sparrow Hawk, all received from Malacca, and it is much more closely akin to *Nisus* than *Virgatus*. No trace of ferruginous colouring underneath was observable in any of the three. They were of the size of the male of *A. Nisus* or somewhat smaller with the plumage of the non-rufous adult female of that species, combined with the trilineated throat of *Virgatus*; the affinity I repeat being much closer to the former species than to the latter." Now the whole of this is *verbatim* applicable to a female before me, closely resembling the first described by me, having lost the rufous edgings to the feathers, *except* that it has not the *central* stripe, but *each* feather of the whole throat has a dark shaft, or *very* narrow dark shaft stripe. As for the "trilineated throat" of *Virgatus*, the adults have not a trace of it, and out of nineteen specimens of all ages, only three show it distinctly.

Dr. Stoliczka next thought that *he* had obtained a specimen of *A. Gularis*, which he described at length. I shall not quote his description, for it refers very obviously to a *young* male *Nisus, pur et simple.* It appears to be the dimensions which misled him; these he gives, as wing, 8. Tail, 5·75. Tarsus, 2·13. Mid toe, 1·63; and he adds that these dimensions are evidently intermediate between those of *Nisus* and *Nisoides.* This however is a mistake. The wings of a number of male *Nisus*, European specimens, varied from 8·13 to 8·38. An Indian specimen has the wing, 7·6, and he himself sent home a specimen (according to Von. Pelzeln. Ibis, 1868) with the wing 7·25. The tails of the European birds varied from 6·55 to 6·88, that of the Indian bird is 6·4; the tarsus of this latter is 2·2, and its mid toe to root of claw, 1·45; so that his dimensions, though small, are not sufficiently so to induce doubts of the specimen being a *Nisus*, while the plumage he has so accurately described, is unmistakably that of a young, but not *very* young, bird of that species. Von Pelzeln came to the same conclusion; he says "One individual, evidently a male, is ticketed *Accipiter Nisoides*, Blyth (*A. Gularis*, Schlegel;) but in my opinion all the examples belong to the true *A. Nisus.*"

In the same paper in the Asiatic Society's Journal, in which he described the young *Nisus*, he added the following valuable remarks about the type specimens of *A. Nisoides.*

"On comparing Mr. Blyth's originals in the Indian Museum, I found that one of the three originals is lost, the other two very much resemble in the upper dark brown colouring our specimen, and one of them has some of the tips of the scapulars and tertiaries distinctly tipped with rufous brown. The cross bars below are, however, ochreous yellow, only *with a slight ferruginous tint on the sides of the breast*, but not nearly to the extent described in our specimen. This cannot be, however, of very great importance, for the same colour is very variable in *A. Nisus. The throat is white, and so far as the feathers are preserved, they present a few dark streaks about the middle*, though on this point neither of the specimens is quite perfect, and it is only to be regretted that such valuable originals were not better cared for. The measurements given by Mr. Blyth are, wing 7¼ inches; tail 5⅓ inches. The two respective specimens in the Indian Museum have the wings 7½ and 7¾; and the tail 5⅓ and 5⅝ inches. Mr. Blyth supposed the specimens to be females, but they could with as much reason be regarded as males. Still it cannot be questioned that the typical specimens referred to, are remarkably small as compared with usual specimens of *A. Nisus.* I found this difference especially apparent after having a short time previously procured in the lower hills several specimens of the last species. The claws appear remarkably strong, compared with the size of the bird, and the general deep brown colour is always very conspicuous, when compared with the ashy hue of *A. Nisus;* still I think it wants further proof, until the species is firmly established.

Mr. Blyth in his commentary (Ibis, 1866, p. 239) says, "Dr. Jerdon writes word, that *A. Nisoides* is not rare in the interior of the Himalaya," and it is not unlikely that Dr. Jerdon observed it in the same portion of the hills, where my specimen was procured, for he visited the Sutlej valley in 1864. The species cannot be easily mistaken for *A. Virgatus*, which is comparatively very common and much larger."

The passages italicized, seem to me to point to these specimens being *Virgatus* after all, and in regard to Dr. Stoliczka's concluding sentence, I can only say that I have above given *maxima* and *minima* dimensions, derived from a large series, and that these sufficiently prove that *Virgatus* is not only, not much larger, but often not *at all* larger.

I hope having said this much, that our numerous observers will thoroughly work the question out. *N. Gularis*, Schlegel, Japan, may be a good species, but Schlegel's Nipal specimen renders this *dubious*. In the distinctness of *A. Virgatus* and *A. Nisoides*, Blyth, I confess that I have at present no great belief.

No. 26. **Aquila Chrysætus,** Lin.

The Golden Eagle.

As to the breeding of this noble bird within our limits, I have no information. During all the many trips that I have myself made in the interior of the Himalayas, and in all the collections of Himalayan birds that I have examined, I have never seen a specimen. Every so called Golden Eagle, which has as yet been sent me, has proved to be *A. Imperialis*, in the dark third stage of plumage. Capt. Cock and others feel sure that they have seen it, but none of them seem as yet to have bagged one. Mr. Hodgson, I am told, sent specimens from Nepal; but I have been unable to learn whether they were shot there or brought in from Thibet.

As far as I yet know, this bird is of such excessive rarity in the Himalayas, south of the snows, as scarcely to deserve a place in our list. Mr. R. Thompson says—"I have seen a large Eagle very similar in size to the adult *A. Chrysætus*, but of a dark brown colour with two large moon-shaped whitish spots on each wing, near the base of the primaries; also with the tail white, ringed with a band of dark brown. These I think must be the young of *A. Chrysætus.* They were observed close under the snow line." A supposed *A. Chrysætus*, however, sent me by Mr. Thompson proved to be a huge female *Imperialis.*

Dr. Stoliczka tells us that this species "is often seen about Kotegurh and further east," but although I have at Kotegurh a regular establishment for shooting and preserving birds,—from whom I have received more than one thousand specimens,—who have special injunctions to shoot all large Eagles and who have sent me several *A. Imperialis*, I have as yet received no example of this species; and that although I have tried to stimulate my men by promises of large rewards should they secure a specimen, they say that there is no species, but the one sent, *A. Imperialis.*

Of the breeding of the Golden Eagle in Europe, Mr. Yarrell says, "The Golden Eagle makes a flattened platform nest, or rather, a collection of strong sticks, on high and inaccessible rocks, occupying a space of several square feet. The female bird which is considerably larger than the male, lays two and sometimes three eggs, towards the end of the month of March or the beginning of April. If the eggs are removed, it is said that the bird does not lay any more that season. The egg is about three inches long, by two inches and five lines broad, of a dirty white colour, slightly mottled nearly all over with pale reddish brown. Incubation with the Golden Eagle, according to Mr. Mudie, lasts thirty days, and the young Eaglets are at first covered with greyish white down."

Mr. Hewitson, quoting chiefly from Mr. Wolley, tells us, that the Golden Eagle begins to breed in March or early in April, and will return to the same eyrie for many successive years. It makes a nest of great size composed of sticks, (or in Shetland, where it would be difficult to find sticks, of long rope-like pieces of seaweed) lined with roots, dry grass, heather, moss, fern or other *vegetable*, not animal, materials. The nests, though usually on rocky ledges of precipices, are by no means always in inaccessible places, but may often be climbed to, from above or below without ropes and with little difficulty. The usual number of eggs is two, but three are sometimes found in the same nest; they are laid at intervals of several days. The hen sits very close after she begins to lay, so that the first egg is ready to hatch before the second.

The eggs are broad, very perfect ovals; slightly compressed towards one end; they vary very much in colour, some being as above described by Mr. Yarrell; some having reddish white grounds, richly blotched and spotted, or thickly mottled, streaked, and clouded with varying shades of red, and reddish brown; a few are pure white, (then hardly distinguishable from the sea

Eagle's); one egg is described as mottled closely throughout with ochreous brown, but the ordinary type Mr. Hewitson seems to consider to be a closely mottled, dingy reddish ground with more or less deep red, specks, spots, and small blotches. Three eggs figured by this gentleman, measure according to his figures (usually very exact) 3 × 2·35, 3·13 × 2·3, 2·95 × 2·35.

To Dr. Jerdon's range of this species, we must add N. W. Africa. Col. Drummond Hay, I think, mentioned it as being found in Tangiers, and Mr. Tyrwhitt in the Ibis for 1867 remarks, that "it breeds at Tetuan, though not in great numbers." Mr. Tristram found it throughout the Barbary provinces, chiefly in the various *dayats*, or unimproveable oases, where it was breeding *on Terebinth trees* (*Pistacia Atlantica*,) making a huge platform of sticks on the topmost boughs. In one *dayat* in particular, that of Terebinet, a day's journey north of Berragan in the Nizab, the birds were almost gregarious, no less than seven pairs having their nests in one wood, described as "extending over many *acres*."

I append measurements and a description of a magnificent young female, shot in the south of France, and now in Col. Tytler's collection, in what is known in England as the ring-tail stage of plumage.

Dimensions. Length, 41. (?) Wing, 27·63. Tail, 16·25. Tarsus, 4·38. Mid toe (to root of claw), 0.3. Inner toe, 1·94. Hind toe, 1·81. The two latter, with the tarsus, enormously stout.

	Mid toe claw.	Outer toe claw.	Inner toe claw.	Hind toe claw.
Length along curve,	1·81	1·31	2·44	2·75
Circumference at base,	1·13	0·88	1·5	1·53

Bill along curve, from edge of cere, 2; from gape, 2·75. Height at edge of cere, 1. Width at gape, 1·94 (?) Length of cere, 0·91.

Description. The bird is rich purplish brown, the feathers of the occiput and nape, narrowly pointed and tipped with rufous fawn. Scapulars and secondaries much darker, the coverts lighter, primaries almost black. Basal half of the tail pure white, (hence the English name of ring-tail) then a broad, irregular, mottled grey band and the rest nearly black. All but the first three primaries have much white at the base. Underneath, the same purple brown, much variegated, especially on the breast, and lower tail coverts with white, all the feathers being pure white at the base.

The enormous strength of the tarsi, feet, and claws, distinguish it at once from the finest *Imperialis*, but the bill is not, it seems to me, proportionally stronger.

No. 27. **Aquila Imperialis,** Bechst.

The Imperial Eagle.

The majority of the Imperial Eagles, that visit Upper India in such great numbers during the cold season, leave us early in March. A very few remain to breed in the Upper Punjaub, and possibly in the Dhoon; the rest breed in the Himalayas, and not improbably, some of them even further north and west.

As yet, I have no particulars of their nidification in the hills, I have myself only found them breeding in the Upper Punjaub, and there only on three occasions. They lay (in the plains) in February and March, and possibly April; building a large stick platform, on, or near the tops of trees; Peepul trees, in all the instances in which I found the nests; but also at times, like the Tawny Eagle, on Babool and other thorny trees. The nests that I saw, were from 2 feet to 2·5, in diameter, some 6 to 8 inches thick, composed of rather small sticks and lined with a few green leaves. One nest contained two hard set, another three fresh eggs, and the third only one, but from accounts received from Mr. W. Blewitt and others, two appears the normal number.

Mr. Blewitt took a nest of this species near Hansie, in the Dhana Beer (a sort of preserved wilderness) on the 22nd February, 1868. The female, shot on the nest, was sent to me, an old, unmistakeable, black *Imperialis,* with conspicuous white scapular patches, and yellowish head and nape. Mr. Blewitt describes the nest as very dense and compact, 7 inches thick, by 18 only, in diameter; composed entirely of Keekur (*Acacia Arabica*) twigs and without *lining.* The nest was placed like that of *A. Fulvescens,* on the top of a Keekur tree; some 18 feet from the ground and contained two fresh eggs.

The eggs of this eagle vary much, in size, and shape. I have one nearly as large as any one of the Golden Eagle's, figured by Hewitson, but most of them, are little, if anything, above the size of an average *Fulvescens.*

They have the usual pale, greyish white ground, unspotted in most; faintly spotted, and streaked with very pale brown, in others; and in one, richly blotched with purplish brown. They seem normally of a somewhat broad oval, but one or two are a good deal lengthened; and one which is considerably larger than the figure in Bree, which I took early in February; (a solitary egg in a huge nest) is absolutely pyriform. Placing together specimens of *Imperialis, Nævia, Fulvescens, Bonelli, Gallicus,* and *Leucoryphus,* I am unable, so far as texture goes, to point out any certain difference. There is scarcely any gloss on any of the eggs of these various species, but on a few of the *Fulvescens*, there is a slight trace of this.

In size, the eggs vary from 3, to 2·6 in length; and from 2·15 to 1·95, in breadth, but the average of nine eggs measured, was 2·7 × 2·09.

The figure of this bird's egg, in Bree, measures 2·88 × 2·05. The egg is represented as white, clouded with pale dingy yellow, over the greater portion of the surface.

Of its breeding elsewhere, Mr. Tristram gives us several notices. In Northern Africa he remarks—"This rare and magnificent bird appears to prefer the forests to the cliffs, for the purpose of nidification. It occurs very sparingly in Algeria, but is well known to the Arabs, as distinct from the Golden Eagle. The eggs, seem scarcely ever to have any but the faintest clouding, or a few obsolete spots."

Again, in his notes on the Holy Land, he tells us: "This truly imperial bird, is more abundant in Palestine, than in any country which I have visited. It may be said (in summer at least) in great measure, to replace the Golden Eagle of Europe. There is a beauty, and majesty in its movements, and in its greater fearlessness of man, when in search of food, which at once attracts one; while the very distinct white scapulars, and the light head, show conspicuously on the wing. Unlike the Golden Eagle, it was as common at one time of the year as another, though we never took a nest."

To Mr. W. H. Simpson, we owe the following account (vide Ibis, 1860) of the nidification of this species on the banks of the Danube—

"Late in the afternoon of the 26th of April last, having driven across the treeless plain of the Dobrudska, I descended from the open plateau, which, in the part now alluded to, has a breadth of about forty miles, upon one of the small valleys communicating with the Danube. Our attention was immediately drawn to a large nest, that completely filled the boll of one of the aforesaid pollards. It was not very conspicuously apparent, as the branches, now thickening and becoming greener every day, formed a sort of leafy screen round the nest, which would have been well concealed a fortnight later. The nest was of a good size, its exterior circumference being, at a guess, 15 feet; the interior was slightly depressed, but only enough to keep the eggs (two in number) from rolling out. It was lined with wool, which rested upon an immense circular platform of sticks, entirely filling up the boll of the pollard, from which, the young willow branches sprang upwards in a circle, all round the nest. By this means the entire structure was enclosed in a sort of arbour, which would screen the birds from the wind and sun, and from general observation. The eggs, which were slightly incubated, resemble each other considerably; measuring about 2·9 in. by 2·3 in. and being of a uniform dull white colour, with frequent marks and scratches, and occasionally larger blotches of pale brownish grey."

An extra tropical species, this bird occurs throughout the old world, north of the tropic of Cancer, (Swinhoe obtained it at Takow, Formosa,* and I have seen a specimen said to have been killed near Muscat, and have one from near Kurrachee); northward it extends as far as 42° north latitude towards the west of the continent, and probably as far as 50° north longitude on the east; Radde at any rate, got it in Tarei-nos. According to Radde, I note, this species (if I understand him correctly) occupies a broad zone; reaching to, and even passing southwards of the 10° north latitude; but though stragglers may occur further south, especially where mountain chains, or high tablelands run southwards, out-liers in tropical regions of cooler climes, the Imperial Eagle, is I think, essentially a bird of the temperate zone, and the Tropic of Cancer may be most properly assumed as its southern boundary.

North of this, throughout Northern Africa right up to the shores (if I may so speak) of the great Sahara, throughout the whole of Southern Europe, Syria, Persia, Northern Arabia, the basins of the Black and Caspian Seas, the Caucasus, the southern ranges of the Oural, and Altai Mountains, Tartary, China, the Himalayas, the highlands of Central, and the plains of Upper India, (and *nowhere* more common than in these latter), this species is found, and though not entirely migratory, always most numerous southwards, in the winter, and least so in the summer.

Much has been written about the daring and fierceness of this species: I can only say that, in India, (where possibly the climate is subversive of courage), I have never seen the slightest indications of these qualities, I have driven the female off hard set eggs, and plundered the nest before the eyes of the pair,

* Vide Ibis, 1867.

"The other day, half-way up Apis Hill, on a white patch caused by a heavy landslip, I observed what I took to be a black tree stump; but a shining white spot on it excited my wonderment. As we ascended the mass of coralliferous debris, the stump-like object took wing, and slowly flapped away amid the hoots and grunts of several monkeys that were sporting on the hill side. I then saw that it was an adult Imperial Eagle (*Aquila heliaca*,) the white spot being one of the conspicuous shoulder patches this bird carries in the mature plumage."

without either flapping a pinion, even to defend, what even a little shrike will swoop at once to save. I have seen a couple of Crows, thrash one of them soundly; and, whether it be that familiarity breeds contempt, I am bound to record, that after having seen many hundreds and shot, I dare say, a good hundred myself (I killed seven one *morning* in the Etawah district) I look upon the "Königs adler" as no better than a great hulking Kite. As a rule, this species is, with us, an ignoble feeder. I have generally found them gorged with carrion; after a good meal they will sit stupidly on a tree, or any little mud pillar, and permit you to walk within thirty yards of them; but before feeding, they are somewhat wary, and can by no means always be secured, even when seen sitting. On more than one occasion, I have found desert Rats (*Gerbillus Erythrourus*) in their crops, and I once shot one of a pair, which were busy on the line of Rail, at Etawah, devouring a Bandicoot Rat, (*Mus Bandicota*,) which some passing train had cut in two. Occasionally, but rarely, I found that they had eaten Quails, and other birds! Once I shot a male, which was dancing about on the ground in such an astounding fashion, that I killed it to see what the matter was. The bird proved to have been choking, it had swallowed a whole, *dry*, shin bone and foot of an Antelope; the bone apparently could not be got down altogether, and in trying to void it, the sharp points of the hoof, had stuck into the back of the roof of the mouth.

I noticed above that this species only breed in the *Plains of India*, in the far North West; but I once had reason to think that occasional stragglers, may nest lower down country, even in the plains. On the 5th of February, 1867, my head stuffer at Etawah returned with a male Imperial Eagle, and an egg, (white, a rather dull coarse texture, with barely perceptible, faint, yellowish, streaks and spots, and a few tiny darker specks) measuring 2·63 × 2·06, which he professed to have obtained as follows. He saw a female *Imperialis*, sitting on a nest on a large Peepul tree, as he approached, she flew off, he fired at her, but failed to bring her down. He then hid at the foot of the tree and waited. After some time, the male returned, and finding the nest empty, settled on it, when he shot him. The nest, which I afterwards examined, was some two feet in diameter, lined with leaves, and the feathers of wild Geese, and Ducks; my reasons for somewhat doubting this account are; 1st, My stuffer's general want of veracity; 2nd, Our never having met with any other examples of this species, breeding so low down; 3rd, My finding, when I visited the nest fifteen days later, a Snake Eagle (*Circatus Gallicus*) sitting near it. At the same time it must be noted, that I was then particularly anxious to find a Snake Eagle's nest, none of which I had then taken, and that it is very improbable that had my stuffer found a nest of *that* bird, he would *knowingly* have represented it as belonging to any other; *he might* make a *mistake*, but, born and bred a fowler, he *very* rarely blundered, though he often lied. On the whole, the balance of probabilities were in favour of the authenticity of the egg, which, however, in common with all other suspected specimens, I long ago threw away.

In the High Table Land of Southern India, and the Nielgherries, this Eagle doubtless breeds, Jerdon mentions having seen a nest in a lofty tree in the Dekhan; but of its nidification there, I have received no detailed account.

These Eagles, like *Fulvescens*, can run very well; I have particularly noted this on many occasions. In one place I say, "This was a winged bird, and several times ran from twenty to thirty yards with very great rapidity and cleverness, and but for the fact of its having dropped in a newly ploughed* field, and there having been rain during the night, would have given a great chase; as it was, the soft clods tripped it up every twenty or thirty yards, giving it heavy falls."

Captain Hutton sends me the following note on this species:

"This is a common bird about Mussooree, and in the Dhoon, from October to near the rainy season. The young (*A. bifasciata ?*) is by far the handsomer bird of the two, and likewise hereabouts the most common; in October we have sometimes seen as many as fifty together, sailing leisurely in a widespread flock, if such it can be called, and coming from the west, leaving individuals at intervals along the line of march. These appear to be all in the plumage of *A. bifasciata*, and judging from the few adults procurable here, they may almost be called rare. If a carcase be exposed as a bait, it will not lie long without a visit from five or six of them (*A. bifasciata*); and strychnine, rubbed into gashes in the thighs of the bait, is sure to secure some of them. I do not think they breed here."

The changes of plumage in this species are so great, and hitherto appear to have been so imperfectly described, that it is necessary to particularize them, in some detail. When I say that the changes of plumage are very great, it is under the assumption that all the different forms observed are really stages of one and the same species; but of this there is, as yet, *apparently* no entirely conclusive proof.

* These, with us in India, are not like ploughed fields at home. Here ridge and furrow *together* barely exceed 5 inches, as a rule.

Very few of this species remain in the plains of India during the summer, and these few only in the extreme North West.

The specimens usually seen in museums, and all those contained in my own collection, (with the exception of two old birds killed from the nest) have been obtained in November, December, January, or February; hence the connecting links between the various stages, the changes from one to the other of which, probably take place during the summer, are altogether wanting.

There are four very distinct stages of plumage, each of which is represented in my collection by from ten to twelve specimens, and of each stage there are specimens, killed, from early in November, to the beginning of March, and that, without the latest killed specimens of any stage, exhibiting any marked approach to the plumage of any other stage. In fact, during these winter months, the plumage of each stage appears to remain nearly stationary. There are variations in each, but these cannot in any way be chronologically connected; for instance, one bird of a particular stage will be observed in some respect to approximate to the plumage of some other stage; while other birds belonging to the first mentioned stage, killed both earlier and later than the individual specimen referred to, less nearly approximate to the said other stage.

One thing is certain, namely, that if all these four forms are really, as seems probable, stages of one and the same species, they each represent a year, in the bird's growth; but till specimens are obtained, killed during the summer months, or until young ones are brought up in captivity, and the changes of their plumage carefully noted, I do not see how these matters can be definitely settled.

From certain indications, observable in some of my birds, I think I know which are the third and fourth stages; but in regard to the other two, I am somewhat doubtful which is the earlier.

I will briefly describe them in the order in which I believe they should be placed.

1st. The general character of this stage is *lineated.* The under parts, with broader, or narrower pale centres to the feathers, and the upper parts, with pale central stripes. What I take to be the earliest form of this stage has the head and nape, brown; the feathers tipped, and margined, with pale yellowish brown. The upper back scapulars, and lesser wing coverts, darker brown, most of them showing faint traces of paler centres, and tips; and some faintly margined slightly paler.

The lower back is buffy, a patch on the rump being mottled

with brown. The upper tail coverts, fulvous white. The tail feathers, pale wood brown, much abraded, with dirty fulvous tips, and showing, towards the bases, traces of a mottled paler, and darker barring. The primary quills are dark brown, almost black. The secondaries and tertiaries paler, and dingier brown, with a mere trace of a fulvous white tipping, but the tertiaries are a good deal mottled with fulvous white. The median, and greater wing coverts are, here and there, tipped with fulvous white, but many are not so. The chin, throat, sides of the neck, breast, and abdomen, are pale buffy brown. The feathers margined with darker brown, which latter, however, is very narrow, and almost wanting on most of the throat feathers, while it occupies the greater portion of the feathers on the lower breast, and abdomen. The tibial plumes, vent, and lower tail coverts are dingy reddish buff; the lesser and median lower wing coverts, are reddish buff, more or less centred with brown, and the greater lower wing coverts, are mingled white and blackish brown. The lineation of the lower surface, is more obscure and ill-defined than in what I take to be later forms of this same stage. In the next form of this stage, every feather of the head, nape, and upper back, is brown; (a sort of hair brown,) darker than in the form above described, with a conspicuous narrow, fulvous, central stripe. All the wing coverts, and scapulars, are tipped with fulvous, or fulvous white, the lesser ones, narrowly, in fact with a mere spot at the tip; the larger ones, more broadly. The rump, back, and upper tail coverts, are as above described; but the tail is a dingy, wood brown, without any trace of bars, and broadly tipped with fulvous white.

The secondaries are conspicuously tipped with white, or fulvous white. The chin, throat, and ear coverts are unstreaked fulvous; the breast, and upper two thirds of the abdomen, are a warm, somewhat purplish brown, with conspicuous, well defined, narrow, central, fulvous stripes. The lesser, and median lower wing coverts, are more mingled with brown, than in the specimen above described, and the larger lower coverts are greyish white, mottled with blackish brown, and the axillaries, which in the form first described, were reddish buff, mottled with brown, are in this one, similar to the feathers of the breast. In another form of this stage, the head, and back resemble the form first described; the tail, and wings, the second; while the chin, throat and ear coverts are very pale buff, and the breast, and abdomon, are of the same colour; each feather narrowly margined with the warm purplish brown;—noticed as the prevailing colour of these feathers, in the second form.

I believe, that the last described bird is the nearest approach I possess to the second stage, and that the change to it, would be accomplished by the central stripes disappearing from the upper surface; and in the lower surface, gradually extending over the whole feather.

Specimens in this stage vary greatly, independent of the points noted above; in the colour of the thighs, vent, and lower tail coverts, (which in some are nearly white, in others rufous buff,) and in the extent and purity of the white, or fulvous white tipping, to the tail and secondaries. The difficulty is, that these various differences do not go together. If the birds be arranged in a series, with reference to the comparative width of the central stripes of the breast feathers, which width varies, as above noticed, from less than one-fifth to nearly four-fifths of the total width of the feathers; and then turned back upwards, no corresponding progression in the lineation of the upper surface is observable, and in order to obtain a regular series, according to the amount and extent of the lineations of the upper feathers, a totally different arrangement will be necessary. Adopting either of these arrangements, we shall still have no regular progression in the extent, or purity of the white tipping of the tail, or secondaries; or in the colour of the lower abdomen, vent, and leg feathers.

Two birds, whose heads, necks, and upper backs correspond, differ entirely where the lower plumage, or perhaps tail feathers are concerned, and *vice versâ*. It is clear therefore, that whatever be the general sequence of changes, some birds change first below, others above; some earlier on the heads, and others on the tails; thus rendering the determination of the comparative priority of the various forms, doubly difficult.

2nd. The leading character of this second stage, is to have two conspicuous white, or fulvous white, wing bands; one of these at any rate, exists, more or less perceptibly in the first stage, the pale tippings of the tertiaries, and secondaries being generally present, and in some specimens there being traces of the second band, formed by pale tips to the greater wing coverts; but in the first stage, these bands (even where both exist, which they rarely do,) are very inconspicuous. In the second stage, they are strongly marked, and are the first features that attract attention. In this second stage, the whole of the head, neck, chin, throat, back, lesser scapulars, lesser wing coverts, breast, abdomen, sides, leg feathers, axillaries, wing lining, except the greater lower wing coverts, are a nearly uniform brown. The upper tail coverts are clear, slightly yellowish white, the tail dark brown, more or less conspicuously tipped with fulvous white, and with, or without, narrow, transverse, irregular, grey bands. The quills, and greater wing coverts, are dark brown; the latter with the secondaries and tertiaries, broadly tipped with fulvous white; the greater lower wing coverts are pure white, or white mingled with brown, slightly darker than the rest of the wing lining.

The specimens in this stage, vary greatly in the prevailing shade of brown, some are very pale, almost whity brown; others moderately pale hair brown; some are entirely destitute of bars on the tail; others, exhibit them conspicuously; and in the specimens before me, the very lightest bird, and one of the darkest, have no bars whatsoever on the tail. The lower tail coverts, in almost all the specimens, are white, or slightly fulvous white; but in one specimen, they are mottled with the same brown as the rest of the lower parts.

In some, the pale tippings to the tail feathers, are obsolete, in others, conspicuous. The lesser, and median lower wing coverts, in one or two specimens, are narrowly tipped with white; generally, they are of the same uniform brown, as the breast, abdomen, etc. In both these forms, the lower surface of the primaries, are but faintly mottled with greyish white.

One specimen alone seems changing to the third form; in this the wing bands have nearly disappeared, the tail feathers show the irregular, narrow bars, more strongly than in any of the others; the whole of the brown is darker, the pale tipping of the tail, is almost obsolete; many of the median lower wing coverts, are rufous buff, and the longer scapulars, and a few of the feathers of the back are a deep chocolate brown.

The 3rd stage is characteristically of a dark hair, or even at times, umber brown, darkest above, and chocolate brown, on the scapulars, with no pale bands on the wings, or tips to the tail feathers, and with numerous, narrow, transverse, irregular, grey bars on the latter; and with much brown, mingled with the lower tail coverts.

Some specimens shew traces of the wing bars, characteristic of the preceding stage, but more of them shew a few reddish buff feathers on the nape, and pale margins to the lesser wing coverts, obviously incipient changes towards the perfect adult.

A good many, which I suppose to be those nearest to the second form, besides showing traces of the wing bars, have all the feathers of the lower abdomen, narrowly tipped with dingy fulvous white.

Those again which appear to lead to the perfect stage, have the upper tail coverts dark brown, only slightly tipped with white.

That this is really the 3rd stage, there can be little doubt; but even here the changes are most confusing, because, one bird for instance, having a most conspicuous orange buff patch on the nape, has the whole of the upper tail coverts, a clear fulvous white, as in the second stage; while another, though of a deeper brown, shews no trace of buff upon the nape, and has the upper tail coverts, uniform blackish brown, as in the adult.

The wing lining, also varies very much in this stage. In some, and these by no means the most advanced, it is altogether deep brown, as in the perfect adult, while in others, by no means the least advanced, it is a rufous buff, or a rufous buff mingled with dark brown. In one, and that a bird shewing the incipient orange buff head, they are precisely as in the second stage, the lesser and median lower wing coverts being uniform pale hair brown, and the larger lower wing coverts white.

The 4th stage is well known. The whole head, nape, cheeks, ear coverts, and sides of the neck, buff or orange buff, the back, scapulars, (except a few which are pure white) upper tail coverts, wing coverts, primaries and secondaries, chin, throat, breast, abdomen, leg feathers, sides, axillaries, and wing lining, deep blackish brown. The lesser wing coverts margined, and and the upper tail coverts tipped, with fulvous white. The lower tail coverts, white, and a good deal of white mottling about the tertiaries, which are a pale brown. The tail, gray; with a very broad terminal black band, occupying fully two-fifths of its visible surface, and above this, a number of more or less broad, irregular mottled, and imperfect transverse dark, brown bands, which sometimes do, and sometimes do not, coincide exactly at the shaft.

This is what I take to be the perfect adult. In less advanced examples of this stage, the forehead, and more or less of the crown are blackish brown. The feathers of the chin, and throat, as well as the upper breast, are margined, more or less broadly with the same orange buff as the head and nape.

The axillaries, and lower wing coverts, are more or less mottled with rufous, the lower tail coverts with rufous brown; and the ground colour of the tail, above the black tip, is pale yellowish stone colour rather than grey. The upper tail coverts likewise are paler brown, and more broadly tipped with fulvous white. In this stage too, the changes are not synchronous; birds most advanced about the head, being often least so about the tails; those most advanced on the upper, least so on the under surface, and *vice versâ*.

The amount of white on the scapulars too, varies greatly. Some have only a single feather, others nearly the whole scapulars white, and I have some specimens, perfect adults, as regards the plumage on every other point, but exhibiting no trace whatsoever of white on the scapulars.

Although individuals of each stage differ, as above indicated, very greatly *inter se*, still the examples of each stage, taken as a body, are sharply separated from those of every other stage; and connecting links, between the four stages, are greatly needed. At present, we have four types; 1st, the striped; 2nd, the uniform pale brown, with double wing bands; 3rd, the uniform dark brown, without wing bands; 4th, the blackish brown with orange buff head, and nape; but no really intermediate forms, such as are absolutely necessary, to enable us to compile a correct history of the various changes of plumage.

In Europe, the changes of plumage seem even less known than here. In the Ibis for October, 1868, the Rev. Mr. Smith, in his note on the birds of Portugal remarks:

"I entertain considerable doubts whether the only specimen of this bird in the Museum of Lisbon is a genuine Imperial Eagle, inasmuch as there is not a single trace of white on the scapulary feathers; and though Professor du Bocage, whose attention I called to the fact, accounted for it, by declaring the bird in question to be immature, I cannot find that this distinctive characteristic of the species is ever wholly absent, though doubtless it is more conspicuous in adult birds."

To this latter sentence, the editor appends the remarks, "It has usually been supposed that the contrary was the case!" Now my review of the bird's various stages of plumage, shows pretty clearly; 1st, that at any rate until its fourth year, this species never shows *any* white on the scapulars, and 2nd, that it is the fully adult, and these only, that exhibit this specific character. To assist comparison, I subjoin further on, detailed measurements and descriptions, taken from fresh birds, in different stages of plumage. I shall be anxious to learn, whether European Museums contain specimens of the European Imperial Eagle, in all the four above described stages. Here and there a bird in each stage, seems to present some connecting link, with some other stage; but these links, except between the 3rd and 4th stages, are very weak, and my only good reason for believing that all four belong to one and the same species, is, that after examining nearly a hundred freshly killed specimens in one stage or another, I have been unable to detect any structural difference; the dimensions vary, in the same sex, very widely; but the differences are as great between examples of the same stage, as between those of different stages. The bills are longer, broader, or higher, nostrils larger, or rounder, feet more powerful, claws more curved, or the reverse; but of each such variation, as many examples are found in the specimens of any one stage, as of any other; and hence my difficulty in believing that these are not all one and the same species. I may add, that in each stage I have males and females in precisely similar plumage, and that I am unable to discover any constant difference, except that of size, between the sexes.

Radde, in Vol. II. of his travels in South East Siberia, (page 81,) seems to have got hold of very erroneous notions about this species. He says "According to S'ewerzoff's investigations, the white scapulars ought to appear after the first moult, in the females of this species, while in the males, these are not assumed until after the second moult;" and then he goes on to say, referring to an Orenburgh specimen, (which he takes to be in first plumage, changing to second; but which I gather to be really third changing to fourth) exhibiting one white scapular feather, that this decidedly confirms S'ewerzoff's views and contradicts Nauman Junior's statements; who holds that the adult plumage is usually not assumed till the fourth moult in the bird's sixth year.

I had never seen Radde's work, when I wrote the above descriptions of the four stages; but it will be seen, that according to my own original observations, Nauman Junior is right, and Radde and his friend S'ewerzoff altogether wrong, *so far as our Indian race* is concerned. But here the question arises, is the Indian bird really identical with that of the South of Europe, North Africa, Palestine, and the Caucasus?

In the case of *A. Nævioides*, and *A. Fulvescens* one distinguishing feature is said to be, that the changes of plumage are much greater and more numerous in the latter, than in the former; can any similar difference exist between the European and Asiatic race of the "Königadler," as Radde designates it? Radde and Eversmann I see, (as I have myself noticed) correctly point out, that the number of the transverse *scutæ* on the ends of the toes is variable, and affords no real specific character.

Radde further infers that while *A. Chrysætus* avoids the treeless steppes, preferring the wooded country, *A. Imperialis* is of extreme rarity in the forest-clad hills, which the former affects. It is doubtful whether this distinction *generally* holds good.

The following are the results of a large number of measurements recorded from freshly killed specimens :—

	Male.		Female.	
	From	To	From	To
Length, ...	28·5	30·5	30·0	32·63
Expanse, ...	69·0	76·0	70·0	85·0
Wing, ...	20·75	23·0	23·0	24·5
Tail, ...	10·5	12·5	12·0	14·0
Tarsus, ...	3·38	4·0	3·75	4·06
Foot, greatest length, ...	5·25	6·0	6·0	6·63
" " width, ...	4·25	5·0	5·0	5·75
Mid toe, ...	2·37	2·63	2·6	2·88
Its claw, along curve, ...	1·25	1·31	1·63	1·75
Hind toe, ...	1·0	1·13	1·06	1·31
Its claw, along curve, ...	1·63	1·75	1·88	2·13
Bill, including cere, straight, from forehead to point, ...	2·03	2·13	2·19	2·38
Bill, including cere along curve from forehead to point, ...	2·5	2·75	2·81	3·0
Bill, from gape, ...	2·13	2·63	2·75	3·13
Width, at gape, ...	2·0	2·25	2·19	2·44
Height of bill at margin of cere, ...	0·81	0·97	0·94	1·0
Length of cere on culmen, ...	0·63	0·81	0·75	0·88
Distance by which other primaries fall short of 4th or 5th whichever is longest, ...	1st 4·0	4·75	5·0	5·7
	2nd 1·5	2·0	1·5	2·0
	3rd 0·25	0·5	0·44	0·75
Distance by which closed wings fall short of end of tail, ...	0·2	2·25	0·2	2·75
Distance by which lower tail coverts, do., ...	4·0	5·0	5·0	6·0
Weight (in lbs.)	4·0	5·5	6·25	8·75

I now proceed to give full descriptions of the bird in various stages.

1st. What I take to be the earliest form of the *First, or lineated stage.*

Male. Shot, January 7th.

Description. Legs and feet, pale slightly greenish yellow,* four transverse *scutæ* (the 4th in one or two, partially divided) at the ends of all the toes, but the exterior, where there are only three; claws black.

Irides pale yellow, here and there, with a tinge of brownish; bare shelf above eye, pale greenish grey; margins of lids very pale yellowish, lids greyish white.

* Dr. Bree lays stress upon the number of transverse *scutæ* on the ends of the toes; it will be seen from this and subsequent descriptions that this is variable in the extreme, even in the two feet of the same bird, and can therefore, in *no way* be relied upon, as a specific character.

Cere and gape, pale greenish, yellower on culmen: upper mandible at margin of cere, and basal half of lower mandible, very pale blue; tips of mandibles, bluish horny black.

Tongue, rather thick and fleshy; entire, oval at tip, of nearly uniform width, which is very small as compared with that of the gape.

Plumage. Lores, whitish, densely clothed with tiny white feathers, having greatly elongated, naked, black, or dark brown, bristle-like shafts. A trace of a dark brown stripe, over the eye, continued backwards over the ear coverts. Forehead, top and back of the head, and nape, the feathers white at the base, umber brown in the middle, and pale fulvous brown at the tips; the white bases do not show through, and immediately over the eye streak, the feathers so overlap, as to show little, but the pale fulvous brown; all the feathers of the head are very narrow; and sharp pointed, and more and more elongated as they approach the nape. The ear coverts, and cheeks, fulvous brown. The chin, and throat, and upper part of the neck in front, pale fulvous brown, with here and there faint traces of a darker edging. The feathers of the back, sides of the neck, lower neck in front, breast, and upper abdomen, fulvous brown, pale brown, or in some feathers, almost white, broadly and conspicuously edged with dark umber brown. All these, except those of the abdomen, very pointed, and narrow; feathers of the upper back, of a similar character, a lighter central streak, and a dark margin; but the shade of both centre and margin darker than in the case of the feathers previously mentioned. The lower back, rump, and upper tail coverts, palish umber brown, of various shades, each feather very broadly tipped with fulvous white, pure white, or pale rufous, the shade varying in different feathers. The scapulars, and lesser, and median wing coverts, a mixture of several shades of brown, some of the longest exterior scapulars almost black, but the general character of most of the feathers, is to have a paler tipping, or a pale patch at the tips; a few of the median and lesser coverts near the carpal joint, tipped, and margined towards the tip, with pure white. The bird obviously changing its plumage, and the old and new feathers amongst the winglets, greater coverts, and quills, contrasting strongly; the former being a sort of dingy deep olive brown, the latter almost black. The greater coverts of the last few primaries, and first few secondaries, conspicuously margined towards the tip with white. The first six primaries conspicuously emarginate on the inner webs, the points below these emarginations almost black; above this, the inner web is mottled, or obscurely barred with grey, or greyish brown. In the succeeding primaries, and secondaries, there is a trace of mottling, and incomplete barring (very distinct in the new, and less so on the old feathers) on both webs. The new secondaries are almost perfectly black, narrowly margined at the tip with white, and with about seven transverse irregular, and ill-defined bars of grey, or brownish grey, across both webs; but not reaching quite to the margin of either. The old secondaries are a sort of umber, or dark, dirty olive brown, obscurely barred, and mottled with a paler shade, and with traces of a pale tipping. The tertials are brown, obscurely mottled and barred with a darker shade of brown, and grey, and broadly tipped with white, and fulvous white. The tail feathers are of several shades of brown; from sandy, to almost black; none of the feathers very new, but some much older, and more abraded than others, and these are the lightest. All have a pale tipping, and the central ones which are very old, and abraded, seem to have had pale margins; and all show traces of six or seven transverse bars, (on both webs in *most* of them,) of pale fulvous, in the case of the lighter; and brownish grey, in that of the darker ones. The lower abdomen, vent, and lower tail coverts are nearly uniform pale fulvous, and though here and there, a few feathers show traces of a darker brown, these parts contrast strongly, with the broadly dark margined feathers of the breast and upper abdomen. Axillaries, and wing lining, except larger lower coverts, a mixture of brown, and pale rufous; the former predominating in the axillaries; greater lower coverts, brown, greyish brown, and greyish white.

2nd. What I take to be a more advanced form of the *First, or lineated stage.*

Female. Shot, 22nd February.

Description. The feet, and upper surface of toes, a pale wax yellow, feet as usual, dirty and dingy; claws, horn black; scutæ, small, convex, hexagonal, or nearly circular, with four large, thick, transverse ones at the tip of each toe. Inner edge of mid claw, a little dilated.

Irides *very* clear, and pale brown; edges of lids, wax yellow; eye shelf, greyish white, with a faint yellowish tinge.

Cere, wax yellow, with a faint tinge of green near the margin of the cere, at *commissure;* base of both mandibles, bluish grey, the rest of the bill horny brown, and blackish.

Plumage. The lores, point of chin, and the points of the tongues of feathers, which run down each side of the lower mandible, clad with tiny white feathers, with greatly elongated bristle-like, naked, black shafts. Forehead, top and back of the head, the feathers a sort of wood brown, tipped and centred towards the tips, with a pale sandy, or whity brown ; chin, throat, and cheeks including ear coverts, about the same colour as the tippings of the feathers of the head, with traces of a darker tint on cheeks. The neck, all round, shoulders, scapulars (all but the few longest) upper half of back, breast, abdomen, sides, axillaries, and the lesser, and median lower wing coverts, all with pale central stripes, (which are narrower, and more fulvous above; and broader and more nearly pure white below) and darker margins, which above are a sort of wood brown, and below more of an umber brown. The few longer scapulars, are a dark umber brown, with a central whitish spot at the tips. The lower half of the back, rump, and upper tail coverts, are white; the feathers more or less broadly margined towards the tips, with wood brown, or buffy. The longest tail coverts are nearly pure white. Tail, uniform, rather rusty, wood brown ; the tips much abraded, and with a terminal fulvous white band, which, when the feathers were fresh, must have been one inch in width. The lesser, and median (upper) wing coverts are brown, paler towards the centres; the median, with white spots on the tips at the shafts, most conspicuous towards the carpal joint, and most of the rest of the coverts, with more or less traces of such central terminal spots. Feathers under the winglet white, mingled with buffy; winglet, primary, and greater coverts, dark brown tipped with white; secondary, and tertiary greater coverts, also conspicuously tipped white ; but of a lighter brown hue, changing gradually as they recede into the brown of the median and lesser coverts. The first six primaries conspicuously notched on the inner web, and the second to sixth inclusive, conspicuously, and the first slightly, emarginate, on outer web. Beyond the notches and the emarginations (which are very high up, that of the 2nd being hidden by the greater coverts), the first six primaries are nearly black; above the emarginations, the outer webs are a deep brown, and above the notches the inner webs are greyish brown; with broad, incomplete, ill-defined grey transverse bars. The seventh is a deep brown, with the basal two-thirds of the inner web, as in preceding; all seven have the merest trace of a pale tip. The last three primaries and all the secondaries, are broadly tipped with white. The last three primaries are a lighter brown than any of the preceding feathers, or than the secondaries; and are much silvered over with grey, the tenth being almost pure grey. The secondaries are a deep umber brown, but with some traces of grey mottling on the outer, and inner webs of the earlier ones, and the same is observable on the tertiaries. Below, it remains to notice that the pale, or whitish central stripes become so broad towards the lower part of the abdomen, that the feathers there are nearly unmixed fulvous white. The feathers immediately below the vent, and the lower tail coverts, are white; but some of the largest of the latter have a buffy tinge. The thigh coverts are a dingy white tinged on the upper portion with pale rufous. The tarsus feathers, are a dirty white. The larger lower wing coverts, are mottled greyish brown, and greyish white.

Of a third bird in this stage, I find noted, that the feet have four large scales, at points of mid toes, and three on all the others; that the irides were very pale yellowish brown; the margins of the lids dusky; the eye shelf yellowish; the cere and gape wax yellow; the base of both mandibles greyish blue, and their tips horny black.

3rd. What I consider a good typical specimen of the *second, or twin barred light brown stage*. Male shot, January 4th.

Description. Legs and feet a pure, deep, somewhat orange yellow. Scutæ, reticulate, with four large scutæ at the end of the mid toe, and three at the end of the others. Claws, black, inner edge of claw of centre toe dilated. Other claws, with a somewhat sharp cutting edge beneath, on both sides.

Irides, dark brown; the membrane of the bare shelf overhanging the eye, dingy greenish; lower eyelid, pale greenish white, sparsely feathered with whitish down.

Bill, horn black; cere, gape, and base of lower mandible, rich, somewhat deep yellow.

Plumage. The whole of the lores pale brown, thickly covered with long, soft, blackish brown bristles, one set of which, curve outwards, and upwards, towards the nostrils and forehead, and the other set of which, go straight down over the *commissure;* there are few bristles also on the tip of the chin, and on each side of the lower mandible, about half way between the gape, and the tip. A narrow, indistinct, dark brown eye streak above the bare projecting shelf, from the forehead continued backwards over the ear coverts. The whole of the front, and top, and back of the head, pure brown; the feathers white at their bases but this not showing through. The feathers lanceolate, and the shafts somewhat darker; on some few, there is the faintest trace of a paler tipping. The nape, and upper part of the back of the neck, of the same colour, but paler tipped; the feathers long and pointed. Lower part of the back of the neck, back, rump, scapulars, (except a few of the longest) and whole of the lesser and median wing coverts (except a few of the longest of those of the primaries,) a slightly lighter brown, than the crown, and very broadly and ill-definedly tipped with a slightly paler shade of brown, which owing to the over-lapping of the feathers, is for the most part, the only colour seen. The longest of the scapulars, a deep umber brown; in some lights, almost black. Upper tail coverts white, with a slight tinge of rufous, or fulvous. Tail feathers, blackish brown, obscurely mottled in places, with a lighter brown, and narrowly tipped with dingy white; their shafts white at the base, brownish for the terminal half. The coverts under the winglet a mixture of white, pale brown, and rufous white; the winglet itself, blackish brown, narrowly tipped with rufous white, and tinged on the edge of exterior web with brown. The primaries and greater coverts, very dark brown, tipped with fulvous white; the first seven primaries nearly black, all but the first emarginate, and strongly tinged on the outer web above the emargination, with grey, or grayish brown; the first six conspicuously notched on the inner webs, and mottled with greyish above the notches; the last three primaries are mottled brown and gray, the outer webs being almost entirely gray; the first narrowly, the second less narrowly, and the third broadly tipped with rufous white. The secondaries dark brown, all conspicuously, and broadly tipped with rufous white, and obscurely barred with a darker brown. The tertials similar, but their general hue is lighter. The whole of the greater coverts of the secondaries, as well as of the last three primaries dark brown, conspicuously and broadly tipped with rufous white, and as is often the case with the secondaries themselves, and the primaries greater coverts, with a sort of greyish patch on the brown above the tipping. The tips of the median coverts, of the primaries, and some few of the first secondaries, pale rufous white. The entire under surface of the body, throat, neck, ear coverts, axillaries and lesser lower wing coverts, uniform pale brown, much the same colour as the upper parts; but many of the feathers especially of the breast, and abdomen, very faintly margined with a slightly darker tint; vent feathers, and lower tail coverts, fulvous white. Greater lower wing coverts, white with a faint rufous tinge. The wings when closed, reach as far as the end of the exterior tail feathers, which are 1⅝th shorter than the centre ones.

4th. A fairly typical specimen of the *third, or barless dark brown stage. Female.* Shot, January 17th.

Description. Legs, feet rather dingy wax yellow; claws, black; feet, with convex reticulated scales; mid toe of left foot, with three large transverse scutæ, all above being reticulated; mid toe of right foot, with five transverse scutæ; inner toe of left foot, with three and what would have been a fourth had it not been divided down the centre; inner toe of right foot, and hind toes of both feet, with four, outer toes of both feet with three transverse scutæ. Irides, brown; edge of lower lid, plumbeous; of upper lid, yellowish; bare shelf above the eye, dingy, pale, slightly greenish yellow; lower lid, greyish white, sparsely clothed with brownish white down. Cere, gape, and base of lower mandible, full butter-cup yellow, but with a tinge of green, near the nostrils, and on lower mandible. Bill, pale, bluish grey at junction of cere, and near base of lower mandible, bluish horny beyond.

Plumage. Lores greyish white, thickly clad with tiny down-like feathers, with elongated naked dark brown shafts, looking like fine bristles. There is a small patch of similar feathers at the tip of the chin, and at the point of the sort of tongue of feathers, which runs down the basal half of the sides of the lower mandible. The forehead, and front of the top of the head, umber brown, only one or two feathers of a slightly lighter hue. The feathers of the occiput, and nape, of the same umber brown, elongated and narrow pointed; and all conspicuously tipped and margined towards the tips, with a pale, somewhat fulvous brown, which colour, owing to the over-lapping of the feathers, perhaps predominates. The whole of the back of the neck, upper back, scapulars, and lesser and median wing coverts, a mixture of paler and darker brown, some feathers being of the one colour and some of the other, the dark being most numerous on the upper back, and back of neck, and least so, on the lesser wing coverts. The longer scapulars are almost all of the darker hue: *(the darkest hue is not nearly so dark, as that of the adult Imperialis, but the lighter is darker than that of the Bifasciata, my 2nd, stage).*

The *middle back* is chiefly of the paler hue, one of the feathers being nearly wholly greyish white, and three others tipped with the same. The lower back, and rump, are uniform dark brown. The upper tail coverts, are a somewhat fulvous white, broadly tipped, and irregularly barred, with palish fulvous brown. The tail feathers, are a mixture of new and old; the former darker, and more umber, the latter somewhat more sandy; all with traces of five or six irregular, ill-defined, wavy, transverse, greyish bars, conspicuous on the new feathers, and least visible on the outer webs of all the feathers new and old. The winglet, and all the greater coverts, are very dark brown, except the last two or three of the greater coverts of the primaries, which are paler brown. The inner webs of all these feathers, are more or less mottled, or obscurely barred with grey. The coverts below the winglet, are mostly a lighter brown. The first six primaries, of which all but the first are conspicuously emarginate on the outer web, are all black, or blackish brown, below the emarginations; but, except the two first, the rest are a paler brownish on the outer web, above the emarginations. All six are notched on the inner web, (the sixth least manifestly so), all are blackish brown on the inner webs below the notches, and all are much mottled, or obscurely though broadly barred, with greyish on the inner web above the notches. The last four primaries, are not quite alike in the two wings, all have dark tips, longest in the seventh, shortest in the tenth; but the outer webs above this, are three of them grey and one somewhat fulvous brown, in one wing; and two of them grey and two fulvous brown in the other; the grey showing *traces* of incomplete, broad, brownish bars, and the inner webs of all, being of a somewhat lighter brown, lightest in the tenth, broadly but incompletely barred throughout with grey. The secondaries are dark brown, but of somewhat varying shades, all with ill-defined, broad, grey bars on the inner webs, and traces of the same, in a good light, on the outer webs of some.

The tertials are similarly barred, but are a (somewhat) lighter and more sandy brown than the secondaries. The whole of the chin, throat, sides of the neck, and ear coverts, are a nearly uniform and rather dark umber brown. The feathers of the chin, and part of the throat, are rather scanty, and show the white of their bases through, more or less. The whole of the breast, abdomen, sides, and thigh coverts, are a warm, but light umber brown, a shade darker than the light colour of the upper parts, mingled with dark feathers, of the same shade as the darker colour of the back, &c. The dark feathers are most numerous on the breast, and amongst the longer thigh coverts. The axillaries, and the whole of the wing lining, except the lower greater coverts, (which are a greyish brown, many of them more or less barred in both webs with greyish white), are a rich umber brown, intermediate between the two shades of the lower parts. The vent feathers, and those of the lower tail coverts, are a lighter brown, and their whitish basal portions, show through, more or less.

Of the 4th stage, well known in Europe; I think it unnecessary to give a detailed description; but I note that Dr. Bree's figure, is very defective, insomuch as the whole interscapulary region, by him shown as a yellowish brown, little darker than the head and nape, is really, an intense, almost black brown, and this too is the colour of the lesser, and median wing coverts, and leg plumes, given in his plate as a rich reddish brown. I add, that I never yet saw a specimen with such huge white scapular patches, as he represents.

Since the above was written, the following remarks on the nidification of this species by Mr. C. Farman, have appeared in the Ibis for 1869.

"Of all the Eagles to be met with in this country, this is by far the most common, and it breeds in great numbers in all parts of Central Bulgaria.

"Nidification commences at the end of March or beginning of April, the 8th of April being the earliest date at which I have found the eggs (some thirty of which I have taken). I have, however, taken fresh eggs of this bird as late as the first week in May. Its favourite place for building its eyrie is on an isolated tree, or where the trees are scattered about at some distance from one another, or a clump of two or three, at the most, standing alone in the open country, but where there is little or no cultivation.

"The nest is little more than a large flat platform of coarse sticks, about three feet six inches in diameter and piled up to the height of eighteen inches or two feet, but in some old nests much higher. The interior is slightly concave, and lined with a few smaller twigs and a little dry grass, wool, pieces of old rag, or any other small rubbish that comes within their ken; in most instances, however, the lining is very scanty.

"The number of eggs in a nest is generally two, sometimes three, never more, and not unfrequently only one.

"The Imperial Eagle, always a shy bird and difficult to approach, is ever more so during the breeding season; the male bird is always on the watch, either flying in graceful circles at some height above and about the nest, or seated on some neighbouring tree, whence, on the slightest appearance of danger, he comes swooping down towards his eyrie, uttering a hoarse croaking noise, as a warning to the female, who instantly leaves the nest and joins her partner in his circling evolutions high up above their eyrie."

No. 28. **Aquila Nævia**, Gmel.

The Spotted Eagle.

The Spotted Eagle breeds commonly throughout the Oudh and Rohilcund Terai, the Dhoon and the northern portion of the Saharunpoor district, (and probably in many other suitable localities) but I have never myself had the good fortune to see or take a nest. My friend, Capt. Marshall, R. E., furnishes me with the following note on the nidification of this species.

" Builds in the Saharunpoor district in the end of May and beginning of June. The nest is commenced about the end of April and the young are hatched by the middle of June.

" The nest is placed in a fork near the top of a large tree, about thirty-five or forty feet from the ground. All that I have found, have been in the line of trees along the bank of the Eastern Jumna Canal, on the outside ones farthest from the water, and always in Sheesum trees. I found four nests, one with young (on the 10th June) and three with eggs on the 22nd of May and 3rd and 11th of June. All the eggs were hard set. The nest is a large circular platform-like structure of sticks, with a few dead leaves in the egg receptacle, but no other lining. I noticed no remains of food in any of them. The diameter of the whole nest was about twenty inches, and the interior depth about two inches. I have never found more than one egg in any nest; the egg now before me is a perfect, but very blunt oval; of a slightly yellowish white ground, somewhat profusely spotted and blotched with rather faint yellowish brown, and a pale washed-out purplish brown, which latter colour greatly predominates; the egg is absolutely glossless."

An egg which I owe to Capt. Marshall's kindness, is a broad oval in shape, and has a greyish white ground, richly blotched and spotted with pale purple. This egg is somewhat larger in every way than that figured by Mr. Hewitson; it has no gloss, and when held up against the light, the shell, as in all these Eagles, is a bright sea-green.

This egg and the one above described by Capt. Marshall, measure respectively $2·7 \times 2·2$ and $2·5 \times 1·96$.

The egg figured by Mr. Hewitson from Mr. Wolley's collection, measures 2·44 by 2·02.

Without pretending to dogmatize in regard to a matter which I have not by any means fully investigated, I am inclined to think, that the changes of plumage in this species, have not yet been satisfactorily determined.

There are two supposed races of this bird, one the western, or smaller form, *A. Nævia*, Gmel. and the other the eastern and robuster form, *A. Clanga*, Pallas. Now whether this latter be really a form of *Nævia*, or whether as I suspect, it really represents the second stage of *A. Imperialis* (q. v.) it seems certain to me that our bird is the feebler or eastern form, the true *Nævia* of most European authors.

Further on I shall give exact, and more or less detailed,

measurements, and descriptions taken from eleven fresh specimens of this species, but I wish first to premise that, according to my views, this Eagle has three well marked stages of plumage.

1st. The buffy, or buffy fulvous.

2nd. The purple brown, white spotted.

3rd. The uniform deep brown stage.

In all these stages, where the sexes have been ascertained, this species can at once be separated, by its much smaller size, from, *A. Imperialis*, while from *A. Fulvescens*, it may be distinguished; first, by its invariably barless tail; secondly by its more silky, and soft plumage, and thirdly by its rounder nostrils.

The utmost confusion seems to prevail amongst some, at least, of the continental ornithologists as to this, and kindred species. Radde, I find, boldly uniting *A. Nævia*, *A. Nævioides*, *A. Clanga*, *A. Bifasciata*, and *A. Fulvescens*. The best of it is, that the measurements and descriptions (such as they are) that he gives, clearly prove to me that with *one* exception, his supposed *Nævias* are *all* forms of *A. Imperialis*, more or less intermediate, (because killed in April and May) between the four stages described by me when dealing with that species.

That *Bifasciata* is a form of *Imperialis* is I think certain.

That *Nævia* is utterly distinct from *Nævioides* and *Fulvescens* is equally certain.

That *Fulvescens*, *Fusca*, and *Punctata*, are one and the same, is beyond doubt; but whether these are, or are not, distinct from *Nævioides* is yet doubtful, though I incline to believe them so.

That our common upper Indian Spotted Eagle is identical with that of western and southern Europe, the true *Nævia*, figured by Yarrel, the detailed dimensions and descriptions given further on, will, I believe, sufficiently establish.

Whether *A. Clanga* is a true species, or whether Pallas like Radde, ignorant of the four-fold change of plumage in *A. Imperialis*, obtained specimens of this latter, between the 1st and 2nd, and 2nd and 3rd stages, and to these gave the name of *Clanga*, I cannot decide, but I am strongly disposed to think that this is the real origin of the supposed more robust form of *A. Nævia*.

The absolutely unbarred tail, is at all ages, characteristic of the Spotted Eagle; I can show a sequence of some forty odd birds, from the pale buff, to the deepest umber or liver brown, not one of which exhibits a trace of barring on the tail; while per contra, I can show a still larger series of *Fulvescens*, every bird in which (except three in which the tails are terribly abraded and bleached), shows unmistakable barrings on the *centre* tail feathers. Besides this, the difference in the texture of the plumage, (that of *Fulvescens* being comparatively stiff, harsh, and thin, that of *Nœvia*, soft, silky, and dense) in the strength of the bills, feet and legs, and in the shape of the nostrils, suffice to separate these two species conclusively. Both go through, it is true, not very dissimilar changes of plumage, and individuals of both races may be found so similar in general appearance, that even *good* figures of them might wholly fail to prove them different, but a mere glance at the tails, the first touch almost of the plumage, or a comparison of the bills, nostrils and feet (supposing the sexes to be known) would unmistakably show how distinct they were.

Nœvia, with us, at any rate, is a bird frequenting moist localities. Where large jheels abound, or where canal irrigation is extensively resorted to, there *Nœvia* (in upper India at any rate) is very common, but in the dry sandy plains, which occupy so vast a portion of the surface of Continental India, this species is extremely rare.

A remarkable fact as to change of geographic distribution, resulting from modification of the physical aspect of a country by human industry, came under my own notice in connection with this species. The Etawah District between Cawnpore and Agra, belonged essentially to the dry sandy class. For years I shot through this district without ever obtaining a single specimen of the Spotted Eagle. After a time the Ganges Canal, with innumerable, minor channels was opened out through the district. Huge tracts came under irrigation. A year or two passed away, when suddenly one day, shooting with Mr. Brookes, along the canal, we found the Spotted Eagle common. Subsequently, numerous specimens were obtained at various localities in the district in the neighbourhood of the canal. I thought I *might* possibly have overlooked this species in past years; but this seemed unlikely, because winter and summer I daily had one or two men out shooting, and even had I always passed it over, one or other of them must have killed it. However, this matter was set at rest, by several *Aheriahs*, (native hunters and bird-catchers by caste), spontaneously pointing out this bird to me, as having only appeared in the district during the last two years. This species has always been plentiful in the Dhoon and the northern portion of the Suharunpoor District, in which the Ganges Canal has its origin, and there can be little doubt that as the canal, year by year, was opened out further and further, developing tracts suited to their tastes, the Spotted

Eagles (whose favourite food with us is unquestionably* frogs,) rapidly followed its course.

This bird, generally sits in a very slouching kite-like fashion, across a branch, half way up a tree. *Fulvescens*, on the other hand, more commonly sits bolt upright, in the centre of the very *top* of a tree; so that, when looking from a distance, you see his head and half his body, against the clear sky above the very top of the tree, while when close to the tree, you cannot see him at all. *Imperialis* too, often adopts a similar position.

If *Clanga* be a true species, and *not* a form of *Imperialis*, as I cannot help suspecting, it is curious that the true *Nævia* should occur in India and western Europe and *Clanga* in Palestine. Mr. Tristram (Ibis, 1865) tells us, that the Spotted Eagle is "much more common in winter than in summer on the plains. We observed it only two or three times in the Lebanon in spring. Mr. Gurney has pronounced a specimen I showed to him, to belong to the large form described by Pallas as *Aquila Clanga*. I found one nest in a tree, between Nazareth and Caiffa."

I now give, in a tabular form, exact measurements of eleven specimens. These are not perhaps well chosen, but they are all I have by me, and they were all recorded from the fresh bird, with the utmost care.

As in the case with *Imperialis*, so here, one of my reasons for believing in the specific identity of all the various forms hereafter to be described, (and the dimensions of whose representatives, I am now about to give) is the close structural resemblance of all these latter in every minute detail.

---

* I have unfortunately not preserved a record of the contents of the stomachs in more than thirteen cases. In eleven of these "Frogs and Toads, chiefly small" are recorded. One I shot in the act of eating part of the liver of an Antelope we had killed, and one had eaten a Rat.

DIMENSIONS.	1 Male.	2 Male.	3 Male.	4 Female.	5 Female.	6 Female.	7 Female.	8 Female	9 Female.	10 Female.	11 Female.
Length,	26·5	25·5	26·0	27·75	27·5	27·88	26·75	27·5	28·0	28·5	27·5
Expanse,	61·0	63·0	64·0	67·0	68·0	69·0	69·5	68·0	69·0	72·0	73·0
Weight in lbs.,	3·94	3·38	3·81	3·5	3·56	3·81	3·56	4·16	4·19	4·2	3·98
Wing,	19·25	19·0	19·75	19·5	20·0	20·5	20·0	20·75	21·0	20·5	21·0
Which primary the longest,	4th	4th&5th	5th	4th	4th&5th	4th	5th	4th	5th	4th	4th
By how much other Primaries fall short of longest,	1st 4·13	3·88	3·75	4·13	4·63	4·0	4·88	4·63	4·5	3·9	4·5
	2nd 1·5	1·19	1·25	0·88	1·38	1·75	1·38	1·38	1·5	1·6	0·9
	3rd 0·5	0·38	0·44	0·13	0·5	0·43	0·38	0·38	0·7	0·2	0·37
Length of tail from vent,	10·63	11·0	11·0	11·75	11·5	12·0	11·5	12·0	12·0	12·2	11·5
By how much longest feathers exceed shortest,	1·13	1·13	1·0	1·13	1·13	1·0	1·0	1·0	1·1	1·2	1·3
Tarsus,	4·06	3·94	3·92	3·5	4·25	4·0	3·94	4·0	3·8	3·82	4·0
Foot, greatest length,	5·5	5·25	5·3	5·75	5·63	6·0	5·38	5·63	6·0	5·88	5·7
Ditto, greatest width,	4·75	4·75	4·68	5·0	4·88	5·25	4·5	5·0	5·07	5·0	4·65
Mid toe,	2·19	2·13	2·17	2·13	2.25	2·44	2·22	2·44	2·5	2·37	2·5
Its claw, along curve,	1·25	1·25	1·3	1·25	1·25	1·19	1·13	1·13	1·38	1·25	1·25
Hind toe,	1·13	1·13	1·1	1·13	1·13	1·19	1·09	1·19	1·16	1·08	1·15
Its claw, along curve,	1·56	1·5	1·6	1·63	1·56	1·31	1·44	1·56	1·75	1·38	1·5
Inner toe,	1·21	1·3	1·28	1·4	1·43	1·5	1·4	1·52	1·51	1·49	1·5
Its claw, along curve,	1·4	1·37	1·38	1·42	1·53	1·63	1·4	1·61	1·6	1·47	1·37
Bill, straight, including cere,	1·81	1·88	1·9	1·97	1·88	2·0	1·94	1·81	1·94	1·94	1·9
Ditto, along curve, ditto ditto,	2·25	2·25	2·27	2·38	2·31	2·47	2·38	2·38	2·37	2·4	2·5
Ditto, from gape,	2·28	2·63	2·7	2·38	2·31	2·38	2·49	2·38	2·44	2·4	2·3
Ditto, width at gape,	1·69	1·75	1·76	1·75	1·75	1·88	1·69	1·88	1·89	1·78	2·0
Ditto, height at margin of cere,	0·66	0·69	0·7	0·69	0·72	0·75	0·69	0·72	0·78	0·72	0·75
Length of cere,	0·69	0·75	0·73	0·75	0·75	0·75	0·69	0·66	0·69	0·78	0·75
Distance by which the closed wings fall short of end of tail,	1·0	0·5	Nil.	0·88	0·88	end of tail.	0·25 beyond end of tail.	0·25	0·25	Nil.	0·2
Distance by which lower tail coverts fall short ditto,	3·25	3·5	3·6	3·63	3·5	3·5	3·0	3·25	3·75	4·0	3·9

Description. I first take No. 1 male, as fairly typical of the first stage of plumage.

Feet, pale dingy yellow; claws, darkish brown; iris, pale yellowish brown. The whole lower mandible and basal half of upper mandible, greyish white, with a tinge of blue; tip of upper mandible, horny brown; cere and gape, pale dingy yellow.

Plumage. The whole head, throat, neck all round, breast, sides, abdomen, and thigh coverts, a pure buff. Most of the feathers, darker shafted, and those of the top of the head conspicuously so; a narrow dusky, ill-defined supercilium running backwards over and behind the ear coverts. Upper back and scapulars, light brown, the longest of the latter only somewhat darker, and all but these broadly margined with fulvous white, and with the margins much abraded. The middle of the back, buff, the bases of the feathers, white, and showing through. The feathers of the rump, light brown, broadly margined with buffy white and white. The upper tail coverts pure white. The tail brown, paler towards the tips, the margins of which are almost white. The lesser and median coverts, light brown each broadly margined with buff towards the base, and white towards the tip.

The greater coverts, except those of the first three or four primaries, a rather darker brown than the median, margined towards the tips with white, and those of the last three primaries margined with white the whole way up the outer webs. The first seven primaries as in the adult; but the outer webs above the emarginations a redder brown. The last three primaries not only tipped with white, but with a broad white margin all the way up the outer web. The winglet, the greater coverts of the first three primaries and the secondaries a rich umber brown, showing in some lights a purple gloss; the secondaries narrowly tipped with white. The axillaries, and the whole of the lower lesser wing coverts and median coverts, except just at the carpal joint, a warmer buff than even the breast; a sort of rufous salmon colour, I might almost call it; feathers below the vent, and lower tail coverts a slightly buffy white; (as in the adult) longest thigh coverts, and tarsus feathers, dirty fulvous, or buffy white.

Next as typical of the second stage, I take No. 4 a female, shot at Rahun, February 20th, (the male above described, was shot at the same place, on the same date, in company with this very female).

Description. Feet, pale wax yellow; claws, black above, horny brown beneath, *scutæ* reticulate, inconspicuous, 5-4 well marked transverse *scutæ* at the ends of the mid toes, and 4-3 at the ends of the others, inner edge of mid claw a little dilated. Irides, a rather light brown. Eye shelf and edges of lids plumbeous, lower lid nearly white, with a few tiny tufts of down. Bill, bluish grey at base of both mandibles, and horny black at tips, cere and gape pale wax yellow.

Plumage. The skin of the lores pale bluish, pretty thickly set with tiny pale brown feathers, the dark naked prolonged shafts of which at front curl upwards and outwards towards the nostrils and forehead like soft bristles. Forehead, top, and back of the head, a rather light umber brown, the feathers specially of the hind head, very narrow, sharp pointed, and *paling* towards the tip. From the gape, under the eye and over the ear coverts, a patch of brown lighter than the top of the head. Below this from the side of the lower mandible a slightly darker band, than either the above mentioned ear patch, or the throat, which latter with the chin, is about the same colour as the ear patch, but looks lighter, as the feathers are rather sparsely set, and allow the white bases to show through a good deal. The neck all round, upper back, scapulars, and lesser wing coverts an uniform rich umber brown, a shade darker than the top of the head; a few of the longer scapulars have a central fulvous white spot on the tips, two or three of the median scapulars on one side have a trace of the same kind of spot. Lower back and rump the same rich umber brown, but each feather with a conspicuous somewhat pear-shaped, brownish or fulvous white spot at the tip. The upper tail coverts slightly-fulvous white. The tail feathers nearly uniform blackish brown, the shafts of the basal one-third white, or whitish. Near the tips, the colour fades to a sort of sandy brown, and there is a trace of a pale tipping. The median and greater coverts much the same colour as the lesser coverts, but all the greater coverts, except the first three or four (which with the winglet are a rather darker brown still) conspicuously tipped with fulvous white, and all the longest, and a few of the other median coverts with central, fulvous white spots at the tips. The secondary greater coverts are conspicuously mucronate, and abraded at the tips. The second to the sixth primaries are emarginate on the outer webs, the emarginations being high up, in the second hidden by the coverts. The first to the fifth are strongly notched on the inner webs, the notches being almost equally high up. The first six primaries are blackish brown below the emarginations and notches; above they are umber brown on the outer web, and greyish, mottled with brown, on the inner web. The rest of the primaries and secondaries are tipped inconspicuously with brownish white, have the outer webs umber brown, and the inner pale greyish brown, with numerous close, rather narrow, ill-defined, brown transverse bars. The whole upper surface has, in a good light, a certain purplish gloss. Breast, sides and upper abdomen, the same rich umber brown as the neck, but each feather with a narrow, paler, somewhat sandy, central streak, these becoming larger and more conspicuous as the feathers recede from the neck; on the lower abdomen, the central streak occupies nearly the whole feather, and the feathers immediately above the vent, are wholly of this sandy brown hue. The thigh coverts are the same rich deep umber, but the longest are tipped with fulvous white, and those above them have central fulvous white spots at the tips. The whole of the feathers below the vent, and lower tail coverts, rather dirty, or slightly fulvous white. The lesser and median lower wing coverts the same rich umber brown, a few of the latter over the first few primaries with terminal fulvous spots. The larger lower wing coverts greyish brown, faintly and irregularly mottled, with greyish white. Tarsus a paler brown than the thigh coverts, mottled behind with dingy white, and with the terminal feathers in front of the same colour.

I next take No. 11, a female, as typical of the third or *uniform deep* brown stage. Shot on 27th December.

Description. Feet bright orange yellow. Irides deep brown. Cere and gape, orange yellow. Bill, blue dusky at tips. Tongue rather long and narrow, of nearly equal width throughout, obtuse ended, with conspicuous central groove.

Plumage. The whole bird a nearly uniform rich umber, or deep liver brown, the quills and tail feathers almost black, and these and the longer scapulars with a perceptible purple gloss. A narrow white tipping to the longest upper tail coverts, and a few of the feathers near the vent, a little mottled with white; no trace of white tipping or mottling to *any* other portion of the plumage. The bases of all the feathers are white, but the bird is so well feathered that these nowhere show through. The brown of the head, neck and throat is slightly paler than that of the rest of the body, and the feathers of both head and nape have traces of slightly paler brown, narrow central stripes. A few of the lesser and median wing coverts, old abraded feathers, are a somewhat paler brown. I have another bird before me *very* similar to this one, except that the whole plumage is a still darker brown, there is no admixture of paler feathers in the wing coverts, the faintly paler centres of the hackles are almost wanting and the tarsal feathers are *pure white*. This I take to be the oldest form. I have seen and preserved several such, but have unfortunately failed to record measurements from the fresh bird in any of these. As far as can be ascertained from the skins, they correspond precisely with the dimensions above recorded.

In the second stage considerable variations occur. Of No. 10, a bulky looking female shot near Juggernathpoor in March, and which is decidedly in younger plumage than the one which I have described as typical, I have the following note :—

The whole bird is a lighter and duller brown, and its spots are a duller fawn or dingier fulvous white than those of the No. 4 type. There is no purple gloss. The chin is darker and more the colour of the front and top of the head, where there is little trace of the pale tippings. On the other hand, the pale brown tippings are more conspicuous on the feathers of the hind head and upper part of the neck. The breast, abdomen and sides are nearly uniform dull pale wood brown, with only here and there faint traces of the rich dark umber brown margins so characteristic of this stage. The longer thigh coverts again, are almost wholly dingy fulvous white, with only a mottling of dingy umber brown on the basal halves. Lastly, the rump is mostly a dingy fulvous, the feathers only having narrow dingy umber brown margins, which do not extend to the tips. The bird, though much nearest to No. 4, appears intermediate between it and No. 1.

Of another, I say, No. 5, female resembled No. 4 closely, but there was a much richer purple gloss on the whole upper surface, which also was somewhat darker ; the ear patch was not so light, the spots on the scapulars and lower back and rump were larger and more conspicuous, and in the case of the scapulars far more numerous. The upper back and base of the neck behind, of uniform colour in the first, have in this specimen terminal, central buffy spots. The pale tippings to the feathers of the head were far more conspicuous, every one of the median wing coverts had its terminal spot, and most of the lesser have also a minute buffy white linear spot, or speck at the tip. There was somewhat less white about the upper tail coverts. Below, the surface generally darker and the central streaks lighter and far more strongly marked. A patch of feathers on the breast, a sandy brown, (though not so pale as the central streaks of the lower feathers) only narrowly margined with the deep umber brown. There was rather more white about the tarsus above the foot. The pale tipping of the tail feathers was also more conspicuous.

No. 3 male, was an older bird, intermediate between the second and third stages, " not a speck or spot on back of neck, upper back, shoulders, lesser and median wing coverts, except at the very tips of the longest of the latter. None of the quills, except the last three primaries with more than the faintest trace of pale tippings, only a few minute specks on the scapulars. Scarcely any pale centering to the breast feathers, and far less of this on the abdomen than in any of the preceding" (*viz.* Nos. 2, 4, 5—10).

Further I may add that No. 2 male, and No. 6 female, were identical in plumage with No. 4, though No. 2 was smaller and No. 6 a little larger. No. 7, a female, the smallest obtained, was much the same type as No. 5 as regards the amount of spotting; in other respects differed from Nos. 2, 4 and 6, but little. The longer thigh coverts were, however, almost wholly fulvous white, the spots being so large as to occupy nearly the whole surface of the feathers. Nos. 8 and 9 were between No. 7 and Nos. 2, 4 and 6) the throats and breasts being perhaps a purer and darker brown.

In all the specimens of the first and second stages of plumage that I have examined, the ovaries and testicles have been so little developed, as to render the discrimination of the sexes, a matter requiring *care* and a magnifying glass. In all specimens of the third stage of plumage, they have been well developed.

I think I ought to note, that my valued friend, Mr. Brookes, differs from me as to the first stage described, really pertaining to this species. He believes it to be distinct. For my part, the exact structural correspondence, the possession of more or less intermediate forms, and the fact that in a part of the country where the Spotted Eagle is common, these pale buff birds were pointed out by native fowlers, as the young of the species, incline me to the opinion already expressed of the specific identity of the two forms.

Mr. C. Farman, in the Ibis for 1869 gives the following particulars in regard to the nidification of the Spotted Eagle in Bulgaria.

"In the spring of 1865, I observed a nest of this bird placed on an Ash tree overhanging the stream at the southern entrance of the Pravidy valley: it was more neatly put together than most of the Eagles' nests, and was warmly and softly lined with the blossoms of the Ash tree; it contained one young bird just hatched, and two eggs already cracked by the young birds within. On the edge of the nest were the two fore legs of a Leveret."

No. 29. **Aquila Fulvescens.** Gray.

The Indian Tawny Eagle.

This species breeds in different parts of upper India, from the middle of November to the middle of June, but the great majority I think, lay in January. Out of one hundred and fifty-nine eggs of which I have a record, eighty-three were taken in January, thirty-eight in December, twenty-eight in February, the rest in November, March, April and June. Only *one* in this latter month, and none at all in May. The very hot dry weather puts a stop to the laying of most species. The nest is always, as far as my experience goes, placed on trees. I have never met with one placed on rocky ledges, although I have found them on trees at the foot of, or near to precipices, which contained apparently most "eligible sites."

They build a large flat nest of sticks between two and three and a half feet in diameter, and from four inches to one foot in thickness, according to situation. The nests are generally lined with green leaves, sometimes with straw or grass intermingled with a few feathers, and sometimes have no lining at all. They are generally placed at the very top of the tree, and though I have found them occasionally on Peepul and Tamarind trees, the great majority were on moderate sized, but dense, Babool trees, standing apart in the midst of fields or low jungles.

The normal number of eggs seems to be two, but it is by no means uncommon to find three. The eggs of this species appear to me, to vary prodigiously in size and shape; but it is not improbable, as already remarked, when treating of *Gyps Bengalensis*, that this excessive apparent variation, is due to the enormous series I have before me. I have taken more than a hundred of this bird's eggs myself, and from first to last, have had more than double this number sent me by other observers. Normally this bird's egg is a somewhat broad oval, slightly pointed towards one end, and answering both in size and shape very well to Dr. Bree's figure of the Tawny Eagle's egg; very often, however, the eggs are somewhat smaller than this, and occasionally a great deal larger; some are very long and pointed. A pair which I took in the Goorgaon district, (shooting the old bird) are fully as broad as the egg in Bree's figure, and as long as his figure of the Lammergeyer's egg; so that they appear a long and narrow egg; the cubic contents of these must be fully twice that of some of the smaller specimens; they each contained a fully developed chick, ready to hatch off. A few of the eggs are nearly spherical, but the broad oval greatly predominates. The ground colour of the eggs is the usual greyish white, unspotted in about half the specimens and exhibiting more or less conspicuous markings in others. Of the markings, the most common are a few large blotches and splashes of yellowish brown accompanied by pretty numerous specks or spots of the same colour, distributed pretty evenly, over the whole egg. In some, the blotches are more extensive and numerous, and exhibit a tendency to cluster towards one end more than the other, and the colour becomes a reddish brown or in some a purplish brown, while in others all three colours are mingled. In no egg that I possess is more than one-third of the surface covered with markings, and as a rule, even the richest coloured eggs (and these are comparatively rare) have not above a seventh or eighth of the surface of the egg covered with markings.

Elsewhere I have remarked, "The eggs vary extraordinarily both in size and shape from a very long oval, much pointed at one end, to almost a sphere; but the ordinary type, is a rather broad oval, slightly narrower at one end. In colour, they are most commonly white, with a *very* faint tinge of bluish green; but many of them are more or less streaked, spotted, or blotched, with different shades of brown, or reddish brown, and occasionally purple of varying intensity, and here and there, one may be found richly marked with sharply defined spots and blotches of bright, though slightly brownish, red. Many of the eggs, when taken from the nest, have a faint gloss on them; but they lose this by washing, and the eggs become so soiled during incubation, that it usually *is* necessary to wash them. The texture is generally close and compact, the egg lining is a pure sea-green."

In size the eggs vary from 2·35 to 3·25 in length and from 1·8 to 2·25 in breadth; but the average of one huudred and fifty-nine eggs measured, was 2·63 by 2·11.

Mr. William Blewitt remarks, that he found great numbers of the nests of this bird, in the neighbourhood of Hansie, during January, February, March, and April 1868. None contained more than two eggs, and many of these latter were considerably incubated. The nests were without exception in *dense* Keekur trees (*Acacia Arabica*) at heights of from sixteen to twenty-four feet from the ground. The nests, sometimes loosely and at others densely constructed, were composed of twigs and small branches of Keekur, Ber *(Z. Jujube)* and similar thorny trees; more than one had a thin lining of grass or leaves, but the majority had no lining. In diameter (excluding straggling ends) the nests varied from sixteen inches to nearly two feet, and in depth from barely four to nearly nine inches.

During the latter part of 1868, great scarcity prevailed in Hansie and the whole neighbouring country, owing to the failure of the rains. Fodder, especially, was unprocurable, and throughout vast tracts, all the Babool, Ber, and Peepul trees were entirely denuded of their foliage, in order to feed the cattle. The result has been that *A. Fulvescens* has entirely deserted the neighbourhood, and where in 1868, with but little trouble Mr. Blewitt met with *scores* of nests, he has this year only succeeded in finding two!

My friend, Mr. G. F. L. Marshall, R. E., writing of this species, says, "Very common in the Saharunpoor District. Is said to catch fish by all the natives; but I do not believe it. The native name is Machopa, or Machoka. It builds on trees, a nest of sticks, and lays two white eggs, sometimes pure, sometimes blotched with dusky and brownish. It commences building in the end of March, but the eggs are not laid, till the end of May; and I have taken fresh eggs up to the middle of June, and at Shamlee, in the Mozuffernugger District, I took five nests early in June, all with fresh eggs."

It is a curious fact, that in many parts of the country, the natives believe that the "*Ruggur*," as they usually designate it, catches fish. I have examined the stomachs of probably some fifty specimens, but though I have often found them full of small frogs, I have never detected any remains of fish.

Most birds when they have eggs, even before they begin to sit, watch their nests closely. I have, however, repeatedly found nests of this Eagle, containing one or more eggs, with no parent bird any where near. I have several notes of this, I quote one.

"On the Western Jumna Canal, near Hissar, on the 15th December, I found a large nest on the top of a Babool tree. The nest seemed rather fresh and therefore, though there was no bird near, I sent up a man to examine it. It proved to contain two large eggs. Whilst the man was near the nest, no bird made its appearance, only after we had waited about a quarter of an hour, a large *Fulvescens* in dark plumage, soared slowly past, at a great height over head. This was about 2 o'clock in the afternoon. We did not touch the eggs, called the man down, and withdrew to watch the nest; hiding ourselves carefully some little distance off. It was not till the sun was setting that this same *Fulvescens* suddenly made its appearance, and descended to the nest, where it was shot. It was a female, and from first to last, we saw nothing of the male."

The plumage of the young is very pale. I find a note of one

we met with "February 18th, 1867, a fine young one in a nest, a nice plump little white woolly chap, as Brookes said, for all the world like a well-washed poodle dog!"

Great differences of opinion exist, as to the identity or otherwise, of this species and *Nœvioides;* and as to the changes of plumage, whether the dark, or the light birds are the oldest, &c.

As regards its identity with *Nœvioides*, Mr. Blyth says, "This species is united with the African *A. Nœvioides* by Mr. G. R. Gray (B. M. Cat. B. Nepal, 2nd Edition); but it is a considerably smaller bird, and varies much more in its colouring. I have had many alive, three or four of them together; but never saw any approaching the size of the three fine specimens of *A. Nœvioides*, at present in the Zoological Gardens."

I am not in a position to decide this point, but I subjoin a number of accurate measurements from the fresh bird, which will facilitate the decision of this question elsewhere.

As regards changes of plumage. The young one in the nest is yellowish white, and the young of the first year are little else but whity brown. In the second stage, early in their 2nd year, they become wood brown, and in this stage are found breeding although *rarely*. In an intermediate stage, as I take it, late in the 2nd, or early in the 3rd year, they are about half wood brown, and half deep brown, and in the last or third stage, as I take it, by the beginning of the 4th year (or the end of the 3rd) they are throughout, deep umber, or in some, liver brown; which is perhaps not so dark in the first year it is assumed, as it becomes later. In both the intermediate and third stages, they are commonly found breeding, but according to my notes, out of every ten breeding birds, about one is in the second plumage, three in the intermediate, and six in the more or less dark garb. In all stages, there is a more or less apparent transverse barring in the central tail feathers, often mottled, irregular and ill-defined, but still distinctly visible in all but three of the enormous series in my museum; and in these three, the feathers in question are so abraded and bleached, that they very probably may have originally exhibited the bars.

I regret extremely, that most of my notes* on this species have been lost, and that I have now at hand, full details of only four specimens.

---

* I take this opportunity of again remarking, that one of my chief reasons for printing these crude, ill-digested notes, is my inability to find time to arrange them properly, and my fear, that if I delay putting them on permanent record, they may be lost altogether. In May 1857, I had com-

	1 Male.	2 Female.	3 Female.	4 Female.
Length,	24·0	28·0	27·0	27·0
Expanse,	60·0	67·0	69·0	67·0
Weight (in lbs.),	......	4·6	4·0	4·06
Wing,	18·0	21·0	19·5	19·5
Which primary longest,	5th	5th	4th & 5th	4th & 5th
1st Primary falls short of longest by	5·0	......	4·75	4·78
2nd „ „ „ ...	......	......	1·75	1·5
3rd „ „ „ ...	......	......	0·75	0·6
Length of tail from vent,	10·0	11·25	10·0	10·0
Tarsus,	2·75	3·25	3·31	3·25
Foot, greatest length,	5·0	6·0	5·75	5·5
„ „ width,	4·38	5·0	5·0	4·63
Mid toe to root of claw,	2·0	2·5	2·5	2·38
Its claw along curve,	1·25	1·38	1·25	1·25
Hind toe to root of claw,	1·0	1·13	1·13	1·06
Its claw along curve,	1·5	1·75	1·75	1·5
Bill, including cere from forehead straight to point,	1·5	1·8	2·0	2·0
„ „ along curve „	2·44	2 56	2·63	2·63
Bill, from gape,	2·25	2·5	2·56	2·56
„ width at gape,	2·13	2·25	2·0	2·06
„ height at margin of cere,	......	......	0·75	0·78
Cere, length on culmen,	......	......	0·75	0·81

Besides this, the great majority of my specimens have recorded on their tickets, certain leading measurements, taken from the fresh bird, before skinning, (along with date, place, colours of soft parts, contents of stomach, and sex,) and from these I transcribe a number of measurements.

---

pleted a work on Indian ornithology, *very* inferior to Dr. Jerdon's subsequently published one, and therefore on this account not to be regretted; but still containing much that his volumes do not supply about the Birds of the Punjaub and the N. W. Provinces, and the first work of its kind. The fair copy, *en route* to the printer, was destroyed, with the rest of the contents of the mail bags, by rebels; while the original notes, with my vast collections, including nearly 2000 species of Asiatic and Australian birds were burnt a few weeks later at Etawah by mutineers. I see nothing improbable in the recurrence of an equally serious cataclysm, in the event of England's becoming involved in a general European war.

	Length.	Expanse.	Wing.	Tail.	Wings when closed reached to within how much of end of tail.	Weight in lbs.
Male 1st, ...	25·25	66·5	20·4	10·25	0·5	4·0
„ 2nd, ...	25·5	65·0	20·0	10·0	......	3·0
„ 3rd, ...	26·0	64·0	19·5	10·5	......	2·75
„ 4th, ...	26·0	64·0	20·7	10·4	......	3·0
„ 5th, ...	25·25	64·25	19·5	11·0	1·75	3·0
Female 1st,...	27·5	69·0	21·4	12·0	1·5	4·5
„ 2nd,...	27·63	70·0	21·3	11·0	1·25	4·75
„ 3rd,...	28·0	73·0	21·75	12·0	1·55	4·5
„ 4th,...	27·5	70·5	21·0	11·5	1·75	4·5
„ 5th,...	28·5	73·25	22·0	11·13	0·5	4·5
„ 6th,...	27·38	69·25	20·75	11·5	2·13	4·5
„ 7th,...	28·0	69·5	21·6	11·75	2·0	5·0

I have selected these, as small, large, and average examples out of over forty ticketed birds, and this set of measurements, with the more detailed ones given above, ought to enable European naturalists to decide, whether there is really, in point of size, any great difference between *A. Nævioides* and *A. Fulvescens*.

The female No. 3 (killed near Etawah, January 4th) of which I have above given *detailed* measurements, was a characteristic enough example of a bird changing from what I consider the second, into the third stage; as I have it by me, I give an exact description of this specimen.

Description. Legs and feet, dirty greenish white; claws, black; feet and toes, with reticulate scales, but with five large transverse *scutæ* at the tip of the middle, and hind toe, and four at the tips of each of the lateral ones.

Irides, brown; edges of lids, bluish; orbits, bluish white, sparsely feathered with white down; membrane of bare eye-shelf, pale bluish grey.

Cere and gape, dirty cream colour, bluish about nostrils; upper mandible, at junction with cere, and lower mandible except at the tip, pale bluish grey; tips of both black.

Tongue, thick, fleshy, entire, slightly bilobed, of nearly uniform width throughout, very narrow in proportion to width of gape.

Plumage. Lores, greyish white, densely clothed with long, fine, dark brown, hair-like feathers. A patch on the forehead, on each side, dark brown, the feathers narrowly edged with pale brown. The whole of the rest of the top of the head a sandy brown, mingled or mottled with a somewhat darker hue. Feathers of the nape, and upper hind neck, much elongated, lanceolate, and mingled fulvous white, and pale brown. Base of the neck behind, and upper back, somewhat light umber brown, each feather tipped and margined with whitish brown. Lower back, pale brown, the white bases of the feathers showing through in places; rump, a rather darker brown. Upper tail coverts, lighter again, and whitish towards the tips. Scapulars mingled three shades of brown, from very dark to light fulvous brown. Tail feathers dingy greyish brown, tipped paler; very narrowly, and closely but obscurely, barred with very dark brown. Lower wing coverts, pale whitey brown, irregularly blotched with patches of rich dark brown. The median wing coverts pale brown, tipped and margined still lighter. Coverts under winglet, mingled white, fulvous and brown. Winglet very dark brown, the interior feather whitish on the inner web; greater coverts of primaries brown, those of the first few primaries very dark brown, especially on the outer webs, and scarcely perceptibly tipped with white. Those of the later primaries a lighter brown and conspicuously tipped with white; and all of them with a good deal of greyish white on the inner web, which, however, is not visible without raising the feathers. Greater coverts of secondaries brown, some darker and some lighter, but all much darker than the median coverts. All of them with a good deal of greyish white on the inner web, and many of them more or less noticeably tipped with white. The primaries beyond the emarginations, which are conspicuous from 2nd to 7th, nearly black. Above the emarginations, the general colour is a lighter brown, barred, and freckled with greyish white, obscurely on the outer, and conspicuously on the inner web. The last three primaries, however, have the ground colour grey, with dark brown, wavy, transverse bars on both webs. The secondaries dark brown on the outer web, tipped greyish; and with a number of large transverse oval spots or incomplete bars of grey, on the inner webs. Below the gape, and behind the eye, a brown patch. Chin and centre of upper part of throat, darkish brown, the sides being pale fulvous brown. Lower part of throat and neck in front, dark brown, each feather with a narrow, central, fulvous white streak. Sides of neck, pale fulvous brown, with a few dark feathers intermingled. Breast, abdomen, sides, thigh coverts, and axillaries, dingy fulvous brown, some feathers rather darker than others; vent feathers, and lower tail coverts, white, tipped with fulvous; some almost entirely light fulvous. Lesser lower wing coverts, pale fulvous brown with, here and there, a single, very dark feather. Greater lower wing coverts, brownish grey. First five or six .primaries, conspicuously notched on inner web. These, above the notches, and the rest of the quills throughout their whole lengths, have the lower surfaces obscurely barred greyish white and blackish brown. A faint trace of similar barring observable on the lower surface of tail feathers. The wings extend to tips of exterior tail feathers, which are 1⅓ inch shorter than central ones.

Of the female, No. 4, shot on the same date, in nearly the full adult plumage, I have the following note:

" Almost exactly the same size as preceding and with the lores, quills and tail feathers much the same, though the latter were somewhat darker, but the whole of the rest of the plumage was a nearly uniform umber brown, darkest on rump, some of the largest scapulars, eye streak, and breast, and palest, on middle of back, upper and lower tail coverts, and lesser and median wing coverts (the former of which have a trace of sandy). There is some white about the chin, throat, and vent, owing to the bases of the feathers showing through. The feathers of the top of the head *very* narrowly, and inconspicuously margined paler, and the elongated lanceolate ones of the nape, and back of neck, with tiny, inconspicuous paler tips."

No. 30. **Aquila Hastata.** Less.

The Long-Legged Eagle.

I know nothing of the nidification of this Eagle, nay more, I am sorry to say, I know nothing of the bird itself. To the best of my belief, this species does not occur in Upper India, and I do not think that I have ever seen an *undoubted* example of it.

Col. Tytler has a specimen, (male) shot near Jessore, which he *calls Hastata*, and which he assured me, both Mr. Blyth and Dr. Jerdon had seen, and named, as *Hastata*. It is vastly like *A. Fulvescens*, a pretty uniform dingy, *slightly* rufous brown, throughout. Longer scapulars, secondaries, and tail, a deep purplish chocolate brown; primaries, almost black at the tips; longer upper tail coverts, and lower tail coverts yellowish white; a few of the tibial plumes with terminal fawn coloured dots. In a very strong light, a faint trace of lighter bars is discernable on some of the lateral tail feathers. None of the feathers of the upper plumage are tipped with white. The upper tail coverts are not *barred* with white, though the longest *are* yellowish white. There is scarcely a trace of obsolete barring; no white tip to the tail, though of some feathers, the abraded terminal one-eighth is slightly paler. There is not a trace of pale fawn, or of any bar, on either breast, abdomen, feathers of the leg, under wing coverts, or under tail coverts. There are no spots on the wings, and no pale tippings to the tertiaries. It is therefore not the adult *Hastata* of Jerdon, and still less the young. The beak is feebler, the tarsi slenderer, and longer than in *Fulvescens*, and this seems the only point in which it resembles *Hastata*. The following are the dimensions taken from the skin. Length, 24. Tail, 10. Wing, 18·75. Cere, 0·63. Bill, along curve from margin of cere to tip, 1·5 scant; from gape, 2·25; width at gape, 1·81; height at margin of cere, 0·63. Tarsus, 3·63. Mid toe, 2; its claw, 1·06; hind toe, 1·09; its claw, 1·25 full.

Mr. Blyth remarks, (Ibis, 1866) "This species is well figured by Mr. Hodgson, as I pointed out to Mr. G. R. Gray, who does not include it in the second edition of his Catalogue of that gentleman's collection. I have had many fresh specimens of all ages, and could always easily distinguish it from *A. Clanga*. Though nearly of the same linear dimensions, it is considerably less robust, with smaller bill, and feet; and there is a recognizable difference in the plumage in all its phases; while in its habits, it partakes (in a prominent degree) of the nest-plundering propensities of *Neopus Malaiensis*."

I should like to see a good series of this, to me, somewhat doubtful species. As regards the lesser robustness, and smaller bill, and feet, these can scarcely be relied on, when we have to deal with a species so excessively variable in these respects, as is *A. Nævia*. I do not for one moment presume to assert, that *Hastata* is not a good species, but I am sure, that the majority of the specimens that bear the title are *Nævias*, pur et simple. This was the case with several supposed *Hastatas* sent me from Lower Bengal. Moreover, the only specimen I could *find** in

---

* It must not be supposed, that this is any reflection on Mr. Blyth. This gentleman *made* the Calcutta Museum, and for some twenty years *his* talents shed a lustre on the Asiatic Society, which its then members did but little to merit. From the day *he* left Calcutta, the Museum has been disgracefully neglected; numbers of specimens, as far as I could judge, in the confused state in which the whole collection was when I visited it in 1868, have had their tickets changed, or have disappeared altogether; and it in no way follows, that the misnamed specimen that I saw, was one of Mr. Blyth's

the Asiatic Society's Museum ticketed *Hastata* was unmistakeably *Nœvia*.

No. 31. Hieraetus Pennatus. Gmel.

The Booted Eagle.

Of the nidification of this species in India, we know but little, and yet it is by *no* means an uncommon bird, in Upper India at any rate. Mr. Brookes says, "I have seen several at a time near Chunar in company with *Milvus Govinda*, they were seated on the ground during the heat of the day, near a shallow tank in which they had been bathing; allowing me to go within twenty yards of them as they did, I could easily distinguish them from the Kites."

Mr. R. Thompson writes: "I have commonly met with these birds in Gurhwal and Kumaon. The young are distinguished by having a deal of white underneath. I once saw one dash into a tree in which a number of Parrakeets were assembled and catch and kill one. I have also seen them fly down to a Rat, and try and catch it on the ground."

I have shot them myself, in the Goorgaon district and near Umritsur in the Punjaub.

Of their breeding elsewhere, I have seen but few detailed accounts. Lord Lilford has the following note on their nidification in Spain.

"A little further on in the forest, we found a large nest on the lower branch of a Pine. Manuel crept cautiously up towards it, and shot a fine female Booted Eagle as she dashed off. He then made a *cache* with Pine boughs within shot of the nest, and in about half an hour another shot proclaimed to us that the male bird also had fallen. The nest contained two eggs;

Hastatas. Let us hope, that under the new regime, this noble collection may be restored to something like its former condition.

Talking of Mr. Blyth's great services in the cause of science, during his twenty years' *slavery* (for it was little else) in Calcutta, one cannot help feeling, that there is a sort of retributive justice, even in this world. The pompous Jacks in office, who alternately neglected, and attempted to patronize Mr. Blyth, (whose invaluable services they pretended to remunerate by a pittance less than they would have presumed to offer to their French cooks) are now either dead, or dragging out their crotchety existence in some old-Indian-peopled watering-place; in either case, unknown and unhonoured; while the name of Blyth, the naturalist, is known, and respected by men of science throughout the civilized globe.

this appears to be the invariable number laid by this Eagle, which is one of the most common of the raptorial family in this district, arriving about the end of April, and remaining in the country till October. The nests, of which we found several, were generally placed on the lowest branches of a tall Pine, at their junction with the main trunk, and were built of sticks, but inside invariably contained fresh twigs with the green leaves adhering to them. This Eagle has a shrill piercing scream, different from that of any other raptorial bird with which I am acquainted."

In Spain they appear to lay in the latter part of April, May and June. Two of Lord Lilford's eggs, figured in the Ibis, have greyish white grounds; the one has only the faintest trace here and there of pale yellowish clouds, the other is more richly streaked, clouded and blotched with a dull ferruginous red. The former is a rather perfect broad oval measuring 2·05 by 1·7; the other, a large egg, still a broad oval, but somewhat pointed and compressed towards one end, measures 2·25 by 1·83.

Of the breeding of a *very nearly* allied (if *really* distinct) species, *H. Morphnoides* in Australia, Mr. Gould gives the following account:—

"I was led to the discovery of the bird by finding its nest, containing a single egg, upon which it had been sitting for some time. The nest was of a large size, and was placed close to the bole, about one-fourth of the height from the top of one of the highest gum-trees; the egg was bluish white with very faint traces of brown blotchings; two inches and two lines long, by one inch and nine lines broad. Very recently I have received a second specimen of the egg of this species which, although very similar to the one above described, differs in being more extensively blotched with yellowish brown and pale purple, the latter hue appearing as if beneath the surface of the shell."

As to the distinctness of *H. Morphnoides*, the nidification and eggs of which are, it will have been observed, similar in many respects to those of *H. Pennatus*, Mr. Blyth had the following remarks in the Ibis for 1867:—

"I have already remarked (Ibis, 1866, p. 241) that a rudimentary crest is always observable in Indian specimens, at least I found it so in all which I obtained in Bengal, in one which I shot near Moulmein, and in one or two South Indian specimens received from Dr. Jerdon; but I cannot perceive a trace of rudimentary crest in two mounted Nepal specimens in the British Museum, received from Mr. Hodgson. The rudimentary crest referred to, resembles that of *Spizaetus Limnaetus* of Bengal, and also of many Bengal examples of *Pernis Cristatus*, and as the subcrested *Hieraetus* averages a rather larger size than the European *H. Pennatus*, I do not think that it can be distinguished from the Australian *H. Morphnoides*, Gould. Mr. Swinhoe's crested specimen of *Poliornis Poliogenys* (Ibis, 1864, p. 429) should here be borne in mind. Mr. H. E. Dresser agrees with me in the opinion, that the white-breasted specimens of *H. Pennatus* are adults, as in *Eutolmaetus Bonellii;* whereas in *Spizaetus Limnaetus* and *S. Cirrhatus*, the white-breasted birds are the young."

As regards the second point raised by Mr. Blyth, *viz.* as to whether the dark plumage is that of the adult or young, I think further investigation is necessary. Mr. Tayler, in his notes on the Birds of Egypt, which appeared in the Ibis for 1867, has the following remarks in regard to this species:—

"This pretty little Eagle, which is by no means common in Egypt, is subject to considerable variation in colour, for a specimen shot by one of our party, which showed no sign of immaturity, was of a uniform dark brown."

This statement I can confirm, from a careful examination of a specimen in the dark plumage, now in Col. Tytler's museum, which is, I consider, manifestly an old bird. A female, apparently an old one, shot from the nest and off the egg which I shall notice later, was also of an uniform dark brown colour.

I subjoin detailed measurements and description, taken from the fresh bird, of a male which I shot in the Goorgaon district on the 12th December. In company with this bird were three others; two in the dark plumage which seemed to me to take the lead and be the old birds, and the other similar to this one.

Dimensions. Length, 18·75. Expanse, 49. Weight, 1·75lbs. Wing, 15; the 4th primary the longest, 1st, 4·53; 2nd, 1·85; 3rd, 0·45 shorter. Length of tail from vent, 8·25; the longest tail feathers exceeds shortest by 0·25. Tarsus, 2·3. Foot, greatest length, 3·48; greatest width, 3·5; mid toe, 1·58; its claw, straight, 0·8; hind toe, 0·78; its claw, straight, 0·1; inner toe, 0·9; its claw, straight, 0·9. Bill, straight from edge of cere, 0·88; along curve, 1·05; from gape, 1·4; width at gape, 1·1; height at front at margin of cere, 0·5; length of cere, 0·45; Wings when closed reach to within 1 of end of tail. Distance by which lower tail coverts fall short of end of tail, 3·43.

Description. Legs and feet, pale wax yellow. Irides, somewhat pale brown. Bill, bluish black at tip, pale blue at base. Cere and gape, bright wax yellow. Lores and forehead, pale buffy white, a very narrow blackish streak, running at the lower border of the lores, between the lores and the eyes, and over the eyes, and a somewhat similar stripe running immediately under the eye. Cheeks and ear coverts, dull rufous, the feathers with narrow central blackish brown streaks. Crown, occiput, nape, sides and back of neck, pale rufous buff, the feathers centered with umber brown, broadly on the centre of the crown and occiput, where there is a trace of a rudimentary crest; and narrowly elsewhere, and most of the feathers paling off at their margins.

Upper back and inter-scapulary regions, rather pale umber brown. Mid back, a pale wood brown; middle of rump, umber brown; sides of rump and upper tail coverts, buffy, or rufous white. Scapulars, mingled fulvous white and pale wood brown; a few of the longest scapulars only being a rich umber brown. Lesser wing coverts, a rather rufous umber brown, the feathers conspicuously darker centered; median wing coverts, wood brown, broadly margined with fulvous white; secondary greater wing coverts, a rather pale umber brown, very narrowly tipped with fulvous white. Secondaries a deep umber brown, narrowly tipped with fulvous white; primaries and their greater coverts, very deep umber brown; some of the hinder primaries somewhat lighter brown, and narrowly margined towards the tips with fulvous white. Tertiaries, pale wood brown, exterior webs nearly entirely buffy white. Tail feathers, pale dingy umber brown, very narrowly tipped with fulvous white, and with *traces* of a terminal and three or four other, darker, transverse bands. Chin, throat, breast, and whole lower parts, fulvous or buffy white, palest on the leg feathers, lower tail coverts, and wing lining. The feathers of the chin, throat, and sides of the breast more rufous, and with long, narrow, central, dark brown streaks, broadest on the sides of the breast. Axillaries, wing lining, and sides, white, mostly with dark shafts, and with irregularly shaped, more or less cordate, spots, on the shaft near the tip. Some of the axillaries have three or four such spots along the shaft. The lower surface of the earlier primaries, is a peculiarly glossy bronze brown; the first five have *most conspicuous* notches on the inner webs, and the second to the sixth have well marked emarginations on the outer web.

In examining this bird, one is impressed by the fact, that all the light wood brown feathers of the scapulars, and wing coverts, are old and abraded ones, whilst all the deeper coloured ones, are new.

So far as this and another similar example, now before me, go, I should be inclined to say, that the dark brown form was the older one. Of this darker form, Col. Tytler has a specimen, killed at Umballa, a female, and to my notion clearly an old bird. The dimensions of this specimen, *taken from the skin*, are as follow. Length, 21·5. Tail, 9·25. Wing, 15·88. Cere on culmen, 0·56. Bill from edge of cere to point along curve, 1·13; from gape, 1·5; height at margin of cere, 0·53. Tarsus, 2·25. Mid toe, to root of claw, 1·88; its claw along curve, 1·06; inner toe, 1·0; its claw along curve, 1·34; hind toe, 0·88; its claw along curve, 1·47.

Description. The head and neck are dingy brown with dark shafts and traces of dark central streaks, the rest of the upper surface is a dull brown, (except the longer upper tail coverts which are white); the upper back, longer scapulars and secondaries (which are narrowly tipped yellowish white) being darker than the rest; tertials and lesser and median coverts paler, and tail, (also narrowly tipped yellowish white) with all but the uropygials (and even on these a trace of the same is discernable) exhibiting obscure, irregular, clouded bars of a darker colour. Beneath, a more rufous brown, slightly paler on vent and lower tail coverts; tibial plumes and the feathers of the throat, breast, abdomen and sides, darker shafted. Lower surface of tail, greyish white, with the brown bars showing through more or less, on all but the outer laterals. Traces of banding on the inner webs of all the primaries *above* the notch.

I can see no trace of a rudimentary crest, no superciliary stripe, no band from the angle of the mouth, no dark central stripe to the chin.

Mr. Layard, who gives this species from South Africa, says, "The only specimen I have seen is a *young* bird shot by Mr. Jackson at Nel's Port. It is entirely of a dark brown colour, in some places inclining to black. He tells me he was attracted to it by its peculiar cry."

The shrill note of this Eagle, which has, as noticed by Lord Lilford, a peculiar intensity of character, was what first drew my attention to the bird which I shot in the Goorgaon district and have above described.

Mr. Blyth tells us, that this species occurs in the Indo-Chinese sub-region. Mr. Wallace does *not* include it in the *Raptores* of the Malay Archipelago.

Since the major portion of the above was written, my collector, Mr. Theobald, found a nest of *H. Pennatus* on the 21st February, 1869, at Hurroor in the district of Salem and from it shot the old brown birds, above noticed. "The nest," he says, "was on the branch of a high Banyan tree (*Ficus Indica,*) about forty or fifty feet from the ground. It consisted of dry twigs, and was in shape a circular platform, with a slight depression in the centre, devoid of lining." The eggs were two in number, only one of which reached me in safety. This one is a very broad oval, almost exactly the same size as the one figured by Mr. Bree. The ground is a dead white, devoid of gloss and pretty thickly blotched and streaked throughout with reddish brown. The egg reminds one much of some of the richer coloured eggs of *Milvus Govinda*, but the markings are smaller, and the shell when held up against the light is a very pale sea-green, much lighter than in any of the numerous specimens of *M. Govinda* that I have yet examined. It measures 2·13 by 1·78.

Mr. Howard Saunders, in the Ibis for April, 1869, gives us some further particulars of the nidification of this species in Spain. He says, " The Coto del Rey, which we first entered, is principally covered with scrub and small timber, mingled with clumps of large size, generally in a ring with a marshy clearing in the centre.................................I cautiously crept round to the front, and stood out to give myself as fair a shot as possible. Off went the bird, and down came a very old female Booted Eagle (*Aquila pennata*,) just as I expected. The nest was lined with green boughs, and contained two eggs, very hard set. This was on the 1st of May."

No. 32. Neopus Malaiensis, Reinw.

The Black Kite Eagle.

This is another species, in regard to whose nidification we are profoundly ignorant. The structure of this bird is very peculiar, and its eggs would materially aid in elucidating its true affinities.

I have seen it in the Himalayas as far west as Simlah, and have shot it, not far from, but several thousand feet below, Nynee Tal. It is doubtful whether it breeds westwards of Nepal. Mr. R. Thompson, writing from Kumaon, says: " They appear to come into the lower spurs of the Himalayas about the middle of September, and to stay with us till about April, when they disappear; where they go to, I can't say, but they are not to be found during the summer either on the frontier, or in the interior of the Himalayas here, as far as I am aware."

I am by no means sure that Mr. Thompson is right; I believe I have seen it in Kumaon in June, and I certainly saw one near Simlah in the middle of July; it is to be hoped that ornithologists in the Himalayas will watch this bird a little more closely.

There has been a rather amusing difference of opinion about a supposed young bird of this species. Dr. Stoliczka shot a young Eagle, at Rogi near Chini. Capt. Beavan and Col. Tytler who saw it, pronounced it to be a young *Neopus*, and Capt. Beavan thus announced the fact in the Ibis :—

"Perhaps the best thing he has, or at least the greatest novelty to me, is a young *Neopus Malaiensis*, Reinwardt, in a phase of plumage, never before I believe recorded. Beneath, entirely dark brown, like the under parts of *Milvus Govinda*, each feather black shafted; the top of the head rufous, (the feathers also black shafted) a conspicuous shoulder spot of a pure white; primaries of wings, black; secondaries and tertiaries, dark brown, their coverts being broadly margined with ashy grey; tail, the same. The upper back is dark brown, with here and there a purplish gloss; legs, dark yellow, with black claws; bill, horny; cere, yellow. This specimen cannot have long left the nest, judging from the but partial development of the tail."

Dr. Stoliczka, per contra, affirms, that this bird is a young *Pennatus;* he says, "The only species which I have obtained in the beginning of August, 1866, in a forest near Chini, was a young specimen of what I believe to be *Aquila Pennata*, Gmel. (Jerd. Vol. I. p. 63.) The specimen is only about three-fourths grown; in colouring it exactly agrees with the old bird, except that the inner webs of the tail feathers are not barred; a white shoulder tuft is distinctly traceable. Dr. Jerdon says, that the young bird of *A. Pennata* is white beneath. This makes the question of the identity of our bird doubtful, although, as I have said, there is no difference in its colouring from that of an old *A. Pennata*. The specimen is not a young *Neopus*, which always has the beak in proportion somewhat more slender."

Von Pelzeln, (Ibis, 1868) confirms Dr. Stoliczka's view, remarking that the plumage is very like that of a young *A. Pennata* shot in Lower Austria. Whichever is right, what strikes one is, that both parties dwell on the plumage, whereas the structure of *N. Malaiensis* is so peculiar, that a single glance at the feet would have settled the matter conclusively. The inner toe in this species is nearly as long and much thicker than the mid toe, while its claw is *considerably* larger than that of even the hind toe; moreover, the claws are not merely, as Dr. Jerdon describes them, "moderately curved." They are so little curved that, for the claws of an Eagle, one might designate them as almost straight. I cannot conceive how *Hieratus Pennatus* and *Neopus Malaiensis* could possibly be confounded at *any* stage of their existence; I shrewdly suspect that even chicks, extracted from eggs nearly ready to hatch off, would be at once distinguishable by their characteristic feet.

Besides India, Burmah and Malayana proper, Wallace notes the occurrence of this species in Java, Sumatra, Celebes and Ternate; but it must be rare in the Archipelago, as our author, himself, has never met with it there.

I subjoin dimensions of a female. Length, 31·5. Expanse, 75·0. Wing, 25·5; the 6th primary the longest, the 1st, 8·4; the 2nd, 3·92; the 3rd, 1·55; the 4th, 0·8; and the 5th, 0·3 shorter. Length of tail, 14·75; the longest tail feather, 0·75 longer than the shortest. Tarsus, 3·62. Length of foot, 6·3; greatest width, 5·2; mid toe to root of claw, 1·87; its claw along curve, 1·25; hind toe, 1·4; its claw along curve, 1·63; inner toe, 1·63; its claw along curve, 1·78. Bill, straight from margin of cere, 1·15; along curve from margin of cere, 1·37; from gape, 2; width at gape, 1·6; height at front at margin of cere, 0·6; length of cere, 0·58; distance by which the lower tail coverts fall short of end of tail, 6·2; weight 4 lbs.

Of a male (from a skin). Length, 27·0. Wing, 21·75. Tail, 13·38. Tarsus, 3·25. Mid toe to root of claw, 1·69; its claw along curve, 1; inner toe, 1·44; its claw along curve, 1·56; hind toe, 1·25; its claw along curve, 1·38. Bill, along curve from margin of cere to point, 1·19; from gape, 2; height of bill at margin of cere, 0·55; length of cere, 0·5.

No. 33. **Eutolmaetus Bonellii**. Temm.*

Bonelli's Eagle.

This Eagle, in the plains of India, lays in the latter half of December and in January; but in the Himalayas, it lays, I believe, in April and May. The nest is usually placed on ledges of precipitous earthen or rocky cliffs, and in the plains I think preferentially in the immediate neighbourhood of some large river or jheel. I have repeatedly seen their nests in the high clay cliffs of the Jumna and Chumbal in the Etawah districts, and I found a pair breeding in the ruined and cyclopean walls of the ancient Togluckabad, south of Delhi. Occasionally, however, they build on trees; and I found a nest

---

* It seems probable that Vieillot's specific name, *Fasciatus*, has the priority, but I have not the necessary works by me to enable me to decide this point.

containing a single egg in a large Peepul tree near Bhurtpore. The nest (as I said before, commonly placed on some convenient ledge or suitable recess in the cliff's face) is very large, from four to six feet in diameter, and is composed of thickish and moderate-sized sticks, varying from 1·5 to 0·5 in diameter. The nest itself varies in thickness from a few inches to a couple of feet, and being always finished off to a level; when placed, as often happens, on a more or less shelving declivity, is much thicker exteriorly than interiorly. In the nests that I have examined, branches and twigs of various kinds of thorny *Acacias* were the chief materials used. In no nest that I have seen, not even in that one mentioned as found on a Peepul tree, was there any very perceptible depression in the interior of the nest. In the centre of the platform, a circular space, of some eighteen inches in diameter, is commonly smoothed over with a thin layer of green twigs; and in the centre of this again, a smaller space of perhaps one foot in diameter is carefully carpeted with green leaves, those of the Neem, Peepul, Peeloo, and other trees being apparently indifferently made use of.

Normally, they lay two eggs, but I have once found three in a nest, and on two occasions have known of a single, much incubated egg being met with.

I have not seen many eggs of this species. All I have seen were oval, varying slightly in size and in the comparative length of the minor axis. Many are unspotted, the rest are more or less faintly blotched, streaked, or spotted with pale yellowish or reddish brown. I have never seen a richly coloured egg of this species. The ground colour is that of all Eagles of this type, a pale greyish or bluish white, often becoming, during the course of incubation, much soiled and discoloured.

In size they vary from 2·56 to 3 in length and from 1·95 to 2·22 in breadth, but the average of nine eggs was 2·83 by 2·1.

My friend, Mr. Brookes, whom I first put up to the breeding places of this bird in the Etawah district, and who has since taken many eggs there, I believe, writes, (this has since appeared in the Ibis) :—

"The eggs were usually two, but in two instances only one. Two were white, unmarked, but all the others sparingly blotched and spotted with bright reddish brown, and sometimes intermixed with blotches of light reddish grey. The largest egg measures 2·96 inches by 2·16 inches, and the smallest 2·79 inches by 2·04 inches. I have a pair of eggs out of the same nest, one plain white, the other well marked."

Capt. Hutton, writing from Mussooree, says "*Eutolmaetus Bonellii* remains here all the year, breeding in places similar to those selected by *G. Barbatus*, but although we have several times found the nests, we never could get at them. It stoops to fowls and is destructive to the larger game birds."

Mr. R. Thompson has the following note in regard to this species in Kumaon and Gurhwal. "I have never been up to examine the nests of these birds, because they are always placed on the most inaccessible precipices, but I can vouch for the time of their breeding, *viz.* from April to June. I had a nest for several years in view, but never could get at it; it was on a steep precipice and none would volunteer to assist me. That the birds had their nests there, was more than established, because during other periods of the year, the pair used to carry off my poultry and eat it wherever they found a place suitable; but in the breeding season they always carried their plunder to the nest.

"One year I caught the young birds, two in number, the first in July, and the second in August.

"I have subsequently caught young nestling birds at Nynee Tal along with the old ones, thus taking the whole family. This was in the month of August.

"In February last, I saw a pair apparently courting, which flew to and out of a large nest placed in a tree in the forest, at a place called Bunderjewrah, eight miles east of Ramnuggur."

Elsewhere (in the Ibis) I have thus described the taking of a nest of this species.

"About a mile above the confluence of the clear blue waters of the Chumbal and the muddy stream of the Jumna, in a range of bold perpendicular clay cliffs, that rise more than a hundred feet above the cold weather level of the former river, I took my first nest of Bonelli's Eagle. In the rainy season, water trickling from above, had, in a way trickling water often does, worn a deep recess into the face of the cliff, about one-third of the way down. Above and below, it had merely broadly groved the surface, but here, finding a softer bed I suppose, it had worn in a recess some five feet high and three feet deep and broad. The bottom of this recess sloped downwards, but the birds, by using branches with large *twiggy* extremities, had built up a level platform that projected some two feet beyond the face of the cliff. It was a great mass of sticks, fully half a ton in weight, and on this platform (with only her head visible from where we stood at the water's edge) an old female Eagle sat in state. This was on Christmas day! It is not many holidays a really working official gets in India, or at least can afford to give himself, and part of mine are generally spent in the open air, gun in hand.

"At the foot of the cliffs is a talus of rough blocks of clay, that it will take many a flood yet to amalgamate, and up this I crept until I was only about sixty feet below the nest. Here, however, I could see nothing of the bird, I shouted and kicked the cliff, the men below screamed, threw fragments of kunker (one of which very nearly blinded me) and by various signs attempted to indicate to Mrs. Bonelli that a change of locality was desirable. Serenely sublime in the discharge of her maternal duties, that lady took no notice whatsoever of the uproar below; accustomed to the passage of noisy boat crews, and, like some other sovereigns who sit calmly aloft, unable to realize that it is really against their sacred selves that the mob beneath is howling, the Eagle never moved. Beaten at our first move, we changed our plan. I crept down the talus, and sent up a man to throw down dust and small pieces of earth, (we were afraid of breaking the eggs), in the hopes of driving her off the nest. Luckily the very first piece of earth hit her, then came a shower of sand, and concluding I suppose that the cliff was (as it often does) about to fall, she flew off the nest with a rapid swoop. Bang, bang, both barrels, 12 bore, No. 3 green cartridge, full in the chest, (as the body showed when we skinned it), and yet with a half fall, like a tumbler Pigeon, through some fifteen or twenty feet she recovered herself and swooped away as if unhurt, close along the face of the cliff; a hundred yards further I saw a tremor, then in a moment it was clear that she was in the death struggle, she began to sink, and an instant after fell over and over on to a flat block of clay with almost incredible violence. The dust flew up from where she fell, as if a shell had dropt there, but as a specimen, the bird was scarcely injured.

"We had hardly secured the female, after the manner of bird-stuffers, plugging nostrils and shot holes, stuffing throat and smoothing feathers, when we heard a shrill creaking cry and saw the male coming straight for the nest with a bird, (which turned out to be a *Turtur Cambayensis*) in his talons. Coming to the nest, the bird seemed surprised to find it empty, it took no notice whatsoever of us, nor did it apparently catch sight of its mate, stretched out with her white breast uppermost on the deck-like platform of our barge, but it straightway settled itself down in the centre of the nest and became entirely invisible. Again tiny stones were thrown down and after standing up, staring proudly round and stalking to the edge of the platform, where he was hailed with shouts, the male bird flew off slowly, swooping down to within twenty yards of where I sat, and the next moment dropped stone dead with only a loose charge of No. 6 through him.

He was a much less bird than the female. She measured 29 inches in length, nearly 70 in expanse, and weighed close on 6 lbs. He was only 26 in length, 62 in expanse, and about 4 lbs. in weight.

We had now to get the eggs, if eggs there were, because as yet we could only guess and surmise in regard to these. Just above the recess, the cliff bosomed out with a full swell for some two or three feet, effectually preventing any one's looking down into the nest from above, or, except by an accidental cannon in the broad groove, such as my boatman had made by a fluke at the very first shot, from even throwing anything down into it. Above the swell, the cliff was as nearly perpendicular as might be, and it really did seem as if getting into that nest would be no easy matter. However, some six feet east of the nest, passed a sort of fault or crack which traversed the cliff at an angle of about 45 degrees and down this, a stout rope round the waist, with infinite trouble and no little danger, a way was found after all to the nest. Once there, it was a firm platform of sticks at least five feet by three and a half. In the centre of this, a circle of about twenty inches in diameter was smoothed over with fine green twigs of the Peeloo, *(Salvadora Persica)*, and on this again, a circle of about a foot in diameter was smoothly spread with the green leathery leaves of the same tree, and on these reposed the coveted treasures, two fresh eggs. One of these eggs was bluish white, blotched and speckled very feebly, but thickly towards the larger end, with *pale* reddish brown. It measured 3 in length by 2·19 in breadth. The other was almost pure bluish white, with scarcely any traces of markings any where, and measured 2·81 in length by 2·13 in breadth. I had always felt morally certain, that the egg figured as this bird's by Dr. Bree never belonged to this species, but was probably only a well coloured *Neophrons*, but now the thing was certain. No aquiline bird that laid the eggs I had in my hand could ever have laid an egg similar to that given in the "Birds of Europe not observed &c."

A few days later in similar cliffs a few miles higher up, I found another nest. This time, however, the platform was much larger, and was only about six feet below the top of the cliff. One could look into it without the slightest difficulty, and a Jackal could assuredly have made his way there with ease, as even I got down to it without help and without a rope. The platform of sticks was fully five feet in diameter, there was the same smooth patch of twigs and smaller smooth circle of green leaves, this time of the Peepul *(Ficus Religiosa)* and, as in the former case, on the leaves, about five inches, apart lay two fresh eggs. These had a bluish white ground blotched all over, but thinly and very feebly, with pale dingy reddish brown; and they measured, the one, 2·62 by 2, and the other 2·51 by 2. The eggs were therefore considerably smaller than those above described, while the female, which I shot as she left the nest, was a much younger and smaller one than the magnificent bird first killed."

Mr. Tyrwhitt Drake, in his notes on the Birds of Tangiers and Eastern Morocco, tells us that this species breeds at Tetuan and also at Cape Spartel.

Mr. Tristram in the Ibis for 1865, writing of Palestine, remarks—

"Bonelli's Eagle is rather common in every part of the country; but seems to avoid the plains, being much attached to the wadys and rocky terraces with which the country abounds. Most of the birds we saw were in the adult plumage; but in early spring we noted several with the ruddy breast of the second year's plumage, which evidently had not paired. It frequents the gardens behind Sidon and Jaffa, but is more generally found in the wooded hill regions about Carmel, Tabor, and the Lake of Galilee, from which places we procured the eggs in April, as well as two nests of one egg each in the neighbourhood of Gerasch, east of the mountains of Gilead. It does not appear to lay till the end of March; and then generally a single egg. These are either white, or with the faintest russet spots. One nest, which contained two eggs, both fairly coloured, baffled all our attempts at its capture. It was comfortably placed under an overhanging piece of rock near the top of the cliffs of Wady Hamam, in such a position that no rope could be thrown over to let down an adventurous climber; and yet from another point, which projected nearly parallel to it, we could look into the nest with longing eyes."

Mr. W. H. Simpson, in his notes on the birds of Mesolonghi and Southern Etolia, gives the following account of the nest and eggs of a Bonelli's Eagle which he took on the 27th of February.

"This done I was in possession, and able to make a closer inspection of the nest itself, which consisted principally of branches of wild olive, terebinth and thorn, arranged according to their size. There was no lining of wool, as is usual in Eagles' nests, but the eggs lay on a thin layer of olive leaves. The eggs themselves, which I retain in my collection, are slightly unequal in size. The larger is of a smooth texture and bluish white ground colour, very sparingly marked with rust-coloured spots and minute dottings."

This Eagle is pretty common in the plains of Upper India, and is generally distributed through the country, though, (except in the North Western Provinces,) it is chiefly found in hilly and woody tracts. Layard found it in Ceylon, but it does not appear to go eastward. I can nowhere find it recorded from Burmah, and Wallace did not meet with it in the Indian Archipelago.

Swinhoe does not appear to have met with it anywhere in China north or south; it is not amongst the Birds of Japan, and Radde does not include it in his Avi-fauna of south-east Siberia. Throughout the south of Europe, it is found, though nowhere common, and in Palestine as we have seen, it is plentiful. I do not find it noticed from Egypt, nor from the Red Sea coast country. In the north of Africa, it occurs in Morocco, Algeria and Tunis, but not it would seem further east. Layard gives it from South Africa, on the strength of a single specimen identified by Mr. Gurney, but the latter gentleman has since avowed grave doubts of the correctness of this identification, and it seems in the highest degree improbable that this species should occur in Southern Africa.

On the whole, the range of this noble and powerful, though short-winged, Eagle, appears to be comparatively restricted.

I subjoin exact dimensions of three fine females, recorded from fresh birds. Similar measurements of males have unfortunately been lost.

	No. 1.	No. 2.	No. 3.
Length,	28·5	28·0	27·5
Expanse,	64·5	64·5	67·0
Weight (in lbs.),	4·75	5·25	5·0
Wing,	20·0	19·63	19·65
Which primary the longest,	4th	4th	4th
1st Primary falls short of longest by ..	6·0	5·75	5·0
2nd „ „ „ ..	2·0	2·5	2·0
3rd „ „ „ ..	1·0	0·75	0·2
Tail, length from vent,	12·0	12·0	12·75
Tarsus,	3·75	3·69	4·0
Foot, greatest length,	6·63	7·0	7·0
Foot, greatest width,	5·25	5·75	6·0
Mid toe to root of claw,	2·5	2·69	2·63
Its claw along curve,	1·5	1·5	1·69
Hind toe to root of claw,	1·5	1·31	1·5
Its claw along curve,	2·13	2·06	2·25
Bill, straight, including cere, from forehead to point,	1·88	1·94	1·94
„ along curve „ „ ..	2·25	2·38	2·38

Bill, from gape " " ..	2·13	2·19	2·13
" width at gape " " ..	1·31	1·38	1·56
Height at front, at edge of cere,........	0·94	0·81	0·75
Length of cere only, ...	0·69	0·75	0·71
Lower tail coverts fall short of end of tail by	5·25	5·0	5·3
Wings, when closed, fall short of end of tail by	2·7	2·95	3·0

In all these, the feet were pale, dingy, whitish brown, with a tinge of yellow, most distinct on the first joint of the mid toe. Five, or rarely four, large transverse *scutæ* at the end of the inner, hind, and mid toes; three, or rarely four of these on the end of the exterior toe. Claws, black. Irides, in some bright yellow, in the others brownish yellow; orbits, greenish with small down-like white feathers; edges of lids, fleshy plumbeous; eye-shelf dingy green or in some plumbeous; bill, bluish gray at base, horny black or blackish brown towards the tips; cere and gape, pale dingy, or in some dingy yellow, bluish about nostrils.

Plumage. No. 1, female, shot from the nest. Banks of Chumbal, Mohwa Sonda, December 26th, 1866. The whole of the lores and portion under the eye densely clothed with tiny white feathers, the long naked black shafts of which, project like bristles. The forehead and the whole top of the head, rich dark brown, here and there slightly mottled with white owing to the white bases of the feathers showing through. A few of the feathers of the hind head narrowly and inconspicuously margined with white. The whole of the back of the neck and upper back, dark brown, more or less mottled with white, owing to the tips only of the feathers being brown, and the white of the basal portions showing through. Scapulars dark brown, the longest ones darker and richer coloured. The whole of the lesser coverts, and the greater coverts of the tertiaries and of a few of the secondaries, dark brown. Winglet, greater coverts of primaries, and of most of the secondaries, very dark, almost blackish, brown. Feathers under the winglet deep brown, tipped or mottled with white. Upper tail coverts very dark brown, some of the longest obscurely barred with greyish, and here and there some of the white of the basal portion of the feathers showing through. Tail feathers, dull grey, with a broad band of dusky at the tip, and several other narrower indistinct wavy bands, most clearly seen on the inner webs of all but the central feathers. Ear coverts whitish, and tipped brown. Chin and throat pure white, a few only of the feathers with dark shafts. The whole of the breast and abdomen, pure white; most of the feathers with a narrow, linear ovate patch, of dark brown along the shafts. Thigh-coverts dark brown, a little speckled and mottled with white. Feathers of the tarsus mingled pale brown, and white, with dark shafts. Under tail coverts pale brown, with ill-defined and irregular bars of pure white. Lesser lower coverts of the wing, white, with very dark brown patches. The rest of the wing lining nearly pure dark brown, with only here and there a few specks of white. The first six primaries conspicuously notched on the inner web, and the inner webs of these primaries, above the notches, much mottled with white. Lower surface of the tail feathers, greyish white, with brownish tips, somewhat mottled with dusky especially on the inner web. Axillaries dark brown, irregularly blotched with pure white.

No. 2, female, (shot on the banks of the Chumbal near Chicknee, December 29th, 1866, beside the nest which was ready for laying in,) had the whole top and crown of the head moderately dark brown, only a few of the feathers towards the front of the head having assumed the rich dark brown hue, described in the first bird. The two central tail feathers also were a pale sandy brown, tipped with a broad band of dusky brown, and with five or six transverse, wavy, indistinct bars of the same, across both webs. The rest of the feathers being of the same hue as those described in the first specimen, except the second and third exterior on one side, which were also, of the sandy brown tint, indicative of an earlier stage of plumage. The ear coverts were nearly entirely dull brown with scarcely a trace of white about them, and the whole chin, throat, breast and abdomen were white, every feather with a conspicuous central linear stripe of a somewhat dark brown, larger and more conspicuous on the sides and abdomen, and some of the feathers of these parts with traces of edgings or imperfect bars of the same colour. The thigh coverts were a paler brown, conspicuously dark shafted and mottled with fulvous. Feathers of the tarsus were slightly fulvous white with dark shafts. There was more white in the wing lining than in No. 1. The axillaries were of a paler hue, and more variegated with white; a few of the feathers of the point of the chin have elongated naked bristle-like shafts.

No. 3, female, shot on the banks of the Senghur near Chuchowlee, January 10th, 1867. The hue of the upper parts in this, was darker on the whole, than in No. 1, and the plumage was closer and firmer, moreover, almost the whole of the feathers of the head, back of neck, upper back, lesser scapulars and lesser wing coverts, were margined inconspicuously, with a *somewhat* paler and more rufous brown; in the feathers of the sides of the neck and a patch behind the ear coverts, running back and almost meeting at the nape, the contrast between the margin and centre is considerable, but in the parts previously enumerated, it is very slight, and might pass unnoticed by a careless eye. Except in the middle of the back, the white bases of the feathers scarcely show through any where. The tail feathers are of two shades, the one set grey, as in No. 1, the others a sort of olive brown, with darker brown tips and wavy bars. The ear coverts are pale rufous, each feather centered with dark brown. The whole of the chin, throat, breast, sides and abdomen, *white*, the feathers with broad central stripes (narrowest on chin and throat) of darkish umber brown, and many of those of the breast, sides and abdomen, with traces of somewhat paler brown borders. The thigh coverts are mostly dull brown, with darker brown central stripes and with but a trace here and there towards the base of the tibia of white mottling. The tarsus feathers are pale fulvous brown, with darker centres and shafts. The smaller lower wing coverts in this, may be most properly said *to be brown*, with white patches, though some few, just about the carpal joint, are more white than brown. There is much less white, and more of the rich dark brown about the whole lower surface of the bird's body and wings than in No. 1.

Of these, No. 3 was the oldest, and No. 2 the youngest bird.

No. 34. **Spizaetus Caligatus.** Raffles.

The Changeable Hawk-Eagle.

My collection contains no egg of this species, and I have never yet myself succeeded in finding a nest. My friend, Mr. R. Thompson, furnishes me with the following notes:—

"The breeding season commences in March, and lasts until the end of June, but they mostly lay in April and May. The nest is placed at a height of from forty to fifty feet from the ground, on large trees, in dense woods, usually in a good game locality. The nest is a large round structure from 2·5 to 3 feet in diameter, much resembling that of the common *Aquila Nævia*, a thick clumsy platform, composed of thick dry twigs and roots, with a central depression from four to five inches deep, lined with fine roots, and stems. The eggs are usually two, but I have preserved no record of their appearance, and I have no specimens by me to measure or describe.

"Our *Moorhaitah* or 'Peacock-killer' as he is always called by the paharees, is a common bird in our province, (Gurhwal) they are known as famous destroyers of game, and many a fine

Peacock with a magnificent train, has my *mahout* rescued from their clutches, only to die by the knife instead of by the Hawk's claws. I once saw a single *Spizaetus*, stoop at a Peacock which was on the ground, and strike at his head ; the Peacock dodged, rose and flew into a patch of tall grass where he lay concealed. The Eagle betook himself to a tree close by, whence he quietly watched the movements of the other. After a while, the Peacock began to move from his place of concealment, the moment he was well out of the grass, the Eagle darted down and caught him by the neck. When I got up to the place, having been a witness to the whole proceeding, the Eagle left his quarry and flew up into a tree; the Peacock was quite dead.

"I have often put up black Partridge for these birds, and have had much sport watching them flying after the game. These birds are first rate at jungle Fowl in the wild state. I have caught several, and tried to train them; but all my falconers, either refused to keep them, or destroyed them shortly after they were put in their possession. A small Chicken, or in its place a grown up Hen or Cock, is a capital bait for catching this bird. The net used is a vertical one, about eight feet square with large and stout meshes. The Hawk dashes into this like fury, and is always caught.

"I have taken the young from the nest, one always; but I have frequently seen the wild birds feeding two young ones.

"Both young and adult utter a peculiarly loud cry, which may be thus rendered; whee-whik, whee-whik. This cry is sometimes uttered whilst on the wing, but most commonly, whilst perching on trees.

"Another and most common cry is something like this and resembles a whistle—toot, toot, toot, toot twee, uttered at intervals.

"The young are most noisy, though the adults at the pairing time, are particularly so. All the *Spizaeti* that I know, utter very similar notes, a perfect imitator of their notes is *Edolius Paradiseus ; Cissa Sinensis* and *Garrulus Lanceolatus* sometimes imitate it finely. Many Drongoes do the same."

With reference to the above, I should remark, that Mr. Thompson furnished me with a fine series of the birds referred to, and they undoubtedly belonged to this species.

In regard to the *Spizaeti*, Mr. Blyth (Ibis, 1866,) has the following interesting remarks:

"With respect to *S. Caligatus* and *S. Alboniger* mentioned under the head of *S. Kieneri*, see Mr. Gurney's enumeration of the species of this genus, (for which he accepts the name *Spizaetus*) accompanying Mr. Gould's figure, (Birds of Asia, part

XV.) of *S. Alboniger* (*S. Borneonensis*, Gray,) I have to remark that the species common in Lower Bengal (and there the only one) is *S. Limnaetus* (*Falco Caligatus* of Raffles,) identical with the common Malayan race, similarly assuming the black plumage with full maturity, and very rarely exhibiting more than the rudiment of an occipital crest, as distinguished from *S. Cirrhatus* of other parts of India and Ceylon. The latter never attains the black plumage, and has always a long occipital crest. Horsfield's type specimen of his *Falco Limnaetus* from Java, is identical with the Bengal bird, but Professor Schlegel (Mus. P. B. *Astures*, pp. 10, 11) describes a long-crested specimen from Western Java which seems to agree with *S. Cirrhatus* of India, while his other Javan specimens are clearly *S. Limnaetus*. Even the large and very conspicuously distinguished *S. Nipalensis*, Hodgson, is considered by Professor Schlegel to be merely a variety of this *S. Cirrhatus*. Yet he discriminates *Spilornis Cheela* from *S. Bacha*, which most assuredly are less strongly characterized apart, than are *Spizaetus Nipalensis* and *S. Cirrhatus*. *S. Nipalensis* should occur rarely in the mountainous parts of Southern India, as it was obtained by the late Dr. Kelaart, at an altitude of about 4000 feet in Ceylon. Professor Schlegel notes *S. Kieneri* from the Philippines. It may be remarked, that the black, final plumage of *S. Limnaetus* is analogous to that of the North American *Archibuteo Sanctijohannis*, if not also to that of *Astur Melanoleucus*, A. Smith (Zool. S. Africa, *Aves*, pl. 18); but see Mr. Gurney's remarks (Ibis, 1864, p. 357)."

The following are Mr. Gurney's observations, which I transcribe from Mr. Gould's magnificent work.

"SPIZAETUS ALBONIGER, Blyth; *S. Borneonensis*, Gray. This very distinct species, the smallest of the Asiatic Spizaeti with which we are at present acquainted, was first described by Mr. Blyth (A. D. 1845) in the fourteenth volume of the 'Journal of the Asiatic Society of Bengal,' p. 173, in the following terms:—'A smaller species than either of those from India, measuring about 21½ inches in length; wing, 13 inches, and tail, 9½ inches; tarsus, 3 inches; occipital crest, 3¼ inches. Adult: black above, with a purple gloss; the large alars embrowned, and distinctly banded with black; tail black, with a broad, light greyish brown bar occupying about its third quarter from the base; the longer upper tail coverts have each two cross-bands of the same, lower parts pure white, with a black mesial line on throat; large intense black drops on the breast. The belly, vent, lower tail coverts, tibial plumes, and short tarsal feathers are throughout closely barred black and white;

beak black, and toes wax yellow. A younger specimen has the drops fewer and smaller on the breast, an admixture of rufous about the head. 'Several unmoulted brown feathers among the wing coverts, and one unmoulted tail feather which has three narrowish dark bars, with two or more at the base, closer and less defined: a remarkably handsome species from Malacca, the Tenasserim provinces, and Borneo.

"The following species are also found on the continent of Asia and in the adjacent islands.

"*Spizaetus Lanceolatus*, Temminck, and Schlegel, Fauna Japonica, p. 7.

" ———— *fasciolatus*, Schlegel, Museum des Pays Bas, p. 9.

Professor Schlegel, though citing the above synonym for this species, appears to doubt its being specifically distinct; it is, however, a very well-defined species, differing from *S. Albo-niger* in its larger size, in the absence of a crest, and in the strong rufous colouring of the upper portion of the breast in the adult bird. It inhabits the Celebes, and, according to the authors of the 'Fauna Japonica,' is also found in Borneo. This species, of which the British and Norwich Museums contain fine examples, brought from the Celebes by Mr. Wallace, has not yet been figured.

"*Spizaetus Kieneri*, De Sparre, Magasin de Zoologie, 1835, pl. 35 (adult).

"A specimen in immature plumage, said to have been killed on the coast of Scotland, near Aberdeen, in the year 1828, is figured in Jardine and Selby's 'Illustrations of Ornithology,' pl. 66. This species has been observed in Northern and in Central India, and it also occurs in the islands of Java and Borneo; but both there and in India, it appears to be a bird of considerable rarity.

"*Spizaetus Philippensis*. This specific name I would propose for a species of *Spizaetus* inhabiting the Philippine Islands, which appears to me to be undoubtedly distinct, though not admitted as such by Professor Schlegel, who is disposed to consider it as referable to *S. Kieneri* (Vide Museum des Pays Bas, p. 12,) an opinion in which I am unable to agree. As this *Spizaetus* is at present unfigured, I add the description of a specimen in the Norwich Museum, which I suppose to be an adult female:—

"Total length, 25 inches; wing, from carpal joint, 14$\frac{3}{4}$; tail, 11$\frac{1}{2}$; crest, 2$\frac{1}{2}$; tarsus, 3$\frac{1}{2}$; middle toe and claw 3.

"The general colour of the upper surface in this species is a dark umber brown; but the base of the feathers of the crest is white, and the margins of the other occipital feathers are of a light yellowish brown. Some of the scapulars and upper alar feathers (especially the latter) are slightly tipped with the same; the tail, which is of a somewhat lighter brown than the back, is tipped with a very narrow edging of white, and is also crossed by seven blackish brown bars, the upper one being, however, somewhat indistinct, and the two lower being separated by an interval which is twice the breadth of the spaces between the other bars. The throat has a broad blackish band running down its centre, with two similar and nearly parallel bands proceeding from the corners of the mouth, the three bands all merging in a cluster of dark brown lanceolate marks upon the upper portion of the breast, the intervals between these markings and also the whole plumage of the lower sternal and abdominal regions being tinged with a yellowish rufous; the under tail coverts are barred with brown and white, the former bars being much broader than the latter; and the thighs and tarsi are marked throughout their length with narrow equidistant transverse bars of the same colours.

" A second and apparently less adult specimen in the Norwich Museum resembles the one above described, except in the crest being less developed and in the colours generally being somewhat lighter, particularly on the head, and the markings, especially on the lower part of the tarsi, being paler and less distinct.

" *Spizaetus Nipalensis*, Hodgson. *(Here Dr. Jerdon's description &c., is quoted from the Birds of India.)*

" *Spizaetus Cirrhatus*, Gmel. This species (the common Crested Eagle of India and Ceylon) differs from S. *Nipalensis* in its somewhat smaller and much more variable size, in the paler character of the transverse markings on the abdomen and thighs, in the entire absence of the white abdominal ovate spots, and especially in the less powerful development of its talons generally, and of the inner and hinder claws in particular, these being very decidedly smaller and feebler in this species than in *S. Nipalensis*.

" *S. Cirrhatus* is figured in the Pl. Col. pl. 282, under the name of *Falco Cristatellus*.

" *Spizaetus Caligatus*, Raffles. This species is very nearly allied to the preceding (with which many Ornithologists consider it to be identical,) but appears to differ from it in the following particulars, viz., first by the non-development of the crest, which is a marked feature in most specimens of *S. Cirrhatus*, but which is entirely absent in the great majority of specimens of *S. Caligatus* and when it does appear, is much less elongated than it usually is in *S. Cirrhatus;* second, by the bill being somewhat deeper and more powerful, and the tarsi somewhat shorter, in *S. Caligatus* than in *S. Cirrhatus*, the comparison being, of course, made between individuals of equal general size; third, by the wider geographical range of *S. Caligatus*, which is found not only in India and Ceylon, but also in Burmah, the Malay Peninsula, Sumatra, Borneo, and Java; fourth, by the tendency to melanism, which is of constant occurrence in *S. Caligatus*, while in *S. Cirrhatus* such a variety is very rare. This black variety of *S. Caligatus* has been observed in Java, to be permanent and hereditary, and to be commoner in that island than the paler race. Some naturalists have indeed, considered it as specifically distinct; and such is the opinion expressed by Dr. Bernstein (a resident in Java) in a very interesting paper published in Cabanis's Journal of Ornithology, Vol. VIII. p. 417. The adult of the paler race is figured by Temminck in the Pl. Col. pl. 127, under the title of '*Falco Niveus;*' and the same work contains a figure, in pl. 134, of the dark variety, under the name of '*Falco Limnaetus;*' the latter is also figured in Horsfield's Zoological Researches in Java, Aves, pl. 3.

"In conclusion I may recapitulate the species of Asiatic *Spizaetus* which I have above enumerated, and which, in my opinion, may be considered as distinct:—

"*Spizaetus Alboniger*, Blyth; *S. Lanceolatus*, Temminck; *S. Kieneri*, De Sparre; *S. Philippensis*, nobis; *S. Nipalensis*, Hodgson; *S. Cirrhatus*, Gmelin; *S. Caligatus*, Raffles."

Dr. Jerdon remarks that he is not aware that that *S. Caligatus* (described by him under the name of *Limnætus Niveus*) occurs in Upper India. I have already put on record Mr. Thompson's remarks as to its occurrence in the Gurhwal and Babur forests, and I may note, that I have killed it myself in various portions of the Sub-Himalayan ranges, as far west as the Jumna.

No. 34(*bis*). Spizaetus Andamanensis.* Tytler.

The Andaman Hawk-Eagle.

I have never myself seen this species in a wild state, but my friend, Col. Tytler, has furnished me with the following note in regard to it.

---

* In these notes, I intend to include, where I have such by me, brief descriptions and notices of Andamanese and Cingalese species, not given in Dr. Jerdon's work.

Dimensions.	Adult Male.	Adult Female.
Length,	24·0	25·25
Expanse,	40·5	40·45
Wing,	13·75	14·25
Which primary longest,	5th	5th
Amount by which other primaries fall short of longest,	1st 4	1st 3·75
" " "	2nd 1·0	2nd 1·5
Length of tail from vent,	10·15	10·25
By how much longest tail feathers exceed shortest,	0·5	1·5
Tarsus, (feathered to feet,)	3·65	3·6
Foot, greatest length,	3·3	3·45
" " width,	3·2	2·8
Mid toe,	1·95	1·8
Its claw, along curve,	0·85	0·85
Hind toe,	1·1	1·1
Its claw, along curve,	1·1	1·1
Inner toe,	1·05	1·3
Its claw, along curve,	1·1	1·1
Bill, straight (from edge of cere),	1·2	1·23
" along curve, do.	1·37	1·4
" from gape,	1·65	1·6
" width at gape,	1·1	1·1
" height at margin of cere,	0·65	0·55
Length of cere,	0·4	0·35
Distance by which lower tail coverts fall short of end of tail,	3·8	3·9

" *Spizætus Andamanensis*, Tytler. First, male adult; head with the traces of a crest, and of a light brown colour, striped with dark brown; each feather is, for the basal three-fourths white, and one-fourth from the tip light brown with a longitudinal dark brown stripe in the centre, which gives an appearance of light brown to the head, but on the feathers being in the slightest ruffled, the head assumes an albescent appearance. Back, wings and tail brown, but from the greater portion of the base of each feather being white or light brown, the upper surface of the bird assumes a mottled appearance of brown and white, the brown being darkest in the centre of the back, quill feathers and tail. The greatest portion of the inner web of the quill feathers is white, which gives a white appearance to the under surface of the wing which is most striking when the bird is flying. The primaries are dark towards their points, but all the wing feathers are more or less conspicuously banded with four or five dark brown bars. This is also the case with the feathers of the tail. All the under surface is white, streaked with longitudinal brown marks on the breast, flanks and centre of abdomen. Some of the under wing coverts have three or four dark brown bands, and immediately under the bend the feathers of the wing are streaked with rufous; this is also the case with the thighs and some of the lower tail coverts, and white feathers of the densely feathered tarsus. The toes are yellowish, with black claws; cere greenish slaty; bill dark blackish slaty; irides, dark reddish brown. The two outermost lateral tail feathers, when observed from beneath have a very albescent appearance, with dark dots near the tips, and traces of spots of the same colour at intervals going towards the base.

"Two female adults very similar to the last, but the markings on the lower wing coverts are more, and those on the abdomen less numerous than in No. 1; but the thighs and tarsi are richly banded with rufous brown, and white.

"These birds are not uncommon amongst the mangrove swamps of the Andamans; but I have never seen them soaring, or even flying about, until disturbed. They are with great difficulty obtained, for it is impossible for a boat to approach them in such situations, and equally so to get at them by land, for the mangrove trees grow in the water, and when the tide goes out, the soil is too soft to bear the weight of a man, so I found it very difficult to procure specimens of this by no means uncommon bird. I have never seen more than one or two together. The Andaman bird is considerably smaller than the Indian *S. Limnætus* to which is bears a striking resemblance."

Capt. Beavan had the following remarks on this species in the Ibis for 1867 :—

"This species was originally described in the 'Proceedings' of the Asiatic Society of Bengal for 1865, p. 112. The following description is taken from specimens in Col. Tytler's collection.

Length,	25·5 in.	Wing,	13·5 in.	Tarsus,	3·5 in.	Tail	10·25 in.
„	24·5 „	„	13·5 „	„	3·5 „	„	10·25
„	23·12 „	„	14 „	„	3·75 „	„	18·25

"Bill and claws, slaty horn coloured; legs feathered to the toes, which latter are of a dirty yellow colour. The tail usually has seven transverse bars of a darker hue than the rest. The general colour of the bird is creamy white, somewhat inclining to rufous on the head, upper tail coverts, and interior of thighs. The wings, tail, and lower nape are brown, the head in some specimens is slightly marked with longitudinal brown striæ, and the under wing coverts of all, spotted with the same. This species will probably be classed next to *Spizactus Limnactus* of

Lower Bengal and the Burmese countries, from which, however, it differs conspicuously in the colour of the plumage."

The specimens that I have seen, were minatures of *S. Caligatus*, except that the heads, necks and under parts, were nearly spotless yellowish white, a sign doubtless of nonage. There *were* spots and dark central stripes, but they were few and far between. The tails had broad, dark brown, subterminal bands, narrowly tipped with yellowish white and besides these four (*not* seven, as in those described by Capt. Beavan,) broad, transverse dark brown bars.

Is it possible that this species should be identical with *S. Lanceolatus*, Bp. Consp. Av. I. p. 28, of which Wallace gives the Celebes and Sula Islands as the habitat? The dimensions are not very dissimilar.

No. 35. **Spizaetus Cirrhatus,** Gmel.

The Crested Hawk-Eagle.

I know nothing of the nidification of this species, nor am I likely I fear to do so, until observers generally learn to discriminate it better.

With the exception of 4 specimens recently received from Mr. R. Thompson, every skin yet sent me as belonging to *S. Cirrhatus* (*S. Cristatellus*, Tem.) has proved on close examination to pertain to *S. Nipalensis.*

Blyth as already quoted (No. 34. q. v.) tells us, that "even the large and very conspicuously distinguished *S. Nipalensis*, Hodgson, is considered by Professor Schlege, to be merely a variety of his *Cirrhatus*." Had Schlegel said that *Nipalensis* was only the adult of the bird commonly received as *Cirrhatus*, he would have been perfectly correct. I have seen, and possessed specimens, of the so-called *Cirrhatus*, from Ceylon, the Puchmurree Hills, Etawah and Kumaon, and these were all unmistakeably immature examples of *L. Nipalensis*, as was proved by comparing them with young ones captured in the Himalayas, whose parents were known and whose nests had been watched.

Dr. Jerdon has not described the young of *Spizaetus Nipalensis.* This I have done at length, and my descriptions and measurements will I hope throw some light upon the matter.

It is these immature *Nipalensis* that are always mistaken for *Cirrhatus*; the mature birds no one, who knows *both* species

(Prof. Schlegel must excuse me, but it is a fact,) can possibly confound together.

In *Cirrhatus*, the upper surface of the adult is considerably lighter than in *Nipalensis*, and the feathers, of the head, nape, and upper back are *comparatively* light brown, centred more or less broadly, with dark brown ; while in the adult *Nipalensis* there is scarcely a trace of paler edgings in the feathers of the head, and none in those of the upper back. In *Cirrhatus*, the cheeks, and ear coverts are pale brown, each feather with a very narrow central dark brown stripe, while in the same parts in *Nipalensis*, the blackish central stripes occupy nearly the whole feather. In *Cirrhatus*, the breast and upper abdomen are pure white, each feather with a huge broad, dark brown central stripe on the terminal half. The whole of the lower abdomen, vent, lower tail coverts, sides, flanks, and tibial plumes are nearly uniform umber brown, without in the *adult*, even a trace of white mottling. In *Nipalensis* on the other hand the whole of the breast, except the extreme upper portion, the sides, flanks, abdomen, vent, lower tail coverts, and tibial plumes, are deep umber brown, paling on the abdomen and towards the vent, every where broadly, regularly and conspicuously, transversely barred with white; the bars being broadest and least numerous on the sides and body, and narrowest and most numerous on the tibiæ. The axillaries of the fully adult *Cirrhatus* are of a pale umber brown slightly darker towards the centre, without a trace of bar or mottling, while the axillaries of *Nipalensis* are broadly and conspicuously barred with white.

The crests in these two species are excessively similar ; quite as long in one as in the other, both black and more or less conspicuously tipped with white, but really, with this exception, no two birds of the same genus, can well be more unlike each other than are the perfect adults of *Cirrhatus* and *Nipalensis*.

I should mention also another difference which will I think be found constant ; viz. in the bandings of the tail. In *Cirrhatus* and *Limnaetus*, the space between the broad terminal bar and the next one is always considerably broader than the terminal bar itself, while the succeeding bars are generally narrower than the interspaces. In *Nipalensis* on the other hand the first space is narrower, or, at any rate, not broader, than the terminal band, while the succeeding spaces are narrower than the bars. Moreover there is a greater contrast in colour between the bars and interspaces and a somewhat sharper definition of these in *Nipalensis*, than in the other two species.

From the adult of *Caligatus*, *Cirrhatus* is at once distinguished by the long, black white edged, or in some only white tipped, crest. A rudimentary crest, more or less elongated, is doubtless met with in some specimens of *Caligaetus*, but it is never more than half the length of that of *Cirrhatus*, and very frequently altogether wanting.

The young of *Cirrhatus* undoubtedly closely resemble those of *Nipalensis*. But where the sexes have been ascertained, the much greater size of the wing would alone enable us certainly to separate the birds. In *Cirrhatus*, the wing of the female, averages according to my experience, 17·62, while in no instance have I found the wing to exceed 18 inches; the male appears to have the wing on an average 16·5. The smallest male *Nipalensis* that I possess, or have measured, measured 17·75, and I have now in my Museum a female, whose wing measures 19·5.

Besides the difference in size, there is another little difference which appears to me to be constant and which would alone enable us to separate either *Cirrhatus* or *Caligatus* at *any* stage, from *Nipalensis*. I say appears to me, because I have only had an opportunity of closely examining nine specimens of *Nipalensis*, six of *Cirrhatus*, and about a dozen of *Caligatus*. In all these, the distinction I am about to point out held good; whether it does so universally is for other ornithologists to determine. In *Cirrhatus* and *Caligatus*, the feathering of the foot ends, more or less, above the division of the toes. In some specimens fully an eighth of an inch of the foot is left bare, in others the feathering especially of the centre portion of the foot, comes down all but level with the division of the toes. In *Nipalensis* on the other hand, the feathering runs distinctly down the middle toe, reaching furthest down exteriorly; so that in some specimens fully, and in all nearly, one-half of the outer portion of the first joint, of the mid toe, is plumed.

Admitting that the young of both *Nipalensis* and *Cirrhatus* do generally so resemble each other, that, although the practised eye will at once separate specimens, it is difficult to express the difference by any verbal descriptions, I yet think that the difference in size, coupled with the difference of the pluming of the feet, just noticed, is sufficient to enable even a tyro to discriminate between them.

To some practised ornithologists, this detailed demonstration that *Cirrhatus* and *Nipalensis are* different, will seem superfluous and they may be tempted to exclaim in Cornish fashion "Who said they wor'nt! do you wish to argue, you beggar?" but I can assure them, that in India, the majority of our field ornithologists, not only fail to discriminate between the young of *Cirrhatus* and *Nipalensis*, but actually disbelieve (as I did at one time myself) in the existence of any distinct species, *S. Cristatellus* vel *Cirrhatus*.

I cannot here do better than quote the remarks of Mr. R. Thompson, who, without any communication on this subject with me, scarcely a year ago sent me the following—

"Jerdon does not give a description of the young state of *L. Nipalensis*, but from his description of the early and later state of *L. Cristatellus*, (*S. Cirrhatus*,) I am inclined to think that he has mistaken *L. Nipalensis* for it; any how, his descriptions hold correct for the young and somewhat later stages of *L. Nipalensis*. The long occipital crest nearly five inches long, deep black, tipped with white, is exactly it. The *L. Niveus* (*S. Caligatus*) though sometimes with the crest, has it not so long, nor is it black, but a dark brown, edged on the upper margin with earthy white. Jerdon's description of the young state of *L. Cristatellus* is positively precise with the actual state of the young *L. Nipalensis*, excepting that beneath, this latter is not pure white, but a very light rusty with some few black centre markings."

"Last year I obtained two authenticated live specimens of the young *L. Nipalensis*. Photographs of these birds were sent to Mr. Hume. I have now a live one in the second stage of plumage, which would agree with Jerdon's adult *L. Cristatellus* only that it is very light ferruginous below, instead of pure white, as in adults of the *L. Niveus*." Later, Mr. Thompson after further opportunities of observation, altered his opinion and writing from Jubbulpoor in May 1869, he says, "I have got a couple of skins of *Limnaetus Cristatellus*, just as Dr. Jerdon describes it and I feel with him that the two races (*L. Niveus* and *Cristatellus*) are distinct. The cries of both birds are precisely similar and no ordinary observation would enable one to point out where the difference lies; but this, as Dr. J. says, will be found in the long black crest pointed white, which is always present. I have seen several, all with the black, white tipped, full crest. I only found one nest, which contained a half fledged young one, which I took and kept for some days till the heat killed it. Young as it was, the little wretch used to seize and clutch hard a chicken offered to it."

Mr. R. Thompson also says, "*S. Caligatus* is the bird which holds sway in the lower forests. In the Himalayas it is succeeded by *S. Nipalensis;* but in the more open country in the lower plains, there occurs a small semi-crested Eagle, the minature of *S. Caligatus*, which Jerdon nowhere describes. My specimen was shot in the act of feeding on a grey horn bill which it had chased and killed. It was not *Astur Trivirgatus*. It had the tarsi well feathered to the toes. The skin was sent home."

Can this bird be the *F. Lathami* of Tickell, referred to by Jerdon? and is this by any chance *S. Nanus* of Wallace, Ibis, 1868, page 14? I wish some one would procure and send me specimens of this supposed dwarf Hawk Eagle. It has been repeatedly mentioned to me by sportsmen, but I have never felt sure that the young of *Hieraetus Pennatus* was not really what they referred to, although when shown specimens of this, I have on two occasions been told, that their bird had shorter wings and a longer tail.

It is noteworthy that Blyth remarks, that *Cirrhatus* never attains the black plumage. Wallace, however, who gives as habitats of the species, Java, Penang, Sumatra, and Borneo, says, "My specimen from Java is nearly black, and that from Penang very white underneath."

To judge, however, from his synonymes, he refers to the species which I have given as *S. Caligatus*, and it may happen, that the *Cirrhatus* of some authors, is no other than *S. Caligatus*, while of other and specially Indian authors, the *Cirrhatus* is only the young of *Nipalensis*.

No. 36. **Spizaetus Nipalensis**, Hodgson.

Hodgson's Hawk Eagle.

This beautiful species breeds, as far as I yet *know*, only in the Himalayas, laying during March, April, and the early part of May.

Its nest, a large coarse stick structure, is placed upon some large tree, either hidden in a dense forest, or projecting from the face of some inaccessible cliff.

It lays two eggs I think as a rule, but single eggs are often found much incubated.

Although I have, in former years, seen several of its nests, the only specimen that I now possess of the eggs of this species I owe to Capt. Hutton. In shape it is a broad regular oval, almost symmetrical at both ends. The shell is coarse, dull and glossless, the ground colour a slightly greenish white, spotted thinly with reddish brown, and with numerous large blotches and streaks of very pale inky purple. It measures 3·78 by 2·23.

My friend, Capt. Hutton, favours me with the following note:

"This species is common at Mussoorie and occurs also during winter in the Doon; at Mussoorie it is a permanent resident, and most destructive to pigeons, fowls and game; its loud shrill musical whistle may often be heard far up in the heavens even when the bird itself is lost to sight. It breeds at about 5,500 feet of elevation, constructing a thick basket-like nest of twigs and small branches, placed on a lofty tree often growing out of the fissure of a rock overhanging a precipice, which is apt to turn the head of any but a mountaineer, and to look into which reminds one of the bottomless pit! Nevertheless we have on more than one occasion contrived to rob the nest. One of these was found on the 5th of March and contained one egg, which was left for the purpose of ascertaining whether the bird would lay another. A few days afterwards, on finding no addition, a man ascended the tree which was of tolerably easy access and the old bird making no warlike demonstration, the prize was secured. On attempting to clean it, however, it was found to contain a fully formed young bird. On another occasion we did not rob a nest so easily. It was found on the 18th March, and contained two eggs, which were left to hatch. On the 1st of April, the nest was again visited and found to contain two youug ones covered with a rufous coloured down; on the 16th April, finding that one young one had fallen from the nest, preparations were made for lowering a man down the precipice to the root of the tree, which leaned ominously out of a cleft in the rock obliquely overhanging an awful chasm. On reaching the tree, the man began to ascend, but before he had reached the nest, one of the old birds made a dash at him, and struck him sharply on the shoulder, causing the blood to flow. Nothing daunted, the man proceeded on his perilous course, under cover of one or two shots from above to scare the old birds away; but without the desired effect, for on the man's arrival at the nest, another charge was made by the female who struck the poor fellow on the head and again caused blood to flow, but luckily the man's greasy linen skull-cap became firmly fixed upon the talons of the bird, which scared her to such a degree, that uttering a loud scream of alarm she sailed away, rapidly followed by her mate, and the young one was then brought in safety from the nest. It was nearly half fledged with small slaty coloured feathers, and grew to maturity in a large roomy cage, when it was set at liberty, and after hanging about the place to be fed for several days, finally took unto itself the wings of the morning and disappeared. These birds sometimes breed in the same nest for two or three years, and apparently only abandon it when it becomes old and rotten, when they select another tree whereon to construct a new habitation at no great distance from the other."

Mr. R. Thompson says "I have always found two young with

this bird, which is the most beautiful Hawk of the kind we have. He is great at poultry, when living in the vicinity of a station. I have caught them regularly with the vertical net. On an Oak tree on the Ayarpatta hill, a pair bred this year, the result, two young ones. I have not seen their eggs. The notes of this bird are similar to those of *S. Caligatus*.

I once saw one fly at some wild Kalij Pheasants. The difference in habits between this bird and *S. Caligatus* is this. The one is generally confined to the deep wooded hills ascending far into the interior of the Himalayas to almost the snow line, feeds much on Pheasants, Hares, Black Partridge, Monaul and Cheer Pheasants, and sometimes on young Deer. Whereas the other, *S. Caligatus*, is always found in the Bhabur forests and *does not* ascend the hills to any great height, and *never* is found in the interior of them. It chiefly lives on Pea-hens, Jungle Fowl, Partridge and Hares, and I have seen it kill and eat a full grown Civet Cat. I have also seen young birds watching and taking Rats near corn stacks in the Bhabur cultivated tracts, and more than once, have seen one dash into a tree in which a lot of Parrakeets were assembled for the night, and take a bird. I might sum up with the following:

" *S. Nipalensis* is a shy forest bird, not at all common except in suitable localities, and even there, more than a single couple are rarely seen. *S. Caligatus* is a common, bold bird, found in very many localities, and in the hills entirely confined to the very outside range of the Himalayas. I saw one the other day in South Mirzapore."

I subjoin exact measurements of four specimens, three young and one adult, and I would remark that one matter which may have contributed to lead some observers to class young specimens of *Nipalensis* as *Cirrhatus*, is the excessive variability of dimensions in the former species. To give an instance of this I would refer to the measurements of No. 3; here the inner toe claw is given as 2·63. Looking through the measurements, this struck me as excessive, and I had the very specimen brought out of the Museum. On measuring the claw in question on one foot, the original measurement proved correct, *but* the corresponding claw of the other foot measured only 2·1. Testing other figures, and the measurements of other specimens, all of which are still in my Museum, I found similar though not such striking diversities, in corresponding parts of the same birds. This may explain the extraordinary discrepancies in the following dimensions, all of which were *carefully* recorded at the time; I may mention that I have a larger specimen than any of these; a female with the wing 19·5, but no measurements are recorded of this.

	Young.			Adult.
	No. 1 Male.	No. 2 Female.	No. 3 Female.	No. 4 Female.
Length,	27·5	29·0	28·5	29·25
Expanse,	51·0	55·0	54·0	56·0
Wing,	17·87	18·3	18·87	18·5
Which primary longest,	5th	4th & 5th	5th	5th
Amt. by which other primaries fall,	1st 4·0	5·4	5·8	5·7
" " " short of longest,	2nd 1·5	2·3	2·9	2·7
" " " " ...	3rd 0·6	0·95	1·15	1·3
Length of tail from vent,	12·75	12·75	13·5	12·63
Longest tail feathers exceed shortest,	0·9	1·0	......	1·0
Tarsus,	4·2	3·7	3·75	4·4
Foot, greatest length,	6·4	7·25	6·87	6·6
" width,	5·75	5·5	5·19	5·13
Mid toe,	2·13	2·25	2·88	2·25
Its claw, along curve,	1·44	1·44	1·25	1·37
Hind toe,	1·3	1·37	1·37	1·25
Its claw, along curve,	1·87	2·13	2·05	2·25
Inner toe,	1·24	1·37	1·25	1·37
Its claw, along curve,	1·69	2·0	2·63	2·17
Bill, straight, from edge of cere, ...	1·2	1·2	1·18	1·3
" along curve, ditto,	1·41	1·44	1·25	1·5
" from gape,	1·62	1·72	1·6	1·9
" width at gape,	1·28	1·22	1·33	1·1
" height at margin of cere,	0·65	0·72	0·7	0·7
Length of cere (if any),	0·36	0·43	0·35	0·4
Lower tail coverts fall short of end of tail,	5·75	6·4	6·4	6·25
Longest crest feather,	4·2	4·0	3·5	4·5

No. 1, a young male, shot on the 17th November, had the bill black; the cere, hoary black; the irides, yellow; the feet, dirty yellowish white. The whole of the head, back and sides of the neck, and ear coverts, rufous buff, each feather with a narrow dark brown central stripe, a long, conspicuous, occipital crest, black, narrowly tipped with white; scapulars and inter scapulary region, hair brown, the feathers paling at the margins, and towards their bases to a pale wood brown; rump and upper tail coverts, dingy somewhat rufous wood brown; central tail feathers, a sort of olive brown, very narrowly tipped with white, with a one inch subterminal, and four other half inch broad, transverse, dark brown bars. Lateral tail feathers, remains of nesting plumage, much abraded, with sandy brown grounds, and barred like the central feathers. Wing coverts, except the greater primary coverts, a rather pale wood brown, most of them, especially the smaller ones, with dark brown centres, not sharply defined, but fading into the paler margins. Most of the secondary greater coverts almost wholly white on the inner webs. Quills and primary greater coverts, umber brown, darkest on the points of the earlier primaries where it is almost black, paling to a wood brown on the tertiaries. The second to the fifth primaries with conspicuous emarginations on the outer webs, above which they are paler, and obscurely barred with dingy buff. The first five primaries conspicuously notched on the inner web; white on the under surface above the notches; below the notches greyish white, tipped, and strongly barred with blackish brown. Chin and throat spotless white, base of neck in front, breast, and abdomen, pure white, the shafts of each feather blackish brown, but only towards the tip, and the feathers either tipped with rufous buff, or with a spot of that colour near the tip. Vent feathers and lower tail coverts dingy rufous or pale rufous brown, obscurely barred with fulvous white; tarsus yellowish white with a few faint brownish spots; sides pale, more or less rufous brown, with here and there a trace of white mottling. Flanks and tibial plumes pale rufous brown, distinctly though irregularly barred with white. Axillaries pale dingy rufous with a series of double white spots or imperfect transverse bars. Wing lining white, barred, the larger lower coverts with blackish brown, the smaller ones with mingled, dingy rufous and hair, brown.

No. 2, a female, killed 1st November. In its upper plumage, it greatly resembles the preceding, but from the nostril right over the eye it had a broad stripe of buffy fawn, without any dark centres to the feathers. The feathers of the top and back of the head and nape, instead of having narrow blackish brown central stripes, had the whole centres of this colour, leaving only moderately broad rufous buff borders. The back was slightly darker brown, as were also the wings and rump; the longest upper tail coverts were narrowly tipped with white and showed traces of one or two transverse white bars higher up. The central tail feathers were wood brown *without a trace of any bars*, and on the lateral tail feathers which were a dingy umber brown, the dark brown bars so conspicuous in No. 1 were obscure and almost obsolete. The crest is slightly fuller and the white tipping broader. The cheeks, ear-coverts and sides of the neck have a more spotty and less lineated appearance than in the preceding bird. The chin and throat is a pure pale buff, or rufous white with the faintest trace of a dark brown line down the centre. The upper part of the breast is rufous or buffy white, each feather with a conspicuous linear ovate central brown stripe. Lower breast, abdomen, vent, and tibial plumes, sides and axillaries, a sort of pale rufous buff, salmon coloured on the axillaries. Two feathers on the abdomen and one or two on the flanks a wood brown, each with two rather conspicuous fulvous white transverse bars. The axillaries and the rest of the lower parts above mentioned are entirely unbarred and unspotted, except the tibial plumes which here and there contained brown feathers with obscure rufous white transverse bands. Tarsus, fulvous white, with a few pale rufous brown spots, lower tail coverts pale, slightly rufous, brown, with conspicuous broad transverse fulvous white bars. Wing lining rufous white with only a few small brown spots towards the ends of the longer ones.

No. 3, a female, shot December 15th, in its general upper plumage is intermediate between No. 1 and No. 2, but the tail is yellowish brown with one terminal and six other broad, transverse, umber brown bars, the terminal being no broader than the others. Underneath, the bird closely resembles No. 2, but, there is no trace of a central throat stripe and only some dozen feathers of quite the upper breast, have narrow, central, dark brown stripes. Per contra, the sides and an irregular broad band, across the abdomen have the feathers pale wood brown, with well marked broad transverse, whitish bars. The barrings on the lower tail coverts and tibial plumes are very obscure, mere nothings. The wing lining, axillaries &c. correspond with No. 2.

These three are all of known parentage, undeniable specimens of *S. Nipalensis*, shot in the interior of Kumaon, near Mussourie and above Kotegurh, and might easily, so far as general appearance goes, be mistaken for *S. Cirrhatus*. The extreme variability of the tail markings is remarkable.

The fully adult female, No. 4, has the whole top of the head, nape, ear coverts, cheeks and sides of the neck blackish brown, in some lights almost black. The feathers especially of the hind head and sides of the neck, narrowly margined with rufous fawn, and the bases of the feathers of the same colour more or less tinged with brown, showing through a good deal, here and there. The scapulars and back, are deep umber brown. The larger scapulars, with traces of broad, darker brown transverse bars and the longer upper tail coverts narrowly tipped with white, and with broad and conspicuous transverse white bars. The tail very narrowly tipped with white, with a greyish brown ground, a very broad subterminal, and four other broad transverse deep brown bands; the fourth lost under the upper tail coverts, and the bars being considerably broader than the interspaces. The chin and throat, fulvous white; base of the neck in front, and upper breast a mixture of brownish and fulvous white, the feathers broadly centred with blackish brown, so broadly towards the sides as to have only a narrow margin of the paler colour. The lower part of the breast, abdomen, vent, sides, flanks, axillaries, tibial and tarsal plumes, and lower tail coverts, brown of various shades; in some places yellower, in others more of an umber tint, with conspicuous, transverse, white, or fulvous white bars, narrowest and closest on the tibial plumes, broadest and furthest apart on the sides. Larger lower wing coverts white, broadly banded with blackish brown; lesser lower wing coverts, buffy white, broadly barred with somewhat buffy brown.

No. 37. **Spizaetus Kieneri,** DeSparre.

The Rufous-Belled Hawk-Eagle.

Nothing is known of the nidification of this species, I myself have never even seen a specimen.

Mr. R. Thompson, (whom I look to for specimens) remarks, "I enter this bird here because I have seen it come in at the end of April and remain for some time on the lower well wooded hills.

It has a rapid and elegant flight, mounts well, better than *S. Caligatus* or *S. Nipalensis*, which soar very awkwardly. Its cry is also somewhat different from the latter, and resembles a chirrup more than a clear metallic note."

Mr. Wallace has the following brief note on this species (Ibis 1868).

"Spizætus Kieneri, Gervais, Mag. de Zools. 1835, Ois. pl. 35; Schleg. Mus. P. B. Astures, p. 11.

Hab. Borneo (Wall.); Philippines? (Mus. Lugd.); India (Jerdon).

I obtained a single specimen of this small Eagle in Borneo. It had seized a Pigeon, which it was devouring when I shot it. Wing, 13 inches, the point, 4 inches; tail, 7·5 inches; tarsus, 2·5 inches; middle toe, 1·625 inch; inner toe, 1 inch."

No. 38. **Circaetus Gallicus,** GMEL.

THE SHORT-TOED EAGLE.

The Short-toed Eagle lays in the plains of Upper India in January, February, and March, and, according to Mr. R. Thompson, in April and May in the Gurhwal forests.

As a rule, its nest is placed on trees, but on two occasions in the Etawah district, we have found this species breeding on small platforms, in the face of the high clay cliffs of the Jumna.

In different localities, it varies in its choice of trees; where trees are plentiful, it will build on the topmost boughs of a very tall one, while in the bare country, in Hurriana, and in Western Rajpootana, you will find the nest not half way up some stunted Neem tree, or scraggy thorny *Acacia*, a mere apology for a tree.

The nest is a large circular stick structure, some two to three feet in diameter and from six inches to a foot in depth, externally very loose and straggling, but composed of rather slighter materials than *Fulvescens* generally uses, and with a rather deeper internal depression.

Some nests are entirely devoid of lining, rather finer twigs compose the floor of the internal depression and on these the egg reposes. Some nests again have the egg *bedded* in straw and grass, positively as if packed to travel; under some I have found a few green leaves spread, after the fashion of Bonelli's Eagle, and under many, a little grass. There appears to be no rule in this matter, season does not affect the question, nor, as far as I can see, locality; in the early part of January, and late in March, in the Agra and Sirsa districts, and in the far west beyond Jodhpoor, I have observed the same diversities in the "internal arrangements" of the nests.

I have taken a great number of the nests of this species, and many of my friends have found them also, but in no instance out of between forty and fifty recorded cases, did any of us meet with more than a single egg in the same nest.

The eggs of this bird are typically broad ovals with a slightly pyriform tendency. They are of a pale bluish white colour; bluer than those of any other of our Indian species of Eagle, and are, to judge from a very large series, invariably spotless: moreover they seldom appear to be discoloured during the process of incubation in the way most other Eagles' eggs are. In my whole collection, only one egg is in any way as small as that figured by Dr. Bree, and more than one are all but as large as the egg of the bald Eagle figured on the same page. The colour of the shell in this species when held up to the light is a peculiarly bright sap green, very different from the deep green of *Haliœtus Leucoryphus*, or the sea green of *Fulvescens*. In size they vary from 2·65 to 3·15 in length and from 2·05 to 2·45 in breadth, but of twenty eggs measured the average was 2·91 by 2·31.

When deprived of their egg, the short-toed Eagles, will hang for weeks about their desolated homestead, but apparently they never lay a second time, as many other species do.

Mr. W. Blewitt informs me, that he took nine nests of this bird in the neighbourhood of Hansie between the 18th January and the 26th February and four between the 6th and 26th of March, some of the eggs were fresh, some more or less incubated; but no nest contained more than a single egg. Eleven of the nests were on Keekur (*Acacia Arabica*) trees, one on a Jhand (*Prosopis spicigna*) tree and one on a Seeshum (*Dalbergia Seesoo.*) The nests were placed at heights varying from fourteen to twenty-two feet from the ground.

They were composed of twigs of the Keekur (*Acacia Arabica*), Kheyr (*Acacia Catechu*) native plum, (*Zyzyphus Jujube*). They varied in diameter from fourteen to twenty-four inches, excluding straggling ends, and in thickness from four to eight inches. Some were slightly and loosely put together, others were very densely and closely constructed. Most of them appeared to have no lining; but three were thinly lined with straw, two with leaves and one with fine grass.

Mr. G. Marshall, R. E., writes to me—

"Of this bird I have found but one nest. I found it on the 13th of March with one egg, and left it till the 6th April, in hopes that more would be laid, and when I took it at last, it was rather hard set, so that probably the bird lays but one egg. The nest was in a Seeshum tree, so high up among the smaller branches that I reached it with difficulty; it was made of twigs and so loose in structure, that I could see that there was only one egg from below, before I had reached the nest. The egg was well shaped and pure dull white."

Mr. R. Thompson writing from Gurhwal says that the situation of the nest is "usually on the highest branches of a tall tree, in a moderately wooded country, and mostly in one standing by itself." He adds: "Breeds in the Patla Dhoon, and all along the lower open forests. During the pairing season, utters a loud and plaintive cry, usually when the pair are mounted high in the air, when they may be observed tumbling about and darting at each other in a most remarkable manner."

In Mr. Salvin's "Bird-nesting in the Eastern Atlas" we have the following:

"The first nest of this species we obtained, was brought from Blad el Ghua, a village to the south of Djebel Kekma; it contained two eggs, both of which had been incubated sometime, so that the long bare tarsi and large eyes of the embryo left little doubt as to the identity of the species. Of these eggs, one had slight indications of colouring; a feature I have never observed in other specimens. The eggs are usually deposited in March; but some birds defer laying till April. The Arabs call this bird 'White Eagle.'"

Mr. Tristram in his ornithology of Palestine (Ibis, 1865) remarks.—

"In its breeding habits it varies, choosing generally some low ledge in a wady, but sometimes also building a great platform of sticks in the top of a large Oak or Terebinth. The first egg we took was in a wady on Carmel, on March 23rd, quite fresh, the second in a wady near Heshbon, east of the Dead Sea, on April 30th, equally fresh; after which we obtained several others, not yet incubated, so late as to the 10th of May. One egg we took was prettily spotted, all the others were white. On one occasion, the sitting bird we shot from the nest was ascertained by dissection to be a male. In Africa, I have found two eggs in the nest, but in Palestine we never found more than one. The same rule seems to hold throughout all the Raptors, that wherever the species is abundant, the number of young is proportionally fewer than when the individuals are scarce."

As I have already remarked, when speaking of another species, I rather question, this plausible little generalization with which the most charming of all ornithological writers, rounds off the above passage. The short-toed Eagle is certainly scarcer in the south of France than in the north of Africa, so that if there are two eggs in the latter place, to one in Palestine and India, there ought surely to be three in the former locality. The best account, however, that I can find of the nidification of this species in the south of France is that quoted by Bree. 'Dr. Alexander Savatier wrote to me from Beauvais, Sur Matha, (Charente-inférieure) "I have killed on its nest, in a forest in our neighbourhood, a female of Jean-le-Blanc. This nest was placed upon a very high tree, it was sixty or seventy centimetres in diameter; it was composed of dry twigs; it only contained one egg, half sat upon. It was May the 16th. The shell was a dirty white and rugose. The peasants assured me, they had seen other nests always with only one egg, and that this was never spotted."

I have noticed that this bird may often be seen soaring high over a nearly dry jheel, then descending and hovering from place to place almost like a Kestril, but with a scarcely perceptible movement of the wings. When on the wing they are readily distinguished, by the white, slightly spotted or barred under surface, and broad rounded wings.

When they come down on their prey, they drop on it softly and silently, and not with a rush like the *Fulviventer*, or *Imperialis*. The feet are covered with Armadillo-like scales, of which a few seem to be shed from time to time; new ones (at first of a pure pearly white) growing up from below to replace them. The bird by its enormous head and eyes, and huge ear holes, and by its inner toe claw larger than any of the others; small cere and comparatively silent flight, reminds one much of the larger Owls.

Although this present species extends, according to Mr. Wallace, as far east as Timor and Floris, and is found throughout India, Syria, and the south of Europe as well as in the north of Africa, this latter continent is par excellence, the head quarters of the dry plains-loving *Circacti*. Besides *C. Gallicus*, *C. Pectoralis*, *Zonurus*, *Fasciolatus* and *Beaudoni* are enumerated by Verreaux from various parts of Africa, and I have seen subsequently notices of two other distinct species, whose names I have unfortunately forgotten.

Dr Jerdon's measurements strike me as too large to represent average examples. I subjoin measurements recorded from fresh birds, of which Nos. 1 and 2 were old birds, Nos. 3 and 5, two-year old, and No. 4 a yearling.

	Length.	Expanse.	Tail.	Wings fall short of tail by	Weight.	Wing.
No. 1 Female,......	29·5	76·5	13·25	1·25	4 lbs.	22·5
No. 2 Female,......	27·25	70·0	12·25	1·13	4 lbs.	21·5
No. 3 Male,.........	25·75	70·0	11·75	0·25	3 lbs.	20·8
No. 4 Y. Female, ..	27·69	71·0	12·0	0·0	2·5 lbs.	21·25
No. 5 Female,......	27·75	70·0	?	0·5	3·25 lbs.	21·0

I will add detailed measurements and descriptions of two other females, the one No. 6, a very old, the other No. 7, quite a young bird; in weight they differed vastly, in linear dimensions very little.

No. 6, an old female, shot 23rd February. No. 7, young female, shot 26th February.

Dimensions (those first given are of No. 6, the second ones those of No. 7.)

Length, 28·75-27·5. Expanse, 68-69. Weight in lbs., 4·19-2·81. Wing, 20·75-20·63. In both, the 3rd and 4th primaries were the longest, and these exceeded the first primary by 5·63-4·63; and the second by 1-1·25. Length of tail from vent, 12-12·25. Tarsus (feathered in front for I inch) 3·69-3·69. Foot, greatest length, 5-4·88; greatest width, 4·75-4·38; mid toe to root of claw, 2·19-2·06; its claw along curve, 1·38-1·19; hind toe, 1·13-1, its claw, along curve, 1·5-1·19; inner toe, 1·72-1·7, its claw, along curve 1·56-1·53. Bill including cere, from forehead to point, straight, 1·88-1·75; along curve, 2·5-2·25; from gape, 2·5-2·25; width at gape, 1·81-1·69; height at front, at margin of cere, 0·88-0·81; length of cere on culmen, 0·44-0·5. In both, the wings when closed reach to within 0·5 of end of tail; and the lower tail coverts to within 4·25 of end of tail.

Description of No. 6.

The legs and feet are a pale earthy greyish brown, covered with prominent, sharp-edged, armour plate, overlapping, loose-looking, hexagonal scales. Three large scales at the end of each toe, the upper generally divided, claws black, inner edge of middle one, conspicuously dilated into a cutting edge.

Irides, bright orange yellow; orbits thickly covered with white down.

Bill, pale greyish blue at base, blackish horny at tips; cere which is small, whitish, with a tinge of bluish grey in places.

Tongue large, fleshy, hastate, obtuse ended.

The forehead, lores, chin and patch on each side of lower mandible whitish, and, except on the forehead, with black, naked, much prolonged, bristle-like shafts. The whole top and back of head, throat, neck all round, back, rump, upper tail coverts, scapulars, and upper wing coverts, except primary greater coverts, a sort of earthy brown, of more shades than one; the throat and neck in front being the palest and most fulvous, (all the feathers conspicuously dark-shafted,) and the scapulars (the longest of which are a dark, almost umber, brown) and mid back the darkest. Many of the feathers especially of the back of the neck, and lesser wing coverts inconspicuously margined paler. Winglet, primaries and their greater coverts, a dark brown, but the primaries from the 2nd to the 6th emarginate on the outer webs and with a greyish shade on the outer web above the emarginations. First three primaries conspicuously notched, and the 4th and 5th with a trace of similar notches on the inner webs, which in all five are nearly wholly white above the said notches. The later primaries and the secondaries, (the brown of which latter pales as they recede from the primaries, until, like the tertials, they are nearly concolourous with their coverts) with half the inner webs diagonally white; and with four conspicuous, broad, dark brown, transverse bars.

In the new feathers, the white runs as a narrow band round the tip, and the transverse bars are obscurely visible on the outer, as well as the inner webs; all the tail feathers are white at the base; but this is hid, except in the lateral ones, by the upper tail coverts; all are narrowly tipped with white; all have a broad subterminal, and two other conspicuous, transverse, dark brown bars. The ground colour of the whole of the central feathers is pale brown, but in the lateral feathers, nearly the whole ground of the inner web is pure white, and in the exterior feather, more than the basal one-fourth is white on the outer web also. The bars decrease slightly in width and strength, as the feathers recede from the centre.

There is an inconspicuous blackish brown supercilium, and a good deal of faint blackish brown is mingled in the ear coverts. The whole breast, sides, abdomen, thigh coverts, lower tail and wing coverts pure white, each feather with a broad subterminal bar, (or in some of the wing coverts, spot,) of pale earthy brown. The axillaries are similar, but have two or even three of the brown transverse bars.

Description of No. 7.

Feet and legs almost a pearl grey, irides a gamboge yellow. The whole of the head, chin, throat, and neck all round is white, but all the feathers have the shafts, a sort of fulvous brown; there is a little dusky and fulvous mingled with the ear coverts, and many of the feathers of the back of the neck, and most of those at the base of the same all round, are tinged at the tips with fawn colour or pale fulvous brown. The breast, abdomen, thigh coverts, sides, axillaries, lower wing, and tail coverts are pure white, not a few of the feathers, however, having inconspicuous, subterminal, transverse bands of a sort of fawn, or pale fulvous brown. The rest of the bird is much as in the adult, but everywhere of a lighter shade; there are only two or at most three bars on the inner webs of the last five primaries and the secondaries, and these are much less conspicuous, and feebler than in the adult. On the tail, the white tipping and broad dark subterminal band are barely to be traced; while the other bars ure feebler than in the adult.

No. 39. **Spilornis Cheela,** DAUDIN.

THE CRESTED SERPENT EAGLE.

This very handsome bird, which should perhaps more properly stand as the Indian Harrier Eagle, breeds throughout the

Sub-Himalayan ranges and regions, as far west at any rate as Kangra, at heights of from 2500 to 5500 above the sea level, laying in March, April and May.

The nest is, I believe, always placed on trees in the immediate vicinity of water, not at the top of the tree, but in some fork, as Capt. Cock says, "like the common Kite."

It is circular, loosely made of thicker or thinner sticks and twigs, and lined with fresh leaves or fine twigs, and roots of grass; it varies in size from 1·5 to 2 feet in diameter and from 4 to 8 inches in thickness.

They lay, I believe, usually only one egg, but in the Dhoon, where they are plentiful, natives assert that they not unfrequently have two young ones, and must therefore, if this be true, occasionally at least lay two eggs.

The only two eggs that I have yet seen of this species, both of which were taken by Capt. Cock near Dhurumsalla, differed much in appearance. The one, though considerably larger than average specimens, and with a closer and less chalky texture, greatly reminded one of a common type of the eggs of *Neophron Ginginianus;* while the other, though of course smaller, in shape and richness of colouring, resembled some of the more brilliantly coloured eggs of the Golden Eagle, such as Mr. Hewitson's second figure, in his third edition. The first egg had a dingy reddish white ground, with at the large end a ragged cap of dingy brick red, mottled with deep, blackish, blood-red. Beyond the cap, which was of the size of a rupee, streaks, specks and splashes, all having a longitudinal direction and looking much like a dense reddish brown shower falling from the cap, thickly covered the whole of the rest of the egg, growing less and less dense towards the small end.

The other had a *pure* white ground, and was thickly blotched, mottled and clouded with the richest blood and brick red. The big end for the space of about a rupee exhibited no markings, but a few specks and spots, and though the rest of the egg is every where pretty thickly covered, the markings are most dense at the small end. In shape, the one egg is a nearly perfect ellipse, slightly pointed towards the small end, but the other egg is a very broad oval, very obtuse at the large end and scarcely less so at the smaller extremity.

These two eggs measure 2·8 by 2·25 and 2·79 by 2·15. Capt. Cock, of Dhurumsalla, to whom I owe these eggs and many others, as well as much valuable information, sends me the following note in regard to the nidification of this species.

"I have taken, or rather found, four nests of this species in the neighbourhood of Dhurumsalla, at heights of from 4000 to

4200 feet above the sea. The first, which I found on the 3rd of April, contained one semi-incubated egg, and was placed on a Mangoe tree, one of a clump of four, situated on the banks of a stream in tolerably well-wooded country. The second, found April 8th, contained one hard set egg, and was also in a Mangoe tree, one belonging to a small grove, overhanging a tiny stream, in a dark, well-shaded situation.

"The third, found April 11th, contained a perfectly fresh egg, it was in a thick grove, beside which a stream runs, and in which two old nests of this same species were also found.

"The fourth contained no egg, but on the 19th of April was complete and ready to lay in; this too was in a grove, overhanging a stream.

"The nest is about half way up the tree, not on the top, but placed more like the nest of the common Kite, on some fork.

"It builds a peculiar and not very large nest. The nests are always made of the twigs of the tree on which it is placed, fresh twigs broken off by the bird, and the lining of the nest is of leaves of the same tree. No feathers, mud or other material are used in the construction of the nest, which is about 1·5 feet across; the hollow in which the eggs are laid, is rather deeper than is usual with birds of this class.

Capt. Hutton sends the following note:

"*Spilornis Cheela.* The nest was found on the 10th of March at 5500 feet of elevation; it was composed of dry sticks and small branches interlaced on a tall tree; on visiting it again, we found that some mischievous urchin had pulled it to pieces, which they are constantly in the habit of doing. This bird is common both in the Dhoon and hills, and where a pair take up their quarters, no Fowl or Pigeon can escape; I have had a Dove cot cleaned out over and over again by them. They are cunning hunters, one sweeping over the hill side at no great elevation, while the other takes a higher line, so that let the Pigeon ascend or descend, he always finds himself between two fires, and unless he can find shelter in a tree, he is sure to be caught, as the pursuers decrease the distance between their lines and meet their victim at the point."

Mr. Thompson says—

"This species breeds from April to June, building a coarse circular nest some two feet in diameter, composed of thick roots and stems, and lined with finer twigs and grass roots. The nest is usually placed on lofty trees, in well wooded, shady and watered ravines, or in the low Himalayan rice-lands and warmer valleys.

I have found the nests of these birds in the lower valleys. They contained one young, usually. I have never got the eggs; the young I have reared and kept tame about me. The parent birds often succeed in destroying Pheasants and bringing them to the nest. Snakes, Lizards and Frogs they are very fond of. A young tame one, kept along with two *Athena Brahmas*, one Carrion Crow, and three of the large green Woodpeckers (*Gecinus Squamatus*) killed and eat every one of the latter, although well supplied with other fresh meat."

Mr. Blyth remarks, that this species will probably be found to extend to all suitable localities, throughout the Indo-Chinese sub-region.

"The true *Circaeti* frequent dry open country, where they prey chiefly on Snakes and Lizards. The species of *Spilornis* are found more about wet places, where they subsist mainly on large Frogs (which they clutch in the mud) and on the more or less aquatic Snakes (as the *Tropidonoti* and *Homolopsides*); hence their feet are almost always more or less clotted with sediment, which may render them frequent agents for transporting to a distance the germs of aquatic organisms."

He adds, that it abounds in Lower Bengal and along the Terai at the foot of the Himalayas, and that Professor Schlegel notes it from China. "Mr. Gurney observes that *S. Orientalis*, obtained by Mr. Swinhoe in Formosa, appears to be identical with *S. Cheela*, and that specimens from that island and from Northern India, are rather larger than those from Southern India, Siam, and the Malay peninsula."

With reference to this latter remark, I note, that Wallace, who gives this species as from Borneo, records the whole length at twenty-three inches; the wing at fourteen, and the tail at nine. Can this be the same species as ours with a length of 29; wing 21; tail 14 inches? I have recently killed and most carefully measured several of these birds, and shall, to facilitate comparison, give the results further on.

These specimens I obtained in the Saharunpoor district, along the Western Jumna Canal, where they are excessively common, and where in a morning's walk three or four might be seen, sitting slouchingly, and kite-like, on branches about half way up the tree, not quite at the end of the branch, but about half way between the end and the trunk of the tree.

All the specimens I obtained had eaten small Snakes; there were fully fifty little Serpents in the stomach of one, things scarcely bigger than large worms, and a gentleman who used to collect for me, sent me a specimen, that he had killed near Syree (below Simlah), along with the skin of a Cobra some two and a half feet long, which Cobra, he wrote to me, he had himself taken out of the bird's stomach, *dead*, but without marks of injury.

Those interested in Indian Oology are familiar with that remarkable passage in Gould's century of Himalayan birds which runs: "The Hon'ble F. J. Shore gives the following notes, (on *Ascalaphia Bengalensis*). 'Builds in trees, the nest being composed of large and small sticks, the female laying two large eggs mottled with black, reddish brown and white. Its native name in the Dhoon is Hokra Cheel, the natives considering it among the Cheel or Kite genus, and affirming that it is strong enough, and does, in fact, attack and kill wild Cats.'" Now as *A. Bengalensis* invariably, like every respectable Owl, lays white eggs, and, to the best of my belief, always on ledges of cliffs or banks, I mentally classed the Honourable author with Le Vaillant and one or two other well known writers of fiction. The other day in the Saharunpoor district, on the borders of the Dhoon, I heard *Spilornis Cheela* called a *Dogra Cheel*, and so was able to absolve Mr. Shore of every thing, *except* writing about what he did not understand.*

The following are the dimensions of four of the Sharunpoor specimens:—

	Female. No. 1.	Male. No. 2.	Male. No. 3.	Male. No. 4.
Length,................	29·0	27·5	28·2	26·5
Expanse, ...	67·5	62·0	63·5	58·7
Wing, ...	21·0	19·5	20·25	19·245
Which primary longest, ..		4 & 5	3 & 4	4 & 5
Amount by which other primaries fall short of longest,.............	1st 4·8	1st 4·0	1st 4·4	1st 3·5
" " "	2nd 1·8	2nd 1·3	2nd 1·25	2nd 3
" " "	3rd 0·8	3rd 0·3		3rd 0·3
Length of tail from vent, ..	14·25	12·8	13·2	12·3

* But how are we to explain that other stupendous Munchhausenism, which Gould in the same work inserts on this same Mr. Shore's authority, viz. that *Ceryle Guttata* "constructs its nest among large stones, composed of mud, lined with grasses, adhering to the sides of a stone, similar to the nest of the Swallow, and lays four eggs coloured, like itself;" *i. e.*, an it please you, *black* and *white?* I should like to see *C. Guttata* do it! The fact is, this much maligned bird, an orthodox Kingfisher of good connections, lays pure white eggs in a hole in a bank. But how *are* we to explain this story? what Indian bird? what bird in the whole world I might probably say, lays jet black and satin white eggs? It requires no little charity not to set this down as fiction, *pur et simple!*

Longest tail feathers exceed	No. 1.	No. 2.	No. 3.	No. 4.
shortest, ...	1·85	2·5	0·2	0·8
Tarsus, ...	4·15	3·9	4·3	4·0
Foot, greatest length, ...	5·6	5·5	5·0	5·0
" " width, ...	4·3	4·0	4·0	4·1
Mid toe, ...	2·5	2·0	2·25	2·0
Its claw, along curve, ...	1·37	1·06	1·25	1·25
Hind toe, ...	1·0	1·25	0·87	0·87
Its claw, along curve, ...	1·15	1·25	1·5	1·25
Inner toe, ...	1·45	1·13	1·06	1·25
Its claw, along curve, ...	1·31	1·31	1·37	1·25
Bill, straight from edge of cere to point, ...	1·35	1·32	1·4	1·32
" along curve, ditto, ...	1·56	1·51	1·63	1·5
" from gape, ...	2·12	1·9	1·95	1·9
" width at gape, ...	1·32	1·2	1·3	1·18
" height at margin of cere, ...	0·7	0·62	0·7	0·65
Length of cere, ...	0·4	0·32	0·55	0·32
Closed wings fall short of end of tail, ...	2·3	2·5	3·3	2·5
Lower tail coverts fall short of tail, ...	6·2	5·75	6·4	5·4

The colouring of the soft parts was as follows : Irides, intense yellow ; cere, skin of lores and gape, bright, or in some, dingy lemon yellow ; legs and feet, pale dingy yellow. Claws, black. Bill, slaty, or pale plumbeous at base, bluish black at tips and on culmen.

Though common near the foot of the hills, this species is rare in the plains of India ; Mr Brooks mentions having shot it in the Baidar jungles and near the Sirsa station, of the East Indian Railway. He shot one too in the Etawah district, near the canal ; and Mr. Carleylle, the curator of the Riddell Museum, Agra, shot one at a small tank below the museum ; but in the course of twenty years, I have myself never met with one in the plains of India, a hundred miles distant from the foot of the hills.

Of the specimen referred to, Mr. Carleylle sent me the following very full* description. "Male, shot March 1st, 1868. Greatest length of feathers of crest, 3¼ inches. The wings reach to within two inches of the end of the tail. Upper surface of the feathers of the head and crest, jet black. Base of the feathers of the head and crest for about two-thirds of their length white. Feathers of occiput, also tipped narrowly

* This may be useful for comparison with the alleged Borneo specimens.

with white. Chin, black. Feathers of ears and lores, smoky black; the tips very narrowly mottled lighter.

"There are bristles at the sides of the base of the upper mandible, and in front of the eyes; and there are still more numerous bristles at the base of lower mandible, at its sides and underneath.

"There is bare yellow skin, above and in front of the eyes, which is of a nearly golden yellow colour, with a very slight greenish tinge, in front of the eyes, and orange yellow above the eyes. Skin at base of lower mandible also bare for a short distance towards the chin, and of a dull yellowish tinge. Eye-lids deep yellow. Irides, bright golden yellow. Upper mandible, dark horn-colour, with a bluish ash-coloured patch at the sides of its base. Cere, yellow. Lower mandible, bluish ash-coloured, with a darker tip. Base of lower mandible, of a dirty yellow colour.

"Feathers of the nape and upper part of the back, hair brown, or umber brown, mottled towards their extremities, with a narrow edging of a dirty, fulvous ashy-white, or earthy-white colour. Sides of neck, of a dark, or blackish chocolate brown colour. Medial part of back and scapulars, dark blackish brown, very narrowly tipped with fulvous earthy whitish colour. Upper tail coverts, the same colour as the medial portion of the back; but the shorter anterior feathers are tipped with a terminal edging of small white spots, and the longer, posterior feathers are tipped with a narrow white edging. Tail, for about nearly half its length from the base, black, but becoming a little lighter, or of a brownish colour, towards the base; a few of the feathers, near their base, having solitary, exceptional blotches of a light fulvous, or dirty ash colour, mostly on the inner webs. Then follows, towards the centre of the tail, a broad transverse bar, with rather jagged, or undulating edges, which is white, mottled and marbled with ash colour, on the upper side of the tail, and white, marbled white, or watered pearl ash white, on the under side of the tail. Breadth of this bar about two and a half inches. Rest of tail, towards the tip, for about two and three quarter inches, black. The tail is then tipped with ash colour, and finally, (very narrowly), with white.

"The throat and breast have a very finely barred and mottled appearance; the base colour of the feathers appears to be pale fulvous, which is closely and narrowly barred with dark blackish brown on the throat, and barred with paler brown on the breast. I can best describe the colouring of the throat and breast of my specimen, by saying that it most nearly resembles the style of the colouring of the breast feathers of *Syrnium Newarense*.

"Feathers of the whole abdomen, sides and thighs, of a bright fulvous colour with a rufescent tinge, paler on the thighs; each feather with two longitudinal rows of beautiful large oval white ocelli; each ocellus surrounded by an edging of dark, brown; these ocelli very much resembling those which mark the plumage of the Argus Pheasant. The plumage of the abdomen and thighs, is very considerably unwebbed and setaceous, or rather crinose; the feathers having the appearance of being composed of long, limp, setaceous hairs, (such as the bleached hempen-looking hairs one sees on the sides of the Mongoose and young Porcupine,) and are of an earthy fulvous colour towards the thighs, somewhat tinged with rufescent on the sides of the belly. Under-tail coverts, of a most beautiful bright rufous fulvous colour; each feather with two rows of transversely oblong-shaped, jagged-edged, large white ocelli, each ocellus surrounded with an edging of dark blackish brown, shaded off lighter, which gives to these beautiful large ocelli, the appearance of the spots on a Leopard's skin. Some of the central pairs of ocelli are transversely confluent, forming a bar across the feathers.

"Lesser upper wing coverts, blackish brown, sprinkled, here and there sparsely, with rather smallish, clear white spots. Greater upper wing coverts, brown tipped, here and there, with a few white specks. Winglet, (or little false wing) ashy black, marbled with white at the base of the feathers on their outer webs, and with ashy-white on the inner webs. The feathers are plain black towards their termination; the points slightly tipped with pure white.

"The primary feathers have their quills of an umber brown colour. Outer webs of the primaries, for half their length, brown. Inner webs ashy brown, marbled with white and ash colour; the second, third, fourth, fifth and sixth quill feathers having, on their inner webs, on the upper side, only at half length, a large conspicuous light spot, half white towards the edge, and half ash colour towards the quill. Then there follows next below this, a broad nebulous fulvescent, or fulvous ashy coloured bar, about three inches in breadth, which crosses the whole seven primary feathers; on the under side of the wing, this bar is of a whitish ashy colour. The remainder of the primary feathers, for about four to four and a half inches to their tips, are black or dark blackish brown; the first primary, which is much shorter than the rest, is very slightly tipped at the very apex with white; the fourth, fifth, and sixth primaries, narrowly tipped with white; the second and third *not* tipped, but ending black.

"The same description will almost answer for the secondaries. With regard to the tertiaries, I mentioned before a fulvous ashy bar as crossing the whole of the *primaries*: this bar continues across the *secondaries* also; but when it reaches the tertiaries, only the outer webs receive the termination of the bar, which is here much darker, with a rufescent tinge, while the inner webs (in the same line) are very conspicuouly marbled and mottled with white. Under side of the wings, at about one quarter of their length from the tips, crossed entirely from side to side, with a broad pearl-ashy white bar, which becomes somewhat mottled on the under side of the secondaries and tertiaries. Above this, or higher up the under side of the wing, along its centre, a sort of irregular double or treble row of rather smallish white spots traverses, in broken order, the whole wing from side to side.

"Lesser under wing coverts, of a beautiful rufous tawny colour; each feather with two longitudinal rows of clear white ocelli: each ocellus surrounded with an edging of blackish brown. Larger under wing coverts, of a beautiful pearly grey colour, each feather with two longitudinal rows of large oval, and oblong, clear white ocelli; each ocellus surrounded with an edging of brown; some of the central pairs of ocelli, more transversely extended towards each other, than others, so as almost to have the appearance of a sort of broken bar on some of the feathers. These ocelli, on the under wing coverts, are even still more like those on the plumage of the Argus Pheasant. Tarsi naked, with large hexagonal scales and of a dirty earthy yellowish, or pale horn colour, tinged blotchily, towards the lower parts, with a sort of aureous or saffron colour.

"Feet, with smaller scales, and of a dirty yellow colour. Upper scales of toes, very large, and of an aureous yellow colour. Claws, black."

No. 39 (BIS.) **Spilornis Bacha,** DAUDIN.

THE MALAY HARRIER EAGLE.

[*S. Spilogaster*, Blyth. *Hæmatornis Elgini*, Tytler. *Falco Bido*, Horsf. *Circaetus Bacha*, Schlegel.]

I know nothing myself of the nidification of this species, which I have never seen alive; but Mr. Layard who knew this species well (though he gives the wing eighteen inches!) in Ceylon where it is common, remarks, "They were very plentiful at Point Pedro, in the north of Ceylon, and frequented the jungle-dotted plains throughout the Northern provinces. It was no uncommon thing to see three or four on the wing at once, wheeling round in airy circles; and from their peculiar markings they could be recognized at a great distance. They built on Banyan trees, usually a large, strong nest of sticks, without any lining, and laid three eggs, of dull white colour, with a few, dried blood coloured blotches at the obtuse end. Axis, 2″ 7.″ Diameter 2. They fed on Snakes, Lizards, and other reptiles and insects. They were particularly partial to the large trees on the banks of tanks, and from them swooped down on the Frogs which came up to sun themselves on the floating logs or weeds."

Col. Tytler very kindly furnishes me with the following dimensions *(taken from the dry skins)*, and descriptions of Andamanese examples, with some notes on the habits of the species :—

Dimensions.	Adult Male.	Young Male.	Adult Female.	Young Female.
Length, ...	21·62	23·25	22·5	22·75
Expanse, ...	44·0	40·0	46·0	41·0
Wing, ...	14·25	14·25	14·25	14·0
Which primary longest,	4 & 5	5th	3rd	5th
Amount by which other primaries fall short of longest, ...	1st 3·5 2nd 1·1	1st 3·65 3rd 0·5	1st 1·3 2nd 6·0	1st 1·4 2nd 1·37
Length of tail from vent,	10·0	10·0	9·6	9·8
By how much longest tail feathers exceed shortest,	0·7	1·0	0·8	1·2
Tarsus, ...	3·2	3·2	3·2	3·15
Foot, greatest length,....	3·5	3·5	3·2	3·0
Foot, greatest width, ...	2·9	2·55	2·45	2·35
Mid toe, ...	1·6	1·65	1·7	1·7
Its claw straight, ...	0·8	0·8	0·85	0·75
Hind toe,..............	0·7	0·85	0·8	0·85
Its claw straight, ...	0·9	0·9	0·95	0·85
Inner toe, ...	0·9	1·1	0·95	1·05
Its claw straight, ...	0·85	0·9	0·9	0·85
Bill straight from edge of cere,..............	1·15	1·15	0·9	1·1
Do. along curve ditto,	1·37		0·9	1·25
Do. from gape, ...	5·7	1·5	1·6	1·75
Do. width at gape, ..	1·05	0·92	1·05	0·85
Do. height (or at margin of cere),........	0·55	0·55	0·55	0·57
Length of cere (if any),	0·4	0·35	0·45	0·45
Distance by which lower tail coverts fall short of tail, ...	4·5	4·65	4·5	4·8

Description. Adult, Male. Head blackish brown, as also the primaries; neck, back, rump, upper tail coverts, scapularies, secondaries and tertiaries, dark brown, all the under surface of a lighter brown than the upper; tail blackish with the tips albescent greyish brown, with two broad bands of the same colour on each tail feather, and the rudiments of a third at the base; the bands of the two centre tail feathers are perhaps more albescent than those on the lateral ones; the rump and upper tail coverts are spotted with white, as also some of the upper wing coverts. Breast, abdomen, flanks, vent, lower tail coverts, under wing coverts, and thighs dotted profusely with roundish spots, largest on some of the under wing coverts, and abdomen, and smallest under the head of the wing, and thighs. Chin and throat unspotted, the feathers on the head forming a full broad crest nearly two inches in length, each feather of the head more or less margined with light rufous brown, a trace of which is perceptible in all the feathers of the back. All the feathers of the head and crest have their basal half white. All the primaries, which are of a blackish brown, the secondaries, and tertiaries have white greyish bands, beginning with a white tip to most of the feathers; the first primary has two bars, the second four, the third four. A yellow naked skin passes from the cere, which is also yellow, through the lores to over, and under the eyes, the portion over the eye being slight. Bill at point dark slate, basal portions of both mandibles, yellow; feet, yellow; claws, black; irides, dark brown.

2. Adult, female, similar to the last in all its markings, colours, &c.

3. Young female, lighter brown than Nos. 1 and 2, the margins of the feathers on the head more albescent rufous; the spots on the wing coverts and rump, larger, rounder and more numerous than in either of the two preceding specimens, otherwise very like them.

4. Young male, in colour very like No. 3, as also in all its markings, but being a much younger bird, the head is more albescent, each feather being margined with white, then a dark brown band 0·3, the rest of the feather white; a few dark blackish brown feathers on the forehead of the same hue as the head of the adult No. 1, the rump and upper tail coverts are less spotted than in No. 3.

Remarks. This species is by no means uncommon on all the islands of the Andaman group, but being the first new bird discovered there by me, I named it after the then reigning Viceroy of India, the Earl of Elgin. By the measurements and colouring, it will at once be seen how different it is from

S. Cheela of India. I am not familiar with *Bacha*, not having a specimen of that bird in my museum, to compare the Andaman birds with, so on this head I am unable to make any remarks, though I have reason to believe it is a totally different bird from *Falco Bacha*, Daud., which is the type of *Spilornis*, G. R. Gr. 1840.

"The *Spilornis Elgini* frequents swampy grounds, particularly where there are abundance of trees; here they feed on Frogs, Reptiles and Fish, the two former being their principal food. I have never seen more than one, or occasionally two together; on being disturbed they fly up at once into a tree, and remain so stationary amongst the branches and foliage, that notwithstanding being a large-sized bird they are difficult to discover. I have never seen them, on Pass, Chatham or Viper island, but constantly on all other parts of the settlement, particularly in the vicinity of Phœnix Bay, nor have I ever seen this species soaring in the air, which I have on some few occasions seen the Indian *S. Cheela* doing."

In uniting *Spilogaster*, *Elgini*, and *Bacha*, I am merely following the best authority on these points, I mean of course Mr. Gurney; knowing the bird only by the specimens in the Asiatic Society's and Col. Tytler's museums, I am not competent to form any independent opinion. Mr. Blyth had the following remarks on this species in the Ibis :—

"*S. Spilogaster*, nobis (J. A. S. B. XXI. p. 353.) *Hæmatornis Elgini*, Tytler (J. A. S. B. XXXII. p.87,) from the Andaman Islands, where it occurs together with the preceding; also *H. Bacha* of Colonel Sykes's list of the birds of the Dukhun (*P. Z. S.* 1832, p. 79,) as identified from a specimen in the India Museum presented by Colonel Sykes, being doubtless that referred to *(loc. cit.)*. This well-marked race inhabits the Indian peninsula and Ceylon, and also the Andamans, from which last named locality a fine pair are now living in the Zoological Gardens. It is a smaller bird and not so handsome as *S. Cheela*, with less developed crest and much less of black upon the crown, the tail markings quite different, having the black subterminal band conspicuously much less broad. Some individuals may very probably show considerable similarity to the Malayan *S. Bacha*, which would account for Professor Schlegel identifying a Cinghalese specimen with the Malayan bird; still the tail bands should be differently placed." On this the edition had the following note :—

"We learn from Mr. Gurney that he has never seen an Indian example of this bird, but that specimens from Ceylon and the Andamans appear to be absolutely identical with S

Bacha, (Falco Bido, Horsf.) from Java, Sumatra, Borneo, and Singapoor."

Two specimens of the Andaman bird were sent by Colonel Tytler, when he was Governor of the settlement, to Calcutta, for the Zoological Society, which birds seem somehow to have been presented to the Society in Mr. Grote's name; in regard to these, Blyth tells us in the Ibis for 1868 :—

"The live birds sent to the Zoological Gardens by Mr. Grote belong not to this species, as stated, but to the next *H. Elgini,* which Mr. Gurney considers to be identical with *H. Bacha* of the Malay countries, described by me, from Ceylon, as *H. Spilogaster* (Cf. Ibis, 1866, pp. 242, 243)."

For the present we may, therefore, safely assume the identity of the Ceylonese, Andaman, Malayan &c., forms.

As the head quarters of the *Circaeti* are to the west, so those of *Spilornis* are to the east. The Indo-Chinese region, besides *S. Cheela* and *Bacha,* includes three other species, *S. Holospilus,* Vigors, from the Phillippines and South China, *S. Rufipectus,* Gould, from Celebes, and *S. Salaensis,* Schlegel, from the Sala Island, which latter species, however, Wallace considers to be "hardly more than a slight local modification," though where exactly distinct species begin, and local modifications end, is more than I pretend to know.

No. 40. **Pandion Haliaetus,** Linn.

The Osprey.

I have no particulars of the nidification of this species in India, but I saw the nest of one on a large tree, in the valley of the Surjoo, in Kumaon.

Mr. R. Thompson says—

"I insert this bird here, because I believe its nest is to be found on the Ganges above Hurdwar, where I have seen the birds as late in the season as the middle of May. I think I shall be able to lay my hands on the nest at some time or other."

Of its breeding in the British Isles, Mr. Yarrell remarks—

"The Osprey makes a large nest, sometimes on high trees, at others, on rocks or about old ruins near large pieces of water, and lays two or three eggs, which are generally hatched in June. The eggs are about two inches and four lines long, by one inch ten lines in breadth, blotched and spotted over the larger end with reddish brown on a white ground. In some specimens, the secondary colour is of a paler yellowish red."

Mr. Hewitson gives us the following particulars: "Sir William Jardine says, that a pair or two may be found about most of the Highland Lochs, where they build on the ruined towers, so common on the edges, or insulated rocks, of these wild waters. The nest is an immense fabric of rotten sticks, and is generally placed, if such exists, on the top of the chimney, and if this be wanting, on the highest summit of the building. And aged tree may sometimes be chosen, but ruins are always preferred, if near. Mr. Wolley remarks, that there is something in the general appearance of the nest, which reminds one of the nests of the Wood Ants; it is usually in the form of a cone cut off at the top; the sticks project very slightly beyond the sides, and are built up with turf and other compact materials; the summit is of moss, very flat and even, and the cavity occupies a comparatively small part of it. Wilson says that, in America, the nest of the Fish Hawk is usually built on the top of a dead or decaying tree, sometimes not more than fifteen, often upwards of fifty feet from the ground. I ascended to several of these nests that had been built in from year to year, and found them constructed as follows;—externally large sticks, from half an inch to an inch and a half in diameter, and two or three in length, piled to the height of four or five feet, and from two to three feet in breadth, these were intermixed with corn-stalks, seaweed, pieces of wet turf in large quantities, and lined with dry sea-grass, the whole forming a mass observable at half a mile's distance, and large enough to fill a cart: and formed no inconsiderable load for a horse. These materials are so well put together, as often to adhere in large fragments after being blown down by the wind. During the time the female is sitting, the male frequently supplies her with fish, though she occasionally takes a short circuit to the sea herself, but quickly returns again."

Mr. Hewitson adds: "The Osprey, in England as in America, lays its eggs in the beginning of May; they are sometimes two, almost always three in number. Wilson says, rarely four.

"They are more oval in form, than those of any of our British *Falconidæ;* they do not usually differ much."

The egg which Mr. Hewitson figures as typical has a white ground, here and there clouded with pale purple, and very richly blotched and streaked, most densely towards the large end, with deep red, becoming in its intensity almost black. His figures measure 2·52 by 1·89; and 2·43 by 1·93.

Of the nidification of the Australian form of this bird, which, after comparison of several specimens, appears to me identical with our Indian race, Mr. Gould furnishes the following particulars: "The nest being of great size, is a very conspicuous object; it is composed of sticks varying from the thickness of a finger to that of the wrist and lined with the softer kinds of sea-weed. It is usually placed on the summit of a rock, but is sometimes constructed on the top of a large *Eucalyptus*, always in the vicinity of water. A nest observed by Gilbert in Rottnest Island, measured fifteen feet in circumference.

"The eggs are two in number, of a yellowish white, boldly spotted and blotched, with deep rich reddish brown, which colour, in some specimens, is so dark as to be nearly black, other specimens, again, are clouded with large blotches of purple, which appears as if beneath the surface of the shell. The medium length of the eggs is two inches and five lines, and the breadth one inch and nine lines."

The Osprey is found throughout the lower ranges of the Himalayas, in the rocky gorges of all the larger streams, and along the course of the Ganges and the Jumna, from their mouths almost to their sources. I have from time to time observed it in the Cawnpoor, Etawah, Agra and Allyghur districts. I met with it also on the Sutledge, at the Sambhur Lake, and the Nujjufgurh jheel, and I recently shot a very fine one close to Saharunpoor, on the Western Jumna Canal. Mr. Brooks says, that this species is "common on the river Tonse, also inland in the Mirzapoor district where there are jheels and tanks. I shot one at night off a post in the middle of a tank."

Though thus widely distributed, this species is nowhere I believe in India numerically abundant.

Out of India, this species (or very closely allied representative races) is found throughout the greater portion of the globe.

As to the specific identity of the various races of the Fish Hawk, Mr. Gurney, our greatest living authority in such matters, remarked in the Ibis for 1868:

"The Norwich Museum possesses an extensive series of Ospreys from various parts of the world, and I have no hesitation in expressing my belief that the species is identical not only on the coasts of North America, and of Europe, but also on those of Africa, Asia and Australia."

I subjoin measurements, &c., of a fine female, killed near Saharunpoor on the 7th November. Length, 21·15. Expanse, 0·65. Weight in lbs. 2·69. Wing, 19; the third primary the longest, the first primary falls short of the longest by 2·6; the second by 0·2; and the fourth by 0·8. Tail, from vent, 9·3; longest tail feather exceed shortest by 0·4. Tarsus (feathered in front for 0·8), 2·4. Foot, greatest length, 4·6; greatest width, 4·15; mid toe, to root of claw, 1·85; its claw, along curve, 1·5; hind toe, 1·25; its claw, 1·4; inner toe, 1·1; its claw, 1·5; outer toe, 1·4; its claw, 1·55. Bill, straight from edge of cere to point, 1·2; along curve from edge of cere, 1·45: from gape, 1·57; width at gape, 1·13; height at margin of cere, 0·55; length of cere, 0·3. Closed wings exceed the end of the tail by 0·1. Lower tail coverts fall short of end of tail by 0·3. The legs and feet were a very pale delicate sea-green, the scales very rough and shagreen-like. The claws, black; the irides, bright yellow. Bill, black. Gape and base of lower mandible, pale lavender plumbeous. Cere and skin of lores, (which are very thinly feathered), dark lead colour. Inside of mouth, purplish pink.

MY SCRAP BOOK:

OR

ROUGH NOTES

ON

INDIAN OOLOGY AND ORNITHOLOGY.

EDITED BY

ALLAN HUME.

Part I., No. 2.

CALCUTTA:

PRINTED BY C. B. LEWIS, BAPTIST MISSION PRESS.

1870.

PREFACE TO NO. 2.

No. 3 being a supplement to Nos. 1 and 2, and which will complete PART I. RAPTORES, will, D. V., appear immediately.

No. 3 will contain additions to, and corrections of, the notes that have already appeared, as well as notices of several species not included in numbers 1 and 2.

I have already to thank Mr. J. H. Gurney, M. P., for a most valuable series of notes on No. 1. which will appear in No. 3, and I would earnestly entreat all my coadjutors and friends to furnish me, with the least possible delay, with any remarks or information that they may desire to appear in No. 3.

No. 3 will contain an index to the three Nos. as well as an errata list, and any assistance in the preparation of this latter, will be thankfully received.

I have now to tender my most sincere thanks to Miss M. B. Cockburn and the following gentlemen, for the valuable information and numerous specimens with which they have furnished me since Part 1 appeared; Mr. F. R. BLEWITT, the Rev. H. BRUCE, Mr. W. E. BROOKS, Mr. E. BUCK, Mr. H. R. P. CARTER, Capt. COCK, Mr. T. COX, Dr. EDDOWES, the Rev. S. B. FAIRBANK, Major FISHER, Capt. GARSTIN, Capt. HUTTON, Mr. R. D. HIME, Mr. V. IRWIN, Dr. JERDON, Dr. KING, Col. MAISTER, Capt. C. H. T. MARSHALL, Capt. G. F. L. MARSHALL, Capt. MASSON, Capt. MAYNARD, Capt. MITCHELL, Capt. NAIRNE, Dr. NEWMAN, Major DELME RADCLIFE, Mr. C. SHILLINGFORD, Mr. F. B. SIMSON, Dr. SLAUGHTER, Mr. R. THOMPSON, Col. TYTLER, Capt. UNWIN, Mr. WAIT.

Of the 1360 species which it is proposed to notice in these rough notes, 1063 species are represented already in our

Museum by over 8000 specimens (obtained within our limits*) while the eggs of 323 species are represented by 5700 specimens. There is still therefore enormous room for improvement, especially where eggs (and nests) are concerned, and I trust, that all my kind coadjutors above enumerated, as well as many others who have *promised* assistance, will, so far as they conveniently can, aid in perfecting the collection and in completing our information in regard to all this vast array of species.

I may mention that it is most especially in the avi Fauna of BURMAH and CEYLON (in which provinces *alone* I have as yet no correspondent) that I need assistance.

Lists of desiderata, will be furnished on application, and specimens, and information as to food, habits and nidification, will be equally gratefully received and acknowledged by

ALLAN HUME,

AGRA.

N. W. Provinces, India.

* Rather more than 100 other species are represented by specimens from Europe, Africa and Australia.

ROUGH NOTES

ON

Indian Oology and Ornithology.

No. 41. **Polioaetus Ichthyaetus.** HORSF.

THE EASTERN WHITE TAILED EAGLE.*

This species generally, I believe, lays in January; but in the valleys of Kumaon and Gurhwal, where it is, I know, far from uncommon, it is said to lay as late as April.

It builds, invariably, as far as I have yet observed, on large trees, situated on the bank of some river, or in the immediate proximity of some considerable piece of water. It constructs its own nest, returning like the Golden Eagle, year after year, to the same spot, and each year adding fresh materials, so that the nest, a very large one to begin with, grows in time to an enormous size, reminding one of Wilson's descriptions of those of the Osprey. Stout sticks, and small branches mingled with twigs and grass roots, are the principal materials, but weeds and coarse grass help to fill up the interior, in which, as in the case of Bonelli's Eagle and others, a thin layer of green† leaves

---

* I am obliged to add the word "Eastern" to the English name given by Dr. Jerdon, because the "White Tailed" Eagle, or Sea Eagle, is the name by which a very different species, the European, *H. Albicilla,* is universally known.

† It is probable that the object of laying the eggs on green leaves, is to secure a certain amount of moisture for the shells.

Eggs artificially hatched, have, we know, to be daily sponged with a moist cloth. Great numbers of birds leave their eggs for a short time about sunrise, to feed in grass and jungle, and return all "dewy breasted" to their nests, so that I have taken Pea-fowls' eggs, quite wet from this cause. But how is sufficient moisture secured for eggs laid, like those of the Sand-grouse, on the bare, absolutely dry sand, whose parents feed in the dryest ground, (never, even when they drink, wetting their feathers in the slightest) and return dry-breasted to their eggs?

is commonly spread, for the eggs to rest on. The eggs are normally three in number; but I have twice seen only two eggs in a nest, in both cases fully incubated. The only egg that I now possess, (which I owe to Captain Cock,) is a broad and very perfect oval in shape. In texture, it is rough and pitted, but it nevertheless has a slight gloss. It is a perfectly unspotted egg, and though in places somewhat soiled and discoloured, must, when fresh, have been a nearly, pure, milk white. Held up against the light, the shell is even a darker green than that of *H. Leucoryphus*, in fact it is almost black. Whether this character is general, or peculiar to the single specimen I now possess, I cannot of course decide. I have had many of these eggs in former years; but I did not then, unfortunately, collect specimens.

Five eggs, of which I have recorded measurements, varied from 2·72 to 2·8 in length, and from 2·1 to 2·15 in breadth.

Captain Cock sends me the following note:—

"The nest of *Polioaetus Ichthyaetus* is a very large structure of sticks, in fact the biggest nest that I have known of. I found one on the top of a high thorn tree, on the banks of a river. When I first visited the nest, it was empty, but the bird was sitting on the tree near it. I again visited the nest about a fortnight later, and found three eggs in it. The nest was about 5½ feet in height, about 4½ in diameter, and but slightly hollow. There were a quantity of leaves in the nest quite fresh. The leaves belonged to some small shrub (the leaf itself was a very small one) and were evidently placed there to make a softer bed for the eggs. The birds had built in the same tree for an immense time, but at length the tree was blown down, and they built on the next biggest tree to it, and have continued for the last few years to nidificate there. The eggs were dirty white, similar in shape and size to the one sent to you *(above described.)* The birds did not exhibit any anger when their eggs were taken, but the female flew round and round a few times."

Captain Unwin remarks,

"I found a nest of *Polioaetus Ichthyaetus* in the neighbourhood of Huzara on the 27th February, 1869. The nest was situated in a large, Tulip tree, about 35 feet from the ground. It was built of sticks, stubble, weeds, and coarse grasses, and was about 2½ to 3 feet in diameter. It contained two young birds. The villagers stated, that the old birds arrived every year, about November. The probable age of the young was four or five weeks; they were unable to fly, though one was pushed outside the nest. I subjoin the dimensions* and a brief description of one of these young birds which I took from the nest. Later, while watching the tree, through a glass, from a distance of some 150 yards, I saw one of the old birds arrive, with a fish, I should think nearly 2℔s. in weight, in its claws."

Horsfield (Zool. Res. in Java) tells us of this species, that "their nest was built on the top of a large tree, and was constructed in a rude manner, of branches of trees. The branches which were placed on the exterior, were more than an inch in diameter: the inside was lined with small twigs. It was irregularly round, and very slightly excavated."

My friend, Mr. Thompson, writes to me from Gurhwal that these birds "breed from March to May. The nest, which is a large structure of small sticks and twigs loosely put together, is usually placed in a tree at a convenient distance from the water, and at no great height from the ground. I have found their nests on the Kosilla river, at Oomta Dabee, in the Patlee Dhoon, on the Ramgunga river; Kotree Dhoon on the Sunnai river; and lastly above Hurdwar on the river Ganges. They lay from two to three large white eggs, smaller than those of *Haliactus Fulviventer*. Three appears to be the normal number of their eggs. During the breeding season, the birds utter at intervals, a loud yet plaintive cry, especially whenever one of them approaches the nest whilst the other is sitting in it. The male during this time is assiduous in his attentions, and the meeting of the pair on his return from fishing excursions always appears to call forth fresh cries. About the middle of April the eggs are laid, and are hatched during the following month. These birds are generally distributed over the rivers and larger streams of the Sub-Himalayas, remaining on them throughout the year."

Mr. Blyth had the following note in the Ibis for 1865; "*Haliaetus Lineatus*, Gray (Hardwicke's Ill. Ind. Zool.) is erroneously assigned in the Ibis, (1863, p. 23) to the young of *Milvus Govinda*, it being decidedly the young of *Pontoaetus Ichthyaetus* (Horsf.) in abraded, spotted plumage; for the young of this bird, and of *M. Govinda* are quite similarly speckled."

---

* Expanse, 64 inches; wing 17; length 25; tail 8·25; bill at gape, 3·5; Tarsus 3·5. *Description*—Irides dark brown; cere brownish; gape and orbital skin, pale yellow; legs and feet pale yellowish white; bill and claws horny black; lores naked and whitish, thinly covered by blue hairs. Plumage, above, dark brown, primaries and tail blackish, 3rd and 4th quills longest, Secondaries on inner web pale fulvous, slightly speckled with dusky. Beneath of a somewhat lighter brown throughout.

This does not exactly agree with Captain Unwin's description, recorded on the spot from a live young one, taken from the nest to sit for his portrait, and for my part I am inclined to believe, that *H. Lineatus*, Gray, is the young *not* of *this* species, but *possibly* of the *next*, *H. Leucoryphus*. This species occurs not only all over India, Burmah and Malay, but also as we learn from Mr. Wallace* (Ibis 1868) in Sumatra *(Wall)* and Borneo. (Mus. Lugd.)

No. 42. **Haliaetus Leucoryphus.**† PALLAS.

PALLAS'S SEA EAGLE.

I have taken the eggs of this species during the latter‡ half of November, in December, and January, and once or twice, in

---

* Mr. Wallace gives the following brief note of a male obtained by him. "Total length, 26 inches. Wing, 17·5 in. Mid toe, 2 in. Bill black, cere dusky, feet white."

† Haliaetus Leucoryphus.

DIMENSIONS.

		Length.	Expanse.	Wing.	Tail.	Tarsus.	Foot, greatest length.	" " width.	Mid Toe to root of Claw.	Its Claw along Curve.	Hind Toe to root of Claw.	Its Claw along Curve.	Inner Toe.	Its Claw along Curve.	Bill straight.	" along Curve.	" from gape.	" width at gape.	" height at margin of Cere.	Length of Cere on Culmen.	Wings when closed fall short of end of Tail by how much.	Lower Tail Coverts fall short of end of Tail by how much.	Weight in lbs.
MALE.	From	29	75	21	11	3·75	6·00	5·25	2·56	1·47	1·3	1·8	1·4	1·7	2·00	2·75	2·25	1·67	0·78	0·62	1·4	4	5·4
	To	31	79	22	12	4·00	6·5	5·6	2·75	1·52	1·4	1·9	1·5	1·8	2·25	2·9	2·43	1·75	0·82	0·73	1·6	5	5·12
FEMALE.	From	32·0	82	23	13	4·00	6·75	5·95	2·87	1·59	1·5	2·1	1·6	2·00	2·25	2·8	2·65	1·75	0·85	0·69	1·37	4	6·8
	To	34·25	85	24	14	4·5	7·25	6·1	2·94	1·63	1·6	2·2	1·75	2·1	2·44	3·12	2·88	1·94	0·92	0·75	1·67	5	8·12

(Three males, four females, measured and weighed).

‡ Mr. Brooks has found eggs as early as the 11th of November.

the early part of February. The greater number of these birds, however, lay in December, and most of the nests that I have examined later than the 15th of January, have contained young ones.

The 3rd, 4th, or 3rd and 4th primaries are the longest. The 5th nearly as long. The 1st from 4·5 to 6 shorter, the 2nd from 0·25 to 1·3 shorter. Exterior tail feathers from 1 to 1·5 shorter than central ones.

DESCRIPTION. Legs and feet, greyish white, sometimes with a faint bluish tinge, usually much stained and discoloured about the toes. The inner toe and claw are very large and thick, very nearly the same size as the hind toe. The pads, especially of these toes, are large, and the whole surface of the sole rough and shagreen-like. The claws black, all very large and sharp; a few large scales on the front of the tarsus, (which is feathered *in front* for the upper one-third and sometimes nearly one-half) just below the feathered portion, the rest coarsely reticulate. Nearly the whole ridge of the middle toe is covered with large transverse scales, and there are about seven of these on the exterior, and five or six on the interior and hind toes. The scales just above the claws, especially on the inner and hind toes, large and *very* thick.

Irides. Pale brownish yellow, in some lights almost silvery.

Bill. Cere, pale bluish green. Nostrils, gape and base of lower mandible bluish. Upper mandible greenish horny, dusky at tip. Tip of lower mandible, brownish as a rule, but in some the whole lower mandible is a sort of bluish or greenish horny.

Tongue. Rather long, thick, fleshy, of nearly uniform width throughout, obtuse ended, with a conspicuous groove down the centre.

Plumage (Adults). Forehead and a streak continued nearly the whole way over the eyes, somewhat dingy white. The whole of the rest of the front and top of the head and occiput, palish whitey brown. The feathers somewhat abraded and slightly darker shafted. Feathers of the nape, and upper part of the back of the neck, paler and slightly more rufous; the feathers much elongated and pointed. The feathers of the base of the back of the neck rather browner again: broad, sharp pointed, and somewhat paler edged. Upper back a somewhat darker brown again, feathers sometimes narrowly paler edged. Middle and lower back, rump and upper tail coverts, dark, sometimes *very* dark, brown. Feathers of the tail darker brown, almost black, with a 4½ (in males) to 5½ (in females) inch broad, transverse, pure white bar on both webs. The scapulars, and the whole of the wings, very dark rich brown. The second to sixth primary conspicuously emarginate on the outer webs, and sometimes slightly greyish just above the emargination. Lores, chin, cheeks, ear coverts, and throat pure white, the feathers of the throat very narrow, greatly lengthened, and with the webs much disunited. Feathers of the side of the neck, beyond the white, of the same fulvous brown, and lengthened in the same way as the feathers of the back of the neck. The lower neck, breast, and abdomen, dull, somewhat rufous brown, darker on each side, just above the thighs. Feathers below the vent, and lower tail feathers dark brown, the longest obscurely tipped, or mottled with fulvous white. The axillaries, and lesser under coverts of the wing, very dark, almost blackish brown. Under surface of the quills, and their greater lower coverts, with a bluish or slaty tinge in some lights. Upper portion of the thigh coverts, dark brown. Lower portion, paler and more rufous brown.

They build on large trees, on the Peepul (*Ficus Religiosa*) by preference I think, but also on many other kinds, Sheeshum (*Dalbergia Seesoo*) Banyan (*F. Indicus*) &c. The trees that they select, are almost invariably solitary ones, situated either on the banks of some river, or beside some considerable Jheel. In Upper India, I do not know a single large jheel, which retains water in it as late as February, where a pair of this species does not breed, and all down the Jumna, Ganges, Chambul and Sutledge, wherever I have been, I have invariably met with at least one pair every three or four miles, and in particular localities every *half* mile!

The nest is a huge platform of sticks, some of which are often as thick as a man's arm, with a superstructure of thinner

---

The inner webs of the first 4 or 5 primaries, conspicuously notched, and generally greyish above the notches, and the tips of the secondaries mucronate.

Sometimes a feather will be found in the tail with only half the inner web, of the white bar portion, white, the rest almost black.

Somewhat younger birds have the crown and occiput rather darker, and the forehead, chin, throat, &c. whity brown, instead of pure white, indicating a less mature plumage.

A very fine young female, shot near Suman, on the 27th February, 1867, was throughout, a dull brown of different shades. The head, neck and under parts, light fulvous brown, the chin and throat much paler, with a dark patch behind the eye, and over the ear coverts. The hackles of the hind head and neck paling towards the tip, and mostly inconspicuously pale, centred. The back of the neck, upper back, lesser scapulars, and median and lesser wing coverts, a rather darker brown, all the feathers, but specially the coverts, faintly and narrowly margined paler. The middle back very dark umber; rump and upper tail coverts, about the same brown as the upper back, the whole much mingled with dirty white, some of the feathers being almost entirely of this colour, some having only the outer webs so, and some only the bases, which are but partially seen, white. The inner lesser scapulars are similarly varied. The longer scapulars, tail feathers, and most of the quills, the winglet, and primary greater coverts, are a very deep (almost black) umber brown. A few of the quills, old ones not yet moulted, are a pale, somewhat rufous, umber. The centre tail feather has the broad white bar, but still imperfect on one web, and three of the other feathers have a few small inconspicuous whitish spots where the bar would be in the adult. Below, the axillaries and some of the side feathers are white, tinged with fulvous or pale brown, and there is a good deal of mottling with white, or fulvous, on some of the under wing coverts, and the inner webs of some of the primaries. There are traces of white on many of the feathers of the mid breast. The lower tail coverts are a pale brown, mottled more or less with fulvous white. The upper portion of the thigh coverts are a darker brown than the rest of the under surface of the body.

A nestling female nearly able to fly, taken out of a nest at Rahun on the 21st February, 1867, weighed 5lbs. 14oz. was a nearly uniform dark brown above, and rather lighter below. The legs and feet were a clear pale lemon yellow.

sticks and twigs, and with only a slight depression towards the interior, which is lined with fine twigs and green leaves, occasionally intermingled with rushes and straw.

The nest is usually placed in a broad fork, near the very top of the tree, on branches that seem scarcely strong enough to support the huge mass, and is sometimes occupied by the same pair for many successive seasons.

I do not think that this species ever takes possession of other birds' nests. It either builds a new one for itself, or repairs one formerly belonging to it, even though this may in the interim have been usurped by *Vultur Calvus* or *Ketupa Ceylonensis*, both much addicted to annexing the poor Sea Eagle's laboriously constructed nest. I say laboriously constructed, because I once watched a young pair constantly occupied for a full month, building a new nest, which they were still at work finishing off when I left. Nothing can seem rougher or more rugged than their nest when finished, and yet out of every four sticks and branches that they brought, they rejected and threw down at least three. Both birds brought materials, and side by side, the pair would work away, throwing down almost as many sticks as they had brought; then apparently they would quarrel over the matter, there would be a great squealing, and one would fly away and sit sulky on some cliff point near at hand; after a time the one left on the nest would go off in quest of materials. Immediately, the other would drop softly on to the nest and be very busy (though what they did except lift a stick and put it down in the same place it was impossible, even with a good glass, to make out) till the absent bird returned, not unfrequently with a fish instead of a stick. It is a curious fact, but I observed it repeatedly, that if the female, which is much the largest, brought the fish to the nest, the male set to work on it at once, without so much as, By your leave; while if the male brought it, the female used to eye it, sidle gradually up, and only take slow and modest mouthfuls. When, however, the female begins to sit, the male will bring her fish or fowl, and go off for other food for himself, not attempting to share it with her: and when not on the nest, neither seems to presume to interfere with the other's captures without permission (vide infra).

The usual number of eggs laid by this species is three, but I have myself twice found four, and it is not at all uncommon to meet with only two eggs, fully incubated, or two young ones, in a nest.

One curious point about these birds is, that unlike most Eagles, they do not always desert a plundered nest. I have twice taken single eggs out of nests, and ten or twelve days later, on re-examining the same nests, in consequence of observing the birds still hanging about the place, found that a couple more eggs had been laid since my last visit.

Typically the eggs of this species are a rather broad oval, but a good deal of variation both in size and shape occurs. I have one or two very long and one very broad pyriform egg, but these are exceptions. The colour is greyish white, and every specimen that I have yet seen (and some fifty have passed through my hands) has been absolutely unspotted. No doubt, as incubation proceeds, like most other Eagles' eggs, they become much soiled and stained with dingy yellow, but none have exhibited any trace of the markings shewn in Dr. Bree's figures. As far as size goes, his figure pretty correctly represents an average specimen, but fully half are a good deal larger.

The eggs of this species can, I think, generally be separated from those of almost all our other Indian Eagles, except those of *P. Ichthyaetus*, by the intensely dark green of the shell when held against the light. If it is possible to separate any of our Eagle's eggs by the texture. I should say, that as a rule, there is generally a certain smoothness in the feel of these eggs, which distinguishes them from those of other species; but this is by no means an invariable test.

The eggs vary from 2·55 to 3 in length, and from 2·02 to 2·27 in breadth, but the average of 26 eggs measured was 2·77 × 2·18.

It does not do to dogmatize about the habits of birds. I have examined fully fifty nests of this species, some containing eggs, and some young ones, and were I to trust to my own personal experience alone, I should certainly assert that the old birds *never* show the least fight in defence of their homes and progeny. Nevertheless one of our most accurate observers certifies to their excessive pugnacity when they have young: Captain Hutton in the J. A. S. remarks:—

"I notice this species, because Captain Tickell states, that it never makes the slightest attempt at defending its nest, a striking contrast to the marvellous tales we read of, concerning the Golden Eagle in the Highlands of Scotland, &c. This remark is correct only, so long as there are eggs in the nest, for no sooner are these hatched, than the temper of the bird becomes wholly changed, and it will then defend its young with fierceness and determination. The nests I have repeatedly found, and robbed, both on the banks of the Ganges, and of the Sutledge, and in all cases where they contained only eggs, not the least show of resistance was made, the old birds either sailing off with a loud querulous cry, or sullenly remaining on an adjacent tree, watching the robbery that was going on. On one occasion, however, I met with a very different reception, when my servant was attacked with an unexpected ferocity, from which nothing but my gun could have saved him. The circumstance occurred in January 1832, when on my way up the country. The nest was placed near the summit of a tree, growing on one of the Colgong rocks, in the middle of the Ganges, and contained two half-fledged young ones. The old birds offered a most determined resistance, and without the aid of fire arms we should decidedly have been defeated, as they dashed fiercely and fearlessly at the man in the tree, who prayed hard to be allowed to descend, and was only kept at his post by the promise of reward and fear of the cudgel. At first we had to contend with the female only, but after one or two rapid stoops and dashes at the robber's head, which he avoided by bobbing under the nest, finding she could make no impression, she suddenly uttered a shrill cry, which was responded to in the distance, and in an instant after, her mate was seen swiftly gliding to her aid, from the opposite bank of the river. The two then charged together towards the nest with the rage and fierceness of despair, and so terrified the man in the tree, hampered as he was with the young ones, that had I not fired at and wounded the Eagles as they advanced, they would assuredly have hurled him into the river. In this manner, however, after repeated attempts to come to the rescue, we managed at last to drive off the old birds and secure the booty. At the end of five weeks the young ones exhibited as nearly as possible the plumage of the bird figured by Hardwicke and Gray as "*H. Lineatus.*"

Recently Captain Hutton* has sent me the following further remarks in regard to this species. "In the Dhera Dhoon this

---

* I am indebted to Captain Hutton for many interesting notes on the nidification of our Indian Birds.

The following are some general remarks by the same well known naturalist in regard to the locality whence the information that he furnishes has been chiefly drawn.

"The tract of country in which the following observations have been made, comprises the Dhoon, and the greater portion of the mountain district of Ghurwal, being enclosed between the Ganges and the Jumna, on the east and west, and the snowy ranges and the Siwaliks, on the north and south.

In proceeding from the Plains proper, south of the last mentioned range, up to the snows, it is usual for convenience sake, to divide the tract into three distinct regions, termed the Southern or Terai region, the Central or Forest region, and the Northern or Snowy region. As might naturally be expected

bird is extremely common, but it merely skirts the outer hills; about 5500 feet, without entering them. I have seen six to eight

---

the Southern forests are the richest and most varied, both in respect to vegetation, and in animal life, and from the warmth and moisture of the climate, are more particularly the resort of the soft-billed or insectivorous birds, those numerically far outweighing the granivorous species. This remark, however, more particularly applies to the summer months, for in the cold season, many of the former travel farther south, and give place to numerous species of Finches, Thrushes, Pigeons, &c., from the central and northern regions. Among the feathered tribes, in fact, there is a constant change, and succession of genera and species, throughout the year, many appearing to visit us from the south for three or four months in summer, for the sole purpose of breeding: retiring again as soon as the periodical rains are at an end, and their progeny is old enough to travel. So great is the influx of northern species into the Terai, during the winter months, that we should almost be justified in saying that, at that season, our fauna, as regards the feathered tribes, is exchanged for those of the central and northern regions. The Doves, the Cuckoos and smaller insectivorous species of the summer, giving place to more northern types, reminding us poor exiles, of our boyhood's days, when the leafless trees and hedge-rows of our dear old fatherland were enlivened by the sharp quick chirp of the Fieldfare, the quivering tail of the Redstart, or the creeping Hedge Sparrow, threading its way through, and seeking concealment in each snow-covered bush and thicket.

And yet, notwithstanding the multitude of species resorting to these hills, it is by no means an uncommon thing, to hear collectors, and even naturalists remark, that they have searched in vain through the forests and brushwood, without finding a single nest to reward them for their toil, and it becomes a perfect mystery to them where the several species actually breed, or whether they breed at all in these localities. The fault here lies entirely with the collector, who, if he be not a practical naturalist, seldom gives himself the trouble to consider which are the most likely resorts of the particular species he may desire to procure. To seek for *Nucifraga*, *Cocothraustes*, the Siskin, and various others among forests composed of oaks, rhododendrons, andromeda, and the like, would be as absurd as to hunt for them among the copsewood tracts of the outer southern mountains; each species has its own peculiar resort, whether it be for food, for shelter, or for a breeding-place, and it will probably, at particular seasons, be found no where else, except when it performs its periodical migration from one region to another. Thus the Pine forests will furnish species that are to be met with nowhere else; the mixed forest of oaks, rhododendrons, laurels, and andromeda, &c., will harbour other kinds, while the dense southern brushwood tracts are especially devoted to the insectivorous tribes. Climate, soil, and elevation, will always be found to exercise a very material influence in the productions of the vegetable world, and according to the nature of those productions, so will be the nature of the food, and of the species which depend upon it. Warmth and moisture, are indispensible to the production of insect life, and the higher we ascend, the more attenuated and dry becomes the atmosphere, the consequence being the decrease or cessation of insect life, and in such situations therefore, it would be absurd to seek for insectivorous birds, their place being occupied by granivorous, frugivorous and root-eating species. It is in the damp warm brushwood jungles, of the southern tracts, that the soft-billed birds are to be sought for, and there my own experience tells me they are to be found abundantly, so abundantly in fact, that this tract

together passing along the side of the hills below Mussoorie for some distance, and then returning again together in like manner; but what the object can be I cannot make out, for there is no fishing-ground along that route. They build in lofty trees, on the banks of the larger Dhoon streams, laying one or two, large, white eggs. The nest, I have described in the J. A. S. of Bengal. The cry of this bird is loud and harsh, and somewhat querulous; it may be heard at a great distance,

---

might almost be termed par excellence, 'the region of birds nests,' so numerous are these during the breeding season of the summer months.

With respect to Hawks and Eagles, although the nests of many species are not difficult to discover, yet, being found, it is often entirely impossible to gain access to them. Some of these are built in lofty trees, overhanging the sides of precipices, which make one shudder to look into the yawning depth below; such is generally the spot selected by that beautiful Hawk, the *Spizaetus Nipalensis*, while the Vulture Eagle, selects a ledge of rock, to which one can only descend by a rope, and with a strong chance of being hurled into eternity, should the old birds be any where near at hand; nevertheless I have succeeded in robbing both these nests. In the Dehra Dhoon the nests of *Haliaetus Leucoryphus* and of various Vultures are far from uncommon.

Another important point is likewise to be considered in the selection of breeding localities, and one I imagine which rarely enters into the head of the collector, for as with molluscous animals, limestone tracts are ever more productive than others, so precisely is it with the feathered tribes; the snail must have an abundant supply of lime, or it cannot properly secrete its calcareous shell, and without calcareous matter, the bird would be equally unable to secrete the shell, which encloses and protects the egg, a fact which may often be seen in the farm-yard, where Hens that have been unable to procure a sufficient supply of lime, with their food, will lay their eggs without a shell and surrounded only by a strong transparent membrane. It is likewise this craving for lime, and salt, that prompts domestic Pigeons to pick the mortar out of walls.

A limestone formation will consequently always be found to be more densely populated by the feathered tribes, than regions of siliceous rocks. The Falcon tribe are rendered somewhat more independent in this respect, because the smaller bones of animals which constitute their prey, furnish abundant material for the construction of the egg shell.

Now it so happens that the lower Terai region, of the southern range between the Jumma and the Ganges, is just such a district as birds of the soft-billed kind especially delight in, for the rock formation consists chiefly of large beds and shattered blocks of limestone, from the crevices and hollows of which, springs up a dense jungle of brushwood, sometimes interspersed with forest trees, at other times without them; the locality is moreover well watered by numerous rills and streams of pure fresh water, along the mossy margins of which, are found the nests of many species that delight to build in such situations, while as the streams increase in size, as they debouche from the dark glens and ravines, to enter upon and fertilize the Dhoon, the deepening banks of silt will often furnish nests of the various species of King-fishers, which deposit their eggs in holes, bored in the crumbling banks above the water line."

and, on more than one occasion, has guided me to its nest. Often have I watched this handsome bird seated high, perched in solitude, upon the dry and leafless branch of some tall tree, that overlooked a river's bank—or oftener, seated on the bank itself, watching perchance for the appearance of its prey. Uttering its shrill and clamorous cry, half croak, half scream, it would suddenly spread out its wings and sweep across the water, rising gradually in wide gyrations, until nearly lost to sight, and taking a keen survey of the plain beneath; then gradually descending in circles as before, until with a sudden downward headlong rush, it would dash upon a Partridge or a Hare, and bear it off in triumph. I have seen it hawking on the Ganges after Ducks and Teal, which are sometimes found in the rains breeding with swarms of Paddy birds, on the Colgong rocks, in the middle of the river. The Duck would quietly paddle along about the centre of the stream, and the Eagle would follow the same course far above, but gradually and slily descending along the line, until with a sudden downward dash, it would nearly reach the Duck, and, then slowly and gradually sweep upwards again as the wary little Duck plunged deeply beneath the surface to rise again, before or behind the Eagle, which would pursue it over and over again in like manner, without a chance of success, until weary of the chase, he would wing his way to shore, doubtless to inform his mate that no 'ducks and green peas' were forthcoming for that day's dinner!"

Where, however, the Duck is a wounded one, and I have but rarely seen these Eagles strike at those that were not so, the result is often different, as my own notes, which I proceed to transcribe, will show.

"This is essentially a water bird, and as far as I know, is never found far from the banks of large rivers, lakes or jheels. Early in the morning, even in the cold weather, it goes down to the water side, and has a good bathe. It is amusing to watch this large bird standing up to its belly in water, sitting down, first on one side, then on the other, so as to wash the wings and back, ducking the head in and out, and splashing, spluttering, and fluttering the wings, for all the world like a Pigeon or a Sparrow. After its bath, it resorts to the top of some tree, or along the banks of large rivers, to some craggy point, where it sits awhile sunning itself, generally with its wings half outspread. Thence it flies heavily off to seek a meal. A large fish near the surface attracts its attention, as it flies pretty low over the river, down it swoops with more activity and rapidity than its habitual demeanour and method of flight would lead one to expect, and strikes for a breakfast, dashing its huge feet and long legs into the water right up to its body. Very often (far more often than he succeeds) the Ringtail is baulked by the Roohoo, (*Cyprinus Rohita* and *Mrigala*) his favourite fishy food, and has to try again and again before he breaks his fast. If anywhere he spy a wounded Goose, or other water bird, he is down on him or after him in a moment. The bird, even if only slightly wounded, and flying more or less well when the Eagle takes up the chase, drops at once into the water. Down swoops the Eagle, its long legs extended to the utmost, and just as his claws are within a yard of the victim's head, down dives the Goose, only to rise when its pursuer has swept past; round comes the Ringtail again, down dives the Goose; again and again these manœuvres are repeated, and at last either the Eagle gives up the chase, or the Goose, (and this, I think, is most generally the case,) diving a little too slowly, gets caught by the long legs (which are each time dashed their whole length into the water) before it has got deep enough down, and the Eagle then flies slowly to the shore, bearing its prey in its talons. A grey Goose will weigh on the average 7lbs., (much heavier are recorded,) but I have repeatedly seen good sized grey Geese carried off in the claws of one of these Eagles, the bird flying slowly and low over the surface of the water, but still quite steadily. Once, many years ago, one of these birds procured me a fine fish for breakfast. Standing on the high clay cliff on the Meerut side of the river, at Baghput on the Jumna, a little above the ghat, I saw one of these Eagles capture a fish, so large, that the bird only with great difficulty succeeded in reaching a low sand bank, in the river, with its prey. As it flew to this bank, it flew so low, and with such difficulty, that the writhing fish in its claws, struck the water every few yards, and twice seemed likely to pull its persecutor under water. At last, however, the sand, some 250 yards away from where I stood, was reached. Directly the shore was gained, I fired a heavy rifle at the Eagle, the bullet passing just above it. For a minute it struggled to rise again with the fish, but a second bullet closer still, compelled it to rise without the fish; and though it circled round above, uttering its shrill scream, to be joined in a few minutes by its mate, they neither of them ventured down, and a boatman crossed and brought the spoil over to me. This was a Roohoo (*C. Rohita*) and weighed 13lbs. 2oz., and was perfectly uninjured except a gash at the back of the head, four deep claw wounds on the back of the neck, and four more about half way down the back. I have often tried this plan since, but never with success, the captured fish in every other case having proved light enough for the bird to fly away with when shot at."

As soon as one bird has made a capture, it is generally joined by its mate. The latter usually stands a little apart for a moment or two, as if to allow the capturer to satisfy the first cravings of hunger, then sidles slowly up and begins with evident diffidence to feed too. This, however, is only the case if the spoil is large. If the fish or the bird be small, the second comer does not attempt to approach; but after a few minutes flies off.

The scream of the Ringtail is very loud, shrill and thrilling, and its peculiar accents can never be mistaken after being once heard.

To judge from the rough shagreen-like soles of their feet, fish is perhaps their natural food, but wounded or freshly killed Geese, Ducks, and even Snipe, and Sandpipers, are greedily seized, and devoured. It is noticeable, that when eating a Goose, or other large bird, this Eagle usually holds it on the ground, somewhere near the edge of the water, breast downwards and breaking through the back, eats out the entrails, liver, &c., not touching the breast.

Captain Hutton tells me, that they capture all kinds of game, Hares, and even young Foxes; but where I have observed them, water-fowl and fish have been their chief diet. Although in the Dhoon this species does not, Captain Hutton says, enter the Himalayahs, I have found them in Kumaon, far up the valleys of the Kosila, Ramgunga, and Surjoo, at least an hundred miles in a direct line from the southern outskirts of the Hills.

Professor Schlegel identifies our Indian species *H. Fulviventer* of Vieillot, with Pallas's bird, and I have no doubt correctly so, but one of the dimensions given by him "length 24 inches" is absurd, and must have been taken from a dried skin; the smallest adult male that I have yet seen measured 29 inches in length, while females run up to 34. His dimensions of wings and tail will do well enough; but he has both tarsus and mid toe, exceptionally small, and the feet are *not* yellowish (at any rate in the adult) as he says, but greyish white, sometimes with a faint bluish tinge. I note that both feet and cere are wrongly coloured in Dr. Bree's otherwise very tolerable figure.

Professor Newton, from the examination of (I believe) a single sternum, was disposed to separate our Indian and the Crimean races, but the sterna of Eagles differ greatly at times in the same species, while other specimens may be obtained belonging to clearly distinct species, which are utterly undistinguishable; and so far as my experience goes, no reliable conclusions as to the specific distinctness, or identity of nearly allied forms can be arrived at, amongst the Eagles at any rate, merely from an examination of sterna.

In the Etawah district, this bird is known as the "Dhenk" and "Putras."

---

42 BIS. Haliaetus? Pelagicus. PALLAS.

(Kitll. Kupf. der. vog. t. 2. f. 1.—*Falco Leucopterus*, Temm. Pl. Col. 489. The type of *Thallassætus*, Kaup. (1844.) Grays Gen. Vol. I.)

It is with much hesitation, that I provisionally refer to the above-named species, two* examples, now in my museum, of an *Haliaetus*, differing apparently from any species yet recorded from India.

---

* HALIAETUS PELAGICUS ?

DIMENSIONS.	Length.	Expanse.	Wing.	Tail from vent.	Tarsus.	Mid toe to root of claw.	Its claw, straight.	Hind toe.	Its claw, straight.	Inner toe.	Its claw, straight.	Bill, straight.	a long curve.	from gape.	width at gape.	height at front at margin of cere.	Length of cere only.	Distance by which lower tail coverts fall short of end of tail.
MALE.	32·8	86·25	24·8	12·5	3·52	2·1	1·3	1·4	1·52	1·45	1·48	2·0	2·5	2·6	1·7	1·05	0·68	4·0
FEMALE.	34·0	88·0	26·0	13·0	4·2	2·5	1·35	1·55	1·52	1·52	1·5	2·05	2·6	3·05	2·0	1·12	0·85	4·7

The 4th primary is the longest. The 3rd is subequal, the 2nd is 1·4 shorter, the 1st, 4·5, and the 5th 0·6, shorter. Exterior tail feather; M. 1·4 F. 2·2, shorter then the central ones.

DESCRIPTION.

Male. The legs and feet were bright orange yellow, the gape, and a portion of the cere yellow, the upper portion of the cere yellowish brown. Bill blackish horny. Irides, (?) (not recorded). The head, nape, cheeks, ear coverts, and sides of the neck, hair brown; all the feathers white at their

I shot these birds, the one in February 1866, and the other in February 1867, in the neighbourhood of one of the huge jheels which, situated between Mynpooree and Etawah, are a favourite resort of all descriptions of waterfowl and waders, as well as of birds of prey.

They are both young birds; in both, the plumage is mottled and obviously in a transition stage, and in the absence of speci-

---

bases; in some, for the basal half, in some for fully the basal two-thirds, but very little of the white shewing through, the feathers being densely set; all the feathers of these parts long, and linear, those of the occiput especially. The back of the neck, the whole of the back and rump, scapulars, and wing coverts, except the greater primary coverts, as well as the feathers of the breast, and abdomen, a warm buffy fawn color, changing to white at their bases, and more or less broadly tipped with hair brown. The longer scapulars and the upper tail coverts, which latter are very broad, and come down to within some $4\frac{1}{2}$ inches of the tip of the tail, a mixture of yellowish and hair brown, mottled and freckled with white, and yellowish white. Tail, which is very wedge-shaped, reminding one of that of the Lammergeyer, dark brown, mottled all over with dingy yellowish white, which color predominates on the inner webs. The quills, winglet, and greater primary coverts, chocolate brown. The second to the fifth primaries, conspicuously emarginate on the outer web, and with a grey silvery tinge above the emarginations. The first to the fifth primaries, conspicuously notched on the inner webs. The chin and throat, pale buffy brown, the feathers whitish at the base and darker at the tips. The flanks, and thigh coverts, pale yellowish brown, the feathers tipped darker, the lower tail coverts, dingy white, broadly tipped with brown, which in the longer ones is a dark hair brown, in the shorter a dull yellowish brown. Wing lining a sort of umber brown, the bases of all the feathers paler, some of them fawn-colored, and some of them white.

Female. The legs, feet, cere and gape, a sort of brownish yellow. The upper mandible, and claws, blackish horny. The tip of the lower mandible, yellowish horny. The whole of the head, nape, sides of the neck, cheeks, chin, and throat, pale yellowish brown, the feathers white, tipped with yellowish brown, which, owing to the feathers being closely set, is the predominent color, especially on the top of the head. The ear coverts a darker brown, the whole of the back of the neck, back, rump, and upper tail coverts, breast, sides, abdomen, vent, and lower tail coverts, white, comparatively narrowly tipped with yellowish brown, and many of the feathers, with a narrow linear ovate, hair brown, shaft spot, near the tip. As in the male the upper tail coverts are ovate lanceolate, very broad, and long, and reach to within less than six inches of the end of the long wedge-shaped tail. Most of the scapulars, and the tail feathers, are a mixture of dull dark, and pale dingy yellowish brown, every where mottled and freckled with dirty white, which occupies almost the whole of the inner webs of the lateral tail feathers. The wing coverts, except the greater primary coverts, are wood brown, shewing little or nothing of the white bases; most of the tertiaries are mottled white, and dingy yellowish brown, like the tail. The secondaries are a dull, slightly rufous brown, much mottled on the interior webs with white, and the primaries are dark chocolate brown, greyish above the emarginations. Some of the primary greater coverts, are dark chocolate brown, and others are a pale rufous brown.

mens with which to compare them, I can only conjecturally refer them to *H. Pelagicus.*

The shape of the bill and feet, and the excessively rough shagreen-like soles to the feet, would sufficiently prove that they were sea, or fishing Eagles, even if I had not myself observed them in the act of striking at, and capturing, fish.

Their huge size, (female; length, 34; wing 26: male; length 32·8; wing, 25·0) would alone preclude the possibility of their belonging, either to, *Polioaetus Ichthaetus*, or *Pontoaetus Leucogaster*. Besides, they are true *Haliaeti*, and not *Pontoaeti*, the tarsi covered posteriorly (as on the sides) with *small*, (and not *large*,) irregularly placed scales. In *this* respect, their tarsi correspond precisely with those of *H. Leucoryphus*. Again, Dr. Jerdon tells us, that *Pontoaetus Leucogaster* has been separated by Hodgson, as *Cuncuma*, differing, in the tarsi being less feathered in front, than the true *Haliaeti*, whereas these birds have the tarsi considerably more feathered than *Haliaetus Leucoryphus* ever has. Moreover, the transverse scutation does not descend on to the foot, as in *Pontoaetus*, in fact, there is even less of this on the front of the tarsi, in these two specimens, than in *H. Leucoryphus*.

From this latter species they differ, first, in the much deeper and far less sinuated* upper mandible; 2nd, in the tarsus, feathered in front, for from five-eighths to three-fifths of the length; 3rd, in the excessively rounded, or in fact, wedge-shaped tail, and 4th, in the very long and broad upper tail coverts. Moreover, I have specimens of *H. Leucoryphus*, in every stage of plumage, from the half-fledged nestling, to the old adult, and the plumage of the two birds that I provisionally identify with *Pelagicus*, differs, most conspicuously, from *any* stage of *Leucoryphus*.

So far as the very slight sinuation of the bill goes, these birds correspond apparently, with *H. Albicilla*. I have no specimen of this latter species, but the large figures of the head, in Macgillivray, (Fig. 217, Vol. III.) and in Gray's genera of birds, (Aquilinæ, Details, No. 8,) agree in this respect, although, it must be admitted that, in every other respect, they differ so widely, that no one would imagine, that they were intended to represent the same species.

These Eagles, be they what species they may, (and if not *Pelagicus*, they may be new, in which case I name them *Brooksi*, after my valued friend and coadjutor W. E. Brooks, C. E.,) are excessively wary. I have seen *many* examples,

---

* According to Dr. Jerdon, *Pontoaetus Leucogaster* has a *more* sinuated bill than even *H. Leucoryphus*.

always in the neighbourhood of very large jheels, and on two occasions, apparently in company, with one, or two huge, sea-gull looking Eagles. I never could get within a quarter of a mile of these latter, but from what I could make out of them, with binoculars, they appeared to correspond well with *Cuncuma Leucogaster*, and it was to this species, that I formerly referred these young birds.

The size, however, (females, even, of this latter species, never apparently exceeding 31 inches in length, with wing 24·5,) the scarcely sinuated bill, the tarsus feathered in front, for nearly three-fifths, the bare portion of the tarsus, with only 4, (in one specimen), or 5, (in the other), rather broad, transverse scutæ, render any such identification impossible.

Whenever I have observed them, these birds have either been sitting on some post in the middle of, or on the bare branch of some high tree overlooking some large sheet of water, or else, busy fishing, circling round and round, at no great height above the water, and after a time suddenly striking with great rapidity at some fish. Although there were multitudes of Teal and water fowl, I never saw them attempt to capture any.

These birds are known to the native fowlers, at the Najjuffgurh jheel, but only as occasional visitants, in the cold weather, and they must be rare, as the natives have no proper distinctive name for them, that I could learn, though they recognized their distinctness from the common *H. Fulviventer*, some twenty pairs of which, breed usually in the neighbourhood of the jheel.

Temminck figures this species, *(Pelagicus)* (Pl. Col. 489) under the name of *Falco Leucopterus*, and the bill as shown in his plate, (the upper mandible very high, the lower comparatively slender, and the commissure almost perfectly straight,) corresponds exactly with our Indian specimens.

He thus describes the adults. Bill, cere, bare orbital space, bare portion of tarsus and feet, bright yellow; irides golden; a broad frontal band, the upper half of the wings from the carpal joint, to the greater coverts, the tibial and tarsal plumes, vent, lower tail coverts and tail, pure white. The whole of the rest of the plumage, blackish brown. He adds, that the old female attains a length of 38 inches, but these being French inches, and equal, each to 1·06577 English inches, are equivalent to 40·5 English inches. His measurements, however, were mostly taken from skins, and are in many cases excessive, so that this difference in size, (our young female only measuring 34 inches) does not bar the possibility, of our birds being really *Peiagicus*. What, however, puzzles me is, that in his figure, the tail is shown as almost square, while in our bird, it is not merely conspicuously rounded, but is actually wedge-shaped, recalling the tails of the Lammergeyer, or of the Australian *Aquila Audax*, which latter, however, is smaller, and has the tarsi feathered to the feet.

I have sometimes fancied, that these birds might belong to the European species *H. Albicilla.* This latter species, is found not only throughout Enrope, extending to Sicily and Corfu to the South, and Iceland and Greenland to the North, but almost throughout Siberia, at Lake Baikal, in the upper and middle Amoor where Radde procured it, and in the lower Amoor, and generally the east coast of northern Asia, where H. L. v. Schrenk obtained it, but only, if I remember rightly, in the winter months. *Pelagicus*, on the other hand, has only as yet, I believe, been obtained in Japan, and the extreme east of Siberia; Middendorf procured it in Stanawoi, and Pallas originally described it, I believe, from Kamschatska, so that, of the two, probabilities would be in favour of our birds being the young of *Albicilla*. With the plumage of these, as described by European writers, they agree well enough, but then the bills are so much higher, in proportion to their length, than those of the European species, as figured by Gray, and Macgillivray,* that I cannot help doubting their belonging to it.

Since the above was written, I have learnt from Mr. Brooks, that he has obtained a specimen, precisely similar to one of mine. Others will doubtless occur, and I therefore, to aid other observers, in determining the species to which any specimens that they may obtain, belong, append full descriptions, and measurements, of *H. Albicilla*, taken from Macgillivray.

"MALE. The cere and bill are pale yellow, the iris bright yellow; the tarsi and toes gamboge, the claws black, with a tinge of greyish blue. The plumage of the head, neck, fore-part of the back and breast, with the upper wing coverts greyish yellow, the feathers all greyish brown at the base; of the other parts greyish brown, edged with yellowish grey, the scapulars and feathers of the rump glossed with purple, those of the abdomen, tibiæ, and sub-caudal region inclining to chocolate brown; the quills and alular feathers brownish black, with a tinge of grey, the inner secondaries inclining to greyish brown; the shafts of all, white towards the base; the lower surface of the quills, and the large coverts tinged with greyish blue. The upper tail coverts and the tail are white (generally freckled with dusky grey at the base). The down on the breast is pale grey, that on the sides darker.

---

* But then while *figuring* a long, comparatively low bill, Macgillivray *tells* us, that "the bill is *larger* and *higher*, than in any species known, excepting *Haliaetus Washingtoni!*"

Length, to end of tail, 36 inches; extent of wings, 72; bill, along the ridge, 3·41 inches, along the edge of lower mandible, 3, its height, 1·41; wing from flexure, 24; tail, 11·5; tarsus, 4; first toe, 1·33, its claw, 2·16; second toe, 1·58, its claw, 2·16; third toe, 3, its claw, 1·41; fourth toe, 2·08, its claw, 1·58.

FEMALE. The female does not differ from the male in color, and her superiority in size is often not very remarkable.

Length to end of tail, 40 inches; extent of wings, 80; bill along the ridge, 3·91, along the edge of lower mandible, 3·33, its height, 1·66; wing from flexure, 27·5; tail, 12; tarsus, 4·5; first toe, 1·5, its claw, 2·25; second toe, 1·16, its claw, 2·33; third toe, 3·08, its claw, 1·64; fourth toe, 1·66, its claw, 1·41.

YOUNG. The bill is brownish black, the base of the lower mandible yellow, the cere greenish yellow; the feet yellow, the claws black. The bases of all the feathers are brownish white, their middle parts light reddish brown, their tips only blackish brown. The head and nape are dark brown, each feather with a minute, brownish white spot on the tip. On the middle of the back, and on the wings, light reddish brown is the prevalent color, the black tips of comparatively small extent; on the third part of the back, there is much white, that color extending farther from the base. The quills and larger wing coverts, are blackish brown, with a tinge of grey; the tail feathers brownish white in the centre, black towards the margins, with irregular white dots, the lower parts are of the same colors as the back, or are pale reddish brown, marked with longitudinal streaks and spots of dark brown; the lower wing coverts brown, the tail coverts white, with light brown tips.

PROGRESS TOWARD MATURITY. In the second year, the young exhibit little difference, being, however, of a darker tint on the back and wings. An individual at this age, has the bill brownish black, tinged with blue, its base and the cere greenish yellow; the iris hazel brown; the feet gamboge, the claws brownish black. The head and nape are dark brown, the base of all the feathers, on the upper parts, is white: on the hind neck and fore-parts of the back that colour, tinged with yellowish brown, prevails, a lanceolate or obovate deep brown spot, being on each feather towards the end; on the middle of the back, the brown prevails, on the hind part white, and the rump and upper tail coverts are light brown, tipped with darker. The scapulars are dark brown, with a purplish tinge, the wing coverts dark brown at the end, but most of the larger pale brown in the greater part of their extent; the quills black, with a purplish grey tinge, the secondaries gradually becoming more brown, and all faintly variegated with light grey and brown on the inner webs. The tail is brownish black, with a tinge of grey, and more or less finely mottled with whitish. The lower parts may be described as brownish white, longitudinally streaked with dark brown, there being a lanceolate patch of the latter on each feather; the lower wing coverts and feathers of the legs dark brown; the lower surface of the quills bluish grey; the lower tail coverts white, tipped with brown; the down on the breast pure white.

REMARKS. In this species, the bill and iris change from dusky brown to pale yellow, and the plumage, at first white at the base, and dark brown at the end, gradually loses its white, while the dark parts become paler and more extended, the final colouring being more uniform.

The tail forms no exception, for its basal white also diminishes; but the white which is gradually substituted for the brownish black, spreads from near the end to the base."

---

43. Cuncuma Leucogaster, GMEL.

THE WHITE-BELLIED SEA EAGLE.

Dr. Jerdon's description of the soft parts of this Eagle, hardly corresponds with those of other authorities. He gives the irides, brownish yellow, the cere, pale greenish yellow, and the legs, dirty white. Mr. Wallace (Ibis 1868) gives the "Bill, black, base and cere, lead colour; feet, very pale yellow; iris olive brown. Length, 26 to 29 inches."

Mr. Gould again, in his hand-book to the birds of Australia, p. 16, says that, "the cere, lores and horny space over the eye, are bluish lead colour, slightly tinged with green, and the legs and feet yellowish white."

I have never killed this bird myself, nor found its nest; Dr. Jerdon tells us that they breed at Pigeon Island, (thirty miles or so south of Honawr, on the western coast), in December, January, and February, and my friend Mr. H. R. P. Carter, has verified this observation, through a correspondent, and, I believe, procured eggs thence, but I have not yet received these.

Mr. Gould (loc. cit) has the following interesting remarks, on the breeding of this species.

"With regard to the nidification of the white-bellied Sea Eagle, I could not fail to remark how readily the birds accommodate themselves to the different circumstances in which they are placed; for while, on the mainland, they invariably construct their large flat nest on a fork of the most lofty trees, on the islands, where not a tree is to be found, it is placed on the flat surface of a large stone, the materials of which it is formed, being twigs and branches of the Barilla, a low shrub which is there plentiful. The eggs are almost invariably two in number, of a dull white, faintly stained with reddish brown, two inches and nine lines long, by two inches and three lines broad."

This bird occurs, but only, apparently, near the sea coast, throughout India, Burmah, the Andaman Islands, (Tytler) Malacca, Celebes, Gilolo, Batchian, Morty, Aru Is. (Wallace) Sumatra, Java, and Timor (Mus. Lugd.) In upper, or continental India, it is excessively rare, if indeed it ever occur. Mr. R. Thompson it is true, tells me, that he feels confident that this bird breeds on the Himalayan rivers, and that he has frequently met with it on the smaller streams of the Ram Gunga valley, but I cannot help suspecting that he has mistaken for this species, the bird that I have provisionally identified with *H. Pelagicus*, and which I have described under No. 42 Bis.

Mr. Gould remarks, that this species " depends almost entirely for its subsistence upon the dead Cetacea, fish, etc. that may be thrown up by the sea, and left on the shore, by the receding waves, to which in all probability are added, living moluscas and other lower marine animals." The following interesting notes by Colonel Tytler show, that when fish are eccentric enough to move about on the top of, instead of *in* the sea, they form a favorite food of this Eagle.

" This species is not uncommon, throughout all the islands of the Andaman group. At Port Blair, it is often called the Duck Eagle, from the quacking sound it emits, (very similar to the quack of a Duck,) when flying, and particularly when fighting with another of the same species, about some captured fish.

" The harbour of Port Blair swarms with a species of Pipe-fish; these are constantly seen skimming along the surface of the water, (apparently on their tails,) for long distances, and it is a beautiful sight to see this fine Sea Eagle, whilst soaring high in air, dash down like a falling cannon ball on one of these wave-walking fishes, almost to a certainty capturing it, before it has time to sink into its natural element. No sooner, however, does one of these Eagles capture a fish, than another is sure to be down upon him, eager to rob him of his prey. A series of skirmishes, ending in a regular chase, takes place, and away go the Eagles, each quacking louder than the other, until both disappear far out at sea, leaving the result of the contest uncertain.

" Whilst passing in the steamer near the island of Narkandam (between Burmah and the Andamans) for the purpose of stocking it with Pigs, Goats, and Fowls, for the benefit of any future cast-aways on that lonely island, I observed a very great number of these Sea Eagles on the rocks and trees, and as they must be there perfectly undisturbed, this doubtless, is one of their breeding-places. At Barren Island, I also observed numbers of this Eagle, and for this, the great abundance of dead fish generally strewing its shores would account. There is a volcano on this island, which is always in a more or less active state of eruption; sulphur and sulphur springs abound in it, and there is said to be a boiling spring, in one place, under water, near the shore, and either owing to the heat of the water, or to noxious gases or substances finding their way into the sea in its neighbourhood, the shores of this island are almost always strewn with dead and decaying fish; a rather objectionable locality to human visitors, but a perfect paradise to the white-bellied Sea Eagle."

---

44. Buteo Vulgaris, Bechstein.

The Common Buzzard, *(of Europe)*.

I have never seen any specimen, of this species, which had been obtained in India. The specimen to which Dr. Jerdon refers, (Birds of India, Vol. I. p. 87) as killed on the Neilgherries, and which he figured, (Ill. Ind. Orn. pl. 27) belonged to a different species, *B. Desertorum ?* (No. 44 bis.) I very much question, whether the common Buzzard of Europe, really does occur in India; every Indian killed example, as yet sent me, as belonging to this species has proved to belong to that next to be noticed.

Mr. Blyth says, that this species "certainly occurs in the N. W. Himalayas, near Mussouree, where several specimens were collected by Dr. Stewart." I saw two of the specimens, to which I believe Mr. Blyth refers, and though not then acquainted with the difference between the two species, remember these specimens well, and believe them to have belonged to the next species. In another place, Mr. Blyth says "numerous examples from the N. W. Himalayas, several of which are in the same collection" (the Calcutta Museum) "I consider to be unmistakeably *B. Vulgaris*." When I visited it early in 1868, the Calcutta Museum only contained two Indian killed specimens, labelled *B. Vulgaris*, one from Darjeeling and the other from Nepal, (none at all from the N. W. Himalayas,) and both these two I should refer to the next species.

After all, this species may occur in the Himalayas, and,

indeed, the natural presumption is, that Blyth is right, and that I am wrong, and that it *does* so occur. Still I have thought it necessary to put my own doubts on the subject prominently forward, in view to stimulating enquiry.

Of the nidification of the common Buzzard in India, nothing has been recorded. Of its nidification in Great Britain, I take the following from Mr. Yarrell: "In Scotland, the Buzzard forms its nest on rocks, or on the edges of steep scars or beds of torrents; one nest described by Mr. MacGillivray, was placed on the top of a steep bank or rut of a stream, and was composed of twigs, heath, wool and some other substances. In England, the Buzzard usually builds, or takes to a nest, in the forked branches of a tree in a large wood; the materials with which the nest is made, or repaired, are similar to those that have been already named.

The female lays two or three, and sometimes, four eggs, of a short oval form, two inches three lines in length, by one inch and ten lines in breadth, of a soiled white colour, slightly spotted with pale brown."

Mr. Hewitson tells us that, where trees are available, its nest is built on them, and is composed of sticks lined with a quantity of wool, fur and such like soft materials, but that in Scotland, where it inhabits treeless districts, it makes its nest, (which is very much like an Eagle's, except in size,and lined with the same kind of dry grass,) upon the ledges of rocks. He further tells us, that the eggs, which are three or four in number, vary according to the age of the bird, (I wonder whether this is a *well* ascertained fact) and are sometimes spotless white. He mentions one egg as beautifully colored, with different tints of lilac and purple, as also that eggs were brought to a friend of his, for several successive years from the same locality, and doubtless the produce of the same pair, which the first year were white, or nearly so, the second year slightly marked with indistinct yellowish brown, increasing each year in the intensity of their colouring, till the spots became of a rich dark brown. The two eggs which he figures are broad ovals, (one of them indeed is almost spherical) and measure 2·33 × 1·84, and 2·08 × 1·77. The one is boldly blotched and spotted, with clear brownish red, (in which a few dark lines are mingled) and reddish fawn colour, on a pale bluish white, but somewhat soiled ground, the markings being almost exclusively confined, to the broad-end half of the egg; and the other is more thickly clouded, streaked and spotted, with pale brownish red and purplish black, on a ground almost entirely over clouded with reddish fawn.

Dr. Jerdon gives the wing of the female of this species at 18 inches; this seems to me too large. Mr. Yarrell gives it at

14·37, and those of two specimens in my collection, from Europe, marked females, measure,* 15·1, and 15 inches respectively.

I find the following description in the Naturalist's Library, which may be useful to observers in India. "The common Buzzard varies considerably in the colouring of the plumage, scarcely two specimens being similar. The difference consists chiefly, in the intensity of the tint of the upper parts, and in the presence of a greater or lesser degree of marking below. The general colour above, is some shade of umber brown, varying to hair brown, and brocoli brown; the feathers darker in the centre, often edged with a paler tint, or with reddish yellow, and generally glossed with a rich shining purple, which is most prevalent in dark coloured specimens. Wings at the tips are deep umber brown, shading into pure white at the base, where the feather becomes soft and downy; they are crossed with irregular, clouded, dark bars, which decrease in breadth and intensity, towards the roots. The under parts are sometimes pale yellowish white, streaked on the throat and breast, with shades of brown, of different intensity, and on the belly and vent crossed by broad irregular bars: sometimes they are of a uniform tint, nearly as dark as the upper surface of the body, and very little interrupted, and sometimes a very dark and deep band, tinted with purple, occupies the whole belly, while the other parts are streaked and marked with a moderate proportion of brown; the plumes of the thighs are generally dark, crossed with reddish; the tail is slightly rounded, the ground colour whitish, of a chaste grey tinted with ochraceous, or of a reddish yellow; it is crossed by a broad bar of umber brown, near the tip, and by seven or eight narrow ones, of the same colour. In many of its variations it is extremely beautiful. The length of a male specimen before us is twenty inches, that of a female, nearly twenty-three."

Mr. Yarrell's description is as follows:

"The beak is bluish black, darkest in colour towards the point, the cere yellow, the irides generally yellow; but as the common Buzzard, and indeed all the Buzzards, are subject to considerable variation in the colour of their plumage, the irides are observed to vary also. presenting some reference to the prevailing tone of the colour of the feathers. The upper part of the head, occiput, and cheeks, pale brown, streaked longitudinally with darker brown; the whole of the back, wing coverts, upper tail coverts, and upper surface of the tail feathers, dark clove

* The wings of two specimens in Colonel Tytler's collection, measure 16·25, and 15 inches respectively.

brown, the latter barred with lighter brown, the feathers of the former named parts having lighter coloured edges ; the wing primaries, brownish black ; the chin and throat, almost white ; front of the neck, breast, under wing coverts, belly and thighs, greyish white, spotted and streaked with brocoli brown ; under tail coverts, white ; under surface of the tail feathers, greyish white, barred transversely with dark wood brown ; legs and toes yellow ; the claws black."

As it seems most essential to afford observers in the Hills, the utmost assistance possible, in determining, whether any of the Buzzards that they may obtain, really belong to this species or not, I proceed further to quote largely from Mr. Macgillivray's admirable history of British Birds.

The following are his characters of the species :

"Male, with the upper parts, deep brown, the feathers margined with paler, the lower parts, yellowish-white, with longitudinal, oblong, brown spots, the tail with numerous brown and pale bands. Female, deep brown above, and beneath the throat streaked with whitish, the breast spotted with the same. Young, with the feathers margined with light red.

He gives the following detailed description of the male, female, and young.

Male. The wings are large and rounded, with twenty-five quills, the first four primaries abruptly cut out on the inner web, the first six attenuated on the outer ; the first quill four inches shorter than the third, which is longest, but exceeds the fourth only by one-twelfth of an inch, the fifth very little shorter, the second intermediate between the fifth and sixth, the first equal to the eighth. The tail is rather long, broad, and slightly rounded, the middle feather being about three quarters of an inch longer than the lateral.

The bill is black, at the base greyish blue, its soft margins at the base, yellow, the cere and bare space over the eye, greenish-yellow; the irides, brownish yellow ; the feet, bright yellow, the claws black, tinged with blue at the base. The general colour of the upper parts is umber brown, glossed with a tinge of purple ; but on the head and hind neck streaked with yellowish-white, the bases and margins of the feathers being of that colour. The feathers of the back and wings with the margins pale, or brownish-grey ; they and the scapulars barred with white in their concealed parts, the bases of all being white, which becomes apparent on the lined neck when they are raised ; the upper tail coverts are barred with whitish. The primary quills are brownish-black towards the end, the secondaries brown, a great part of the inner webs towards the base white, barred with brown, the bars more extended on the secondaries. The tail is marked with ten or twelve brown bars, alternating with others of a pale greyish-brown, the tips whitish. The cheeks and sides of the neck are yellowish-white, with brown lunar or oblong markings; the throat, fore-neck, and middle of the breast yellowish-white, with the shafts brown; the ground color of the other parts the same, but each feather with an oblong, brown, longitudinal mark; the lower tail coverts barred, the feathers of the legs tinged with reddish, and barred or patched with brown. The lower wings-coverts yellowish-white, spotted and barred with brown; and the white of the inner webs of the primaries forming a conspicuous patch.

Length to end of tail 19·5 inches; extent of wings, 49; wing from flexure, 16·5; tail, 9; bill along the ridge, 1·58, along the edge of lower mandible, 1·55; tarsus, 2·83; hind toe 0·74, its claw 1; second toe, 1, its claw, 1·08; third toe 1·55; its claw, 0·83; fourth toe, 1, its claw, 0·581.

Female. The female is considerably larger than the male, and although similar in colouring, differs in several respects. The colors of the bill, iris, and feet are the same as in the male. The upper parts are of a darker and more uniform brown, the bases of the feathers dull grey; and only white on the hind-neck; the whitish bands on the scapulars more obscure. The wings and tail are colored as in the male, only the last brown bar, on the latter, is much broader than the rest. The predominant color of the lower parts is chocolate-brown; but the cheeks and throat are streaked with dull brownish-white, the fore-neck obscurely, the middle of the breast conspicuously, transversely spotted or barred with yellowish white, intermixed with reddish; the inner and anterior feathers of the legs barred with brownish-red; the lower tail-coverts white, barred with brown, the lower surface of the wing as in the male, but much darker, the white patch, consequently, more conspicuous.

Length to end of tail, 22 inches; extent of wing, 61; wing from flexure, 17; tail, 9·75; bill along the ridge, 1·58; tarsus, 3; first toe, 1, its claw, 1·25; second toe, 0·91, its claw, 1·25; third toe, 1·5, its claw, 1·08; fourth toe, 1·08, its claw, 0·83.

Another individual, shot in Aberdeenshire, in May, 1817, was similar to the above; the whole upper surface, rich brown; on the upper part of the back, the feathers laterally margined with light ferruginous, the scapulars and wing coverts with that colour and white; the primary quills nearly black, glossed with purple toward the end; the secondaries nearly of the general tint; all with the inner webs edged with white, and barred with a deeper shade of brown; on its lower surface, the wing much lighter, there being a white patch, including part of the inner webs of the five outer quills; the coverts barred with white, their ground colour being, toward the base, light ferruginous, toward the end deep brown; the tail deep brown, barred with greyish and reddish, or marked with alternate bars of brown and brownish grey, the last dark bar being the broadest, and the tips reddish-white; nine dark bars on the middle, and ten on the lateral feathers; on the lower surface the prevailing colour brown, of a lighter shade than the upper; on the fore-neck spotted, on the breast barred, with white; the tibial feathers brown, tipped with ferruginous.

Length, 21·5 inches; extent of wings, 50.

These differences between the adult male, and the adult female, I have found to be very constant, although individuals of each sex vary considerably.

Variations. Males vary, in having the white of the lower parts, more or less extended, and the streaks and spots of greater or less breadth. Sometimes the white is so extended on both surfaces, that it might be said to form the ground colour, which is then merely spotted with brown. Females differ also in the extent of the white spots and bars beneath, but they are always darker and more uniformly coloured than the males. Great differences are observed in the number of the scutella, and I have seen a male, which had none on the fore part of the tibia, it having been covered with small scales. When the feathers are old, they become very ragged and pointed, change from deep glossy brown to greyish-brown, with the edges yellowish or even whitish-brown; so that individuals in this state, seem very different from those of which the plumage is fresh, and in those which are moulting, the contrast between the old and new feathers is very conspicuous.

Young. A male shot in October, having its plumage complete, and known to be a young bird by the softness and vascularity of its bones, was as follows:

The cere and soft margins of the bill greenish-yellow, the iris hazel, the tarsi and toes, yellow with a tinge of green, the bills and claws black. The upper part of the head, and the hind-neck are dark brown, longitudinally streaked with yellowish-white, the lateral margins of the feathers being of that colour. The rest of the upper parts deep brown, glossed with purple, all the feathers laterally margined with light-red; the scapulars and some of the large wing-coverts, with several bands of white on their inner webs, of which the edge is mottled with reddish. The hind part of the back is of a uniform dark brown; but the upper tail coverts are barred with light red. The primary quills are brownish black, with the outer webs tinged with grey toward the end, the inner white from the base to beyond the middle, and having several irregular dusky bands. Tail banded with brownish-grey and blackish brown, there being ten bands on the middle feathers, and twelve on the outer, the last dark band little larger than the next, the tips whitish. The sides of the head and throat are yellowish white streaked with brown; the rest of the lower parts yellowish white, longitudinally marked with oblong brown spots, the sides chiefly brown; the lower tail-coverts with a brown spot; the plumage of the legs and tarsi irregularly banded with brown and light red. The dull light red edgings of the feathers are characteristic of the young, as is also the case in the Sparrow-Hawk, Merlin, and many other species.

A female of the same age, differs chiefly, in having less white on the lower parts, the breast being of a nearly uniform brown, although on many of the feathers, there are large reddish-white spots. The feathers of the legs and tarsi are variegated with brown, white, and light red, as are those of the abdomen, and the lower tail-coverts yellowish, barred with brown.

Progress with Maturity.—At the next moult, the bird assumes a more uniform brown colour on the upper parts, the light red markings becoming light brown, or brownish-white. It appears that, as it advances in age, the marginal white of the feathers extends, until the lower parts in the males become nearly white, there being merely an oblong brown spot on each feather, and the white predominates over the brown on the upper parts. In the females, similar changes take place, but the lower parts are always more brown than in the males. I have seen some individuals that had the plumage white, with the exception of the quills, tail and some oblong spots on the upper parts and breast. It thus appears that at first the colors of the plumage are darker than when the bird has attained maturity, and that the white predominates over the brown in old age; but it must be confessed that sufficiently correct observations have not been made on this subject, and that much remains to be done, before the variations of color, in the species, are well understood. The iris, in young birds is brown, in adult birds yellow.

Mr. Temminck states, that in adult individuals, the upper parts, the neck and breast, are dark brown; the throat and belly brownish grey but variegated with spots of a darker brown, the tail with twelve transverse bands, the bill lead-colour, the cere, iris and feet yellow. Very old individuals, he says, have the plumage very deep brown, or chocolate colour, the throat whitish with small longitudinal brown streaks, some white transverse bands on the belly, and yellowish bands towards the abdomen. The young of the year, according to him, have the general colour light brown, variegated with whitish and yellowish, the throat white with longitudinal spots, the feathers of the breast bordered with white, the middle of the belly whitish, with large longitudinal oval or cordate spots. Birds of this latter kind, I think, are old males, those described in the preceding sentence, old females.

---

44 BIS. Buteo Desertorum, DAUDIN.

THE AFRICAN BUZZARD.

Buteo Rufiventer, Jerdon.
„ Capensis, Schlegel.
„ Cirtensis, Le Vaill. Junr.
Falco Vulpinus, Licht.

I have already ventured to express some doubts as to the occurrence of *Buteo Vulgaris* in India, and it is certain that whether this species does or does not occur, the present species figured by Jerdon as *Rufiventer* (Ill. In. Orn. plate 27,) which is common in the Himalayas, is the one that in most Indian collections, does duty for it. This is the species which Dr. Jerdon describes at page 87 of the "Birds of India," when he mentions the specimen shot in the Neilgherries; this is the species to which belong specimens obtained in Cashmere by Dr. Jerdon, and given to Colonel Tytler and myself, by him, as *B. Vulgaris;* and this also, is certainly the species of which Dr. Stewart obtained *some* specimens near Mussourie, *(vide Mr. Blyth's remarks already quoted, page* 261*)* though I cannot assert that he may not have procured others of the true *B. Vulgaris.* Whether this Indian species, be really identical with *B. Desortorum*, Daudin; and *B. Cirtensis*, Le Vaill. Jun., figured by Mr. Bree as *B. Tachardus*, Daudin, I cannot pretend* to say. In this identifi-

---

* My own private belief is, that ours is a larger bird. Layard gives the wing of the South African species, as 14 inches. For comparison, I quote his description &c.

"Upper parts brown; each feather having pale edges, and a black shaft. Head, pale fulvous, streaked with brown. Wing feathers dark brown. Tail feathers fulvous, inclined to rufous, and narrowly barred with brown; the broadest bar at the tip. Under parts, pale fulvous; almost white on the chin and throat; streaked on the two latter, and blotched on the former

cation I merely follow Mr. Gurney, admittedly the best authority in such matters. I quote his remarks on the subject from the Ibis. (1862, p. 361.)

"I have myself no doubt that the "Tachard" of Le Vaillant, and consequently the *Buteo Tachardus* of Daudin, is identical with *Pernis apivorus*, a species which I have twice received from the colony of Natal."

Most ornithologists have erroneously attributed the name of *Buteo tachardus* of Daudin, to the Lesser Buzzard of South Africa, for which M. Des Murs now suggests the new specific appellation of *Buteo delalandi*. This is, as it seems to me, unnecessary; for I cannot but think, that this small Buzzard is the "Rougri" of Le Vaillant, (*Buteo desertorum* of Daudin,) the description and figure of which appear to me to agree with the species now under consideration in all points except one, namely, that the cere and bill are *both* described as yellow, instead of the cere *only*. But may not this have been a mere *lapsus calami* of the author, copied by the artist into his drawing, which was probably made from a skin, of which the bill was faded, or (as is frequently the case in skins, brought from hot countries) in which the horny covering of the upper mandible had shelled off?

Such at least seems to me the probability, and with that view, I consider the small Buzzard of South Africa, as entitled to the specific name *desertorum*.

M. Des Murs expresses a strong opinion, that the small Buzzard of South Africa, is specifically distinct, from that of North Africa, (*Buteo Cirtensis* of the "Exploration de l' Algerie,") but the only difference I can perceive between them is, that the South African bird is usually less rufous, and is somewhat paler on the breast, which are hardly sufficient grounds for a specific distinction.

The geographical range of *Buteo Cirtensis*, (even if it be distinct from its South African Congener) is still very extensive,

---

with brown. Thighs rufous, faintly blotched with fulvous. Vent feathers pale fulvous. Length 1′ 8″; wing, 14″; tail, 7.″ Irides yellow." Fully adult birds become throughout, of a deep rufous brown, blotched with dark markings. In this stage they constitute Le Vaillaint's species, called *Le Rougri*, Ois d' Af., Pl. 17."

I may add that a particularly fine male, unquestionably *B. Desertorum*, from South Africa, now in Colonel Tytler's museum, measured—Length 22, wing 14·5, tail 8·38, tarsus 2·5, feathered in front for one inch. In plumage it greatly resembled some of our Himalayan birds, but, was *much* smaller than *any* of these. Personally, I feel by no means satisfied that our Indian bird is *Desertorum*.

as it is found generally in North Africa, from Mogador to Egypt; and it also occurs in European Turkey, in Southern Russia on the Volga, at Smyrna, at Erzeroum, in Madras, and in Nepal.

The Indian specimens which I have seen, and also that from Erzeroum, are less rufous and more chocolate coloured, especially on the under parts, than more western specimens. This darker form of colouring, would seem to be as worthy of specific distinction, as the paler breasted race of South Africa, and it has been figured and described, as distinct, by Mr. Jerdon, in his 'Illustrations of Indian Ornithology,' (pl. 27,) under the title of *Buteo rufiventer*.

M. Des Murs well remarks, that *Buteo Cirtensis* is closely allied to the large rufous Buzzard of North Eastern Africa, South Eastern Europe and Asia."

The present species, (I mean the Indian race,) so far as I yet know, is confined to the Neilgherries, and the Himalayas. A very large number of specimens from the Himalayas, have passed through my hands, and though I have never shot one myself, the bird appears to be not uncommon anywhere in these Hills from Murree to Darjeeling.

In size, they appear to differ little from the common Buzzard of Europe, though their form seems somewhat slenderer, but the wings which reach to or very near to, the end of the tail, are proportionally longer I think. Unfortunately, European writers as a rule, give very few dimensions, and I cannot therefore be sure in regard to this latter point.

Mr. Yarrell gives the wing of the female European Buzzard, at 14·37 inches; those of two specimens in my collections measure 15 and 15·1, and of two in Colonel Tytler's, 16·25 and 15, while the wings of the present species, measure from 15·5 in males, up to 17·0 in females. Dr. Bree, whose figure, *tolerably* well accords with some of my specimens, gives the wing as only 14·5, but none of the numerous Indian examples that I have examined, have had the wings so short. I note that Dr. Bree correctly represents, (p. 97, Vol. I.) the wings as reaching to the end of the tail; while in Jerdon's figure (above referred to) they are drawn out of position, the carpal joint being advanced too high upon the neck, and the tips of the wings falling considerably short of the end of the tail.

Besides the greater length of wing, this species appears to differ from the common Buzzard, in the prevailing rufous character of its under surface. There is often a yellow tinge in these parts, in *B. Vulgaris*, and the tibial and tarsal plumes are banded reddish, but in no specimen of the common Buzzard that I have yet seen, or can find described, does there appear that predominance of rufous, which characterizes the present species. Again, the adult of this species, (herein resembling *Ferox*) always has the outer webs of the second to the sixth or seventh primary, *silvered* above the emarginations, and this would not appear to be the case in *B. Vulgaris*. From *B. Ferox*, its smaller size distinguishes it; the wings in this latter species varying from 16·25 and upwards in males, to fully 19 inches in large females. The feet and claws too are smaller, and while in no instance have I found the tarsus of *Ferox* less than 3·2, (and it is no less than 3·7 in one large female now before me) in no instance have I found the tarsus of the present species to exceed 2·9, and in the males it often barely exceeds 2·7. I am aware that Bree gives the tarsus 3; but in no one, out of 21 Indian killed specimens, has it exceeded 2·9 scant.

Mr. Gurney, quoted by Dr. Bree says: "The appearance of this bird when alive, is less heavy and more elegant than that of *B. Vulgaris*. My living specimen, which was dull brown when I bought it a year ago, has moulted into a rich rufous plumage, and one that was alive in the Zoological Gardens, a few years ago, underwent a similar change."

This bird of Mr. Gurney's, is described as having "the crown of the head, back, and scapulars a dark ashy brown, each feather having a narrow streak of brown down the centre, shadowed with a rusty red." The tail, tibial and tarsal plumes are figured an uniform dark cinnamon red. "The cere, feet and tarsi," Mr. Gurney tells us, "are lemon yellow, and the iris is sometimes a light hazel, and sometimes yellow, probably assuming the latter colour as the bird advances in age: a similar variation, which exists in the iris of the common Buzzard, is, however, not always referable to age, as I have ascertained by experience. The bill is dark lead colour, but somewhat lighter adjoining the throat and cere."

The plumage of our Himalayan birds, varies most remarkably, but no single specimen that I have yet seen, agrees *very* closely with either Dr. Bree's figure, or any description of *B. Desertorum* or *B. Cirtensis* to which I have access.

One common type of plumage is as follows. The whole of the top of the head, occiput, nape and back of the neck dark brown, (the shafts almost black) each feather more or less narrowly margined at the sides, (*not* at the extreme tips) with bright rufous fawn. The interscapular region similar, but a still darker brown, often glossed with purple and but little of the rufous showing, owing to the close overlapping of the feathers, leaving little but their tips visible. The middle of the back deep hair brown, the rump and upper tail coverts very pure, deep, cinnamon rufous, with conspicuous white shafts. The central tail feathers, a slightly paler cinnamon rufous, somewhat infuscated towards the margins, and with freckled and mottled traces of a single, broad, subterminal, umber brown, transverse bar. The lateral tail feathers similar, but, with the subterminal bar somewhat better marked, and running up the outer margins for an inch or so, and paling on the inner webs towards the bases. (One specimen in this stage has two or three, much abraded, unmoulted feathers in the tail, these have a dirty yellowish white ground, tinged with cinnamon towards the tips, which for the terminal one inch, are dull hair brown, above which are traces of three or four, wavy, irregular, more or less mottled, quarter inch, transverse bars of the same colour.) The wings and scapulars are umber brown, many of the feathers with a purple gloss, and all the shorter scapulars, and lesser coverts, margined, except quite at the tips, with bright rufous, or in some, rufous fawn. The outer webs of the second, and succeeding primaries, above the emarginations, are silver grey, tinged, and in some cases freckled, and mottled, with cinnamon rufous, and the white on the upper surfaces, of the inner webs of all the later primaries, and most of the secondaries, replaced by the same colour, with which even the earlier primaries are tinged. The ear coverts are fulvous white, each feather with a dull, rufous brown, shaft stripe. There is a dark brown cheek stripe from the base of the lower mandible, running under the ear coverts, and this is more or less distinctly marked, in every stage of plumage. The chin and throat are yellowish white, the feathers with narrow dark brown shaft stripes. The whole of the breast, and upper abdomen is buffy white, the shafts rufous, and the feathers of the sides of the breast, with broad, rather pale, and somewhat brownish, rufous centres. The lower portion of the abdomen, vent, flanks, tibial and tarsal plumes, rich ferruginous, deepest on the tibial plumes which are dark shafted, and on the lower abdomen somewhat mottled with rufous, or in some yellowish white. The lower tail coverts are white, altogether unbarred, greyish towards the tips, yellowish towards the bases; the axillaries, and the greater portion of the wing lining, bright cinnamon rufous, some of the larger lower coverts, however, being mingled deep brown and deep ferruginous.

In another type, the general appearance of whose upper surface closely resembles that above described, the rump and upper tail coverts are deep purplish umber brown, only narrowly margined with ferruginous. The central tail feathers are dull brownish grey, slightly tinged with rufous near the shafts, with from seven to eight moderately broad, transverse, hair brown bars, broadest at the tips, where the terminal bar may be nearly three-quarters of an inch broad, and narrowest towards the bases of the feathers, where they may be about three-eighths of an inch; the lateral feathers are similar, but the grey of the inner webs is less tinged with brown, and slightly more rufescent. The silver grey on the outer webs of the primaries, is replaced by ashy brown, and the bright rufous mottling there, and tinting of the inner webs of the quills, by dingy rufous buff, or dull fulvous. The chin is whitish, the feathers with dull, dark brown, central stripes, and the whole of the rest of the lower parts a dull uniform umber brown, (in some specimens suffused with ferruginous,) the feathers of the breast and upper abdomen, narrowly, and not very conspicuously, margined with a dingy rufous buff, or pale ferruginous, and the tibial and tarsal plumes, and lower tail coverts spotted, or imperfectly barred, with dingy fulvous or rufescent white. The axillaries and wing lining, are a deep hair brown, more or less mottled, and margined, with ferruginous, the amount of which, varies very greatly, in specimens of this type.

A third type, has the brown of the upper surface exceedingly dark, and the rufous edgings of the feathers more ferruginous; the rump and upper tail coverts deep chocolate brown, with a rich purple gloss, and no trace of rufous edgings. The tail somewhat as in the last, but much more strongly tinged with ferruginous, with one huge, terminal, blackish brown band, and above this, eight or nine very narrow, and irregular, wavy, transverse bars of the same colour, but paling towards the bases of the feathers. Below, the whole breast, axillaries, sides, flanks, tibial and tarsal plumes intense ferruginous, brightest and most *rusty* on the centre of the breast, deepest and tinged with chocolate in the tibial and tarsal feathers. The whole of the abdomen, vent, and lower tail coverts, yellowish or rusty white, more or less densely banded, or mottled, in twin spots, with deep ferruginous, (which in some specimens, so far predominates, that it might more properly be called the ground colour, and the white the barring,) which in some is bright and rusty, and in others deep, and tinged with umber, or chocolate. Some specimens have the heads paler than I have described, and in these the foreheads, an ill-defined streak over the eye, the ear coverts, chin, and throat are nearly pure white, all the feathers, however, having dark shafts. Where this is the case, the whole tone of colouring is somewhat paler, than I have above described, but all the specimens that I have yet examined, are referable to, or are clearly intermediate between one or other of these three types, that I have attempted to sketch.

Of the nidification of this species in India, I as yet know nothing; Dr. Bree tells us that "according to M. Favier, it nests among the rocks, and the male takes its turn in sitting." It seems a pity that M. Favier was not a little more communicative. He sent an egg, alleged to belong to this species, (no particulars are vouchsafed of how, when, or where it was obtained) in regard to which, Dr. Bree who figures it, remarks, that "it bears a strong resemblance to the egg of the Black Kite, but it is a little more pointed, and has the ground colour a creamy white, while that of the former has a greenish tinge." According to the figure, the egg is a broad oval, a good deal compressed towards one end, is sparingly blotched, and spotted, with a sort of burnt umber brown, and measures 2·17 by 1·8.

No. 45. **Buteo Ferox.*** GMELIN.

THE LONG LEGGED BUZZARD.

This large and handsome Buzzard breeds in great numbers, in March and April, in the N. W. Punjab, the lower hills of

---

* BUTEO FEROX.

DIMENSIONS.		Length.	Expanse.	Wing.	Tail from vent.	Tarsus.	Foot, greatest length.	„ greatest breadth.	Mid toe to root of claw.	Its claw, straight.	Hind toe.	Its claw, straight.	Inner toe.	Its claw, straight.	Bill, straight, from edge of cere to point.	a long curve, do.	from gape.	width at gape.	height at margin of cere.	Distance by which closed wings fall short of end of tail.	Distance by which lower tail coverts fall short of end of tail.	Weight.	Length of cere on culmen.
MALE.	From	20·75	50·25	16·00	9·25	3·20	3·80	3·50	1·45	0 75	0·78	0·90	0·78	0 88	0·90	1·10	1·80	1·40	0 45	nil	2 82	lb oz 1 15	0·45
	To	23 50	59·00	17·00	10·50	3 75	4 40	3 70	1·72	0 85	1 12	1·05	1·08	1 02	1·00	1 25	2·00	1·69	0·53	1·25	4 00	2 12	0·55
FEMALE.	From	22 75	56·25	18 20	10 18	3·20	4·50	3·65	1·50	0 75	0·90	1 02	0·90	0 97	1·03	1 20	1·90	1·35	0·50	nil	3 30	lb oz 2 4	0·44
	To	25·00	62·00	19 75	10·75	3 80	4 70	3 85	1·82	0 90	1·10	1·20	1·12	1·12	1 20	1 35	2 08	1·75	0·60	2·00	3 90	3 8	0·55

the N. W. Himalayas, and Kashmeer. East of the Jheelum, so far as I have yet been able to gather, very few pairs remain to breed in the plains.

(Eight males and females measured and weighed.)

Males. The 3rd, or 3rd and 4th primaries the longest. The 1st is from 3·9 to 5·21 shorter, the 2nd from 0·82 to 1·7, and the 3rd from 0·4 to 0·43, shorter. Exterior tail feathers, 0·2 to 0·88, shorter than interior ones.

Females. The 3rd, 4th, or 5th primaries the longest. The 1st is from 4·2 to 5·5 shorter, the 2nd, from 1·15 to 2, and the 3rd, from 0·15 to 0·6, shorter. Exterior tail feathers 0·7 to 1·3, shorter than interior ones.

DESCRIPTION. *(Of a very fine male, in the light stage of plumage, shot on the 11th January, 1867.)*

Legs and Feet. A dingy, rather pale lemon yellow; a row of large transverse scutæ, on the front of the tarsus, below the feathered portion, nearly to the foot; a row of still larger transverse scutæ, at the back of the tarsus, from the foot to about half way up; three, four and five scutæ at tip of toes, rest of scutellation reticulate, well marked, with the small plates rather convex; claws black, well curved, sharp; inner edge of mid toe claw much dilated.

Irides. Brownish yellow. Edges of lids, and small bare shelf above eye, dusky greenish.

Bill. Upper mandible at junction with cere, and base of lower mandible, brownish plumbeous; tips of both mandibles horny black, gape more yellow; cere yellowish green.

Tongue. Moderate, fleshy, entire, hastate, obtuse tipped, ciliated or finely serrated on posterior margin.

PLUMAGE. Lores thickly clothed with tiny white feathers, with greatly elongated, naked, dark brown or black, hair-like shafts, some of which, as usual, curve up, over the nostrils and front of forehead, while the rest point down over commissure, some being sloped away over the gape. Orbits feathered white. A trace of a very narrow dark brown streak, just above the bare shelf of the eye; the whole of the forehead, crown and occiput, a pale sandy brown, the feathers shafted darker, and with more or less white at the base, which shows through more or less in different places, most, in a patch above each nostril, and slightly above each eye, and least on the crown. Nape and back of the neck, a somewhat darker brown, very much mottled with white, owing to a great deal of the basal portions of the feathers showing through. Upper back, scapulars, and lesser wing coverts a sort of umber brown; somewhat rufous on the lesser scapulars, which with the feathers of the upper back, are faintly, while the lesser coverts are distinctly, margined with rufous or pale rufous brown. The lower and middle back, and rump, are a nearly uniform umber brown. The upper tail coverts are paler, the tips and exterior webs, much mottled, blotched, or imperfectly barred, with buffy or pale rufous. Tail feathers umber brown, narrowly tipped paler. Centre feathers with traces of about eight darker, and somewhat wavy, transverse, brown bars, with the interspaces, (specially on the inner web) near the shafts, mottled with pale rufous, or fulvous white, all the lateral tail feathers, with the greater portions of the inner webs, white, incompletely barred towards the tips, with wavy blotches of brown and pale rufous. The three exterior, on each side, with some white on the outer webs, also at the bases, and beyond this an inch or so of mottling or freckling, with pale rufous, chiefly close to the shaft. On the dark portion of the exterior webs of all, there are in a

During the cold season, they swarm all over the N. W. P., the Punjab, and Rajpootana, making their way far down into Central India, throughout Oudh, and into Behar, but although, as Jerdon says, they are found much in low cultivated lands, especially irrigated fields, edges of jheels, &c., (where they prey mostly on Frogs) their winter quarters, par excellence, is in the half desert tracts of Northern and Western India, amongst the interminable colonies of the Desert Rat, *(Gerbellus Erythrourus)* which is unquestionably their favourite food. In these localities, they occur during the winter in surprising numbers; a dozen may be seen sitting within a circle of half a mile, and fifty counted in a morning's ride. Directly, however, the hot weather begins to set in, their numbers decrease, and by the first of April, all, but solitary stragglers, have retreated northwards, to the Himalayas, or westwards, across the Sutledge.

---

good light, faint traces of darker bars. The medium wing coverts, are a uniform, but rather pale, umber brown, palest towards the edges, while the winglet and greater coverts are an equally uniform, but rather darker shade, the coverts with traces of paler tippings.

The first five primaries (of which the 3rd, 4th and 5th are emarginate on the outer webs) are grey on the outer webs, except the last two, just below their larger coverts, where they are a rather pale umber brown. They are all five conspicuously emarginate or notched on the inner webs, on which, below these emarginations or notches, they are nearly black, while above these, they are nearly pure white, with only a little pale brown, running along the shaft.

The rest of the primaries and secondaries, are dark brown on the outer webs, and tips; and pure white, and pale brown towards the shafts, on the inner webs, with four or five rather ill-defined, and incomplete, darker brown, transverse bars. The ear coverts, chin and throat are white, the feathers have pale, rufous brown shafts. There is a trace of an uniform, rufous brown streak from the posterior angle of the eye, along the tops of the ear coverts. The feathers from the base of the lower mandible, below the ear coverts, and behind them, with small central streaks of the pale rufous brown, as well as the shafts of that colour. The centre of the neck in front, and breast, white, the feathers with darker shafts, and many of them with linear, or narrowly, oval streaks of rufous brown towards the tips, these being most conspicuous on the lower part of the breast. A patch on each side of neck, feathers rufous brown, dark shafted, margined rather narrowly, with fulvous white; centre and lower part of abdomen, vent and lower tail coverts, unspotted, yellowish or dirtyish white; sides uniform umber brown, with darker shafts and feeble whitish margins. Thigh coverts a still darker brown, with a greyish bloom on one web in a good light, darker shafted, and margined, with rufous above, and fulvous white towards the tarsus. Axillaries bright rufous, somewhat mottled, and shafted, with umber brown. Lesser and median, lower wing coverts, pale rufous, to rufous white, with dark shafts, and a narrow rufous brown streak. Coverts beyond carpal joints, umber brown, mottled, and blotched with rufous. Greater lesser coverts, of primaries and secondaries, pale greyish brown, variegated towards the margins, the former with white, the latter with pale rufous.

I have never seen or taken a nest myself, but have had them often described to me by others who have, as large clumsy stick structures, placed usually, high up, in the fork of some large tree, and lined with hair, wool and rags. They lay usually, I am informed, three eggs, but many lay only two, and four are sometimes found. The eggs that I have seen, said to belong to this species, appeared to me undistinguishable from large eggs of the common Kite. I did not, unfortunately, record an exact description, or the dimensions at the time, and my collection contains no specimens at present.

Mr. W. Theobald makes the following note of this bird's breeding, in the neighbourhood of Pind Dadan Khan, and Katas, in the Salt Range.

"Lays in the first and fourth weeks of March. Eggs two to three. Shape *ovato pyriform*. Size, varies from 2·00 to 2·19 inches in length, and 1·66 inches in breadth. Colour greenish white, or white, blotched with red or claret brown, vary greatly. Nest large in trees, sticks lined with cotton, rags, &c., and daubed with mud."

Of their breeding in the valley of Kashmeer, he says, "Lays in the fourth week of April. Eggs two in number, *ovato pyriform*, measuring from 2·10 to 2·40 inches in length, and from 1·77 to 1·80 inches in breadth. Nest and eggs as in plains."

A pair or two may occasionally breed, well down into the plains, as in the case mentioned in the following note; but such an occurrence is quite exceptional. Mr. F. R. Blewitt says, "In 1845 and 1846 when at Bunchari Z. Gourgaon, I well remember seeing a pair of birds during the two hot and rainy seasons. In a clump of high trees, to the left of the road, as you come from Pulwul, just near to Bunchari, there was one of remarkable size, of which each year they took possession, about May, reared their young, and with the young birds, departed in October. The third year, as I was subsequently told, the tree was struck by lightning, and the birds killed."

Of the breeding of this species in Palestine, Mr. Tristram had the following remarks in the Ibis for 1865—"We found the nests, both on trees, and on rocks, generally on the latter. The complement of eggs is two, or three, generally the latter. The first nest we took was on Mount Carmel, on a rocky ledge, easy of access, on March 22nd, and which contained three eggs, quite fresh and beautifully marked; the last fresh eggs we found, were a pair near Mount Tabor on May 1st. The eggs are of course larger than, but no way differently coloured from, those of the Common Buzzard. The nest is large, but more neatly made than those of the Eagles, and well lined with woollen rags,and the soft withered leaves of bull-rushes, and flags, and plastered with mud. The plumage of the Palestine specimen is very rufous, and we shot breeding birds, both with and without the bars on their tails."

There seems now no reason to doubt, that our Indian species, named *Canescens*, by Hodgson, and *Longipes*,* by Jerdon, is really identical, with *Ferox* of Gmelin, *Rufinus* of Rüppel, and *Leucurus* of Naumann. It occurs throughout northern and central India, in Afghanistan, and Persia; Palestine, and North Eastern Africa. Mr. Gurney has received specimens from the mouths of the Volga, and Radde procured it in the Baikal, and Daurian districts of Asiatic Russia, where also he took several nests in April and May, the eggs of those taken in the latter month being hard set. He gives the dimensions of the largest and smallest of 19 eggs as 2·73 by 2·05 and 2·4 by 1·83.

There are two very distinct forms, so far as plumage goes, which, as well as I am able yet to judge, are both referable to this species. The dimensions are identical, and the shape, and contour of wings, tail, bill, legs and feet, are the same, but the plumage is so very widely different, that in the absence of clearly intermediate stages, I cannot feel *perfectly* certain that both forms belong to one and the same species. Moreover, while the one form (the one usually brown, and described as *Buteo Canescens* and *Ferox)* occurs in vast numbers all over the North West Provinces, Punjab, and Rajpootana, the other, which I characterized in the Ibis as *Fuliginosus*, no where, as far as I have yet ascertained, occurs, except as a mere straggler, east of the Jumna, and is only plentiful from about Hansie, northwards and westwards. Nowhere does it appear to be so plentiful as the other form, and to judge from the plumage, bills and feet, if it really be identical with *Ferox*, it is the old bird, and these we know in many species, extend their migrations considerably less than the young. Dr. Jerdon tells me, *(in epist.)* that "a very dark colored Buzzard is not rare near Hissar and Sirsa, in the cold weather. The tail is generally conspicuously albescent; I unfortunately did not procure a specimen to ascertain if it differed, (as I think it does) from the common Buzzard or not." Mr. Gurney writing of *B. Ferox* says, "This

---

* Von Pelzeln, says of a specimen sent from the neighbourhood of Kotegurh, (Himalayahs) by Dr. Stoliczka.

"The specimen sent belongs to the variety *B. rufinus*, and agrees with the examples of the adult birds of that variety collected by Herr Kotschy in Nubia (compare my 'Uebersicht der Geier und Falken, 147 D) only that the Himalayan bird has the tail banded, and consequently must be considered somewhat younger."

species is sometimes of an uniform, dark chocolate brown, all over. I have seen only two such examples, one from India, and one from Abyssinia. This is out of, at least, thirty specimens of the bird, which I have at different times seen; whether this is accidental, or a regular plumage, I cannot tell; but being so rare, in proportion to those in the usual dress, I am disposed to consider it an accidental variation."

Clearly, the Buzzards thus referred to are identical with my supposed *Fuliginosus*, of which I have now twelve specimens before me, varying a good deal in many respects, but only one of them approaching at all closely any (and those only the most dingily colored) of the enormous series of the typical *Canescens* that my collection contains.

The plumage of this Buzzard varies of course very considerably, even in the pale or *Canescens* stage, just as it does in that which constitutes my supposed *Fuliginosus*, but the specimens representing these two stages, (if they really are only stages), constitute groups so separate, that in scarcely any case can a moment's doubt exist as to which group they are to be referred to. The only explanation I can give of this, is, that all my specimens have been obtained between the 1st of November, and the end of March, with the exception of two of the very dark ones, obtained in the Himalayas during the summer.

In the typical *Ferox*, (assuming *Ferox* and *Canescens* to be *really* identical,) the chief variations in plumage are as follows: At one end of the series, the whole of the chin, throat, breast, abdomen, vent, and lower tail coverts, in fact, the whole lower parts are white, with only the faintest possible fulvous tinge in some places, and a few only of the feathers with dark shafts. A few of the feathers of the sides have irregular, patchy, rufous brown bars. The axillaries are pure white, with a faint rufous spot towards the tips; the tibial plumes are pale rufous, mottled with rufous white; and the tarsal plumes are white, broadly barred with pale rufous. At the other end of the series, the chin, throat, breast, and lower tail coverts, are a rich rufous buff, all the feathers, except those of the lower tail coverts, with conspicuous dark shafts, and rich brown, or rufous brown, linear, lanceolate, shaft stripes. The whole of the sides, abdomen, vent, tibial and tarsal plumes, a very rich rufous brown, edged with brighter rufous, and the axillaries pure cinnamon colour. Between these two extremes, there is every intermediate type of colouring of the lower parts. Then again of the upper parts, especially of the tail, there is an equally marked amount of variation. Taking the tail first; in some, the whole of the tail feathers are pure pale cinnamon colour, becoming albescent at the shaft, towards the base of the central feathers, and pure white there, on the inner webs of the lateral feathers; and with a faint silvery greyish shade or bloom, about the middle of the exterior webs. In the perfect form of this type there is not the faintest trace of any bar, on any of the feathers. Then there is precisely the same tail, as it were bleached, the cinnamon being confined to the tips and the outer margins of both webs of the central feathers, and to the tips and outer margins of the exterior webs only, of the lateral feathers; all the rest being pure white. Then there is the same tail as the last described, with the white on the central feathers; and the external webs of the lateral feathers, replaced by a silver grey, only slightly browner, than that of the exterior webs of the earlier primaries. Then we have each of these three forms of tail, more or less barred, with every intermediate form between a mere trace of a single narrow brown bar, near the tip, up to ten narrow, well marked but wavy, and irregular, transverse brown bars. There is still another type of tail, in which the central feathers are a uniform, dull, earthy brown, except along the shafts, where alternate, irregular patches, of a slightly darker brown, and dingy fulvous, remain as it were traces of the fully barred tail. The outer webs of the lateral tail feathers, are in this form, a nearly uniform brown, with but little traces of the markings exhibited by the central tail feathers, but the inner webs are dull fulvous, growing white towards the bases, with numerous, broad, irregular, freckled, brown bars, becoming obsolete towards their bases. Between this form, and the grey banded one, every intermediate stage occurs. The rest of the upper plumage, in specimens exhibiting this latter form of tail, is a uniform, dull, pale, hair brown, without a trace of rufous anywhere, but darker on the rump, the longer scapulars, and primaries, and somewhat paler on the head, (where owing to the white bases of the feathers showing through, a good deal of white is intermingled) and the median wing coverts. The silvery grey tinge, of the outer webs of the primaries, of this form, is inconspicuous, and overlaid with brown. The upper plumage of the specimens with bar-less tails, is much richer, and in fact so different from that just described, that but for the existence of intermediate links, one could scarcely believe in the identity of the two forms. Here we have the whole head, neck, and mantle, a rich rufous buff, the feathers with conspicuous dark brown centres; the feathers of the occiput conspicuously tipped blackish brown, so as to produce the effect of a sub-crest. The rump rich blackish or deep chocolate brown, the upper tail coverts rich rufous, with traces of blackish brown bars. The outer webs of the first four or five primaries conspicuously silvered, reminding one of the wings of the adult *Circus Ærugi-*

nosus, and many of the lesser scapulars with patches of silver grey. The longer scapulars, and secondaries, tipped conspicuously, and the former obscurely mottled, with greyish brown. In other forms of the same plumage, these tippings and mottlings are wanting, as are the grey patchings on the lesser scapulars, while the dark centres of the feathers are so broad, as to reduce the rufous buff to broad edgings. In some again, the rump, instead of being blackish brown, is rufous brown, broadly edged with deep rufous; and in others, the upper tail coverts, instead of being bright rufous, with traces of brown bars, are deep brown, tipped with pale rufous. As the bars on the tail begin to appear, the colours of the upper surface appear to grow dingier; the bright rufous buff becomes rufous white, then dingy buff, and dingy yellowish white; the brown growing paler and more earthy, and as the tail begins to assume the dingy earth brown tinge, the rufous or fulvous edgings to the feathers begin to disappear altogether, and we get to that nearly uniform, dull brown, upper surface, (whitened about the head, owing to the white feathers showing through,) already described.

The great difficulty we meet with, in assigning any chronological value to these changes is, that the changes on the upper surface, do not correspond with those on the lower.

It is easy enough to arrange any number of specimens, in what, looking at the upper or under surfaces only, appears a very perfect series, in which no links are wanting, but directly we turn the specimens over, all traces of any arrangement seems to vanish, and birds at the opposite ends of the chain, when arranged by the plumage of one surface, ought, if arranged according to that of the other, to be placed side by side. This provoking want of correspondence, in the changes of the plumage, of the two surfaces, has already been noticed, page 147, when treating of *Aquila Imperialis*, but it is much more conspicuous and perplexing in the present species. The only points in which the changes in the upper and lower surfaces correspond, is, that as we approach the uniform, dull brown, upper surface stage, the whole of the colours of the lower surface, grow duller, and lose the rufous tinge.

Taking now the typical form, of what I have styled *B. Fuliginosus*, the whole of the head, neck, cheeks, ear coverts, throat and breast, is a deep hair or umber brown, narrowly, and indistinctly margined, with dingy rufous, and the whole of the rest of the bird, except the primaries and tail feathers, are a more or less rich and deep hair brown, tinged with umber on the lower surface, and glossed with purple on the rump, upper tail coverts, longer scapulars and tertiaries. The tail is silver grey, with a very broad, subterminal, blackish brown band, beyond which, there is a narrow, pale tipping, and above which, there are five other, somewhat irregular, and wavy, transverse, dark-brown bars; the grey becoming albescent, on the inner webs of the lateral tail feathers. In all specimens, both of this, and the *Canescens* type, the bases of the primaries, I may mention, are white, forming a very large and conspicuous pure white patch, on the lower surface of the wing.

In another form of my supposed *Fuliginosus*, the whole head, neck, chin, throat, and breast, may be said to be a rich, deep rufous, broadly centred with umber brown. The rest of the lower parts, are an excessively rich, deep, umber brown, with here and there, rufous white spots, or imperfect bars, most conspicuous and numerous on the lower tail coverts.

The upper surface is a darker brown even than that of the first form described, and the longer upper tail coverts, are conspicuously tipped with rufous, while the tail feathers are much tinged with rufous towards the tip, have the terminal bar considerably reduced in width, the grey ground more albescent, and the other bars more or less obsolete.

I have one specimen which appears to be intermediate, between *Fuliginosus* and *Canescens*, the tail is precisely similar to that first described, as typical of *Fuliginosus*, but the whole of the rest of the upper surface, is that of the uniform, dull, earth brown stage, of *Canescens;* the lower surface, however, is unlike any of those which I have described as *Canescens.* It has the chin and throat yellowish white, with brown central stripes, but the whole of the rest of the lower surface, a very dull, rather pale, umber brown, more or less margined on the breast, with rufous.

There are other specimens again, more or less intermediate between this example and the typical *Fuliginosus*, and though I can express no *positive* opinion on the subject as yet, my conviction is, founded chiefly on their perfect structural identity, that both the dark and light forms, (*Fuliginosus* and *Canescens*) must be referred to one and the same species.

No. 46. ? Buteo Asiaticus, Latham.

Buteo Aquilinus
Butaquila Leucocephala. } Hodgson.

? *Buteo Hemilasius*, Schlegel (*Fauna Japonica, Aves, Tab.* 7.)

The Upland Buzzard.

This species is so excessively rare, that no specimen of it exists, I believe, in India, and only one has, as far as I can ascertain, ever been sent from this country. Not only is it a rare, but also to my mind a very doubtful species.

Dr. Jerdon, in his description, follows Blyth, J. A. S. XIV. 176, almost verbatim, he only omits to note the length of the bill from gape, which Blyth gives as 2·12, and to state that the dark bars on the tail "*alternate* on the two webs" (misprinted shafts) "of each feather."

The following were Mr. Blyth's remarks on the single specimen above referred to. Dr. Jerdon of course never saw the bird.

"This bird might be mistaken, on a cursory view, for a variety of *B. Canescens*, J. A. S. XII. 308, were it not for its half-feathered tarsi; and the beak also, is larger, and more aquiline, so that the name is felicitously bestowed. It is by no means a common species in Nepal, as I learned from Mr. Hodgson's people, and as might be inferred from the circumstance of Mr. Hodgson's requiring the only specimen he had sent, to take with him to England. Not improbably, it may prove identical with the *Falco asiaticus* of Latham, described as nearly similar to the European Buzzard, in the colour of its body and wings; the under parts white, with stripes on the breast, tail silver grey, the outer feather marked by obscure bars; bill bluish black, and legs yellow and *half feathered*. Length twenty-two inches. Inhabits China. From the circumstance of its partially feathered tarsi, it might be presumed, that the present species would fall under the division *Archibuteo* of Brehm, but the general character of the bird is not that of the 'Rough-legged Buzzard' of Northern regions."

I have obtained specimens of *B. Ferox*, pertaining to the dark form, answering very closely to Blyth's description, especially where the tail is concerned. The differences dwelt on by Blyth are, it will be observed, the pluming anteriorly of half the tarsus and the larger and more aquiline bill. As regards the former, I find more than one *B. Ferox*, with the tarsus plumed in front, for 1·75 inches; and as regards the latter, I may remark, that the bills of this species vary a good deal in size and strength.

That further researches are necessary, before we conclusively admit either the existence of such a species as *Buteo Aquilinus*, Hodgson, or its identity with *B. asiaticus*, Latham, and *B. Hemelasius*, Schlegel, is pretty clear.

Mr. Blyth (Ibis for 1866) tells us, that in his first catalogue of Mr. Hodgson's specimens, presented to the British Museum, (pub. 1846) Mr. G. R. Gray assented to these identifications, but Mr. Blyth goes on to say, that "in his second edition of that catalogue, (1863) Mr. Gray writes *B. Leucocephala* with *B. Ferox*, and *B. Aquilinus* with *Archibuteo Stropheatus*, Hodgson, the latter being decidedly identical with *Hieraetus Pennatus!* The specimen which I described as *Aquilinus*, was sent by Mr. Hodgson, as his *Butaquila Leucocephala*; but as it had not a sign of white about the head, I suggested to that gentleman, the better name *Aquilinus*, from its robust form. Either this, or *B. plumipes* can hardly be other than *Falco asiaticus* of Latham. His description on the whole, applies better to the former, while the 'half-feathered legs (*pedibus semilanatis*') preclude its identification with *B. Ferox*. Both this species and the next, *B. Plumipes*, have the tarsi feathered half-way down; while in *Archibuteo hemiptilopus* (No. 49) the tarsi are plumed to the toes, in front and externally, and are bare and scutellated behind. I suspect that both *B. asiaticus* and *A. hemiptilopus* inhabit chiefly the Mongolian region, and should be considered stragglers any where away from it."

It seems to me very doubtful, whether *both Butaquila Leucocephala* and *B. Aquilinus*, are not forms of *B. Ferox*; as for the expression "*pedibus semilanatis*" not being applicable to *B. Ferox*, I must demur. The tarsi, in this species, are often feathered for half their length; one now before me, with the tarsus 3·3, is feathered for 1·8; another, a small male, with the tarsus barely 3·2, is feathered for 1·75. Doubtless, in the majority of specimens, tarsi of these lengths would only be feathered for from 1·3 to 1·5, but the amount of feathering varies in different specimens. The fact of the tarsus in Mr. Hodgson's specimen, being feathered in front for 1·75, constitutes no good ground for separating it from *B. Ferox*.

It *may* very likely be distinct, but I have, as yet, seen no sufficient reasons for making sure that it is so. I ought, however, to note that Mr. Hodgson in a letter to Blyth (J. A. S. XV. p. 2, note) remarks of this supposed species, "this is not a typical *Buteo* or *Archibuteo*, witness its reticulate tarsi," if by this is meant that the tarsi have *no* transverse scuta, we have here a difference, enabling us to separate *Aquilinus* at once, from *Ferox*. It is to be hoped, that naturalists at home will carefully re-examine Mr. Hodgson's specimen.

No. 47. **Buteo Plumipes**, Hodgson.

*? Buteo Japonicus (*Schlegel. *Fauna Japon. Aves, Tab. VI et VII A.)*

The Harrier Buzzard.

This is another species of which we have no satisfactory knowledge. One single specimen exists in Mr. Hodgson's collection, in the British Museum. The following are Mr. Blyth's remarks on this species in the Ibis for 1866.

" Mr. Hodgson's specimen in the British Museum is certainly of a uniform dark brown ; but most Buzzards vary exceedingly in colour, and I see no reason why *B. Japonicus* should not be identified with *B. plumipes*, notwithstanding that Mr. Swinhoe expressly asserts, that the former never acquires the dark plumage, of the oviduct, of *B. vulgaris* (P. Z. S. 1863, p. 260). Only that *one* specimen was procured by Mr. Hodgson ; so that undoubtedly, it must be considered an exceedingly rare straggler within the area of his researches. My *B. pygmæus* (J. A. S. B. XIV. p. 217), which Dr. Jerdon thought was not unlikely to prove identical with *plumipes*, is the same as *Poliornis Poliogenys*." (Vide No. 48 Bis.) Dr. Jerdon, quoting, I suppose, though he does not say so, from Mr. Hodgson, (for he had never seen the bird,) remarks, that this is certainly an osculant form, having the bill and wings of a *Circus*, with the short feet of a Buzzard, but Mr. Blyth, more correctly, I think, demurs to any such osculant form, and says " This species I have never seen, but must confess to theoretical doubts, of its truly connecting *Circus* with *Buteo ;* the latter genus and *Aquila* on the other hand, are very closely allied, in fact, but slight modifications of the same immediate subtype, and species of intermediate character, might have been looked for.

No. 48. **Poliornis Teesa,*** FRANKLIN.

THE WHITE-EYED BUZZARD.

This species, in Upper India, lays almost exclusively in April. I have one record of a single egg, taken on the 27th of

---

* *Poliornis Teesa.*

DIMENSIONS. [*The sexes appear to differ little in size. The females are generally larger, but some males (by dissection) that I have measured, exceed other equally well ascertained females. I do not therefore give the dimensions of the sexes separately*].

Length, 16 to 18·2. Expanse, 36 to 39. Wing 11 to 12·5; the 3rd or 4th primary the longest, or these two sub-equal; the 1st from 2·9 to 3·15, and the second from 0·65 to 0.85 shorter. Tail, from 6·65 to 7·5; exterior tail feathers from 0·2 to 0·7 shorter than central ones. Tarsus from 2 to 2·15; and feathered in front for from 0·4 to 0·9. Foot, greatest length, from 2·88 to 3·38; greatest width from 2·5 to 3·15; mid toe 1·29 to 1·32; its claw, straight, from 0.56, to 0·75; mid toe, from 0·65 to 0·75; its claw, straight, from 0·69 to 0·75. Bill, straight, from edge of cere to point, from 0·80 to 0·83; ditto along curve, from 0·86 to 0·9; from gape, from 0·4 to 0·44; width at gape, 1 to 1·1; height at front, at margin of cere, 0·4 to 0·48; length of cere only, from 0·35 to 0·4; the wings, when closed, reach to within about 0·9 of end of tail, and lower tail coverts reach to within from 3 to 3·4 of ditto.

DESCRIPTION. *Legs and feet,* dingy orange yellow; claws black; scutæ conspicuous; a row of somewhat hexagonal ones on front of tarsus, exteriorly, rest of tarsal scales, somewhat small and reticulate. *Irides,* pale yellowish white; orbits, feathered white, a conspicuous row of dark eyelashes; edges of lids, orange yellow, bare shelf above eye dingy yellowish, *Bill,* cere and gape, and base of lower mandible, bright orange; upper mandible, immediately at junction with cere, and lower mandible just beyond the orange patch, fleshy, or pale brownish white, the rest of both mandibles horn black. *Tongue,* moderate, hastate, entire, with a faint central depression. Lores white, the clothing feathers with elongated, dark brown, naked, hair-like shafts. A patch on either side of the culmen, and a line above it, on the forehead white. The whole of the rest of the top and back of the head, a sort of umber brown, the feathers faintly margined paler, and shafted darker. A triangular or diamond-shaped patch of white feathers on the nape, most of which have the shafts brown at the tips, and many of which, towards the centre of the patch, have brown spots towards the tips. The ear coverts very lax, a nearly uniform brown. Sides and back of neck, and upper back, and most of the scapulars, a slightly lighter brown than the crown, with conspicuously darker shafts, obscurely tipped with a slightly paler and more sandy brown, and with the trace of a greyish shade towards the base, in some specimens these parts have a decidedly rufous tinge. Rest of back, rump and upper tail coverts, rufous brown, most rufous on the latter, all with dark brown shafts, and the coverts narrowly tipped with fulvous white, or paler rufous brown, and with a trace of a grey mottled bar just inside the tipping. All the tail feathers tipped fulvous white, and with a subterminal blackish brown band. Centre tail feathers above this band, chestnut, in some tinged grey rufous, with the trace of a broad, longitudinal, grey bar down each web more or less, and faint traces of from 1 to 5, narrow, transverse, dark brown bands.

March, and several of more or less incubated ones found during the first ten days of May, but the great majority of the nests

---

The next 4 on either side similar, but the grey occupying more and more of the inner webs, which have 5, somewhat incomplete, transverse bars, of dark brown. The 2 exterior have the tipping and subterminal band, faint. A narrow streak of rufous, along the shaft, on either side. A considerable portion of both webs at the base white, and the rest a greyish brown, with here and there a trace of darker mottling. The whole of the lesser and median wing coverts, a paler brown than the rest of the body, all with dark brown shafts, narrowly margined with fulvous or pure white, most conspicuously on the longer feathers; the inner webs of many of the median coverts, a good deal mottled with white. Winglet, and primary greater coverts, dark brown, the feathers excessively narrowly margined towards the tips with white, most of them paler, and even white on the inner web towards the base, and the first feather of the winglet, and the first 2 coverts, with a manifest tinge of grey on the outer web. The greater coverts of the secondaries, a sort of sandy or fulvous brown, the shafts darker, and both webs indistinctly tinged with grey, towards the shaft, above the tips. The primaries dark brown at the tips with very narrow whitish margins. The outer webs darkish brown, (lighter towards the secondaries) more or less tinged, or frosted over, in the first 5, with silver grey, purest on the 1st. The first 4 feathers are conspicuously emarginate on the inner web; below these emarginations, and above the dark tipping, the inner web is a sort of greyish brown, with a few faint darkish brown blotches, or incomplete bars; above the emarginations, they are pure white. The rest of the primaries, which have an obscure rufous tinge along the shafts, have about half the inner webs greyish brown, with 4 or 5 transverse darker brown bars, and the other half white, the line of junction being oblique, there being less white towards tips, and less brown towards base. The inner webs of the secondaries are similar, but their outer webs are chiefly greyish brown, the white margins of the tips are broader than in any but the first few primaries, and the broad dark brown tip of the primaries is replaced by an inconspicuous patch of a lighter brown on the tip of the inner web only. The chin and throat are pure white, the feathers very lax, bordered by a broad stripe of darkish brown from the base of the lower mandible on each side, and with a similar stripe down the centre of the chin and throat. The rest of the neck in front, in some specimens, a rather pale fulvous brown, tipped inconspicuously with white, dark shafted, and somewhat mottled with a fulvous white. The breast and the greater part of the sides and upper abdomen, white, the feathers irregularly but broadly barred, with a pale rufous or fulvous brown. In other specimens the whole of the rest of the neck, breast, abdomen, and sides are a nearly uniform, pale but somewhat rufous umber brown, the feathers dark shafted, and with traces of imperfect fulvous white bars, nowhere extending to the shafts.

Thigh coverts pale rufous, whitish towards the tip; most of the feathers, in some specimens, with a triangular patch of rufous brown towards the tips. Lower abdomen, white, or fulvous white, the feathers, with only a more or less faint, triangular patch of pale rufous, or rufous brown towards the tip. Vent feathers and lower tail coverts white, tinged, more or less distinctly, with very pale yellowish brown. Under surface of tail feathers, greyish white, the subterminal dark band showing through in all but the exterior feather. Under surface of the quills white, the broad dark tips of the primaries, and the dark patches at the tips of the secondaries, and the dark transverse bars on the inner halves, of the inner webs, of all the quills, (except in some specimens in the first five primaries,) showing through. The wing lining beyond

examined in this month, by myself and correspondents, have contained young ones. They prepare their nests, as a rule, some considerable time before they lay; a nest examined, and ultimately taken, in Etawah, was completed twenty-four days before the first egg was laid.

They make their own nests, (a new one, as far as my experience goes) each season; never, I believe, appropriating those of other species; but they will at times, pull these to pieces, for materials. The nest is usually placed in a fork, pretty high up in some thickish foliaged tree; mangoes, in some localities at any rate, being decidedly their favourites. I *have* found a nest in a solitary tree; but more commonly they choose one of the outer trees of some small clump or grove.

The nest is a loose structure of twigs and sticks, very much like a Crow's, and without any lining. Normally, they lay three eggs; but I have once found four, and on several occasions, have taken nests containing only two, both fully incubated.

The affinities of this bird, to judge by its eggs *only*, are rather with the Goss Hawk, and the Harriers, than with the Buzzards, or the Kites. The eggs are pure greyish or pale bluish white, absolutely without speck or spot; at least not one, of nearly 40 specimens that I have possessed, has exhibited any traces. of markings. In shape they are a broad oval, but some are slight-

---

the carpal joint, and the greater lower secondary coverts, white, either pure, or with a subterminal, arrow-headed, greyish brown, or pale rufous spot. Rest of wing lining, pale rufous brown, blotched, or incompletely barred with white, the brown predominating more and more, as the feathers approach the axilla, and the sides just above this spot, and the axillaries themselves, having no white, except an excessively faint tipping, but with dark shafts, and having their somewhat rufous, brown ground colour, faintly mottled with a more fulvous tint.

In the young, the forehead, a broad superciliary stripe, the ear-coverts and a patch above them, the chin, cheeks, throat and all the lower parts, except the sides, yellowish white, more or less tinged with rufous buff on the breast, thigh coverts and vent, with very faint traces of the two mandibular, and the central throat stripes, and all the feathers of the breast and abdomen, with very narrow, brown, shaft stripes. The sides are a sort of hair-brown, broadly but imperfectly barred with fulvous white. The crown and oc ciput, sides and back of the neck, fulvous white, with central, hair-brown stripes, which on the crown and occiput, occupy the greater portion of the feathers. The scapulars and interscapulary region, and the lesser coverts, immediately adjoining the scapulars, a rich umber brown, with darker brown stripes, or patches, on the shafts, towards the tips. The tail feathers are obscurely barred with dingy rufous, and dark greyish brown. The central feathers being most rufous and the exterior ones greyest, and all being tipped with rufous white. The wings are much as in the adult, but have the dark bars on the inner webs, much less conspicuous, and in some specimens entirely wanting,on the earlier primaries.

ly pyriform. Mr. Hewitson's figure of the marsh Harrier's egg might do for the largest specimens, while his figure of the egg of Montague's Harrier, exactly represents a peculiarly small specimen that I took in Etawah. Held up against the light, the shell is a sea-green, much of the same hue as that of the eggs of *A. Fulvescens.*

The eggs vary from 1·75 to 2·0 in length, and from 1·4 to 1·62 in breadth, but the average of 31 eggs measured, was 1·85 × 1·52.

These birds are much attached to their nests, and hang about them for many days after they have been robbed, and at times will lay in them a second time. On the 11th April, 1867, I took a single perfectly fresh egg, out of a nest, which a few days before, had been cleared by Mr. Brooks.

Mr. W. Theobald makes the following note, of this bird's breeding, in the neighbourhood of Pind Dadan Khan, and Katas, in the Salt Range.

"Lays in the 2nd week of April. Eggs four only. Shape varies from ovate pyriform, to blunt ovate pyriform. Size, from 1·80 to 1·93 inches in length, and 1·50 inches in breadth. Colour, pure greyish or plumbeous white. Nest, small, of twigs, in trees, near cultivation."

Mr. G. Marshall, R. E., writes from Saharunpoor. "This bird breeds in May, making a small rudely constructed nest of twigs and sticks in the fork of a tree about 25 feet from the ground, and without lining of any sort; the eggs are hatched in the beginning of June, they are generally three in number, but I have never seen more than two young ones in a nest.

"In one nest I found a half-fledged young one, another dead with its stomach eaten away, and two live lizards, one of them partially eaten; on March 27th, I noticed one of these birds commencing its nest, and another on the 7th April; the latter nest I took on the 10th May, and it then had 3 hard set eggs." On another occasion, he says—"This species is very common in these parts, it builds in the forks of trees, generally Sheeshum or Khirna, a very rude and small nest of twigs. I have noticed this bird pulling to pieces the nest of a pied Starling, but I imagine it was only to get the materials, as the nest was empty at the time."

No. 48 bis. Poliornis Poliogenys. Temm. P. C. 325.

Buteo Pyrrhogenys, Faun. Jap. VII. *b.*
„ *Pygmæus*, Blyth.

The Grey-cheeked Buzzard.

This species, first obtained by Dussumier, in the Island of Luzon, (Phillipines) and figured by Temminck as the "Buse á joues grises," has now occurred on several occasions, in Southern Burmah, and must therefore find a place in these notes.

Temminck's original remarks and description of this species are as follows:—

"This little species of Buzzard is less than the European Buzzard by one half, and the beak is somewhat slenderer, and straighter, than that of this latter species. The long wings reach to within a short distance of the end of the tail, which is long and slightly rounded; the toes are nearly similar to those of the Cymindes Buzzards, (of Brazil etc.) or the Honey Buzzard of Europe; the tarsi, however, are long and slender, as in the Asturs; the beak, though smaller, is similar to that of the Honey Buzzard, but the feathers of the lores, and orbital region, are hair-like, as in other Buzzards, and the wing feathers are graduated, as in the Common Buzzard.

"The clear grey colour of the cheek feathers, and the white throat with the central ashy stripe, suffice to distinguish the adult. The mantle is reddish brown, the shafts of the feathers being brown; the quills whitish on the inner webs, and blackish towards the tips, are barred at wide distances, with little black bands; the tail bears four, transverse, blackish bands, on a clear brown ground. The supercilia are white, mingled with greyish; the breast is a uniform brown; the vent, flanks, and abdomen are pure white, broadly barred with reddish brown. The base of the bill and the cere yellow, the tips of both mandibles being black. The feet probably yellow. The whole length 18·1.* The tarsi 2·7. A male only 16 inches in length, retains some of the feathers of the young bird, which shew that in the young, the lower parts are spotted with long brown streaks, bordered on either side with reddish white; the breast is brown mottled with red, each feather with four, more or less rounded, white spots, the white predominates on the vent and flanks, where the brown bars, more or less regularly marked, are much further

* These are the English equivalents of Temminck's measurements given in the old Paris, feet and inches.

apart than in the adult. It seems also that the bands on the tail are more numerous in the young than the adult."

Mr. Blyth remarks, in the Ibis for 1866, that this species was also obtained in the Phillipines, by the late Hugh Cuming, and that an interesting notice of it is given in the Ornithological report, accompanying the narrative of Commodore Perry's exploring expedition to the China Seas and Japan. He adds, " a single specimen was procured by the late Dr. Helfer somewhere in the Tenasserim provinces, which I described as *Buteo pygmæus* in 1845." This description of Mr. Blyth's, is a far better one than I could hope to write, and I therefore transcribe it from that treasury of ornithology, (and indeed Natural History generally) the Journal of the Asiatic Society of Bengal. "Length 18 inches, or perhaps rather more; of wing, 13 inches, and tail 8 inches; bill to forehead (including cere) 0·94 of an inch in a straight line, and 1·25 from point of upper mandible to gape: tarsi, 2 inches; and feathered for nearly its upper third. Colour of the beak blackish, the cere and base of both mandibles, appearing to have been yellow; legs and toes also yellowish, and talons black. General hue of the upper parts, uniform hair-brown, the scapularies and coverts slightly tipped with rufous white: nape white, tipped with brown, and slightly edged laterally with rufous, which colour increases on the sides of the neck, and tinges the wings, the greater feathers of which have their outer webs uniform brown, and the inner, rufescent near the shaft, and white towards the margin, being barred with the same brown as that colouring the outer web; the coverts are slightly edged, and more largely tipped, with dull rufous; the longer upper tail coverts are tipped with whitish; and the tail is nearly of the same brown with the back, but rather paler and more greyish, its middle feathers having four broad dusky bars, the last subterminal, and a rudiment of a fifth which becomes gradually more obscure to the outermost: over and beyond the eye is a conspicuous whitish streak: the under-parts are rufescent whitish, palest on the throat and lower tail coverts, which are without markings, excepting a slight dusky mesial line along the throat; the breast has a broad mesial dusky streak to each feather, assuming on the belly and flanks, more or less, the appearance of transverse bands, which are united along the shafts of the feathers, leaving oval intervals of white, and the feathers being externally margined with pale fulvous; tibial plumes very pale buff, or with rufous central markings; and forepart of the under surface of the wings similarly coloured, the quills albescent underneath and obscurely barred, but dusky towards their tips."

Mr. Swinhoe, in the Ibis for 1864, notices the occurrence of this species in Formosa, and makes the following remarks in regard to his specimen:

"Bill blue black, pale on the gonys and lower portion of base of upper mandible; cere and over the eye dull olive green; eyelids and commissure-angle gamboge;* legs and toes of a deep rich chrome-yellow; claws black, more or less patched with pale brown, chiefly about their middle portions. Total length, 16·5 inches; tail, 9 inches; of twelve even feathers, obtuse at the ends, and somewhat graduated outwardly, so as to give the tail a rounded appearance when expanded; wing, 9·25 inches, the fourth and fifth quills equal and longest. Margin of bill with a single deep festoon on each side. Appearance of bird, between Buzzard and Sparrow Hawk; so that Hodgson's generic name, Butastur, is very aptly applied to it. Some feathers of the hind head long and subacuminate, forming a crest protruding about half an inch."

I have never myself seen this species alive, and have no notes in regard to its habits or nidification.

No. 49. **Archibuteo Hemiptilopus**, Blyth.

The Brown Eagle Buzzard.

Nothing appears to be known in regard to the nidification of this species, of which only three or four specimens are, I believe, in existence.

Dr. Jerdon's description and dimensions are taken from Mr. Blyth's notice, in the J. A. S. Mr. Blyth had only seen a single specimen, so that, as in most species of Buzzards, we may expect to meet with other examples, in very different stages of plumage. The dimensions given, are those of this single specimen, "probably," says Mr. Blyth, "a fine female," and the males will consequently, if this *was* a female, prove considerably smaller.

In regard to the breeding of the nearly allied European species, *A. Lagopus*, the only notice I have met with, is the following, in Yarrell's British Birds. "According to M. Temminck, this bird generally builds on high trees, and lays three or four eggs. A coloured figure of the egg will be found in the first part of Dr. Thieneman's work on the Eggs of the Birds of Europe, tab. III, fig. 2: this representation is two inches two

* In the Ibis, for 1868, he gives the "iris bright clear yellow with a black outer circle.

lines in length, by one inch eight lines in breadth, of a pale brownish white, blotched over the larger end with darker brown."

Of the nearly allied *A. Ferrugineus*, Captain Blackiston records finding nests in April and July, between the north and south branches of the Saskatchewan river in the interior of British North America. One nest, he says, which contained four eggs, placed in an Aspen tree, some twenty feet from the ground, was composed of sticks, lined with Buffaloe wool, and measured 2½ feet across; another nest contained five eggs, and was situated in a tree, only ten feet above a lake, a third nest contained two eggs." The eggs, he says, are of a white colour, plain, or more or less blotched with reddish brown.

Mr. Blyth considers our Indian species to be a mere straggler from the Mongolian Region, but it does not seem to have been procured either in Northern China, or in any part of Siberia, or the Amoor land, by Radde, Middendorf, Pallas, &c.

No. 50. Circus Cyaneus,* Lin.

The Hen Harrier.

As far as is yet known, this species does not breed in India, south of the Snowy Range, but I have been assured, that a fe-

---

* *Circus Cyaneus.*

Dimensions.		Length.	Expanse.	Wing.	Tail from vent.	Tarsus.	Foot, greatest length.	" breadth.	Mid Toe to root of Claw.	Its Claw, straight.	Hind Toe.	Its Claw, straight.	Inner Toe.	Its Claw, straight.	Bill, straight from edge of cere to point.	" along Curve, ditto.	" from gape.	" width at gape.	" height at margin of cere.	Distance by which closed wings fall short of end of tail.	Distance by which lower tail coverts fall short of end of tail.	Weight.	Length of cere on culmen.
Male.	From	17·1	37·4	12·2	8·1	2·55	2·9	2·48	1·20	0·52	0·62	0·64	0·72	0 61	0·6	0·7	1·08	0·96	0·33	1 9	3·3	oz. 10	0·42
	To	18·9	40·2	13·4	8·8	2·78	3·2	2 57	1·31	0·67	0·71	0·73	0·84	0·70	0·7	0·8	1·16	1·04	0·39	2 3	3·8	oz. 13	0·49
Female.	From	19·7	44·2	14·3	9·2	2·92	3·7	3·2	1·47	0·62	0·7	0·76	0 82	0·76	0 71	0·8	1·25	1·5	0·38	2 06	4·3	oz. 15	0·45
	To	21·6	47·2	15·7	10·4	3·17	4·1	3 6	1·53	0·71	0·8	0·83	0·88	0·82	0·77	0·86	1·39	1·9	0·42	2 61	4·9	lboz. 1·3	0 51

male of this species, or the next, was observed sitting on eggs in a marshy plain, at the end of Lake Tsoomourari in Thibet.

(Five males and seven females, measured and weighed.)

The fourth primary is the longest. The 1st is from 3·4 to 3·8 shorter, the 2nd from 0·85 to 1·25, and the 3rd from 0·05 to 0·21, shorter than the 4th. Exterior tail feathers from 0·7 to 1·4, shorter than central feathers.

DESCRIPTION.—*Legs and feet*, bright, somewhat orange yellow, claws black. *Irides* yellow. *Bill* bluish black; cere, yellow, in some a wax yellow, in others tinged greenish.

PLUMAGE.—*Adult male.* The upper parts, (except the first six primaries and the upper tail coverts,) together with the chin, throat, cheeks, ear-coverts, sides of the neck, and a portion of the upper part of the breast, greyish blue, varying in tint according to age, (the young birds being darker,) but always palest on the wing-coverts and tail, purest on the sides of the neck, and more or less tinged with fuscous on the scapulars, crown of the head and nape; the feathers of the nape pure white, except just at the tip, the white bases showing through more or less; the feathers of the top of the head and nape often with narrow, central, somewhat indistinct, brown centres, the traces probably of immature plumage; the forehead, and a line over the eye, whitish; traces of a silvery line under the eye, and over the ear-coverts, and tiny silvery streaks, are mingled with the pure blue grey of the ear-coverts and cheeks; the upper tail coverts pure white, the lateral tail feathers growing paler on the outer webs, until these in the two exterior feathers are pure white except just at the tips; the inner webs of all but the two central feathers white, less and less strongly tinged with brownish grey, as they recede from the centre, and with from 6 to 8 imperfect, transverse, brownish grey, bars, which in old birds become almost obsolete, and traces of some of which are generally to be met with, on the outer webs also, of the two or three exterior feathers, on each side. The lower breast and the rest of the under parts, are white. suffused most strongly on the breast, and faintly elsewhere (except in quite old birds which are sometimes pure white below) with very pale bluish grey. The first 6 primaries are black or blackish brown, the outer webs, (especially towards the tips) and often the tips themselves, more or less suffused with silver grey; the inner webs white at the bases; the rest of the primaries and secondaries, silver grey on the outer webs and tips, white or greyish white on the inner webs above the tips, in some mottled with grey, and mostly shewing traces, near the shafts, of imperfect brown, transverse bars.

Female.—The forehead, a narrow band over the eyes, the lores, cheeks and a line over the ear-coverts fulvous white. The crown of the head, occiput and nape, reddish fawn, the feathers with long, rich brown, central stripes. The ear-coverts and a line from them to the gape, similar, but of a somewhat duller colour. The feathers of the nape, white for the basal two-thirds; the white often shewing through. The feathers of the ruff a somewhat lighter reddish fawn, with narrow, dark brown, central stripes, the hind-neck, and upper back, a mixture of reddish and yellowish fawn colour, the feathers with broad, umber brown, central streaks; the scapulars, interscapulary region, lower back, and rump, umber brown, more or less glossed with purple, lighter in the old birds, darker in the young. The feathers of the rump, generally narrowly tipped with pale rufous; the upper tail coverts, as a rule, pure white but in some cases exhibiting lanceolate, rufous, or rufous brown spots on the shaft. The tail which, quite at the base, is white, has the central feathers brown; *deep* brown in younger birds, and greyer and paler in older ones, narrowly tipped, with white or slightly rufous white, and with four

In Europe, its nidification is well known. Mr. Yarrell says, "The nest is placed on the ground; the materials collected to form it are but few, consisting of small sticks and coarse grass; the eggs are four or five in number, white or of a pale skimmed milk blue, one inch eight lines long, (1·67) against one inch four lines (1·33) in breadth. The male sits occasionally during the period of incubation, and has been shot on the nest. The young are hatched early in June, and are, at first, covered with white down."

Mr. Hewitson says that in England, it breeds chiefly in marshy districts, and that the nest, when situated in low lands, is formed of so large a quantity of flags, sedge, and reed, as to raise it eighteen inches or two feet above the surface, so as to protect the young and eggs against sudden floods. Sir William Jardine tells us, that in a country possessing a considerable proportion of plain and mountain, they always retire at the commencement of the breeding season, to the wildest hills, and that

---

or five, broad, transverse, bars of grey, or greyish brown. The lateral tail feathers are similar but more broadly tipped with white, and with the grey or brownish grey bars changing generally as the feathers recede from the centre, into more or less clear, rufous, white, and the external feathers of all being often much tinged with rufous on their external webs towards their bases, and the brown inter-spaces being generally darker and purer on their inner webs. The lower part of the neck and breast is a mixture of rufous, and yellowish white, each feather with a broad, central, brown, or rufous brown, stripe; the shades of colour in the lower parts varying much in different individuals. The abdomen, vent, and lower tail coverts, yellowish white with brown shafts, and a more or less conspicuous ovate, rufous brown spot at the tips; the sides and flanks, are rufous or rufous brown with large white or fulvous white, double spots or imperfect bars; the tibial plumes hanging down over the tarsus, are similar to the lower tail coverts. The lesser wing-coverts, are more or less tipped with pale rufous fawn; many of the Indian ones, are broadly but imperfectly barred with the same colour; and many of the exterior scapulars have one or two large roundish spots of fulvous white on the outer webs, not very visible until the over-laying feathers are lifted.

The quills are a somewhat pale umber brown, more or less tinged with grey, on the outer webs, below the emarginations, in the first few quills, and white or rufous white on the inner webs above the notches, and with from three to five dark brown, transverse, irregular bars on the inner webs, traces of which are visible on the outer webs also.

Young.—The young resemble the female pretty closely, but have the irides brown, and the colours more marked, the brown being deeper, and the rufous of the head and neck brighter; the upper tail coverts have a reddish brown, linear, lanceolate, central streak, and the tail banded with rufous. The males do not commence to assume their distinctive plumage until the autumn of the second year, and in its transition stage according to Montague, the plumage of the female, remains about the neck, the smaller coverts of the wings, the thighs and part of the abdomen intermixed with the male plumage, after the change has been elsewhere effected.

during this time, not one individual will be found in the low country. The nest is made very frequently in a heath bush, by the edge of some ravine, and is composed of sticks, with a very slender lining ; it is sometimes also formed in one of those places called Scars, or where there has been a rush on the side of a steep hill, after a mountain thunder shower : here little or no nest is made, and the eggs are merely laid, on the bare ground, which has been scraped hollow. In a flat or level country, some common is generally chosen, and the nest is found in a whin or other scrubby bush, sometimes a little way from the ground.

Mr. Hewitson adds, that the eggs which are most frequently of a spotless, bluish white, are yet often slightly marked with yellowish brown, mixed with a purplish hue, and in some specimens with more distinctly defined spots of light brown. His figure of an egg of this species measures 1·79 × 1·43. The average dimensions appear to be about 1·75 by 1·33.

The Hen Harrier appears to occur throughout Europe, in North America,* in North Eastern Africa, Syria, and Turkey in Asia, from Smyrna to Babylon, in Afghanistan, throughout the more temperate portions of the Russian possessions in Asia, and in Northern China.†

In India the Hen Harrier, is pretty common, in the cold weather at any rate, about the outer ranges of the Himalayahs, from Abottabad to Kumaon, and possibly further east, and stragglers have been obtained in Baraitch (Oudh,) Meerut, Bareilly, Gourgaon, Etawah, Saugor, Nagpoor, Chandah and Goona, but except in the Himalayahs, or within 20 miles or so of their feet, its occurrence appears to be somewhat exceptional. The adult male of this species can always be distinguished from that of *Swainsoni*, by its perfectly pure, unbarred, and unspotted, upper tail coverts, and by its full coloured grey blue throat, foreneck, ear coverts, cheeks and sides of the neck, all of which parts, in *Swainsoni*, are pale grey or greyish white. The females are more difficult to separate ; as a rule, however, the upper tail coverts in these also are pure white, and where this is not the case, what markings there are, lanceolate central stripes, very different from the broad bar, or cross bar-like spot at the ends of the upper tail coverts of both the adult male and female of of *Swainsoni*. True that in the young *Swainsoni*, these marks on the upper tail coverts are often obsolete, but then the

* Some ornithologists contend, however, for the specific distinctness of the North American birds.

† Mr. Swinhoe gives it, I see, from Amoy and Takoo.

young of *Swainsoni*, differ altogether in plumage from the adult females, (while those of *Cyaneus* closely resemble that of the old females of that species,) and have the whole under parts uniform, streakless, rufous buff, or rufous. Moreover, the facis, if I may use the expression, of the females of the Hen, and pale-chested Harrier, are as a rule very different to the eye, although it may not be easy to explain the difference in words. In both, there is a large yellowish white patch, below the eye, purest in the pale-chested Harrier, and below this, from the base of the lower mandible, reaching to, and enveloping the whole of the ear coverts, there is a broad dark band, contrasting more or less with the pale patch below the eye, above, and the pale throat below. Now in the Hen Harrier, the contrast is *generally* much less marked than in the other, because the eye patch is not so white, and because the feathers of the band are only a pale dull rufous, with narrow, commonly *very* narrow central brown streaks, giving the band a streaky, or striated appearance, while in the pale-chested Harrier, the contrast is usually very marked, the eye patch is often pure white, and the feathers of the dark band, are deep brown, only very narrowly margined, with rufous, which margins, are insufficient, unless the patch be looked closely into, to break the general uniformity of the colour.—As for the difference commonly pointed out, *viz.*, that the female of *Swainsoni* has six brown bands, and that of *Cyaneus* four, (Bree,) on the tail, it holds good in many cases, but I do not find it *constant ;* I have now before me two Hen Harriers, one from England, and the other from Mussouree, each with six brown bars, including the one nearly hidden by the upper tail coverts, and two pale chested Harriers, with only five such bars, similarly including the one nearly hidden by the coverts.

The tarsus of the Hen Harrier doubtless averages considerably more than that of the pale-chested one, while as I shall notice further, that of Montague's Harrier is so much shorter, that this alone suffices to separate it from all our other Indian species. Another apparently constant difference between the Hen Harrier and the pale-chested Harrier in both sexes, and at all ages, when the wings are perfect, is that in the former, the fourth quill is always the longest, while in the latter, the fourth quill is always shorter than the third, often by fully half an inch.

No. 51. **Circus Swainsoni,*** A. SMITH.

THE PALE CHESTED HARRIER.

Of the nidification of this species, nothing certain seems known. Bree figures an egg, said to belong to this species, from

---

* *Circus Swainsoni.*

DIMENSIONS.		Length.	Expanse.	Wing.	Tail from vent.	Tarsus.	Foot, greatest length.	,, ,, breadth.	Mid toe to root of claw.	Its claw, straight.	Hind toe to root of claw.	Its claw, straight	Inner Toe, to root of claw.	Its claw, straight.	Bill, straight from margin of cere.	,, along curve.	,, from gape.	,, width at gape.	,, height, at point, at edge of cere.	Distance by which closed wings fall short of end of tail.	Distance by which lower tail coverts fall short of end of tail.	Weight.
MALE.	From	17·60	41·00	13·50	9·00	2·64	3·30	2·70	1·10	0·55	0·56	0·65	0·50	0·63	0·57	0 64	0·99	0·86	0·34	1·00	3·80	oz. 10
	To	18·50	42·25	13·95	10·00	2·8	3·45	2·90	1·30	0·66	0·62	0·71	0·60	0·72	0·69	0·77	1·15	0·91	0·39	1·75	4·75	oz 14
FEMALE.	From	18·65	40·00	13·75	9·50	2·65	3·38	2·79	1·31	0·62	0·68	0·75	0·55	0·70	0·70	0·8	1·20	1·00	0·37	1·75	4·00	oz 15·5
	To	20·65	47·50	15·15	11·25	2·92	3·59	3·00	1·50	0·67	0·76	0·82	0·68	0·78	0·78	0·86	1·38	1·09	0·42	2·75	5·00	oz. 1·3

(Eight males and eight females measured and weighed.)

The 3rd primary tbe longest. The 1st is from 3·25 to 4·25 shorter, the 2nd from 0·75 to 1·18 and the 4th from 0·10 to 0·50, shorter. Exterior tail feathers from 0·50, to 1·50 shorter than central feathers.

DESCRIPTION.—*Legs and feet,* bright orange to lemon yellow, according to age. Claws black. Irides bright yellow in adults, dark brown in the young, Orbits yellow, dingier in the young. *Bill.* Cere greenish, or dusky greenish in the adult, somewhat yellower in the young, especially on the culmen, and hidden at sides by the bristles of the lore. Gape, and base of lower mandible, blue, or sometimes greenish blue. Upper mandible and tip of lower mandible, bluish or horn-black.

PLUMAGE.—*Male.* Lores closely clothed with tiny white feathers, with elongated, naked, black brown, hair-like shafts. Forehead, and streak above eyes, and feathers of orbits greyish white, slightly paler than surrounding parts, the whole of the rest of the top of head and nape, to where the ruff joins

Thienemann, but furnishes no particulars. The figure represents a somewhat broad, oval egg, of an uniform, pale bluish

---

in, grey, tinged with brown, most strongly so on nape feathers, and with dark shafts. Cheeks and ear coverts grey, the feathers broadly edged with greyish white, so as to produce a striated appearance. Feathers of ruff, which as regards colour is very conspicuous greyish white, with narrow, central, grey streaks, back of the neck, below brownish grey patch of nape, greyish white, the feathers slightly darker shafted, and some of them with the greyish traces of faint, brownish grey, transverse, subterminal spots. The whole of the base of the neck behind, upper back and scapulars, a sort of ash grey, more or less tinged towards the tips with brownish grey, and the longer scapulars frosted with a purer grey. The middle and lower back, a shade lighter grey, the white bases of the feathers showing through, more or less. Upper tail coverts pure white, with regular, broad, transverse, grey or slightly brownish grey, bars. The whole of the wing coverts, winglet tertials, and outer webs of secondaries and last four primaries, grey, more silvery on quills, and browner on lesser coverts. The median coverts narrowly pale margined, and most of the other feathers of the corners narrowly paler tipped. The second, and last four primaries, have the central halves of the inner webs pure grey, and the marginal halves white The first primary is silver grey on the outer web, dusky grey on the inner, as far as the notch, and above this chiefly white. The next four are nearly black, with a good deal of silver grey however, on the outer webs of the first two, and of white, more or less mottled with dusky, on the inner webs of all towards the base ; the sixth is dusky grey on the outer web and tip, and paler and browner grey on inner web, which has a broad marginal stripe broadest towards base, where it occupies nearly the whole web, of white, irregularly mottled with grey. The central tail feathers are a uniform silver grey, slightly shaded, with dusky on the terminal half. The next feather, on each side, is similar, but there are six or five white patches on the shafts, and traces of corresponding, paler bars, on the inner webs, which are very narrowly, paler margined, in each succeeding feather, the white patches on the shaft are better marked, and extend further and further across the outer webs, while the corresponding broad pale bars, on the inner webs at first only mottled with white, become pure white, and larger, and at the same time, the white margin of the inner webs spreads inward, so that the two exterior feathers have the inner webs pure white, with only four or five, somewhat narrow bars of grey, or brownish grey, (which do not extend to the margin,) and here and there a little freckling, chiefly towards the base of the same colour. Chin, throat and front of the neck pearl grey, whitish on chin. Breast, abdomen, vent, sides, wing lining and thigh coverts pure white, with just the faintest possible grey mottling, or freckling, in places on sides, and base of thighs. Lower tail coverts white, with rather brownish grey, broad, incomplete, rather wavy, transverse bars ; about one or two on each feather. Inner surface of the wings, mingled white and very pale grey, only the terminal $\frac{1}{3}$ to $\frac{1}{2}$ of the second to the fifth primaries, blackish brown. The first to the third quills are conspicuously notched on inner web, the second to the fourth, emarginated on outer webs.

Female.—The lores dusky, covered with black bristle-like hairs, as is also the point of the chin. A patch (scarcely noticeable in some specimens) over the eye, and in front of it, white, tipped with brownish. Below the eye, and front of the ear coverts, somewhat purer, while a band, inside the ruff, from the base of the lower mandible, over the ear coverts to the sides of the nape, dark

white, measuring 1·62 by 1·63. In the plains of India, this bird certainly does not breed. We first see them in Upper In-

---

umber brown, usually darkest towards the nape, the feathers narrowly edged with rufous, and centred darker. A dark streak from the posterior corner of the eye, meeting the top of this band. Forehead, and a line from the forehead over the eye, and the last mentioned dark streak, nearly unstriated rufous brown. The rest of the forehead, and top and back of the head, and nape, where the ruff joins in, and back and sides of the neck, rufous, the feathers all more or less, broadly centred with umber brown. The centres being larger, proportionably, at the base of the neck. Upper back and smaller scapulars umber brown, most of the feathers, usually slightly tipped with rufous. The longest scapulars, somewhat lighter coloured, with scarcely a trace of the rufous tipping; middle back often of a somewhat lighter brown than the upper back, and the feathers, with conspicuous rufous tips or margins. Rump feathers slightly darker, and with somewhat less conspicuous rufous tips. Upper tail coverts pure white, with only a spot or incomplete bar, of dark or pale brown, or rufous, towards the tips. Centre tail feathers dark umber brown, inconspicuously tipped with grey, scarcely perceptible in some and with four or five, transverse, grey bars, the broadest bars towards the tip. The next feather darker brown, conspicuously tipped with white or rufous white, and with one broad, and two or three narrow, pale rufous, and greyish transverse bars, the rufous being chiefly next the shaft. The next feather much the same, but the white or rufous (some are whiter some more rufous) of the bar, and tipping, purer, and a considerable patch at the base, on the outer web, mingled white and rufous, with only a tinge of brown. The second, exterior feather, nearly pure white, or a pale rufous, as the case may be, with subterminal, central, and basal bands of brown, which are more or less rufous in the two latter, on the outer web. The exterior feather has almost the whole outer web rufous white, and the interior more or less rufous white, with traces of a subterminal and two other bands, of mingled, darkish rufous, and brown. The whole of the lesser wing coverts umber brown, broadly margined with rufous, or rufous white. The median coverts the same colour, in some conspicuously, in some faintly tipped with the same rufous white tint. The greater coverts of the secondaries, and the tertials themselves, still the same umber brown, but only very narrowly (in some not at all) tipped with rufous white. The winglet, primaries and their greater coverts, and secondaries, slightly darker brown, all but the first four primaries, and most of the secondaries, with a very narrow, whitish tipping and the outer webs of the first primary, and the next three, which are conspicuously marginate, below the margination more or less silvered with grey. The inner webs of all the primaries above the tips, more or less white or rufous white, with conspicuous, broad, dark brown bars. In some specimens the brown bars are so broad that the ground of the web appears brown, and the rufous interspaces appear like pale bars. There are traces of similar markings on the secondaries, most conspicuous in those nearest the primaries, and less so in those adjoining the tertials. Chin white or rufous white. The ruff in front, and on either side towards the nape, white or rufous white, the feathers centred darkish brown. The whole of the front of the throat, breast and abdomen white or fulvous or pale rufous white, the feathers all broadly, or conspicuously centred with brown and rufous. The feathers of the vent, lower tail coverts, and external thigh coverts, pure white or pale rufous brown, shafted, and with two or more irregular spots of pale rufous along the shafts. The axillaries mostly light rufous brown, with indistinct

dia early in October, (I have twice seen specimens in the last week of September,) and the great majority leave by the close of

---

incomplete fulvous white bars, the lesser under wing coverts fulvous, or pale rufous white, the feathers mostly darker centred. The greater lower wing coverts mostly a brown or rufous brown, and for the most part, edged and tipped with fulvous white or pale rufous. The longest of the lower tail coverts are rather conspicuously tipped with pale rufous.

Females differ considerably, in the amount of rufous, on the top and back of the head, back and sides of neck, etc. In some, the prevailing line is rufous, there being only very narrow brown centres to the feathers, but in others, the brown much predominates, the feathers having only somewhat narrow rufous margins. The extent and amount of the rufous tippings to the feathers of the back and rump varies much, as also the extent and depth of rufous in the tail, and on the lower parts.

Young.— Lores, forehead, a patch under the eyes, a streak over the eyes, to upper corner of the ruff, and a broad patch on the nape, (which latter has several of the central feathers brown tipped, white. Bristles of the lores black. A patch in the anterior corner of the eye, continued as a very narrow streak over the eye, under the white line, and beyond the posterior angle of the eye, backwards, till it joins the top of the ear coverts, dark umber brown. The whole top of the head warm umber brown, faintly margined with rufous, where it infringes on the white supercilium, and white nape patch. The whole of the nape, upper back, scapulars, and wings (except in some specimens some of the median coverts) nearly uniform umber brown, but the quills with a trace of darker banding. Most of the median wing coverts in some specimens so broadly edged with pale ferruginous or buff, as to show but little of the brown: these edgings entirely wanting in others. The winglet, greater coverts, secondaries, and most of the primaries very narrowly paler tipped. Feathers of the lower back and rump, the same brown as the rest of the upper parts, but each feather distinctly tipped with buff. The upper tail coverts often pure white. One or two of them only, with an ill-defined brown patch: in other cases marked as in the adult female. Two centre tail feathers dark umber brown, with four bars of lighter greyish brown. The next four feathers the same dark brown, but tipped and barred with ferruginous or buff, which is brighter and more extensive, as the feathers recede from the centre. Exterior tail feather almost entirely rufous buff, with two, irregular, dark brown bars, and a trace of a third. Patch from the lower mandible, over the cheeks, and embracing the ear coverts, rich dark umber brown. Round this, posteriorly, the ruff uniform pale rufous buff, except just where it separates the white eye streak from the white nape patch, where the feathers are mingled with dark brown. Sides of the neck, below the ruff, which is thus clearly defined, dark umber brown. Chin whitish, with black bristles at the tip. Whole lower parts of the body, including lower tail coverts, uniform, rufous, fawn or pale ferruginous. The lining of the wing the same, but paler, and the largest of the lower wing coverts mottled with brown.

The lower surface of the quills greyish brown. The primaries very distinctly barred, and with more or less white replacing the brown. The first three primaries conspicuously emarginate on the inner webs, and the third and fourth on the outer webs. Lower surface of the tail exterior feathers nearly uniform pale fawn, with only an indistinct trace of three ill-defined bars. The four next feathers umber brown, with fulvous white tips, and two well marked, fulvous white, broad bars. The two centre feathers with scarcely a trace of paler tipping, and with three narrower greyish bars.

March, or early in April, according as the season is a early or late one. In the Terai and Dhoon, they may linger somewhat longer, as I have a specimen from the latter, killed on the 20th of April.

Whether they breed in the Himalayahs, on this side of the Snowy Range, I cannot say ; I have never met with a single one, during my summer rambles in the Hills, and very much doubt their breeding south of the snows.

This bird apparently unknown in Northern Europe and Asia, (where neither Radhe, Pallas, Middendorf nor Schrenk appears to have met with it,) is found alike in North Eastern and Southern Africa and Palestine, occurs in Burmah, and has been procured on the Yangtzee, by Captain Blackeston, but it does not seem to find its way either eastwards to Japan, or southwards to Malayana, or the Archipelago.

The livery of the young is rather peculiar, the whole under parts being a uniform, unstreaked, rufous buff, such as is met with in the young of *Cineraceus*, and in one stage of *Ranivores*. Dr. Jerdon has not noticed this stage, in which I have numerous specimens, and I have therefore, as will be seen in the note, described it at length.

No. 52. Circus Cineraceus.* MONTAGUE.

MONTAGUE'S HARRIER.

I cannot say that I myself believe that this species breeds in India, but my collector, Mr. A. G. R. Theobald, who sent me

* CIRCUS CINERACEUS.

Dimensions.	Length.	Expanse.	Wing.	Tail from vent.	Tarsus.	Foot, greatest length.	,, greatest width.	Mid toe to root of claw.	Its claw straight.	Hind toe to root of claw.	Its claw, straight.	Inner toe to root of claw.	Its claw, straight.	Bill straight from margin of cere.	along curve ditto.	from gape.	width at gape.	height at front, at edge of cere.	Distance by which closed wings exceed end of tail.	Distance by which lower tail coverts fall short of end of tail.	Weight.	Length of cere only.
From	16·5	40·00	14·50	9·30	2·17	2·45	2·12	1·02	0·45	0·50	0·43	0·56	0·48	0·56	0·70	1·00	0·79	0·28	0·05	4·25	8 oz.	0·33
To	17·7	43·50	15·30	10·20	2·35	2·82	2·32	1·14	0·50	0·62	6·55	0·62	0·54	0·62	0·70	1·12	0·82	0·31	0·21	4·9	10 oz.	)·37
From	18·60	41·8	15·00	9·87	2·28	2·87	2·22	1·22	0·56	0·56	0·51	0·59	0·50	0·60	0·69	1·07	0·80	0·30	0·6	4·4	10 oz.	0·32
To	19·50	43·9	16·00	10·5	2·46	3·19	2 35	1·31	0·62	0·63	0·60	0·65	0·59	0·70	0·81	1·20	0·87	0·33	0·9	4·8	13 oz.	0·33

(Four males and three females measured and weighed.)

The third primary is the longest. The first is from three to four inches shorter, the second from 0·6 to 0·9, and the fourth from 0·7 to 1 shorter. Exterior tail feathers from 0·4 to 1 shorter than the central ones.

DESCRIPTION. *Legs and feet* yellow, claws black. *Irides*, Bright yellow in the adult, sometimes brownish yellow in the female, almost white in one young one examined. *Bill* black, dusky in the young. Cere, greenish yellow, yellower in the young.

PLUMAGE. *Adult male.* The whole head, chin, throat, neck all round, breast, back, scapulars, wings (except the first seven primaries which are blackish) and central tail feathers, gray of different shades. The neck, cheeks and ear coverts, bluish; crown of the head, and occiput (below which there is a white mottled nape patch owing to the white bases of the feathers showing through) here and there tinged with rufous brown; the scapulars infuscated and brownish; the back, darker and more ashy, and the wings and centre tail feathers more silvery. The secondaries have a broad, blackish, transverse band, across both webs, forming a conspicuous wing band (not unlike that of the common pigeon, *C. Intermedia)* and with traces of another, or, in some specimens, two other bands on the inner webs. The central tail feathers unbarred, the laterals with four, very broad, transverse, dark bars on the inner webs, and *traces* of the same on the outer webs of some of the feathers. The grey fading, as the feathers recede from the central ones, to pure white

specimens of the bird, correctly named, and measured in the flesh, forwarded at the same time, the following note on its nidification:

---

on the exterior ones, and the dark brown bands changing gradually to dull chestnut on the latter. A broad circle round the eye whitish. The lower parts from the breast downwards, and the whole wing lining (except a few of the longer lower coverts which are ashy grey with large white spots) pure white; the feathers of the abdomen with narrow, rather pale chestnut central streaks; there are lanceolate chestnut dashes in the wing lining, the axillaries are broadly and irregularly barred with blotches, and lower tail and thigh coverts, have the shafts of the same colour, a few faint streaks of which are also generally to be seen mingling with the blue gray of the breast.

Adult female. Forehead and a band round the eye slightly rufous white. Crown and occiput rufous brown, streaked with dark hair brown. A streak from the base of the lower mandible, widening so as to involve the whole ear coverts, darkish brown, in some very dark. Some of the feathers, commonly, very narrowly margined rufous. Back, wings, scapulars and central tail feathers dark umber brown, the quills and central tail feathers, darkest. The lateral tail feathers, paling as they recede from the central ones, which are unbarred, with four or five broad transverse, lighter and generally more rufous brown, bars, often more or less obsolete on the outer webs. The whole of the lower parts are light rufous buff, with narrow, deeper rufous, shaft stripes. Rump and upper tail coverts, mingled white, rufous buff and reddish brown.

Young male of the 2nd year, *(I quote this from Yarrell, I have never obtained a specimen in this stage)* killed while undergoing his second moult.

"The top of the head and the feathers round the cheeks a mixture of brown and rufous, ear coverts grey; occiput varied with white; the nape, back, scapulars, tertials, and upper tail coverts, lead grey; upper surface of all the tail feathers, except the two in the middle, barred with shades of brown and rufous; middle tail feathers, with the outer webs uniform pearl grey; the inner webs with fine dark brown bands on a greyish ground; wing primaries and secondaries blackish brown; greater wing coverts dark brown; lesser wing coverts lighter brown, varied with rufous and two or three grey feathers: chin, and front of neck, pearl grey; breast, belly, thighs, and under tail coverts white, with a longitudinal rufous stripe on the centre of each feather; under surface of tail feathers barred with greyish white and brown; legs, toes and claws as in the adult male."

A young male of the year; a narrow frontal band, a line above, and a patch below and behind the eye, and two broad patches on either side of the nape, white, the feathers of the latter with brown shafts. Chin and throat whitish, bristles, at point of chin black. The top of the head rusty rufous, the feathers, with more or less narrow, lanceolate or linear, dark brown shaft stripes. Ear coverts and a line extending to them from the base of the lower mandible dark brown, the feathers mostly narrowly margined with ferruginous. Wings, back, and scapulars rich brown of different shades, palest on the upper back, rump and lesser wing coverts, more umber on the secondaries and longer scapulars, and greyer, except at the extreme tips, on the primaries; all the quills, the primary greater coverts, back, rump, and scapulars, narrowly but conspicuously margined at the tips with rufous buff, or faintly rufous white. The lesser and most of the median coverts more

"Breeds on the top of high trees. I took the nest of one in December, (Christmas day) which was placed in the fork of a Tamarind tree, about 25 to 30 feet from the ground."

This is not at all in accordance with the habits of this species elsewhere, and I cannot help thinking that Mr. Theobald must be in error, but in another note, still writing from Salem, (Madras) he says,—"It frequents open jungles and cultivated fields, and flies low in search of prey. On one occasion the first one (measurements given,) made a dart at one of my young Pigeons, but failed in its attempt; it did not return to the attack, but was going away, when I shot it. It is not a shy bird when on the wing. On one occasion, I took a nest of one, with three young ones which were of a brindled color on the wings, tail and back, ashy on the other parts; they lived for a fortnight, when they died one after another; they fed greedily on raw mutton."

"The young birds had a sort of shrill whistle."

And speaking of two specimens which he forwarded, he further says,—"Both of these birds were shot in Salem; they are most common about here from December to May or June. I found locusts in the stomachs of both."

All my enquiries and observations lead me to believe that Mr. Theobald is in error, but his assertions are so positive and circumstantial, that being, as he is, familiar with the species, I have thought it only right to direct attention to the subject, by inserting his remarks.

Of the nidification of this species in England, Mr. Yarrell gives the following notice: "The nest is placed on the ground, generally among furze; the eggs, seldom exceeding four in number, are very similar, as might be expected to those of the Hen Harrier; they are white, one inch seven lines (1·58) in

---

broadly margined with brighter rufous. The first few primaries silvered on their outer webs towards their bases, and with three or more irregular, dark, transverse bars on the inner webs, (which are mostly brownish white above the notches,) and faint traces of these on the grey brown, outer webs, above the emarginations; all the tail feathers tipped with pale rufous, most broadly in the external feathers. The central tail feathers deep brown, with four broad, transverse, greyish brown bars, greyer at the bases and browner towards the tips. The lateral tail feathers similar in character, but the grey brown bars change, as the feathers recede from the central ones, to rufous grey, rufous and rufous white; and the deep brown interspaces change similarly to nearly pure cinnamon rufous. The upper tail coverts are absolutely pure white in some, in others with very narrow, rufous brown, shaft stripes. From the throat, the whole lower parts including the wing lining, are pure, pale cinnamon rufous. Some of the feathers of the sides of the breast with dark, linear, brown, shaft stripes, and all the feathers with the shafts slightly deeper coloured than the webs.

length, and one inch four lines (1·33) in breadth. The young, according to Mr. Jenyns, are hatched about the second week in June."

Mr. Hewitson says that "the nest, which is placed upon the ground, is more slight than that of the marsh or Hen Harrier, but is composed, like theirs, of flags, sedge, and rushes. The eggs are usually four or five in number, but six were found in a nest which was forwarded to me; the eggs are of a clear white, distinctly tinted with light blue, and are never, to the best of my information, spotted. The time of incubation is early in May. Mr. Alfred Newton informs me that the Harriers, like the Owls, the Eagles, and probably all the Hawk tribe, begin to sit upon the first egg, and as there is also most likely an interval of some days between the production of each egg, the young are of very different ages, and much more easily supplied with food."

This species is at once distinguished, at all ages, and in both sexes, from all our other Indian species of Harriers, by its extremely short tarsus and by its short fourth primary. In the Hen Harrier, the fourth quill is the longest; in the other three species, the third is the longest; in the pied and pale-chested Harrier the fourth quill averages probably 0·25 inches shorter, while in the present species it averages nearly 0·75 of an inch shorter. As regards the tarsus, Dr. Jerdon gives it at 2.75" in the male, and 3" in the female, but in no female even that I have yet examined, has it exceeded 2·5 inches, and I am pretty confident that there must be some mistake in Dr. Jerdon's measurements.

This species occurs in England; (where at one time it bred freely,) in Scandinavia, in fact almost throughout Europe; in Algeria, Egypt, South Africa, Babylon, Persia and Afghanistan. I do not find it noticed from Northern Asia, nor from China, nor does it seem to extend to Malayana or the Archipelago. In Ceylon, British Burmah and throughout India, it is found, but very locally distributed, always, I think, affecting damp and more or less wooded localities, and scarcely ever found, in the comparatively dry, though richly cultivated plains, of the N. W. Provinces and the Punjaub, and almost, if not entirely unknown in Rajpootana, where the pale chested Harrier is not uncommon. It is most numerous as far as my experience goes, in damp cultivated lands, lying at the bases or on the lower slopes of tho Himalayahs, (the Dhoon is a great place for it,) or the Nielgherries, and feeds much, to judge from the specimens I have killed, on large insects.

No. 53. Circus Melanoleucus.* Gmel.

The Pied Harrier.

Nothing seems to be known of the nidification of this species, in India or elsewhere.

---

* Circus Melanoleucus.

Dimensions.		Length.	Expanse.	Wing.	Tail from vent.	Tarsus.	Mid toe to root of claw.	Its claw.	Hind toe.	Its claw.	Inner toe.	Its claw.	Bill, straight.	along curve.	from gape.	width at gape.	height.	Distance by which lower tail coverts fall short of end of tail.	Length of cere on culmen.
Male.	From	16·00	39·00	13·70	8·00	2 98	1·25	0 55	0·62	0·57	0·62	0·56	0 65	0·68	1·05	0·82	0·36	3 00	0·3
	To	17 15	43·00	14·83	9·20	3·13	1·4	0·58	0·73	0·61	0·74	0·61	0·75	0·77	1·25	0·95	0·41	4·50	0·4

(Five males, 2 adults and 3 young, measured.)

The 3rd primary the longest. The 1st is 3·1 to 3·6 shorter, the 2nd 0·7 to 0·8, and the 4th 0·08 to 0·25 shorter. Exterior tail feathers 0·2 to 0·7 shorter than central ones.

Description.—In all, the legs and feet were yellow, the bill, black, and the cere, blackish horny. The irides in the adults were yellow, in the young yellowish white.

Plumage *Adult male.* The whole head, chin, throat, neck all round, upper breast, upper half, or in some two-thirds, of the back, the scapulars, (all but the undermost one or two) the first 6 primaries and a broad band across the wing (commencing on the carpal joint and involving some of the small coverts, and most of the median and larger coverts of the secondaries and tertiaries) black, (or blackish brown in a somewhat earlier stage of plumage). Lower portion of the back, (except a broad central line, usually black), rump and upper tail coverts, pure white, the latter with large, subterminal, grey spots, or broad imperfect bars, in some specimens, almost obsolete. Winglet, primary greater coverts, last 4 primaries and secondaries silver grey, often broadly tipped with brown, and with a considerable portion of the inner webs white. Tertiaries and some of their greater coverts, dark brown. Undermost scapulars a mixture of dark brown and grey. Shoulder of wing and all the lesser coverts (except those involved

It probably breeds in Bengal and Assam; Col. Tytler tells me that he feels almost certain that he has procured it all

---

near the carpal joint in the black bar), pure white, in some specimens fulvous white, in others tinged grey. Tail feathers pale, greyish, dove colour, or very pale, silvery brown, narrowly tipped white, and all but the central feathers, broadly margined interiorly with white. Lower breast, abdomen, sides, flanks, lower tail coverts, wing lining, and axillaries pure white. Lower surface of tail and quills, except the first six primaries (which are black) albescent or white.

A somewhat younger specimen, had the black everywhere more or less intermingled with dusky brown. This stage is correctly figured by Le Vaillant, (Birds of Africa, p. 32) and Radde mentions a similar specimen, in the Vienna Museum.

Young Male. The whole head, nape and back of neck, clove brown, each feather broadly margined with pale rufous. Upper back and scapulars, uniform, clove brown. Lower back and wings, a slightly lighter shade of the same colour. Some of the longest feathers of the back, with two obscure, terminal, rufous spots, (one on each web); the edge of the wing rufous white and many of the lesser coverts faintly or boldly (it varies in different specimens) margined, with fulvous or rufous white. Upper tail coverts pure white, (in one fulvous white) dark shafted, and with a conspicuous, oval, rufous brown, subterminal spot. The tail feathers a somewhat greyish, pale brown, narrowly tipped with fulvous white, and with broad, rather darker brown, transverse bars. The exterior lateral feathers have the ground colour much paler and tinged rufous, and the transverse bars narrower and less perfect. The whole of the lower parts, are buffy or rufous white, with central, rufous brown stripes, broad on the lower breast and upper abdomen, almost obsolete on the chin and thigh coverts. The cheeks and ear coverts are dull, rather sandy rufous, some of the longer feathers centered darker towards the tips, and (in *some* specimens) all darker shafted. The primaries have the greater portion of the inner webs, pale rufous white; they are barred with darker brown, the bars being wide apart and most conspicuous on the lower surface of the wing. The lower surface of the quills is grey brown on the terminal halves, with darker brown tips and bars, while the basal halves are a somewhat rufous buff, with traces of a few transverse brown bars. The wing lining, is rufous buff, many of the feathers with rufous brown centerings; the axillaries are rufous buff, the shafts darker, and two or more very broad, irregular, transverse, red brown bars, which, in some specimens, run into one another, and occupy nearly the whole surface of the feather. The winglet, greater primary coverts, and the exterior webs towards their bases of some of the later primaries, grey, all with broad, transverse, brown bars.

Other young males are altogether less rufous below, the ground colour being almost white, and the central stripes narrower. In these the tail is greyer, and the bands narrower, and the winglet, primary greater coverts and exterior webs of primaries, are more decidedly grey, (quite silver grey on the two former) and the brown transverse bars more conspicuous. Most of the axillaries are pure white, with large brown spots, or imperfect, transverse bars.

These descriptions of the young males were originally taken from specimens in "Tytler's Museum," but have subsequently been compared with others.

As regards the quills, Radde remarks, that the second and fifth are almost equal, the second only exceeding the 5th by about 0·08, but in a very fine specimen now before me, the second exceeds the 5th by 0·9. The sixth he

the year round at Barrackpoor, and that he believes it to breed somewhere in that neighbourhood. Dr. Jerdon remarks (in his Appendix): "This Harrier, I have every reason to believe, breeds in Northern India. I saw several in Purneah in July, (some of them in a garb resembling that of the females of the other species) and shot one bird in a state of change from the female garb to the black and white ordinary plumage. This was apparently not a young bird of the year, for the tail feathers were much worn. Can this bird, then, have a double moult? It would appear so, unless I was mistaken in considering it not a bird of the year. If so, they have the ordinary female garb of Harriers at first, and shortly afterwards, assume the peculiar pied livery of this species."

The specimen referred to by Dr. Jerdon, he recently showed me, and I have little hesitation in saying that I believe it to be undoubtedly referable to *C. Melanoleucus*. We both agreed that it exactly resembled the grey-winged and grey-tailed, left hand figure, of *Circus Spilonotus* (Ibis, 1863, Pl. V,) but while he assigned it to this species, I contend that either it does not belong to it, or that if it does, this so-called species is merely a form of *C. Melanoleucus*. Of this I shall say more further on. At present I would wish first to notice, that up to the present time, as far as I know, no description of the young of this species has been published. Col. Tytler was, I believe, the first to procure the young, in the 1st year's livery, a stage of plumage in which it much resembles the young of the other, already described, species,—I have therefore given (see footnote) full descriptions of the young, taken originally from Col. Tytler's specimens, but subsequently compared with others from Tipperah.

In all stages of plumage, the males (for I have as yet seen no *authenticated* female of *Melanoleucus*), may be distinguished from those of *Cyaneus*, *Swainsoni* and *Cineraceus*, by the length of the tarsus, which averages over 3 inches, and in no specimen that I have examined, fell short of 2·98 (in a young bird) and in one (a fine adult) measured 3·13.

I am aware that Mr. Gurney (Ibis, 1863, p. 214) gives the average of the tarsus, in three specimens, at 2·87, but possibly, he

---

says exceeds the first by 0·6, but in a specimen now before me, it only exceeds it by 0·3. The proportions of the quills therefore, vary considerably, even in the adults. The second to the fifth, as he points out, are conspicuously emarginate on the outer web, and the first four are notched, but somewhat feebly, on the inner webs. The tail he gives as *even*, only the external lateral feather being slightly shorter than the others, but in some specimens, as my measurements shew, the tail is perceptibly rounded. These, however, were young birds.

measures differently to what I do; any how, out of nine Indian specimens, whose tarsi I have recorded, (measuring most accurately with compasses and a decimal rule,) in no single case did I find the tarsus less than I have mentioned, and it certainly averages, in adults, fully 3·06; similarly measured, 2·8 may be taken as a maximum for *Swainsoni* and *Cyaneus*, and 2·4 for *Cineraceus*.

There is one possible flaw: I have never killed this species myself, and am dependant, for the identification of the sex, and many of the measurements (not of course of the tarsus, or other parts, that do not alter in the dried skin,) on Col. Tytler, Mr. Irwin and others, but taking the whole of the evidence collectively, I entertain no doubt that all the specimens that I have examined, all *but one* (of which the sex was not ascertained) professing to be males, and agreeing closely in all their measurements, *were* really males.

It still is open to any one to suggest, that as Dr. Jerdon's bird is by him believed to belong to a separate species, *Spilonotus* (of which more anon,) these young birds that I have described, may belong to this, and not to *Melanoleucus*. But two at least of these young birds were shot in company with with full-plumaged *Melanoleucus*, and they are one and all somewhat smaller in their dimensions, than undoubted adult Pied Harriers, whereas the supposed *Spilonotus* is said by Mr. Gurney, to be a decidedly *larger* bird, with *longer* tarsi.

I believe we may rest assured that the birds described by me, are *bonâ fide* young males of this species, and it seems not improbable that these may be the birds referred to by Mr. Gurney in the following notice which appeared in the Ibis for 1868.

" A third undescribed Harrier, of the Philippine Island, is of the same size and configuration as the last mentioned, but of very similar colouring to the adult male of *C. hudsonius* (Linn.) which Professor Schlegel (Museum des Pays Bas, Circi, p. 3) mentions as a species inhabiting the Philippine Islands, but which I have never seen thence. It is, however, decidedly a smaller species than *C. hudsonius*, and may perhaps prove to be a hitherto undescribed state of *C. Melanoleucus*, a possibility which has hitherto restrained me from describing it as a distinct species." As regards the females, I have no positive information, but, I feel certain myself, that Dr. Jerdon's specimen was *Circus Melanoleucus*, in plumage intermediate between those stages which I have described, and I cannot doubt, that it exactly corresponded with the figure of the supposed *Spilonotus* in the Ibis for 1863.

The following were Mr. Swinhoe's remarks in regard to this plate:—

"I observed a pair of Harriers beating over the rush-grown delta of the Tamsay river, about the gorge, in March. I watched them for some time, but was unable to get within shot of them. The male appeared of a pied plumage; but the female was brown. I concluded, therefore, that it must have been the species that prevails in the neighbourhood of Amoy, rather than the true *C. Melanoleucus*, Gmel., which ranges in Asia, from India to Peking, and which I have also seen from the Philippines; for Mr. Gurney tells me, that he is informed by Mr. Blyth that this latter species has, in the adult form, both sexes coloured alike. In the broad, flat, open country of the south west, near Taiwanfoo, I observed another Harrier, which I took to be *C. Cyaneus*, L.; but of the species I cannot be sure, as it might have been one of two cognate forms which are hard to distinguish from it at a distance, except by a most experienced eye. These are the Pale Harrier (*Circus Swainsoni*, Smith) and the American Harrier (*C. hudsonius*, L.) The former of these has lately been procured by Captain Blakiston on the Yangtsze river; and of the latter, specimens may be seen in the Leyden Museum, from the Philippines and Kamtschatka.

"I procured no specimens of Harriers in Formosa; but, as Mr. Gurney was anxious to have the *Circus spilonotus* figured, I have supplied a male and female from the neighbourhood of Amoy for that purpose. With reference to this species, Mr. Gurney writes, 'I have just compared three male specimens of *C. Spilonotus*, with three males of *C. Melanoleucus*, and enclose you the measurements, by which you will see that *C. Spilonotus* considerably exceeds *C. Melanoleucus* in all its measurements; in addition to which it has a much larger bill and stronger tarsi. In all these respects (as also in some degree in colouring) it approaches to an allied but still larger species, *C. Assimilis*, Gould, of Australia. I do not think that *C. Spilonotus* ever assumes the black plumage which characterizes the head, neck, back, and a portion of the wings of the adult male of *C. Melanoleucus*. I have not been able to compare your female of *C. Spilonotus* with a female of *C. Melanoleucus*, the only (supposed) female which I have of the latter, being an individual of the sex of which I do not feel sure.

	Total Length (inches.)	Wing from Carpus.	Tarsus.	Middle toe and claw.
Circus Spilonotus ♂ (3 specimens.)	22 23·75	17·25 17·75	3·37	2·75
Circus Melanoleucus ♂ (3 specimens	18	14·5 15·00	2·87	2·00'

"I have unfortunately no measurements of *C. Spilonotus* taken from birds in a fresh state. The only note I can find in my Journals is the following, made on a male, shot at Amoy, the 27th December, 1859:—'Bill, bluish black, paler on the base; cere, light greenish yellow; eyes, fine waxen or primrose, yellow; inside of mouth, leaden blue; legs, yellow ochre, with black claws.' The females of this species have yellowish brown irides, and so much resemble those of the Marsh Harrier (*C. Œruginosus*) that Mr. Blyth identified an example I sent him, as of that species; but as I had frequently seen individual, brown birds, in company with the pied ones, I was led to doubt the assertion. On the rush-grown sand flats, at the mouth of the Changchow river, near Amoy, these birds are particularly common during winter, but they are nearly always females. I do not know for what reason; but in this locality, the adult male is peculiarly rare until the spring, when a few may occasionally be met with. In many points of habit, this bird seems to connect the Harriers with the Govinda Kites, feeding largely on offal and carrion, as well as on Batrachians and small mammals. All these objects I have found in the stomachs of those I have dissected; but remains of birds never. In its heavy sailing flight, this species also more resembles Kites than a Harrier. They are such offensive birds, that I did not care to preserve more than a few for identification.

"Mr. Gurney writes me, that he has seen specimens of *C. Spilonotus* from Singapore, as well as from the Philippines."

Now, in the first place, I must remark that I do not think that it has as yet been satisfactorily determined by dissection, that the adult females of *Melanoleucus are* identical in plumage, with the males.—If any one has done so, I wish they would let me know. Every black and white bird examined by Tytler at a time when he shot many, was a male. Both specimens in the Asiatic Society's Museum were males. The adult female *may* be like the male, but it has not I conceive been as yet *proved*.

Secondly, even if this be conceded, this is no reason why the supposed *Spilonotus* (I refer here not to Kaup's bird, but to the figure in the Ibis) should not be a *female*, in the transitional stage, between the young and old. Mr. Gurney sets them down as males; but the context leaves it doubtful, whether Mr. Swinhoe himself ascertained the sexes; and supposing them to be females, the dimensions given by Mr. Gurney are not very unlike what we might have expected, with reference to the size of the males, while the bill and tarsus would of *course* be stronger. Dr. Jerdon's bird though larger than a very fine male *Melanoleucus* in my Museum, with which I compared it, was rather smaller than those described by Mr. Gurney. As matters now stand, either we must accept the mottled grey bird, as a stage of *Melanoleucus*, or we must include *Spilonotus*, as figured in the Ibis, as an Indian species. It is just possible that Dr. Jerdon's bird may be *Melanoleucus*, and although in plumage exactly similar to Mr. Swinhoe's bird, nevertheless structurally and specially distinct. This, however, is not likely. If some of my correspondents would kindly procure two or three undoubted females of *Melanoleucus*, the matter might probably be set at rest at once.

It remains to be noticed that all this time, the bird figured in the Ibis *may* be a state of *Melanoleucus*, and not *Spilonotus* of Kaup at all. He describes his species thus, "Head, black; wings and tail, without bars; beneath white, with black oblong spots on the crop." He gives this species as from Asia, and places it in the same subgroup as *Ranivorus* and *Æruginosus*, which he classes as Buteonine types, while he keeps *Cyaneus* and *Melanoleucus* as Falconine, and *Cineraceus* and *Swainsoni*, as Milvine types.

Col. Tytler tells me that "this species," *(Melanoleucus)* about Barrackpore (where he says they are quite as common, as *C. Swainsoni* is in the Upper Provinces) "was always found in open ground, small brushwood and fields, not near jheels and swamps as in the case of *Æruginosus;* also, that they are never solitary, and that where one is shot, several others are sure to be seen in the immediate neighbourhood."

The Pied Harrier is a truly Asiatic species; Pallas, or rather Sokoloff, who accompanied him, observed it in Argunj, Radde in the middle Amoor, at Mogotui, Akschinsk, and other places in south east Siberia. In China, it is common in many localities; it has been sent from the Philippine islands. It occurs in Ceylon, Burmah, Assam and Eastern Bengal generally (extending westwards at least as far as Mirzapore*) and although Radde rightly says, that like all the species of this genus, it loves widely extended plains and the neighbourhood of water, it has been found almost throughout the Himalayahs, from the valley of the Burhampooter, right up to Afghanistan, where Griffiths procured a specimen. In the dry plains of Central and Upper India, it seems to be unknown, and it neither extends, as far as I yet know, to Japan on the one hand, or the Malayan Archipelago on the other.

---

* Mr. Brooks says—"I have seen it once on the Kurnouta, which runs into the Ganges near Mirzapore, and several times on the Balen river 30 to 40 miles south of Mirzapore: I never saw it away from water."

No. 54. **Circus Æruginosus.*** Lin.

The Marsh Harrier.

It seems probable, that this species breeds in the plains of India, in suitable localities. In the jheel-studded tract of coun-

* Circus Æruginosus.

Dimensions.		Length.	Expanse.	Wing.	Tail from vent.	Tarsus.	Mid toe to root of claw.	Its claw, straight.	Hind toe, to root of claw.	Its claw, straight.	Inner toe, to root of claw.	Its claw, straight.	Bill, straight, from edge of cere	along curve, do. do.	from gape.	width at gape.	height, at front, at margin of cere	Distance by which closed wings fall short of end of tail.	Distance by which lower tail coverts fall short of end of tail.	Weight.	Length of cere on culmen.
Male.	From	20 70	47·00	15·60	9·4	3·40	1·55	0·80	0·66	0 96	0·81	0·97	0·84	0·92	1·40	1·10	0·41	0·70	4·00	15 oz.	0·35
	To	21·70	50·00	16 75	10·2	3 86	1·59	0·87	0·73	1·05	0 88	1·03	0·88	0 99	1·50	1·20	0·44	1·80	5·00	lb. oz. 1 3	0·39
Female.	From	21 00	50·00	16·20	9·75	3·55	1·65	0 80	0·82	0·90	0·90	0 82	0·90	1·15	1 50	0·93	0·45	0 50	3·70	lb. oz 1 7	0 42
	To	24·00	54·00	17·10	10 22	3·90	1·90	1·00	0·98	1·15	0.96	1·13	1·05	1·19	1·68	1·28	0 52	2·30	4·40	lb. oz. 2 1	0 49

(Six males and eight females measured and weighed.)

The fourth or third and fourth primaries the longest. The first is 3·20 to 4·00 shorter, the second 0·70 to 0·90, and the third equal to or not more than 0·20 shorter than the fourth. Exterior tail feathers 0·50 to 0·98 shorter than interior feathers.

Description. The legs and feet are rich yellow, dingy or pale greenish yellow in the young, the claws brownish black. The irides are orange yellow, sometimes with a pink tinge, deep brown, or brownish yellow in the young. The bill is blackish or brownish black, yellowish at the base, and bluish there in the young. The cere is greenish yellow, or sometimes pale greenish, in the young.

Plumage. I have little to add to Dr. Jerdon's description, except that as the young bird advances towards maturity, there first appears a large rufous fawn, or rufous white patch upon the breast; then the rufous, or yellowish white of the head and nape, begins to run down the back of the neck, and margins of a similar colour begin to make their appearance on the feathers of the upper back and the smaller wing coverts. The colour of the upper parts slightly fades, and a greyish tinge begins to overspread the outer webs of the primaries.

Further I should note, that the adult plumage described by Dr. Jerdon, in which the shoulders, secondaries and tail are silver grey, is according to European writers, never assumed except by the male, and though I cannot speak positively to this point myself, it is a fact that my large collection contry lying partly in the Mynpooree and partly in the Etawah district, I, many years ago, shot a large adult and saw several others quite at the close of May. An unusually heavy rainfall had filled all the lakes, or, as we should call them in Norfolk, *broads*, to overflowing, and the unsettled state of the country had, in a great measure prevented the customary agricultural drain on them, and many of them, commonly dry at this season, were still extensive sheets of water. I can scarcely doubt that these birds bred there that year.

In Oudh, native fowlers informed me, that they bred in swampy grounds, trans-Gogra. Mr. F. R. Blewitt writing from Jhansie, in the neighbourhood of which there are several considerable lakes, says that he has procured the Marsh Harrier there throughout the hot weather and rains.

I cannot find any record of its eggs having as yet been found in India: of its nidification in the British Isles, Mr. Yarrell says, "The nest is placed on the ground, among long coarse grass, in a bunch of rushes, fern or furze, or at the base of a bush. The nest is formed of small sticks, rushes, or long grass: the eggs are three or four in number, of an oval shape, rather pointed at one end, white, two inches one line (2·08) in length, and one inch six lines (1·5) in breadth."

Mr. Hewitson says, "The eggs of the Marsh Harrier, although for the most part white, or slightly tinted with blue, are sometimes also spotted and smeared with brown, in the same manner as those of the Hen Harrier."

This species "almost always breeds on the ground, but will sometimes, assuming the habits of the Common Buzzard, breed in the fork of a large tree, in which place, Montague says, he has himself found it; in such a situation, the nest would, as he describes it, be formed of sticks and such like material. In the fen countries, its usual resort, the nest is composed of so large a quantity of flags, reeds and sedges, as to raise it a foot or a foot and a half above the ground. The eggs are usually four, sometimes, though not often, five in number." Mr. Hewitt considers the dimensions above quoted, from Mr. Yarrell, as too large. His own figure represents a very round, oval egg measuring 1·93 × 1·59.

This species, occurs in every country in Europe, from north to south; in all the Islands of the Mediterranean; throughout

---

tains no single specimen of a female in this stage of plumage. I note that in some old males, the chin and breast are almost pale fawn colour, with darker streaks, while in others the ground colour of these parts is a rich and very red brown.

northern Africa, including Egypt; in Palestine and Asia Minor; Mesopotamia and Afghanistan: eastwards, it has been procured in China, at least as far south as Amoy, and in Japan. Northwards, Radde met with a single example in Tareinor, and Pallas gives it as a visitant to all parts of Siberia, but this seems doubtful. In India, it is to be found in suitable localities, such as its trivial name indicates, throughout the length and breadth of the land; Layard notices its occurrence in Ceylon, and it is not uncommon in British Burmah, but it does not appear to extend to the Malay Peninsular or the Archipelego, in which latter *C. Jardini* seems to replace it.

No. 55. **Haliastur Indus.*** Bodd.

The Brahminy Kite.

The Brahminy Kite lays in March, the latter half of February, or the early part of April, according to season and locality. Like many other species, it breeds earlier in Lower Bengal than

---

* *Haliastur Indus.*—Young female, (about 5 months old).

Dimensions.—Length, 19; Expanse, 57; Wing, 15; Tarsus, 2; Tail, 7·5; Mid toe, 1·35; its claw, 0·7; Hind toe, 0·75; its claw, 0·72; Inner toe, 0·7; its claw, 0·7; Bill, straight, from edge of cere to point, 0·9; from gape, 1·4; width at gape, 1; height at front, at margin of cere, 0·5; Length of cere, on culmen, 0·46. The 4th primary the longest; the 1st 4·3, the 2nd 1·4, and the 3rd 0·2 shorter. The wings when closed reach to 0·5 beyond end of tail. The exterior tail feathers fall short by 0·7 of the central tail feathers; the lower tail coverts reach to within 3 inches of end of tail.

Description.—Bill and cere horny blackish brown. Legs and feet, light greenish yellow. Irides, brown.

Plumage.—The forehead whitish, the feathers dark shafted; a dark brown streak, commencing at the anterior angle of the eye and running backwards over the eye to the top of the ear coverts; chin and throat with the cheeks fulvous white, the shafts brown. The ear coverts pale brown. Feathers of the top of the head, nape, and back of the neck, slightly reddish brown, margined with pale whity brown, and the shafts dark brown. Upper back and scapulars umber brown, many of the feathers paler and abraded at the tips. Rump umber brown, some of the feathers faintly tipped rufous. Upper tail coverts similarly but not conspicuously tipped with ferruginous towards the tip. Tail brown, all the feathers tipped narrowly with whitey brown, the brown, greyish in patches, and all the feathers marginally tinged with ferruginous towards their bases, on the outer webs. First 6 primaries brownish black, with more or less of rufous white or grey on the inner webs towards the bases, the rest of the quills darker or lighter umber brown, narrowly tipped with fulvous white, and the outer webs of the last few primaries much tinged with pale chesnut, and with a good deal of the inner webs, towards the base, of the same colour. The tertiaries a paler brown. The greater primary coverts and winglet deep brown, tipped with reddish white and strongly

up-country. In Upper India, where it is comparatively rare, it almost invariably makes its nest in the neighbourhood of water, building a rather large, loose, stick structure, scarcely if at all distinguishable from the common Kites, *(M. Govinda,)* high up on some large mango, tamarind or peepul tree. The nest which is from eighteen inches to two feet in diameter, and from three to five inches in depth, with a rather considerable depression internally, is sometimes perfectly unlined, at other times, has a few green leaves laid under the eggs, as in an Eagle's nest, but most commonly is more or less lined, or has the materials of the inner part of the nest intermingled with pieces of rag, wool, human hair, and the like.

Most commonly only two eggs are laid, but three are by no means uncommon, and one of my correspondents notes finding four in one nest; a very unusual number.

The eggs vary in shape, of course, but typically are very perfect moderately broad ovals, only slightly compressed towards one end; as a rule they are smaller, and as far as my experience goes, far less richly coloured than those of *M. Govinda.* The ground colour is greyish white, sometimes unspotted, but dingy, sometimes feebly speckled and spotted, at times towards one end only, with pale dingy brown, and sometimes scantily blotched and spotted with reddish brown. In size, the eggs vary, from 1·89 to 2·28 in length and from 1·5 to 1·79 in breadth, but the average of 15 eggs measured was 2·07 × 1·63.

Mr. G. Marshall, R. E. says of this species, "Breeds in the Saharunpoor District. I saw a female on her nest in a huge dry tree in the early part of March, but as the tree was inaccessible, I was obliged to leave it, the nest was of sticks about fifty feet from the ground."

Mr. R. Thompson, remarks:

---

tinged with chesnut towards the tips. The rest of the coverts paler brown, more or less tipped with whitey brown, and tinged with ferruginous, except the lesser ones, in the neighbourhood of the scapulars which are deep brown, strongly tinged with ferruginous; most of the coverts have dark brown shafts as indeed have most of the scapulars; the base of the neck in front, breast, and abdomen, are rufous brown, with narrow, central, fulvous white stripes, which disappear towards the vent, and on the tibial plumes, which instead of a white, central stripe have the shafts dark brown. The larger lower wing coverts are greyish white, with imperfect, greyish brown, clouded bars, and a faint salmon coloured tinge; the rest of the wing lining, is a more or less ferruginous brown, the feathers with darker brown shafts. The lower tail coverts are fulvous or rufous white, the shafts brown.

I think the dimensions given by Dr. Jerdon are too large; I have unfortunately no detailed measurements of adults by me, but I have noted the length of a fine adult male at 18 inches.

"At Shahgunj, Pergunnah Bhurrur, District Mirzapore, I saw on the 6th March, 1869 a pair of these birds building their nest which was placed in a mango tope, in a tall tree. There were no eggs, as the birds had not then laid, but the nest was as complete as it could be.

The nest was like that of *M. Govinda*, and placed on a very high branch."

Of the nidification of the nearly allied *H. Leucosternus* of Australia, Mr. Gould says—"It breeds from the beginning of July to the end of August. I succeeded in finding two nests, each of which contained two eggs; but I am told that three are sometimes found. The nest is formed of sticks, with fine twigs or coarse grass as a lining; it is about two feet in diameter, and built in a strong fork of the dead part of a tree; both of those I found were about thirty feet from the ground, and about two hundred yards from the beach. The eggs which are about 2·17 in length, by 1·67 in breadth, are of a dirty white, having the surface spread over with numerous, hair-like streaks and very minute dots of reddish brown, the former prevailing and assuming the form of hieroglyphics, these singular markings being most numerous at one end, sometimes at the larger, at others at the smaller. The difference even occurring in the two eggs of the same nest."

Mr. E. Ramsay, in regard to the same species, remarks, in the Ibis for 1865—"In almost every instance the examples found by Mr. Rainbird were placed near the tops of the larger trees in belts of mangroves skirting the edges of salt water swamps and marshes in the neighbourhood of Port Denison, They were composed of twigs and dead branches of mangrove, lined with a finer material. One, from which that gentleman shot the bird, and brought me the egg upon which she was sitting, was lined with tufts of lichen; and in this instance, the egg was placed upon various fish-bones, shells and claws of crabs, &c.; the edges and sides were beautifully ornamented with long streamers of bleached sea-weed, which gave the nest a novel and pleasing appearance. The egg has a rough ground of a bluish white colour, with a few minute spots of brownish red near the larger end, it is of an oval form. 2·08 in length by 1·50 in breadth."

This Australian race which differs from the Indian in the absence of the median black stripes of the white feathers, and which was figured by Viellot, as *Haliastus Girrenera* (Gal. d'ois. T. 10) without, however, his discriminating it from the Indian species, extends to Celebes, all the Moluccas and the New Guinea group, while intermediate both as regards geographical position and the intensity of the black shaft stripes, another race appears to occur in Java, Siam, Sumatra, Timor, Flores, Borneo, and the Philippine islands, which is probably *Falco Pondiceria-nus* of Horsf. but which Mr. Gurney considers, should be distinguished as *H. intermedius*. Mr. Wallace, however, as I gather from his paper in the Ibis for 1868, considers this form identical with the Indian.

Mr. Blyth had the following interesting remarks, on these closely allied species.

"According to Pro. Schlegel, this species (*H. Indus*) is spread from Nepaul to the Philippines. *H. Leucosternus*, Gould, he remarks, is founded on the absence of the black median stripes on the feathers of the white portion of the plumage, "a character, purely accidental." This view is irreconcilable with the fact that these marks are *invariably* strongly developed in the Indian race, while in the Javan race (extending to Siam) they are present but only slightly developed, the white feathers being merely black-shafted. Specimens from Bouru, Gilolo, and Aru are of the true Australian race, without even the shafts of the white feathers, black and contrasting. Three Indian specimens and a Javan one were lately to be seen together in the Gardens of the Zoological Society, the difference between them being very conspicuous. Of the immense number which I have examined or beheld close in India, I certainly never saw even one resembling or approximating to the Javanese bird. The intermediate Javan race (*H. intermedius*, 'Ibis,' 1865, p. 28,) is possibly the result of intermixture, and it may be, that there is a greater or less development of the black streaks in the Malayan province according to the proportions of that intermixture, constituting a gradation or transition from the Indian race to the Australian, as in some other instances, where conterminous races blend; and this would lead observers in that particular Zoological province, to suppose the absence, or amount of development of the streaks, to be "purely accidental." The near affinity of the fine large African *Haliastur vocifer* to the "*Brahminy* Kite," noticed by Professor Schlegel, struck me immediately, on beholding the pair of the former, now living in the Zoological Gardens; but the voice is very different, that of *H. indus* being a peculiar sort of *bleat*, quite unlike the shrill cries of most of the *Falconidæ*, and the barking notes of others."

It is the Indian species that occurs in Ceylon; at any rate a specimen received thence is undistinguishable from our up-country birds, and the same may be said of a specimen sent me from Rangoon.

No. 56. **Milvus Govinda.*** SYKES.

THE PARIAH KITE.

This species lays at very different seasons in different localities. In the plains of Upper India and the Punjab, the great

---

* MILVUS GOVINDA.

DIMENSIONS.		Length.	Expanse.	Wing.	Tail from vent.	Tarsus.	Foot, greatest length.	,, greatest breadth.	Mid toe to root of claw.	Its claw, straight.	Hind toe.	Its claw, straight.	Inner toe.	Its claw, straight.	Bill, straight from margin of cere to point.	along curve, do. do.	from gape.	width at gape.	height, at front, at margin of cere.	Distance by which closed wings fall short of end of tail.	Distance by which lower tail coverts fall short of end of tail.	Weight.	Length of cere on culmen.
																						lb oz	
MALE.	From	22·00	51·00	17·00	11·00	2·10	3·75	3·00	1·45	0·70	0·73	0·78	0·78	0·78	1·00	1·20	1·50	1·10	0·48	Nil.	4·40	1 ,, 2	0·4
	To	23·50	56·50	17·80	12·40	2·24	3·90	3·50	1·58	0·78	0·95	0·88	0·80	0·80	1·04	1·25	1·66	1·20	0·52	1·40	5·20	1 ,, 7	0·5
FEMALE.	From	22·10	55·6	18·25	10·90	2·00	3·75	3·25	1·45	0·72	0·80	0·80	0·85	0·80	0·95	1·25	1·48	1·11	0·50	Nil.	3·70	1 ,, 8	0·40
	To	25·00	60·00	19·10	13·70	2·25	4·00	3·50	1·70	0·80	0·95	0·90	0·90	0·90	1·22	1·50	1·85	1·22	0·55	1·50	5·90	2 ,, 2	0·43

(5 *males and* 5 *females measured and weighed.*)

The 4th (3rd rarely sub-equal)primary the longest. The 1st is 4·2 to 5·75 shorter, the 2nd 1·00 to 2·15, and the 3rd nil to 0·78, shorter. Central tail feathers 1·00, to 2·29, shorter than external ones.

DESCRIPTION.—The legs and feet are yellow; wax yellow, in the old birds and pale lemon yellow in somewhat younger ones; very pale greenish grey in young ones. The claws are black. Irides are brown; yellowish brown in some, pale brown in others, and deep brown in others. The bill is black, or blackish horny. The cere and gape in the old bird yellow, in younger birds the cere and gape are greenish grey, and in others again the lower mandible, cere and gape are horny brown.

Plumage.—(I have not sufficiently worked out the different stages of plumage, but there are two leading types.)

1st,—Fully adult. The whole of the top of the head, back and sides of the neck, dingy wood or pale umber brown; the feathers with an exces-

majority lay in February; a few only breeding in the previous and succeeding months. Lower down country, they are, I believe, earlier, and I myself have taken eggs as early as Christmas day. In the districts bordering on the bases of the Himalayahs, March is the more general time, while in the Himalayahs, where our bird is common up to a height of six or seven thousand feet, they mostly lay in April and May. Everywhere, stragglers breed earlier and later, by nearly six weeks, than the great body of the birds do, so that even in the neighbourhood of Agra, we have eggs recorded as early as the 29th December, and as late as the 13th April. In Bareilly, I took a nest of fresh eggs, on the 9th May, and at Simlah found three much-incubated ones, as late as the first week in June. They build almost without exception on trees, but I have found two nests (out of many hundreds that I have examined) placed, Neophron like, on the cornices of ruins.

The nest, mostly placed in a fork, but not uncommonly laid on a flat bough, is a large clumsy mass, of sticks and twigs, the

---

sively narrow, dark, shaft stripe; and with a very narrow, paler stripe, on each side of this, towards the tips. The whole of the rest of the upper parts unstriped brown, very dark upon the first few primaries, and much paler on the tertials and lesser wing coverts. The tail tinged with grey and with obscure traces of transverse darker bars; many of the lesser coverts and of the tertials, as well as most of the upper tail coverts and the tail feathers themselves, narrowly, but somewhat obscurely, tipped paler. The chin and throat whity brown, the shafts more or less conspicuously darker. The breast, abdomen, lower tail coverts, and tibial plumes, dull hair brown, dark shafted, or with narrow, dark, central, shaft stripes; those of the breast, with narrow, pale stripes, on each side of the shaft stripes, towards the tips; the rest, in many birds, with a pale spot towards the tips.

In some specimens, the whole upper plumage is greyer, the chin and throat are white instead of whity brown, under parts are more of an umber brown, and the pale stripes on either side the shaft stripes, are pale dull rufous. The tippings of the feathers of the back, scapulars, upper tail coverts, and tail, a purer white, and better defined, and the paler brown, median coverts of the wing, have a conspicuous, though very narrow, dark brown, shaft stripe. In all, the shafts of the lower tail coverts are dark.

2nd.—The young bird has the whole head, neck, breast, abdomen, and sides, umber brown, each feather with a conspicuous, broad, fulvous yellow or buffy streak. The chin and throat, are dingy fulvous, some of the feathers inconspicuously darker shafted. The back, scapulars, upper tail coverts, and wing, (except the first few primaries which are almost black) a more or less rich umber brown, glossed in many cases with purple, and every feather, more or less narrowly tipped, with rufous or fulvous white; the tail and lower tail coverts, much as in the preceding. In some specimens, the light streaks are almost pure white, in others rufous buff.

All intermediate stages are met with. In some, whilst the upper plumage is nearly that of the adult, the whole of the lower parts exhibit the white, yellowish white, or rufous buff, central stripes characteristic of the young.

various thorny accacias appearing to be the favourite material, lined or intermingled with, rags, leaves, tow, &c. The birds are perfectly fearless, breeding as freely on single stunted trees, situated in the densest populated bazars, or most crowded grain markets, as on the noblest tree in the open fields. The great majority breed in the suburbs of the towns and villages, the offal of which supplies their daily food, but single nests may be found far away from human habitations, in almost virgin jungle.

Two, appears to be the normal number of the eggs, but they often lay three. Twice I have obtained four, and on several occasions, I have met with a single hard-set egg, or young one, in a nest.

When robbed of their eggs, the old birds as *a rule* mope about the place without laying more eggs, or attempting to build a fresh nest, but I have known several instances, in which more eggs were laid in the same nest, and one in which an entirely new nest was constructed by the old birds in an adjoining tree, in which a single egg was laid and hatched.

As regards the eggs themselves, the countless varieties of types of coloration which they exhibit, defy description. I have before me now specimens absolutely devoid of any trace of colour which might well stand for gigantic specimens of *Poliornis Teesa*, but these of course are very exceptional; I have only two such in a series of several hundred. The ground colour is almost invariably a pale greenish or greyish white, more or less blotched, clouded, mottled, streaked, pen-lined, spotted or speckled with various shades of brown and red from a pale buffy brown to purple, and from blood-red to earth brown. Many of the eggs are excessively handsome, having the boldest hieroglyphics, blotched in blood-red, on a clear white or pale green ground. Others again are covered with delicate markings, as if etched on them with a crow quill, but no doubt, the markings in the majority, are more or less smudgy, and but dingily coloured. In some few, the ground colour is a dull mottled purple, clouded over with deeper shades of purplish brown. Compared with many other species, the eggs do not vary so very much, in size or shape; they are normally, a very perfect oval, scarcely more compressed at one end than at the other, but elongated, pointed, spherical and pyriform varieties occur. The color of the shells, when held up to the light, varies a good deal, in some it is as light a green as *Circaetus Gallicus*, in others, as deep as in *Haliaetus Leucoryphus*. I may here note, that Dr. Bree's figure of the egg of the Arabian Kite, correctly enough represents one common variety of the eggs of *Milvus Govinda*.

Although, as a rule, the eggs are glossless, a good many, when freshly laid, bear more or less of a natural glaze, which vastly brightens their colouring.

In size, the eggs vary from 1·9 to 2·35 in length, and from 1·55 to 1·85 in breadth, but the average of 273 eggs measured, was 2·19 by 1·77.

Capt. G. F. L. Marshall, writing from Saharunpoor, remarks that this species "generally breeds in February and March, but I have taken eggs as late as the end of April. It usually lays three eggs, but will lay more, if some of the eggs are taken. I took two out of three eggs from one nest, leaving one to prevent the bird forsaking the place. A short time after, I sent a shikaree to shoot and bring me the bird; he mistook my orders and brought the eggs, there were three then, two more had been laid; after this, one other egg was laid, and then the nest was forsaken; the nest was in my own compound, so that I had ample opportunities for watching it."

Mr. W. E. Brookes remarks, that this species is, "tolerably common both at Nyneetal and Almorah, at both of which places it breeds about two months later than it does in the plains."

That there are certainly two distinct species of Kites in India, my remarks, when treating of the next species (No. 56 bis), will I hope, sufficiently clearly show, but besides this, it seems by no means improbable, that a third species, *M. affinis* of Australia and the Archipelago, also occurs, and further, it appears by no means impossible, that *M. Melanotis* of China and Japan, may also be found within our limits.

The following are Mr. Blyth's remarks on these three species, in the Ibis for 1866.

"Professor Schlegel (Mus. P. B. *Milvi*, p. 2) identifies this with the *M. melanotis*, Schlegel, (Faun. Japon. *Aves*, tab. V. and V. B.) of China and Japan. Of the myriads of Indian Kites, which have been familiarly observed by me for more than twenty-one years, I certainly never saw one even approaching to the rufous colouring represented in the 'Fauna Japonica' (tab. V. B.); and so far as I have seen, the adults of *M. melanotis* exhibit a mottling of the feathers of the upper parts, as shown in the figures cited, which is never seen in adults of the Indian Kite. The Chinese species has, moreover, a rather stouter bill. In former years, I held this opinion in opposition to that of my friend Mr. Swinhoe *(in epistolis)*; but I observe that he now gives *melanotis* (and not *govinda)* in his "Catalogue of the Birds of China" (P. Z. S. 1863, p. 260.) Mr. Gould, in his recently published 'Hand-book to the Birds of Australia,' states of *M. affinis*, that it "appears to enjoy a very wide distribution, since it not only inhabits Australia, but appears to extend its range through the (so-called) Indian Islands, to the peninsula of India. Mr. Gurney informs us, that it occurs in Macassar, and certainly in India as far north as Nipal, though it is generally confounded, in the latter country, with its larger relative *M. govinda*. In every assemblage of Indian Kites, there is much disparity of size, some males being considerably smaller than the largest females, and the former would seem to be undistinguishable from the Australian *Affinis*, but I am not disposed to accept the opinion, that there are two separable races of *Milvus*, in the Indian and Indo-Chinese sub-regions. In Mr. Gould's representations of the Common Pariah Kite of India, (Part IV. of the Birds of Asia) the cere and feet should have been coloured of a much paler or dull light sulphur yellow, or what might rather be termed, dull yellowish white; while the dark iris is correct, and conspicuously distinguishes both this species and *M. melanotis* when alive, from *M. migrans*, as may now be seen in the Zoological gardens."

On this, Mr. Gurney made the following note: "With reference to the question of the supposed occurrence in India of *Milvus affinis*, I may mention, as one distinction between that species and the smaller individuals of *M. govinda*, that so far as I have observed, there is no appreciable difference between the old and young bird in the former, whilst in the latter, it is very strongly marked, as it is also in *M. melanotis*, if we may follow Mr. Blyth in considering this a distinct race."

It is to be hoped, that observers in India, in all parts, will from time to time, kill specimens of all the Kites big and little, that they see about them, and preserve these, recording length, weight, expanse and sex. No collection in the world, contains a really good series of the Indian Kite, not even my own, and until such a series be got together, and carefully examined, it is impossible to say whether *Affinis* and *Melanotis* do, or do not occur in India.

As regards these two species, the following is Mr. Gould's description of *M. affinis* :—

"The sexes are nearly alike in size and colouring. Feathers of the head, and the back and sides of the neck reddish fawn colour, with a central stripe of dark blackish brown; all the upper surface glossy brown inclining to chocolate, and passing into reddish brown on the wing coverts, the shaft of each feather being black, and the extreme tip pale brown; primaries black; secondaries blackish brown; tail which is slightly forked, brown, crossed by several, indistinct bars of a darker tint, and each feather tipped with greyish white; throat brownish fawn colour, with the stem of each feather black; the remainder of the under surface rufous brown, with a central line of dark brown on each feather, which is broadest and most conspicuous on the chest; cere, gape, and base of the lower mandible yellow; upper mandible and point of the lower, black; tarsi of toes yellow; claws, black; irides very dark brown."

He gives no dimensions, (why are European ornithologists invariably so careless about these matters?) but the following are some dimensions *taken from a skin* in my own collection, said to be of a male: length, 24; wing, 16·75; tail, 10·6; tarsus, 1·9; mid toe to root of claw, 1·45; its claw straight, 0·7; hind toe, 0·8; its claw, straight, 0·78; bill from edge of cere to point, straight, 0·98; bill from gape, 1·65; height at front, at margin of cere, 0·5; cere only, 0·5. The central tail feathers are 1·9 shorter than the external one. The fourth primary is the longest; the first is 4·7, the second 1·6, and the third 0·07 shorter.

It is only right to notice, that I have Indian specimens in my collection, to my (perhaps unpractised) eye, *absolutely* undistinguishable from this specimen sent me from Australia, by Gerrard Krefft, Esquire.

As regards *M. Melanotis*, I have neither description nor measurements by me. Radde and Schrenk affirm, that it is not specifically distinct from "*Niger*" *i. e. Migrans*, and say, "If we collate together the described differences of colour, the character of the eastern form *(Melanotis)* will be found to consist in this, that a more pronounced contrast (in the young extending to portions of individual feathers) exists between the clear, yellowish and dark, grey brown shades, while in the western form *(Migrans)* the colours blend into an almost uniform, (and with advancing age, more and more predominating) ferruginous brown." And Radde goes on to affirm, that specimens of the European *Niger*, (or *Migrans*, Bodd, and this latter name has the priority) have been obtained, showing the brighter plumage of *melanotis*.

It is clear from this, that whether distinct or not, *Melanotis* and *Migrans*, cannot differ much in *size*. Of *Migrans* (which he calls *Ater)* Bree gives the length 22 inches, and of a male, 20 inches, with the wing 17.

Layard, who unites both *Affinis* and *Govinda* with *Migrans*, (in which, however, he is clearly wrong, because the latter is distinct, whatever the former two may be) gives the length as 21, the wing at 18 and the tail at 10 inches.

The dimensions of *Melanotis*, must, since the distinctness of the species is disputed by so many writers, be very similar, and it must therefore be a much smaller bird than the one which I have described as *M. Major* (No. 56 bis) and which so far as *plumage* goes, it seems to resemble *very* closely.

The present species, *M. Govinda*, seems (if really distinct from *Affinis)* to be confined to India, Ceylon, and Burmah. In China and Japan, it is replaced by *Melanotis;* in Australia and part, at any rate, of the Archipelago, by *Affinis.* In Arabia, South Eastern Europe, Egypt and South Africa, we have *M. Parasiticus*, and in the latter three localities, and throughout southern and central Europe and northern Africa *M. Migrans*, (from which Radde and others consider *Melanotis* doubtfully distinct,) while in England, and in many parts of Europe, the red Kite *Milvus Regalis* (vel *Vulgaris)* though now perhaps somewhat scarce, was at one time nearly as common, as the Pariah Kite with us.

No. 56 bis. **Milvus Major.*** Sp. Nov.

The Larger Indian Kite.

This new species may be at once distinguished from the Pariah Kite, by its superior size, although approaching more

---

* Milvus Major.

Dimensions.—*(I only have accurate measurements of* 2 *specimens, both females.)* Length 26·75, 27·75; Wing, 21, 21·5; *(Col. Tytler's specimen has the wing* 22.") Tail 13·3, 13·75; length of tarsus. 2·5, 2·4, *(both feathered for* 1·4); mid toe to root of claw 1·62, 1·7; its claw, straight 0·7, 0·82; hind toe, 0·88, 0·91; its claw, straight, 0·8, 0·96; inner toe, 0·85, 0·89; its claw, 0·72, 0·9; bill straight, from edge of cere to point, 1·05, 1·06; from gape, 1·75, 1·78; width at gape, 1·32, 1·38; height at margin of cere, 0·55, 0·58; length of cere on culmen, 0·45, 0·48; lower tail coverts fall short of end of tail by 5, and 5·85. The 4th primary is the longest; the 1st is 5·35, the 2nd 2·00, and the 3rd 0·20, shorter.

(*The smaller of the two birds is in the second stage of plumage, described below, the larger is in the first or adult plumage.*)

Description.—1st adult female. Bill and claws horny black. Legs dull yellow. Toes, mingled dingy greenish and yellow. Cere, pale greenish yellow.

Plumage.—General plumage, much as in the common Kite, but the whole of the upper part with a more or less purple gloss. Forehead and lores whitish, crown, occiput, nape, back of the neck, breast and upper abdomen rich umber brown, dullest on the head, with very narrow, black or blackish brown, shaft stripes, which again are bordered on either side, in some feathers throughout their whole lengths, in others only towards their tips, with narrow, more or less pale, rufous stripes. The lower abdomen and flanks, similar, but the black shaft stripe almost obsolete, and the two rufous stripes broader and blending. A blackish brown stripe, from the posterior angle of the eye, over the top of the ear-coverts. Chin, throat, checks and greater

nearly in its plumage to *M. Melanotis*, and (in a slightly less degree) to *M. Govinda*, it is fully as large as *M. Regalis*, has

---

portion of the ear-coverts white, the feathers black shafted, and, as they approach the breast, tinged with dull rufous. Scapulars, umber brown, beautifully glossed with purple, and tinged with an almost golden yellow towards the extreme tips. The whole of the lesser and median coverts, purplish brown, but with nearly the whole visible portion of the tips, rufous, or orange, with the shafts conspicuously darker. The winglet, the greater primary coverts, and the first few primaries, almost black, but with a purple gloss. The later primaries, secondaries, and tertials, umber brown, all more or less glossed with purple. The secondaries, darkest and most richly glossed. The tail, with *excessively* broad feathers, (central ones 2·5 in breadth) and much forked, (the external tail feathers being fully 2 inches longer, than the central pair,) a dull umber brown, growing deeper in shade as the feathers recede from the centre, all narrowly tipped with white, and obscurely banded with 8 or 9 broad transverse somewhat darker bars. The rump and upper tail coverts like the scapulars, but somewhat paler. The vent, and lower tail coverts, and the tibial and tarsal plumes, are dull rufous buff, some of the feathers more or less mottled with greyish brown, and the tibial plumes faintly streaked with brown. There is a great deal of white, mottled with imperfect greyish brown bars, on the inner webs of the primaries, towards their bases; a few of the larger, lower, wing-coverts are mingled grey and dark brown. The rest of the wing lining and axillaries are a rich, somewhat rufous, umber brown; the feathers more or less tinged towards the tips, or streaked with rufous. The lateral tail feathers, like the primaries, are white or greyish white on the inner webs towards the bases, and on these parts of course, the transverse bars are more apparent.

2*nd. Young Female.*—The forehead and lores whitish, feathers dark shafted, a narrow dark line over the eye, joining the conspicuous blackish brown patch, which runs from the posterior angle of the eye, over the ear coverts. The whole of the feathers of the top and back of the head, back and sides of the neck and upper back, rich purple brown, with a narrow, central, buffy white stripe. The feathers of the top of the head, dark shafted. The whole of the scapulars, tertiaries, rump and upper tail coverts, lesser and median wing coverts, a rich purple brown; all the feathers, more or less conspicuously dark shafted, tinged golden towards the tips, and more or less pure white at the extreme tips. The secondaries, the richest glossy purple brown, tipped similarly to the feathers above described, but to a less extent. The first 6 primaries purplish black, very narrowly tipped with fulvous white, the other primaries similar to the secondaries; but somewhat paler. The central tail feathers, not so broad, as in the adult, being only 2·2, wide; and the tail not so forked; the exterior being only 0·75 longer than the central. The tail is an umber brown, purpler and less grey than in the more adult bird, somewhat broadly tipped with yellowish white, and with traces of dark bars, and much white on the inner webs towards the bases, as in the adult. The chin is whitish, the throat, cheeks, and basal portion of the ear-coverts dull rufous brown, the feathers white at their bases and inconspicuously darker shafted. Breast and upper abdomen and sides, rich umber brown, with moderately broad, rufous, buff, central stripes, the rufous buff, fading to pale fulvous towards the lower abdomen. Lower abdomen, vent, and tibial and tarsal plumes, pale fulvous, with ill-defined, brown stripes towards the margins of the feathers. Lower tail coverts slightly more rufous, a good deal freckled above the tips with pale greyish brown.

quite as strong, bill, feet and claws, and, like it, has the tarsus further feathered than in the common Indian Kite. The tail

The whole of the wing lining and axillaries (except a few of the greater lower primary coverts which are greyish black,) rich purplish umber brown, tipped with rufous buff, or with a stripe of that color running a short distance up the shafts from the tips. There is more white on the inner webs of the quills, and the white is purer, in this stage, than in the adult; in this respect, again, corresponding with *Milvus melanotis*.

3rd Nestling.—Obtained near Mussourie. Male. Measurements *from the skin*. Length 24; wing 19·5; tail 11·5; tarsus 2·4; mid toe, 1·65; its claw, straight, 0·61; hind toe, 0·70; its claw, straight, 0·80; inner toe, 0·75; its claw, straight, 0·78, Bill, straight from margin of cere to point, 1·07; from gape, 1·8; height at front at margin of cere, 0·55; length of cere, on culmen, 0·41. Lower tail coverts fall short of end of tail by 4·5. Quill and tail feathers very much abraded.

DESCRIPTION. *Plumage.*—The general character of the plumage is a mixture of rufous, slightly infuscated, and pale fulvous and fulvous white; only the primaries, secondaries and some of the greater coverts being dark in their visible portions. The whole chin and throat, cheeks, and basal halves of the ear coverts, and generally the under parts, pale fulvous, or dingy yellowish white, the feathers of the breast and abdomen, much tinged towards the sides of the feathers with a slightly brownish or infuscated rufous; the axillaries, and the wing lining in the neighbourhood of the shoulder joint, bright cinnamon rufous, infuscated towards the margins; the rest of the wing lining, (except the greater lower primary coverts which are mingled blackish grey, and rufous white,) a rich rufous umber brown, tipped and tinged towards the tips with cinnamon rufous. Almost the whole of the inner webs of the primaries, above the notches, are pure white in this stage. The lores and forehead are fulvous white. There is a broad, rufous brown stripe from the posterior angle of the eye, over the tips of the ear-coverts. The crown, occiput and nape, brownish rufous, dark-shafted and the feathers margined with yellowish white or pale fulvous; sides and back of the neck and upper back, yellowish white, the feathers, broadly freckled towards the margins with brownish rufous. Lower back and rump, rufous, the feathers dark shafted, tipped paler (almost white in the longer upper tail coverts) and more or less freckled or suffused with greyish brown; the visible portion of the scapulars and tertiaries, a sort of rufous buff, freckled or suffused with greyish brown, tipped paler and with conspicuous dark shafts. Tail feathers, dull, greyish rufous, with traces of 8 or 9, incomplete, irregular, narrow, clouded, transverse, umber brown bars. The lateral tail feathers being less rufous, and their inner webs paler, and towards the bases almost white, but even there, tinged with rufous grey. The visible portion of the lesser and median coverts dingy rufous buff, fading towards the tips, to very pale yellowish or almost pure white. The basal portions of the feathers, umber brown in the median coverts, and more or less freckled with this color in the lesser ones. The greater primary coverts and first five primaries, deep brown, tinged at the tips with rufous and very narrowly tipped with almost pure white; the greater secondary coverts pale umber brown, tinged towards the tips and freckled and mottled towards the margins, with rufous buff, and tipped more or less broadly with very pale yellowish white. The 7th and succeeding primaries, the visible portions, rufous buff narrowly tipped with white, and clouded in obscure bars with purplish brown. Secondaries the richest purple brown, narrowly tipped with rufous buff, fading at the extreme tip to pale yellowish white.

is large and well forked, and the tail feathers very broad; in a specimen before me, the central tail feathers, are 2·5 inches broad, 3 inches from the tip; at present I only know of five specimens, one in Col. Tytler's museum and four in my own (one lent by Mr. W. Brooks).

At all stages, the colouring is richer than in the common type, and the patch behind the eye and over the ear coverts is darker and more strongly marked. This peculiarity, and the fact that Radde's figure of the young of *Melanotis*, almost exactly agrees with one stage of the young of the present species, led me at one time to identify the latter with the former. European naturalists, as a rule, give dimensions but sparingly, but after consulting such works of reference as were available to me, it appeared certain that birds, of which the females measure from 26·75 to 27·75 in length, and of which the wings vary from 21 to 23 inches, measured from the carpal joint, could not possibly belong to any known, old world species of Kite, with the exception of *Regalis*, from which their plumage differ *toto cœlo*, and I have therefore been compelled to consider them as belonging to a distinct species which I have characterized as *Milvus Major*.

It is not only in size and a somewhat richer colouring that the present species differs from *M. Govinda*. The latter is a bold, tame bird, a denizen of the most crowded haunts of man. The greater Kite is a wild wary bird very difficult to approach, and found only in the open fields or in swamp or jungle. Its flight is heavier and more Buzzard-like, and though I have often seen it, since I first began to distinguish it, I have invariably failed to procure specimens. This peculiarity of its habits, has been noticed by others besides myself. The gentleman from whom Col. Tytler years ago received the specimen he now possesses, and which was procured in Lower Bengal, writing of it at the time, said that he had procured it with great difficulty, and had been induced to pursue it persistently, believing it to have been some species of Buzzard. Mr. Brooks has, equally with myself, noticed its extreme wariness, and has failed to obtain a second specimen, though he too has continually seen and pursued it.

It appears to be only a winter visitant to the plains, at which season I procured a specimen near Ajmeer, (Mr. Brooks shot his in Etawah,) but I feel confident that I have observed it throughout the summer and rainy season, in the Himalayahs, from which Capt. Hutton, not long ago, sent me a specimen, with the remark that it was "the finest Kite" he had ever seen.

I know as yet nothing of its nidification, and nothing further of its distribution than I have already mentioned, but doubtless, now that its distinctness has been pointed out, other observers will supply the necessary information.

I cannot think, how, in writing the above, I overlooked the following remarks by Mr. Blanford, in regard to which, I at the time wrote, remarking that the species alluded to, was (as I then thought it) *M. Melanotis*: they obviously refer to this new species.

"*Milvus*, sp. I shot near Woon, north-west of Chanda, a Kite considerably exceeding the common *M. Govinda* in size, but otherwise undistinguishable. It is a male, and measures, closed wing, 20; bill from gape, 1·7; tarsus, 2·5; tail, 13. The bird is evidently young, for the inner portions of the feathers are rich brown; but the feathers of the head and neck are rich brown with dark centres, not whitish, as usually in a young *M. Govinda*, and the abdomen, and lower tail coverts are pale rufous." This I take to be nearly fully adult.

No. 57. **Pernis Cristata.*** Cuvier.

The Crested Honey Buzzard.

(Schleg. Mus. P. B. Pernes, p. 2, Valkv. Nederl. Ind. pl. XXV. fig. 1-3, XXVI. fig. 1-2. Tem. Pl. Col. 44.)

This species lays in May and June, and in the latter and former halves respectively, of April and July. It builds in

---

* Pernis cristata.

Dimensions.		Length.	Expanse.	Wing.	Tail from vent.	Tarsus.	Foot, greatest length.	greatest breadth.	Mid toe to root of claw.	Its claw, straight.	Hind toe to root of claw.	Its claw, straight.	Inner toe to root of claw.	Its claw, straight.	Bill, straight, from edge of cere.	along curve. do. do.	from gape.	width at gape.	height at front, at edge of cere.	Distance by which closed wings fall short of end of tail.	Distance by which lower tail-coverts fall short of end of tail	Weight.	Length of cere.
																						lb oz	
Male	From	24·00	49·00	15·50	10·30	1·90	4·70	4·50	1·80	1·00	1·10	0·88	1·35	0·92	0·80	0·98	1·40	0·95	0·40	1·30	5 00	1 12	0·60
	To	25·50	54·00	16·00	11·00	2·10	4·80	4·60	2·05	1·05	1·20	0·95	1·40	0·95	0·90	1·05	1·45	1·10	0·43	2·50	5 90	2 2	0·64
Female	From	26·00	55·00	15·75	11·50	2·19	5·00	4·75	2·03	0·94	1·06	0·75	1·44	1·09	0·95	1·09	1·63	1·05	0·38	2·25	5 00	2 80	0·50
	To	28·00	57·00	17·25	12·75	2·70	5·25	5·13	2·13	1·19	1·13	1·06	1·54	1·15	1·08	1·20	1·76	1·25	·048	3·00	7 00	2 15	0·69

trees, placing its moderately sized, stick and twig nest, in a fork, usually some considerable height from the ground. In

---

(*Three males and six females measured and weighed.*)

The fourth primary the longest. The first is 3·50 to 5·00 shorter, the second 1·09 to 1·50, and the third nil to 0·50 shorter. Exterior tail feathers 0·37 to 1·00, shorter than central ones.

DESCRIPTION. The legs and feet, which are very full and puffy, vary from dingy yellowish white in the young, to bees-wax yellow in old adults. Scutellation, well marked and reticulate, (the plates somewhat concave, especially at back of tarsus,) except about three or four, transverse scutæ, at the tips of all the toes ; a mere trace of a connecting membrane, between the central and outer toes, at the base. Claws black, and except the mid toe claw, compressed ; hind claw much curved, and mid claw with the interior margin, usually much dilated, especially towards the tip. Irides brilliant yellow, duller or slightly brownish in younger birds. Cere black, greenish at nostrils and towards commissure. Gape and two-thirds of the commissure from gape, and greater portion of lower mandible pale blue; greater portion of upper mandible and tip of lower, black ; a small dingy greenish patch on each side of the lower mandible towards the base. Tongue, moderate, obtuse, entire ; rather stiff and membraneous towards the tip, (where it is slightly emarginate) and margins.

Plumage.—Of one quite young bird, the whole head, neck, and under parts are fawn coloured : the throat and chin paler and unstreaked, the crown of the head and nape more rufous, all the feathers, except those of the chin and throat, darker shafted, and those of the crown, nape and breast with a conspicuous, median, dark brown streak. The whole of the wing coverts and back are a light brown, lighter on the wing coverts many of which are margined paler. The longer scapulars, secondaries, and tertiaries are a somewhat darker brown. The quills are somewhat darker still. The upper tail coverts are of nearly the same pale rufous or fawn that pervades the lower parts. The tail is a light brown, the usual narrow white tip, then there narrow wavy bars of paler hue, banding the terminal five inches of the tail feathers, and showing in one place, about four inches from the end, a small spot of dark brown, on both sides of the shaft. About five inches from the end, is a tolerably well marked bar of darker brown, about half an inch wide, then again nearly an inch of the same brown as the rest of the tail, with three narrow, irregular, pale bars, and then just under the upper tail coverts, a trace of another, half inch broad, ill-defined, darker brown bar. The tail in this instance, presents scarcely a trace of the almost constant, subterminal dark brown band. The lining of the wing is the same colour as the rest of the lower parts, and its feathers similarly darker shafted. There is a faint greyish streak covering the lores and eyes, and extending for about a quarter of an inch behind the eye.

In other specimens of somewhat older birds, the fawn colour is everywhere replaced by a rich rufous, in others by a dingy rufous brown, in others by a very dark wood brown, and lastly, in some, by an almost pure white. To all these the above description would answer *mutatis mutandis*, remembering that the difference in the colour in the under parts, and head, extends, to a certain degree, to the brown of the upper parts. The wing lining, in almost every case, being exactly the same shade of colour as the breast. The tail, however, in most specimens, differs from that of the young bird above described. First, there is the narrow tipping of white, then a bar of more or less dark brown about an inch wide, then about three inches of a

texture, the nests differ much, some are compactly and neatly, others loosely and carelessly put together, but all are more or

---

lighter brown, with five or six narrow wavy bars of a still lighter colour, then a half or three quarter inch of the same dark brown as the subterminal band, then another inch and a half of the paler brown, with two or three of the still lighter wavy bars, and then just under the tips of the upper tail coverts, another half or three quarter inch, darker brown band. Many of the birds have three or four, somewhat lengthened, black brown feathers on the neck, margined with the same colour as the rest of the head, which form a sort of incipient crest. Laying six or seven, well chosen specimens, of the above described type, varying but little except in their shades of colour, beside each other, these shades of colour differ so extraordinarily, that one might almost believe that specimens of the creamy, white-breasted kind had been dipped in a series of dyes of every shade, from the most delicate fawn, to the deepest burnt sienna.

There is, however, a somewhat different type. The crown is brown, the feathers with very dark central stripes, a broad supercillium, the ear coverts and the sides and back of the neck are pale, somewhat rufous brown, the feathers dark shafted, and those towards the base of the neck broadly centered with very dark brown. The whole of the scapulars, upper back, wing coverts, secondaries and tertiaries very dark brown, the back less dark, and the upper tail coverts light brown, the tail of the ordinary type, above described, but altogether much darker. The grey of the lores and eye streak more ashy, the chin, throat, and upper neck nearly pure white, only slightly tinged with fulvous and no dark shafts; a row of feathers on each side of the lower portion of this pale patch, conspicuously tipped with black brown. The breast somewhat pale rufous, or rufous brown, all the feathers with dark brown, linear, central stripes. The whole of the rest of the lower parts nearly uniform fawn, with scarcely a trace of dark shafting to the feathers. The wing lining and the axillaries the same tint as the breast, not dark shafted, but the axillaries distinctly banded with a lighter tint.

In the old bird the tail has the usual white tip, then a two inch band of dark brown, then a similar space of lighter brown, freckled (not barred), with a still paler colour, then another two inch, dark brown band, then an inch or so of the lighter freckled or mottled brown, and then another dark brown band showing just under the upper tail coverts.

In the primaries at all ages, the inner web is white, or nearly so, above the emarginations, with some few pale brown spots or incomplete bars. Beyond the emarginations in the old bird, there is a white tip, two dark, and one light bar, exactly as above described in the tail, which though most conspicuous below, are very visible above, but in younger birds, the dark portion of the primaries are clouded and indistinctly barred like their tails, this barring being often scarcely visible above. In some specimens, as in that first described, scarcely any barring or clouding is visible, even beneath. The secondaries and tertiaries are usually, at all ages, very faintly barred with a slightly lighter shade, and this is most visible when the bird has recently moulted. In some birds whilst the head, neck, and ear coverts are a dark rufous brown, darker centered, and the rest of the upper parts a very dark brown, the chin, throat, breast, and abdomen are pure white, most of the feathers of the two former dark shafted, and the two latter with large, subterminal, dark brown lunules, each set in a round spot of somewhat pale rufous brown, and the axillaries, thigh and lower tail coverts are broadly, though regularly banded, with this latter colour. In some birds, the lesser wing coverts are so broadly marless thickly lined with leaves or occasionally grass. As a rule they lay *two* eggs, but it it not uncommon to find a single, fully incubated egg.

Normally, the shape of the eggs, of this species, is nearly spherical, and even the most aberrant are a very broad oval. Typically, they are very highly coloured eggs, and remind one much of the eggs of the European Honey Buzzard. I have a specimen which corresponds closely with the second figure in Hewitson's Pl. XV. and I have others fully as richly coloured, but of a different type. The ground colour varies from white or pinkish white to buffy yellow, and the markings from reddish brown to intense blood red. In one, the markings are a rather dingy though deep purple. In another, the whole egg is buff brown, faintly but thickly mottled and clouded with yellowish brown. Another egg, with a reddish brown ground, is entirely capped, and thickly mottled, over the whole of the rest of the surface, with a very dull but deep cinnamon red, reminding one forcibly of some of the richest coloured Neophrons. As a rule, these eggs are glossless, but one or two have a trace of gloss about them. The lining, or rather the colour of the egg-shell, when held up against the light, varies from greenish white to dingy yellowish green.

In size, the eggs vary from 1·82 to 2·22 in length, and from 1·55 to 1·85 in breadth, but the average of ten eggs measured was 2·03 by 1·72.

---

gined with fawn or creamy white, that there is almost more of this than the brown visible, and this is not dependant on age or sex, or even altogether on the colour of the lower parts, since, though I have never observed this in any birds which were of a dark hue beneath, I have specimens of which the entire ground of the lower parts is creamy white, the wing coverts of which show no trace of a paler margin. One old bird with tail and wings bearing the signs of maturity above indicated, will have the whole of the lores, forehead, round the eyes, and top of the head dark slaty gray, with a black brown occipital crest of three feathers about an inch long. The occiput and back of the neck, very dark rufous brown, darker shafted, and the rest of the upper parts and sides *dark* brown. The whole lower parts pure white; the feathers of the chin with very narrow, dark brown, longitudinal, central stripes, and those of all the rest of the lower parts with similar, rather wider stripes, and large, broad, subterminal, pale, rufous brown blotches, the axillaries and some of the thigh coverts being distinctly banded. Another old bird not only has the whole lores, forehead, crown, sides of the head and occiput bluish grey, with only a tinge of brown on the occiput, but the whole brown of the upper parts, which is pale compared with the majority of specimens, has more or less of a greyish tint, some feathers being browner and some greyer, but all pale, and with no trace of a crest. The whole lower parts a nearly uniform, wood brown, (paler on the throat) with the shaft (and the shafts only) dark brown.

Almost every possible combination of the varying plumage, and shades of colour, of different parts, above described, may be met with.

I owe to Capt. G. F. L. Marshall, R. E., the following interesting note, on the nidification of this species, in the Saharunpoor district, which renders further remarks of my own on the subject unnecessary. "The Crested Honey Buzzard builds in May, the young being usually hatched in the beginning of June. The season for building is, however, spread over a long period, as in one case, I noticed a bird building on the 23rd *March;* the nest was completed by the end of *April,* but the first egg was not laid till the 12th May, and the second egg on the 14th; I took the nest on the 15th.

"The nest is situated in the stout fork of a tree, generally about two-thirds of the way up; of the ten nests I have taken, one was in a Toon tree (*cedrela toona*) and all the rest in sheeshum trees (*Dalbergia Sissoo.*) The nest is cup-shaped in the first instance, but so filled up with the lining, as to appear more like a flat platform. It is a compact structure, composed entirely of twigs, neatly put together and lined with a thick layer of dead leaves, chiefly Sheeshum leaves, almost filling up the hollow space; in one instance I found the nest lined with perfectly fresh green leaves, and as there were two eggs in it, the lining must have been partially renewed after the eggs were laid. The outer diameter of the nest is about sixteen to eighteen inches, and of the egg receptacle about ten inches; the depth of the structure, including lining, is about nine inches.

"The eggs, *two* in number, are deposited in the middle of the platform, the colour varies greatly, from a white ground, more or less blotched with every shade of reddish brown, to a reddish brown ground, clouded and blotched with a darker shade. Some are exactly like gigantic Falcon's eggs, while others again, closely resemble richly blotched Kite's eggs: in shape they are mostly very round. The shell is thin, and rather brittle, and smoother than is usual among the Raptores.

"The bird is rather familiar in its habits, and by no means shy; I took three of its nests, from compounds in the station of Saharunpoor, and three more from the compounds of the Canal Chokees. It seldom flies far and is easily approached. When the eggs are near the hatching point, the bird sits excessively close; I have found it impossible to drive it off by throwing stones, and on one occasion the female only flew when my hand was actually on the nest, though she had been struck pretty sharply by several of the stones. The male bird assists in building and is more wary than the female.

"On one occasion, I noticed a male bird with a stick in its claws fly into a tree and return without it. I went up to the place, and noticed the commencement of the nest; while I was standing there the male bird returned with another twig, but catching sight of me from the distance he turned off and went into another tree some distance off, and nothing would induce him to come near the place, till I was well away, though the female kept going and coming all the time."

Mr. W. Blewitt says, "We found one nest of this species near Hansie, on the 16th June, which contained a single fresh egg. The nest was placed on a Neem tree, at the height of about sixteen feet from the ground, and was slightly built of Keekur and Zisyphus twigs and scantily lined with a reed grass. It measured ten inches in diameter and four in depth."

In another letter, also from Hansie, he remarks,—"We got two nests, of the Honey Buzzard, on the 5th and 10th July, out of Sheeshum trees on the canal banks. One contained a single, fresh, the other a solitary, fully incubated egg. The nests were respectively, about fifteen and twenty feet from the ground, were constructed of Keekur and Sheeshum twigs, and were lined with leaves."

Mr. R. Thompson, writing from Gurhwal, remarks that "The Honey Buzzard breeds from April to June, building its circular, pan-shaped nest (which no little resembles that of *Spizaetus Caligatus)* in large trees, in open forest country.

"These birds steadily arrive in our forests, along with swarms of bees, in March, when they begin to pair. In April they begin to select trees to build on. During the coupling season, both birds utter a loud yet plaintive cry, very similar to that uttered by *Spizaetus Caligatus*, but from which it is distinctly recognizable. The food of these birds is varied. I have seen them eating frogs and even young birds, and have often found the craw fully distended with honey.

"The flight is rapid and direct, with occasional upward sweeps. Dr. Jerdon is wrong in stating, that it does not soar gracefully. It soars vigorously, rising to a very great height. As many as five or six couples might be seen here, in a single day well mounted in the air. The bird can dart down from a great height very rapidly, which it always does when tired of soaring, and is the cause of terrible alarm to Mainas and Parakeets, who set up awful screams at its approach to their nesting trees. I firmly believe this bird to be an arch robber of nests, having more than once detected him at work hunting about a tree very carefully, to the intense terror of the inhabitants."

In a later letter he adds, "I saw a pair soaring, not only very gracefully, but very high in the air in the Agoree pergunnah, district Mirzapore, and in proof of this, I shot one of the birds which, whilst I was watching the couple, darted down and settled in a tree. The skin was sent to you from Allahabad."

The colouring, of different specimens of the Crested Honey Buzzard, differs so conspicuously, even amongst birds of apparently the same age, that I have thought it necessary to describe several specimens. Dr. Jerdon seems to consider the stages of plumage, at different ages, tolerably well characterized, but after examining a great number of specimens, the only marks by which I could certainly distinguish the older from the younger birds, were,—first, that the old have two, very broad, well marked, dark, brown bands visible on the tail feathers, and the space of paler brown enclosed between them is freckled and mottled with a lighter colour, *but not barred*—while in younger birds, the tail is *invariably banded*, more or less plainly, with *numerous, pale, narrow, wavy streaks*, besides two or more brownish bands of darker brown, which broadish bands however are neither half the width, nor so well defined, nor so dark as in the old; and secondly a very similar difference in the banding of the primaries beyond the emarginations. All other signs of age appear deceptive. Year old birds have at times, the lores, cheeks and face quite gray, while old birds may be seen nearly white below, each feather with a conspicuous, median stripe of the darkest brown. Some young birds too are so dark a brown above, as in some lights to appear almost black, while the old are often a mixture of pale brown and grayish. The light edgings to the feathers of the upper parts are, (contrary to all analogy,) met with occasionally in the old, as well as in the young, and there are really very few points in the plumage of this species, which seem constant in *all* specimens, at all ages.

Capt. Marshall concurs with me in this: he tells us that " the birds vary considerably in plumage even in the adult, as every specimen I have got was shot off a nest, and they vary from dark brown to almost white in the general ground colour, the commonest tinge being brownish ashy. I also noticed that the brown specimens, and the whitish ones, always had a distinct incipient occipital crest of black feathers, whereas in the ashy type there was never even the faintest indication of it."

This species seems to be confined to India, south of the Himalayahs, Burmah, the Malay Peninsular, Sumatra, Bangkok and Java. I have never seen it recorded from Ceylon, nor have I seen any specimen killed at a greater elevation, than 4000 feet in the Himalayahs, or even at this height, any where except along the outer ranges. It is very locally distributed in upper India, but the double lines of trees, that every where border our canals, throughout their whole length, are beyond doubt among its most favourite haunts. It is essentially a wood and water loving species.

Mr. Blyth, at one time, described a specimen of a Crested Honey Buzzard from Mergui, under the name of *Pernis Brachypterus*, in the following terms.

"Colour dark hair brown above; crest simple, broad, two and a half inches long, the feathers composing it, white tipped as are also those adjacent. Lower parts white, with dark central streaks or tears on the breast and flanks."

Does any one know what became of this specimen? and what ultimate verdict, if any, was pronounced as to its specific distinctness?

I cannot find that this supposed new species has ever been confirmed, or suppressed. The description would apply well enough to many examples of *P. Cristata*, that I have seen, except that the crest is longer than any I have yet noticed in this species. If distinct, it should stand as No. 57 bis.

No. 58. **Baza Lophotes.** CUVIER.

THE CRESTED BLACK KITE.

Nothing is known of the nidification of this rare species, of which I have never myself procured a specimen.

Of the nearly allied Australian *B. Subcristata*, all Mr. Gould tells us is, that he has received an egg, procured in the bushes of the Clarence, said to belong to this species, which egg is a pure white, and measures about 1·63 by 1·25.

The crested Black Kites are essentially an Oceanic type. Besides the Australian species, already referred to, we have, according to Wallace, the typical *B. Reinwardti* from Bouru, Amboyna and Ceram, and a somewhat smaller race of the same species from New Guinea, the Aru and Ke Ilds, Salwatty and Timor; *B. Rufa*, from Batchian, and Gilolo; *B. Magnirostris*, from Celebes and the Sula Islands, and possibly Borneo and the Philippines; and *B. Sumatrensis* from Sumatra.

As for the Indian species, it occurs in Ceylon, on the east coast of the Peninsula, in Lower Bengal, Assam, Tipperah, and British Burmah, but as far as I can make out, only as a seasonal visitant, during the latter part of the rains and the early part of the cold season.

Schlegel says, that our bird is found in Malacca, which Mr. Wallace seems to question, but Blyth says, he has repeatedly seen it from thence. As for its being more frequently met with in the lower ranges of the Himalayahs as Dr. Jerdon says, I doubt much its *ever* having been killed in these hills west of Nepal, and we must I suspect prefix "*Eastern*" to "Himalayahs," to make the passage accord with facts.

No. 59. Elanus Melanopterus.* Daud.

The Black Winged Kite.

It is somewhat surprising, that up to the present time, neither I nor any of my numerous correspondents, have succeeded

---

* Elanus Melanopterus.

Dimensions.—The sexes do not appear to differ much in size—The following are the dimensions of 2 males and the average of 3 females.

	M.	M.	F.
Length,	12·25	12·75	13·00
Expanse,	34·75	34·50	34·00
Wing,	10·75	10·50	10·15
Tail,	5·25	5·38	5·62
Tarsus,	1·12	1·20	1·30
Mid toe to root of claw,	1·02	1·06	1·10
Its claw, straight,	0·58	0·53	0·56
Hind toe,	0·50	0·56	0·68
Its claw, straight,	0·65	0·60	0·70
Inner toe,	0·68	0·54	0·72
Its claw,	0·60	0·60	0·68
Bill, straight from margin of cere to point,	0·60	0·62	0·65
„ from gape,	0·95	1·15	1·08
„ height at margin of cere,	0·32	0·32	0·35
Length of cere on culmen	0·21	0·25	0·18
Distance by which closed wings exceed end of tail.	0·38	0·25	0·80
Distance by which lower tail coverts fall short of end of tail,	1·55	2·23	1·75
	oz.	oz.	oz.
Weight,	7·5	6·5	7·5

The 2nd primary is the longest, the 1st is from 0·5 to 0·8 shorter, the 3rd from 0·4 to 0·5 and the 4th from 1·0 to 1·1 shorter. The external tail feathers fall short of the antepenultimates, (which are usually the longest) by from 0·3 to 0·5. The tarsus, bare behind, is feathered in front for 0·7 to 0·75.

Description.—The *legs and feet* are bright yellow, light lemon yellow in some. The claws black. The *bill* is black, the cere, gape and base of lower mandible yellow. The *irides*, bright crimson, or carbuncle coloured in adults, yellowish pink or pure bright yellow in the young.

Plumage. Adult. Forehead, a narrow streak above the dark supercilium, the anterior portion of the lores, the chin, cheeks, ear coverts, throat and whole lower parts, wing lining, edge of the wing, and all but the central tail feathers, white, the external webs of all, but the two exterior on each side

in obtaining the eggs of this species. I have three several records of the birds having been noticed building nests, in different parts of the plains, in the early part of the hot weather, but in every case, they abandoned the nests without laying. My present impression is that they entirely leave the dry plains of upper India during the hot season, and resort to well-wooded and watered localities to breed in.

Mr. R. Thompson tells me, that in lower Gurhwal and Dehra Dhoon "they breed from April to June, choosing low trees, usually one standing by itself, in (for *those* localities) sparsely wooded spots, to build on. The nest is circular, not unlike that of *Corvus Culmenatus*, composed of small sticks and twigs, and lined with fine grass roots and fibres. This species is sparingly found along the foot of the Himalayahs. It does not enter valleys, unless, as in the case of the Patlee and Dehra Dhoons, they happen to be pretty open."

The eggs are figured by Bree from specimens which Mr. Tristram obtained in Algeria, where the bird itself appears to be rare. In Europe, it would not seem to breed, though it is said to be a regular visitant to Greece, and to occur as a straggler throughout the south of Europe.

According to the figure, the eggs measure 1·75 by 1·38 and 1·66 by 1·39. The one has a bluish, the other a dull creamy, white ground, both are somewhat sparingly streaked and blotched with pale yellowish brown, and one exhibits besides, a few deep brownish red blotches.

---

of these, more or less faintly tinged grey. Posterior portion of lores, a narrow supercilium, a small patch of coverts just at the origin of the primaries, nearly hidden by the winglet, (which is *grey* and not *black*, as Dr. Jerdon gives it) and the whole of the lesser coverts, and the median secondary and tertiary coverts, black; the wing patch *more* or less glossy, with the browner bases of the feathers showing through, and usually with more or less of a greyish bloom, most conspicuous over the forearm. The rest of the upper plumage, grey, (of very different shades in different individuals, but always darkest on the primaries, scapulars and interscapulary region) which varies from a full slate grey to a pale almost pearl grey.

A *young male* (shot November the 15th) differed in having the whole head and nape white; all but the frontal feathers, with somewhat narrow, yellowish brown, central, stripes towards the tips. The shorter scapulars and interscapulary region much tinged with yellowish brown. All the scapulars and quills with a conspicuous 0·1 to 0·13 terminal white band. The black wing patch is confined to the lesser coverts, the median coverts are grey like the rest of the wing, but narrowly white tipped. The patch near the bases of the primaries, black in old adults, is dark grey. The upper breast and centre of abdomen, are tinged with pale fulvous. The iris in this bird was bright yellow.

Mr. Tristram remarks that "these eggs are interesting, as corroborating by their character, the position of the species between *Astur* and *Buteo*."

Mr. Allen, who says he found this species common throughout Egypt, at least as far up as Thebes, remarks that "it is said to breed in the Mokattam hills, behind Cairo, but I have never yet been able to meet with the nest."

Mr. Allen had some further interesting remarks, in regard to this species, amongst others (a point not noticed by Dr. Jerdon) referring to the different colours of the iris in the young, which, in a specimen which I shot, at Fazilka, on the Sutledge, on the 15th November, was quite yellow. Mr. Allen says, "The iris in the immature specimen is of a bright salmon colour, in the adult of a brilliant carmine red; and this bird, when recently shot, with its pure white breast, delicate dove-coloured back, and black shoulders, is an exquisitely beautiful object, though the soft, owl-like feathers of the face and throat and breast, invariably lose their delicate gloss when the skin has been prepared some days. This species is crepuscular in its habits, feeding largely on mice and beetles, as well as on small birds. It has the sclerotic ring of the eye very deep, and altogether shows strong *Strigine* affinities."

Of the nidification of the allied *Elanus Scriptus* in Australia, Mr. Gould gives the following account:—"It nests in companies, as near each other as possible. The nest is composed of sticks, lined with the pellets ejected from their stomachs, which are principally composed of the fur of the rats upon which they chiefly subsist. The eggs, which are four or five in number, have a white ground, blotched and marked with reddish brown, darkest at the smaller end; they are one inch and three quarters long, by one inch and three-eighths broad. The markings are easily removed by wetting."

I have often watched these birds hunting over the dry bed of a jheel, catching now and then a mouse, but most generally large grasshoppers.

They hover over the grass, in the fashion of a Kestrel, or perhaps more like a *Circaetus Gallicus*, but in a clumsier and heavier manner. The wings point upwards, so that the tips are within 3″ or 4″ of each other, instead of being retained nearly horizontal as in the Kestrel, and the legs and tail hang down unlike those of any other bird, that I have yet noticed. Thus hovering, they, after a time, slowly descend, and when within a few feet of the ground, generally drop suddenly. They are very tame, bold birds, passing unconcernedly within a few yards of a sportsman, when busy hunting, over fields or grass, and sitting composedly on the bare end of a bough, whilst gun in hand one walks up to within a few paces of their perch.

Mr. H. R. P. Carter, writing from Conoor (Southern India) remarks that "this species frequently perches on telegraph wires, flies quietly off on the approach of an engine, and perches again, a hundred yards or so ahead. With a slow train, I have seen this kept up for two or three miles.

"Sometimes I have seen them remain on the wire within a few yards of the train and let the train pass without moving."

This bird, which is recorded from all parts of India, from Ceylon to the base of the Himalayahs, and from various localities in British Burmah, is seldom seen in any numbers, but I once saw more than a dozen pairs hunting together over the dry reedy bed of a jheel. This was on Christmas Day, near Badlee, (Z. Rohtuk, Punjaub) and in these very reeds, on this same day, I procured the first specimens of *Emberiza Schœnicolus* recorded from India.

As regards the general distribution of this genus and species, I cannot do better than quote some remarks of Mr. Gould, which appeared in the Birds of Asia.

"There is not a more distinct and better defined group of Hawks, than those forming the genus *Elanus*, the members of which are widely spread over both the old and the new world. In America, the *Elanus leucurus* has a wide range, from Mexico to Brazil; Africa, India, and the Indian Islands are inhabited by three others; one, the *E. Melanopterus*, ranges over southern Europe, the whole of Africa, and India; Australia, however, appears to be the head-quarters of the genus, two species at least, the *E. Axillaris* and *E. Scriptus* inhabiting that country. The present bird" (*E. Hypoleucus* from Macassar, north Celebes, Borneo and Java) "differs from all the other members of the genus; it is most nearly allied to *E. Axillaris*, but exceeds that bird in size, and is destitute of the black spot on the under surface of the wing. It is true, some small tippings of black are seen; but they occur on a different part to the spot in *E. Axillaris;* the character, by which it may at all times be distinguished, is the silvery white hue of the under surface of the primaries, throughout their whole length."

No. 60. **Strix Indica.** BLYTH.*

THE INDIAN SCREECH OWL.

The Indian representative of the European Barn Owl lays (apparently,) in Upper India, from the middle of February, to the middle of June; Mr. R. M. Adam obtained the eggs on the 10th June, near Agra; Mr. Brookes obtained them near Etawah on the 17th of February; and I have obtained them on three occasions in March, in Allygurh, near Jeypoor, and near Lucknow.

As far as I yet know, they breed either in holes of old buildings or in wells, the latter being the favourite locality, but at Ajmere, some native fowlers showed me a pair in a small and easily accessible cave, in which they asserted that these birds had bred for years.

In some instances, the eggs appear to be laid on the bare ground with but a few grass stems or feathers about them, in others there is a small stick nest, much like that of a Pigeon's.

According to my experience they lay three eggs, but according to native trappers, *sometimes* as many as six, and *usually* four.

The eggs, like those of all owls, are unspotted white, but most of the specimens that I have seen had, like many of our larger owls, eggs, a very faint creamy tinge. In shape, the eggs appear

---

* STRIX INDICA.

DIMENSIONS.—*The females average larger, but I find some males as large and heavy as any females that I have examined, and I therefore do not give separate dimensions for the sexes.*

Length, 13 to 15·2; expanse, 37 to 43·5; wing, 11·1 to 12·2. Tail from vent, 5·8 to 6·12. Tarsus, 2·45 to 2·85. Foot, greatest length, 3·4 to 3·67; greatest breadth, 3·52 to 3·8. Mid toe, to root of claw, 1·3 to 1·5; its claw, straight, 0·7 to 0·85; hind toe, 0·65 to 0·75; its claw, 0·7 to 0·8; inner toe, 1·08 to 1·35; its claw, 0·83 to 0·95. Bill straight from margin of cere to point, 0·78 to 0·88; from gape, 1·5 to 1·75; width at gape from 0·86 to 0.97. Height at front at margin of cere, 0·38, to 0·43. Length of cere on culmen, 0.5 to 0·6. The second primary is the longest, the first is from 0·12 to 0·8, and the third from 0·05 to 0·3 shorter. The tail is as nearly as possible even. The closed wings extend from 0·25 to 1·2 beyond end of tail.

DESCRIPTION.—The tarsus is feathered to the feet, but the feathers become very sparse and bristly towards the latter, and are little more than bristles at the foot; the toes are fleshy or dirty white, or light brown with a pinkish tinge, thinly covered on the whole upper surface with whitish bristles. The claws horny brown, as a rule, but in some very dark, and in others yellowish horny, tinged only with brown on the ridges.

Bill slightly yellowish white, faintly tinged with pinkish towards the cere, which is fleshy.

Irides. Brown, sometimes almost black.

to be more oval and less round than those of the European *Strix Flammea* to which they closely approximate. Of all our Indian Owls too, so far as my experience goes, this species lays the least spherical egg. The texture is compact and fine, but there is less gloss than in most species of this family.

The eggs vary from 1·68 to 1·79 in length, and from 1·2 to 1·35 in breadth, but the average of nine eggs measured was 1·74 by 1·27.

In regard to this and nearly allied species, I reproduce the following remarks by Mr. Blyth, which appeared in the Ibis for 1866.

"Strix Indica, nobis, n. sp.

Syn. *S. Javanica*, Jerdon, B. Ind. 1. p. 117; *S. Flammea*, Gould, P. Z. S. 1859, p. 151 (ex. Siam)?. Prof. Schlegel (Mus. P. B. *Striges*, p. 4) unites *S. Javanica* with *S. Flammea*, and remarks of "individus des Indes orientales" that "Il parait que leur taille est tant soit peu moins forte que dans ceux de l'Europe, et que le bas de leur tarses est un peu moins emplumé." The late Hugh Strickland identified Horsfield's type Javan specimen with *S. Candida*; and the species which is figured by Gray and Mitchell (Gen. Birds, pl. 15) is considerably more akin to *S. Candida* than it is to *S. Flammea*, and again still less so to *S. Indica* (which I now distinguish) of the Indian and Indo-Chinese subregions. The latter, as Dr. Jerdon remarks, as compared with *S. Flammea*, "differs by being larger, with more robust feet and toes, and in being more spotted beneath." The last character, however, is by no means of constant occurrence. At a time when I erroneously supposed the Indian Screech Owl to be identical with the European, I at once discriminated a specimen of the latter, (from an unknown locality, Egypt, as I afterwards learned), and placed it as a separate species, (No. 172, of my Catalogue of the Birds in the Asiatic Society's Museum, Calcutta, 1849). Subsequently, I named it *S. Pusilla*, (J. A. S. B. XVIII. p. 801) and was not a little surprised, when it proved to be the real *S. Flammea*. The distinction I have ever since found to be constant; and the difference of the two races is so very conspicuously apparent, upon comparison of specimens, that I cannot understand Prof. Schlegel identifying a Nepalese example, (presented by Mr. Hodgson) with his Javan race They belong even to different sections of *Striginæ*, with much difference of habit. *S. Indica* ranking with *S. Flammea* in Strix proper, and *S. Javanica* in *Scelostrix* of Kaup, together with *S. Candida*, and *S. Capensis*. Prof. Kaup considers the Australian *S. Delicatula*, Gould (B. Austr. i. pl. 31,) to be identical with *S. Javanica (vera)*; remarking.

"I cannot find any difference between the examples of this species from Australia, and those from Java (?), and I feel quite sure that *S. Delicatula* and *S. Javanica* belong to one and the same species" (Trans. Zool. Soc. IV. p. 247.) Mr. Cassin, in his 'Catalogue of *Strigidæ*,' keeps *S. Delicatula* apart from *S. Javanica* (Proc. Acad. Nat. Sc. Phil. 1849); but then all his specimens were Indian, and of course *S. Indica:* yet he cites the beautiful and correct figure of *S. Javanica*, published by Messrs. Gray and Mitchell, as representing his supposed *S. Javanica*. Finally, Mr. Gould, in his Handbook to the birds of Australia, retains *S. Delicatula*, but refers to *S. Javanica* "of India" *(i. e. S. Indica)* and not to the true *S. Javanica* of the Malayan sub-region. Numerous specimens of *S. Delicatula* in the British Museum, seem to make a very close approach to *S. Indica* and not to *S. Javanica*, which latter is a small Scelostrix* (as distinguished from Strix) with white bill and claws, like the Indian *Neophron*. *S. Affinis*, nobis (Ibis 1862, p. 388,) from South Africa, proves to the *S. Poensis*, Fraser. Mr. Wallace has a fine true *Strix* from Macassar,† which is still more robust than *S. Indica*, and closely approximates *S. Personata* of Australia (Gould's B. Austr. i. p. 29)."

I have a few remarks to make on this interesting note. In the first place, although the amount of spotting on the lower surface of our Indian bird, varies much, yet out of the fifty odd specimens that I have seen, I have never seen one with the perfectly spotless, almost indescribably pure white, which so often characterizes the whole under surface of the adult European bird. In *Indica* there are always I believe, some few spots and some faint trace of fulvous tinging.

Fortunately, all 3 species, *Delicatula*, *Indica* and *Flammea* are well represented in my museum, and the much greater robustness of the tarsi, toes and claws of *Indica*, as compared with *both* the others, is very conspicuous.

S. Javanica, vera, I have never seen, but *S. Indica*. (*Javanica*, apud Jerdon, &c.) is unmistakeably distinct from *S. Delicatula*, Gould. It differs not only in the much stouter tarsi, toes and claws, but also, in its slightly larger size, longer wings and

---

* The species of *Scelostrix* are distinguished by their long and slender tarsi, which are not feathered on the lower half. They are ground-birds, which conceal themselves in long grass during the day, and affect the open country away from human habitations—habits considerably diverse from those of the birds which constitute the genus *Strix* as here limited.

† The Owl here referred to is apparently—

S. Rosenbergi, Schlegel. N. T. D. iii p. 181, from Celebes, Macassar and Menado. A. H.

decidedly (taking a *series* of each species) more rufous tone of colouring. *Flammea* again, is intermediate in tone between these two, (though decidedly nearest to *Indica*) but has I think, somewhat less of pencilling on the upper surface, than either of them.

As regards the colouring of the claws, it should be noted, that in some specimens even of *Indica*, the claws are yellowish horny, only slightly tinged on the ridge with pale brown.

S. Indica is found throughout India, Ceylon, and Burmah, and probably as Mr. Blyth supposes, extends throughout the Indo-Chinese sub-region.

No. 61. **Scelostrix Candida**. Tickell.

The Grass Owl.

I have never shot this bird myself, and can find no record of its nidification.

It doubtless breeds with us, and very possibly, in holes in the ground. Mr. R. Thompson says—

"As I have frequently shot this bird in open grass lands, both in the hills and just outside of them, I have entered him here, as it is likely we may find his nest too. In the Dehra Dhoon years ago, I shot a young bird of this species, either I think late in March or in the beginning of April. Strange to say, the young bird was flushed out of the deserted hole of a fox-burrow."

I have nothing to add to Dr. Jerdon's description, except that the facial disk is at times strongly tinged with that peculiar pinkish or purplish hue, which many examples of the Australian S. *Castanops* exhibit.

As regards the distribution of this species, I doubt at present its occurring in Oudh, the North-West, Central Provinces, or the Punjaub, except within the belt of jungle and forest land lying near the base of the Himalayahs.

As for its supposed occurrence near Hodul, two gentlemen permanently resident in the immediate neighbourhood of that place, have repeatedly searched all the grass lands, in the vicinity, from the banks of the Jumna westward, for miles, without ever flushing any Owl, but the short eared, or as it is often called at home, the Woodcock Owl. (*Otus Brachyotus*). In the Bijnor and Moradabad Terai, I have seen it put up when I have been Tiger-shooting, but though I have beaten in my time probably thousands of miles of heavy grass, on the banks of the Jumna, Ganges, &c., for one sort of game or another, I never saw a single specimen of this Grass Owl in the plains proper, of Upper India. Moreover, I have never seen a specimen in any of the numerous collections made in those parts, that I have examined. However it *may* occur, but even if it does, it must be only as a straggler and very rarely.

No. 62. **Phodilus Badius**. Horsf.

The Bay Screech Owl.

Nothing is known of the nidification, and next to nothing of the habits, of this most beautiful species. Dr. Horsfield says: "The Wowo-wiwi is rarely met with in Java. It never visits the villages, but resides in the deepest forests, which are the usual resort of the Tiger. The natives even assert, that it approaches this animal, with the same familiarity with which the Jallak (*Pastor Jalla*, Horsf.) approaches the Buffaloe, and that it does not fear to alight on the Tiger's back. The Wowo-wiwi is never seen in confinement; the few individuals which I obtained, were from the densest forests of the district of Pugar, and from the ranges of low hills, south of the capital of Surakarta. Like most other species of this family, it is a nocturnal bird."

The above is all I have been able to find recorded of the habits of this species. Temminick, who figures it (Pl. Col. 318) quotes this passage, and gravely remarks that this habit of roosting on Tigers' backs, requires *further confirmation!* He *says* that the iris is *brown* and figures it bright *yellow;* an ingenious method of getting out of the difficulty, since it can hardly, (the bird being what it is,) help being one *or* the other.

Dr. Jerdon describes the lower parts as pale fulvous yellow, but in the specimen which he himself gave me, they are from the lower breast and downwards, a beautiful salmon pink. All the quills are beautifully banded with black on their inner webs, the first two or three on the outer also; and the first feather of the winglet, the first greater primary covert and the first primary have the outer webs white, with broad transverse bars of the deepest brown, mingled at the extreme margins of the feathers with chesnut.

Dr. Jerdon also omits to notice, (what Temminck's very indifferent figure correctly shows) one of the most notable features in the plumage of this species, viz. that the whole forehead and anterior half of the crown is a pale delicate salmon pink, contrasting strongly with the deep but brilliant chesnut of the posterior portion of the crown, the occiput, &c.

Mr. Blyth, remarked in the Ibis for 1866, that the proper position of this species was with the *Syrniinæ;* "Professor Schlegel refers this species to his *Ulula*, as distinguished from *Strix;* and upon examination of the external ear and other characters, I find that it has no claim to belong to the Screech Owl, sub-family (*Striginæ*), but is distinctly one of the Hooters (*Syrniinæ*). Messrs. Mottley and Dillwyn remark, that it has only a single note, frequently repeated, and which is much like the first note of the common Wood-Owl's cry."

This may be the case, but so far as bill, disk, shape of head, tail, and wings, and the character of the plumage is concerned, it seems to me to be a *Strix*. The legs and feet are perhaps more like those of the hooters, but an osculant type as it avowedly is, its external affinities are more with the barn than the wood Owls.

The whole tone of its colouration is that of the so-called rufous phase of *Scops Pennatus;* it would be curious if a non-rufous phase of this species also were to turn up.

The Bay Owl has been found in Borneo, Sumatra, Java, the Malay Peninsula, Burma Proper, Aracan, Assam, Sikhim and Nepal, and Mr. R. Thompson says, "I have shot one or two specimens of this bird, many years ago, in the Dehra Dhoon, flushing it out of short grass in broken raviny ground." So that Major Boyes' specimen in the Philadelphia Museum need not, (as Mr. Blyth supposes) necessarily have come from Tenasserim.

No. 63. **Bulaca Indranee.** Sykes.

The Brown Wood Owl.

I have been able to discover no record of the nidification of this species, and though it is by no means uncommon in Southern India, I possess no specimens. At present, as I shall more fully explain when dealing with *B. Newarensis*, I very much doubt the specific distinctness of the two forms.

Of the geographical distribution of this present form, I can say nothing; according to Dr. Jerdon, *Indranee* occupies all Southern and Central India, Ceylon, Burmah and the Malayan Peninsular, while *Newarensis*, is confined to the Himalayahs, but I have seen a Burmese specimen wholly undistinguishable from a specimen which I myself shot at Simla, and which ought to be *Newarensis*.

No. 64. Bulaca Newarensis.* Hodgson.

The Nepal Brown Wood Owl.

This species, so far as I yet know, lays in May. I have only seen one nest, which was in a deep, wooded, precipitous little

---

* Bulaca Newarensis.

Dimensions (*of Males.*)

	Old.	Young.
Length,	21·5	21·5
Expanse,	52·5	51·6
Weight,	2 lb. 1 oz.	1 lb. $12\frac{3}{4}$ oz
Wing,	15·5	15·2
Which primary longest,	5th	5th
Amount by which other primaries fall short of longest,	1st 4·5 2nd 2·3	1st 4·7 2nd 2·2
Tail of how many feathers,	12·	12·
Length of tail from vent,	9·5	9·5
By how much longest tail feathers exceed shortest,	1·	0·8
Tarsus (densely feathered),	3·	2·8
Foot, greastest length,	4·5	4·4
„ greatest width,	5·	4·8
Mid Toe,	2·	2·
Its claw, along curve,	1·4	1·25
Hind Toe,	·9	·9
Its claw, along curve,	1·1	1·0
Inner Toe,	1·8	1·6
Its claw, along curve,	1·55	1·3
Bill, straight from base,	1·75	1·65
„ along curve,	1·75	1·9
„ from gape,	1·9	1·8
„ width at gape,	1·45	1·37
„ height at front,	1·00	·9
Length of cere which is indistinct,	·83	·75
Distance by which the closed wings fall short of end of tail,	1·5	0·7
Distance by which lower tail coverts fall short of ditto,	3 9	5·0

Description.—*Legs and feet* densely feathered to the last joints of the toes, which last joints, are pale plumbeous; claws dusky lead colour. *Irides* deep brown. *Bill.*—Greenish horny white, bluish towards base; cere, which is ill-defined, plumbeous. Bare eyelids and eye shelf, very pale, fleshy plumbeous.

Plumage.—The centre of the forehead, crown, and occiput, deep blackish brown, with, in some lights, a marked purple gloss. Bristly feathers in front, and immediately above the anterior angle of the eye, black shafted, and with most of the webs black, but some of them greyish white. Point of the forehead and a broad line on each side, from the forehead, over the eye, very loosely webbed; black at the base, the terminal two-thirds greyish white, more or less distinctly rayed with pale, yellowish

valley or khud, at the back of Mahasoo (near Simla). Contrary to what might have been expected, it was placed on a

---

brown bars, the bars being most distinct on the inner, least so on the outer feathers. This quasi supercilium extends backwards, nearly as far as the posterior angle of the eye; from thence, there is a narrow, ill-defined, dusky, brown band, running behind the posterior angle of the eye and under the eye towards the lores, where it is lost in the dark loral bristles, and dividing the eye as it were from the cheeks and ear coverts, the feathers of which are a very pale yellowish brown, indistinctly banded with rays of a darker brown, the feathers having the webs very much separated. The feathers of the chin and the band of ruff feathers running from the chin, below the light cheek and ear feathers, above described, and upwards, behind the ear coverts, and above the eye, to near the crown—a sort of chocolate brown, a shade darker than even the feathers of the crown. There is an enormous bare patch above and partly behind the eye, hidden in life by the downward projecting feathers of the sides of the crown. Below the chin, the centre of the throat is pure white. Front and sides of the neck, the whole lower surface of the body, wing-lining, lower tail coverts, tibial and tarsal plumes and feathers of foot, buffy or fulvous white, every feather closely and conspicuously banded with very numerous, narrow, brown bars; these bars are rather closer on the upper portion of the breast; wider apart and larger on the lower tail coverts; much closer and somewhat less distinct on tibia, tarsus and foot, and somewhat less distinct on the lower coverts of the secondaries, where also the ground colour is somewhat more rufous. The larger, lower coverts of the first six or eight primaries are more or less broadly tipped with dark brown, above which the barrings are somewhat obsolete. There is a purplish brown tinge, on the feathers at the base of the neck, in front, forming a sort of ill-defined, pectoral gorget, most conspicuous at the sides of the neck. The banded, fulvous white feathers of the rest of the sides of the neck, extend partially backwards, so as nearly to meet behind, and form a sort of ill-defined, imperfect collar. Feathers of the side of the head, behind the ruff feathers, and above the imperfect collar, nape, upper back, central scapulars and lesser wing coverts, a rich, deep, slightly rufous brown, many of the feathers more or less clouded with the deep chocolate brown of the top of the head, and exhibiting in some lights a purple gloss. Longer and exterior scapulars, and some feathers of the centre back, more or less distinctly barred with white or fulvous white on one or both webs; the bars on some feathers, especially on the outer scapulars, being very sharply cut and distinctly marked, while on others, they are freckled irregulars bands. I note that this barring is greatly concealed by the overhanging feathers of the upper back and centre scapulars. The greater and median coverts of the secondaries are a somewhat lighter shade of rufous brown, most of them narrowly tipped with white or fulvous white, and indistinctly freckled or barred with the same colour. The winglet, and greater coverts of the earlier primaries a rich deep velvet brown, with a most peculiarly soft and glossy texture, and in some lights a rich purple gloss. The greater coverts of the later primaries are intermediate in colour and markings between these and the greater coverts of the secondaries. The quills are brown, deeper and purpler on the earlier primaries, and growing lighter and more fulvous towards the later secondaries; all but the first 2 primaries, are distinctly and broadly barred, on both webs, with

shelf projecting from the face of a low precipice; immediately above it, projected a large point of rock, from which depended a perfect curtain of bushes, which reached the tops of the trees, growing at the foot of the precipice. The nest, the Paharees said, (I could not get up to it myself,) was composed of sticks, with a few feathers intermingled, it was completely hidden from sight by the bushes and rocks above and below, and contained on the 6th of June, three very young birds.

The female was fired at, but not obtained at the time; weeks afterwards, her remains were found, hanging in the moss and ferns of a tree, some distance down the valley, utterly rotten and spoiled.

The male brought the young ones up, and on the 10th of October, I shot him and one of the young ones, then as nearly full grown as might be.

---

pale fulvous. The 2nd to the 6th primaries are distinctly emarginate on the outer webs, and the barrings are dull and inconspicuous, and the margins serrated below the emarginations. All the quills are narrowly tipped with rather dull white. The tertiaries are narrowly banded more conspicuously than the greater secondary coverts, less so than the exterior scapulars. The lower back and upper tail coverts are the same dark brown as the central scapulars, faintly and narrowly banded with yellowish white. The tail feathers are also of much the same shade of brown, somewhat deeper on the exterior webs of the lateral feathers; all are conspicuously though not broadly tipped with white, and all have numerous, imperfect bars on both webs, which on the central feathers, the external webs, and terminal one fourth of internal webs of lateral feathers, are somewhat narrow, and pale fulvous in colour, and on the basal three-fourths of the inner webs of the lateral feathers are very broad and nearly pure white. On the inner surface of the wing, the inner webs of the first 6 primaries are conspicuously notched, the seventh exhibiting a trace of the same. The first primary is barless, but on the inner web, above the notching, there is a buffy freckling. All the other primaries, above the notching, in those that have notches, and all the rest of the quills, except the terminal, one fourth, are buffy, with broad, irregular, rather pale, brown bands, more or less freckled with dark brown. The terminal portion of all the quills except the first two, are dark brown, with transverse, fulvous, or buffy bands, more indistinct and wider apart on the third and other earlier primaries, and closer, and more conspicuous, on the later secondaries. The second primary shows very faint traces of similar barrings. The lower surface of the tail is buffy brown, darker towards the tip, somewhat closely and conspicuously barred with yellowish white. Upper portion of the last joint of the toes are pale plumbeous, with 3 or 4 large but soft membraneous scutæ. The claws are very sharp and the inner margin of the central claw is dilated and knife-like. The bill curves almost from the base, the cere is ill-defined and blends almost insensibly with the corneous portion of the bill, and there is a conspicuous notch near the tip of the lower mandible. The ear aperture is enormous. I may add to the dimensions above given, that the third primary is 1·1 shorter than the fifth, and the fourth ·5 shorter than the same.

I very much doubt the distinctness of this and the last species. I give below in great detail, the measurements taken in the flesh of the old and the young males, above referred to. It will be seen that the dimensions very little exceed those given by Dr. Jerdon for *Indranee*, and fall far short of those which he gives for *Newarensis*. A Burmese *skin*, differed in none of its dimensions, by more than a mere fraction, from the skin of the old male above referred to.

Mr. Blyth holds a different opinion, and I reproduce his remarks further on; but I nevertheless still hold, that the distinction of size is, *to say the least*, neither so constant, nor so material as has been asserted, and has by no means been so established as to render (if Dr. Jerdon's measurements of the southern race are reliable)* a specific separation of the northern and southern birds, *certainly* requisite. Dr. Jerdon gives the wing of the southern species at from 13 to 14 inches. The Burmese bird has them 14·8. My two Simla specimens have them 15·2 in the young and 15·5 in the old male. A fine Bussahir specimen has them 16·2, a peculiarly large Kumaon bird 16·7, and this is the largest in my museum. Dr. Stoliczka says, "An unusually large specimen of 21 inches in length, with the wing of a little over 18 inches, and the tail of 10½ inches, was shot at Kotegurh in February, 1866." But Von Pelzeln, says of this same specimen, "The wing in this specimen measures 16″. A specimen received from Baron Hügel and also from the Himalayahs, is decidedly smaller (wing 15″); above it is much redder, and the wavy cross-markings underneath are narrower and paler."

I have no Sikhim or Nepal specimens. Can it be that a larger race inhabits those districts, while in Kumaon and westwards, the race is identical with that of Southern and Central India? Certainly, the evidence before me, leads to the conclusion, that even if the Nepal and Neilgherry birds be distinct, the Burmese, Kumaon, Simlah and Kotegurh birds are intermediate between these two.

The following however are Mr. Blyth's views in regard to *B. Newarensis*.

---

* It is only just to Dr. Jerdon to say, that nothing can, as a rule, be more reliable and accurate, than his *own* descriptions and figures. But a vast number of his descriptions and dimensions, are taken almost if not quite verbatim from other writers in the Asiatic Society's Journal, &c., who were by no means so careful as himself, and as (his work being a *manual*) he did not think it necessary to note quotations of this kind, he often gets credit for errors for which he is really not responsible.

"This species is figured by Gray and Mitchell, (Gen. Birds, pl. 14), with yellow irides, which is a mistake. The species of *Bulaca*, as of *Syrnium*, have dark* irides, while those of *Ptynx* (I suspect) have yellow irides. In the great series of Scops-Owls, there are two groups, one having dark, and the other yellow irides. To the former belong certain African species of considerable size, as the so-called *Bubo lacteus*, (Temm. P. C. 4), also *B. poensis*, Fraser (figured in incompletely mature plumage as *B. fasciolatus*, Temm., in P. Z. S. 1863, pl. 33), and another beautiful species, *B. cinerascens*, now, together with *B. poensis*, in the Zoological Gardens, which seem to differ only from *Bulaca*, (founded on the present species) in having tufts of peculiar and rather flimsy texture, which they have a peculiar mode of displaying, spreading them out laterally like the opening of a wing; and to this group of Scops-Owls also belongs the *Ephialtes lettia*, and its immediate congeners (as noticed in the sequel). A parallel series of yellow-eyed Scops-Owls comprises the so-called *Bubo Africanus* and species akin to it, as also the small European Scops-Owl with others allied to it. Professor Schlegel and also Mr. G. R. Gray, erroneously identify *Bulaca Newarensis* of Hodgson with *B. indrani* of Sykes (*B. monticola*, Jerdon), the Himalayan species being very much larger than the other, and differing more from it than *Spilornis Cheela* does from *S. bacha* As Dr. Jerdon remarks, the Himalayan bird must† weigh fully double that from Southern India."

To my mind neither of Dr. Jerdon's descriptions, *i. e.*, neither that of *Indranee* nor *Newarense*, sufficiently accurately represent our Simla bird, and I have therefore given in the footnote, a detailed description taken from a fresh specimen (the old male) killed near Mahasoo, but I should note that some birds have the whole of the upper parts a paler and more decidedly rufous brown, than in the specimen described, and the feathers of the centre of the forehead, crown, and occiput, absolutely uncolorous with those of the nape, upper back and central scapulars, instead of contrasting with them by their deep chocolate-like tinge.

The feathers of the tarsus and base of the foot are *very* thick and full. So that the lower portion of the tarsus appears fully one and three quarter inches deep, measured from front to back. The arrangement of the toes is somewhat remarkable, almost

* Vide my description of the Simla Bird.

† Our old Simla male weighed 2 lbs. 1 oz. it is to be hoped that some ornithologist in Southern India will weigh some fine male Neilgherry Bird.

scansorial, if I may use the term. When the fresh foot is pulled out, so that the sole is flat and without crease, the mid and hind toes are in one straight line, and the two lateral toes are also in one straight line. The inner and mid toe subtend between them an angle of only 60 degrees, and similarly the outer and hind toe subtend only the same angle, while the outer and middle toe subtend an angle of 120°, as do the hind and inner toe. The soles are very flat, with scarcely any pads and with nearly an inch square of surface, beyond the corners of which the soles of the toes project. In colour they are fleshy white, thickly set with conspicuous, but soft papillæ. It should be remarked, that the hind toe is not absolutely on a level with the three anterior toes, but has its origin a little higher up.

I have shot a good many of this species, at one time or another. I have always found great difficulty in getting them to fly. They are always in well-wooded localities, but so far as my experience goes, affect small precipices, on the sides of wooded hills.

Mr. Thompson sent me the following note, in regard to the large Kumaon specimen already referred to—"During the past winter, I got a specimen of this bird, which I shall send you. It was being mobbed by a gang of Crows at Huldwanee at the foot of the hills, and some boys killed it with pellets from their bows."

A specimen which I secured on Nagteeba (north of Landour and across the Uglas), was set upon, when we did succeed in making it fly by a pair of Falcons, who knocked it down, one of them inflicting a severe wound on the back. As far as I can remember, the Falcons were "*Atriceps;*" at the time, (I had not then distinguished the species,) I considered them to be *Perigrinator*. Of the geographical distribution I have nothing to add to what I said under *B. Indranee.*

No. 65. **Bulaca Ocellata.*** Lesson.

The Mottled Wood Owl.

This species, lays in the plains of the North-Western Provinces and the Punjaub, in March, but I have a note of the eggs having been taken in the Dhoon early in April.

---

* Bulaca Ocellata.

Dimensions. *(I do not find that the sexes differ constantly in size, and I therefore do not give their dimensions separately.)*

Its eggs are deposited at heights of from eight to twenty-five feet from the ground, in some large cavity, or in the depression

---

Length, 17·9 to 19·2; expanse, 45·0 to 50·5; wing, 13·0 to 14·9; tail, 7·3 to 8·4; tarsus (feathered throughout) 2·05 to 2·4; foot, greatest length, 3·4 to 4·1; greatest width, 3·9 to 4·35; mid toe to root of claw, 1·35 to 1·65; its claw straight, 0·9 to 1·03; hind toe, 0·75 to 0·9; its claw, straight, 0·7 to 0·82; inner toe, 1·0 to 1·25; its claw, 0·9 to 1·05; bill, straight from edge of cere to point, 0·85 to 0·98; from forehead, straight to point, 1·17 to 1·42; from gape, 1·6 to 1·7; width at gape, 1·0 to 1·38; height at front at margin of cere, 0·48 to 0·56; length of cere, 0·5 to 0·63; wings, when closed, reach to end of tail or fall short of it by not more than 1″, lower tail coverts fall short of end of tail by from 2·25 to 3·8.

The third, or third and fourth primaries are the longest; the first from 2·5 to 3·0, and the second from 0·6 to 1·1, shorter. The external tail feathers are from 0·45 to 0·9 shorter than the central ones. Weight from 1 lb 6 oz. to 2 lbs., but 1 lb. 8 oz. is about the average.

DESCRIPTION. The front of the *toes* sparsely feathered with dingy white bristly feathers; terminal joints with three, transverse, soft scales, or folds of skin, pale greenish brown; *soles* yellowish white, papillæ conspicuous but soft; *claws*, which though sharp are little curved, and comparatively rather feeble, pale brown at their bases, dark brown at the tips; inner edge of middle claw somewhat dilated.

Irides. Brown, in some light, in some deep.

Bill. Horny black, pale and greyish on lower mandible.

Cere. Dingy, a mixture of dirty, pinkish, brownish, and yellowish, horny—varies a good deal.

Tongue. Thick, fleshy, broad, membraneous and slightly divided at the tip.

Plumage (of an adult male, shot on the nest, March 6th, 1867). Lores with a prominent tuft of white, bristle-like feathers, with widely separated webs, and shafts prolonged some distance beyond webs, such prolongation being black or blackish brown, and a few of the feathers with traces, of one or more, dark brown or blackish bars. A somewhat similar tuft on the end of the chin, but without the black tips. Feathers, of point of forehead, immediately over the eye, behind the eye as far as the ear aperture (which is enormous) and round below the eye to the base of the lower mandible, including the feathers of the eyelids, greyish white with blackish tips and most of them with narrow, transverse, black or blackish brown bars, a stripe of these feathers behind and partly below the eye tinged ferruginous. From the base of the chin, a line of dark brown to blackish feathers runs (bounding the greyish white, barred ones, above described) round the cheeks, behind the ear opening, and behind the eye, to the top of the head, defining the facial disk, which is not very decided; below this line (some of the feathers of which, especially near the chin, are a good deal mottled or at times barred with white, dingy white or rufous) a large, pure white patch on the centre of the throat. Centre of forehead, top and back of the head, back and sides of the neck, the feathers a rich chesnut, more or less broadly tipped with blackish brown, with conspicuous, but somewhat irregular, white spots on the tippings. The whole back, scapulars and wing coverts, except those of the primaries, dingy ferruginous at their bases, the terminal portions (of greater or less extent) white, obscurely barred with irregular and more or less incomplete, dark brown bars and the interspaces closely speckled and mottled with the same colour. In many cases, traces of the barring and mottling extend up the

at the fork of two or more huge branches, of some old peepul or mango tree. There is no nest, so to speak, but a little dry touch wood, a few dead leaves, or a little earth, covering the floor, if I may so call it, of the nesting place, forms a scanty bed for the eggs.

---

feathers, on to the ferruginous portion—in the greater secondary coverts, the white, mottled interspaces are chiefly on the outer web, and in the smallest coverts, the brown altogether predominates at the tips. The winglet much resembles the secondary greater coverts. The primary greater coverts, as a whole, are brown, more or less buff at the base and on inner webs, and with a tipping and two or three broad, transverse bars (chiefly on the outer webs) of mottled white or brown, or mottled buffy and brown. The first four primaries are notched on the inner webs conspicuously, and there is a trace of the same in the fifth and sixth. The second,third and fourth, are also emarginate on the outer web. The extreme tips of all the primaries are mottled fulvous white and a faint brown; above this the ground colour of the tips (as far as the notches and emarginations, where these exist,) is a slightly yellowish brown, and above this the ground colour is a rich buff. All the primaries are barred throughout, on both webs, with transverse, irregular, brown bars, very inconspicuous on the brown tips of the first few primaries. The interspaces on the outer webs, are every where mottled with brown, and on the earlier primaries above the emarginations cover much of or in some nearly the whole, web, and below these, have a paler ground (greyish white) than the corresponding portions of the inner web. The secondaries are regularly barred with brown, broadly on the outer, more narrowly on the inner webs, and with the tips, and interspaces of outer webs, greyish white, mottled and speckled brown, and the interspaces of the inner webs buff, to buffy white, the brown bars growing narrower, and the buff interspaces wider and paler, as they approach the interior margin. The upper tail coverts are ferruginous buff, with greyish white tips, barred and mottled with brown. The tail feathers are brownish buff, with broad, dark brown tips. The tips of *all* the feathers, the whole of the central ones and of the outer webs of the lateral ones, with broad, close, irregular, incomplete, mottled white brown and dark brown bars, and the inner webs of the lateral tail feathers like the inner webs of the secondaries. Base of the neck in front, breast, sides, abdomen, lower tail coverts and lower wing coverts (except greater ditto of primaries which are pale buff with black tips), ferruginous to pale buff at base, the rest being greyish white with several, narrow, clearly defined, transverse, slightly wavy brown bars. The tint of the basal portion diminishes in intensity, as the feathers recede from the base of the neck, and becomes nearly white in the lower tail coverts. The thighs and tarsi are, the former, a dull buff, the latter greyish white, with numerous, close, transverse, narrow, wavy brown bars.

No. 2. A female shot on the nest, March 7th, with all the abdomen bared for incubation.

This corresponded precisely with the above description, yet differed considerably in appearance, owing first, to the dark circumscribing line of the facial disk being less marked; second, to many of the feathers of the white throat patch, having excessively narrow, black tippings; third, to there being a much larger extent of the mottled white, on the whole upper surface; fourth, to the ferruginous or buff of wings, tail, and bases of body feathers, as well as the brown of the tips of primaries and tail feathers being paler.

Two is the ordinary number of eggs laid; indeed there were two eggs (in three instances more or less incubated) in every one of the seven nests of which I have notes.

The eggs of this species are generally a very round oval. White, with in many instances a very delicate creamy tinge. In size and shape, they seem to be scarcely distinguishable from those of the allied *S. Aluco* of Europe. In texture they are coarser than those of *Strix Indica* or any of the *Ephialtes* or *Athenes*, that I know; but they are finer than those of *Ketupa Ceylonensis* or *Ascalaphia Coromanda.* From the eggs of *Ascalaphia Bengalensis*, it is scarcely possible to separate them; although *Bengalensis* is a considerably larger bird, its eggs, as regards size, shape, and texture, seem almost identical with those of the present species. All that I can say, with an ample series of both before me, is, that as a body, the eggs of *Bengalensis* are a mere trifle larger, and have more gloss than those of *Ocellata.* For the size of the bird, the eggs of the present species are somewhat large.

In length, they vary from 1·94 to 2·1, and in breadth, from 1·63 to 1·75, but the average of ten eggs measured, was 2·01 by 1·68.

I have more than once shot the male sitting on the eggs. Mr. W. Blewitt writes, "I found a nest near Hansie in a hollow of a peepul tree about nineteen feet from the ground, on the 16th of March. The nest hole which was lined with leaves, contained two partially incubated eggs."

Mr. Brookes says, that on the 3rd of March, 1867, he "took a pair of eggs out of a nest in a mango tree. The nest was in the fork of two huge branches about twenty feet from the ground. There was a little earth and a few dry mango leaves. The eggs were pure white and very round."

Mr. Blyth, writing of this species says, that it has "conspicuous rose-coloured orbits, though I see that my friend, Dr. Jerdon, has described them as 'orange;' this, however, may depend on the age, the red distinguishing the young." I have recorded the colours of the soft parts, of more than a dozen specimens, in *all* I find this note, "edges of lids reddish." The fact is, different people see colours very differently, and what is more, even if they see them alike, describe them in very different terms; the reader may take his choice, between rose coloured, orange and reddish, without going very far wrong.

This species is found throughout India, east of the Sutledge, and of the Indus below its junction with the former, and west of the Ganges. I have seen specimens from near Aboo, and from Kattiwar, and again from near Fazilka. It occurs, though sparingly, in Lower Bengal, Mr. Blyth having, he says, picked up an unmistakeable feather of one, in a mango tope, thirty miles from Calcutta. I have a specimen from Monghyr. It has not been recorded from Ceylon, and in Assam it is apparently replaced by the next species. West of the Sutledge, I cannot find any record of it, although it may very likely occur there. It is most common in moderately dry country, well furnished with large groves. The large mango topes of the N. W. Provinces are favourite haunts of this species. My own experience is, that it affects neither very damp, nor very dense jungly districts. It certainly occurs in the sub-Himalayan valleys, as I obtained a specimen near Jewlee, below Nynetal. I cannot say whether it ascends the Hills to any height. Mr. Blyth thinks that it does not, and I have never myself met with it at any considerable elevation.

The stomachs of four specimens that I examined, contained exclusively the remains of Rats, Mice and Squirrels !

No. 65 bis. Bulaca Sinensis. Latham.

The Malayan Wood Owl.

Strix.	*Orientalis,*	*Shaw.*	Gen. Zool. VII. 257.
"	*Seloputo.*	*Horsf.*	Trans. Linn. Soc. xiii. p. 140.
"	*Pagodarum.*	*Tem.*	Pl. Col. 230.
Ulula	*Seloputo.*	*Schleg.*	Mus. P. B. Striges, p. 22.

I know nothing personally of this species, and can find nothing recorded of its nidification; I merely follow Mr. Blyth in the above synonymy. He says, that *Strix Sinensis* of Latham, is clearly the *S. Seloputo* of Horsfield, " of the Malayan region, spreading into the Tenasserim provinces and Siam, and doubtless into China; as distinguished from *B. Ocellata (Syrnium ocellatum,* Lesson, Rev. Zool., 1839, p. 289) of India, which has not been observed eastward of the Bay of Bengal. Latham had merely seen a drawing from India (doubtless Hardwicke's) which he thought might refer to his *S. Sinensis* ; but both Latham's and Shaw's descriptions clearly indicate the Malayan species."

Latham's description is, however, to my mind, by no means *clearly* indicative, of *any* particular species, and would answer about equally well for several species. He says:

"Length 17 inches, bill dusky black; face pale, with dusky markings, and the feathers surrounding it, marked with dusky; plumage in general, above, ferruginous chestnut, marked with dusky, spotted irregularly at the back part of the head and neck, with black and white; chin and throat white; the rest of the parts beneath, the same, but crossed with numerous fine dusky lines; quills and tail chestnut, powdered with darker dots, and crossed with bars of the same, at half an inch distance; legs feathered to the toes; claws dusky. Inhabits China. In the collection of General Davies. I observe one very similar if not the same, among the drawings of General Hardwicke, found at Cawnpore, in India, in September."

It is very clear, that Latham did not himself realize the identity of his *Sinensis* and Horsfield's *Seloputo*, for he describes the latter separately, in the following words:

"Length 20 inches. Body above ferruginous bay, crossed with indistinct bands of a paler colour; beneath white, banded with ferruginous bay; chin whitish, throat inclining to yellow, ocular region pale ferruginous; legs crossed with dusky yellow bands. Inhabits Java; called there Selo-puto."

Now it will be observed that "ocular region pale ferruginous" exactly hits the character of this species, whereas "face pale with dusky markings" does not suit it at all.

While therefore, following Mr. Blyth in this identification, I am by no means *certain* myself, that Latham's *Sinensis* and Horsfield's *Seloputo are* one and the same.

Be this, however, as it may, *Seloputo*, Horsf. and *Pagodarum*. Tem. is constantly found in Burmah, and must therefore find a place in these notes.

Temminck thus describes this species, which he says that Dussumier brought from the *continent* of India; though he had received other specimens from Java.

"The tarsi are thickly clad with down, covered over with small feathers; the toes are clothed on their upper surfaces only, and the last joint is bare; the disk is small; the closed wings reach to the end of the tail; the down at all ages is a rufous yellow.

The adult has the crown, and the sides of the neck of a somewhat bright rufous chestnut, each feather with one or two rows of pure white spots, encircled by a black zone. The back, the lesser wing coverts and the scapulars, are coloured much like the nape, but slightly lighter; the white spots are less regular and larger, but are encircled with a black band; the secondaries and the base of the primaries, have wide apart, reddish yellow bars, on a reddish brown ground. The tail, divided by irregular bars, is tipped with white, and paler below. The face and eyebrows are a spotless reddish yellow. The breast is barred with transverse bands of white, and reddish chestnut. The whole of the rest of the lower parts are pure white, intersected by widely separated, very regular, narrow, transverse brown bars.

The iris is yellow. Length 17 to 19, (French) inches, *(equal to from* 18 *to* 20·12 *English inches)*.

Yearling birds have the tarsi clad in whitish down. The face is dusky, and the whole plumage has a light rufous tinge. The lower parts are barred, much as in the adult. The feathers of the upper parts exhibit, regular, transverse, white, and light rufous bands; the white bands are encircled, (as in the adult) but they are much larger than in the latter. The changes effected by successive moults in the shape of these broad enframed bands, produce intermediate varieties. In some the upper parts exhibit brown, white and rufescent, zig-zags. In old birds the white spots are small and isolated."

No. 66. **Syrnium Nivicolum,*** Hodgson.

The Himalayan Wood Owl.

Of the nidification of this species nothing seems to be as yet known. Of the nearly allied *Syrnium Aluco* of Europe *(S. Stridula auct.)* Mr. Hewitson says, "The tawny owl usually

---

* Syrnium Nivicolum.

Dimensions. *(Of an adult female).*

Length, 17·5. Expanse, 42. Wing, 12·15. Tail from vent, 7·9. Tarsus, 2. Foot, greatest length, 3·6; greatest width, 3·75; mid toe, to root of claw, 1·25; its claw straight, to point, 0·81; hind toe, 0·6; its claw, 0·73; inner toe, 0·95; its claw, 0·86. Bill, straight from forehead to point, 1·33; from gape, 1·55; width at gape, 1·1; height at front, 0·6.

The closed wings fell short by 1, and the lower tail coverts by 4 inches, of end of tail.

The fifth primary was the longest. The first was 3·1; the second, 1·35; the third, 0·4; and the fourth, 0·15, shorter. The exterior tail feathers fell short by one inch of the central ones.

Description. The *legs and feet* densely feathered to the terminal joints of the toes, which had two or three moderate transverse scales, of a dull plumbeous colour. Claws, brown, paler at tips and bases. *Irides,* dark brown. *Bill,* pale fleshy yellow. *Cere,* which is very faintly marked, plain brown.

Plumage. Feathers of the face greyish white, dark shafted, more or less tinged with dingy rufous brown, and all but those of the lores more or less distinctly banded with narrow dark brown bars. Feathers of the ruff, deep brown, more or less spotted, or mottled or narrowly barred at the tips with mingled white and pale fawn colour. The top of the head, nape, back, scapulars, lesser and median wing coverts, deep, almost blackish brown, mottled and freckled, with dull, slightly rufous, buff or buffy white. Tail and quills, a duller and somewhat paler brown, with irregular, imperfect, more or less mottled, dull, buffy white, transverse bars, and more or less freckling of the same colour on the interspaces towards the margins of the feathers. The central tail feathers have six, the external eight, transverse

lays its eggs in a hollow tree, sometimes in the holes of rocks and occasionally in the deserted nest of some other bird; they are round, large, bright and glossy, from three to five in number, and are deposited at irregular intervals, the first being sat upon as soon as laid; the young of the same nest differ in consequence very considerably in their size."

He figures an egg 1·95 by 1·6.

Yarrell says, "The eggs of this species are large, compared with those of either of the three Owls *(Otus Vulgaris, O. Brachyotus, Strix Flammea)* last described. They are smooth and white, measuring one inch ten lines (1·83) in length, by one inch six lines (1·5) in breadth."

Montague states, that it breeds in the hollows of trees and sometimes in barns; it prepares very little nest, and at times deposits its eggs merely on the decayed wood. Temminck, on the other hand, affirms that it lays in the deserted nests of Buzzards, Crows and Magpies.

I cannot understand how our Indian species could ever be considered *identical* with the European *Aluco*.

Both species vary a good deal in colour, but the Indian species is invariably considerably darker, and less rufous than the European. Again the Indian species is very markedly larger. The following are dimensions* recorded from fresh specimens of fine females of both species.

	Length.	Expanse.	Wing.	Tail	Tarsus.	Claws straight from root to point. Mid.	Hind.	Inner.	Outer.	Bill straight from anterior margin of nares to point.
S. Nivicolum,...	17·5	42	12·15	7·9	2·0	0·81	0·73	0·86	0·69	0·68
S. Aluco,.........	16·2	35	11·13	7·1	1·9	0·67	0·59	0·72	0·58	0·61

bands; all are narrowly white tipped. Large, irregular, white or buffy white blotches, on the outer webs of the external scapulars, and the earlier, greater, primary coverts. The feathers of the breast and abdomen are mingled pure white and buff coloured, with very deep brown, central stripes, and two or three, narrow, irregular, transverse, brown bars. Sides, flanks and wing lining (except the greater, lower primary coverts which are mingled brown and white) dull, silky buff, more or less imperfectly barred, with brown. Tibial and tarsal plumes dull, more or less infuscated buff, irregularly banded with narrow, imperfect, dull brown, transverse bars. Lower tail coverts similar but paler, and the bars more obscure and further apart. The feathers over the eye are whiter, than the rest of the face, forming a broad, ill-defined, pale, superciliary band.

* I am indebted for these measurements to Messrs. C. L. Gordon, and G. F. L. Marshall respectively. The European specimen, my correspondent informs me, was a particularly fine bird.

Not only is the bird larger as a whole, but the claws and bill are more than proportionally larger and stronger.

There seems to be a difference too in the shape of the wings; in all the specimens of *Aluco*, which I have examined, the fifth primary fell perceptibly short of the fourth, while in *Nivicolum* (I have only examined, however, three examples of each) the fifth quill is either equal to or exceeds, the fourth.

I cannot doubt that the two species are perfectly distinct.

Dr. Stoliczka has the following note on this species:—"I procured one specimen of this species above Chini, at an elevation of 14,000 feet, and another specimen was shot by my shikarees at Kotegurh in winter 1866. It is in this portion of the hills rather a rare bird.

"The greater coverts of the primaries have a white, terminal spot on the outer webs. The spots on the outer webs of the quills are fulvous brown, paler on the inner; the cross bands on the two central tail feathers are indistinct, and the plumage is generally finely mottled with light brown all over; the tips of all tail feathers are white; below, on the sides of the breast, and on the abdomen, most of the feathers are centrally streaked brown, each being marked with three cross bars."

This species, as far as is yet known, is confined to the Himalayahs, I have seen it from as far west as Murree. Eastwards I only know of it as far as Darjeeling. Capt. G. F. L. Marshall shot one at Kussowlee, at a height of only 5000 feet above the sea, and this is the lowest level at which I have known it to occur.

No. 67. **Otus Vulgaris.*** FLEM.

THE LONG EARED OWL.

As yet nothing has been recorded of the breeding of this species in India, but I have reason to believe that it is a per-

---

* OTUS VULGARIS.

DIMENSIONS. Male, (*killed Bhoondsee* 20-3-68.) Length, 14·5. Expanse 36. Wing, 11·1. Tail, 5·6. Tarsus, 1·45. Mid toe to root of claw, 1·1; its claw straight, 0·65; hind toe, 0·65, its claw, 0·53; inner toe, 0·92; its claw 0·63. Bill, straight, from forehead to point, 1·1; along curve 1·33; from gape 1·1; height at front, 0·58. The second primary is the longest; the first, 0·8 and the third, 0·1 shorter. Lateral tail feathers 0·55 shorter than central ones. Wings reach to 0·5 beyond end of tail. Lower tail coverts to within 1·8 of ditto.

Female (*killed Darjeeling* 6-11-69). Length, 16·2. Expanse, 40·5. Wing, 12·2. Tail, 6·0. Tarsus 1·6.

DESCRIPTION. *Bill*, blackish brown. *Cere*, fleshy. *Claws*, horny black, paler at bases. *Irides*, bright yellow, to orange.

manent resident of the forests of the interior of the Himalayahs. Mr. Yarrell gives the following account of its nidification in England: "The long-eared Owl is said not to make a nest for itself, but to take to the deserted habitation of some other bird, when of sufficient size for its own wants; and has been known to rear its young in the old drey of a Squirrel. The eggs are four or five in number, oval, smooth, and white; one inch, eight lines and a half long, (1·7) by one inch three lines and a half in breadth, (1·29). The young are hatched by the end of April, are then covered with white down, and do not quit the nest during the first month."

Mr. Tuke says that, in Yorkshire, "it takes possession, about the middle or end of March, of the deserted nest of the Crow,

---

Plumage. Chin pure white. Lores and feathers over the anterior half of the eye, white, (in some slightly yellowish white) the feathers more or less dark shafted towards the tips or tipped with dark brown; eye-lashes and spot at the anterior angle of the eye, and feathers just above the posterior half of the eye, deep or blackish brown; cheeks and ear coverts, pale yellowish to reddish buff, the feathers white shafted towards the base and often black shafted or blackish brown towards the tips. Forehead, crown and occiput, deep brown, the feathers margined, with pale yellowish or reddish buff, and freckled and mottled with white, often leaving scarcely any portion of the deep brown visible. In some the brown is paler and the amount of white freckling varies much in individuals. The ear tufts are from one-half to two inches in length, deep brown, margined, with buff at their bases, and generally on the inner webs towards the tips, with white. The back of the neck and upper back, varies from pale yellowish white to reddish buff, broadly streaked with a lighter or darker brown. The scapulars, wing coverts, and upper tail coverts deep brown, more or less margined or tinted towards the margins with pale fulvous or reddish buff, and irregularly mottled and freckled with white or greyish white, which in some specimens occupies the greater portion of the surfaces of the feathers. There is generally a very conspicuous edging of buff or buffy white to the outer scapulars, some of the coverts and the outer feathers of the winglet. The tail feathers are buff towards the base, grey or grey brown towards the tips, with irregular, mottled, transverse, brown bars, the interspaces too being similarly freckled and mottled. The quills, similar. The feathers of the ruff are white or buffy white but tipped with blackish brown. The breast and abdomen, pale yellowish, or rufous buff with broad, central, dark brown stripes, and more or less conspicuous but ill-defined, white spots on either web towards the tips, and on the abdomen, with one or more narrow, transverse, wavy, brown bars, and a little freckling of the same colour. The tibial and tarsal plumes are the same colour as the rest of the lower parts but entirely unspotted. The wing lining varies from rufous buff, to pure white, one or two of the feathers at the edge of the wing have dark brown, lanceolate, central stripes.

The tone of colouring varies a good deal in different individuals, as does the amount of the white or greyish white freckling of the upper surface, and the white on the lower surface. In all, the rufous buff, at the base of the first few primaries, is rather conspicuous on the outer webs.

Ringdove, and perhaps that of the Squirrel, in a Scotch or Spruce fir tree, on which, after flattening and sometimes lining with a few feathers, are deposited its two or three beautifully white eggs. It is curious to observe how flat they invariably make their nests, so much so, that in even a slight wind, it is difficult to conceive how the eggs retain their position when the parent bird leaves them." This species, however, is one of those, of which the female begins to sit, from the moment she lays the first egg, and a great difference in the ages of the young, is generally observable.

Macgillivray tells us that "it generally appropriates the deserted nest of a Rook or other large bird, but sometimes forms one for itself, and lays from three to five eggs, which are elliptical, 1·75 in length by 1·33 in breadth, smooth and of a pure white colour."

This species is not entirely nocturnal, nor does it confine its depredations entirely to moles, mice and insects. Mr. Tuke already quoted, remarks:—

"We have met this species in the woods, sailing quietly along, as if hawking, on a bright sunny day, and invariably found in or around the nest, feathers and other remains of the winged race. In one case, a freshly killed Chaffinch, in another the wing of a Snipe, and several smaller birds and in a pellet the indigestible pad of a young Hare or Rabbit."

Of the distribution of this species in India, Dr. Jerdon says *in epist*, "The long-eared Owl is by no means rare in low jungles near Delhi, and thence through the Punjab, during the cold weather. I always found several together."

I can confirm this, having received a specimen killed at Bhoondsee, Zillah Gourgaon, and another from near Hansee, both killed in the cold weather. They are far from uncommon about Darjeeling, at any rate during the early part of the cold weather; whether they remain in the Himalayahs throughout the year I cannot say, but I received a specimen killed near Narkunda in June, and Dr. Stoliczka notices their being found in the forests near Nachar.

Out of India, this species appears to be found throughout Europe, Northern Asia, and the northern and central portions of North America.* It occurs in Northern Africa including Egypt, Asia Minor, and Afghanistan, and specimens from Hakodadi (Japan) are said to be absolutely identical with European ones.

* Some writers have separated the American race, but the birds appear to be identical.

No. 68. **Otus Brachyotus.*** Gmel.

The Short Eared Owl.

This is another species, whose eggs do not as yet appear to have been taken within our limits. Mr. Hoy (I quote Mr. Yarrell) says, of the nidification of this species in Norfolk, "I have known several instances of their eggs and young being found. One situation is, on a dry heathy soil, the nest placed on the ground amongst high heath; the other in low fenny ground, among sedge and rushes; a friend of mine procured some eggs from the latter situation during the last summer."

Mr. Yarrell continues—"The eggs of this bird, seldom exceeding three in number, are smooth and white, one inch eight lines (1·67) in length by one inch three lines and a half (1·29) in breadth."

---

* Otus Brachyotus.

Dimensions.		Length.	Expanse.	Wing.	Tail from vent.	Tarsus.	Mid toe to root of claw.	Its claw, straight.	Hind toe, to root of claw.	Its claw, straight.	Inner toe, to root of claw.	Its claw, straight.	Bill, straight, from edge of cere.	„ from gape.	Distance by which closed wings exceed end of tail	Distance by which lower tail coverts fall short of end of tail.	Weight.
Male.	From	14·50	36·50	11·75	6·00	1 36	1·20	0·62	0·62	0·50	0·62	0 61	0·58	1·05	0 25	1·00	oz. 10
	To	15·00	39·75	12·50	6·80	1·80	1·26	0·72	0·72	0·60	0·80	0·71	0·63	1·25	1·00	1·90	oz. 13
Female.	From	15·00	40·00	12·00	6·25	Other measurements not recorded.											oz. 14
	To	16·00	42·00	13·30	7·10												lboz. 1 1

(Five males measured and weighed.)

The 2nd primary the longest. The 1st is 0·30—0·75 shorter, the 3rd 0·20—0·45, shorter. Exterior tail feathers, 0·30—0·60, shorter than central ones.

Two nests which Sir William Jardine found on an upland moor in Dumfriesshire, and which contained five eggs, were formed upon the ground among the heath, the bottom of the nest scraped, until the fresh earth appeared, on which the eggs were placed, without any lining or other accessory covering.

Audubon says—"The only nest of this kind that I have found contained four eggs of a dull bluish white, and of a somewhat elongated or elliptical form, an inch and a half in length, and one inch and one-eighth in breadth. The nest which was placed under a low bush and covered over by tall grass, through which a path had been made by the bird, was formed of dry grass, raked together in a slovenly manner and quite flat, but covering a large space."

Hewitson figures a broad, oval, bluish white egg, 1·68 in length, by 1·3 in width.

This species, so common throughout India, would not appear to extend to Ceylon; and though by no means uncommon in Lower Bengal, Assam and British Burmah, would not seem to extend southwards to the Malay Peninsula or the Archipelago. One of the most widely distributed of its whole family, this species occurs almost throughout North America, throughout Europe, the islands of the Mediterranean, portions of North Africa, Egypt, Asia Minor, Mesopotamia, in Russian Asia, almost to the mouths of the Amoor, Northern China and Japan. In many of these localities, as in the plains of India, it is merely a winter visitant, and I have been unable to ascertain the most southern limit at which it has been found breeding. Radde mentions, that it is a common bird throughout the south of East Siberia, where he often found it breeding, and that in the Daurian Steppes, he found fresh eggs as early as the 20th April, and others scarcely incubated by the 25th of May.

It seems scarcely likely that this species breeds in India, south of the Snowy Range, but the high grassy table-lands of Thibet are probably the brooding haunts of the myriads of short-eared Owls, which are so widely distributed over the plains of India, during the cold season.

No. 69. Ascalaphia Bengalensis.* FRANKLIN.

THE ROCK HORNED OWL.

This species breeds as a rule, in February, March, and April, but eggs are occasionally met with in both December and

---

* ASCALAPHIA BENGALENSIS.

DIMENSIONS. (*The sexes do not appear to differ sufficiently to make it worth while giving the dimensions separately, but the females are usually somewhat larger.)*

Length 21 to 23. Expanse 52·5 to 58·0. Wing 14·75 to 16·0. Tail 8·25 to 8·75. Tarsus, 2·94 to 3·25. Foot, greatest length, 4·2 to 4·35; greatest width, 4·2 to 4·38; mid toe to root of claw, 1·5 to 1·82; its claw straight, 1·06 to 1·92; hind toe, 0·81 to 1·00; its claw straight, 0·8 to 0·88; inner toe, 1·65 to 1·72; its claw straight 1·05 to 1·12. Bill straight, from margin of cere to point, 1 to 1·06; from gape, 1·7 to 1·76; width at gape 1·45 to 1·56; height at front, at margin of cere, 0·58 to 0·61. Wings when closed, reach to within 1·5 to 1·9 of end of tail. Lower tail coverts reach to within 1 to 1·25 of end of tail. The 4th Primary is the longest; the 1st is from 1·5 to 2; the 2nd from 0·45 to 0·55; and the 3rd from 0·06 to 0·2 shorter. Exterior tail feathers from 0·7 to 0·85 shorter than central ones.

DESCRIPTION. *Legs and feet* feathered; the toes *above* only, but almost to the very points, where there are 3 large transverse scales on the inner, and 2 similar ones on each of the other toes; the scales greyish horny. Soles with prominent pads, thickly covered with prominent papillæ, a sort of buffy white. Claws dusky almost black, lighter at the roots; inner edge of mid-claw dilated into a narrow knife-like edge. *Irides* narrow, of great diameter, intense orange yellow, brightest internally. *Bill* horny black. *Tongue* rather short and broad, fleshy, somewhat spatulate. The tip obtuse and slightly emarginate.

The lores and sides of upper mandible at base are occupied by two dense tufts of nearly pure white bristly feathers having the webs much disunited, and having the extreme tips black; the shafts of most are prolonged as bristles. They completely overhang the nostrils and reach to within from three-eighths to one-fourth of an inch of the end of upper mandible. The edges of the eyelids are brown, the eyelids bluish white and bare, except for 2 dense rows of short feathers near the margins, with very disunited webs, which are white with the tips of most of the shafts, blackish on lower and posterior half of upper lid, and brown on anterior portion of the latter. Feathers of forehead, immediately overhanging the upper mandible, and the anterior one-third of eye very similar to those of the lores. A broad band of similar feathers, but tinged with pale buffy brown, from near the base of the egrets, behind and below the eye, embracing the ear coverts, and every where bounded posteriorly by a narrow dark brown band, which commencing above the eye, runs to the base of the egrets, and thence downwards behind the ear, to a little below the gape. Forehead, top and back of the head a sort of umber brown, with whitish marginal and terminal spots giving a mottled appearance; these spots are much larger proportionally and more buffy towards the front of the forehead, where the brown almost disappears; the warm buffy tint of the bases of the feathers shows through a good deal in some, towards the back of the head. There is an ill-defined, mottled, buffy streak from above the eye, above the dark brown band, to the very base of the egret, up the interior

January, and in the lower valleys of Gurhwal, according to Mr. R. Thompson, may be met with as late as the end of May.

side of which it almost seems to run, since a portion of the inner web of the longest and the outer webs of some of the shorter are buffy or buffy white. The rest of the egrets (which are some $2\frac{5}{8}$ long) are a rather darker brown than the top of the head. The sides of the head and upper part of sides of neck for about 1 inch behind the dark brown band are mingled buff, buffy white and brown, no colour showing clearly, but the feathers if closely examined, are mostly buff at the base, and whitish towards their extremities where there are 2 or 3 narrow, wavy, brown, transverse bars. The chin is occupied by a dense tuft of feathers similar to those of the lores, (but entirely white) which curve out quite to the end of the lower mandible. There is a similar tuft on each side of the lower mandible, and a line of similar feathers round the gape, and running up (overhung and nearly hidden by the buffy, or brownish white feathers below the eye) to the lores; from where the narrow dark brown line terminates a little below the gape, a broad, irregular band of buffy feathers with darker or lighter brown central streaks runs right across the throat, separating the white of the chin from a pure white, somewhat triangular patch in the centre of the throat or upper neck in front. The feathers of the rest of the neck all round are a rich buff colour with more or less white towards the tips, and conspicuous, broader or narrower, central stripes of dark brown. The upper back, shoulders, scapulars, median, secondary and tertiary greater coverts, are brown, varying somewhat in shade but still dark, with two or more, mottled, or even freckled pairs of large spots or incomplete bars, of white, buff or buffy white. The tertiaries are similar, but having a much lighter and more rufous ground colour, and more of the mottled incomplete bars. The extreme edge of the wing is white, and the immediately adjoining feathers much mottled, with a rich buff, but the lesser wing coverts as a whole are a rich dark brown, towards the tips (which alone show) with only one or two pairs of rather small, buff, or fulvous white, irregular, marginal spots, and this is the character of the winglet. The greater coverts of the primaries are a rich rufous buff at the base, and dusky brown at the tip, the centres banded with freckled and mottled bars of both colours. The primaries are the same rich rufous buff, tipped with a lighter shade of dusky brown, which tips are much longer in the first than in the succeeding primaries. The first two primaries have the whole outer webs banded brown and rufous buff, freckled with brown, but in the succeeding primaries the rufous buff above the tips is nearly pure except for two or three, narrow, brown, bands towards the end on the outer, and one or two similar ones on the inner webs. The dusky tips themselves are a good deal banded and freckled, especially towards the secondaries, which want the well marked dusky tips, and, with a less pure rufous buff ground, have about four or five brown bars on the outer and three or four on the inner webs, the interspaces on the outer webs being a good deal dashed with white and mottled and freckled with brown. The central tail feathers resemble the outer webs of the later secondaries, the lateral ones their inner webs. The brown bars growing narrower and narrower on each succeeding feather, as they recede from the centre. The second primary is clearly and the third slightly emarginate on the outer web, and the three first, the first especially, are conspicuously notched on the inner webs. The inner surface of the quills except at the tips or where the bars show through, is a delicate, pale, rufous buff, almost salmon colour, as are also the larger lower primary coverts, which have dusky tips. The edge of the wing, as above noticed, is white, the rest of the wing lining is rufous buff, the median lower coverts

The birds make no nest, but merely scoop a small hollow in the earth, in which to deposit the eggs. Occasionally, they will lay on the level ground under some over-hanging bush or tuft of grass, but almost without exception, they choose some little cave or recess in, or projecting ledge or shelf of, some rocky or earthy cliff in the neighbourhood of water. The precipitous banks of canals and rivers, are perhaps their favorite brooding-places, and as my friend, Capt. G. F. L. Marshall, first pointed out to me, they (in northern India) almost invariably select a cliff face looking westward.

The normal number of the eggs is perhaps four; but I have often found three and, more than once, only two eggs much incubated.

The eggs of this species appear, comparatively speaking, very uniform in size and shape. Very perfect broad ovals, white with a faint creamy tinge, they are, but for a slight superior glossiness, scarcely distinguishable from those of *B. Ocellata.* In texture, they are finer than the eggs of *A. Coromanda,* and for the size of the bird, seem to me decidedly small. I note that I can scarcely believe that the egg figured by Bree as that of *A. Savignyi* really belongs to that nearly allied species. The egg being barely two-thirds the size of the smallest *A. Bengalensis* I have yet seen.

The eggs of the Indian species, vary from 2·05 to 2·20 in length, and from 1·65 to 1·8 in breadth, but the average of ten eggs measured is 2·10 by 1·73. The egg figured by Bree is only 1·54 by 1·34.

This species is very common in the Saharunpoor district, especially towards the North, and from thence Mr. G. Marshall sent me the following account of its nidification.—" The Rock Horned Owl breeds from December to April, the middle of March being the best time for searching for its eggs. On one occasion only, I found the eggs on the level ground, on a plain, at the

---

broadly but irregularly margined with slightly rufous or buffy white, and a few of those near the carpal joint, with ill-defined, brownish, sub-terminal spots. The lesser lower coverts, with faint, narrow, wavy, transverse, brown or rufous brown bars. The breast, abdomen, sides, flanks and lower tail coverts are a rich rufous buff, with very numerous, narrow, transverse, wavy, brown bars, darkest and closest on the sides and feeblest and widest apart on the lower tail coverts, and almost wanting in the immediate vicinity of the vent. The feathers of the upper breast adjoining the base of the neck, with conspicuous very dark brown (in some almost black) central stripes. The thigh coverts the same hue as the rest of the lower part of body, but altogether unspotted and unbarred. The tarsi and toe feathers, buffy white, also unspotted and unbarred.

foot of a tuft of grass; on every other occasion, I have found them on a ledge, in the perpendicular bank of a ravine, generally by the canal and, without exception, on the left bank facing the west. It lays four, very round, pure white eggs, slightly hollowing the ground to receive them, but making no attempt at a nest or even a lining to the hole. I have always found the nest close to water.

"I found	two fresh eggs,	on	16th December.
"	four set eggs,	"	3rd April.
"	two fresh eggs,	"	21st March.
"	two young birds,	"	3rd April.
"	four fresh eggs,	"	16th April.
"	two fresh eggs	"	28th March.
"	four half-fledged young	"	26th March.

"The birds keep close to water as a rule, and the male bird seldom wanders far when the female is sitting; they seldom perch on trees, and, during the breeding season, the male bird may be seen sitting on the top of the bank, somewhere near the nest, at all hours of the day. They are rather shy birds, and leave the nest at once, if approached."

Capt. Hutton remarks, that this species is "common along the foot of the hills in the Doon; I have had the young ones in March from a hole in a steep bank of a ravine, at Rajpur; in April also a man brought word, that he had found a nest, with nothing in it, but it was only just completed; waited for a fortnight, and sent a man to bring the eggs, but it again proved blank. The bird ascends sometimes in the summer to 5,500 feet."

Capt. Cock says, "Coming home on the 17th March, at Dhurumsalla, I took a nest of *Ascalaphia Bengalensis* with eggs. I shot the old bird. The nest was in a little cave in the face of a steep precipice full of little bones of rats and mice, one or two feathers, and only a slight depression in the sandy floor. Eggs hard set."

Mr. Blyth remarked in the Ibis for 1866, that the Indian species is "distinct from *A. Ascalaphus*, though closely approximating to that species. Dr. Jerdon omits to give the colouring of the irides, which are of a redder and deeper flame-yellow than those of a specimen of *A. Ascalaphus* at present in the Zoological Gardens."

Of the nidification of *A. Ascalaphus* (Savigni Tem.,) I quote the following from a paper of Baron Warthausen, which appeared in the Ibis for 1860. "This species has been observed by Heuglin in Upper Egypt and Nubia in pairs and in small companies; it breeds also in Lower Egypt, where Wilke found two nests on the pyramids of Abusir and Lakara on the 26th and 27th of March, 1858. Each of the cavities scratched in the sandy surface, at a shadowy but not dark locality, contained three fresh eggs.

"The eggs of the one brood are more elongated, those of the other more rounded; all having a very regular form, the greatest diameter passing through the centre and the profile descending the poles sometimes in a more gentle, sometimes in a more abrupt, elliptical curve. The length (*given in French lines*) varies between 22 (1·97) and 24 (2·13) lines, the breadth between 18⅓ (1·67) and 20 (1·80); the largest specimen is 24 (2·13) lines long and 20 (1·80) broad, the smallest, 22 (1·97) long and 19 (1·71) broad; the weight is 48 to 60 grains."

It will be observed that the dimensions of these eggs correspond precisely with those of our Indian birds, so that the egg, figured by Bree, must necessarily have belonged to some other species, but it is only fair to state that it is M. Moquin Tandon, who furnished the figure, and not Dr. Bree, who is responsible for this error.

Dr. Jerdon says, that the Indian species is found throughout India and Ceylon; but I cannot find it recorded by any authority from the latter locality. Eastward it certainly extends to British Burmah; but I do not find it noted from Singapore and the Straits, and it probably does not extend, to the Malay Peninsula; westward it has been sent from Afghanistan.

I have already at page 226, noticed the Hon'ble F. J. Shaw's apocryphal account of the breeding of this species. It is only explicable, as there suggested, by supposing that he intended to refer to *Spilornis Cheela.*

No. 70. **Ascalaphia Coromanda.*** LATHAM.

THE DUSKY HORNED OWL.

The vast majority of this species lay (in Upper India at any rate) in December and January, but I have found the eggs on several occasions in February and once early in March.

---

* ASCALAPHIA COROMANDA.

DIMENSIONS.		Length.	Expanse.	Wing.	Tail from vent.	Tarsus.	Mid toe to root of claw.	Its claw, straight.	Hind toe to root of claw.	Its claw, straight.	Inner toe to root of claw.	Its claw, straight.	Bill, straight, from margin of cere to point.	from gape.	width at gape.	height, at front, at margin of cere.	Distance by which closed wings fall short of end of tail.	Distance by which lower tail coverts fall short of end of tail.	Weight.	Length of cere on culmen.
MALE.	From	22·01	54·00	15·75	8·13	2·18	1·83	1·09	1·05	1·00	1·60	1·10	1·05	1·60	1·12	0·58	1·15	1·70	lb 3	0·51
	To	23·50	57·00	16·45	9·00	2·40	1·95	1·16	1·10	1·05	1·70	1·20	1·12	1·70	1·28	0·60	3·75	2·00	4	0·65
FEMALE.	From	23·00	56·00	16·90	8·75	2·30	1·83	1·16	1·01	1·00	1·65	1·20	1·09	1·65	1·12	0·59	1·75	2·00	4	0·60
	To	25·00	60·00	17·50	9·25	2·56	2·00	1·25	1·13	1·12	1·80	1·30	1·18	1·68	1·32	0·62	2·75	2·23	6	0·70

(Three males and three females, measured, and weighed.)

The third, fourth, or third and fourth primaries the longest. The first is 2·70 to 3·20 shorter, the second 0·90 to 1·10, and the third nil to 0·90 shorter. Exterior tail feathers 0·25 to 0·60 shorter than central ones.

DESCRIPTION. *Legs and feet* feathered; the latter sparsely; terminal joint bare, pale grey, with one or two, large, soft, transverse scales. Claws, black. Irides, deep yellow. Bill, greyish white, or pale lavender, with the tips and culmen, pale yellowish horny.

Plumage. Upper parts, except primaries and tail feathers, earthy brown; in some specimens greyer, in others more umber; often considerably darker on the head, lesser scapulars, and interscapulary region. The feathers of the head, nape, interscapulary region, and often many of the scapulars and lesser coverts with narrow, ill-defined, dark brown, shaft stripes; all the feathers, more or less vermicillated very finely with excessively narrow, irregular, imperfect, wavy bars of a paler colour, producing a freckled appearance. This pale colour, is in some a dull fulvous white, in others grey, in others pale greyish brown; in some this marking is very conspicuous; in others, it is almost obsolete, especially about the shoulders. The long ear tufts, which in some specimens are fully 2·75 inches long, are of the same dark brown as the narrow, central, shaft stripes, which brown varies much in shade, in different

As a rule, they construct stick nests (which from the same pair resorting to them for many successive seasons, and adding to them yearly, are at times enormous) in the fork of some large tree. At times they appropriate some old nest of the Tawny Eagle *(A. Fulvescens)* placed in some thick and thorny, but comparatively low Acacia tree. In most cases, the nests contain some lining of more or less green leaves, and a few feathers or a little grass. Occasionally I have found the eggs laid in the hollow of some huge stump, or in the depression at the fork of three or more large branches, with no stick nest, and only a few dry leaves as a bed, but out of more than thirty nests that I found one December in trees along the banks of the canal near Hansee and Hissar, all but one were regular stick structures. One nest contained no lining but a little dry earth. The great majority of the nests, that I have examined, contained two eggs, often much incubated, but I once found three, and have heard of four being met with. In two instances, I see by my notes that single fully incubated eggs were found. The eggs of this bird vary surprisingly in size and shape. Typically they are a broad oval, comparatively very large for the size of the bird, but long, oval, pyriform and nearly spherical varieties occur. I have taken a very great number of these eggs myself, and have extreme sizes of which the cubic contents of the one are fully double those of the other. In colour they are a decidedly creamy white, in texture often somewhat coarse, but, withall, more or less glossy. I have many specimens greatly exceeding

---

specimens, being in some, very dark, almost black, in others a moderately dark hair brown. There are large white, or pale yellowish white patches, on the outer webs of the exterior scapulars, and towards the tips of most of the larger and median coverts. The tail is a dull rufous fawn, nearly pure white towards the tip, with four, and on the central feathers, generally five, broad, transverse, umber brown bands, darker in some, lighter in others, and the pale interspaces on the central tail feathers are much freckled, and in some cases entirely suffused with the same colour; this freckling occurs, though in a less degree on the succeeding feathers, the interspaces growing clearer and brighter as they recede from the centre. The primaries are similar to the tail feathers, the tips infuscated or freckled like the central ones, and the interspaces clearer and brighter towards the bases.

The lower parts are greyish white, with a faint yellow tinge, everywhere except on the middle of the throat, each feather with a narrow dark brown shaft stripe, and with numerous very fine, wavy and freckled transverse greyish brown bars, or vermicillations. The extent and depth of colour of these delicate markings vary much in different specimens, in some almost entirely obscuring the ground colour on the breast and abdomen.

Tibial and tarsal plumes yellowish or pale fulvous white, in some specimens with faint, longitudinal, dark brown streaks, and in others with narrow, clouded, imperfect, transverse bars of the same colour.

in size the egg of *Bubo Maximus* figured by Hewitson, while I have one specimen scarcely exceeding the egg of *S. Stridula* which he figures.

The eggs vary from 2·2 to 2·55 in length, and from 1·75 to 2 in breadth, but the average of 56 eggs measured was 2·33 by 1·89.

In this species I have invariably found the female sitting, but the male is always near at hand, and very commonly sitting on some branch immediately above the nest. I once shot a female, sitting on a partly incubated egg and on skinning her, found a second egg in the oviduct ready for expulsion, I have repeatedly taken one perfectly fresh, and one partially incubated egg out of the same nest, and it seems clear that these birds, like the Harriers and many Owls, begin to sit directly the first egg is laid.

Capt. G. Marshall remarks,—"The Dusky Horned Owl is rather rare in the Saharunpoor district. I shot one at Seengrah, one at Shamlee, one at Kulsea and one at Dhalapie; this last I shot at *four o'clock in the afternoon*, it had a freshly killed Teal in its claws, which it was eating from the head downwards when it was killed. It breeds in hollow trees in February. I have taken but one egg, round and white, it was in a hollow formed by a rotten stump of a Toon tree in the Kulsea compound, about fifteen feet from the ground."

I can, from personal observation, confirm the above remarks, as to this Owl's being by no means strictly nocturnal. I have on several occasions killed it in the act of devouring birds, or rats, early in the afternoon, and have repeatedly seen it hunting along the banks of the canal, a good hour before sunset.

This well-marked species has been most unaccountably confounded by European writers with other distinct species or grouped, with very different types. Mr. Blyth had the following remarks on this subject in the Ibis for 1866. "The late Prince Bonaparte associated this bird with *Huhua Orientalis* (erroneously placing *H. Pectoralis*, Jerdon, as a synonym of the latter,) in the 'Revue de Zoologie' for 1854 (p. 542). Prof. Kaup also, as strangely associates *A. Coromanda* with *Huhua Nipalensis* and *H. Orientalis*, as also the African *Bubo (?) lacteus* (Temm.,) in his division *Urrua*, while *A. Bengalensis* and *A. Ascalaphus* are assigned by him to typical *Bubo! A. Bengalensis* happens to be the type of *Urrua* of Hodgson. The irides of *A. Coromanda*, in all that I have seen and kept alive, were of a bright deep yellow, rather than 'orange-yellow' as Dr. Jerdon asserts."

Mr. Blyth is certainly correct in giving the irides as deep yellow.

This is perhaps, if we except *Athene Brama*, the most common species of Owl in the North West Provinces. As far as my experience goes, it is most common in comparatively open country, greatly affecting mango topes, so common in Upper India. It is perhaps most numerous in the narrow belts of trees which fringe our canals. In such localities about Christmas time, a nest may be found, on an average, in every mile of canal, and in the Western Jumna Canal where the trees are somewhat old, I have met with half a dozen pairs in a morning's walk. The birds seem to be omnivorous; no doubt rats and birds, especially the latter, are their favourite food, but I have found in their stomachs remains of both frogs and jungle lizards *(Uromastix)*.

They doubtless occur, as Dr. Jerdon says, in the lower ranges of the Himalayahs, but I have never happened to come across them in the North Western portions of the hills (they have I know been sent from Nepaul) and my impression is, that they somewhat eschew dense forests, and much prefer open and well cultivated, and watered, though of course tolerably well-wooded, country.

Eastward they extend to Tipperah and into British Burmah, but not, it would appear into the Malayan Peninsula or further south. In Rajpootana, and the North-West Punjab they are excessively rare, and I can find no record of their having been found west of the Indus.

No. 70 BIS. **Bubo Maximus**,* SIBBALD.

THR GREAT EARED, HORNED OR EAGLE OWL.

Strix Bubo, LINN. LATH. *&c.*, *&c.*
Bubo Atheniensis, DAUDIN—*B. Europæus*, LESSON.

Dr. Jerdon says in his appendix, "*Bubo Maximus* of Europe, or a pale variety of that bird, occurs in the higher region of the

---

* BUBO MAXIMUS.

DIMENSIONS.—(From Macgillivray.)

Male.—Length, 24. Expanse, 58. Wing, 19. Tail, 11. Tarsus, 2·75. Bill, along ridge, 2·5. Cere, 0·92.

Female.—Length, 26. Expanse, 61. Wing, 20. Tail, 10. (somewhat worn). Tarsus, 2·75. Bill, along ridge, 2·42. The 3rd primary the longest; the 1st 1·67; the 2nd, 0·17; and the 4th, 0·08 shorter. Central tail feathers exceed external do. by 1 inch.

Himalayas, but apparently along the snow line. A specimen was sent to the Museum of the Asiatic Society by Capt. Smyth

---

DESCRIPTION.—*From Macgillivray.*) *Bill* greyish blue at base, bluish black towards the end; the cere dusky; soft edges of the mandibles flesh coloured, as is the inside of the mouth. *Irides* bright orange; bare edges of the eyelids and margins of the nictitant membrane dusky. Scutella pale greyish blue; claws of the same color as the bill; soles, pale flesh colour.

The bill is short, very robust, considerably compressed; the cere rather large, and nearly bare, although concealed by the feathers in the neighbourhood.—The nostrils are large, broadly elliptical, oblique, divided by a soft projecting ridge, their greatest diameter four-twelfths of an inch.

The tibia is rather short, the tarsus short, robust, and with the toes feathered. The first toe very short, the second considerably longer than the fourth, and in about the same degree exceeded by the third; the two latter connected by a short web; all with three terminal scutellæ, and their lower surface padded and papillate.

Plumage.—The plumage is very full, soft, blended and elastic.

The facial disks extend round two-thirds of the eye, leaving the upper part covered with shorter feathers; those at the base of the cere are linear, with strong shafts and bristly filaments.

The ruff extends from a little above the ear to the chin, and is formed of oblong, slightly curved feathers. Over and above the eye, on each side is a double series of elongated feathers, of which there are nine in each row, the longest projecting upwards of two inches beyond the rest of the plumage.—On the outer side of the tibia is a tuft of very soft elongated feathers.—The facial disks are pale yellowish brown, faintly barred with dusky; their anterior part greyish white, with the shafts black at the end. The feathers of the lower eyelid are greyish white, of the upper chiefly black. Those over the eye, and the long tufts, are brownish black, internally edged or mottled with reddish. The general colour of the upper parts is reddish yellow, spotted, barred, and minutely dotted with dark brown. On the lower part of the hind neck, most of the feathers have only a median longitudinal blackish brown band. The small wing coverts at the flexure, the alula, and the primary coverts, are almost entirely dusky. The quills are barred with brownish black, and in the intervals yellowish red, nearly pure on the inner webs, but on the outer closely and minutely undulated with brown. The tail is similar, but with less yellow. The feathers on the upper part of the throat are white; a band of barred and mottled feathers then crosses the throat, being continuous with the ruff; and on the middle of the neck is a white patch with some dusky spots. The rest of the neck is reddish yellow, each feather with an oblong, brownish black, longitudinal band, and transverse, lateral, undulated bars. On the thorax and sides, the feathers are similar, the central dusky patch gradually becoming narrower, and on those farthest back ceasing; while the narrow, transverse bars become numerous in the same proportion. The large tibial feathers and lower tail coverts are greyish yellow, mixed with red, and barred with dusky; those of the tibiæ more tinged with yellow, and more faintly barred. The downy or concealed part of the plumage is dark greyish blue.

The following description is extracted for comparison from the Naturalist's Library. "The disk and ruff are small and incomplete, greyish black, tinted with ochraceous, and margined round the occipital edges with black. The egrets which are fully two inches long, are deep black, slightly edged with ochraceous

of Almorah. Blyth, however, informed me that Hodgson's Shikarees, when in Calcutta, recognised *Bubo Maximus*, as a species which they knew."

I have never seen an Indian-killed specimen of this species, but the Shikarees who yearly shoot birds in Spiti, Kooloo, and Lahoul, assert the existence of a large Horned Owl, feathered to the claws, which can scarcely be other than *B. Maximus*. For convenience of reference, I extract from European writers some accounts of the nidification of this species, and append dimensions and description.

Mr. Yarrell says,—"The nest of this bird is large, the materials collected being spread over a surface of several square feet, among rocks or the walls of old ruins. The female is larger than the male, and produces two or three eggs of a short oval shape, two inches five lines (2·42) long, by one inch ten lines (1·83) wide, and perfectly white."

Mr. Hewitson tells us that the Eagle Owl breeds in the north of Europe, making its nest upon the bleak and unsheltered summit of some lofty mountain; in such situations Linnæus found their nests and young ones, and he quotes from Linnæus' journal of May 17th, the finding three young birds, and an egg, on a little grassy plot encircled on three sides by rocks, but open to the south, on the steep southern side of the

---

yellow on the inner sides. The whole upper parts, including the wings and tail, have a ground shade of ochraceous yellow, with the centre of the feathers black, which broadens at the tips, and at the sides is shaded off in light wavy mottles of a similar tint. On the greater coverts and secondaries, the markings assume the form of indistinct bars from their greater crowding, while along the shaft, the dark colour is continuous. The quills on the inner webs are of a brighter tint of ochraceous, and are there crossed with distinct narrow bars of black; on the outer webs, the bars, though distinct, are yellowish brown, clouded with a darker shade, and generally edged next the ground colour with an irregular darker margin; towards the tips the dark colour predominates, and is there mingled with gray. The ground colour of the tail is paler than that of the quills, and it is crossed with mottled bars of brownish black; the pale spaces towards the tips, and on the centre feathers, being also thinly mottled; on the inner webs the bars are very narrow. When viewed from the lower side, it is much paler in colour, the bars appear all narrow, and the mottling on the intermediate spaces scarcely appears. On the under parts of the body, the same ochraceous tint prevails; the chin is white; on the throat, breast, and belly, the feathers are broadly streaked with black, which breaks off to the sides in interrupted bars; on the other parts of the belly, vent, flanks, and under tail coverts, the shaft is black, and the feather is crossed with numerous irregular bars of brownish black, nine or ten sometimes being counted on one feather. The tarsi and toes are clothed as in *Otus*, and are crossed with indistinct bars of brownish black. The irides are brilliant and bronzed orange.

highest mountain in Medalpad. Mr. Wolley, whom he also quotes, gives an account of finding two young ones and an egg, on the 20th of May, on a ledge of a rocky precipice. The young and the egg "lying upon a small quantity of compressed fur, principally of rats, the remains of the castings of the parent birds, their bed nearly flat, for there was not more than two inches of soil. The ledge was not more than two feet wide, and terminated abruptly just beyond the nest. I have visited three other sites of nests of this bird, and they were all of similar character, upon ledges in, or over cliffs. They were all unsheltered over head, sunshine seeming rather to be courted than avoided."

Eagle Owls, in confinement, have bred, laying, in all the cases noticed by Mr. Gurney, three eggs; "which may be assumed," that gentleman remarks, "to be the normal number of their eggs."

Mr. Hewitson figures a pure white egg, 2·17 in length, by 1·94 in breadth.

Little seems to be known, of the habits of this species, except that it affects mountainous and wooded countries, and preys upon quadrupeds and birds, such as fawns, hares, and grouse.

As to its distribution I can, at present, add nothing to the following remarks of Mr. Yarrell.—"The bird inhabits Denmark, Sweden, Norway, Lapland, Russia, and the Continent of Europe generally, but particularly the fir-covered mountains of Switzerland, and the high rocky country of Aragon, extending southward as far as Italy, Turkey, Corfu, and Sicily. Mr. Strickland saw specimens at Smyrna, and it is recorded as inhabiting the Morea. Pennant says, it is found as far to the eastward as Lake Baikal and Astrakan; and Mr. Gould has seen skins of this bird in collections from China."

No. 71. **Huhua Nipalensis.** HODGSON.

THE FOREST EAGLE OWL.

Nothing seems to be known about the nidification of this species.

I have never myself killed the bird, nor can I throw any light upon the question of the identity or distinctness of the Northern *Nipalensis* and the Southern *Pectoralis*, Jerdon. Dr. Jerdon himself is now, I believe, inclined to consider them distinct. Mr. Blyth made the following remarks on these two races, and the allied *H. Orientalis* (Horsf. in the Ibis for 1866.) "The *Bubo pectoralis* of Cassin's 'Catalogue of *Strigidæ*' is distinguished from his *B. Nipalensis*, which latter is placed as a synonym of *B. Orientalis*, and is moreover from the Himalaya. Now *Huhua Nipalensis* is a very much larger bird than *H. Orientalis*, and is, otherwise conspicuously distinct from it The only question that remains is, whether *H. Pectoralis* of Jerdon, figured in the 'Madras Journal of Literature and Science' (Vol. X. p. 89, pl. 1,) from Southern India, be distinct from *H. Nipalensis* of the Himalaya. A juvenile Tenasserim specimen of this genus forwarded by Col. Tickell to the Asiatic Society's Museum, Calcutta, was incorrectly assigned by me to *H. Orientalis* (J. A. S., B. XXVIII. p. 411) as corresponding to the description of *Strix Sumatrana*, Raffles, (Trans. Linn. Soc. Vol. XIII. p. 279) and also Temminck's figure of the immature plumage of *Orientalis* (P. C. 289); but I erroneously added *H. Nipalensis* and *H. Pectoralis* as synonyms, as again in the Ibis for 1863, p. 26. The same nestling bird was described* by Col. Tickell as *Ptiloskelos Amherstii*. It should be referred decidedly to *H. Nipalensis*."

---

* The following is Tickell's description of the young bird.

"Nestling—Sex not distinguishable. Length, 15·5. Wing, 10·5. Tarsus, 1·75. Femur, 4·25. Bill, 1·81. Iris sepia. Bill and feet, pale flesh colour, the latter with a yellowish tinge. Claws, blackish horny. Head, neck and body, including scapulars and wing coverts dirty white tinged more or less deeply with orange tawny. Each feather marked near its end with an arrow-headed bar of sepia. Head and nape with spots of the same. On the breast these marks take the form of wide, broken bars, lapping round the neck. Wing coverts also, irregularly barred. All the plumage is immature and deciduous, but the remiges (which usually at once assume the permanent colouring) are ashy sepia, barred broadly and softly with full sepia, with marbled interspaces. Downy plumes of legs white."

No. 72. *Ketupa Ceylonensis. Gmel.

The Brown Fish Owl.

This species breeds from December to March, but the majority lay I think in February. They always nest in the vicinity of

---

* Ketupa Ceylonensis.

Dimensions.		Length.	Expanse.	Wing.	Tail from vent.	Tarsus.	Foot, greatest length.	,, greatest breadth.	Mid toe to root of claw.	Its claw, straight.	Hind toe, to root of claw.	Its claw, straight	Inner toe, to root of claw.	Its claw, straight.	Bill, straight from edge of cere.	from gape.	width at gape.	height, at front, at edge of cere.	Distance by which closed wings fall short of end of tail.	Distance by which lower tail coverts fall short of end of tail.	Weight.	Length of cere.
																					lboz	
Male.	From	21·00	54·00	15·00	7·60	2·80	4·60	4·90	1·75	1·03	1·00	0·90	1·40	1·10	1·10	2·00	1·65	0·60	Nil.	2·00	2 ,, 4	0·65
	To	22·00	56·00	15·70	8·00	3·10	4·80	5·10	1·85	1·13	1·10	1·00	1·55	1·22	1·25	2·10	1·80	0·70	Nil.	3·00	3 ,, 2	0·81
Female.	From	22·00	56·00	16·50	7·80	2·80	4·75	4·9	1·75	0·98	1·00	1·00	1·45	1·10	1·15	1·95	1·65	0·65	Nil.	2·00	3 ,, 0	0·68
	To	23·50	59·00	18·00	8·50	3·25	4·90	5·2	1·98	1·13	1·10	1·06	1·60	1·35	1·42	2·20	1·81	0·72	Nil.	3·00	4 ,, 4	0·80

(Three males and three females measured and weighed.)

The fifth primary the longest (fourth and sometimes third and fourth subequal. The first is 2·5 to 4·75 shorter, the second 0·70 to 1·40, and the third nil to 0·50, shorter. Exterior tail feathers 0·45 to 1·3 shorter than central ones.

Description. *Legs and feet,* (tarsus feathered in front, for from 0·5 to 1·00, but the leg bare behind for from 0·25 to 0·6 above the joint), a dingy greenish grey, light greenish, or sometimes plumbeous. Three large scutæ at the end of each toe, the rest of the upper surface of the toes, and tarsus, with small prominent reticulated scales. Papillæ of the soles of the feet harsh and much developed, reminding one of the soles of an Osprey. Inner toe and claw, nearly as long and stouter than the mid toe. Claws bluish grey at the base, horny black beyond; mid claw with two sharp edges developed, one on the inner side, and one beneath; other claws round or elliptical in section with a sharp knife-like ridge developed below. *Irides*

water, sometimes choosing a cleft in rocks overhanging a mountain stream, sometimes a broad shelf in the clay cliffs of some

---

bright yellow. Iris very narrow, but of large diameter. Orbits, with a dense double row of bristly, black shafted, white feathers, with the bare shafts considerably elongated. The rest of the eyelids bare; the upper greenish, the lower greyish brown.

Cere greenish grey. *Bill* dingy greenish; point of the upper mandible blackish horny; of the lower mandible yellowish.

Plumage. Lores with a huge patch of bristle-like white feathers with greatly elongated black bare shafts overhanging the commissure and meeting over the base of the cere; some of them almost if not quite as long as the bill itself. The whole of the forehead, top and back of the head are a somewhat pale pinkish brown, each feather centred darker. The feathers above the ear coverts on each side, behind the eye, lengthened so as to form aigretttes or ear tufts from an inch and a half to two inches in length. The feathers of the back of the neck often a *somewhat* darker shade, more broadly shafted with a still darker brown, and most of the feathers with a trace of wavy mottling or obscure bars especially towards the tips on the lighter brown portion. Upper back and scapulars much the same hue, and dark centred in the same manner, as the feathers of the back of the neck, but most of the exterior feathers of the scapulars where they overhang the lesser wing coverts with nearly the whole outer webs white, and the lighter brown of the scapulars and in a less degree of the feathers of the upper back very much mottled and variegated with tiny wavy lines and small irregular blotches of fulvous white. Lower back, rump, and upper tail coverts much the same hue as the upper back, but with only a central line of dark brown and very feebly mottled with fulvous white. All the lesser wing coverts, the same brown as the upper back, with similar broad dark brown centres, with a few spots of fulvous white on some of the longest. The median coverts mostly dark brown towards the shafts and on the inner webs, with one or two well marked spots of white or fulvous white on the latter, and the outer webs mostly white or fulvous white, freckled or mottled with paler brown. The winglet and primary coverts chiefly dark brown with two or more imperfect transverse bars of fulvous white or paler brown. The greater coverts of the secondaries much the same as the preceding, but the outer webs much tinged with pale fulvous brown, and there is more white and more mottling about them than the preceding. The primaries are dark brown tipped with fulvous white and with four or five $\frac{1}{4}$ to $\frac{3}{4}$ inch transverse bars, of white, fulvous or rufescent white, on the outer, and pale brown across the inner webs. The secondaries have much the same character as the primaries, but the bars are closer and larger in proportion and are more conspicuously mottled, and as a whole generally appear to have more white upon them than the primaries. The tertiaries and their coverts like the greater coverts of the secondaries are a paler and more fulvous brown, much marked with imperfect bars or blotches of fulvous white mottled with brown. The tail feathers are dark, somewhat umber, brown tipped with rufous or fulvous white, and with three or four comparatively narrow transverse bars of the same hue, most of the bars showing marks of faint mottling with a darker colour. Under the eyes and ear coverts, is a conspicuous patch of elongated, bristle-like rufous brown feathers with dark shafts; on the point of the chin is a patch of white bristle-like feathers, with elongated bare black pointed shafts, which curl up round, and are nearly as long as the lower mandible. The feathers of the rest of the chin and a patch

river, sometimes a huge cavity in some old Banyan tree, and at times appropriating an old nest of *Haliaetus Leucoryphus.*

Where they make their own nest, on a ledge or recess of a cliff, it consists of little but a few sticks, mingled with a few feathers, or when in holes of trees, of a few feathers and dead leaves, but when they annex an old nest of the fishing Eagles, (and I have several records of this) they seem to line it more carefully with finer twigs, grass and feathers. I have never found green leaves under the eggs of this species.

Normally they lay two eggs; I have altogether records of nine nests, and in none of these were there more than two eggs or young ones.

The eggs are very perfect, broad ovals, white with, in most specimens, the faintest possible creamy tinge. The shell close-grained and compact, freely pitted all over its surface, but nevertheless more or less glossy. They seem to me undistinguishable from many of those of *Ascalaphia Coromanda.* In size they vary from 2·29 to 2·44 in length, and from 1·84 to 1·94 in breadth, but the average of nine eggs measured was 2·3 by 1·88.

Mr. G. Marshall writes: "This bird is pretty common in the Saharunpoor district, it lays two, round, white eggs, and returns year after year to the same nest. I found one nest in a hollow in the fork of a Banyan tree about twenty-five feet from the ground, the hollow being so deep, that the parent bird, sitting, could not be seen from the ground on any side. I found it accidentally, as I was climbing the tree for another nest. I watched it for three years; in 1866, on the 10th April, I found

---

on the throat immediately below it, pure white, with, towards the tips, a dark brown central streak, and three or four narrow wavy bars of reddish brown; the feathers on each side of this patch, on the sides and front of the neck, breast, abdomen and flanks, a somewhat rufous or pinkish brown, each feather with a narrow well defined central streak of very dark brown and closely barred throughout its whole length on both webs with narrow transverse wavy bars of a somewhat darker brown than the ground colour, though much lighter than the central streak. Thigh coverts and evnt feathers uniform fulvous or brownish white. Lower tail coverts very pale brown or fulvous white, streaked and barred like the body feathers. I note that the bars are closer and more numerous on the breast, where the general tint is also more vivacious, and the reverse of this, on the flanks and lower tail coverts. The wing lining somewhat, similar to the body feathers, but much less narrowly banded and altogether lighter; the greater lower coverts, however, of the primaries are pure white, broadly tipped with blackish brown. Lower surface of the quills glossy brown, darkest on the primaries, tipped with greyish white and with three or four transverse bars, of greyish white, growing yellower as they approach the bases, where the inner webs are mostly yellowish white.

it with two young ones; in 1867, I visited it on the 17th March, and again found young ones; in 1868, on the 24th February, I found two eggs, the first of which was hatched on 14th March, the other egg I took. The tree in which the nest was, was a very large one, in a small grove of Jamun trees, on the bank of an extensive jheel near Sirsawar."

Mr. Brookes mentions that he "shot a female on the 25th of February, sitting on two addled eggs. What little nest there was, consisted of sticks, and was placed on a shelf of the clay cliffs of the Jumna, in the Etawah district. The shelf was slightly overhung, and on it, within twenty yards of the Fish Owl, a Neophron had her nest." Towards the end of July, I found a pair of these Owls with two fully grown young ones, in a tiny cave in the rocky and precipitous banks of the Kosila, near Kakuree Ghat. The cave, the mouth of which was veiled by a large down-trailing Andromeda bush, had obviously been their nesting place, and though well concealed, was easy of access. There were a few sticks covered over with castings and remains of numerous birds and bones of small mammals. I turned the whole family out of their quarters, but did not otherwise molest them, an act of forbearance which I later had cause to regret, as they ceased not, the livelong night through, to give forth the most vociferous protests (from the cliff face, immediately above my tent) against, as I *suppose*, my neglect to honour them with a place in my museum.

On January 11th, 1867, I visited a large nest in a Peepul tree overhanging the Jumna below Sheregurh, in which, both in 1865 and 1866, to my personal knowledge, a pair of *H. Leucoryphus* had reared their young. To my surprise, it was tenanted by a pair of *Ketupa Ceylonensis*, which had carefully relined the nest, and had at that time a solitary young one in it, some seven days old, a ball of whitish down. On the nest we found two Quails, a Pigeon, Doves and a Mynah, all with the heads, necks and breasts eaten away, but with the wings, back, feet and tail remaining almost intact. Two or three of them were quite dry, and one which I still have, is quite as good a specimen, as most of those that I owe to an eminent naturalist, who appears to preserve his birds by first pulling out half the feathers and then having what remains, carefully run over, on very dirty ground, by a heavy cart wheel!

On the banks of the Sutledge and again near Bhurtpoor I found nests which I had been led to as those of *H. Leucoryphus*, occupied by *K. Ceylonensis*.

I have never yet had certain evidence of their feeding on fish.

I have invariably found the remains of birds or small animals, about their breeding places.

This species is nowhere I believe numerically *very* common, and in the plains of Upper India it is rare as compared with *A. Bengalensis*, or *Coromanda*. I have generally found it in rocky, broken or raviny ground, and it most affects, according to my experience, the craggy banks of streams and rivers, where it roosts, during the day, near the base of some dense bush growing out of the face of the cliff.

It occurs pretty well throughout India, from Ceylon to Afghanistan on the one hand, and Darjeeling on the other, extending into Assam and British Burmah, where Mason mentions that it "often lifts up its boding notes of *tee-douk*, uttered with sepulchral tones at midnight, and like a ventriloquist, seems to throw its voice to any point of the compass at pleasure."

There are, however, wide tracts in the continent of India, in central Rajpootana for instance, where it appears never to be met with, dry almost treeless, sandy plains, or bare rocky ridges, that do not suit the fancy of this water loving Owl.

Westwards it *probably* will be found in Persia and Mesopotamia; in Palestine it *has* been obtained; but on this head I shall content myself with reproducing the remarks of Mr. Tristram, its discoverer there, "We can only point to one locality as the certain residence of this bird in Palestine. It is perhaps the most interesting addition, as well as the most unexpected, which we made to the fauna of the country, and was found by us in the wild wooded glen of Wady el Kurn, running up from the Plain of Acre. We discovered it accidentally, and at first took it for the *Bubo Ascalaphus*, when it bolted out of the dense foliage of a great Carob tree, under which we were standing; we thus put up no less than four individuals in two days. When disturbed, the bird was more than ordinarily perplexed, even for an Owl; but owing to the difficulty of crossing the gully and the dense jungle, we were only able to secure a single specimen which had been put up from a Carob tree by Mr. Bartlett, and was marked by me, on to a ledge of rocks on the opposite side of the Wady. The Wady possesses a perennial stream, well-shaded by ever-green timber, and swarming with fish and crabs, the favorite and probably exclusive food of the *Ketupa*." This appeared in 1866. Writing on the same subject in 1868—Mr. Tristram says, "The most interesting of the Indian non-Ethiopian species, is *Ketupa Ceylonensis;* and the occurrence of this great fish-eating Owl is the more exceptional, as there are no *strigidæ* in Africa bearing the least affinity to this well marked genus, and since it has not yet been found in the Jordan valley, but only sedentary by the streams of the coast."

Eastwards, Mr. Swinhoe informs us that, this species is a constant tenant of the dark rocky ravines of Hong Kong. He sent a specimen home, which was identified by Dr. Sclater as *K. Ceylonensis*, so that no doubt can remain as to this point. Southwards in Malayana, it seems to be replaced by the two following species *K. Flavipes* and *Javanensis*.

No. 72. BIS. Ketupa Javanensis.* LESSON.

THE MALAY FISH OWL.

Strix. Ketupa. Horsf. Trans. Lin. Soc. xiii. p. 141.
„ Ceylonensis. Tem. P. C. 74.
Scops Ketupa. Cuv. Reg. An. I. p. 347.

Nothing has been recorded apparently of the nidification of this species. It occurs in Burmah certainly, and must, therefore, find a place in these notes. Mr. Blyth says, that it is a species "which occurs (perhaps as a straggler) on the eastern side of the Bay of Bengal as high as Arakan, in Ramri Island, together with *K. Ceylonensis;* but further southward, it is the common Fishing Owl of the Malayan Peninsula, and undoubtedly the supposed *K. Flavipes* referred to as "common in the Indian islands and Siam" by Mr. F. Moore. Prof. Schlegel does not assign either *K. Ceylonensis* or *K. Flavipes* to the Malayan sub-region; but Mr. Cassin notes a specimen of *K. Ceylonensis* from Java, which is doubtless a mistake. Col. Tytler has inadvertently written *Javanensis* for *Ceylonensis* in

---

* KETUPA JAVANENSIS.

DIMENSIONS AND DESCRIPTIONS *(adapted from Temminck)*. Length 16 to 19·25.

Legs and feet yellowish. *Bill* dusky. *Irides*, yellow?

Plumage. The general colour is a somewhat orange, light rufous (or bright rufous buff). The lower parts, with long, blackish brown, central stripes; the throat pure white; the head, egrets, and back of the neck, similarly marked to the breast, but the stripes broader and closer set; the back, scapulars, and wing coverts, with broad, very closely set, imperfect, transverse, black or blackish brown, bars. The quills and tail feathers, blackish brown, intersected at wide intervals by somewhat narrow, rufous yellow bars, and all tipped whitish. The face, reddish buff, the feathers dark shafted, and at the sides of the disk tipped with blackish brown.

his remarks on the fauna of Barrackpore near Calcutta, (Ann. and Mag. Nat. His. 1854, XIII., 366)." In a note to this, the Editor of the Ibis remarked that Mr. S. H. Gurney agrees with Mr. Blyth in considering *Ketupa Flavipes* of North Eastern India, distinct from *K. Javanensis* of the Malay Archipelago, as though the colouring of the two is similar, the former is fully a third larger than the latter. Mr. Blyth added that besides the difference in size, the upper portion of the tarsus of *Flavipes* is clad with short downy feathers. As I shall notice when dealing with the latter, the front and exterior of the tarsus in that species are feathered to within less than an inch of the foot in a specimen in my museum, while in a specimen of Javanensis, I find only the front of the tarsus feathered downwards for less than 0·75 from the tibia-tarsal articulation.

The following passage, occurs in Finlayson's MS. (quoted in Horsfield's Catalogue, as referring to *Flavipes*) in regard to the present species.

"This is a heavy, clumsy bird, but very powerful. It is usually seen on the wing in the twilight. It is common in the Indian Islands and at Siam."

This species does not extend far into the Archipelago, but is confined, out of Burmah, Siam and the Malay Peninsula, to the Indo-Malay Islands, Sumatra, Java and Borneo, not extending apparently to the Philippines.

No. 73. Ketupa Flavipes. Hodgson.

The Tawny Fish Owl.

Dr. Jerdon tells us (quoting from Mr. Hodgson,) that this species breeds in February and March, which is highly probable, but I have not been able to find any more circumstantial account of its nidification.

Mr. Hodgson says, "This species is common in the several regions of Nepaul, notwithstanding the great diversity of climate. They fly well by day, and are constantly found on the banks of rivers. I have procured specimens with the stomach full of fish, and they also prey on crabs. Their weight is about three and a half pounds. These birds moult once a year between June and October inclusive."

I notice that in this species, the tarsi are feathered much further down than in *Ceylonensis*. In the only specimen which I possess, the whole tarsus is feathered in front and exteriorly to within less than an inch of the foot.

As far as is yet known, this species is confined to Nepaul and Sikhim. I cannot learn that it has ever been procured in Kumaon; but I have recently been informed that it has been killed near Cherapoonjee, but as I have not seen the specimen, I cannot vouch for the fact. Mr. Blyth remarks that it is *K. Javanensis*, and not the present species, as Mr. Finlayson's Manuscript notes, quoted in Horsfield's Catalogue, assert, that is common in the Indian islands and Siam.

No. 74. **Ephialtes Pennatus.*** HODGSON.

THE INDIAN SCOPS OWL.

The Indian species of Scops Owls are, as Kaup justly remarks, exceedingly difficult to discriminate, and my collection

---

* The following are the dimensions and description of a specimen in the rufous stage.

DIMENSIONS. Length, 8·25; expanse, 15·5; wing, 5·7; third and fourth primaries longest; first 1·1, and the second 0·3 shorter; tail, 2·5; tarsus, 1·0; mid. toe to root of claw, 0·8; its claw straight, 0·39; hind toe, 0·39; its claw, 0·32; inner toe, 0·65; its claw straight, 0·4; bill straight, from edge of cere, 0·5; from gape, 0·8; width at gape, 0·65; height at margin of cere, 0·32; length of cere, 0·32; closed wings reach to end of tail; lower tail coverts fall short of end of tail by 0·7.

DESCRIPTION. The legs and feet dingy fleshy; irides, yellow; bill, greenish horny, and yellowish on lower mandible.

Plumage. The prevailing colour is a very bright chestnut, a few of the feathers on the forehead and above the eye, are greyish white, and the loral bristles are white, tipped with chestnut and black, a few of the feathers of the crown have the shafts dark brown, one row of the exterior scapulars are tipped blackish brown, and have the outer webs yellowish white. The primaries which are of a duller and paler chestnut towards the tips, have the outer webs above the tips broadly barred with yellowish white and dark brown; the brown bars being, if I may so term it, hollow, namely dark at their margins, and chestnut coloured or buffy inside. The inner webs are mottled and barred with dusky and yellowish fawn, the secondaries and tertiaries are more or less barred, irregularly and cloudily about the tips. The tail chesnut like the rest, though somewhat paler than the back, with four or five, ill-defined, narrow, dusky, transverse bars. The edge of the wing at the carpal joint is white; the outer webs of one or two of the feathers of the winglet are white, barred brown and chesnut. The chin is whitish, the whole of the throat, neck, and ruff, chesnut like the upper parts, only one or two of the feathers of the ruff broadly dark shafted towards the tips. Feathers of the breast and sides, chesnut, dark shafted at the tips where also they are mottled and freckled with pure white. The whole of the feathers of the abdomen, flanks, and vent, with dark shaft stripes, and with delicately mottled and freckled, chesnut and rufous brown, transverse bars upon a pure white

is too weak to permit of my solving *all* difficulties as I should wish. The plumage in all, varies so much in different individuals of the same species, and is of a nature so difficult to convey a really correct idea of, by mere verbal description, that the confusion that appears hitherto to have existed, in regard to this beautiful little group, can be no matter for surprise. As far as the specimens before me enable me to judge, we have six distinct species in India. Two with slender tarsi of the *Pennatus* type, and four with stouter tarsi, larger birds of the *Lempigi* type.

I shall now briefly enumerate these six species, noticing one or two of the chief points of difference.

(A) with slender tarsi.—

1 EPHIALTES PENNATUS Hodg. *Feet feathered to base of toes. Wing 5·5 to 5·75, reaches to end of tail; third and fourth primaries longest.*

2 „ GYMNOPODUS. Gray.? *Feet and extreme point of tarsus, bare. Wing 5·25 to 5·5, extends over three-fourths of tail; fourth and fifth primaries longest.*

(B) with stout tarsi.—

3 EPHIALTES LETTIA. Hodg. *Toes quite bare, or only just over-hung at their bases by the feet feathers. Wing 6·6 to 7·2.*

4 „ PLUMIPES. Nobis. *Toes feathered, in some, half way down the terminal point, in all, to end of sub-terminal point. Wing, 6·7 to 7·3.*

5 „ GRISEUS. Jerdon. *General tone of plumage greyer and more silvery. Wing, 5·6 to 6·63.*

6 „ MALABARICUS. Jerdon. *General plumage darker and more rufous. Wing 5·5 to 6·0.*

Other differences are noticeable in tone of color, proportional length of primaries, &c., which I shall notice, in dealing with each species, the above will, I believe, suffice to enable any one to determine to which species any specimen he possesses may belong: that is, provided that there are no *other* Indian species of Scops Owl, but as my collection at present only contains twenty-three representatives of this group, I cannot feel at all certain as to this point.

Of the present species *(E. Pennatus)* I have never yet taken the eggs, but Mr. R. Thompson to whom I owe an undoubted

---

ground. Tarsal and tibial plumes plain rufous fawn colour, with a few tiny brown spots towards the ends of the tarsi. The wing lining is chesnut and buffy white, indistinctly barred with dusky brown.

specimen of this species in the rufous phase, informs me that "they breed from March till August, in holes of trees, usually at no great height from the ground." He adds, "this is a common bird in our forests, (Gurhwal,) but I never yet took the trouble to take their eggs. Several pairs used to breed in the Botanical Gardens at Seharunpore. A pair has been breeding for three seasons in a small tree in front of the forest Bungalow at Kotedwara. Four years ago, a young one, in the rufous phase, was brought to me in the month of July."

Dr. Jerdon's description of this species in both phases of plumage appears to me sufficiently correct, and the specimens that I possess agree, so far as the quills are concerned, with Kaup's subgenus Scops. The third and fourth quills are the longest, the first is emarginate on the inner web, and the second and third only slightly so. The wing, which is comparatively long and pointed, reaches to the end of the tail, whereas in the next species, as I shall notice further when dealing with that, the fourth and fifth quills are the longest, and the wing which is much rounded only extends over, at most, three-fourths of the tail.

Capt. Hutton remarks that *Ephialtes* "as a genus, was long since pre-occupied in Entomology, and ought, therefore, to be changed, unless it has been banished from the nomenclature of that branch of Natural History." I hope that some of my English correspondents will decide this question for us.

I reproduce Mr. Blyth's remarks on this species, which appeared in the Ibis for 1866; premising merely, that *E. Gymnopodus*, Gray, is I believe a good species (*vide* No. 74 Bis) and Indian, and that I am almost certain, for reasons that I shall explain when dealing with that species, that Mr. Blyth's own *E. Spilocephalus* is in reality identical, *not* with *Pennatus*, but with *Gymnopodus*.

"74. Ephialtes Bakkamæna (Pennant); *Otus Scops Japonicus*, Schlegel (Faun. Japon. *Aves* tab. IX.); *Scops Zorca Asiatica*, Idem. Mus. P. B. *Oti*, p. 30.

Of this small Indian Scops Owl, the Calcutta Museum can show a very complete gradation from the grey *Scops Pennatus* to the bright chestnut or ferruginous *S. Sunia* of Hodgson; or if one semilink in the chain be wanting, it is supplied by an Indian specimen referred to the European Scops Owl by Mr. F. Moore. The specific identity of *S. Pennatus* and *S. Sunia* is certain, and they cannot even be admitted as different races; yet Mr. G. R. Gray (in his B. M. Cat. of Birds of Nipal, 2nd edit., 1863) adopts *S. Sunia* for the rufous bird, while the grey bird (with *S. Malayensis*, A. Hay, and *S. Spilocephalus*, nobis, as synonyms) he refers to the European *E. Scops*. Mr. F.

Moore makes the same confusion. I am decidedly of opinion, as I have before stated (Ibis., 1863, p. 27), that the proper name for the Indian bird, whether grey or rufous) is *E. Bakkamæna* (Pennant.) It is the only Scops Owl which I know of as an inhabitant of Lower Bengal, and I have occasionally obtained specimens in a curious way; they would lodge by day within the moveable "leaves" of a *jilmil* (or "Jalousie"), in which singular retreat I have captured them. I have also known *Mus. Flavescens* to resort by day (with the vain notion of concealing itself) to the same very insufficient hiding place. Of course the *jilmils* being a little open, to permit of their ensconcing themselves, the animals intercept the light from without, and are so discovered.

The Indian (or more probably Chinese) *E. Gymnopodus*, Gray, is surely no other than *E. Bakkamæna* (*vide* Ibis, 1863, p. 27); but the Malacca race (*S. Malayensis*, A. Hay) seems to be somewhat different, and I have not found it to vary in shade of hue; while in India the rufous specimens are certainly more common than the grey; I even think, considerably so."

I have not as yet adopted Pennant's specific name, because I have been as yet unable to satisfy myself that *E. Bakkamæna* is really identical with *Pennatus*.

Whether the supposed rufous phase of this species be *really* a mere phase of plumage, and *not* a characteristic of a distinct species, I am by no means certain. My friend Capt. Hutton (who, however, mis-calls this species *Lempigi*, while he calls *E. Gymnopodus*, *E. Pennatus*) informs me that he has on several occasions obtained the nestling as rufous as the parents. Further observation is necessary, and should the rufous variety prove entitled to specific separation, it will form a seventh species of Indian *Ephialtes*, under the name of *E. Sunia*, Hodgson. As for what Mr. Blyth says about the Calcutta Museum exhibiting a complete series between *Pennatus* and *Sunia*, I can only say that I could find nothing of the kind in February, 1868; the rufous and grey specimens that I saw, exhibited no indication of grading the one into the other; every single example being separable at a glance, as pertaining unquestionably to the one or other race. Of course this in no way proves that Mr. Blyth is wrong, or that the rufous is *not* merely one phase of plumage; specimens that existed in Mr. Blyth's time may have been lost, or may have been put away where the Baboo in charge could not find them: all I mean is that I do not consider the identity of the two forms established, and that I hope ornithologists will endeavour to settle the question satisfactorily one way or the other.

I have seen this bird from various localities in the lower ranges of the Himalayahs from Kussowlee to Darjeeling, and concur in Capt. Hutton's remarks to me (*in Epist.*) that, "it is less common in its own haunts" than *E. Gymnopodus*, "it frequents valleys at about 3500 to 4000 feet, and generally near a stream of water."

It has a low soft call, very different from the bell-like notes of *E. Gymnopodus* and *Glaucidium Brodiei*, which, as Capt. Hutton has proved, are very similar, both being low, sweet, whistled ejaculations, if I may use the phrase.

This bird doubtless occurs in the Hilly ranges of Southern India, but all the specimens as yet sent me thence were either *E. Griseus*, or *E. Malabaricus*, which latter, it should be noted, *Mr. Blyth* identifies, and possibly correctly, with *E. Lempigi.*

No. 74. bis. **Ephialtes Gymnopodus.*** Gray ? (E. **Spilocephalus.** Blyth ?)

The Bare-foot Scops Owl.

I first received specimens of this species from Capt. Hutton, who had named it *E. Pennatus*, and my reason for believing it

---

* Dimensions. Length, 7 to 7·75; expanse, 14·5 to 15; wing, 5·4 to 5·6; fourth and fifth primaries the longest, the first 1·75, the second 0·9; and the third 0·35 shorter than the longest; tail 2·75; exterior tail feathers 0·4 shorter than the interior; tarsus, 1·2; mid. toe to root of claw, 0·7; its claw straight, 0·32; hind toe, 0·33; its claw, 0·27; inner toe, 0·6; its claw 0·38 bill straight from edge of cere, 0·4; bill from gape, 0·68, width at gape, 0·68; height at margin of cere, 0·26; length of cere only, 0·3; closed wings fall short of end of tail by 0·75; lower tail coverts fall short of end of tail by 1·1.

Description. The forehead and a broad stripe over the eye, pale rufous white or fawn colour, some of the feathers with a few minute brown spots towards the tip; loral bristles, pale fawn colour, more rufous *towards* the tips, and black *at* the tips. Feathers under the eye and ear coverts pale fawn colour, more or less tinged rufous, and freckled and mottled or imperfectly barred with brown; the top of the head, back of the neck, back, scapulars, rump and upper tail coverts and lesser wing coverts, with a more or less dark, rufous, fawn ground, very finely and closely freckled with dark, in some almost blackish, brown, the frecklings becoming confluent towards the tips of all the feathers of the head, and most of the feathers of the lesser wing coverts, and some of those at the back of the neck producing, especially on the first named parts, a regularly spotted appearance. An irregular, ill-defined, broad, white or yellowish white half collar at the base of the neck; most of the exterior row of scapulars, with the outer webs white or yellowish white, and tipped dark brown. The tail, rufous fawn, with about seven, broad,

to be identical with Mr. Blyth's *Spilocephalus*, is, that Capt. Hutton has a specimen, on the wrapper of which, Mr. Blyth himself wrote the name of *Spilocephalus*. Moreover, laid amongst specimens of all the other five Indian species of *Ephialtes*, it is the only one of which the head is truly and conspicuously spotted, recalling by the way, to a certain extent, the markings on the head of *Scotopelia Peli*, as figured by Mr. Wolf in Vol. I. of the Ibis.

Capt. Hutton gives the following account of the nidification of this species. He calls it *Pennatus*, it is true; but he has sent me beautiful specimens of the birds, which leave no doubt that the species referred to is the present one.

"This Owl occurs on the Himalayas, in the neighbourhood of Mussoorie, at an elevation of five thousand feet, and nidificates in hollow trees, laying three pure white eggs, of a rounded form, on the rotten wood, without any preparation of a nest. Diameter of egg, 1·19 × 1 inch. The nest was found on the 19th of March."

In some respects this species approximates to Athene, the fourth and fifth quills are equal and longest (and not the third and fourth as according to Jerdon they should be in *Ephialtes*) while the note is almost identical with, or at any rate is of precisely the same character as that of *G. Brodiei*. Capt. Hutton, who quite independently noticed the peculiar rounded shape of the wing, but from want of works of reference, identified this species

---

somewhat freckled, transverse, brown bars, most strongly marked towards the bases of the feathers, and becoming more or less obsolete towards the tips. The quills, rufous fawn, broadly barred and clouded with dusky brown, which, above the tips, suffuses the greater portion of the inner webs. The rufous fawn being replaced in three or four of the interspaces, of the outer webs, of the third to the sixth or seventh primaries, by slightly rufous or buffy white. The carpal joint of the wing whitish; the outer webs of the outer feather of the winglet and the tips of some of the secondary greater and median coverts, white, or faintly buffy white, with broad, irregular, brown bars. The chin and throat, rufous white, or pale fawn color, some of the feathers of the throat with narrow, somewhat irregular, transverse, brown bars, and all the feathers of the ruff tipped with the same colour. The breast, abdomen, and flank, pale rufous white or fawn colour very thickly freckled and vermicillated with dark brown, most thickly on the breast, somewhat more sparingly so on the abdomen and flanks, the markings becoming confluent in spots, towards the tips of some of the feathers. Tarsal plumes, more or less ferruginous, tibial ditto, rufous white; the whole more or less spotted or obscurely barred with dusky. The wing lining and axillaries silky yellowish white, except towards the edge of the wing, near the carpal joint, where the feathers are mingled rufous and dusky brown.

The general tone of colouring in some specimen, is darker and more rufous, in others paler and more buffy.

with *Pennatus*, proposed (*in Epist.*) to separate it under a new genus as *Athenoptera*, and should such separation be deemed expedient, the name is an appropriate one. The plumage, ear tufts and bare bristle-less feet, are, however, those of *Ephialtes*, while as far as my experience goes in *Lettia*, *Plumipes*, and *Griseus*, the fourth and fifth primaries are most commonly longest, and *not* the third and fourth. For the present, I prefer to retain it under *Ephialtes*.

Capt. Hutton remarks of this species :—

"This bird, if it be truly *Ephialtes Spilocephalus* of Blyth, and he wrote that name on the paper wrapper with his own hand, cannot stand under that genus if Jerdon's generic characters are correct, for while he gives third and fourth quills longest, this Mussooree bird has the fourth and fifth longest, as in Athene. I have lately examined six good specimens, and this character is apparent in all. It is a curious fact, moreover, that I have fully ascertained the double whistle so often heard in the hills, to belong, not to *Glaucidium Brodiei*, as has always been supposed, but to the present species; four have been shot while uttering the whistle "*who-who*" close to my house in fine moonlight nights, and three or four specimens of *G. Brodiei*, uttering a somewhat similar note of four syllables, have also been shot while uttering it; there is in fact no shadow of a mistake about it, and yet I, for one, have for many years attributed both notes to *G. Brodiei*, and could have sworn that the latter bird uttered the double note of "*who-who*," and that I had shot it while doing so. The fact is, however, that the two species being common, are often either found in the same tree or very near each other, and the collector following the sound, shoots whichever bird he sees first, and so confounds the notes.

"I do not believe in any red phase of plumage in this species, as we have taken the young from the nest, and found them and the parents alike,—while as regards *Ephialtes Lempiji*" (*this is really E. Pennatus*) "or what I take to be such from Jerdon's description, with which it agrees tolerably well, the nestling is red like the parent. The wing of *E. Lempiji*" (*should be E. Pennatus*) "however differs *toto cœlo* from that of the present species," (*viz.*, *E. Gymnopodus*). "In the former bird, the third and fourth quills are longest, and the wing reaches to the end of the tail, if not beyond it, whereas in the present species, the fourth and fifth quills are longest, and the wing is short, not far over-reaching two-thirds of the tail; in the former, the quills are pointed, in the latter, broad and obtusely rounded. At all events, whatever the true specific names, and I am by no means certain of these, they cannot stand under the same generic characters. Our present bird occurs abundantly at 5,500 feet, and probably higher; and the other species is not, by any means, so common, nor does it come up so high as this, and seems to be far more shy."

Again in another letter he says: "The note of *Glaucidium* is also a low whistle, but runs thus slowly like the other, 'hoo–hoo–hoo–hoo,' the middle note pronounced quicker, and joined while there is a pause between it and the others, as— 'o–o, o–o;' this I always knew belonged to *G. Brodiei*, but thought the other belonged to it also, until we shot the other birds uttering it."

He also remarks of the present species, that "it extends far into the hills, as I have procured it north of the Tyne range corresponding to Simla; Blyth was surely wrong in giving '*Noctua, auribarbis*, Hodg.' as a synonym of this bird, for Gray says that this was *A. Cuculoides*. The wing, however, is rounded, with the fourth and fifth quill longest, and the plumage and ear tufts those of *Ephialtes*. I took the eggs in April at Mussooree, at 5,500 feet."

The only specimens that I have seen of this species, some nine or ten in number, had all been procured in the Himalayahs, near Mussooree, in Gurhwal, and below Simla.

The entirely naked feet, feathered, if I might so express it, (though anatomically it is a misapplication of terms) only to the ancle, the conspicuously spotted plumage of the head, the short wings with the fourth and fifth primaries longest, alone suffice to distinguish this species, which, if *not*, as *I* believe it, *Gymnopodus* of Gray, must stand as *E. Huttoni*, in honour of the noble old naturalist, whose accurate observations I so often have to refer to, and whose life-long devotion to the study of God's glorious works, has scarcely yet been appreciated as it deserves. Fortunately he is one of those who look for something higher and better than "the praise of men."

No. 75. **Ephialtes Lettia,*** Hodgson.

The Nepal Scops Owl.

Two comparatively large species of Scops Owls are found in the Himalayas, the first *E. Lettia*, altogether paler and some-

---

* E. Lettia.

Dimensions. Length, 10 to 10·5. Expanse, 19 to 20. Wing, 6·6 to 7·2; fourth and fifth primaries the longest;—first, 1·6 to 1·9 shorter; second, 0·7 to 0·9 shorter; third, 0·25 to 0·4 shorter; length of tail, 3·2; longest tail

what more rufous in its tints; the eastern form, apparently not going further west than Kumaon, and most plentiful at Darjeeling; with toes quite bare or only just overhung at their

---

feathers exceed shortest, which are the exterior ones, by 0·2. Tarsus, which is densely and fully feathered, 1·4 to 1·5. Mid toe to root of claw, 0·95 to 1; its claw straight, 0·5; hind toe, 0·5; its claw straight, 0·4; inner toe, 0·8 to 0·9; its claw straight, 0·55. Bill straight, from edge of cere, 0·6 to 0·7; from gape, 1·0 to 1·05; height at front, at margin of cere, 0·35 to 0·39; length of cere, 0·3. Lower tail coverts fall short of end of tail by 1·5.

DESCRIPTION. The feet, in some greenish horny, in some yellowish fleshy; bill, yellowish horny, brown at tip and on side of upper mandible, and edge of lower mandible.

Plumage. The forehead, a broad streak over the eye running down the interior web of the aigrettes, feathers under the eye and most of the ear coverts, loral bristles and chin, white, with a greyish or yellowish tinge, most of the feathers tipped and some imperfectly barred with dark brown. The ear coverts in most specimens, much suffused with rufous, and the longest of them broadly tipped with a deep umber brown, which tippings form a continuation of the ruff band. The whole of the top of the head, and back of the neck, and the exterior webs of the aigrettes, back, scapulars, tertiaries, lesser wing coverts, rump, and upper tail coverts with a rufous fawn, or in some buffy yellow ground colour, everywhere (except on the outer webs of the outer scapulars, and in a broad irregular half collar at the base of the neck,) very closely and finely freckled, or irregularly barred, with minute, zig-zag lines of dark brown. Many of the feathers, specially of the head and aigrettes, with large, deep brown blotches, or irregular stripes or spots towards the tips, confined in the aigrettes to the outer webs. In some specimens these dark brown spots are peculiarly conspicuous on the tips of the comparatively unmarked feathers, which form the irregular half collar already referred to. The outer webs of the quills have the same ground colour, but as usual, palest on the first few primaries, with five or six broad, irregular, mottled and imperfect, transverse, brown bars, which are continued as perfect bars, on to the inner webs, where the interspaces are much mottled, and instead of having the clear fawn colored or buffy tint of the outer webs, are much suffused with brown, and towards the bases become almost obsolete. The outer webs of the secondaries also, have the buffy portions much freckled and mottled with brown. The tail might perhaps be best described as brown, with five or six imperfect and irregular, transverse, rufous fawn bars. The interspaces much freckled with the same color; the brown predominating at the bases, the rufous fawn towards the tips. The throat and feathers of the ruff are white, suffused with rufous fawn towards the tips, those of the throat with two or three, very narrow, transverse, brown bars towards the end, and those of the ruff broadly blotched at the tips with deep brown. The breast and the abdomen, are white, pale yellowish, or rufous white, closely but irregularly barred, with delicate, wavy, brown lines, and many of the feathers with irregular, dark brown, shaft stripes or lengthened blotches. The vent feathers and lower tail coverts are white with, in most specimens, one or more imperfect bars, at the tip. The tibial and tarsal plumes are similar, but the former are generally much more rufous, and the latter more purely white than the ground color of the breast, and the markings, always coarser than those of that part, are, in some specimens, close and regular, in others mere spots.

bases by the feet feathers; and the second *E. Plumipes* (Sp. nov.) as I provisionally designate it, altogether a darker and browner bird; the western form it would seem, from Dhurmsalla, Kotgurh and Simlah, extending to Gurhwal, with the toes *feathered*, (not *bristled* as in the Athene's), in some specimens, half way down the terminal joint, and in all, to the end of the *subterminal* one.

In size they do not differ greatly, but from the three* specimens of each that I possess, *Lettia* seems somewhat the bulkier bird, and *Plumipes* to have the longest wings and most powerful claws.

The only eggs that I have seen, unmistakably pertaining to this species, were taken on the 22nd May, 1869, out of a narrow cleft (completely hidden by a small drooping shrub) in an overhanging precipice, in the valley of the Surjoo, between Petoragurh and Almora, in Kumaon. They were described as laid on a few small sticks, or twigs, amongst which a few feathers were interspersed. In all other instances in which I have myself found, or have known of the finding of, the eggs of any species of Scops Owl in India, they have been in hollows of trees, but both parent birds were sent me in this instance with the eggs, and I had no reason for doubting my collector's good faith, who, although a native, is a very tolerable ornithologist, and so far as my experience goes, very careful and reliable. The eggs, three in number, were very spherical in shape, pure white and very glossy, and varied from 1·33 to 1·38 in length, and from 1·18 to 1·2 in breadth.

Two other eggs, *purporting* to belong to this species, were sent me from near Darjeeling. I cannot vouch for their authenticity. They measured 1·28 and 1·3 respectively in length, and 1·4 and 1·15 in breadth.

Mr. Blyth had the following remarks on this sub-group in the Ibis for 1866.

"Although Prof. Schlegel does not know of this species (*E. Lempiji*) as Indian, it is nevertheless common in Malabar and Ceylon, where it is undistinguishable from examples from the Malayan sub-region. It differs from the series next to be noted by its yellow irides.

This species is always paler and more rufous or more buffy than the next (*E. Plumipes*) and the dark blotches of the head, back, ruff and lower parts, are always smaller and much less conspicuous, but *inter se*, the specimens of this present species, vary a good deal in general tone of colouring, some being decidedly browner, some more rufous, and some more buffy.

* Since the above was written I have obtained several other specimens.

There is a series of three, very similar, dark-eyed races, of different sizes, and each having its respective range of distribution. The largest is *E. Rufitorques*, Bonap. (Faun. Japon. *Aves.*, tab. 8, where it is figured with yellow irides, which I suspect is a mistake): wing, 7 to 7·5 inches. The next is *E. Lettia*, Hodgson, of the Indo-Chinese sub-region, spreading westward along the lower regions of the Himalaya; wing, 6·5 to 7 inches. The third and smallest is *E. Griseus*, Jerdon, (*E. Lettioides*, nobis,) from the Coromandel or eastern Ghats of the Indian peninsula, where only it has been observed as yet, being replaced in the western or Malabar Ghats and in Ceylon by the golden-eyed *E. Lempiji:* wing, 5·5 to 6 inches only. I believe that all of these will have to be eventually recognized as specific races, as also *E. Rufescens* (Horsf.) (*E. Mantis*, S. Muller) from Sumatra, Java, and Borneo, and a much larger species which is otherwise very like it, *E. Sagittatus*, Cassin (Journ. Acad. Phil. II. pl. 12,) of which I have seen several specimens not differing in color, all of them from the Malayan peninsula. This fine Scops Owl bears just that relationship to *E. Rufescens* which *E. Rufitorques* does to *E. Griseus* (*E. Lettioides*,) and I should long ago have named it, had I not been under the impression that it was the true *Rufescens* of Horsfield."*

In regard to the above I must remark, first, that I somewhat doubt the identity of the Malabar Scops Owl (*vide 75 quatuor*) with *E. Lempiji*, Horsfield; secondly, that I do not attach much importance to the colour of the irides in this sub-group, this being unquestionably variable, in one species at least, *viz. E. Griseus*, in which I have observed them, dark brown, brownish yellow, and almost pure yellow; and, thirdly, that, as I shall more particularly note when speaking of that species, (75 tris) *Griseus* is not by any means confined to the Eastern Ghats, but

---

* "I have looked over Mr. Wallace's collection of Scops Owls (obtained by himself) and found no difficulty in resolving them into six species, *viz.*:—

(1.) *E. Sylvicolus* (Wallace,) Flores. The largest of them, a young specimen having the closed wing, 8·5 inches.

(2.) *E. Magicus* (Muller); *E. Leucospila*, G. R. Gray. From the Moluccas. Since identifying these, I have found that Professor Schlegel has likewise done the same.

(3.) *E. Menadensis* (Quoy and Gaim.) From Celebes and Flores.

(4.) *E. Lempiji*, Horsfield (*Strix noctula*, Reinw. and Temm.) Malayan sub-region, Ceylon and Malabar.

(5.) *E. Rufescens*, Horsf. (*Otus mantis*, Muller.) Sumatra, Java, Borneo.

(6.) *E. Malayanus* (A. Hay.) Malayan peninusula." (*See further*, p. 403.)

occurs in the Central and N. W. Provinces, the Punjaub and Rajpootana, in suitable localities.

As for the present species, *E. Lettia*, although very probably it does, as Mr. Blyth remarks, occur throughout the Indo-Chinese sub-region, all the specimens that I have yet seen were procured in the Himalayahs, in Sikhim, Nepaul and Kumaon at heights of from 3,000 to 5,000 feet above the sea; it seems to affect the warmer and more wooded valleys and preys largely on beetles and insects, these being the only contents of the stomachs of three specimens that I myself examined.

No. 75 bis. Ephialtes Plumipes.* (Spec. Nov.)

The Plume-foot Scops Owl.

Four eggs of this species, together with the female birds, were sent me from Kotegurh, where the latter had been captured on the eggs, in a hole in a tree. The eggs were taken on the 13th of May, and were partly incubated. They are intermediate in size between those of *Athene Brama* and *Athene Cuculoides*, but they are more spherical than either. They are of course pure white and slightly glossy. They do not appear to be quite as large as some of those of *E. Griseus* that I possess.

---

* E. Plumipes.

Dimensions. Length, 9·5 to 10. Expanse, 20. Wing, 6·7 to 7·3. The 4th Primary the longest; the 1st, 1·7 shorter; 2d, 0·8; and the 3rd, 0·2 shorter. Length of tail, 3; exterior tail feathers, 0·2 to 0·4 shorter than the interior feathers. Tarsus, 1·6 to 1·7. Mid toe to root of claw (feathered to base or middle of terminal joint) 1; its claw straight, 0·55: hind toe, 0·5; its claw, 0·5: inner toe, 0·8; its claw, 0·57. Bill straight, from edge of cere, 0·6; from gape, 0·92; width at gape, 0·92; height at front at margin of cere, 0·33; length of cere, 0 38; lower tail coverts fall short of end of tail, by 1·1 to 1·3.

Description. The full description given of *E. Lettia*, renders it unnecessary to describe this species at length. The toes fully feathered to the base of, or even half way down the terminal joint, alone suffice to separate it from all our other Indian Scops Owls, but I may remark that the general tint of colouring is darker, and as a rule less rufous or buffy, and the dark blotches on the head, back, ruff feathers, breast and abdomen, are larger and more conspicuous. The feathers of the throat and front of the ruff are also much more barred. I have never myself seen this bird alive, and therefore cannot give the colours of the irides and other parts which change in the dry specimens, nor can I, not having recorded them myself, *vouch* for the accuracy of those dimensions which cannot be checked from the dry skins, but I have no reason to doubt the correctness of those above recorded.

In size, they vary from 1·25 to 1·28 in length, and from 1·1 to 1·5 in breadth.

I have only seen four specimens of this species, one from near Murree, two from Kotegurh, and one from Gurhwal. I do not think, notwithstanding the marked and unmistakeable difference in their feet, (which in this species are feathered quite to the base of, and in some half way down, the terminal joints of the toes) that any one has hitherto discriminated this present species from *Lettia*, but now that the distinction has been pointed out, I hope that some of my co-adjutors will watch for it, and furnish further information about its habits and distribution.

No. 75 TRIS. Ephialtes Griseus.* JERDON.

This species breeds in the spring, laying three or four very round white eggs, in holes of trees, commonly more or less

---

* EPHIALTES GRISEUS.

DIMENSIONS. (*The sexes do not appear to differ in size. I have recorded numerous measurements of both males and females, and though the majority of the females are slightly larger than the majority of the males, I have measured males quite as large as any females, and females as small as any males.*)

Length, 7·88 to 8·5. Expanse, 20·5 to 21·5. Weight, 4 oz. to 6·25 oz. Wing, 5·6 to 6·63; the fourth primary the longest; sometimes the fifth and rarely the third sub-equal; the first, 1·25 to 1·63 shorter; the second, 0·5 to 0·65 shorter; the third from sub-equal to 0·06 shorter. Tail of twelve feathers; length from vent, 2·5 to 3·37; exterior tail feathers about 0·35 shorter than central ones. Tarsus from 1·06 to 1·19. Foot, greatest length, 1·63 to 1·94; greatest width, 1·63 to 2·06; mid toe to root of claw, 0·69 to 0·81; its claw, straight, 0·36 to 0·44; hind toe, 0·38 to 0·46; its claw, 0·31 to 0·38. Bill, straight, from edge of cere, 0·56 to 0·63; from gape, 0·88 to 0·94; width at gape, 0·75 to 0·78; height at front at margin of cere, 0·31 to 0·38; length of cere, 0·3 to 0·4. Wings when closed reach to within 0·31 to 0·75 of end of tail; lower tail coverts reach to within 0·9 to 1 of end of tail.

DESCRIPTION. Toes and claws very pale greyish brown, the latter darker at the points and not much curved, soles creamy white, pads and papillæ much developed and soft, scutellation obscure, three or four transverse quasi scales at the end of each toe; interior ridge of mid claw slightly dilated. Irides, in some, brownish yellow, in others, dark brown; in one nearly pure yellow. (*All the specimens whose irides I have described are now before me; these belong unmistakably to one and the same species, and are quite distinct from any of our other five species of Scops Owls, specimens of all of which are also before me.*) Bill; upper mandible dark brown, lower mandible paler especially towards the chin. Cere, dusky greyish, swollen and with circular nares pierced at the edge of the swollen ridge. Tongue, moderate, rather thin, of

lined with leaves and straw. The eggs are pure white, glossy, and very spherical.

---

equal width as far as the triangular tip, hastate at the base, and slightly divided at the tip.

Plumage. (A female caught on her eggs at Puhpoondh, Zillah Etawah, March 10th, 1867). A prominent tuft of disunited-webbed, bristly, white feathers (with dark naked tips to the shafts, and traces on those nearest the eye, of dark cross bars,) on each side of the upper mandible at its base. A faint tinge of buffy at the anterior angle of the eye, rest of lores, feathers below and behind eye, including ear coverts, loose webbed, silky, greyish white with traces of faint, minute, transverse, brown bars; chin white, the feathers of the extreme tip somewhat bristly and curving upwards round lower mandible. Across the throat and upwards immediately behind the ear orifice, as far as the base of the aigrettes, a band of creamy or pale buff feathers, with numerous, minute, transverse, wavy, brown pencillings and bars, those from the aigrettes to the sides of the throat with conspicuous, dark brown tippings, which form the defining line of the disk, and a few of those in the centre of the throat with similarly colored spots at the tips. Forehead and a broad supercilium running up the inside webs of the aigrette feathers, and a curved band at the back of the head, extending from the point of one aigrette, to the point of the other (when laid flat on the head), a silvery grey or greyish white, the feathers with dark brown shafts, and numerous, minute, transverse, pencillings of that colour, and some of them with terminal spots. Centre of forehead and top of head, a triangular space surrounded by this grey band, a rich dark brown, purest on the centre of the forehead, with small twin spots or imperfect transverse bars, and mottlings, to a greater or less extent, of pale buff. The outside webs of the aigrettes are similar, as are the feathers of the band, outside and contiguous to the curved grey band, which latter seems continuous with the dark line of the outer webs of the aigrette, while the former seems to start immediately above the centre of the eye. Below the dark band, at the base of the back of the neck, is another band of very similarly marked feathers, but whereas the dark brown predominates in the former, the buff much predominates in the latter. The back, rump, upper tail coverts, scapulars, wing coverts, except the greater ones of the primaries, a mixture of pale brownish grey, and pale buffy; with dark brown, central streaks, and numerous, transverse, wavy, brown pencillings, and mottlings. In the outside line of the scapulars, the buff is very pure, and in some positions conspicuous, and while the rump, upper tail and lesser wing coverts are dingier and greyer, the centre of the upper back and the median and secondary wing coverts show more of a pale buff. The primary greater coverts are very dark brown, with broad, transverse, buffy, mottled bars. The quills are darkish brown, with numerous, broad, transverse, greyish, more or less dingy, white bars, much more conspicuous on the outer webs; with the exception of a few bars on the upper portion of the outer webs of the earlier primaries, which are unmottled and slightly tinged with creamy, all the rest of these bars are closely mottled and pencilled with brown. The second, third and fourth primaries are just perceptibly emarginate on the outer webs, and the first to the fourth are conspicuously notched on the inner webs. The sides of the neck behind the dark line, the breast, sides, abdomen and thigh coverts, a sort of creamy grey, very soft and silky, the feathers with narrow, rich, brown, central streaks, and numerous, minute, irregular, wavy, transverse pencillings. Greater portion of wing lining, vent feathers, and lower tail coverts, silky greyish white, the latter, some of them,

Although I have taken the eggs of this species several times, I have, I regret to say, only one note on the subject "Puhpoondh" (Z. Etawah,) "March 10th, 1867. I caught a female *Scops Griseus* to-day on her nest, at least, on one egg, in a hole in a mango tree, which also contained about a dozen dry leaves and a few feathers, whether blown in by accident or placed there by the bird, I cannot say. The little animal bit and scratched so vigorously, that I had to use a cloth to get her out; she fought so valiantly for her penates, that I was sorry to sacrifice her, but it was important to preserve her skin to prevent future doubts as to the species to which the egg really belongs. She contained another fully developed egg, which my stuffer stupidly broke in skinning her. The egg was quite fresh, it looked a large egg as compared with those of *A. Brahma* (though it is shorter than some of these latter), owing to its great width. It is pure white, without any tinge, either of blue or cream colour, fine in texture, and almost as glossy as a dove's egg. In size and shape though a trifle more spherical than this latter, it corresponds almost exactly with Hewitson's figure of the egg of *Scops Aldrovandi*. It measures 1·25 by 1·15."

Mr. W. Blewitt found two nests, both in Sheeshum trees on the canal bank near Hansi. Both nests were in holes, the one contained one, the other two fresh eggs, a bed of leaves and straw being placed under the eggs. The nests were found on the 25th March and 2nd April. Mr. Blewitt shot, preserved, and sent me one of the parent birds, which belonged unmistakeably to Jerdon's *Griseus*, and exhibited the pale greyish plumage,

---

with dark central streaks towards the tips. Tarsus feathers silky greyish white, with a faint buffy tinge towards the joint, and with several, narrow, somewhat irregular, transverse, brown bars. Tail feathers, greyish brown, with imperfect, transverse, mottled bars of very pale dingy buff, and with the interspaces too, more or less mottled with the same colour.

Other specimens killed at Bareilly in May, answered well to the above description, except that in some specimens, the whole of the colours were dingier, while the white of the lower abdomen, vent, lower tail and thigh coverts was purer. The tarsal plumes in some were entirely unbarred, and generally, the markings were less pronounced, and clear, than in the first described specimen. Specimens from numerous other localities, undistinguishable with these. In most birds (six out of eight of those now before me) the tarsal plumes are entirely unbarred.

Very few of the specimens show the silvery half collar on the neck described in the Puhpoondh specimen, in most, the deep brown of the top of the head is continuous down to the broad buffy collar, at most a few feathers on the nape, being greyish towards the tips.

On the whole, however, the coloration of specimens from the most distant localities differs but little.

unbarred legs, and six-inch wing, characteristic, according to him, of that species.

The eggs are very round, considerably larger than those of *Athene Brahma*, and than the egg of this species already described. They are fairly glossy and, of course, pure white, and only vary from 1·32 to 1·36 in length, and from 1·15 to 1·18 in breadth.

As I have pointed out in the description, the absence of bars on the tarsi, although the *rule* in this species, is by no means an invariable characteristic. The female which I captured on the egg has the tarsi barred. Of a pair which I caught at Bareilly in May in a hole, with three half grown young ones, one had the tarsi barred, while in the other they were pure white and absolutely spotless. Judging from my notes, at least one in every six specimens has the tarsi more or less clearly barred, and at least two more out of the six, exhibit *traces* of the same. I have not been able to satisfy myself, whether these differences are accidental, or depend upon age or sex.

This species is widely distributed in India, and though rarely *seen* is really by no means uncommon. Jerdon gives it from the Eastern Ghats, whence I also have received a specimen, and I have before me now specimens from Saugor, Jhansee, Etawah, Bareilly, a low valley near Almora, Dehli, Hansie, and Mount Aboo, all of which though varying *slightly* in size and colour, are manifestly one species, and clearly distinct from the five other species that I have separately noticed.

All the specimens that I have hitherto examined in the flesh, had fed exclusively on beetles, crickets and the like.

This species (and very possibly all the other *Ephialtes*, but this is the only one that I have had opportunities of watching closely), is entirely nocturnal in its habits, and except when disturbed from some hiding-place, will never be seen abroad, so long as there is the least bit of daylight about. During the day, they roost in holes of trees, or, where the foliage is very dense and the branches very close, on some leaf embowered branch A pair that I used to watch at Bareilly, roosted in a dense clump of young Sakoo trees ((*Shorea Robusta*) which grow in the public gardens. They always sat in the same places, about three feet apart. At night, long after *Athene Brahma* was chattering angrily every where, and perching out openly on bare boughs and telegraph wires and posts, long after the two horned Eagle Owls (*Ascalaphia Bengalensis* and *Coromanda)* were about, and *Bulaca Ocelata* was busy trying to awake the echoes (there did not happen to *be* any there to wake unfortunately); the two little Scops Owls would still sit motionless, and never once did they leave their retreats whilst light enough remained to see them. In the early morning, it was the same thing; no matter how early I went, as soon as it was light enough to distinguish them from the leaves, (in which except from one single point of observation they were completely hidden,) there they were, looking for all the world as if they had never moved since the preceding evening. Their cry or at least what I believe to be their cry, for I heard it very often in Bareilly where this species is very plentiful, is a low, monotonous, double note, a sort of bell sound, or low, short whistled, *tew, tew*, repeated for hours together at short intervals; it much resembles the note of the so-called Bell Bird of the Himalayahs, *one* of the utterers of which at any rate, Capt. Hutton has proved to be *E. Gymnopodus*, (74 bis,) but it is somewhat louder and less musical.

As far as my experience goes, this species is exclusively confined to localities in which there are plenty of trees, and where either from natural or artificial causes, the soil is more or less damp and insects are plentiful. Trees on canal banks, and canal irrigated lands, are, in upper India at any rate, their favourite haunts.

No. 75 QUATUOR.—Ephialtes Malabaricus,* JERDON.

THE MALABAR SCOPS OWL.

The only specimens that I possess of this species I owe to Mr. H. R. P. Carter (who killed his at Coonoor) and Mr. Jenkyns, (who killed his on the Western Ghats).

---

* EPHIALTES MALABARICUS.

DIMENSIONS. Females (two specimens only, measured in the flesh by Mr. H. R. P. Carter) length, 8·0 to 8·24. Expanse 16·5. Wing, 5·95. The 4th primary the longest; the 1st 1·7; the 2nd 0·65 and the 3rd 0·15 shorter. Length of tail 2·75; exterior tail feathers 0·25 shorter than the central. Tarsus 1·05 to 1·08. Mid toe; 0·73 to 0·9; its claw, straight 0·32 to 0·35; hind toe, 0·35 to 0·43; its claw, straight 0·3 to 0·32; inner toe 0·68 to 0·75; its claw 0·36 to 0·42. Bill, straight, to edge of cere, 0·43 to 0·5; from gape, 0·8; width at gape 0·62 to 0·7; height at front, at margin of cere, 0·25 to 0·3. Length of cere, 0·35. Wings when closed reach nearly to end of tail. Lower tail coverts fall short of end of tail by about 1.″

DESCRIPTION. Feet yellow. Irides dark yellow. Bill yellowish horny, darker above.

As to the nidification of this species I know nothing; I have had eggs said to belong to *E. Lempigi* sent me from the Neilgherries, but the greatest confusion as to the nomenclature of this little group, has hitherto prevailed amongst Indian naturalists, and it has been customary in the south to call every thing *not E. Pennatus*, *E. Lempigi;* while in the north *E. Gymnopodus* has generally done duty as *Pennatus*, and every thing else has gone down as *Lempigi*.

It is impossible therefore to decide to what species the eggs sent may have belonged.

Whether *E. Malabaricus*, Jerdon, be really identical with *E. Lempigi*, Horsf. is a matter for future decision; Mr. Blyth, it will have been seen, considers that they are so, but I somewhat doubt the fact. The plumage is very similar, but *Lempigi* appears to be a much larger bird.

Strix Noctula (Reinw.) figured by Tem. Pl. Col. 99, from Java, is clearly identical with *E. Lempigi*, Horsf. Temminck gives the length at 9·75 English* inches, while a large female *Malabaricus*, from the Ghats measured only 8·4. Mr. Carter's obviously adult female was only 8·25.

Admitting the great similarity of the plumage, it appears to me, that the marked difference in size, would render the specific union of these two races, inhabiting widely different localities, very questionable, especially in a genus which in India and elsewhere varies locally so much.

Of course Temminck's dimensions may be excessive, (Bonaparte gives the wing as under 6 English inches) and I have no other measurements to refer to, but if the true *Lempigi* be from 9·5 to 9·75 in length, it must I think be held to be distinct from *E. Malabaricus*.

Malabaricus extends to Ceylon; I have seen a specimen from Ceylon, undistinguishable from my Malabar and Neilgherry birds.

Besides the Indian Scops Owls already enumerated, Malayana and the Archipelago furnish, as Mr. Wallace tells us the following—

PLUMAGE. The full description of *E. Griseus* already given, renders any minute description of this species unnecessary.

Generally it may be said that only the point of the forehead and a narrow streak over the eye, is white; and these parts instead of being silvery white as in *Griseus*, are fulvous. Again the chin, throat, ruff feathers, breast, and abdomen, instead of being white or creamy white as in *Griseus*, are a rich buffy fawn. Altogether, the bird is a good deal smaller, and the lower parts conspicuously more buffy than in any specimen of *E. Griseus*.

* *I. e.* nine inches two lines, French.

E. Menadensis, Quoy; from Celebes and Flores.

E. Leucospila, Gray; from Batchian, Morty Island, Boru, Ternate and Celebes.

E. Sylvicola, Wallace, from Flores.

E. Magicus, Bon; from Ceram and Amboyna.

E. Mantis,* Bon; from the Malay Peninsular, Sumatra and Borneo.

I ought perhaps to have included in these notes *E. Lempigi*, Horsf., as two years ago, I was shown a Rangoon specimen apparently (I had not then examined this group) belonging to that species, but I am by no means *sure* of its occurrence (the bird I saw *may* have been *Lettia*) within our limits, or indeed north of the Straits, where, as also in Sumatra, Java and Borneo, it is common.

No. 76. Athene Brama,† Tem.

The Spotted Owlet.

This species breeds in February, March and April; but the great majority of the birds lay in March.

---

* This latter, probably confounded with *Lempigi*, is said to have occurred in Burmah. I quote Bonaparte's description "Affinis praecedente (*Lempigi*) sed minor, alis vix quinque pollicaribus (say 5·35 Eng.). Ferrugineus, albo-rufescente fuscoque varius, maculis supra parvis, pallidis, sagittatis, subtus minimis, elongatis; fronte albo-rufescente."

Note. Col. Tytler showed me specimens of an *Ephialtes* from Barrackpore, which he called *Lempigi* and which (I had not then studied the group) may have been so; but what was most remarkable was, that these were altogether undistinguishable from specimens which he had received from Mons Verreaux as *Braziliensis* from South America.

† Athene Brama.

Dimensions. *(Sexes vary but little in size, but the female weighs considerably heavier.)*

Length, 8·0 to 9·5. Expanse, 21 to 22·5. Wing, 6·15 to 6·65. Tail, 2·75 to 3. Tarsus, 1 to 1·1. Foot greatest length, 2·1 to 2·2; greatest width, 2·15 to 2·23; mid toe to root of claw, 0·72 to 0·82; its claw straight, 0·4 to 0·45; hind toe to root of claw, 0·38 to 0·42; its claw, 0·36 to 0·41; inner toe to root of claw, 0·6 to 0·65; its claw, 0·38 to 0·4. Bill straight from margin of cere to point, 0·48 to 0·52; from gape, 0·78 to 0·84; width at gape, 0·64 to 0·72; height at front at margin of cere, 0·30 to 0·36; length of cere, on culmen, 0·25 to 0·31. Wings when closed reach to end of tail or fall short of them by not more than 0·5 inch. Lower tail coverts reach to within 0·75 to 1·5 of end of tail. The third and fourth primaries are the longest. The first from 0·9 to 1·1; and the second from 0·2 to 0·35 shorter. The exterior tail feathers are from 0·13 to 0·42 shorter than the central ones. The weight

Holes in old trees, (scantily lined with a few dry leaves and feathers, decayed wood, or a little grass,) are their favourite laying places, but holes in old buildings, and clefts in rocks are sometimes resorted to. I remember Mr. Brookes telling me, that in his office at Etawah two Rollers (*C. Indica*) had chosen a

---

is from 3·5 to 6 oz. A particularly large female from Saugor, weighed 7·5 ounces.

DESCRIPTION. *Feet,* dingy greenish, front of toes sparsely clad with whity brown bristles. Claws, very sharp, blackish horny; inner edge of mid claw a good deal dilated. Papillæ of soles, small distinct, soft. *Irides* bright pale yellow. *Bill,* horny green. *Cere,* dusky, much swollen above the nares. Tongue, obtusely hastate; slightly membraneous and emarginate at the tip.

Plumage. Facial disk, which is nearly obsolete, partially defined, by a dark, earthy, brown tipped, row of feathers, running right across the throat and upwards behind the ear coverts. The general colour of the facial disk or space enclosed, by the above line, including apex of forehead, and broad supercilium, white, but the ear coverts themselves are *very* pale brown, obscurely barred with darker brown; there is a dusky patch in front and below the anterior angle of the eye; most of the bristle-like feathers of the prominent lore tufts are only dingy white, and the naked tips of their elongated shafts are dark brown. Middle of forehead, top and back of head, and sides of ditto behind facial disk line, dull earthy brown, the feathers with pairs of small white spots, or narrow incomplete white bars. These spots are most numerous, on the forehead, and largest on the sides of the head. The back of the neck is generally the same dull earthy brown, but at the base of the occiput, and down the back of neck, there is an ill-defined and mottled, white, triangular patch, owing to some of the feathers being broadly tipped, or marked near the tip, with white; this is only clearly seen, when the neck is extended. The neck in front, below the brown disk line, is white, and this colour extends as a sort of collar, backwards, but does not quite meet at the back. The whole back, scapulars, upper tail coverts, and wing coverts are the same dull earthy brown, the upper back nearly spotless, the feathers of the other parts with numerous pairs of white spots towards the tips and more or less imperfect white bars higher up, which latter are hidden by the overlapping of the feathers. The ground colour of the tail feathers, and quills, is the same, as that of the back. The tail feathers have about four transverse white bars, narrow on the centre tail feathers, and the outer webs of the lateral ones, but broad, and somewhat scallop-like on the inner webs of the latter. The first five quills are notched on the inner webs, the second to the fourth slightly emarginate, on the outer ones. The first five primaries, and the secondaries, have several white spots on the outer webs, and the last five primaries exhibit traces of the same, and all (but the first five primaries below the notches, where there are only faint traces of them) have large, broad, pure white scallops, on the inner webs, corresponding with the white spots, on the outer webs, which, with them may be considered, portions of incomplete bars. The base of the neck in front the breast, sides, flanks, and thigh coverts, white, the feathers with subterminal, brown bands and triangular spots, which at the base of the neck predominate, owing to the overlapping of the feathers, and form a sort of mottled zone. The middle of the abdomen, vent, lower tail coverts, and tarsi feathers, a slightly dingy white.

hole, or rather spot to build in, on the top of the central wall of a gable roof, just under the main longitudinal beam. Two of these Owlets came and determined to breed there, and after a couple of days' fighting and screeching, &c., the Owls took possession of the Rollers' comfortable nest and there laid. The Rollers went round the corner of the same house, chose a new hole, built a new nest and bred there. Generally when met with out of holes in trees, their nests are more substantial, than when in the latter, and in such cases, I suspect the nests are more often theirs by right of conquest than by construction.

They lay four or five eggs: most commonly the former. All are when blown a beautifully pure white, but until blown, have, when quite fresh, a beautiful pink tinge, and when a good deal incubated, are an opaque marble white. Most of them are of a close, uniform, satiny texture, but a good many are thickly covered in part or whole with minute pimples, if I may use the word, white, but owing to the shell there being thicker, of a rather deader white than the ground.

Typically the eggs of *Athene Brama* are oval. In some cases broad and approaching the normal Owl shape, but more commonly a moderately broad oval, differing little in colour, size and texture from those of some of our green pigeons, and some of the smaller specimens are positively undistinguishable from large eggs of *Turtur Risoria*. The largest specimen I have seen is smaller than the eggs of *Noctua Tegmalmi* figured by Hewitson and as above remarked much less spherical. Out of some hundreds, I have only one specimen nearly as spherical as his figure.

The eggs vary from 1·15 to 1·45 in length and from 0·93 to 1·1 in breadth, but the average of 54 eggs measured was 1·25 by 1·04.

Mr. W. Blewitt writes, "I took four nests of this bird between the 16th and 21st March. Two contained three and two four eggs, one set of the latter only being at all incubated. The nests were in decayed hollows of Sheeshum, Jamun (*Eugènium Jambolanum*) and Neem trees, the eggs were in each case more or less bedded in dry leaves, or feathers, or both." On another occasion he wrote, "I found several nests of this species near Hansie in the latter half of April. They were in holes of Peepul and Siriss trees, and each contained three eggs laid upon a few blades of straw with a few dry leaves or feathers."

This is a very bold little bird, and always issues from its diurnal roosting-place long before dusk. It is one of the birds which really seem to think that Telegraph wires were erected for their sole and especial benefit, and the numbers that one sometimes sees, perched on these in a run of two or three miles down a railway line on a trolly about sunset, is surprising. Very often it will not even move for a train, or if it does, only takes a short undulating flight, alternately opening the wings widely and closing them again entirely, and then re-alights on the wire. It is a great bird for a kind of whispered chattering, which the natives try to imitate in its name "Khoosuttia," which recalls to us the French word for the same sound, "*chuchoter*."

As regards its geographical distribution out of India, Mr. Blyth remarked in the Ibis for 1866—"I believe that Dr. Jerdon is mistaken in noting this bird from Ceylon, as also from 'Persia and other parts of Asia,' west of India. *Noctua indica*, one of the synonyms of this species, is described as being 'common about the foot of the mountains near the town of Erzeroum,' (P. Z. S. 1839, p. 119). This, I believe, is the only authority for noting it from Persia; and the species was doubtless *A. Persica* (Vieillot.)"

No. 76 bis. Athene Persica.* Vieillot.

The Persian Owlet, or Southern Little Owl.

Noctua Meridionalis, Risse.
,, *Glaux*, Savigny.
Strix Noctua, Forskal.
,, *Passerina*, Ruppell.
,, *Numida*, Levaillant, *Junr.*
(?) *Athene Gymnopodus*, Hodgson.
,, *Bactriana*, Blyth.

Mr. Blyth says that this species "inhabits Middle and Western Asia, Southern Europe, and Africa, north of the Atlas;

---

* Athene Persica.

I have unfortunately no detailed measurements of this species. The following is a note which I made from one of the Swat specimens; unfortunately at the time, I did not know what the bird was. "It appears to be about 6·75 or 7 long. Wing, 5·0. Tail, 2·5. Tarsus, 0·9. Feet *feathered* not completely so it is true, but far more so than in *Brama*, than which it is much smaller. The whole upper surface, a dingy rufous ashy brown, much the same colour as in some specimens of *Ninox Scutellatus*. There are numerous greyish white blotches on the head, nape and base of the back of the neck. The tail has three, conspicuous, narrow, transverse, greyish white bands visible, with a fourth nearly hidden by the upper tail coverts. The chin, cheeks, ear coverts, middle of throat, upper breast, lower abdomen, breast and lower tail coverts, dingy fulvous white, unspotted. The sides of the neck, lower

and is common in Afghanistan, but does not enter the Indian sub-region, nor even the Himalayan province of the South Turanian sub-region, Mr. Hodgson's specimens having been obtained north of the snow."

As a matter of fact, however, I have now seen two specimens shot in the Peshawar valley. I have seen two more from Afghanistan, and have had in Col. Tytler's museum, the opportunity of comparing North African specimens of, apparently, the same bird, with *Noctua* of Europe.

Mr. Bree tells us that this species "is generally believed by naturalists to be only a pale variety of our little Owl *Strix Noctua*," but it appears to me, undoubtedly distinct from this latter species, though of course not so clearly so, as it is from *A. Brahma.*

The dimensions of *Athene Persica* (I have only seen skins) seem identical with those of Brahma, (the one I first saw, however, was much smaller) but in the general tone of colour, the size and character of the markings, and the distance to which the true feathers extend on to the feet, there are clearly appreciable differences. First, the colour appears to be more rufous, in some specimens almost a dingy chestnut brown, far more rufous, in every case, than are 99 out of every 100 individuals of *A. Brama*, although I *have* seen *somewhat* rufous specimens of these latter from Barrackpore.

Secondly, the markings of the head are larger, longer and

---

breast, upper abdomen, sides and flanks, and tarsal plumes a more rufous white, with numerous, irregular, central streaks and blotches of a rufous brown brighter than the upper parts, and some of the breast feathers with imperfect sub-terminal bands."

Mr. Blyth described this species under the name of *Bactrianus* in the J. A. S. for 1847, from one of Capt. Hutton's Candahar specimens, as follows, his dimensions, it will be observed, are much greater than those of the bird I first saw.

"Length about nine inches, of wing, 6·25, and tail, 3·5 inches. Tarsi, 1·25 inch. Plumage of the upper parts somewhat rufescent clay brown, with large, round, white spots on the feathers, more or less concealed, and wholly so on those of the middle of the back: coronal feathers with medial whitish streaks: face white; some of the radiating feathers on the sides of the beak, terminating in the black vibrissæ; chin, throat, lower tail coverts, and the tibial and tarsal plumes, white, also the fore-part of the under-surface of the wing; a longitudinal broad streak on each feather of the breast and abdomen; on the hind neck, the white so predominates upon the feathers as to give the appearance of a half collar. The great wing feathers have broad incomplete pale bands, disposed alternately on their two webs; and the middle tail feathers have a double row of some alternating pale spots, passing into dull bands on the outer tail feathers: beak (in the dry specimen) whitish; and claws pale horn colour.

more pear-shaped, the spots on the wing coverts and scapulars are much larger, the bars on the tail are broader and less perfect, more like broad double spots, and the markings of the under part are much more blotchy and streaky. In *Brama* the whole feet and toes are clad in bristle-like feathers, in *Persica* only the toes, the *feet* being covered with *true* feathers like the tarsi, and even the toe bristles being somewhat more feather-like than in *Brama*.

Noctua, no doubt is very close to *Persica*, closer than the latter to *Brama*, but it is *browner* and less rufous (while *Brama* is *greyer*) and the spots on the head and nape (and elsewhere) are still longer and larger, and even the toes, may be more properly said to be feathered than bristled.

In Candahar, Capt. Hutton tells us that it is common amongst the rocks and ruins. In India it occurs, probably as a mere straggler, only on our extreme North Western frontier. In Egypt, Mr. Taylor tells us (Ibis, 1867) that it is "very abundant, and equally at home, in town, and country. Breeds in March. Flies freely and well in broad day-light. Differs very little from the *A. Noctua* of Europe."

No. 77. **Athene Radiata.** Tickell.

The Jungle Owlet.

The Jungle Owlet breeds in the early part of the hot weather, laying in April and May, in holes in trees. Though I have twice found nests containing young ones, neither I myself nor any of my numerous correspondents, have yet, it would seem, obtained the eggs, which, however, we may safely prophesy, will prove to be three or four in number, pure white, sphero-ovoidal, measuring some 1·25 by 1 or thereabouts. Mr. R. Thompson, writing from Gurhwal, says—"This species breeds in May and June, in holes in small trees. It is very common in all the warmer valleys. Young birds are quite fledged in June, from three to four young ones at a time. I have never seen them living in families as Dr. Jerdon asserts. I have always found them either in pairs or single. The males of this species are considerably smaller than the females, so much so, that one would easily take them to belong to another species. The cry is a too–roo–roo–roo–roo, &c., drawn out to a considerable length, and resembling that of the common Goanna lizard. This cry is sometimes terminated with double or treble notes, resembling somewhat those of *A. Brama*.

Its flight is both rapid and strong, with closed wings, like that of the Besrah. It kills and devours all kinds of small birds, even taking them in the day-time. I had one caught which came down at a chicken three times all by itself, and killed it in broad daylight. The chicken was set in a trap for *Limnaetus Niveus.*"

Dr. Jerdon describes the soft parts differently to what I should; the feet are *yellow*, bristled to the toes, the bill light yellowish horny and the irides, bright yellow. He is wrong in saying, "beneath, throat white, the rest of the body &c."; in good fresh specimens, the lores and chin are white, the ends of the bristle-like elongated shafts, blackish. From the base of the lower mandible, joining into the white of the chin, runs a broad white stripe under the ear coverts and round the lower half of the posterior margin of the aural orifice, this latter portion of the stripe, not being visible in the dry skin, unless the ear coverts are lifted, but being very conspicuous in the living bird, who, especially when teased, sets the ear coverts out, nearly at right angles to the bill. Between these white stripes, and below them, joining the feathers of the neck, the throat feathers are closely barred rufous or rufescent white and dusky brown, precisely unicolorous with the sides of the neck; below this there is a large white patch at the base of the neck in front. Most of my skins show all this, but in some, in which owing to the size of the head, the skin, and feathers of the throat have been injured in turning, it is not so apparent, but it is invariably found in fresh specimens, and in living birds of which I have kept several.

These birds in confinement tame readily, and eat raw or cooked meat, insects, frogs, in fact any thing, animal. I have seen them in the day-time, in the shady verandah in which they were kept, kill and eat crickets, ants and butterflies. A pair of sparrows made a nest on the interior cornice of the enclosed end of the verandah, in which they lived. At first, the sparrows, teased, and bothered the Owls, the whole day long at intervals, the Owls merely retreating inside their box, chattering angrily, but one night two of the three got loose, killed both sparrows, eating their breasts and entrails, and all the young ones, of which not a trace was left. They did not attempt to leave the place, (this was at Dehra) and I let the third loose, after which they gradually grew wilder, (returning, however, for some weeks for the day to their box,) and at last left the house altogether, although, when I gave it up they were still hanging about the trees in the very jungly compound. They were excessively noisy birds, both by night and even at intervals by day, in fact at times a perfect nuisance. Dogs were their abomination and the way in which, menaced by a puppy of mine, who evidently thought it famous fun, they would lower their heads, set out their wings and ear coverts, and "curse and swear," (a mixture of hissing and chattering utterly indescribable in words) was really quite 'edifying!'

Specimens from Dehra, Saharunpoor, Kumaon, and Kaladoongee, in fact (as far as I have had the opportunity of observing them) northern birds, differ apparently constantly in tint from those sent me from the Madras Presidency, Aboo and other comparatively southern localities. The whole of the barred portions of the upper half of the body, breast, throat, head, neck, upper back and lesser coverts, in the northern birds are more rufous, the light bars conspicuously so, than in the southern birds, in some specimens of the former, the light bars are bright rufous buff, and in no specimens can they be called merely "rufescent *whitish*," (a correct description of those of the southern birds) being in every case distinctly *rufous*, although it may in some birds be rather pale, dull or slightly fulvous. Again, in the southern birds the bars of the longer scapulars are either pure white or greyish white, while in the northern they are tinged with rufous or fulvous. It is true I have only five of each before me now, and I have only now noticed the difference in comparing the whole series, but it is constant in all these and seems very marked. There is more white too in the lower parts, and the rufous of the primaries is brighter and clearer in the southern than the northern specimens, and generally the whole tone of colouring in the two races differs markedly to the eye, and if really constant, is noteworthy.

This genus, or perhaps I should say the type form of this genus, is one which appears to have a great tendency to vary; the species it contains are very numerous, each for the most part restricted to a natural territorial division, in many instances of very limited extent. The present species does not extend, I believe southwards far beyond the Neilgherries. Further south and on the west coast, it is replaced by *Malabaricus* and in Ceylon by *Castaneonotus*. It does not appear to be found in lower or Eastern Bengal, nor in Burmah, although Dr. Cantor procured "a single specimen of this pretty little Owl, at Keddah (Malayan Peninsula) agreeing in every respect with those obtained from India." Westwards in upper India, I do not find it noticed from Cashmere, and though it may be found there, it has not occurred in any of the many collections that I have examined from thence, and the neighbourhood of Murree. Even within the limits, within which it is known to occur, it is very locally distributed, affecting forests and jungles, intermingled with rocky ridges or broken ground, and almost if not quite unknown in the level open portions of the Punjaub, Rajpootana, the North-West and Central Provinces. Throughout the sub-himalayan country and the lower ranges of the hills themselves, as far west as Mandi; (rarely if ever ascending above 3000 feet in height) in the Rajmahal hills, the Siwalikhs and the more considerable ridges of the Aravallis, where these are not bare, the Jungle Owlet, is more or less common, according to the supply of insects, which in a wild state, to judge from those that I have examined, form its chief food.

No. 77 BIS. **Athene Castaneonotus.*** BLYTH.

THE CEYLON OWLET.

This species, first discriminated by Mr. Blyth, is admitted by Professor Schlegel to be distinct from *A. Castanoptera* Horsfield, (No. 77 tris.). Mr. Layard gives the following account, of its "manners and customs." (Ann. and Mag. of N. H., 1858, XII., pp. 105, 106.) "Its hoot is not unlike the cry of the cuckoo, though, more shrill and abrupt; indeed when I first heard it one morning, I thought it was the note of our annual visitor, the European Cuckoo. It hoots as late as 9 or 10 o'clock in the morning, in shady situations; is silent during the heat and glare of the day, but begins again at 4 or 5 P. M. It is most on the alert during moonlight nights, feeding on *Coleoptera* and geckoids, securing the latter while creeping up the bark of trees, seizing them in its claws, * * * it sees very clearly by day, being even then most difficult to approach."

I have had no opportunities myself of observing this species, which seems to be confined to Ceylon, although Mr. Blyth suggests, that this may be the species which Dr. Helfer noticed under the name of *Castanoptera* as occurring in Tenasserim.

---

* The following is Mr. Blyth's original description. "Entire mantle and wings deep chestnut rufous, more or less obscurely barred with subdued dusky. Primaries, light dusky, faintly barred with rufous on the inner webs, and with a series of spots of bright rufous on the outer webs. Tail dusky, with eight or nine, narrow, white, or whitish bars, the last of these terminal; head and neck closely barred with bright rufescent on a dusky ground, contrasting strongly with the rufous of the back; breast nearly similar but the colors deeper. Abdomen, white, with longitudinal dusky streaks; vent and lower tail coverts, pure white; bill, pale yellow; irides, *red brown?* Wing, about 5."

No. 77 TRIS. Athene Castanoptera.* HORSF.

THE JAVANESE OWLET.

Strix. Spadicea Reinw. TEM. Pl. Col. Pl. 98.
Noctua Castanoptera, SCHLEG. Mus. P. B. Striges, p. 34.
Strix „ HORSFIELD, Trans. Linn. Soc. XIII. p. 140.

Mr. Blyth tells us, that Dr. Helfer notes this species from the Tenasserim Provinces, as also that it might be expected to inhabit the Malayan Peninsular. I know nothing of the species myself, but as it is very likely to occur, and is actually noted (although by a "somewhat loose authority" according to Blyth) as having occurred within our limits, I think it best to append Temminck's description.

Horsfield first described it from Java, and it is doubtful whether it has ever been obtained elsewhere.

No. 78. Athene Malabarica. BLYTH.

THE MALABAR OWLET.

This is another species whose nidification has not been observed.

I have nothing to add to Mr. Blyth's full description of this species which Dr. Jerdon has quoted verbatim.

---

* Temminck's remarks on this species are to the following effect:

"The wing covers a great portion of the tail, of which the feathers are equal, the tarsi are feathered, but the toes are only sparsely covered with bristles. This species is well characterized and easily recognized by the rich chestnut or nut brown purple of the back, wings and tail. The whole head, nape, sides and front of the neck, as well as of the breast, are transversely barred, at equal intervals with brown and dull yellowish bands. The region of the thorax, and the flanks are coloured like the back, and there are some purplish blotches on the tibial plumes; the rest of the lower parts are pure white. Large white blotches, cover the exterior webs of the scapulars, and of some of the coverts, placed near the fold of the wings. Bands of yellowish rufous appear on the quills, and there are five, narrow bars of this colour on the tail feathers, which are narrowly tipped with the same. The sexes differ little." The length is from 7·4 to nearly 8 inches, (English).

No. 79. **Athene Cuculoides.***

The Large Barred Owlet.

The large Barred Owlet lays from March to May; its eggs, four in number, are always deposited in some hollow or hole in a tree, without any nest or at most, a mere apology for one in the shape of a few dead leaves, or a little dry touchwood.

---

* Athene Cuculoides.

The females, accord with Dr. Jerdon's measurements. The males are smaller; the following are the dimensions of a fine male killed near Nyneetal.

Length, 8·88. Expanse, 20. Wing, 5·7. Tail from vent, 3·38. Tarsus, 1·02. Mid toe, to root of claw, 0·84; its claw straight, 0·51; hind toe, 0·45; its claw, 0·4; inner toe, 0·63; its claw, 0·48. Bill straight, from edge of cere to point, 0·52; from gape, 0·85; height at front, at margin of cere, 0·38. The closed wings reach to within, 1·38 of end of tail; the 4th primary is longest, the 5th, 0·08, the 1st, 1·5; the 2nd, 0·55; and the 3rd, 0·1, shorter. The exterior tail feathers are 0·4 shorter than the central ones, and the lower tail coverts reach to within 1·05 of the end of the tail.

Description. The feet, sparsely bristled, are light yellow; claws brown, yellowish horny at base; the irides, bright amber yellow; the bill light yellowish horny.

The lores, (some of the feathers of which are tipped dusky) a band over the eye, the chin, and two broad stripes, running from the chin and base of lower mandible, under the ear coverts and round the lower half of the posterior margin of the aural orifice, (where it is hidden in dry specimens by the ear coverts,) a broad band at the base of the neck in front, an ill-defined streak down the centre of the breast and abdomen, the vent feathers and lower tail coverts, white; the tail and quills, brown, of varying shade, corresponding with but rather darker and purer, than that of the back; the former with six or seven narrow, transverse, white, fulvous or rufous white bars, (according to the general tone of colouring of the specimen) averaging about 0·1 in width and 0·4 apart, one of which is terminal and another more or less hidden by the upper tail coverts; the quills with conspicuous spots or imperfect bars, of white or fulvous white on the outer webs and traces of corresponding pale bars on the inner webs, and the secondaries tipped with the same colour. The rest of the plumage, brown (varying in different specimens from greyish or earthy, to hair or even rufous brown) every where regularly banded with narrow, white (or greyish, or fulvous, or rufous white as the case may be in different individuals) bars, closest on the ear coverts and front of neck, (where they may average 0·1 apart) and widest apart on the scapulars (where the interspaces may average 0·25).

The exterior webs of some of the outer smaller scapulars and of some of the coverts near the fold of the wing, with large blotches of white or rufous white which are much more developed in some specimens than in others. Inner webs of all but of the first four quills, yellowish or rufous white towards the bases. Wing lining and axillaries, chiefly yellowish white. Tarsal feathers mottled or irregularly barred whitish and brown. Bars often irregular, and much white intermingled on the abdominal region and flanks.

The eggs which, as might be expected, are pure white and glossy, are rather large for the size of the bird. In shape they vary from almost perfect spheres to broad ovals and are as nearly as possible like those of the little Owl of Europe *(A. Nudipes)*.

The few eggs that I have measured, varied from 1·38 to 1·48 in length, and from 1·17 to 1·24, the average of six eggs being 1·42 by 1·19.

Capt. Hutton says, "I have found the nest of this species, which I at the time erroneously identified with "*Nudipes*," in the neighbourhood of Mussouree, at elevations of between five and six thousand feet. The eggs, three (or four) in number, round and pure white, are deposited in holes in trees, without nest."

Capt. Cock, writing from Dhurumsalla, says, "I found their nests on three occasions, always in a hollow tree. On two occasions there were four eggs in each nest, and the other time four young ones. Nests in hollow hill oaks some twenty to thirty feet from the ground. There was no lining to the nest, just a few dead leaves that might have been in the hollow accidentally. Eggs on each occasion varied in shape, but each nest of eggs retained its own characteristics, thus in one the eggs were all more spherical, in the other more oval."

Mr. R. Thompson writing from Gurhwal, says that this species "breeds in May and June, in holes, in large trees. It is quite as common as *A. Radiata* in these forests, but has not the active sanguinary habits of the other. Many breed in the oak and fir woods above Khoorpatal. I had the young brought once in June some three years ago."

This species is confined, so far as we yet *certainly* know, to the Himalayahs; it is very doubtful whether the Indo-Chinese bird, is really identical with the Himalayan. It seems most probable that the Burmese bird either corresponds with the Japanese race or is a distinct species, (vide 79 bis).

No. 79 bis. **Athene Whiteleyi.** Blyth.

The Japanese Barred Owlet.

I know nothing of this species, but merely introduce it because Mr. Blyth thinks it probable that this and *not Cuculoides* (vera) is the Burmese species, a question that may be easily decided by residents in Burmah.*

* In this case as in all others, I shall always be happy to examine, name, and *return* any specimens that may be sent me; small birds travel well by post, in little tin cases, or even in one joint of a bamboo.

This is what Mr. Blyth says,

"Mr. Gurney has called my attention to certain distinctions observable in a Japanese race supposed hitherto to be this species. The tail has only six narrow white bars, one terminal, and another of them at the extreme base of the feathers, so that four only remain to constitute the conspicuous barring of the rectrices; the markings of the wing primaries and secondaries are also fewer and further apart than in the common Himalayan bird. In India, the latter is quite peculiar to the Himalaya, whereas in Burmah, the race considered hitherto as identical, extends down to the level of the sea shore; a pair had their abode in the verandah of Col. Phayre's residence in Rangoon. This Indo-Chinese bird requires now to be compared with the Japanese race, which latter seems to be sufficiently distinct to warrant the application of a new name; and I therefore propose to designate it *Athene Whiteleyi*. Except in the comparative fewness of the markings upon the flight feathers of the wings, and more especially the rectrices, it entirely resembles the *A. Cuculoides*. The Chinese species hitherto referred to *A. Cuculoides* is probably identical with that of Japan."

Besides the Indian species, already enumerated, numerous other *Athene's*, (even restricting the genus, as I would, and excluding *Ninox* and *Glaucidium*,) occur in Malayana, in many cases, each Island having its own distinct form of Owlet, the extreme proneness to vary in the type form of this genus being as remarkable as in *Accipiter*.

I notice a remark of Mr. Blyth's in the Ibis about another species of *Athene*. He says "*A. sonnerati* (Temm. Pl. Col. 21) is stated to have been sent from Pondicherry by *M. Leschenault*, but no such bird is known in India or Burma. Dr. Pucheran identifies it with *Strix superciliaris*, Vieillot (Rev. Zool. 1849, p. 19,) which is therefore different from *Ephialtes Sagittatus*, Cassin, (Ibis, 1863, p. 21): and Prof. Kaup designates it *Ieroglaux Superciliaris*, but without mentioning its particular habitat which was unknown to Mr. Vieillot. The same individual specimen in the Paris Museum was described by Temminck, Vieillot, and Lesson."

Temminck, I note, says that this bird was sent from Pondicherry by *Sonnerat*.

It seems to me by no means *certain* that this species may not occur in India. Scarcely a week passes without some hitherto unrecorded species turning up, and I therefore quote Temminck's remarks and description. "This species is nearly allied to *Strix Passerina* and *Tegmalmi* of Europe; the tail is much longer than the wings, exceeding them by more than 2·1, (*English*,) and the tarsi and toes are feathered. The length is 11·7, (*English*).

"The whole of the upper parts are rufous brown, the feathers of the head being dotted with very small white spots, and those of the coverts and the secondaries (?) with large, round, ones. The primaries and tail feathers are unbarred and unspotted, unicolorous with the back; the orbital region, face and throat, are rufous white, the lower parts are pure white, intersected by transverse, widely separated, brown bars; feathers of the tarsi and toes, rufous; claws and bill yellow."

According to the plate, the secondaries and the primaries above the emarginations are paler, a white spot is shown on the outer web of the second primary just above the emargination.

No. 80. **Glaucidium Brodiei.*** BURTON.

THE PIGMY COLLARED OWLET.

This species lays in May and June, in hollows of trees. It makes little or no nest, though a hole that I examined in

---

* G. BRODIEI.

(I have unfortunately mislaid my paper of the measurements of this species.)

DESCRIPTION. Lores, (the elongated bristle-like shafts of the feathers brownish black towards the tips,) a supercilium continued backwards over the ear coverts, (obscure in skins but well marked in the live bird,) a band under the eye, the chin, and a broad stripe running thence, and from the base of the lower mandible below the ear coverts, and round the lower half of the posterior margin of the aural orifice, (where in dry skins it is more or less hidden by the ear coverts,) the lower part of the throat, and a broad band at the base of the neck in front, a broad streak running down the centre of the breast and abdomen, and the lower tail coverts, (the latter with a subterminal brown band,) pure white. The ear coverts, top of the head, nape, sides of the neck and a broad band across the throat, in some greyish, in some rufous, brown, thickly spotted, or in some irregularly banded with tiny imperfect bars, of greyish, rufous, or fulvous white. A broad, rufous buff, half collar at the base of the neck behind, including in it two large black or blackish brown blotches. The back, scapulars, wing coverts, rump and upper tail coverts, a somewhat clearer brown, of the same shade as the head, regularly barred at intervals, at distances of about 0·2 with very narrow bars, nearly unicolorous with the spots on the head. The tail, darker brown, with about seven, narrow, transverse bars, of the same colour as those on the back, and the feathers narrowly tipped with the same. In some specimens, a few of the coverts and of the exterior scapulars, have large, white, or fulvous blotches on the outer webs, but I have others which do not exhibit a trace of these.

July, containing four young ones, seemed to have been sparsely lined with feathers.

The eggs are doubtless four in number, nearly round and pure white, but I have never yet myself obtained any.

The following is Capt. Hutton's account of its nidification: "It lays its eggs in hollow trees without any preparation of a nest. On the 11th May, 1848, I found three young ones and an egg just ready to hatch, in a hole of a wild cherry tree. The egg was nearly round and pure white; but, being broken, I could take no measurement of it. The young ones were clothed in a soft and pure white down. The old female remained in the hole while we cut into the tree, and allowed herself to be captured."

Mr. R. Thompson writes, "This species breeds from May to July, usually in holes, in oak trees. I have usually met this bird with three young ones. In September the young are quite fledged. The note is a *took took, took, took, took, took*, repeated often. Another cry said to be uttered by this bird is the plaintive and melancholy whistle one hears after the breaking up of the rainy season, in well-wooded hilly districts, somewhat like the following, *twee-twee*, repeated at intervals, and most usually heard at night. This Owlet feeds on young birds, mice and cicadæ. I shot one which had just caught and was eating an adult specimen of *Zosterops Palpebrosus*. Awful is the chattering among the many hill tits we have up here, when they discover the whereabouts of their small though vigorous enemy. His greatest torment is the little *Siva Cyanouroptera* who, with his incessant chattering, causes him considerable annoyance. The flight is rapid and vigorous, and the bird is quite as active in the day as it is at night."

Capt. Hutton writes,—"The twin whistled note, commonly attributed to this bird, is really that of the Scops Owl; like yourself I could have declared that I had shot *Brodici*, in the act of uttering the "*wheu-whoo*" note, but in these cases, there must have been a Scops Owl at hand, and unobserved, for closer attention teaches me that *G. Brodiei* has four notes in its

---

The quills are brown, with rufous or fulvous white spots on the outer, and imperfect white bars on the inner webs (except quite at the tips of the primaries) towards the margins. The breast on either side of the white stripe, and the sides are brown, usually a good deal more rufous than on the upper parts, with narrow, transverse, fulvous or rufous white bars. The abdomen, vent and flanks, *white*, mottled, not barred, with a more or less rufous brown, the feathers being white with a large blotch on one or both webs towards the tips, and not unfrequently, if carefully examined, with a circular white spot in the middle of the brown.

whistle, slowly uttered like the other, but the middle note double, thus, "*whew—whew-whew—whew;* my boys too who are keen observers of these things and prowl about, gun in hand, sometimes till 10 o'clock at night, positively insist upon it that the double note belongs to *Ephialtes* alone, and that *G. Brodiei* has only the four notes "*whew—whew-whew—whew.*"

I am by no means sure that this species *does* as Dr. Jerdon remarks, live chiefly on insects. One shot in the valley of the Surjoo, about sundown, had a *Phylloscopus* in his claws, the head so mauled, that the species could not be made out, and none of the stomachs of three other specimens of which I have notes contained insects.

This little Owl is very watchful; by day at any rate he sits motionless, doubled up on a considerable sized branch, looking like a knot or excrescence; but, point in his direction, and he is off like a shot, nay as a rule, the moment your eyes fix on him, he is aware that he has been recognized and darts away.

These wee birds are as daring as the Falconets. I once witnessed a curious encounter between one and a Jay. I was sitting on Lurya Kanta, beyond Nyneetal, watching one, from behind another tree. A Jay (*G. Bispecularis*) was threading in and out of the branches, as is their wont, when arriving on the bough where the Owlet sat, he, for some reason best known to himself, gave three or four lolloping, sideway hops, and for all the world like a school boy at play with a comrade, went bump up against the little ball of feathers. He did not peck at her, or attack her, as being a corvine bird he was bound to do, but *flopped* against her sideways. This upset the diminutive Minerva's sense of propriety and gravity, she opened her wings, to avoid falling, swore at large, (a squeaky, scratchy, combination of hiss and chatter) flew about a yard, wheeled round and fell on the Jay's head in a style, that sent him to the right about screaming, after which with sundry ejaculations and many shakes of her feathers, the pigmy settled down again exactly on her former perch. Nothing more was seen of the Jay; but I expect he went and told tales, for soon after a mob of *Pari* and *Machlolophi* worked their way up into the tree, and soon began reviling her ladyship, in such very improper language, that with a sudden dart, she disappeared down the khud, almost without a second flap of her wings.

As far as is yet known, this species is a purely Indian one, and is found only on the Himalayahs, the Khasya Hills, (whence I have received a specimen) and the "mountainous interior of the Tenasserim Provinces where Col. Tickell obtained it."

I am somewhat inclined to believe that a second species of this exists, which I named *G. immaculatus*, owing to the almost total absence of spots on the upper surface, but my only specimen has not yet been returned by Mons. Verreaux to whom I sent it, and it *may* be only the young of the present species.

Capt. Hutton I may mention, thinks also that there is *decidedly* a second species, the one being very much more spotted than the other.

No. 81. **Ninox Scutellatus.*** Raffl.

The Brown Hawk Owl.

Comparatively common as this Owl doubtless is in some localities, I have been unable to find any record of its nidification.

---

* Ninox Scutellatus.

Dimensions. (*I have measured no specimens of this in the flesh, the following are from Mr. F. R. Blewitt.*)

Female. Length, 11 to 12·1 inches. Expanse, 27 to 29. Wing, 8·6 to 9 25. Tail, 5·1 to 5·4. Mid toe to root of claw, 1·2 to 1·25; its claw, straight, 0·52 to 0·55; hind toe, 0·6 to 0·72; its claw, 0·44 to 0·47; inner toe, 0·8 to 1·0; its claw, 0·55 to 0·61. Bill, straight, from edge of cere to point, 0·5 to 0·56; from gape, 0·9 to 1·00; width at gape, 0·8 to 0·9; height at front, at margin of cere, 0·3; length of cere on culmen, 0·32 to 0·36; closed wings reach to, from within 1 of, to, end of tail. Lower tail coverts fall short of end of tail, by from 1·82 to 2·25. The 4th primary is the longest. The 1st is from 2 to 2·2, the 2nd from 0·68 to 0·82, and the 3rd, 0·05 to 0·16 shorter. Exterior tail feathers, 0·15 to 0·4 shorter than central ones.

Description. *Legs* and *feet* yellow to reddish yellow, in some specimens, probably young birds, greenish grey, *Irides* bright yellow. *Bill,* blackish; the ridge of the culmen, pale horny yellow. *Cere,* greenish; in one specimen tinged with yellow.

Plumage. Lores, forehead, and chin, white; the elongated bristle-like shafts of some of the feathers blackish. Ear coverts, brown, ashy at the base. Top of the head, back and sides of the neck, ashy brown. Throat and front of the neck, slightly more rufous brown, streaked with fulvous. In some specimens, the fulvous greatly predominates, and these parts may then be said to be light fulvous streaked with greyish brown. Back, scapulars, lesser and median, and greater secondary wing coverts, tertiaries, and most of the secondaries, rump and upper tail coverts, brown, varying much in shade in different individuals. Some being a greyer and more dove brown, others more rufous, but always more rufous on the coverts, and generally palest or clearest on the tertiaries. The exterior scapulars with larger or smaller, pure white bars, sometimes on both, and sometimes upon one web only. In some specimens conspicuous even when the bird is at rest, in others only visible by lifting the feathers. The tertiaries are barred on both webs with white; the tail is pale grey, greyish brown, or pale brown,

Mr. R. Thompson tells me that it is "common in parts of the deep-wooded valleys of the Paltee and Kotree Dhoons, where I dare say the bird breeds. I have frequently heard the mournful cries which Jerdon has stated to be uttered by this bird. I have also I think heard similar cries uttered by the same bird, or by *Otus Vulgaris*, at Nyneetal and Paoree."

As regards geographic distribution out of India, I think a careful comparison of specimens will be necessary, before we can conclusively assume the specific identity of all the eastern Asiatic races. At the same time as my description will show, Indian specimens vary very greatly, both in the general tone of colour, and in the extent of the white on the scapulars.

As regards size too, the differences are considerable, and although (not having by me any measurements recorded in the flesh of this sex,) I am not sure of the fact, my impression is, that the males are *very* much smaller than the females, not exceeding 10·5 inches in length.

Throughout the plains of the N. W. Provinces, the Punjaub and Rajpootana, this species is almost unknown. Once and once only I killed a specimen, in a large, jungly grove in the Etawah district, when busy hawking insects after dusk.

No. 81 BIS. **Ninox Affinis.*** TYTLER.

THE ANDAMAN HAWK OWL.

I admit this bird as a distinct species, with some hesitation. I am by no means convinced, that Col. Tytler's bird is really

---

white at the extreme tip, with five, regular, transverse, brown bars, darker or lighter in different individuals, the basal one of which is more or less completely hidden by the upper tail coverts, and which average about 0·4 in breadth. The primaries, their greater coverts and the winglet, are generally somewhat darker brown than the rest of the wing, but the former are paler on the outer webs. All the quills are banded paler, somewhat obsoletely towards the tips and on the outer webs, but very conspicuously on the inner webs above the tips. The breast, abdomen, sides, flanks, vent and lower tail coverts are pure white, the breast with broad, rufous brown stripes, and the flanks and abdomen with large, more or less heart-shaped, spots of the same colour towards the tips of the feathers. The lower tail coverts, sometimes spotless, and sometimes with traces of a few pale brown, arrow-head, transverse bars; tarsal and tibial plumes, mottled white, pale fulvous and brown. One or other of these colours in some specimens the white, in others the fulvous or the brown greatly predominating. Axillaries, white or pale fulvous, more or less imperfectly but broadly barred with brown or pale rufous brown. Edge of the wing just above the base of the primaries, white. Wing, lining, mingled white, brown, and pale fulvous.

* NINOX AFFINIS.

(I am indebted to my friend Col. Tytler, for the following dimensions and description, taken by him from a skin in his museum.)

smaller than the males of the Indian race are, and though the appearance of the lower surface of the Andaman bird does differ somewhat from specimens of the Indian bird in Col. Tytler's museum, I should like to compare a series of the one, with a series of the other before finally assenting to the validity of the new species. Let, however, Col. Tytler, (who has most obligingly furnished me with notes on this and other Andamanese species) speak for himself.

"This species was first procured at Haddoa Point, Port Blair, Andamans. I named it *Affinis* from its strong resemblance to the Indian *N. Scutellatus*, which latter is larger in all its proportions than the Andaman bird, and in its general colour is lighter; the feet of the Indian bird are larger and coarser, and the whole of the under surface, considerably less rufous than *N. Affinis*, but the most striking difference is in the markings of the abdomen, and flanks of the Indian bird, which from the points of each feather being brown, gives those parts a spotted instead of a streaked appearance which the Andaman bird has," *(vide detailed description)*.

Capt. Beavan says in the Ibis, "Closely allied to *Ninox Scutellatus*, (Raffles) but very considerably smaller, and differing also in being much more rufous on the under parts, and darker generally above. Not uncommon at Aberdeen point, Port Blair, in heavy jungles, and thick forests."

Nothing is known of the nidification, and nothing further of the habits of this species.

Dimensions. Length, 10. Expanse, 18·3? Wing, 6·9. Tail from vent, 4·4. Tarsus (*covered with hair-like feathers,*) 1. Foot, (*covered with stiff bristles,*) greatest length, 2·1 (?); greatest width, 2·2 (?); mid toe to root of claw, 1·05; its claw, along curve, 0·55; hind toe, 0·55; its claw, along curve, 0·45; inner toe, 0·85; its claw along curve 0·45. Bill from gape, 0·8; width at gape, 0·7. The 4th primary is the longest, the first is 2·1 and the 2nd 0·7 shorter. The lower tail coverts fall short by 2·4 of the end of the tail.

Description. All the upper surface, rufous brown with the slaty bases of the lax feathers shewing through in many places, thus giving it more or less, a slaty tinge. In the tail feathers, there are six well defined blackish bars, the tips of all are brown; the inner webs of the quill feathers are dark; chin, albescent; throat, breast, and abdomen rufous; breast, abdomen and flanks, striped, that is to say, each feather being albescent at the margins, rufous at the tips and darker near the shaft, gives the appearance of being streaked; vent, and under tail coverts, pure white; thighs, tarsi and under wing coverts, rufous; toes, thickly covered with thick strong bristles, of an albescent brown color. Claws at the base, albescent, the rest, blackish slate, the inner webs, of all the primaries, excepting the first feather are faintly barred with dark towards the point half, and with albescent buff towards the basal half, giving the wings from beneath a speckled albescent appearance; the face and a little of the forehead, albescent; nostrils and base of upper mandible protected by stiff lax feathers, white, with a black shaft. Bill, yellowish horny at point, greenish slate towards the base, irides, bright yellow.